CHALLENGES OF PERSONAL ADJUSTMENT

William C. Coe

Fresno State College

Rinehart Press · San Francisco

Excerpts by F. Barron from Chapter 14 of *Creative Person and Creative Process*. Copyright © 1969 by Holt, Rinehart and Winston, Inc. Reprinted by permission of Holt, Rinehart and Winston, Inc.

Excerpt by S. Freud from the Standard Edition (Volume VII) of the *Complete Psychological Works of Sigmund Freud*, revised and edited by James Strachey, used courtesy of Sigmund Freud Copyrights Ltd., The Institute of Psycho-Analysis and the Hogarth Press Ltd. American rights for the excerpt by S. Freud from Volume 3 of *The Collected Papers of Sigmund Freud*, edited by Ernest Jones, M.D., Basic Books, Inc., Publishers, New York, 1959.

Excerpt by W. C. Schutz from *Joy: Expanding Human Awareness*, reprinted by permission of Grove Press, Inc. Copyright © 1967 by William C. Schutz.

Excerpts by C. Rogers from *Client-Centered Therapy* used by permission of Houghton Mifflin Co.

Excerpts by C. Rogers and B. Stevens used by permission.

Excerpts by J. Wolpe used by permission of Pergamon Press and Stanford University Press.

Excerpt by G. W. Fairweather used by permission of John Wiley & Sons, Inc.

Excerpt by A. Button from *The Authentic Child* used by permission of the author and Random House, Inc.

Excerpt by F. D. Cox used by permission of William C. Brown Co.

Excerpt by J. L. McCary used by permission.

Table 4–1 adapted by Coleman from L. E. Hollister and E. D. Luby et al. Used with the permission of the *Annals of The New York Academy of Sciences*. © The New York Academy of Sciences, 1962; reprinted by permission.

*To my children
Karen and Bill*

Preface

This book was written to meet the requirements of a textbook in courses variously called Personal Adjustment, Psychological Adjustment, and Mental Hygiene. The reader needs no previous knowledge of psychology in order to understand the material, but an attempt has been made to organize the topics so that they will be interesting to those with formal backgrounds in psychology as well.

Many difficulties confront the author of a textbook on human adjustment. What material should be included? In how much detail? What topics are relevant to the student? To the instructor? To both? One of the knottiest problems is to find material that is interesting, relevant, or entertaining to the student and that also demonstrates the empirical nature of psychology as a science. To introduce clinical data while avoiding the naïveté of telling "how to do it" and to present research data without the dryness of much technical writing offer formidable challenges. The majority of students are interested in what psychological findings can tell them about themselves as developing individuals. At the same time the instructor wants to make it clear that valid knowledge results from careful, well-planned research. At this stage of its development psychology can offer only tentative explanations of human behavior. Furthermore, reliable psychological techniques for coping with living problems are just beginning to be developed. This textbook is thus an attempt to steer between the extremes of "techniques and advice" on one side and "hard-core experimentation" on the other. The reader will find a combination of theoretical, empirical, and clinical material throughout, presented with emphasis on their interrelatedness and relevance to human adjustment. Case studies and personal accounts have frequently been included to illustrate theory and research, as well as to stimulate the reader to personal reflection. The extent to which the book achieves my goals remains for the reader to judge.

I have tried to present information on most of the important theoretical orientations of modern psychologists. In that sense the book is "eclectic." Although no one school of psychological thought dominates the book, it is only fair to inform the reader of my personal preferences. In my opinion the psychosocial view of man holds the most promise for advancing scientific knowledge and alleviating human suffering. Other psychologists may agree with me only in part or not at all. Given our present knowledge, however, there can be few certainties in psychology, and there is certainly ample room for disagreement. The student who becomes aware of this fact has learned an important lesson. He should feel free to criticize *any* investigator's formulations, to question the data, and to draw his own conclusions.

The organization of the book has been designed to enhance the learning process. In general, the content moves from general concepts (like motivation) to more specific instances of personal adjustment. Cross references among chapters are frequent, so that teachers can alter the order of chapters without undue confusion to the student. Of course, I have tried to make all material interesting and pertinent to the concept of human adjustment.

The book consists of three major parts. The first introduces the reader to some basic notions related to adjustment. Its purpose is to acquaint the student with the concept of adjustment and basic psychological processes (like inheritance, motives, emotions, and perception) involved in it. Some of this material may overlap with what is taught in courses on introductory psychology, but here the general concepts are directly related to tasks of adjustment. For example, in discussing heredity I point out the importance of physical characteristics in an individual's relations with others and his culture; in the section on motivation I discuss the acquired need that can develop into alcoholism; and in discussing perception I examine the phenomena of "psiland" (extrasensory perception, clairvoyance, psychokinesis).

In Part II I shift to an examination of the theoretical views of man that are widely held by psychologists today. The techniques (psychotherapies) associated with each of these theories are described in some detail, and case material further demonstrates the applications of these techniques. Four basic theoretical views are described: psychoanalysis and ego psychology, humanism (including existentialism and Rogerian theory), learning theory and behavior modification, and the psychosocial view (including role theory and experimental social innovation).

Part III will familiarize the student with the various tasks of adjustment, within the framework of developmental psychology. To this end, important tasks at different periods of growth are discussed, beginning with prenatal development. The final chapters deal with the challenges of childhood, adolescence, and adulthood. Adolescence and early adulthood are emphasized because they are most relevant to the prospective reader. The challenges of these periods are likely to play a major part in students' current experiences.

Several features of this textbook have been planned to aid the student. A rather complete outline will be found at the beginning of each chapter. It should serve as an overview of the material to be learned and should help to orient the student's thinking and expectations. It should also serve as a useful framework for review. A summary at the end of each chapter should also help to refresh and clarify the student's memory of the chapter contents. In order that the writing flow more smoothly, I have generally omitted detailed references from the text itself and have consolidated them at the end of the book.

Acknowledgments

It would be virtually impossible to acknowledge all those who have contributed indirectly to the writing of this textbook. My gratitude goes to all my former students and clients who have added, bit by bit, to my understanding of human adjustment. Episodes from the lives of some of them have been included in the text, with pseudonyms to protect their privacy. To them I am doubly grateful.

I am also indebted to the many publishers and authors who have permitted me to reproduce their material in this volume. Specific acknowledgments are included where excerpts appear in the text. Fresno State College gave me a semester's leave of absence from teaching duties, during which a large portion of this manuscript was prepared.

Several people have helped in the arduous task of preparing the manuscript for publication. I wish to thank Dorothie Scordino, Landa Fong, Vicki Wager, Jeanette Abrahamian, Karen Fulvio, Chris Mayo, Gwenn Wright, and Diane Pilakowski for deciphering my scrawls and putting them into readable form. The secretarial staff of the department of psychology at Fresno State College, especially Martha Raught and Dorothy Adams, assisted greatly in handling the many minute details that are necessary in the publishing of any book. Linda Buckner deserves special recognition for her secretarial efforts, her useful suggestions on organization and style, and, most of all, her personal encouragement and support during the trying stages of preparation.

Some of my colleagues at Fresno State College read portions of the manuscript, offered constructive criticism, or helped in other ways. I am particularly grateful to Ernst Moerk, Frank Powell, Stanley Lindquist, Harrison Madden, Edwin Tenney, Alan Button, and Mitri Shanab.

Especially important was the editorial assistance of Theodore R. Sarbin of the University of California at Santa Cruz. Most of the major revisions in early drafts were direct consequences of his detailed and constructive evaluations. Our work sessions were highly stimulating and productive. I also want to thank his wonderful wife, Genevieve, for her excellent hospitality and warm companionship during these meetings.

William C. Coe

Fresno, California

Contents

Preface   v

Acknowledgments   vii

PART I   BASIC NOTIONS IN THE STUDY OF PERSONAL
         ADJUSTMENT   1
  CHAPTER 1   The Concept of Adjustment   3
  CHAPTER 2   Processes of Adjustment: The Role of Inheritance   21
  CHAPTER 3   Processes of Adjustment: Motives and Emotions   38
  CHAPTER 4   Processes of Adjustment: Perception   63

PART II   THEORETICAL VIEWS OF MAN AND
          ASSOCIATED TECHNIQUES   85
  CHAPTER 5   Classical Psychoanalysis and Ego Psychology   89
  CHAPTER 6   The Humanistic View   127
  CHAPTER 7   Learning, Behavior Modification, and Personality   171
  CHAPTER 8   The Social-Psychological View   213

PART III   ADJUSTMENT: ACCOMPLISHING TASKS IN
           THE LIFE CYCLE   253
  CHAPTER 9   Adjustment in Childhood   255
  CHAPTER 10   Influences on Childhood Development   293
  CHAPTER 11   Adjustment in Early Adolescence   333
  CHAPTER 12   Adjustment in Late Adolescence: Vocations and
               Sexuality   361
  CHAPTER 13   Adjustment in Late Adolescence: Choosing Values   391
  CHAPTER 14   Adjustment in Adulthood   419

References   453
Index   463

PART **I**

BASIC NOTIONS IN THE STUDY OF PERSONAL ADJUSTMENT

The major aim of this part is to suggest the scope of the study of personal adjustment and to present basic knowledge and related material. This information should act as a foundation for the remainder of the book. We shall examine both the concept of adjustment and the basic processes of adjusting.

In Chapter 1, one individual's problems in living serve as a starting point for examination of the more general concept of adjustment. We offer our own view of the adjustment process, then describe several attempts to define the "normal" individual. In the next three chapters we examine the basic characteristics of man: his inheritance, his motivations and emotions, and how he perceives the world. All these factors play important roles in determining the outcome of personal adjustment. In some instances inherited characteristics appear to have primary importance; in others they seem to have almost no effect. An important challenge for the student of human adjustment is to discover in what ways, and to what degrees, genetic background influences human characteristics. The factors motivating behavior and the emotional responses that color our actions are also important. A basic understanding of these processes will be of immeasurable assistance in evaluating the theoretical views of man presented in Part II. A firm understanding of man's ability to register environmental stimuli and to give them meaning (the perceptual process) is crucial to a grasp of the complexity of personal adjustment. Special topics related to perception (sensory deprivation, extra-sensory perception, psychedelic experiences) are treated in Chapter 4. These topics help us to recognize how limited our present knowledge of human behavior is and how many phenomena need to be more precisely understood.

1

The Concept of Adjustment

A. Ron: An Example of Personal Adjustment
B. Adjustment as Relatedness
   1. Self-Relatedness
   2. Interpersonal relatedness
   3. Cultural relatedness
C. Definitions of Normality
   1. Freedom from symptoms
   2. Cultural relativism
   3. The statistical approach
   4. Ideal behavior
   5. Conclusions
D. Summary

As we are interested mainly in the ways in which people adjust to living, it is appropriate to begin by looking at one individual's achievements and failures in adjustment.

RON: AN EXAMPLE OF PERSONAL ADJUSTMENT

Ron found himself in a precarious situation. Something was wrong. He was twenty-five years old, and life seemed to be passing him by. He felt out of control, unable to get hold of himself. He was a nice-looking young man, and he made a good income working in his father's business, but for a month or so he had just been going to work, putting in his time, coming home, and staying in his apartment by himself. He felt tense, upset, and lonely. Why didn't he tell his father that he didn't like what he was doing? He should certainly tell him that he was not training his son right. With all his experience he should be able to teach his son how to be successful. When Ron thought deeply about his predicament it appeared that the main difficulty was a struggle within himself—an inability to face his father with his wish to do something else, an inability to change his customary ways of acting.

He didn't sleep well because he was so tense much of the time. He tried to read a lot, but that didn't really reduce his tension either. Masturbation offered temporary release, though he inevitably felt guilty afterward. It had always been like that. Why couldn't he control it? Why did he have to masturbate when he knew it was wrong? Well, he had to have some release from the nagging tension.

Other difficulties crowded into his mind as well. He was becoming increasingly uncomfortable around people. When he went to a party, something he rarely did any more, he was tense, ill at ease, and unable to enjoy the company of others. It seemed that whatever he did would lead them to think that he was stupid. He didn't know what to talk about. He tried to find what others were interested in and talk about that, but rarely did he feel that he made a positive impression.

His discomfort in relations with people was part of another problem—women. He wanted to be married, to have a wife, to have a family, to be like other young people and find happiness with a mate. Yet he wondered how he could ever do these things. Sure, girls had liked him, he had taken out a few, and he had almost become involved a couple of times—but something kept him from closeness, something forced him away when intimacy threatened. It wasn't that he knew nothing about sex; he had heard the other guys talk about it, and in the army he had even gone along with them to a prostitute to show that he was a man. But prostitutes had only made it worse. He spent his time with them, but it was never enjoyable as it was supposed to be—he performed the act but never reached orgasm. He wondered what he could do. Whenever he was in close contact with a girl he liked, one who

4

also liked him, he had to withdraw if he became sexually aroused. He felt ashamed, he felt embarrassed, and he brought the relationship to an abrupt halt.

There was more to his uneasiness. He questioned what everything meant. The religion of his childhood did not provide him with satisfactory answers. Life appeared to have no meaning; there were no real goals or values to believe in. At times society seemed superficial and hypocritical. Of course, he wanted to make money; he wanted to have possessions—a new car, good clothes, and a well-furnished apartment. But now that he could afford them, they did not seem to make much difference. He still felt empty; he had no life. He felt isolated, alone, angry, unhappy, and guilty.

As he entered the psychologist's office for the first time he thought: "Perhaps this isn't the right thing to do after all? How could someone else change all these things?" A friend had told him of having been helped in his own distress by a psychologist. Maybe one would help Ron too. As he thought back he wondered whether he should not have confided in his friend and told him some of his difficulties—of course, not *all*. But something had to be done. Almost without realizing it he was sitting in the chair, head down, relating his thoughts to a complete stranger.

Ron's parents were of the second generation of immigrant families that had come to the United States in search of a new life. Times had been rough, but the newcomers had managed to get a foothold in their new country. Eventually, however, their children were to benefit from the move. Ron's father had been a strong, hard-working boy whose major goal had been to raise himself from the low social and economic status of his parents. He had had to quit school after the fifth grade to help support his family, but he had worked hard and had continued to advance up the economic ladder. He now owned a successful insurance business. For years he had worked long hours and almost every weekend. Work had, in fact, been almost his entire life. Now that he was older and could take time off he had no other interests—his business remained the center of his life. He was a proud, self-confident man who had reached his goal. He met people on his own terms; he was aggressive and forcible, likable but quick to anger. He was looking forward to Ron's taking over his business, for it was important to him to leave to his son something to show his own worth.

Ron's mother was in many ways typical of the "old fashioned" wife. Her life was centered in her home. She cared for Ron and for the house, respected her husband, and took abuse from him without complaint. She had married at an early age. With her husband she had struggled through the Depression and the hard times when he was starting his business; finally they had achieved many of the material rewards so long out of their reach. Although she admired her husband for his drive, energy, and productiveness, she also felt that something had been missing from her marriage. The emotional closeness that she had always hoped for had not been met. Sometimes she had found herself thinking about leaving her husband and finding a new life. But she had put such thoughts out of her mind because it would be wrong to leave; in fact, it was wrong even to think of it. It was against her religious values and her upbringing.

When Ron, her only child, was born, her whole life had changed. He had become the center of her activities, an outlet for her affections. She believed that she and her son had a wonderful relationship—she cared for him, and in turn he loved her deeply. It had often crossed her mind as Ron was growing up that he ought to mix more with other children, but she had quieted her concern by telling herself that there was no reason for him to put up with nasty children who hit him or took his toys. She decided that it was better for her to show him only happiness, to protect him from a world that she knew could be cruel. At present, however, she was confused, for Ron had changed. He didn't seem to like being with her and even made remarks that hurt her feelings. She wondered why he did not live at home with her where he really belonged—for she wanted only to look after his best interests as she had always done. She thought the problem might be that he did not have a girl friend. It was certainly time that he married and brought home some grandchildren. She had been disappointed that he had not liked her friend's daughter, from such a nice family, with solid ideas *and* financially sound. She had resolved to look around some more.

Ron remembered little of his childhood, but he knew that it had been safe, pleasant, and full of affection from his mother. His father, however, had always been an ambiguous figure. He had always been at work. Ron remembered arguments between his parents about money and how difficult things were, yet his mother had always seemed able to find something for him to enjoy. He had never felt deprived. The one thing about his father that was clear was that he expected Ron to do well—to make something of himself. His father had always wanted to be proud of him, and Ron wanted to do what he could to fulfill his expectations.

Ron recalled that his mother had rarely been angry with him. She had always been a source of comfort except when she had caught him playing with his sex organs. It had felt good, but it had upset her a great deal. She had called him "bad" and "dirty" and had spanked him with strong admonitions never to do it again. He had not understood why so pleasant a thing should be so bad, but as long as he did not do it, at least while his mother was around, she was warm and affectionate toward him. He remembered how interested he and a neighbor girl had been in each other's bodies. They had been only five years old, and the differences between them had been intriguing. He had always been afraid that his mother might find them, but it had seemed worth the risk. They had once played a game of "peep show." Mary had gone into the closet, taken off her clothes, then slid open the door for him to see. When his turn had come he had been afraid and had experienced shame of his body for the first time. He remembered being unable to face Mary when he had opened the door. He stood with his back to her. It seemed to him now that he had never been comfortable with his body, especially his sex organs.

Ron had looked forward to school, but when he had been left alone with all those strange children he had felt afraid. He had not known many children before, and he did not know what to do about these aggressive strangers. He had not been a particularly strong child, and he had usually ended up losing arguments and fights. He recalled how fortunate it had seemed that his teacher had been so much like his mother. She had recognized how he felt and had helped him until he had been able to understand the other children better. He had eventually begun to enjoy their company. He had done his school work to please his teacher and to receive praise from his parents. He had not been the top student, but he had always done as well as most.

Even under these circumstances it had looked as if things were going to work out fairly well until he had become ill with rheumatic fever when he was eight, a disease that could have affected his heart. He had felt very bad for months—feverish, weak, and unable to do much. His mother had cared for him, had made sure that he did not overwork and had probably prevented serious damage to his young body. When he had returned to school, however, he had not been allowed to participate in most of the children's games, which were much too strenuous for his weakened condition.

Ron had thus become a loner at an early age. He had always gone straight home after school, for things had been comfortable there. His mother would keep him occupied whenever he felt lonely. The other children did not dislike him and allowed him to play when he wished, but he felt that he should not, that the exertion might bring back his illness. It was a long time before he had realized that his illness was over and that he would not suffer a relapse if he entered into normal activities. The doctor had pronounced him cured. There was no damage to his heart, and he was able to live a normal life. Still, he had not entered into many school activities. Often he had wanted to participate but was not comfortable around the other children. By the time that Ron had reached early adolescence he still had few friends. Although his peers had not disliked him, he had simply been more comfortable by himself.

Ron had not changed much during his adolescence. The other kids had formed groups, followed fads, and become interested in girls. But he had remained on the sidelines—not shut out but afraid of being let in. Something had happened to him about that time. Accompanying his physical growth were strong sexual urges. He had rediscovered the pleasure of masturbation and pleasant sensations associated with ejaculation. But he had always been ashamed afterward. His parents had never discussed sexual matters with him. He had learned about them slowly by reading in secret, and once in a while he had overheard the other boys' talk.

Girls had seemed to frighten him; he had stayed clear. It was not that they had ignored him, for he had been a good-looking boy. But he had been uncomfortable in relating to them. He remembered that his parents had been concerned about his apparent lack of interest in girls and how easy they had made it for him to go out with the daughter of one of their friends. They had given him the family car and money to take her to dinner and dancing. Ron had liked her at first, but before long she had shown a stronger interest than he had been willing to tolerate. Whenever they were physically close he would become ashamed of feeling sexually aroused. Consequently he had withdrawn from the relationship.

Ron had finished high school and had entered junior college. He had not been sure what he wanted to do, but it had not seemed too important at the time. He had had a number of basic requirements to complete before deciding on a major, and he had been doing well in college until, one night when he was in bed, he had overheard his parents having sexual relations. He had been so disturbed about it that he had joined the army the next day. He had not completely understood his own behavior, but he had felt that if they could have their pleasure he ought to be able to also. It might happen if he left home.

Ron's period in the army had been satisfying. Many of his fellow soldiers had complained about the life and the restrictions placed on them, but to Ron it had been comforting to know just where he stood, where he belonged, and what he was to do. He had even become friends with some of the men in his company. For the first time he had experienced friendships that were not full of tension and insecurity. He knew that wanting to wear the uniform was not "the thing," but secretly he had liked it. It had given him a feeling of belonging to something, of having some purpose in life, a feeling that he had never really experienced before. He had also liked his work. He had been assigned to an office where he had done detailed work and had rarely had to interact with other people. He had been good at it, had worked hard, and had learned the job well.

When his hitch was up, Ron had left the army somewhat reluctantly, but he had felt that there were other things for him to do. He had decided to return to school and to make something of himself. He had moved back home and had picked up his studies where he had left off; he had started doing fairly well. He had also found that he was able to get along better with people his own age than he had been before.

A combination of circumstances had, however, caused him to quit college. He had been doing very poorly in one course and had dreaded the thought of receiving a low grade. At the same time his father had been urging him to help in the business so that eventually he could take it over. Ron had decided that he should; he had told himself that he wanted to. He had studied diligently to learn the business; in fact, he had become more proficient in the details of policy writing than his father was. But he felt that something was lacking, and he was not truly satisfied. He had the nagging feeling that he was not becoming independent, that he was still being taken care of by his parents.

There were also problems with his job. The work he did was satisfactory, but he was not nearly as good at the sales aspects of the business as he wished. He became very anxious when he made business contacts; he rarely felt adequate in this important function. He was also threatened by his father's talk of retiring and turning the business over to him; he really did not feel that he could handle it. He blamed his father for not having trained him properly, for not having taught him what he needed to know to run the business. After a year he had been very dissatisfied and dejected to the point that he had faced his father with his feelings. He had told him that he wanted to quit, to go back to school, and to find something for himself. But his father had not seemed to hear him. The issue had been resolved by making him a full partner so that he would feel that the business was his as well; the solution had satisfied Ron at first. He had worked for almost another year before again becoming dejected and upset; again he was on the verge of confronting his father. It was then that he had revealed some of his difficulties to his friend, who had then suggested that he seek help.

It has been more than a year since Ron decided that he had to change and consulted a psychologist. It has not been easy to convince his father that he has different needs, that he is neither fit for nor satisfied with the type of work that his father does. He has entered training in electronics, is enjoying it, and has found a new job that is pleasant and interesting. He gets along with the people at work, but there is no pressure to sell to them or to depend upon his interpersonal skills for success. He is rather surprised to find that he is more comfortable when he goes to parties. He does not feel that he has to say anything to keep things going. He recognizes that other people like him, even though he is not outspoken and entertaining. He is a serious young man with serious thoughts, and others respect him for it. Perhaps it would always have been that way had he given others a chance. Of course, he still feels uncomfortable at times, and some of the old tensions occasionally return.

There has also been a change in his feelings toward women. Some of the old fear is still there, but he no longer has to run from closeness. Nor does he look on sexual matters as frightening and bad. Although he still has difficulties, he is no longer ashamed of experiencing warmth with his girl—he now has a girl. They have not engaged in sexual intercourse but have become intimate and have explored each other to some degree. They have discussed their feelings about sex, and Ron has been able to explain how it used to be for him. To his surprise he found that his girl has also had misgivings. They have been much more comfortable with each other after having opened up. Ron's future now holds real possibilities. Perhaps he and his girl will be married; they have discussed the matter and it seems possible. They enjoy each other's company and share many of the same values. Ron is a bit surprised to find that a woman can also be a person, that she has feelings as he does, that she also has difficulties, and that she is willing to share them with him.

Ron is even beginning to find some satisfaction in his religious beliefs. Religion is not the same to him as it was when he was younger. He is no longer awe-stricken and fearful of punishment. Now he thinks about the larger meanings of things. Nor is he completely satisfied with society. There appear to be many failures and hypocrisies and they disturb him, but he realizes that other people also have their beliefs about how things should be and that they do not always agree with his own. He does what he can to help the political party that he feels best represents his views.

Ron has changed. Often he thinks of his therapist and wants to thank him for his help, but the important change in Ron has been the assumption of responsibility for his own life, for seeing himself as he really is and doing something about his wishes. His parents are still important to him, but he has come to see them as two other individuals with their own lives. His life is in most ways separate from theirs. His relationships with them have grown closer now. His father is disappointed, but he is getting over it.

Ron still wonders about his future: where he's going, what he will become, and how much he will accomplish. The difference is that now he feels a sense of confidence that he can make satisfactory choices about his life.

ADJUSTMENT AS RELATEDNESS

What can Ron's life teach us about adjustment? If his experiences are an example of personal adjustment, one thing is clear: Adjustment is a *personal* matter. Every individual makes a unique adjustment, and every individual has unique ways of adjusting. No two people have exactly the same experiences in life, nor do they have exactly the same capacities for meeting their experiences.

In a general way personal adjustment is the process by which an individual applies his resources to fulfill his personal needs while at the same time maintaining harmony with his environment. Optimal adjustment may be described in terms like "self-actualization" and achieving the "whole self" or the "unitary personality." At the other end of the spectrum are severe disturbances in adjustment, labeled "mental illness." An individual must adjust simply because he is alive. Forces acting upon him require him to change; he must deal with them with whatever capacities are available to him. These forces originate in his biological needs, other people, and his cultural milieu. The same demands may be pleasurable to one person and obnoxious to another. For example, many find demands for closeness from the opposite sex rewarding, but Ron found them frightening.

Some pressures to adjust arise from outside: from disasters, wars, poverty, bigotry. Others result from choices of occupational, parental, or religious roles. Life is a continuous interplay of such forces, many of which we create ourselves, and many of which we do not; but, regardless of their sources, they demand responses from us.

The question of what is "good" and what is "bad" adjustment inevitably arises: We like to evaluate behavior. But first we must agree on the nature of adjustment and establish criteria for judging specific kinds of behavior or general categories of conduct. It seems easy, for instance, to agree that human suffering is "bad." But what if Christ had not suffered? Or Martin Luther? Perhaps their suffering created the necessary motivation to pursue their beliefs. In the United States and most Western societies striving for financial success is positively valued. The man who lacks ambition and always takes the "easy way" may be little respected by others, even though he seems satisfied with his life. It is not easy to judge a person simply by his behavior, even when it directly contradicts cherished values. Judgment depends upon its frame of reference; when an observer receives more information about a person, he may change his judgment.

Societies set explicit rules (laws) for the behavior that their members may not exhibit without punishment. Still, an individual can choose to break the law and take his chances or to try to change it through procedures established for that purpose. There are limits to the amount of permissible social deviance before a person is segregated from society. Depending upon the nature of his behavior, the individual may be classified as "criminal" or "mentally ill," but in either instance he is separated from the mainstream of society, presumably so that his behavior will not interfere with the lives of others. The question of conformity arises in relation to deviant behavior. To what degree must a person abide by, or conform to, social constraints? When is he judged "bad," and when is he judged "good"? I prefer to treat adjustment separately from moral attitudes. Deciding what value to place on adjusting behavior is the personal responsibility of each individual.

I have chosen to treat adjustment as a process by which the individual responds to certain aspects of life. This view of adjustment is, however, not self-contained. It draws heavily on the existential view of man, which is described in detail in Chapter 6. This combined approach emphasizes the individualism of each man while recognizing that he must deal with the world as he views it from several vantage points. The process of attending to and dealing with the world is defined here as "relating" to the world. Although several types of relating will be described separately here for the sake of clarity, they are all intertwined in reality to shape one organized (or disorganized) personality. Those that are important for personal adjustment involve relations with one's inner workings (self-relatedness), other people (interpersonal relatedness), and the social milieu (cultural relatedness).

This view of adjustment represents an attempt to remain neutral about moral judgments on specific conduct. It also denies the notion of adjustment as mere conformity; adjustment is an active process of coping with the demands of life.

SELF-RELATEDNESS

It is common to speak of one's relationship with himself as his identity—the I or the me, as perceived by the individual. In general, clearer perception of one's self permits greater flexibility in adjustment. Ron's struggles and changes reflected increased acceptance and unification of demands from within himself. An important aspect of personal adjustment is dealing with such demands.

BIOLOGICAL DEMANDS

Biological functioning is an important source of internal demands. One group of demands arises from the necessities of survival: hunger, thirst, and the needs for oxygen, elimination, and physical safety. The products needed to meet these needs (food, shelter, protection) are provided largely through man's social organizations; they become of prime importance mainly when they cannot readily be satisfied. Starving people turn most of their energies to seeking food, a drowning man exerts all his energy fighting for air, and so forth. In times of war or catastrophe, when normal social systems are ineffective, survival demands are likely to tax capacity for adjustment. Ron, however, was little concerned with survival demands. His adjustment to them had been relatively simple because of his status in our social system. Survival demands occupy a more important place in the adjustment of individuals at lower economic levels.

Other demands arise from the necessity for procreation of the species— the "sex drive." Man's adjustment to his sexuality is further complicated by social and cultural inhibitors of free expression and therefore often reflects more prominent demands than simply biological ones. Ron was greatly concerned about sex. Like so many others he was struggling to find a satisfactory release for his sexual tension. Sexual adjustment was very important to him.

Society places many constraints on sexual behavior. Individuals must often seek compromises between their sexual needs and social values that are variable or inconsistent. For example, at one period of life sexual abstinence may be part of adjustment, but almost overnight, through the legal sanction of marriage, a person may be expected to enter into sexual experiences freely and openly.

PHYSICAL APPEARANCE

An individual's physical appearance creates demands. His body image may be an asset or a liability, depending upon cultural and subcultural criteria of beauty. Physical appearance is no small matter to many people, especially during adolescence and early adulthood. Its importance in the United States is reflected in the development of a huge cosmetics industry. Almost any part of the body may now be changed to conform with social definitions of physical beauty. In the 1920s women bound their breasts flat; more recently they wore uplift bras to make their breasts seem full. The adjustment to one's body may thus include changing it in prescribed ways to please others, but it may also include accepting one's appearance as it is.

Heavy demands may be made upon an individual whose physical appearance is regarded as extreme—either deformed or beautiful. Other people's responses to him may be determined primarily by his physical characteristics. At first glance, Ron's physical appearance did not seem to be a major factor in his adjustment. His appearance was acceptable and even attractive to many girls. But a girl's attraction to him raised difficulties by arousing sexual demands, and his attractiveness thus may have intensified his disturbance associated with sexual arousal. Also, although Ron's childhood illness had left no outwardly noticeable signs, his response to it had made other adjustments more difficult.

INTELLECTUAL AND PHYSICAL ABILITIES

Everyone must adjust to his own unique intellectual and physical capacities. Although they can often be used to the fullest, they impose limitations as well. Some abilities that are evaluated positively by others may not facilitate personal adjustment. A boy with high athletic ability may, for example, find himself continually encouraged by others in sports activities. If he prefers to pursue intellectual goals he may have to struggle against pressures directing him toward sports. Individual abilities, however they are judged by others, are thus frequently sources of adjustment demands. Ron's intellectual and physical abilities presented such demands. He had had to adjust to a physical disability that had prevented him from participating in certain activities with his peers. He had also tended to deny personal characteristics and intellectual capacities that reduced his chances of success in his father's business. He was thus prevented from realistically evaluating his own personal attributes that were more suitable for other occupations.

VALUES AND BELIEFS

Other internal demands arise from value and belief systems, one's own acceptance of the "rights" and "wrongs" dictated by society. Values and beliefs are originally learned from people important to the individual during the process of learning a culture (enculturation). Although they result in outside demands (usually parental), they often become internalized. They may then conflict with other demands and call for adjustment. Several internalized demands were creating difficulties for Ron. His values connected with sexual behavior, his attitude toward occupational roles, and his religious beliefs all led to internal conflict. His adjustment was not successful from his own point of view, and he frequently found himself torn among a series of unappealing choices.

Most values are internalized during childhood, when they may serve as positive guides to adjustment. They may, however, become sources of stress in later life as personal roles and the world itself change. Searching for and defining one's personal values and beliefs is one of the primary tasks of late adolescence. Each generation experiences a new world, and old beliefs must often be discarded if the individual is to meet new circumstances satisfactorily.

INTERPERSONAL RELATEDNESS

Other people generate a number of demands for adjustment. Our dependence upon society requires interaction with others, and these interactions require adjustment maneuvers.

CASUAL RELATIONSHIPS

A great many human relationships are simply casual. Little involvement is required, and well-defined social roles afford guidelines for behavior. Buying an object from a clerk, for example, engenders few demands that are not readily fulfilled by customary social gestures. Dining in a restaurant, going to a movie, driving in traffic, and so on create demands that can easily be met; each culture provides fairly clear behavioral codes for such situations. Behavior considered appropriate in one culture may, however, be considered inappropriate in another. Loud belching after a meal is considered flattering in some Asian and African cultures, but in the United States it is impolite. American flyers forced down behind the lines in Europe during World War II were under extreme tension in interpersonal contacts because of cultural differences. The way that they held forks or cigarettes, for instance, might give them away to the enemy. Ron found casual relationships mildly disturbing. They were not of major importance in his adjustment, but they required more of his energy than is usual.

CONTINUING RELATIONSHIPS

The demands of continuing personal relationships are generally more important. They are characterized by greater emotional involvement, deep caring or love for others—friends, family, mate. Often they require a sharing of lives, give and take between two individuals. Trust, dependence, and open recognition of the other's feelings are required. The most common demands arise from conflicts between self-interest and the interests of the other person.

Prejudgment may play a role in the development of close relationships. Values and attitudes based on physical appearance, skin color, nationality, religion, and so on may hinder or encourage continuing relationships with certain other people. For instance, the individual who dislikes "all Roman Catholics" may close himself to a specific relationship before evaluating the possibility of emotional closeness. The object of prejudgment may be under permanent stress in all his close relationships. In our society the black person finds prejudgment a continual source of stress.

Ron's family relationships were a constant source of stress to him. Open-

ness or closeness with other people created excessive demands on his capacity for adjustment. Especially disturbing were the potential demands of a close relationship with a girl; turmoil and indecision characterized his heterosexual relationships.

Cultural Relatedness

Man is not the only organism to have developed an adaptive, integrated social system, but he has developed it the farthest. Modern man has essentially conquered the natural world; there are few areas in which he is not king.

Figure 1-1   The dilemma of man's technical advances. Reproduced by permission of Johnny Hart from *Pace Magazine*, April 1969, pp. 10–11.

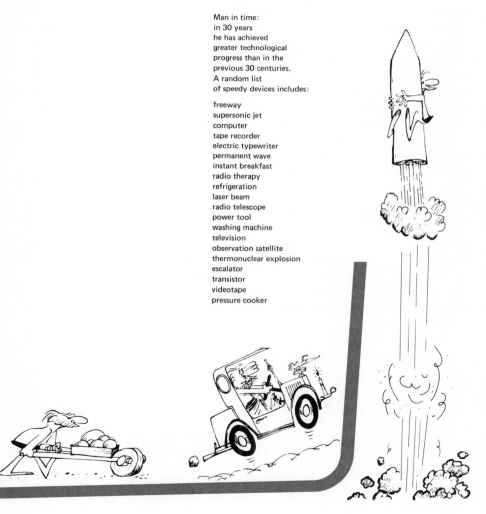

He has made huge strides in health, industrial technology, and financial systems. He has reached the nuclear age with its awesome source of energy potential. As he moves into outer space, the possibility of inhabiting other planets seems near. But man's accomplishment has been lopsided. Great advances in scientific technology and material gains have not been paralleled by advances in social structures and human relationships. Man deserves a "pat on the back" for what he has accomplished, but nevertheless starvation, war, and prejudice are still common, and total destruction of the world is more than a possibility. As Figure 1-1 shows, man currently seems confused and perhaps even frightened by his own successes.

SOCIAL CONSTRAINTS

Some demands for helping to maintain a viable social structure are placed on the individual. The group's "shalls" and "shall nots" take the form of laws, customs, manners, religious values, and other moral systems, all of which change slowly, so that they sometimes seem irrelevant to present times. Individuals find themselves having to choose between accepting constraint and the responsibility for change. Should laws, customs, and values that seem inappropriate be respected? Should one work within the framework of his particular political system to bring about change, or should he seek it in other ways? We are reminded of Patrick Henry's famous saying, "Give me liberty, or give me death!" and we shudder at the possible consequences of the same philosophy today. Deciding on war, on life or death, is no longer always an individual or even a group matter; the choice may affect the entire human race.

GROUP IDENTITIES

One way to meet cultural demands is to identify strongly with a group and to play down individual identity. The pressures to conform to social standards create demands that are frequently difficult to reconcile with personal desires. Ron found himself in a conflict between "respecting one's father" and "respecting one's self." Sexual morality caused him difficulties and he was also under pressure to reconcile social and religious values with his personal needs.

Social mores may work to one's advantage or disadvantage. Prejudices may benefit some people but create excessive demands on others. In our society it is an advantage in most social and vocational pursuits to have white skin.

ORGANIZATIONS AND GROUPS

Community organizations and social groups may also create demands. Although it was not emphasized in the above account, Ron found it necessary to belong to local service clubs for business reasons, even though he was uncomfortable at meetings. Social endeavors, whether for pleasure or vocational advancement, require adjustment from the individual. Even young children find themselves under pressure to belong to the "right" group. Nowhere else are these pressures clearer than in the peer relationships of adolescents, for whom social acceptability has prime importance.

DEFINITIONS OF NORMALITY

Scientists have found it exceedingly difficult to agree upon definitions of normality and the "normal" person. Many psychologists have put forth views, some of which have characteristics in common, and some of which are quite different. Examining some of these views will broaden our understanding of personal adjustment. It is likely that the reader has already himself applied some of the ideas that are described here, and it is probable that some combination of them offers the most realistic view of personal adjustment.

FREEDOM FROM SYMPTOMS

One view of normality has developed from a medical framework: If there is an abnormal, then there must be a normal; a person is normal if he does not show signs of mental illness. The primary criteria for this concept of normality are therefore negative—the attributes that a person does *not* show. In this view one of the clearest signs of normality is not being in a mental hospital; hospitalized patients are abnormal by definition. But at present the symptoms of "abnormality" can include almost any kind of conduct that deviates from general social expectations. Even trained people frequently disagree on whether or not specific symptoms are present. Consequently, classifications of mental illness and symptoms are inadequate criteria for judging normality.

Diagnosis of symptoms may also be based on inferences from observations of behavior in accordance with psychodynamic theories of personality. The same behaviors may, however, indicate different internal processes, some of which may suggest that things are amiss (abnormal) within the psychological system. An apparent unawareness of one's own behavior (unconscious motivation) is the primary criterion of abnormal behavior from this point of view.

Viewing normality as an absence of symptoms is most useful to professionals who limit their practices to severe disturbances. Clients of mental-health clinics or hospitals, for example, are usually not treated unless they can be labeled abnormal. Treatment of one who is not "sick" cannot be justified. Although this approach thus has an institutional function, it can hardly be considered adequate to describe a person who functions normally.

CULTURAL RELATIVISM

Anthropological studies have led to a conception of the normal person that is based on cultural role expectations. The meaning that a culture places on specific behaviors determines whether or not they are normal. Consequently a person may be considered abnormal in one culture but not in another. Vivid imaginings may, for instance, be called "visions" and valued highly in some cultures, but in our own they are usually called "hallucinations" and considered definite signs of mental illness. Even within our culture, however, some groups perceive "visions" as welcome, even divine events.

Similarly, some sociologists consider a person normal when he does not deviate from socially acceptable paths for achieving goals. Those who follow the social codes are defined as normal, whereas deviants are considered abnormal.

Cultural relativism is similar to the symptom approach in that negative criteria define normality. A person who does not show symptoms or deviance is considered normal. Critics of the cultural view believe that normal people do not necessarily accept cultural constraints; simple accommodation to society's standards does not seem to them a sufficient criterion for positive adjustment.

THE STATISTICAL APPROACH

Normality may be defined by the relative frequency with which specific characteristics or types of behavior occur. Normal intelligence, for example, is usually defined as the limits between which 50 percent of the population scores on an I.Q. test (90–110). Higher or lower scores are abnormal. The statistical definition of normality does not involve value judgments, but we are inclined to make them anyway. A high I.Q. is generally evaluated positively, for example, whereas a low I.Q. carries a negative evaluation. Psychological tests typically supply the frequency data used to judge the commonness or uncommonness of the trait being measured.

There are several problems connected with the use of statistics to define normality. First, the average (normal) is usually difficult to specify. What is a normal degree of aggression? There are many circumstances (competitive sports, business, war) that call for high degrees of aggression in successful adjustment. Socially determined roles call for different degrees of aggression; in our society males are usually expected to be more aggressive than are females. As a consequence, it is very difficult to find a sample on which to establish test norms. A second problem is determining how much deviation from the center to consider normal. Limits are arbitrary, and their primary use is in segregating extreme cases. A third problem is that "normal" may not be desirable. For example, individuals who fall within normal limits on all personality traits are generally considered bland, unresponsive, and boring.

IDEAL BEHAVIOR

Those who identify normality as the ideal stress the positive and creative aspects of man, the attributes of each individual and how he makes use of them as measured against an absolute standard. E. J. Shoben, Jr. (1957), for example, has said that behavior is healthy and positive when it reflects the unique attributes of humanity, which in his opinion include:

1. Ability to learn from one's own and others' experiences
2. Foresight and self-imposed discipline through anticipation of outcomes
3. Envisioning ideals and working for their fulfillment.

C. Rogers (1959) has taken a similar approach. He has listed ten values for the person who is continuously striving for self-actualization. As with most such lists the specific characteristics are put in the form of goals. It is rare, however, for an individual to fulfill these goals completely.

This approach, however, also presents difficulties. Each proponent constructs his own list of ideal characteristics. Even though a great deal of agreement can be found among different writers, value judgments are necessarily involved. In addition, all these definitions stress creativity and certain other positive behaviors to the point at which they cannot possibly be experienced by most flesh-and-blood individuals.

CONCLUSIONS

We have seen that it is not simple to arrive at a satisfactory definition of adjustment or normality. My preference is for definitions that reflect the complexity of activity involved in dealing with life and do not involve value judgments of behavior, such as the idea of "adjustment as relatedness" presented earlier.

It seems important that the student recognize the diversity of opinions on these issues and the impossibility of determining once and for all whether or not his or others' conduct is normal. Evaluating oneself and others is certainly an integral part of living, but it is helpful to be aware that judgments are often biased by one's own system of beliefs and values. It should be clear from this chapter that "normal" and "abnormal" are concepts that lack scientific verification. All too often conduct that deviates from an established set of social values is labeled "abnormal." Such labeling tends to dismiss legitimate social complaints and personal differences in the guise of scientific objectivity.

SUMMARY

In this chapter we have examined the concept of adjustment as a process occurring between the individual and various aspects of his world. As a point of departure we took a particular person's adjustment problems and their solutions. The problems that Ron faced and his approach to them illustrated some major aspects of personal adjustment. The study of Ron's life led us to a neutral conceptual scheme for examining adjustment. The adjusting individual is a person who is faced with the problems of relating to himself, to others, and to his culture.

We next examined the ways in which scientists have defined normality, a concept closely related, if not identical, to adjustment. The normal person has been variously viewed as one who is free from symptoms, who conforms to social and cultural roles, who does not deviate significantly from a statistical mean, and who maximizes his own potentials. Each definition has its uses and limitations in the understanding of human behavior.

2

A. General Effects of Inheritance on Adjustment
  1. Physical characteristics
  2. Autonomic reactivity
  3. Energy level
B. Constitutional Theory
  1. Precursors
  2. Somatotypes and measurement
  3. Personality types
  4. Studies and interpretation
C. The Nature-Nurture Problem
  1. Methods of study
  2. The question of intelligence
  3. Final observations
D. Specific Genetic Effects on Adjustment
  1. Mongolism
  2. Phenylketonuria
E. Summary

Processes of Adjustment: The Role of Inheritance

Except for identical twins, it is extremely unlikely that two individuals will begin life with the same genetic background. Genetic factors vary widely and are further modified by interaction with the environment. The combination of individual inheritance and the multifaceted nature of environment means that from the beginning the conditions of each person's adjustment are unique.

The male and female reproductive cells divide to form sperm and eggs, respectively; each sperm or egg contains twenty-three chromosomes. When the sperm and egg cells unite, the chromosomes from each join to form a cell with twenty-three pairs of chromosomes. The growth of a new individual begins as this cell starts reproducing itself.

Each chromosome is composed of genes, each of which determines specific characteristics. As there are probably at least 1,000 genes in each chromosome, it is highly unlikely that two human beings will be born with exactly the same combinations of genes, even though they may have the same parents. Identical twins develop from one fertilized egg that has subsequently divided into two, which accounts for their genetic similarity. Fraternal twins develop from two eggs that happen to be fertilized at the same time; their inheritance is no more nearly identical than is that of ordinary siblings.

The male has a slight disadvantage in heredity because of the nature of the chromosomes that determine sex. The female has two rather large X chromosomes which determine her sexual characteristics. The male, however, has only one X chromosome and a smaller Y chromosome, containing fewer genes. In the female the undesirable effects of any defective genes in one X chromosome may be counteracted by normal genes in the other X chromosome. In the male, however, the defective gene may dominate simply because the Y chromosome has no corresponding gene. Such disorders as hemophilia (bleeding), colorblindness, and baldness in males result from defects in the sex-determining chromosomes. They are much less likely to occur in females because both parents would have to have the same disorder before a female could inherit it. A female may, however, be a "carrier." If both a girl's parents lack the defect, it is impossible for her to have it. If her father has it but her mother is not a carrier, she cannot inherit it because the one normal X chromosome from her mother dominates. If her mother is a carrier and her father has the defect, she still has only a fifty-fifty chance of inheriting the defect because the X chromosome that she receives from her mother may be either the one carrying it or the one without it. A male child whose mother is a carrier has the same fifty-fifty chance of inheriting the defect, regardless of his father's condition. He will inevitably inherit the defect if his mother has it. The male who receives a defective gene will always be born with the disorder.

Recent genetic research has demonstrated that each gene consists of molecules of deoxyribonucleic acid (DNA), which carry specific genetic "instructions." When DNA molecules undergo spontaneous changes or changes caused by external forces, the gene is said to have *mutated*. Mutations generally produce undesirable characteristics, including a wide variety of hereditary diseases, congenital malformations, and constitutional weaknesses. Ionizing radiation from nuclear-weapons tests increases the chances of mutation, as does exposure to X rays. Figure 2-1 is a diagram of the DNA molecule,

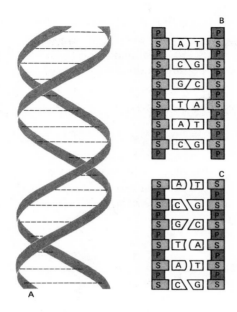

Figure 2-1 Breaking the genetic code. The DNA molecule is a helix, a spiral that looks like a coiled ladder (A). The sides of this "ladder" are chains of alternating sugar and phosphate; the rungs are formed between the sugar groups by combinations of four basic control chemicals—adenine, thymine, guanine, and cytosine— a given rung being formed by a pair of these chemicals (adenine-thymine, thymine-adenine, cytosine-guanine, or guanine-cytosine). It is in the sequence of these rungs (B) that the specific hereditary instructions of the growing organism are encoded. DNA molecules are present not only in germ cells but in the nucleus of every living cell. Each living thing resembles the stock from which it descended because of the DNA which it inherits. . . .

The instructions of the DNA make provision for two main functions—the reproduction of itself, by making exact copies, and the direction of the metabolic activities in each cell, including the building of proteins. Both processes start with a splitting apart of the two halves of the helix (C). To replicate itself, each half then picks up appropriate loose nucleotides available near it until two complete helixes are formed.

To direct metabolic activities in the cell, an intermediary chemical [ribonucleic acid or RNA] is made by the DNA in the nucleus of the cell and sent to various sites in the cell with specific instructions. . . .

If any detail of the DNA instructions is missing or garbled . . . the human organism may be in for trouble. For example, people become ill and die with inherited sickle-cell anemia, in which a single amino acid is wrong out of the 574 that make up a hemoglobin molecule of the blood.

Identifying the exact nature of the communication between the DNA and RNA and between the RNA and the sequence of amino acids manufactured in the cell is known as the "coding problem." Once this genetic code is broken, it will be potentially possible for man either to correct the faulty DNA ladder itself or to bypass the faulty DNA instructions by modifying the RNA, thus giving the cell the correct instructions for normal growth and functioning.

Diagrams from T. M. Sonnenborn, "The New Genetics," *Science & Technology,* 1, no. 9 (1962); reproduced by permission of International Communications, Inc. Text from *Abnormal Psychology and Modern Life,* 3rd Edition, by James C. Coleman, p. 118; copyright © 1964 by Scott, Foresman and Company.

suggesting its potential role in human adjustment once sufficient knowledge has been gathered to permit modification of gene structure.

GENERAL EFFECTS OF INHERITANCE ON ADJUSTMENT

Human characteristics determined by inherited chemical and physiological materials interact with the environment and therefore contribute to deciding the direction of adjustment. As will be pointed out below, the specific effects on the individual will be determined by the nature of his environment, the nature of his biological characteristics, and the interplay between the two.

PHYSICAL CHARACTERISTICS

A person's external characteristics, like physique, height, hair color, and so on, are generally considered to have aesthetic qualities. The individual who inherits physical characteristics associated with his culture's idea of beauty probably will find adjustment simpler, at least early in life. Many of his needs and desires will be more readily met, especially in social circumstances. It is also true, however, that great beauty may isolate him from his fellows or create social pressures directing his behavior into roles that he would not otherwise choose. It is possible that the "handsome" or "pretty" individual will come to overvalue his physical appearance and to ignore aspects of his personality that take on increasing importance as he grows older. We can see this effect in the former movie star who "lives in the past." Nevertheless "ugliness" is usually most distressing to an individual. The unattractive person may be forced to forgo some of his wishes and to compensate by striving toward other goals.

Physical strength and stature may also help to determine the direction of one's adjustment. Short men, for instance, appear to live in a somewhat different world from that of tall men. Shortness may generate feelings of inferiority or a compensating aggressiveness, detracting from a person's ability either to see himself clearly or to act realistically to obtain his desires. Extreme physical malformations may directly affect a person's success in many occupational and social roles and may thus present major problems in adjustment.

AUTONOMIC REACTIVITY

The autonomic nervous system is important in emotional responsiveness. It activates such internal organs as the heart, lungs, gastrointestinal tract, and some glands. Inherited differences in autonomic reactivity may affect adjustment; either an excess or a deficiency can lead to difficulties.

A child's inherited constitution may have no small part in influencing his adjustment. If his autonomic system is highly responsive he is more likely to experience physiological responses he perceives as fear in situations that other children take in stride. Thus, his chances are greater than the less responsive child's to develop conditioned fears or anxieties, which are quite resistant to change. And, his behavior patterns will often be determined by these learned anxieties (Eysenck, 1960). Opposite reactions may occur in children whose autonomic responsiveness is low. They are likely to suffer from too little conditioned learning, and the degree to which they develop socialized conduct may thus be low. They may seem to lack inner controls and may develop antisocial behavior patterns because they have not learned to be wary of responses unacceptable by social standards. It should be pointed out, of course, that other learning can modify the specific outcome for a particular child.

ENERGY LEVEL

An individual's energy level is believed to be determined by his genetic constitution. An energetic person is more likely to require ways of dissipating his energy than is a less energetic person. He is more likely to discharge energy through neuromuscular activity, and under stress he may develop aggressive, escapist, or delinquent behavior patterns. It is at least likely that his interests will turn toward physical activities. A less energetic person tends to discharge energy through fantasy and thought. He may "internalize" his reactions to stress and develop physical (psychosomatic) symptoms.

CONSTITUTIONAL THEORY

PRECURSORS

There have been many attempts to relate inherited physical characteristics and personality traits. In the 1800s the phrenologists attempted to prove that the shape of the skull can be used as an indicator of character traits and attitudes. Their basic hypothesis was that specific areas of the brain control specific personality traits like secretiveness, benevolence, and acquisitiveness. Second, they argued that the skull grows in conformity with the shape of the brain. They believed, therefore, that, by examining the skull, one can find the overdeveloped and underdeveloped portions of the brain. A person's dominant characteristics will be shown by the "bumps" and his weak traits by the "depressions." From the study of famous men and individuals with marked personality traits, the phrenologists developed a schema of specific brain areas controlling the traits. Presumably, by mapping a person's skull they could describe his personality and even offer advice based on his strong and weak traits.

Although phrenology has never received scientific validation it still has followers, as do other theories based on similar hypotheses. The usual procedure of these practitioners is to map the skull, the face, or some other body part, depending upon their specific notions, and then to describe the subject's personality, often including advice on personal or financial undertakings.

A somewhat similar approach is based on the shape of the body. E.

Kretschmer (1925), a psychiatrist, described four body types and related them to categories of mental illness: asthenic (frail, linear physique), athletic (broad-shouldered, strong, slim trunk), pyknic (fat stomach, round body), and dysplastic (striking deviance, rare, surprising, and ugly). By comparing mental patients with their body types he concluded that the asthenic tended to be schizophrenic and the pyknic to be manic-depressive. His methods were not particularly sound or reliable, but they furnished a background for W. H. Sheldon's more detailed and rigorous theory of personality based on body types.

SOMATOTYPES AND MEASUREMENT

Sheldon (1940, 1942, 1954) based his theory on the postulates that heredity is important in determining personality and that personality traits are reflected in physique. His first step was to develop a reliable way to classify physiques, the *somatotypes*. After studies of many individuals he and his coworkers decided that three dimensions were primary in describing a person's somatotype. Each dimension corresponds to the degree to which the three primary tissue layers in the human embryo are proportionately represented in a person's body. Each primary layer develops into specific body parts (see below). Sheldon's body types are labeled according to the tissue layer most highly developed in a person's physique. Thus, comparatively high development of the endoderm is noted by calling the body type endomorphic.

Embryonic Tissue Layer

Endoderm
  (develops into visceral organs and
  fatty tissue)

Mesoderm
  (develops into bone and muscle)

Ectoderm
  (develops into skin and nervous
  system)

Body Type

Endomorphic
  (soft, round)

Mesomorphic
  (strong, angular, muscular)

Ectomorphic
  (slender, fragile)

Sheldon's research team next developed seven-point scales for each of the components. A subject is rated on the degrees of his endomorphy, mesomorphy, and ectomorphy; the result is expressed in a code of three numbers. For example, a subject who is extremely soft, round, and obese (a typical endomorph) might receive a rating of 7 on endomorphy, a rating of 1 (1 being the lowest rating) on mesomorphy, and a rating of 1 on ectomorphy. His somatotype would then be coded 7-1-1. Sheldon has compiled an atlas of somatotypes, in which norms of age, weight, and height are shown in photographs. The examples of persons rated at various ages and so forth help take into account the normal changes in body proportion associated with aging. Given the use of this atlas and proper training, psychologists find that rater agreement is quite high (reliable).

PERSONALITY TYPES

Sheldon's next step was to establish personality types that would correlate with the somatotypes. Beginning with 650 trait descriptions, he and his coworkers reduced them to three clusters of twenty traits each. Those in each cluster were highly interrelated statistically but only weakly related to traits in the other two clusters, thereby establishing three independent traits. Three personality types resulted:

1. *Viscerotonia* is characterized by love of comfort; sociability; gluttony for food, people, and affection; even temper; slow reactions; relaxed posture; and easy relations with others.
2. *Somatotonia* is characterized by love of physical adventure and risk taking; aggression; callousness toward others' feelings; and emphasis on action, power, and dominance.
3. *Cerebrotonia* is characterized by restraint; inhibitions; secretiveness; self-consciousness; very fast reactions; difficulty in sleeping; and preference for solitude.

Once reliable measures of these personality types had been discovered, comparisons of subjects' somatotypes and personality types could be made.

STUDIES AND INTERPRETATION

Sheldon studied 200 college males over a five-year period and found surprisingly high correlations between somatotype and personality type. Each primary somatotype was strongly related to one of the personality types and weakly related to the other two. Endomorphy was related to viscerotonia, mesomorphy to somatotonia, and ectomorphy to cerebrotonia.

The correlations are striking in their magnitude; they are much higher than those in most studies attempting to relate personality characteristics to environmental or other experiential determinants. But other researchers have not always been able to verify Sheldon's findings.

Sheldon has preferred to interpret his results as showing that personality traits are genetically linked to body development. Heredity, glandular functioning, and various early environmental experiences might then account for later personality development.

There are at least two alternative explanations that are equally compelling, however. First is the possibility that physique may be primary in determining the kinds of behavior that are reinforced and are consequently incorporated into personality. An individual endowed with particular physical characteristics is likely to find certain kinds of responses especially effective, whereas a person with a different physique will not. Effective responses are retained and ineffective ones eliminated. A frail child, for example, is likely to find aggression unrewarding, whereas his stronger, more athletic friend will find it rewarding very often. Learning experiences may themselves result from physique in that the latter partially determines what behavior patterns are most adaptive. A second explanation involves cultural role expectations associated with specific physiques. Most cultures have stereotyped expectations for different body types. Fat people, for example, are expected to be jolly, to love food, and so on. The endomorph is therefore likely to exhibit such behavior in order to meet the expectations of those around him. A thin, frail child is often expected to be intellectual, withdrawn, and uninterested in physical activities. Again he will tend to live up to the expectations of those around him. Although Sheldon's results are provocative, a satisfactory explanation of their cause is still to be found.

THE NATURE-NURTURE PROBLEM

One classical conflict in psychology has been that between the "geneticists" and the "environmentalists." The basic issue is the comparative effects of heredity and environment on the development of human characteristics. The development of behavioral genetics, the study of the relation of genetic background to behavioral expression, has brought some pooling of effort; conflict is giving way to concerted attempts to grasp the complexities of human behavior. It is now widely agreed that all human characteristics are influenced to some degree by both environment and genetic background. Rather than asking which is causal, scientists now ask to what extent each plays a part. To answer this question it is necessary to develop methods for experimental control of either the subjects' environments or their genetic composition.

METHODS OF STUDY

THE PEDIGREE METHOD

The *pedigree method,* or *family biography,* was one of the earliest approaches. The history of the generations of one family is traced as completely as possible, and the traits of each member are evaluated to determine whether or not they have been passed on. A frequently cited example was published by H. H. Goddard in 1912. He traced the history of a family, to which he gave the pseudonym Kallikak, and found evidence that feeble-mindedness is inherited. He thought that his study included a control sample because two lines of descent had originated with Martin Kallikak, one through an illegitimate son whom he had sired on a feeble-minded girl, the other through his children by his wife, who had no apparent abnormality. Four hundred and eighty descendants of the feeble-minded mother were studied. Only forty-six of them are definitely known to have been normal; the rest exhibited various kinds of social behavior and signs of low intellect thought to be associated with mental retardedness. Goddard traced 496 descendants of the other branch of the family; 491 were considered normal, and many had been economically or professionally successful.

The obvious weakness in the pedigree method is the lack of control over environmental influences. For example, although Goddard thought he had two groups who differed only in genetic characteristics, their environments cannot be considered equal. The children raised in the environment of the feeble-minded mother are likely to have experienced poverty, antisocial behavioral models, and all the stresses associated with such an environment. On the other hand, the "normal" branch was raised in the middle class and enjoyed higher socioeconomic standards, including emphasis on positive social behavior. It cannot now be determined whether the traits and behavior of Kallikak's descendants resulted from different environmental circumstances or from their genetic backgrounds.

More recently there have been attempts to control the environment by examining the correlations between specific traits at different levels of genetic similarity. For example, the intelligence scores of children may be compared with the intelligence scores of both natural and foster parents. If the correlation between the intelligence of real parents and of their children is higher than that between the intelligence of foster parents and of their children, the hereditary nature of intelligence is demonstrated.

TABLE 2-1   SIBLING METHOD OF COMPARING EFFECTS OF HEREDITY AND ENVIRONMENT

	Heredity	Environment	Evidence for Heredity (Example 1)	Evidence for Environment (Example 2)
Identical twins	Same	Same	.80	.60
Fraternal twins	Different	Same	.40	.60
Other siblings	Different	Different	.40	.30

THE SIBLING METHOD

A more systematic approach is shown in Table 2-1. The scores of siblings with different genetic relationships on particular traits are correlated to establish the relative effects of inheritance and environment; this approach is called the *sibling method*. The table shows that identical twins have the same heredity and presumably the same environment; that is, they develop from one egg and are raised together. The heredity of fraternal twins (two eggs) is no more similar than is that of other siblings, but their environment is assumed to be the same because they are raised together. Finally, siblings of different ages have both different heredity and different environments.

Two hypothetical examples will help to clarify the reasoning behind this design. If we assume that the correlations under Example 1 in the table represent comparisons of I.Q. scores, then they indicate how closely the various pairs of siblings scored on intelligence. Identical twins had a correlation of .80, which is quite high; fraternal twins had .40, and other siblings had .40. The higher correlations between the I.Q.s of identical twins indicate that heredity is more important than environment. Fraternal twins differed from other siblings only on the environmental dimension; their identical correlations indicate that environment had no effect on intelligence. The higher correlation for identical twins indicates that inheritance is important, therefore, the results in Example 1 lead to the conclusion that inheritance plays a large part in intelligence and environment very little.

Example 2 shows results suggesting that environment is critical in determining intellectual level. The comparison of identical and fraternal twins reveals no difference, suggesting that heredity is not important. But normal siblings had a considerably lower correlation, suggesting that the presumably shared environments of fraternal and identical twins may be the primary factor in the development of intelligence.

A similar approach, usually called the *concordance method*, involves comparing pairs of siblings according to whether or not both members show the same trait. The results have been interpreted in the same way as we have interpreted the examples in Table 2-1. For instance, F. J. Kallmann and B. Roth (1956) examined large numbers of identical twins, fraternal twins, and ordinary siblings to determine the percentage of times that one sibling could be diagnosed as schizophrenic when the other was known to have been diagnosed as schizophrenic. He concluded that this form of mental illness has a strong heredity component.

There are still difficulties in this experimental design. The environments of identical twins and fraternal twins are clearly not exactly the same. Identical twins probably have more similar environments than do fraternal twins because they are frequently dressed alike and so on. But they are also treated differently. One is often dominant, some people can tell them apart, and so forth. Fraternal twins have more different environments than do identical twins, though probably not as different as those of normal siblings. At any rate, it is not accurate to say that environmental conditions are adequately controlled by these methods, and the conclusions from these studies must be received with this reservation in mind.

COTWIN CONTROL

Another method is *cotwin control*. Identical twins raised apart are used as subjects in order to control the genetic factor, while environmental conditions vary. A sample of such identical twins is compared with a sample of identical twins who have been raised together. Differences between them must be attributed to dissimilar environments because heredity is controlled.

Again, we will turn to hypothetical findings to understand the reasoning behind this design. In Example 1 of Table 2-2 the same degree of relationship is shown for identical twins reared apart as for those reared together. Conse-

TABLE 2-2   COTWIN CONTROL METHOD OF COMPARING EFFECTS OF HEREDITY
AND ENVIRONMENT

	Heredity	*Environment*	*Example 1*	*Example 2*
Identical twins reared apart	Same	Different	.80	.40
Identical twins reared together	Same	Same	.80	.80

quently, we conclude that the differences in environment have had no effect on whatever trait is being investigated and that inheritance must be the determining factor. In Example 2 the identical twins reared apart show a lower correlation than do those reared together; the environment must therefore have had considerable effect.

Theoretically cotwin control provides definitive answers to the nature-nurture question. In practice, however, it is often doubtful that twins reared apart have extremely dissimilar environments. Adoption agencies, for instance, often try to match socioeconomic levels with those of the real parents; the home environments may thus be similar in many ways. Furthermore, as we have already seen, twins reared together do not have exactly identical environments. Consequently, the effects of environment cannot be described with certainty. Another approach would be to raise children with different inheritance in identical environments, but it is virtually impossible to create environments that are precisely the same.

THE QUESTION OF INTELLIGENCE

Investigators have long been interested in the relative contributions of inheritance and environment to intellect. Table 2-3 (primarily from Hilgard & Atkinson, 1967) summarizes findings on this question. Each of the lines of investigation that we have described is represented. From the comparison of the intelligences of children and those of their natural and foster parents, it seems fairly clear that a heredity component is present. These correlations do not, however, answer the question whether or not the environment affects the *level* of intellectual ability that a child attains but only that children tend to show the same relative order as their real parents more than that of their foster parents. In the same studies, for example, it was found that foster children experienced an average gain of 10 I.Q. points over those that were predicted from the levels of their real parents. It seems that a stable environment favors the maximum development of a child's intellectual performance, but this conclusion is based on the assumption that adoption agencies placed children in homes of higher stability and intellectual standards than those of the homes from which they came.

TABLE 2-3   CORRELATIONS OF INTELLIGENCE-TEST SCORES UNDER DIFFERENT CONDITIONS OF HEREDITY AND ENVIRONMENT

Comparison of child with parents	*Range*
Children and natural parents	.32–.51
Children and foster parents	.00–.26 [1]
Comparison of siblings in same family	*Average*
Ordinary siblings	.50
Fraternal twins	.60
Identical twins	.85
Comparison of twins	*Range*
Identical twins reared together	.88–.92
Identical twins reared apart	.77–.84
Fraternal twins reared together	.53–.63

Source: Data from Hilgard & Atkinson (1967), pp. 450–453.
[1] I.Q. level averaged 10 points above that predicted from the levels of the natural parents.

The portion of Table 2-3 devoted to comparisons of the intelligence of pairs of siblings shows results suggesting that a combination of heredity and environment determines intelligence. Ordinary siblings have the lowest correlation, fraternal twins the next, and identical twins the highest. The difference between identical and fraternal twins is evidence for heredity, but the difference between fraternal twins and ordinary siblings suggests that environment may also have some effect. If heredity were the only factor, ordinary siblings and fraternal twins would have the same correlations and identical twins a higher one, as in Table 2-1, Example 1. If environment were the only factor identical and fraternal twins would have similar correlations, and ordinary siblings a lower one, as in Example 2 in the same table. Furthermore, assuming that the environments of siblings are least alike, those of fraternal twins fairly similar and those of identical twins very similar, we would interpret the results as indicating a direct relationship between correlations of siblings' intelligence and similarity of environment.

The remainder of Table 2-3 shows the evidence obtained by means of cotwin control. Identical twins reared together have an average correlation higher than that of those reared apart, suggesting that the environment is an important factor. Identical twins reared apart are, however, still more alike in intelligence than are fraternal twins reared together, evidence for the importance of inheritance.

The most realistic appraisal of the evidence suggests that both environment and heredity play a part in intellectual development. The organism begins with a biological potential for intellectual development, but the limits on the development of this potential are not firmly set. There will thus be a moderate correspondence between a child's eventual intellectual level and that of his parents, though it is conceivable that parents of very low intelligence will produce a child with potentially high intelligence and the reverse.

If we were to take as a goal the maximization of the intellectual level of an entire population then we could choose one of two paths to this goal. On the assumption that inheritance is important, we could undertake selective breeding to ensure a future race of superior intellects. Such policies have been favored by world leaders in the past, but obviously they are contrary to many current value systems. Selective breeding of animals and plants is common, however, in agriculture. Breed stock is selected according to a specific purpose: beef production, resistance to disease, or the like. Through selective breeding, strains with essentially one genetic structure can be achieved.

A more realistic solution—and a challenge for scientists—is to establish environmental conditions that will encourage maximum intellectual growth. The importance of early experiences in determining later intellectual levels has been demonstrated by investigators (see, for example, Hunt, 1961). In fact, government programs (like the Office of Economic Opportunity's Head Start Program) have been established to help develop the intellectual capacities of children from lower socioeconomic backgrounds so that they can function more satisfactorily as adults in modern industrial society. Before such programs can be successfully integrated into the general educational system, however, much more research on conditions that promote intellectual growth is necessary.

FINAL OBSERVATIONS

The nature-nurture issue is most realistically resolved by recognizing that both heredity and environment contribute to whatever behavior is under study. Furthermore, the degree to which a trait is determined by either factor is a function of the variability of both factors in the population under study. The influences of heredity and environment on any given trait cannot be completely separated.

If the hereditary component of intelligence were exactly the same throughout a given population, so that every child would receive identical genes, and if every child's environment were different, the only way to explain intellectual differences would be as products of environmental differences. On the other hand, if all children were genetically different but raised under exactly the same environmental conditions, variability in intelligence could be accounted for only on a genetic basis.

Other physical and personality traits also depend upon specific combinations of these factors. If we were to attribute inherent aggressiveness, for example, to black children, we could claim it as a basis for race prejudice. When the common environments of black children are taken into consideration, however, aggression may appear highly adaptive. It is clearly more realistic to approach aggression (or any other trait) as a function of a common genetic predisposition of man in interplay with environmental forces.

SPECIFIC GENETIC EFFECTS ON ADJUSTMENT

Some characteristics that are particularly important in adjustment are determined primarily by genetic factors, though they can be modified through changes in the environment. For example, two syndromes associated with mental retardation have been traced to inherited components.

MONGOLISM

Moderate to severe mental retardation occurs in children suffering from mongolism. Characteristically their eyes are slanted, leading to the common label "Mongolian idiot"; the term is unsuitable, however, because mongoloid children are frequently less retarded than it implies. The clinical characteristics were first described by Clifford Down, and the disorder is therefore also called Down's Syndrome.

The cause of this disorder has been traced to chromosome abnormalities (see Figure 2-2). The child receives forty-seven chromosomes instead of the normal complement of forty-six; the extra chromosome is usually associated with pair 21. It appears that either gene mutation occurs in the egg just after fertilization or something goes wrong with the mechanics of growth.

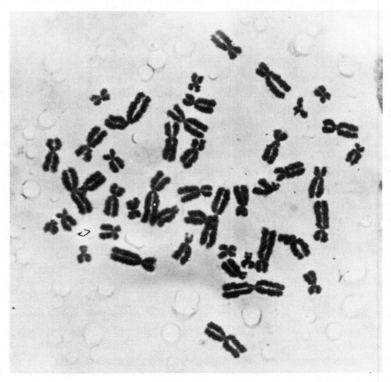

A.

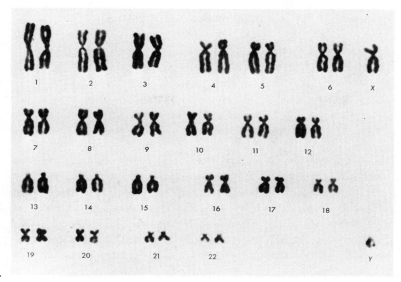

B.

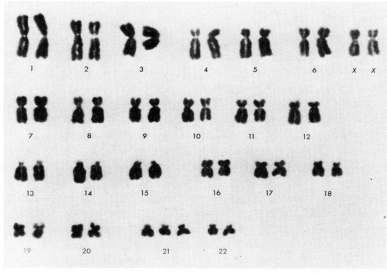

C.

Figure 2-2 Chromosome abnormality in Mongolism. A chromosome count can now be made by treating a cell with a colchicine derivative to stop cell division at the point where the chromosomes are most visible and then applying a salt solution that swells and disperses the chromosomes (A). Treated in this way, chromosomes can then be arranged in pairs. The sample here (B) shows the normal complement of chromosomes for a boy. Such an arrangement also makes it easy to identify certain chromosomal aberrations, such as the trisomy of chromosome 21 common in mongolism (C). Photographs reproduced by permission of J. L. German III from *Scientific American,* November 1961, pp. 67, 74. Text from *Abnormal Psychology and Modern Life,* 3rd Edition, by James C. Coleman, p. 118; copyright © 1964 by Scott, Foresman and Company.

The incidence of mongoloid babies increases with the age of the mother and is especially high in mothers over thirty-five years old. It is possible that metabolic factors associated with aging produce the changes in chromosomes. The chances of exposure to ionizing radiation also increase with age and may explain the higher rate of mutations in the children of older mothers. The disorder is not inherited directly, nor can the birth of a mongoloid child be predicted.

Aside from intellectual retardation, mongoloid children are usually retarded in both gross and fine motor coordination. They are especially susceptible to certain illnesses, which considerably reduces their average life expectancy. There is no known cure, but a healthy, stimulating environment increases life expectancy, and social adjustment can be enhanced by means of special educational techniques (an example of behavior therapy is described in Chapter 7). Environmental changes can thus modify the disadvantages caused by genetic factors but not to the degree that normal adjustment is possible.

PHENYLKETONURIA (PKU)

Another type of mental defect is caused by phenylketonuria (PKU), which has been traced to a recessive gene that has its effect only when coupled with a similar gene. If one parent has this disorder (has a pair of recessive genes) and the other parent is a carrier (has one recessive gene), the chances are only one out of two that their child will have it. If both parents are carriers, there is one chance in four, and if one parent is not a carrier, there is no chance that the child will have it, regardless of the other parent's status. It has been estimated that only one in seventy people is a carrier of PKU; the defect is thus quite rare, occurring once in 10,000–25,000 births.

The immediate cause of the disorder is the lack of an enzyme needed to break down phenylalamine, an amino acid in protein foods. This chemical therefore builds up in the bloodstream and causes damage to the brain.

Since the nature of PKU has been revealed, several tests for early detection have been devised. An infant who shows signs of the disorder is placed on a special diet that is low in phenylalamine. Usually the diet is sufficient to prevent severe damage to the brain. Proper environmental manipulation thus prevents a genetically determined characteristic from affecting adjustment.

SUMMARY

In this chapter we have introduced one of the important processes involved in human adjustment—inheritance of basic biological material. Everyone starts life with certain characteristics, which play varying parts in determining his future adjustment. Inherited attributes include physical characteristics, autonomic reactivity, and energy levels. The effects of such attributes on adjustment are determined largely by their interaction with the environment. The same physical characteristics may, for instance, be deemed "beautiful" in one culture and "ugly" in another.

The importance of inheritance in predetermining personality traits has been emphasized by some investigators. One of the most recent and elaborate of these theories has been proposed by Sheldon. He has developed a reliable system of classifying body forms according to somatotype and for relating them to personality types, which tends to confirm the hypothesis that genetic material is primary in determining personality traits. Although Sheldon's results are intriguing, they are open to alternative explanations.

Another approach taken by investigators is demonstrated by studies of the nature-nurture issue. Scientists have developed special experimental designs to measure the relative contributions of heredity and environment in order to answer such questions as "Is intelligence inherited?" The issue is not easy to resolve, nor are the results so far conclusive. It is a truism, however, that all human characteristics are affected to some degree by both environment and genetic inheritance.

The chapter has closed with an examination of two syndromes of mental retardation known to have genetic bases. The severity of their effects on personal adjustment varies greatly, however, depending upon environmental circumstances.

Introduction

I. Motives
    A. Physiological Motives
        1. Survival needs
        2. Pain
        3. Acquired physiological
            needs
        4. Needs not involving
            survival
    B. Other Apparently Inherent
        Motives
        1. The competence motive
        2. The incongruity-dissonance
            model
    C. Social Motives
        1. Learned motives
        2. Functional autonomy of
            motives
        3. Needs and motivation
        4. The hierarchy of needs
II. Emotions
    A. Labeling Emotions
        1. Physiological and
            psychological interaction
        2. Emotional labeling and
            adjustment
        3. Emotional cues
    B. Emotions as Drives and
        Incentives
    C. Emotional Disorders
        1. Psychophysiological
            disorders
        2. Anxiety reactions
        3. Mood disorders

Summary

3

Processes of Adjustment: Motives and Emotions

INTRODUCTION

Motivation and emotion were briefly described in connection with the definition of adjustment given in Chapter 1. Reasons for Ron's actions and feelings related to them or even causing them were also clearly implied there. It is time now to examine these elements systematically in order to obtain a clearer view of adjustment.

When we speak of motivation we are speaking of the reasons behind a person's actions, why he behaves as he does at certain times. Psychologists call these reasons "motives." A motive serves two functions: It instigates behavior and it directs behavior. Motives are reflected in states of readiness and defined by the ensuing behavior. The student turns his attention to the instructor and readies himself to write. A behavioral pattern is instigated. The circumstances suggest that an "achievement" motive has come into play. The motive determines (directs) the behavior that will bring achievement. The student's attention is oriented toward activity to reach a goal, and subsequent behavior like attentive listening, taking notes, and asking questions confirm his motivation to achieve.

The actions initiated by motives are mostly learned, but some appear to have no basis in previous experience. For example, a newborn baby apparently sucks automatically—without prior learning, as if he is already programmed to reduce his hunger by sucking. It is believed that much behavior in lower animals is unlearned, or instinctive; inborn tendencies to specific behavior operate when specific needs are aroused.

Emotions are subjective experiences of physiological responses. They help to evaluate present circumstances—for example, as pleasurable or unpleasurable—and may thus contribute to modifying behavior. Emotions may serve as motives. Unpleasantness may lead to avoidance, pleasantness to continuation, of contact. Emotions may also serve as incentives; specific circumstances may be sought because they result in desirable emotional experiences. Emotional responses may also reduce the capacity to adjust, and then they are called "emotional disorders."

To understand an individual's adjustment it is necessary to understand the factors that direct his behavior. One of the tasks of a psychotherapist is to analyze motivational patterns. Psychological testing and the assessment interview are tools for understanding a person's motives and emotional reactions; the therapeutic interview is used to bring about changes in these patterns.

MOTIVES

PHYSIOLOGICAL MOTIVES

An important group of motives arises almost entirely from inherent biological needs. Many experiments with animals and human beings have been designed to investigate the physiology of such needs. A general theory of motivation, the *drive-reduction model,* has been developed from the subsequent findings. According to this model, a *need* is aroused by a physiological deficit. The need creates a subjective experience of *tension* and arouses a *drive* that orients the organism toward behavior leading to an *incentive* or a *goal.* When the goal is reached a *consummatory response* occurs. Tension then subsides, and the organism returns to a *quiescent state.*

The drive-reduction model thus reflects a "homeostatic" conception of motivation, the belief that the primary goal of an organism is to maintain a balance of its system. Emotion is intimately connected with the drive-reduction model in that tension is experienced as unpleasantness and the consummatory responses as pleasantness. Although this model seems appropriate for physiological motives its application to human motivation in general has been brought into question.

SURVIVAL MOTIVES

Biological deficiencies that threaten death are an important source of motivation. When physical needs cannot be met the organism is in danger. No matter what other motives may be present, they are not usually expressed until the critical biological deficiency is overcome.

Hunger, thirst, the need for oxygen, the need for temperature control, and the need to eliminate are most frequently listed as physical needs underlying survival motives. The physiological factors that arouse these needs have been studied intensively, but it is beyond the scope of our interest to examine the findings in detail.

Many of the incentives, or goals, related to these basic needs are learned, and they may become quite important in one's overall life plan and adjustment. Many kinds of food, for instance, will satisfy physiological hunger, but people develop highly individual preferences that in turn have great impact on their lives. The gourmet cook offers a good example. Satisfying hunger has become a primary motive in his life. He spends a great deal of time seeking special foods, spices, and so forth and takes great pleasure in exhibiting his culinary skills to his friends. Clearly hunger alone does not explain his behavior; other motives are involved, but they are focused on goals associated with the drive to satisfy hunger. Another example is the obese person's preference for fattening foods. It is not funny for a person who loves sweets and pastries to have to go on a diet that forbids them. His adjustment may be strongly affected by the conflict between his preferences and his attempts to maintain health and achieve physical attractiveness to others. Although his physiological hunger can be met with substitutes, he has learned certain preferences that appear to have their own drive characteristics. An obese person may turn to psychotherapy for aid in changing his motivational patterns so that he can reduce.

PAIN

Pain may be critical to survival, but it is not necessarily so. It serves as a warning that one's body is in danger of physical harm, and therefore acts as a strong motive for human behavior. The sensations aroused by pain usually lead to avoidance and removal of oneself from the painful situation. The psychological equivalent of pain is often loosely labeled "anxiety": it involves recognition of threats to the organism at social, psychological, or personality levels.

Most people learn to avoid circumstances that have previously been associated with pain or that seem likely to have painful outcomes. Behavior therapists (see Chapter 7) use pain to help people break undesirable habits. Stimuli that serve as incentives for such habits are deliberately associated with painful circumstances, usually electric shock, in order to create an avoidance response. For example, an alcoholic looks at a glass of liquor while receiving a painful shock. When he turns his eyes from the glass, the current ceases, thus reinforcing his avoidance response.

The experience of pain is not always perceived as negative. For some people it becomes a goal in itself. People who seek pain are called "masochistic." The term was originally limited to sexual arousal and sexual fulfillment through painful stimulation, like whipping, but its meaning has been broadened to apply to all those who regularly indulge in self-destructive or self-punishing behavior. "Sadism" refers to the opposite tendency, to the taking of pleasure in inflicting pain or punishment on others. Marriage counselors and psychotherapists commonly refer to "sadomasochistic" marriages, in which the partners appear to alternate in hurting each other (not necessarily physically). The stability of the pattern and the partners' unwillingness to dissolve such marriages suggest that they derive pleasure from hurting and from being hurt. A sadomasochistic marriage may last a lifetime and be quite resistant to change.

ACQUIRED PHYSIOLOGICAL NEEDS

Extreme difficulties in adjustment are often associated with physiological needs created by drug addiction. The chronic use of certain drugs can give rise to tissue needs that generate pain if not met. One group of physiologically addictive drugs is the sedatives: alcohol, barbiturates (Nembutal, Seconal, phenobarbital), Doriden, chloral hydrate, meprobamate (Miltown and Equinil). Another is the narcotics: opium, heroin, morphine, codeine, Demerol.

Physiological dependence upon alcohol is the most common addiction in the United States. Alcohol is a socially acceptable sedative that can be purchased rather easily in most states, with only minor restrictions on its use according to age of the user. Other drugs have not presented large-scale social problems in the past, but their distribution and use appear to be increasing at present, especially among the young. Most are legally available only by prescription, but they can also be obtained from illicit traffickers.

Every addiction involves progressive increases in dosage to the point at which the body develops a physiological need for the drug. Cell metabolism adapts itself to the presence of the drug in the bloodstream, and various physiological reactions occur if a certain level is not maintained. These reactions in turn lead to a sense of deprivation and craving for the drug.

At present we know the most about alcoholism, though studies of the effects of other addictive drugs are being carried out. Figure 3-1 is a diagram of the phases of alcohol addiction.

The alcoholic (a loose term that has yet to be satisfactorily defined) experiences withdrawal symptoms when he attempts to stop drinking. They may be relatively mild: perspiration, trembling, weakness, and a craving for alcohol. In other instances they may be quite severe and include nausea, vomiting, an increased heart rate, convulsions, fever, and perhaps even hallucinations. At this point, the alcoholic is actually a victim of his acquired need; it is unlikely that he will be able to stop drinking without assistance. Medical help is necessary to bring him through the withdrawal phase before he can work out the difficulties that originally led him to excessive use of alcohol.

Those addicted to opium or its derivatives (for example, morphine) also develop physiological dependence. Within four to twelve hours after his last dose an addict begins to experience withdrawal symptoms. These symptoms also vary, but they usually become quite severe within forty-eight hours. The first signs are restlessness, irritability, depression, insomnia, muscular weakness, and an increased respiration rate. As time passes these symptoms become more severe, and alternating periods of chills and excessive sweating, vomiting, diarrhea, abdominal cramps, severe headaches, trembling, and pains in the extremities occur. The patient may be unable to take food and water and is likely to become quite dehydrated. Cardiovascular collapse is possible and may result in death if morphine or something similar is not administered. The symptoms disappear rather quickly, within five to thirty minutes after administration of this drug. Otherwise they begin to decline by the fifth day, and withdrawal is usually complete by the eighth day. The patient begins to eat and drink normally and to regain weight. His tolerance for the drug has also disappeared; if he takes the same dosage as before withdrawal he may die.

NEEDS NOT INVOLVING SURVIVAL

Some needs appear to have physiological bases but do not involve survival. The sex drive and the maternal drive are the two most common ones.

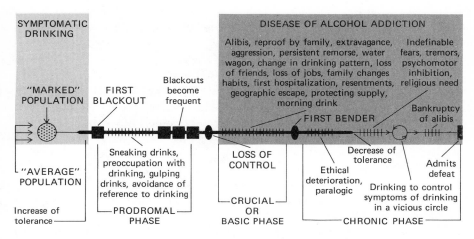

Figure 3-1 Phases of alcohol addiction. This chart is based on a statistical analysis of the drinking histories of 2000 male alcohol addicts and shows the typical sequence in becoming addicted to alcohol. Not all symptoms occur in all cases, and the total time may vary from 7 to 25 years; the average for this group was 15 years.

The dots in the circle at the left represent men and women who are acquainted with each other and use small amounts of alcoholic beverages. Their use of alcohol is a kind of folkway that carries a small social reward. Most have come from the "average" population and get no special reward from alcohol. They make up about 95 percent of all consumers of alcoholic beverages. But occasionally an individual enters the circle from a "marked" population; he suffers from neurotic trends or other personality inadequacies that make alcohol more rewarding to him than to the others, and he may also have an inborn or acquired constitutional liability. In complying with the drinking custom, he experiences considerable relief. So he looks for occasions to drink and may drink fairly heavily; his drinking is symptomatic of some underlying problem and continues until a new symptom appears—his first "blackout."

This marks the beginning of the prodromal phase, during which his drinking still may not be conspicuous and usually is limited to evenings and weekends. The crucial phase begins when the individual loses control over his drinking. Now he still can refrain from starting to drink, but controlled intake is no longer possible for him. During the crucial phase, intoxication becomes the rule but may still be limited to evenings. Solitary drinking begins, and the individual becomes more concerned about how his activities will affect his drinking than about how his drinking will affect his other activities. In the chronic phase, alcohol dominates his life. There is a decrease in physical tolerance and various psychic and physical symptoms may appear. The individual drinks to control his symptoms, but the drinking produces more symptoms. Rationalizations fail, and the individual may finally admit defeat and seek help.

Diagram reproduced by permission of Hillhouse Press from E. M. Jellinek, "The Disease Concept of Alcoholism," 1960. Text from *Abnormal Psychology and Modern Life*, 3rd Edition, by James C. Coleman, p. 118; copyright © 1964 by Scott, Foresman and Company.

THE SEX DRIVE

As the physiological processes involved in sexual arousal become operative, the organism experiences tension, followed by the sexual drive. Many lower forms of animal life have definite cycles of sexual arousal. The females come into heat at specific times of the year or the month, and the males respond to the females' arousal. Although no clear patterns of cyclical arousal have been discovered in the human female, some females, and males too, claim to experience periodic surges of sexual arousal; women often associate them with their menstrual cycles. It is not clear whether such arousal is determined primarily by psychological or by physiological factors.

Direct tactile stimulation of the body is a primary source of human sexual arousal. The genital areas, the penis in the male and the clitoris in the female, are the most responsive to touch, and, of course, they are involved in intercourse. The anus and the breasts are also believed to be sensitive areas in both sexes, though individual preference varies. Other areas susceptible to tactile arousal are the ears, buttocks, thighs, mouth, and, to a lesser degree, almost any area of the skin.

The other major avenue to sexual arousal is psychological. Human beings and other organisms learn to associate specific stimuli with sex and may become aroused simply by perceiving them. Associations between the environment and sexual activity are particularly important in human sexual behavior because of man's greater capacity to learn. Human beings can develop preferences for specific physical characteristics, types of sexual relations, positions in intercourse, ages of partners, and other stimuli. They can also share vicariously in the experiences of others through verbal communication, writing, and the pictorial media. The male seems to be more susceptible to psychological stimuli than is the female. According to A. C. Kinsey and his colleagues (1953), only three of twenty-eight psychological stimuli had equal power to arouse females and males: motion pictures, romantic literature, and erotic biting by partners. There was much individual variation, however. A small proportion of the women in the sample were aroused more by psychological stimuli than were any of the males, and some women were able to achieve orgasm in response to psychological stimuli alone; such reactions were extremely rare in males.

Arousal may not occur in the female for weeks or months; because men are subject to frequent stimulation they can rarely go for long without being aroused. A study related to this point (Epstein and Smith, 1957) revealed that sexual responsiveness in males was correlated with the rate of orgasm rather than with the time since the last orgasm. The findings suggest that the rate of sexual response is determined more by psychological stimuli than by a build-up of physiological tension.

The sex drive has many ramifications in human adjustment because of its close association with cultural values and mores. Each culture has both written and unwritten rules for appropriate sexual behavior. Value judgments are assigned to many aspects of sexuality, including frequency of arousal and the kinds of behavior involved in consummation. Other drives are also subject to cultural values. There are many taboos associated with food products for instance, but most societies place heavier emphasis on the proper sexual activities of their members. A person is likely to find himself torn between his need to express his sex drive and society's definition of "proper" sexual behavior. The resulting stress may take the form of impotency in men and frigidity in women. Some sexual behavior (homosexuality, sodomy, and so on) is widely considered "mental illness" or criminal. Those who engage in such behavior may be subject to punishment (imprisonment or hospitalization) or involuntary psychotherapy, as well as to personal guilt and shame.

THE MATERNAL DRIVE

In lower organisms a drive to care for the young is believed to arise from hormone secretions during pregnancy. A mother rat seems strongly motivated to care for her young. She will return them to the nest if they are taken out, and if they are separated from her she will overcome painful obstacles to bring them back. That other animals also show consistent response patterns toward their infants has led investigators to suggest that this drive is physiologically determined.

Human mothers also experience physiological changes associated with pregnancy and lactation, and their behavior often suggests the presence of a maternal drive. As with most human behavior, however, it is difficult to determine what role learning plays in the expression of this drive. Different cultures have their own methods of child rearing, but it seems generally true across cultures that females care for their young.

Our interest in the maternal drive is aroused by its connections with social values and mores. The woman who chooses a career over having a family or chooses to remain childless is judged by others according to their beliefs about motherhood. Many people in our society would call her "selfish," "manly," even "homosexual." A mother is also likely to be considered "bad" if she does not show "proper" attitudes or take the "right" amount of interest in rearing her children, for example, if she leaves them alone or does not always do what they bid her. Young mothers are keenly aware of the social pressure of others' evaluations of them as mothers—sometimes to the point at which they focus on their children in order to win social approval. The childless wife may experience guilt and shame because of her inability to bear children.

OTHER APPARENTLY INHERENT MOTIVES

Recent investigations have led to the conclusion that some motives are self-generated and not dependent upon physiological needs arising from tissue tensions. As such motives can be observed in very young infants who have had no opportunity to acquire them they are believed to be innate. Recognition of these motives raises doubts about the appropriateness of the drive-reduction model in accounting for all human behavior. Other models have therefore been postulated to explain many of man's actions.

THE COMPETENCE MOTIVE

A number of observations (two of which we shall examine here) suggest that much of an organism's behavior is directed at developing effective ways of interacting with the environment. R. W. White (1959) related this kind of behavior to "competence motives," motives to develop fitness or ability, capacity or proficiency, in dealing with environmental demands. He has suggested that organisms are motivated to learn useful and complex skills—like crawling, walking, language, and thinking—that promote effective adjustment. Effective behavior like grasping, handling, and releasing objects is not a product of random movements expressing excess energy; it is directed and selective and persists because it satisfies an intrinsic need to master the environment.

One such behavior pattern, reflecting the drive to manipulate, has been observed in monkeys (Harlow et al., 1950). Each animal was placed in a cage containing various mechanical devices. He would begin to take the devices apart and would continue working with them until he had become skilled in operating them. He received no reward other than the presumed satisfaction of having performed the task. These observations suggest that animals (including man) need to manipulate objects or situations, that such activity is not random but serves to produce information about a novel set of stimuli. When a young child is handed a ball or other object he is likely to turn it in his hands, to gaze at it, to manipulate it, perhaps to smell and taste it, and so on. His attention and energy are apparently focused on the task of "getting to know" the ball in all its dimensions.

Another example was observed by J. Piaget in his study of the intellectual development of children (1952). He watched his own children at play under semicontrolled conditions. As early as the fourth month they were centering their play on activities that appeared to produce results in the external environment. For example, they seemed to try out purposively their own impacts on a rattle—hitting it, turning it, grasping it, and so on. Piaget's observations led him to believe that the child builds from his initial interest in objects to increasingly complex behavior that is tested in the environment for the purpose of discovery. By the second half of the first year his children had explored different properties of objects and had used the objects as testing grounds for actions that they had learned earlier. When a child was shown a variety of new objects, he would apply familiar behavior patterns and develop increasingly effective methods of examining them. A child who is free from other physiological needs apparently uses his spare time to operate on, or manipulate, his environment. His activities apparently reinforce themselves, for he seems to derive satisfaction from this active exploration.

The need to be effective and the competence motive are considered secondary to the more compelling need for survival, but, when a child is otherwise unoccupied or is only mildly stimulated by his environment, they direct his behavior and reinforce his actions. Even though strongly aroused drives interfere and override manipulative behavior, the competence motive persists between episodes of domination by other physiologically determined motives.

THE INCONGRUITY-DISSONANCE MODEL

J. McV. Hunt (1960) has presented an alternative theoretical model for understanding motivated behavior. He has examined several lines of evidence that challenge the assumptions of the drive-reduction model. First, he has questioned the assumption that all behavior is motivated by homeostatic needs, painful stimulation, or conditioned stimuli. He has cited a number of activities, including the play of young animals, puzzle-solving behavior by monkeys, and those observed in Piaget's work, as indicative of the possibility that behavior is stimulated by other sources. He has argued that organisms are basically active, open energy systems that produce behavior without a preceding deficit or excess. He has also challenged the assumption that returning to a state of equilibrium is reinforcing. He has not denied that reduction of stimulation is frequently reinforcing, but he has cited evidence to indicate that human and subhuman organisms also actively seek stimulation when it is not available. College students who were paid to do nothing, for example, developed strong desires for stimulation. Just experiencing neutral, inactive circumstances was unsatisfactory and led to a desire for activity.

The evidence suggests optimal levels of activation: It is reinforcing to increase activity when the level is too low and to decrease activity when it is too high. The drive-reduction model represents only one aspect of this more general principle. Hunt has further postulated that the quality of stimulation determines its effects. Some stimuli are pleasurable, and others are not. An organism continues (is motivated) to seek things that it likes—candy for example—and to avoid things that it dislikes, like spanking.

Hunt has therefore suggested a general principle of incongruity and dissonance to account for the data. Basically he has conceptualized the nervous system as a perceptual feedback system operating to alert the organism to error. An error is an incongruity between receptor input, on one hand, and expectation based on past experience, on the other. If the inputs are highly incongruent, the drive to bring them within acceptable limits is aroused. Hunt has noted that aspects of this general princple have been incorporated in many physiological and psychological theories of human behavior.

Hunt cited a study of fearfulness in nursery-school children as an example of the working of his model. The results can be accounted for by Hunt's principle, but they are embarrassing to proponents of the drive-reduction model. The latter would predict that children from poorer socioeconomic environments will be more afraid of new circumstances than will middle-class children because they have already experienced more situations evoking fear. Lower-class children have presumably been exposed to (conditioned to) a wider range of stimuli associated with fearful responses. The findings do not, however, support this prediction. Children from middle-class homes actually showed greater fearfulness, as measured by avoidance responses in strange circumstances, than did children from lower-class homes. Hunt has explained this finding: As the lower-class children had had more learning experiences in fearful situations, they were more likely to expect new situations to be fearful. Their expectations were not incongruent with their perceptions. On the other hand, middle-class children had had less exposure to frightening conditions. Their perceptions were therefore more likely to be incongruent with their expectations. When the fearful situation was encountered, the incongruence between perceptions and expectations thus resulted in avoidance.

SOCIAL MOTIVES

Many human motives appear to have no inherent, or biological, basis; they are learned through interaction in society. Most of these motives are unique to human beings, and they are instrumental in much of human behavior. At times their strength appears to overcome all other motives, as is demonstrated by extreme self-sacrifice for religious or social principles.

LEARNED MOTIVES

The drive-reduction model offers one explanation of how social motives are acquired: They depend upon the circumstances associated with the reduction of primary (physiological) needs. A simple example will illustrate. We shall trace the process by which a child acquires achievement motives. As an infant the child's needs for nourishment are met by his mother. As she is constantly associated with drive reduction, her presence in itself becomes comforting; the child comes to value her attention and acquires the motive to please her. If she places high value on achievement, she is likely to reinforce activities that lead to achievement. She may praise the child, for example, when he plays in ways that will be relevant to school learning. When he enters school she pays a great deal of attention to his performance and praises him for scholastic achievement. The activities that please her take on value to the child himself because they are reinforced, and eventually this value becomes independent. When the child grows up his attitudes and behavior will reflect motivation for achievement. On the other hand, a mother may value aggression and dominance and may reinforce behavior like standing up for one's rights, protecting one's toys from others, and so forth. This behavior too eventually takes on independent value.

There are competing theories to explain the acquisition of social motives. We shall examine some of them in a later section. At this point it is sufficient to mention that alternative explanations exist; psychologists do not agree on any one explanation.

FUNCTIONAL AUTONOMY OF MOTIVES

G. W. Allport (1937) postulated the *functional autonomy* of motives. Regardless of how social motives are learned, they can become independent; that is, their initial association with primary (physiological) motives can be lost for all practical purposes. In fact, they may come to dominate motives considered basic to survival. In trying to understand why an individual behaves as he does we must recognize that social motives may be just as powerful, if not more powerful, than the primary motives from which they derive.

Social motives are quite important to professionals in the field of personal adjustment. Therapists must understand their clients' motivations in order to help them understand themselves or discover appropriate means of overcoming difficulties engendered by unrealistic goals. A man with a strong need for achievement, for instance, may have family problems because his overwhelming need to achieve causes him to neglect the needs of those close to him. Needs for love and closeness may be so secondary in his life that he creates stress for others and eventually for himself.

NEEDS AND MOTIVATION

H. A. Murray (1938) attempted to make an exhaustive list of human needs. This list serves to show the wide variety of behavior that must be taken into account in a complete theory of motivation. Needs are divided into two major categories: *viscerogenic needs* based on physiological processes and *psychogenic needs* based on learning experiences. The psychogenic needs most relevant to social motives are

A. Needs associated chiefly with inanimate objects
   1. *Acquisition:* the need to gain possessions and property
   2. *Conservation:* the need to collect, repair, clean, and preserve things
   3. *Orderliness:* the need to arrange, organize, put away objects, to be tidy and clean; to be precise
   4. *Retention:* the need to retain possession of things; to hoard; to be frugal, economical, and miserly
   5. *Construction:* the need to organize and build
B. Needs expressing ambition, will power, desire for accomplishment, and prestige
   6. *Superiority:* the need to excel, a composite of achievement and recognition
   7. *Achievement:* the need to overcome obstacles, to exercise power, to strive to do something difficult as well and as quickly as possible

8. *Recognition:* the need to excite praise and commendation; to demand respect
9. *Exhibition:* the need for self-dramatization; to excite, amuse, stir, shock, thrill others
10. *Inviolacy:* the need to remain inviolate, to prevent a depreciation of self-respect, to preserve one's "good name"
11. *Avoidance of inferiority:* the need to avoid failure, shame, humiliation, ridicule
12. *Defensiveness:* the need to defend oneself against blame or belittlement; to justify one's actions
13. *Counteraction:* the need to overcome defeat by restriving and retaliating

C. Needs having to do with human power exerted, resisted, or yielded to
14. *Dominance:* the need to influence or control others
15. *Deference:* the need to admire and willingly follow a superior; to serve gladly
16. *Similance:* the need to imitate or emulate others; to agree and believe
17. *Autonomy:* the need to resist influence, to strive for independence
18. *Contrariness:* the need to act differently from others, to be unique, to take the opposite side

D. Needs having to do with injuring others or oneself
19. *Aggression:* the need to assault or injure another; to belittle, harm, or maliciously ridicule a person
20. *Abasement:* the need to comply and accept punishment; self-depreciation
21. *Avoidance of blame:* the need to avoid blame, ostracism, or punishment by inhibiting unconventional impulses; to be well behaved and obey the law

E. Needs having to do with affection between people
22. *Affiliation:* the need to form friendships and associations
23. *Rejection:* the need to be discriminating, to snub, ignore, or exclude another
24. *Nurturance:* the need to nourish, aid, or protect another
25. *Succorance:* the need to seek aid, protection, or sympathy; to be dependent

F. Additional socially relevant needs
26. *Play:* the need to relax, amuse oneself, seek diversion and entertainment
27. *Cognizance:* the need to explore, to ask questions, to satisfy curiosity
28. *Exposition:* the need to point and demonstrate; to give information, explain, interpret, lecture

Once a person understands his motives several choices become available to him; that is, if an overwhelming, or unrealistic need can be reduced through psychotherapy, he is freed to experiment with more adaptive patterns. It is also possible to help a person find a more suitable environment for the expression of his needs, through job, educational, and marital changes and so on. More commonly a combination of therapy and environmental change is required. An individual with strong aggressive needs, for example, may reduce them somewhat through psychotherapy and at the same time may take up a socially acceptable sport in which aggression can be expressed constructively.

THE HIERARCHY OF NEEDS

A number of investigators have postulated a single, overriding motive usually called "self-actualization," the need to develop one's potential to the fullest, to become as "complete" a person as possible. The concept of normality as ideal behavior (see Chapter 1) incorporates this idea.

A. H. Maslow (1962) is a "self-actualization theorist" who emphasizes the motivational aspects of behavior (Maslow and Murphy, 1954). He has conceptualized human needs on five levels:

Physiological needs
Safety needs
Needs for love
Needs for esteem
Self-actualization needs

Furthermore, he has suggested that there is a fundamental ordering of human need structure, in which needs are ranged in a hierarchy from basic physiological needs at the bottom to the need for self-actualization at the top. Each higher level represents the needs associated with a successive development of the personality. Lower-level needs must be satisfied before others can be attended to; that is, physiological needs must be met before safety needs, safety needs before needs for love, and so on. If food, water, and protection are unavailable, the lower needs will dominate behavior.

Maslow's proposed hierarchy appears valid in many circumstances and for most people. He is nevertheless aware that there are exceptions, as those who sacrifice or suffer for ethical and religious values demonstrate. Under general conditions of severe and prolonged frustration, however, the lower needs become dominant, and the form of social organization will reflect absence of concern with self-actualization motives. The Donner party, which attempted to cross the Sierra Nevada mountains from Nevada to California in the 1800s is an example. The travelers had set out too late in the year to complete their continental crossing before the heavy snows fell. Trapped with dangerously low supplies, they resorted to eating their dead, and there has been suspicion of murder as well. Higher needs thus gave way to basic physiological needs under stressful conditions.

Maslow's notion has many implications for personal adjustment, especially when applied to society as a whole. Man's higher motivations cannot be realized in a society in which basic needs go unfulfilled. Maslow's solution, an example of the humanistic approach to adjustment (see Chapter 6), is to provide social conditions in which basic needs can be met so that each person has an opportunity to fulfill his higher needs and therefore his potential.

EMOTIONS

Emotions are closely interrelated with motives and can be separated only for convenient discussion. In our discussion of motives we have seen how emotions may instigate and direct behavior.

The subjective experiences labeled "emotional," or "affective," are associated with physiological changes. We do not yet know whether or not the physiological responses accompanying various emotional states (fear, anger, and so on) differ. Does man experience a general state of arousal and label his experience according to stimulus conditions, or does he classify his emotional experiences according to specific neurological and biochemical changes? Attempts to differentiate emotions by the quality of their physiological components have not been especially fruitful. An alternative approach has been to postulate that emotions are differentiated by the *degree* of physiological activation and classified by the intensity of the response. Minimum intensity is represented by sleep and maximum intensity by diffuse excitement.

Investigations more closely geared to studying personal adjustment have dealt with the physiological consequences of fear, anger, and anxiety. The findings are relevant to theories of psychosomatic illness. Some of these problems will be examined later in the chapter.

LABELING EMOTIONS

Labeling an emotional response is a subjective matter. What an individual calls his experience may not agree with what an observer might call it. For example, we watch a man as he encounters a grizzly bear near his backwoods cabin. He stops short, then turns and runs into the cabin. We are likely to think that he has experienced fear. From our vantage point the circumstances appear dangerous; the man's survival seems to have been threatened, and we assume that he has therefore fled in fright. As we continue to watch, however, we see him come out of the cabin and shoot the bear. When questioned he says that the sight of the bear made him extremely angry, for the animal had been destroying his property for some time. In his anger he had run for his gun to end the rascal's mischief. The man has been around wild animals most of his life, and, though he respects their strength, he has learned which circumstances are dangerous and which not. Our error resulted from insufficient knowledge of the context of his actions. Beliefs and expectations interact with circumstances surrounding events to determine the nature of emotional responses.

PHYSIOLOGICAL AND PSYCHOLOGICAL INTERACTION

A study by S. Schachter and I. E. Singer (1962) has thrown some light on the process of labeling emotional states. The findings suggest that emotional experience depends upon physiological arousal plus the subject's perception of circumstances. That is, an individual's understanding of his situation appears to determine the label that he assigns to the physiological changes that he experiences.

Four groups of subjects participated in the experiment. Three groups received adrenaline (a drug that induces symptoms similar to those of emotions), and one group received a saline solution (which has no physiological effects). Each adrenaline group was given different information before the drug was administered. One group was told accurately what physiological changes it would cause: accelerated heart beat, trembling in the limbs, and so on. A second group was given no information about these reactions. The third group was given false information; it was told to expect numbness, itching, and headache. The fourth group was given no information. Two additional experimental manipulations were used to test the effects of cognitive influence on labeling of emotions. Confederates of the experimenters, who were presumably but not actually undergoing the same experiences as were the subjects, were instructed to act either jovial or angry. When acting jovial, they were gay, threw wads of paper into a waste basket, and encouraged the subjects to join them; when acting angry, they complained about the experiment and so forth. Some subjects in each of the four groups were assigned jovial or angry partners.

The experimenters predicted that the confederates' behavior would be most effective in determining the subjects' emotional perceptions when they were most confused about their physiological arousal (had received false information) and least effective for subjects with accurate expectations. The group receiving saline solution was also expected to be little affected by the confederates' behavior. The reports of the subjects after the experiment confirmed these hypotheses. The saline group and the accurately informed group reported little joviality or anger, the uninformed subjects reported more, and the misinformed subjects reported the greatest gaiety. The authors concluded that identical physiological responses are interpreted and labeled according to social setting. What a person thinks about circumstances plays a large part in determining his subjective emotion.

Schachter and Singer's experiment, however, has not supplied a definitive answer to the problem of how emotions are labeled. It is still possible that their subjects' interpretation of circumstances engendered different physiological responses. As the experimenters did not monitor physiological changes in the subjects who experienced anger and gaiety, it is not certain that those changes were identical.

EMOTIONAL LABELING AND ADJUSTMENT

We generally infer emotional states from our ideas about people and their actions under specific conditions. The accuracy of our assessments of the emotional states of others partly determines the effectiveness of our adjustments. Interpersonal relationships are usually enhanced by the ability to gauge the emotional state associated with another's behavior, a process called "empathy." Accurate perception of the emotional responses of others and of oneself may, in fact, be critical to the outcome of an interaction. For example, a threatening robber may be feeling anger or fear. If he feels fear he may easily be frightened away by shouting or resistance; if he feels anger, on the other hand, shouting may bring physical retaliation and the loss of more than one's wallet.

There is some evidence that people whose adjustment has been judged inadequate are relatively unable to infer the emotional states of others. As a result, their reactions often seem inappropriate and maladaptive. L. Krasner and his colleagues (1961) showed a series of stick figures (see Figure 3-2) to a group of hospitalized schizophrenics and an unhospitalized control group of normal people. The figures had been standardized on a normal population to establish consensus upon the moods to be ascribed to each figure: happiness, sadness, anger, thought, and so on. The results showed a large difference between the schizophrenics' ability and the control subjects' to label the

Figure 3-2   Illustrative item from the Stick Figures Test. Reproduced by permission of the American Psychological Association from T. R. Sarbin and C. D. Hardyck, "Conformance in Role Perception as a Personality Variable," *Journal of Consulting Psychology,* **19,** no. 2 (1955).

figures appropriately. The implication is that the patients' social functioning was hampered by their poor perceptions of others' roles.

EMOTIONAL CUES

There is evidence that people from the same culture share a consensus about the emotional states of others. Photographs of actors in feigning emotions have been used to discover the amount of agreement among subjects on classifying these emotions, and six broad categories have been identified with rather high accuracy. Body posture and facial expression apparently furnish cues to emotional responses, and there is also evidence that hand gestures and voice communicate emotions (Carmichael *et al.*, 1937; Dusenbury and Kroner, 1939).

Motion-picture techniques are now being developed to permit minute analysis of behavioral cues that communicate emotional states (Ekman, 1965; Ekman and Freisen, 1967). This approach has revealed that emotional states can be accurately communicated through nonverbal cues. A filmed interview with the sound deleted is shown to subjects, who then judge the mood or feelings of the person interviewed. The only basis for judgment is nonverbal cues. P. Ekman has attempted to discover the details of expressive behavior that communicate emotional states most effectively. One action was deleted from the film each time that it was shown in order to discover whether or not the same emotion continued to be perceived. The effectiveness of different cues could then be established. By slowing the motion picture Ekman could show the observer very rapid changes in facial expressions (micromovements) that were often missed at normal speed. When these movements were deleted from the film, however, the observer did not infer the same emotional states. Fleeting expressions may thus be important in communicating emotions, even though the observer is unconscious of them.

The face is most effective in communicating emotions, though it may be used to simulate them as well. Ekman believes that body gestures reflect cultural learning more closely than do facial expressions, however. The hands help to communicate emotional states, whereas the feet and legs are much less effective.

Another study has suggested that people interpret emotions along three main dimensions (Block, 1957). College students were asked to pair words that denote emotions: weak-strong, active-passive, happy-sad, and so on. Through correlation methods J. Block found that three primary dimensions were used in characterizing these emotional states: pleasantness-unpleasantness, level of physical activation, and interpersonal relatedness. For example, contentment was judged pleasant and guilt unpleasant; anger was considered high in activation and boredom low, and sympathy was rated high in interpersonal relatedness and envy low. Each emotional state was defined by its average rating on all three dimensions. Contentment, for instance, beside its high rating on pleasantness, had a low rating on activation and a moderate rating on interpersonal relatedness.

EMOTIONS AS DRIVES AND INCENTIVES

We have already mentioned that emotions are not always simply responses to behavior; they may serve as drives instigating and directing behavior. Fear and anxiousness represent important drives in personal adjustment. Behavior is often determined by circumstances associated with anxiousness. Breaking the law and failure to conform to social codes, for example, may arouse uneasiness that leads to modification of behavior. Or jealousy, the experience associated with the threat of losing a cherished friend or loved one can cause a person to act in ways that he would normally consider inappropriate. He may go to great lengths to protect his relationship and may even attack a rival.

Emotions may also serve as incentives, as goals in themselves. We have noted that masochism and sadism in sexual behavior appear to have emotional experiences as goals. It is apparent that man seeks activities leading to joy, happiness, and excitement, and it is not uncommon to find that some emotion-producing activities may be carried too far. The child collapses in tears when his roller-coaster ride changes from thrilling to frightening; the teen-ager's exhilaration turns to stark terror when his speeding car hits a slippery spot. Nevertheless, risk taking and stress seeking are frequent in human behavior. The gambler, the businessman, and the entrepreneur all are motivated to some degree by the emotional responses involved in taking risks. Adolescents seem especially eager to test the limits of thrill seeking.

Perhaps thrill seeking can be explained as an extension of the competence motive or of social motives in the service of developing a person's sense of who he is and what he is worth. It is certainly difficult to interpret the behavior of sky divers, skiers, and football players on the hedonistic supposition that man seeks to minimize pain and maximize pleasure, in the sense of comfort. These activities suggest complex interactions between emotional states and man's perception of his own behavior. Although he may not clearly understand his motives, he does seek activities of high risk, apparently for the purpose of experiencing emotional reactions.

EMOTIONAL DISORDERS

Some of the most difficult adjustments to stress engender emotional disturbance sufficiently debilitating to warrant medical or psychotherapeutic treatment.

PSYCHOPHYSIOLOGICAL DISORDERS

A number of physical illnesses are believed to result from inappropriate emotional reactions. The primary difficulty seems to lie in the means by which emotional tensions are dissipated. Most people are able to reduce emotional tension through motor or cognitive activity; talking about frustrations, appropriate anger, and active sports all tend to divert body organs from emotional responses. Instead of discharging tension in these ways, however, some people typically release emotional tension through their viscera, rather than expressing it directly, in order to avoid psychological and interpersonal conflict. They are often unaware that they are doing so. Physical symptoms result

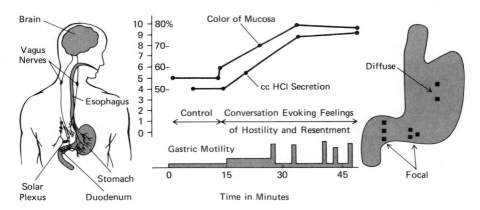

Figure 3-3 Peptic ulcers. It seems that modern civilization may be especially conducive to chronic emotional reactions that lead to peptic ulcers. It is estimated that one out of ten Americans now living will at some time develop a peptic ulcer.

While the causes are not completely known, an interaction between brain excitation and the secretion of stomach acids (which is the direct cause) is suspected. Nervous tension, worry, and general emotional strain bring about a higher flow of stomach secretions than do food and drink. The center chart shows that feelings of resentment, hostility, and anxiety result in an increase of acid production and the engorgement of the stomach with blood. The diagram on the right shows the locations of ulcers which developed in eight of nineteen monkeys that received excessive stimulation of the brain, causing signs of bewilderment, fear, or agitation. Other findings suggest that the electrical activity of the brain of an ulcer patient is more likely to be abnormal than that of the nonulcer subject. Although the relationship between brain disturbance and response to stress is not clear, there seems to be a circular pattern, with stresses of living and higher levels of brain stimulation causing excessive emotional stress in ulcer patients.

Ulcers can usually be controlled and alleviated through diet and various drugs. A more complete freedom from symptoms, however, seems to require psychotherapy aimed at correcting chronic emotional overreaction.

From *Abnormal Psychology and Modern Life*, 3rd Edition, by James C. Coleman, p. 253. Copyright © 1964 by Scott, Foresman and Company.

from exaggerated physiological responses, and organ systems can be damaged by chronic emotional states. Figures 3-3 and 3-4 show the processes presumed to be involved in two psychophysiological disorders, peptic ulcers and migraine headaches.

Three main theories accounting for organ specificity—why one organ, rather than another, is affected—have been developed. One holds that specific personality characteristics are associated with specific organ disorders. "Ulcer types," "hypertensive characters," "asthmatic personalities," and so on are believed to have particular personality traits likely to generate responses affecting particular organ systems. More recent evidence suggests multiple causes, however.

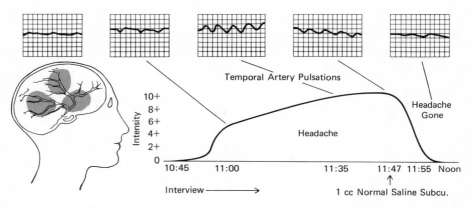

Figure 3-4 Migraine headaches. Migraine headaches are periodic or recurrent, usually occurring on one side of the head, though they may shift or be more general. The cause of the pain has now been attributed to the pain-sensitive arteries of the head, as shown in the above diagram. Migraines may be reproduced by dilating these arteries chemically, and their return to normal size is associated with the cessation of pain.

In recent years attempts have been made to discover conditions that cause vascular dilation. Since migraines run in families it was assumed that heredity is a factor; however, this could not account for the specific onset and recurrent nature of the pain. Experiments showed that stressful circumstances cause vascular dilation in migraine sufferers but not in other persons. The above graph demonstrates the effects of stress. The person was involved in a discussion that evoked feelings of hostility. Changes in the amplitude of artery pulsations and the corresponding intensity of the headache are shown. A saline injection (inactive medication), which the patient believed would stop the headache, was administered with a consequent cessation of pain.

It is believed that these people channel emotional tensions through the vascular system in a way that causes the cranial arteries to dilate. It is not known, however, why their emotional reactions affect this particular physiological system rather than some other.

From *Abnormal Psychology and Modern Life*, 3rd Edition, by James C. Coleman, pp. 256–257. Copyright © 1964 by Scott, Foresman and Company.

Another view is that the nature of the symptoms depends upon the individual's history or constitutional makeup. A high level of emotional tension may affect any organ system, but the way in which an individual reacts to it (his constitutional makeup) determines what his symptoms will be. For instance, some people characteristically respond to emotional strain with rising blood pressure, whereas others tend toward a quickened pulse rate with no increase in blood pressure. Others may have marked respiratory reactions, stomach reactions, and so on. The target organs are likely to be damaged by severe or prolonged emotional stress. Certain organ systems may also be inherently weak or weakened by disease and injury; they are especially vulnerable to stress. The combination of chronic arousal and susceptible organs leads to a specific disorder.

A third theory brings us back to the question of the physiological changes that accompany emotional states. If it can be demonstrated that fear releases one sort of hormone, whereas anxiety does not, then the biochemical nature of the emotional state could determine the organ system that will endure the greatest stress. The type of psychological stress will in turn determine the nature of the emotional response (anger, fear, anxiety). Interactions between stress conditions, emotional quality, and the organ systems is postulated as the cause of specific disorders.

Investigators do not, of course, agree on the causes of psychophysiological reactions. Each theory appears to have merit and warrants further study. Current treatment usually combines medical care for physical symptoms with psychotherapy for the stressful conditions. Medical treatment alone usually provides only temporary resolution.

ANXIETY REACTIONS

One common neurotic disorder is characterized by chronic anxiousness and apprehensiveness. It is punctuated by recurring episodes of acute fright. The victim usually cannot pinpoint the specific source of his stress, and therefore his condition is called "free-floating anxiety." Irritability, difficulties with concentration, and insomnia are common, and physiological responses like increased heart rate and blood pressure occur for no apparent reason. The person seems to suffer from chronic alarm and a state of tension.

An acute attack may be sudden, intense, and brief, accompanied by gasping for breath, dizziness, perspiration, and trembling. General apprehension may balloon into fears of impending catastrophe and possible death. Yet the person usually has no idea what the catastrophe may be or what may cause his death. His tension is visible in muscular tightness, especially around the neck and upper shoulders; overreaction to sudden or unexpected stimuli; digestive upsets; and difficulties in concentration. Heavy use of alcohol and other tranquillizing drugs may further complicate the picture.

Most people in our society experience occasional mild attacks of anxiety. It is a normal reaction to stress situations, and we can understand the discomfort. But the individual suffering from neurotic anxiety has a chronic tendency to overreact to circumstances that most people meet with little difficulty.

MOOD DISORDERS

High levels of elation or depression seriously interfere with personal adjustment. In a *neurotic depressive reaction* the individual responds to distressing circumstances with unusual amounts of dejection for extended periods of time. Typically he becomes discouraged and sad, and much anxiousness and apprehension are often present also. Everyday tasks become quite difficult, if not impossible, and he suffers lessened self-confidence and general loss of initiative. If the response is severe he may be immobilized to the point at which he must be hospitalized; thoughts of suicide are not infrequent.

More severe depressive reactions are called *psychoses*. Combined with the symptoms already described is impaired ability to evaluate reality. In *simple depression* there is a general slowing of mental and physical activity and apathy. General loss of interest often extends to eating so that the person loses weight and experiences digestive difficulties. He usually wants to be alone to contemplate his sins and the darkness of the future. Preoccupation with suicide is common, and attempts are frequent.

All these symptoms are intensified in *acute depression*. The patient may lose contact with reality. He may come to feel that his actions have caused such disasters as plagues, floods, and economic depressions. Or he may have unrealistic fantasies about his body—that his brain is being eaten away, his insides are drying up, and the like. Past sins dominate his thoughts, and he is likely to consider his disorder appropriate punishment.

In the severest stage, *depressive stupor,* the patient is almost completely unresponsive and inactive. He may not eat or speak, and it may be necessary for others to care for his physiological needs. His thinking is very confused; he may have vivid hallucinations and delusions, especially associated with sin, death, and rebirth. He is invariably constipated, has foul breath, and suffers poor general physical health.

Manic reactions lie at the other end of the emotional continuum and are characterized by varying degrees of elation and intense motor activity. As the disorder becomes increasingly serious, the person's manic behavior becomes more frequent and more intense. He seems to have great confidence in his own ability and knowledge, readily expressing his opinions on almost any subject. He thinks rapidly and he may seem witty and entertaining, though he is quick to challenge anyone who suggests that his behavior is inappropriate. He may throw himself into his work and accomplish a great deal because he stays awake almost all the time and expends a great deal of energy. He is full of enthusiasm and wonderful plans; he wants everybody to be enthusiastic along with him. As his pace increases, he may become more irritable and may shift rapidly from gaiety to anger. He may talk at the top of his voice, laugh loudly and readily, and become progressively overbearing in interpersonal relations. In fact, his speech may become so rapid that it is difficult to understand him, as he flits from one topic to another. At this stage he may begin to have delusions—that he is a person of unlimited wealth and ability, for example. He typically lacks insight into his condition and he is likely to threaten those who suggest that he is having difficulties. In the most advanced stages the sufferer becomes confused, wildly excited, and violent. He is incoherent and severely disoriented. He may have vivid auditory and visual hallucinations. It is impossible to hold his attention or to converse with him in a realistic manner, and he is always on the move.

This scene, which took place in the courtyard of a state mental hospital before newer treatment procedures were adopted, illustrates the extreme excitement that can occur:

> A manic patient had climbed upon a small platform in the middle of the yard and was delivering an impassioned lecture to a number of patients sitting on benches which surrounded the platform. Most of the audience were depressed patients who were hallucinating and muttering to themselves and not paying a bit of attention to the speaker. However, the speaker had an "assistant" in the form of a hypomanic patient who would move rapidly around the circle of benches shaking the occupants and exhorting them to pay attention to the speaker. If anyone started to leave, the assistant would plump him back in his seat in no uncertain terms. In the background were a number of apparently schizophrenic patients who were pacing a given number of steps back and forth, and beyond was the high wire fence which surrounded the yard.
>
> The speaker herself was in a state of delirious mania. She had torn her clothing to shreds and was singing and shouting at the top of her voice. So rapidly did her thoughts move from one topic to another that her "speech" was almost a complete word-hash, although occasional sentences such as "You goddamn bitches" and "God loves everybody, do you hear?" could be made out. These points were illustrated by wild gestures, screaming climaxes, and outbursts of song. In the delivery of her talk, she moved restlessly back and forth on the platform, occasionally falling off the platform in her wild excitement. Her ankles and legs were bleeding from rubbing the edge of the platform during these falls, but she was completely oblivious to her injuries.
>
> Fortunately, the degree of excitement in manic reactions can now be markedly reduced by means of various drugs—often in combination with electroshock—and scenes such as this need no longer occur. (Coleman, 1964, p. 328)*

*From *Abnormal Psychology and Modern Life* by James C. Coleman. Copyright © 1964 by Scott, Foresman and Company. Reprinted by permission of the publisher.

SUMMARY

The part that motives and emotions play in adjustment has been considered in this chapter. The instigating and directing forces behind overt behavior are subsumed under the label "motivation." Needs arise which impel us to act. Some of them, like hunger and thirst, arise from chemical deficiencies in the body and serve known physiological functions. Other important physiological needs may be acquired, as drug addictions are.

Other kinds of motives seem, because of their appearance in very young infants, to arise from inherent sources. The presence of drives toward manipulation, activity, and exploration have led to the postulation of a competence motive, which directs behavior so as to increase competence in dealing with the environment. The discovery and investigation of these motives have led to an alternative explanation of motivation, supplementing the theory that man is motivated to reduce the tensions produced by physiological deficiencies. Behavior is considered to be instigated by incongruities between what the individual perceives and what he expects.

Social motives appear to be learned and are highly characteristic of human beings. Men who give up their lives for ideals clearly exemplify the power of social motives. Murray (1938) has listed a number of needs that contribute to human motivation. Maslow (1962) has proposed a hierarchy of such needs and has suggested that man can fulfill his highest needs only after the more basic ones have been met. Furthermore, he has argued that societies are responsible for providing conditions in which man can seek higher goals.

Emotions are obviously important in personal adjustment. They provide qualitative information on events, and they may also stimulate people to act. One question that has still not been satisfactorily answered is how labels become attached to emotional responses. What factors determine whether an emotional experience is considered "happy" or "sad"? Do emotional states differ in the quality of physiological response, do they differ in the quantitative level of arousal, or are they determined by the circumstances associated with their arousal? Research on these questions is still being carried out. Nonverbal cues communicate emotional responses to others, and the accurate perception of emotional behavior in oneself and others facilitates adjustment.

Emotions also act as drives and incentives. Man chooses activities that result in emotional responses, even though they involve high risks, as in skydiving, drag racing, and so on. Finally, emotional disorders may severely cripple effectiveness. Anxiety reactions and depressive or manic disorders are examples of emotional responses that result in especially difficult adjustment problems.

4

A. Introduction
B. The Perceptual Process
   1. Data input
   2. Data processing
   3. Behavioral output
   4. Alice's experience
C. Special Topics in Perception
   1. Sensory deprivation
   2. Psi phenomena
   3. Chemically induced perceptual changes
D. Summary

Processes of Adjustment: Perception

INTRODUCTION

Perception is the process by which man determines the meanings in his world. It is obviously important that we know what is going on about us if we are to be successful in adapting to it. As a student enters the campus, for example, he scans the environment continuously for cues that will provide guides to his action. Robbed of his senses or the mental ability to organize sensory inputs, a person would cease to function as a human being. His responses might cease altogether or might occur randomly and thus ineffectively, for no means of organizing his behavior to accomplish specific ends would be available. If the messages transmitted to the brain were interrupted it would be necessary to look at one's feet in order to know what they were doing. Without sight as we know, the other senses must be used to find directions. Even when all the sensory organs are intact, inputs are a meaningless jumble of sensations quite useless in directing behavior if the nervous tissue of the brain is not functioning. That is, inputs have no values as *cues* to perception and action.

Perception is an extremely complex process, and scientists are only beginning to devise methods for examining its anatomical and physiological correlates. Specific areas of the brain appear to have prime importance for different sense organs, but the physiological processes involved in selecting actions are still very poorly understood. Of course, the more that we learn about anatomical and physiological aspects, the more likely we are to develop means by which to overcome certain kinds of perceptual disorders. Organ transplants offer some hope of replacing damaged sense organs, but a physical corrective for damaged brain tissue does not yet appear to be feasible. Currently, retraining in substitute skills and control through medication offer some encouragement to individuals with perceptual disorders related to anatomical and physiological antecedents.

Although people's perceptions of many things are quite similar, it is also true that each person has a unique perception of events. A number of personality theorists have emphasized the importance of understanding man on the basis of his unique perceptual field,[1] those events which he perceives as he interacts with the world. An individual's personal interpretation of the world about him is of utmost importance in determining the nature and direction of his adjustment. Each person has a characteristic way of scanning the environment, of selecting inputs, of attaching meanings to them, and of acting upon those meanings. In this sense every individual's perceptual field defines his reality.

[1] In Chapter 6 we shall examine Carl Rogers' client-centered theory.

THE PERCEPTUAL PROCESS

Since the advent of high-speed electronic computers investigators have been interested in drawing analogies between the workings of such machines and the processes of knowing. Although computers accomplish ends similar to those of perceiving and thinking, they should not be taken as exact replicas of human systems. They should, rather, be regarded as potentially helpful models for simplifying our understanding of complex processes. In reality the act of perceiving cannot be separated into distinct steps; it is unitary and continuous. But the computer model provides an understandable framework for studying perception by analogy. Figure 4-1 is a simplified diagram of the perceptual process. We shall consider the three major steps in this process separately: data input, data processing, and behavioral output.

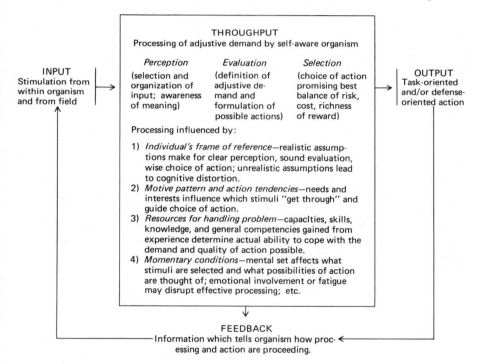

Figure 4-1 Adjustive behavior: Analogy to a computer. Human adjustive behavior has certain obvious similarities to the processing of information by a computer, but the analogy is far from perfect. For example, the stimulation which initiates human action—unlike the input of a computer—does not have an unvarying effect: as the diagram suggests, response varies with changes in the individual's frame of reference, motivational state, and other inner factors. A computer, furthermore, cannot set its own goals or discover ways of processing information for which it has not previously been programmed.

From *Personality Dynamics and Effective Behavior*, by James C. Coleman, p. 187. Copyright © 1960 by Scott, Foresman and Company.

DATA INPUT

The basic input (environmental stimuli) for high-speed computers takes the form of punched cards, magnetic tapes, or magnetic disks. The holes in the cards, for example, are the stimuli for electronic sensors and thus determine the impulses transmitted to the inner workings of the computer. Once inside they are organized, analyzed, and sent on for final manipulations resulting in output.

The human being has various sense organs that "read" environmental stimuli. Each organ receives special kinds of impulses: visual, auditory, kinesthetic, tactile, gustatory, and olfactory. As in the computer, the characteristics of the stimuli determine the information transmitted to higher nervous centers. And, as computer sensors cannot read mutilated cards, human senses are also limited to defined ranges of stimuli. Our eyes cannot sense bacteria because they are too small, our ears cannot receive certain high-pitched sounds, our skin sensors cannot distinguish between two points of touch too close together, and so forth. Even within their ranges the sense organs can process only a fraction of the stimuli available at any one time.

SUBLIMINAL PERCEPTION

There is, however, evidence of *subliminal perception,* unconscious perception of stimuli. Subjects' behavior indicates that they perceive words or objects flashed on a screen at a rate that exceeds their threshold for conscious sensory recognition. At one time the manipulation of subliminal perception was considered for advertising purposes. It was intended that the names of sponsors' products, for instance, would be subliminally presented during a television program. The audience would be unaware of receiving the stimuli, which would still make an impression and affect purchasing habits. Although legislation has been passed to prevent the commercial use of subliminal perception, this kind of perception is likely to occur in everyday life. We have noted, for example, P. Ekman's finding that cues to emotional meaning are not consciously perceived but still affect behavior (see Chapter 3).

FIGURE-GROUND PATTERNING

Stimuli are not necessarily perceived in terms of their measurable characteristics: four lines, red sphere, E flat. They are usually perceived as unitary wholes: square, red ball, "rock and roll." One of the common characteristics of perceptual organization is *figure-ground patterning.* Some stimuli stand apart as the focus of perception (figure), whereas others remain in the background. Contrasting objects seem, depending upon their size, to stand out as figure. For instance, a small, black circle on the wall will stand out as figure: We perceive a black circle on a white wall rather than a white wall covering most of a black background. Figure-ground patterns are also affected by learning. In Figure 4-2, picture A may be viewed as the profile of a young woman or of an old hag. The picture is ambiguous, for either profile may stand forth as figure. When subjects were first shown picture B or picture C before seeing picture A, almost all first saw in picture A the one that they had seen previously (Leeper, 1935). Because our adjustment behavior is influenced by our perceptions of the environment, it is important that stimuli are perceived as organized unities, rather than as random patterns. It is equally important that previous experience can determine what stands out for us.

Figure 4-2   Ambiguous figure-ground effects: The wife and mother-in-law ambiguity. Reproduced by permission of R. W. Leeper.

PERCEPTUAL SELECTIVITY

Selectivity is another important characteristic of sensory perception. An individual selects sensory inputs according to his personal needs and motives. He may reject some stimuli and actively seek out others. All organisms show perceptual selectivity in scanning their environments. A combat pilot continuously scans the sky for signs of other aircraft. Any dark object in his field of vision or the reflection of the sunlight from an object will immediately attract his attention. The same stimuli may be ignored by the casual air traveler. He is more likely to enjoy the cloud formations or to view the landscape calmly.

Most people seek information that will aid them in reaching their goals or reduce threats to their integrity. Vigilance and selective attention may be positive factors in adjustment, but they may also reduce the capacity to perceive the environment realistically. Investigators have postulated the process of *perceptual defense*, the tendency to avoid inputs that stimulate personal conflicts. Such stimuli tend to arouse anxieties and are therefore not recognized. One of the earlier experiments on perceptual defense (McGinnies, 1949) involved flashing words on a screen. At first they were flashed too quickly for accurate perception, but the speed was gradually reduced until they were clear to the subjects. "Taboo" words were interspersed with neutral ones, and the subjects had to wait for lower speeds to recognize them than they did for the neutral words. The investigators concluded that taboo words personally threaten individuals and that consequently they are not perceived as readily as are neutral words.

Although the concept of perceptual defense has been generally accepted, it is not clear whether the subjects actually did not perceive the stimuli or whether they simply did not report their perceptions readily. Did E. McGinnies observe the effects of unconscious factors or of social demands in the experimental situation? L. Postman and his colleagues (1953) performed a similar experiment but with different instructions. To encourage quick responses to taboo words the instructions were framed to imply that ready recognition of taboo words is a positive sign of mental health. Under these conditions taboo words were reported as readily as were the other words. Interpretation of the results as caused by unconscious factors is therefore not completely satisfactory. To understand an individual's behavior it is important to evaluate his social setting, his cultural values, and his previous learning, as well as his possible psychological conflicts.

The more *ambiguous* the stimuli are, the more likely it is that personal needs and motivations will influence perception. The fewer external cues there are to help organize and interpret stimuli, the more a person must depend upon his internal characteristics. The pilot who is set to locate enemy aircraft may react with a start when he notices a dark object which turns out on further inspection to be a bird. A person in an unfamiliar country may perceive the actions of a crowd as hostile when in fact they are merely part of a traditional ceremony. This principle has been applied in the development of projective tests. The test stimuli are purposely unclear, and the subject's responses therefore provide information on his personal needs, motives, and ways of adjusting.

A recent line of research has suggested that personality characteristics are associated with *perceptual styles*. The broader term "cognitive style" describes consistent ways in which individuals differ in drawing inferences from situations. After studying characteristic perceptual styles we can make assumptions about general personality functioning. H. A. Witkin and his colleagues (1962) found that individuals differ in their dependence upon cues from inside their bodies. Subjects took turns seated in a completely darkened room, with a vertical luminous rod at one end. The chair and the rod could both be tilted; the subjects' task was to judge how close the rod was to being vertical. By shifting the rod and the chair the investigators could determine whether the subject was depending mainly upon visual (external) cues or kinesthetic (internal) cues in making his judgments. Those subjects who depended primarily upon visual cues were called "field dependent," and those who depended primarily upon kinesthetic cues were called "body dependent." The same subjects also showed systematic differences in the ways in which they responded to other perceptual tasks like identifying a figure hidden within a more complex figure (embedded figures).

For our purposes it is sufficient to note that input data may differ in characteristic ways, depending upon the individual, and that these differences may reflect personality. Although researchers in this area tend to attribute consistent perceptual modes to personality characteristics, it is not clear, however, which comes first. It is possible that we learn early to perceive in characteristic ways and that our styles of life are conditioned by these perceptions. On the other hand, personality characteristics may determine perceptual styles.

DATA PROCESSING

Once sensory information has been fed into a computer it passes through a series of electronic circuits programmed to assign it meaning. The human brain is also "programmed" to understand sensory inputs in specific ways. Subjective values are assigned to inputs, and cognitive activities establish meaning.

FRAME OF REFERENCE

We decide whether we like or dislike what we see, for example; then we classify it with similar objects in order to decide what action to take. The meaning that an individual assigns to inputs is personal and dependent upon his subjective *frame of reference*, his own characteristic way of viewing the world. Personal motives, past experiences, and specific characteristics of the stimuli are all combined to help determine the meaning assigned to input data.

When a person's perceptions do not agree with those of most individuals he is likely to have difficulty. If, for instance, he perceives the sound of the wind as "the devil's voice," he may be suspected of "hallucinating" and assigned the role of "mental patient." But in another setting he may be considered gifted at coining creative metaphors and assigned the role of "poet."

PREVIOUS EXPERIENCE

A person is constantly attempting to find familiar elements in new situations. These elements can alert him to possibilities relevant to himself: good or bad, dangerous or pleasant, and the like. Consequently, *previous experience* is very important in assigning meaning. Many events are assigned the same meaning by members of a culture because their backgrounds and experiences are similar; each person also has unique experiences that modify meaning, however. It follows that an understanding of the stimulus situation alone is not sufficient to predict individual behavior.

Limited experience can reduce a person's capacity to understand new situations, often to his detriment. Other people can sometimes take advantage of him. For instance, salesmen draw upon information that many of us have not acquired and are unable to evaluate adequately. Political leaders may play upon motives that have little to do with the programs that they propose to initiate. Many people are not sufficiently informed to analyze the implications of a politician's proposals, but because he has associated these proposals with a "good" cause, they may behave in ways that they would oppose if they had all the information. In any event, once the input has been assigned meaning, it provides the person with possible ways for him to act.

CATEGORIZATION

Categorizing information is a highly adaptive activity. Organizing disparate perceptual experiences into meaningful groups reduces a jumble of sensations and thus the complexity of our environment. Verbal symbols are the primary tools of categorization. By assigning labels man can render different things equivalent; he can group objects, events, and people and then respond to them according to their class membership, rather than to their uniqueness.

Although categorizing is useful, it may also result in perceptual errors. One major difficulty in human relations results from too inclusive categorization based on racial, religious, and ethnic differences—from *prejudices.* On the basis of a single cue alone—skin color, last name, or clothing—a person is *stereotyped* and assigned characteristics that have been meaninglessly attributed to a large group. Group stereotypes are usually learned from what others have said about a group, rather than from direct contact and personal experience with members of that group. Because stereotyped attributes often have negative implications, direct experience is then avoided, and the stereotypes are never directly tested.

Stimulus qualities play an important part in prejudice; the clearer they are, the more likely it is that a group will be categorized. If members of a group cannot be perceptually separated it is impossible to classify them. For example, skin color is an obvious cue that may be used to separate people within a society. The simple fact of black skin will cause many people to approach those who have it in predetermined ways. Black people are thus categorized according to minimal information and stereotyped characteristics are attributed to them whether or not they are appropriate.[2]

Stereotyping also results from other cues: sex, age, political party, and so on. When categories are too general they hinder accurate perception and consequently adjustment. For example, if one were to abide by the generalization "all old people are senile and must be treated as if they were children," he would likely often find himself in embarrassing situations.

Our personal needs and motives interact with this tendency to categorize

---

[2] See J. H. Griffin's description (1961) of a white man's experiences after he had chemically changed his skin color.

too broadly. Identifying with groups tends to influence our perceptions of their behavior as "always correct." Although we carefully scrutinize the behavior of opposing groups, our own behavior is likely to be overlooked or always perceived as positive. The more oversimplified or falsely constructed basic categories are, the more likely we are to react to new situations ineffectively. We may be hampered by inability to see shades of gray, or we may become intolerant of the rights of others.

TEMPORARY NEEDS AND CIRCUMSTANCES

Although most of us have rather stable attitudes and values connected with processing information, some sensory input may occur when our responses are not taking their characteristic form. Physiological fatigue or high arousal may distort our perceptions. Individuals are especially prone to reacting "out of character" in conditions of stress. In extreme circumstances faulty labeling may result in behavior that has critical consequences for adjustment. For example, a policeman faced with a threatening mob may perceive a hostile figure pulling an object from his pocket and pointing it at him. He may assign the meaning "weapon" to the object and shoot the other person to protect himself. To his dismay, he may then find that the object was a pipe, and his behavior may result in the loss of his job and criminal proceedings against him.

The temporary effects of sedatives and other drugs also reduce the capacity to process sensory information, and again action may be potentially damaging. Many examples could be cited, but it is sufficient to recognize the added difficulty of predicting behavior when we must take into account the possibility of temporary conditions.

DECIDING ON ACTION

Once the data have been assigned meaning the individual must *decide* what action to take. His decision depends upon the resources available and his success in using them to deal with similar past experiences. The circumstances may be perceived as conflict; therefore whatever action is taken will not be completely satisfactory, for some needs must be denied in order to fulfill others.

Situations also vary in the time allowed for decisions. It may be necessary to decide before all the relevant information is satisfactorily processed; the person has to "take a chance." Given more time he might make a different decision. Again "risky" circumstances are generally those of stress, which further reduce adaptive capacities.

Individuals who have poorly formulated self-concepts often experience stress when they must make decisions. Their overconcern with others' evaluations of their behavior causes them to vacillate between one mode of action and another. In its extreme form doubt about the appropriateness of decisions frequently prevents a person from making them. Stress continues to build, threatening breakdown of adjustment.

Data processing occurs entirely within the organism, as a form of cognitive activity. We know little about man's "circuits" and "programming" compared to what we know of those of the computer. Cognitive processes have traditionally been considered as contained within a "black box," the insides of man, which are unavailable to direct observation.

BEHAVIORAL OUTPUT

The output of data is the final step in a computer. A high-speed machine prints out the results for the operator. This output can also serve as a source of feedback, though obviously the operator must once again prepare it in the form proper for sensory input. At any rate, new information from the machine's output may be fed back into it as input, and then the perception process begins anew. Human behavior is similar. Actions create new sensory information to be perceived and acted upon. Depending upon the nature of the feedback, specific behavior is continued, discontinued, or modified.

A hypothetical example will clarify the entire perceptual process.

ALICE'S EXPERIENCE

Alice, a college sophomore, and her friend had gone to spend the weekend at a mountain resort. The first day had been great. They had met two young men who had invited them to dinner; the men were charming companions and good dancers. Later it became clear that Alice's friend and her young man were becoming quite involved. She told Alice that she had decided to spend the remainder of the night with him and that Alice could do whatever she wished. As Alice disapproved, she decided to return to the campus that night, even though it was late. After driving for about an hour in her open sports car, she noticed that the road was becoming narrower, but as she was still angry with her friend she paid little attention and drove on. Finally the pavement ended, and she realized that she had traveled a great deal farther than she should have without reaching a town; she had lost her way on the unfamiliar mountain roads. She decided to turn around and retrace her path to the main road, but, in her dismay, the engine sputtered and stopped. She was out of gas and stranded late at night in an apparently uninhabited area.

She did not remember having seen a house for some time and wondered what was the best thing to do. It was chilly, dark, and lonely—not a pleasant spot for timid Alice. While trying to decide whether to walk down the road for help or to wait for another car to come along, she heard a distinct sound, the rhythmic crunch suggestive of human footsteps. The darkness reduced her vision, resulting in ambiguity of input. As she continued processing the available information, she decided that she did indeed hear footsteps and, even worse, the heavy and pronounced footsteps of a man. Because of her recent experience with her friend, her present circumstances, and her general attitudes toward sex, Alice immediately ascribed intentions of rape and assault to the unknown figure. How she wished that she had taken her father's advice and bought a car that she could lock instead of her small sports convertible! She could not lock herself in the car, she did not know which way to run, and she felt helpless to defend herself physically. For lack of a better solution she stayed put and awaited further cues. Feedback was quick, for she saw a shape looming out of the darkness. Her initial flash of terror was dissipated when she realized that the figure was wearing a dress. In relief she called out for help. Again feedback was quick—a low, gruff voice answered, "What's the matter, chick, you lost?" Her initial apprehension returned in force, and her mind was torn by doubt and indecision. Should she grab the jack handle from the back seat and fight? Should she run off into the woods? Should she await still further information? Again her conflict was great; none of these actions seemed completely satisfactory. The figure came closer, his pace quickening, and she could hear his heavy breathing—she had to make a decision now! She checked a sob, grabbed the jack handle, and flung herself toward her would-be assailant. Her tears blurred her vision, but she saw that he was big and burly. He sidestepped easily and pinioned her arms to her sides. "Hey, wait a minute lady, I'm not going to hurt you. What's wrong, you nuts or something?" Alice looked up at the badge and hat of a forest ranger, then laughed and cried with relief. After composing herself, she borrowed some gas and received directions to the main road.

Alice's initial perception of the footsteps had been accurate, though their context and her recent experiences had led her to stereotyped expectations, which increased her stress. The ambiguity of the stimuli had caused her to project her own fears and needs onto her perceptions. Her wish to avoid a man alone in the woods late at night had led her to perceive his overcoat as a dress. This misperception had reduced her fear temporarily, but further feedback combined with a short time in which to make her decision had created sufficient stress to reduce her dependence upon outside cues almost completely. It was only after the final reduction of her stress that she was able to perceive circumstances realistically and to respond in an adaptive way.[3]

SPECIAL TOPICS IN PERCEPTION

Sensory Deprivation

Psychologists have studied the effects of reduced sensory input on human functioning. Internal stimuli increasingly dominate the perceptual field when external inputs are reduced. Responses to ambiguous stimuli (for example, Alice's experience as reported in the previous section) or to reduction of

[3] Modified from a case presented by T. R. Sarbin (1968).

sensory stimulation show that perception becomes increasingly distorted as a person relies on internal inputs. Studies of sensory deprivation suggest that stable adjustment depends upon adequate contact with the outside world.

Subjects may be paid to remain in small, dark, soundproof cubicles either a specified time or as long as they can (Vernon, 1963). Other conditions permitting as little sensory input as possible have also been studied (for example, see Solomon *et al.*, 1961). It is, of course, impossible to cut off a subject's sensory inputs completely; he can always detect his own breathing, body movements, and so on.

The results of these studies have been varied but often quite striking. Subjects have typically experienced some disorientation, impairment of ability to solve problems, and reduction of other adaptive capacities. Some have developed delusions and hallucinations, both classical symptoms of serious mental disorder. Subjects also become more responsive to suggestion and prone to accept as fact any information given to them. Reports of increased suggestibility have led some people to draw a parallel between sensory deprivation and "brainwashing" procedures. General Dean's experiences during his captivity by the North Koreans in 1955 provide an example of the use of sensory deprivation to change attitudes and beliefs. He was closely confined for long periods with minimal stimulation aside from the pain of his cramped muscles. His personal solution was to solve calculus problems in his head; in this way he "filled" empty time and maintained his psychological integrity.

Reports from explorers and others in conditions of deprivation have also added to our knowledge. Notable is a report by A. Bombard (1954), who was alone on a life raft crossing the Atlantic Ocean for sixty-five days. He experienced a great need for other people to confirm his impressions. He feared that he was becoming incapable of telling what was real and what was not. A sixteen-year-old boy, R. L. Graham, found himself in similar circumstances sailing around the world alone in a twenty-four-foot sloop, except that he had a cat for company; he, too, noted the terrible loneliness for another person but apparently suffered no perceptual distortions (Graham, 1968). Although experiences like his cannot be considered to involve sensory deprivation, they obviously involve social deprivation.

Caution is indicated, however, in attributing the results of sensory-deprivation experiments to absence of sensory input alone. M. T. Orne and K. Scheibe (1964) designed an experiment to test the effects of expectation on subjects' behavior under conditions of quasi-sensory deprivation. One group of subjects was told that it was participating in a sensory-deprivation study. The experimenters wore white coats, physical examinations were performed by a physician, and the subjects were led to believe that they would probably have disturbing or unusual experiences. They were told that they could press a "panic button" and be released from the experiment if necessary. They were then requested to remain for four hours in a normal office (with desk, chair, lights, and so on), certainly not an environment of sensory deprivation. The control group was not given physical examinations or prepared for unusual experiences, nor was it offered a "panic button." Its members were also told that they were part of a control group. As the investigators had predicted, the "experimental" subjects reported many of the classical phenomena associated with sensory deprivation—perceptual and cognitive changes, anxiousness, and so on. Members of the control group sat out their time in the same environment but experienced little or no stress and reported none of the symptoms of sensory deprivation.

This study should alert us to the possibility that experimental subjects act to please investigators in hopes of furthering science. And, though it raises questions about the causes of behavior and discomfort in isolated conditions, it does not necessarily ignore the reality of the subjects' experiences. Lack of stimulation may heighten need for other human beings, and the insecurity of being alone in strange surroundings may cause sufficient stress to distort subjective experiences. Bombard obviously was not deprived of actual sensory input; on the contrary, the Atlantic Ocean may have offered stimulation that most of us can do without. But communication with other people was not possible. It may be that the stress factor lies in man's dependence upon a stable social system for survival. When it is taken away his integrity is threatened and his perceptions become distorted.

Sensory deprivation has implications for personal adjustment. People labeled "schizophrenic" often have strange ideas (delusions) and perceptions (hallucinations). They characteristically attempt to deal with stress by turning their attention away from the stress-producing circumstances, that is, by "withdrawing" from other people. As a result they attend to the stimuli that are available—their thoughts and fantasies. Their inputs eventually become as "real" as the external inputs, resulting in highly idiosyncratic patterns of behavior. When they come into contact with other people, their deviant behavior may seem shocking; then social institutions responsible for dealing with this kind of deviance (mental hospitals) are brought into the picture. Schizophrenic behavior is explained as symptomatic of disease, and those suffering from it are removed from society. Somewhat less serious effects follow when an individual shuts himself off from everyday personal interaction. He is deprived of a number of learning experiences that would be useful in his adjustment, and he may be considered naïve, "stuffy," or eccentric. As isolated people receive less feedback from their actions than do others, modification of their behavior may be slow.

Psi Phenomena

Phenomena that have been historically associated with the supernatural, the unknown, and the mysterious are now being studied by psychologists under controlled experimental conditions. These investigations are not yet widespread among psychologists, and there is controversy over the genuineness of the phenomena themselves (McConnell, 1969; Rhine & Hall, 1969). This part of the field has therefore been labeled "parapsychology," implying that it is not quite a legitimate field of study within the established limits of psychology. Rather than embroiling the student in these polemics, we shall turn to examination of the kinds of behavior under investigation, to "Psi-land," as it is called by parapsychologists.

EXTRASENSORY PERCEPTION

A response to an event that is not perceived through any of the normal sense modalities is called extrasensory perception (E.S.P.). Three types of phenomena fall into this category: those connected with telepathy, clairvoyance, and precognition.

MENTAL TELEPATHY is the transfer of thought from one person to another without overt communication. Claims to his ability have been made by "mind readers" throughout the ages, but its presence is extremely difficult to test under experimental conditions. One major problem with all the psi phenomena is that they apparently cannot be brought about at will. If they do not appear during experimental investigations, it does not necessarily mean that they do not occur at other times.

Personal reports of telepathy are often exciting and convincing. For instance, an acquaintance of mine described telepathic experiences that he had had with a close friend during adolescence. Neither he nor his friend could explain the capacity of each for knowing what the other was thinking, but he claimed that they carried it to the point of signaling each other's positions when separated on mountainous terrain. Both enjoyed hiking and frequently went on outings in the mountains together. They would go their separate ways with no prearranged meeting place. When it was time to meet, one would concentrate on his position, and the other would read his thoughts. Each received specific kinds of thoughts better than he received others; one therefore thought in words because his friend was able to receive them best, whereas the other would visualize his position because his partner received pictorial imagery best. Examples of telepathy over long distances are particularly striking because all possibility of communication through nonverbal cues is thus eliminated. Whether or not my friend was telling the truth cannot be determined, but there seems no reason for him to have made up the story. Such reports have stimulated investigators to study parapsychological behavior in the laboratory.

CLAIRVOYANCE is another form of E.S.P., the perception of objects or events that do not impinge on the senses. Examples are commonly reported, especially stories of sudden awareness that loved ones many miles away have died. Such experiences just seem to happen and are very difficult to bring under experimental control.

It may be argued that people have many curious thoughts but report only those that impress them because of their association with events. Consequently only events that support the notion of clairvoyance are reported, though in fact their association with specific thoughts occurs by chance. Furthermore, it is not unlikely that many of our thoughts are directed, perhaps unconsciously, at events that are very likely to occur. A mother whose son is away at war may awaken in the middle of the night with the frightening notion that her son is dying. The next morning a telegram verifies her fears, and she is convinced for various reasons that she has been clairvoyant about his death. But his death was somewhat probable, and it is likely that she has had earlier, similar thoughts that were not followed by the event. The subtler the connection between thought and event, the more likely it is to smack of the occult.

PRECOGNITION, the perception of an event that will occur in the future, is probably the most studied form of E.S.P. Some individuals have become quite noted for their predictions. Jeanne Dixon (Montgomery, 1965), for instance, has claimed to predict international events quite accurately through messages received from a supernatural source. Yet J. B. Rhine, the father of research on E.S.P., has questioned such claims: "Lots of people predict things. She happens to have a good press agent, but let me answer impersonally. Unless prophecies are carefully recorded in advance of fulfillment and checked by responsible and trained scientists, they should not be taken seriously" (Rhine & Hall, 1969).

The classical experiment for testing precognition is guessing a card before it is turned up. A pack of twenty-five cards, five cards marked with each of five symbols, is used. The subject guesses the symbol coming as the cards are turned up one at a time. He will make five correct guesses by chance alone. The experimenter who turns the cards is usually out of the subject's view. Subjects who score consistently above chance have been found. Rhine has reported that one man hardly ever failed to do well, no matter what the conditions. He was equally good at "predicting" an event that had already occurred; that is, he could guess what card had already been turned up (clairvoyance). After he had difficulties in a love affair, however, his ability completely disappeared, and he was never again able to score above chance.

Rhine believes that it is characteristic of people with extraordinary psi ability to lose it later; some people also lose it periodically. A "turning of luck" for a man who has been steadily winning at the crap table is attributed to *negative psi*; suddenly he becomes a consistent loser. Most professional gamblers will verify the existence of this phenomena; they recognize when they are "hot" and when they are "cold." Indeed, even many nonprofessionals recognize what appear to be "runs of luck."

Several factors seem associated with negative psi. For instance, other thoughts appear to disturb a subject. If a subject who is scoring well is kept late but is too polite to tell the experimenter that he has a date, his perform-ance invariably drops just as far below chance as he had been scoring above chance.

Belief in E.S.P. also appears to be related to psi ability. Nonbelievers seem to score below chance, whereas believers' scores average above chance. No explanation for this phenomenon is known. It is possible that believing aids concentration and that subjects with high psi ability are preselected on the basis of their belief. It is also possible that belief has developed through successful experiences. Another possibility is that nonbelievers subtly defend their belief by rejecting their best guesses in favor of alternatives that turn out to be incorrect.

PSYCHOKINESES

The other main group of psi phenomena are the *psychokineses* (P.K.). They are defined as mental operations that produce direct effects on material bodies or energy systems. For example, an individual "wills" a certain number to appear on the throw of a die. Classical P.K. phenomena are popularly said to demonstrate the triumph of "mind over matter."

Rhine has reported some recent research on psychic action over plants. A sensitive apparatus registering flow of electrical current is attached to a plant's leaf epidermis. Two such plants are placed before a subject, who is behind a screen so that he cannot breathe on them; he concentrates on the target plant. Subjects are selected because they have "green thumbs." If the current in the target plant fluctuates greatly, compared to that in the control plant, a "hit" is recorded. The studies are showing some moderate positive effects, but they are not yet conclusive.

We do not intend to offer detailed criticism of work with psi phenomena. E. Hilgard and R. Atkinson (1967) have presented a concise critical discussion of this work. But parapsychological topics do suggest the diversity of human experience. The phenomena are very important to those who experience them, regardless of whether or not they can be incorporated into a scientific body of knowledge. They are often cited as support for cherished beliefs and values.

CHEMICALLY INDUCED PERCEPTUAL CHANGES

There is increasing interest among scientists and laymen in drugs that produce unusual changes in perception. Such drugs have been labeled *psychotomimetic* because their effects are thought to mimic the symptoms of serious mental illness, primarily those of schizophrenia. They have also been called "psychedelics," which can be translated literally as "mind manifesting." Three of these drugs have aroused major interest: mescaline and peyote, which are derivatives of certain cactus plants (peyote is less used because it causes nausea after ingestion and "hangover" after it wears off); psilocybin, an artificially manufactured drug similar to derivatives of some mushroom species; and L.S.D.-25 (lysergic acid diethylamide), an artificially manufactured drug.

A SOCIAL ISSUE

Both historically and currently the psychedelics (and other drugs) have been used by thrill seekers and people wishing to escape the pressures of everyday living. There is much controversy over the use of drugs for such purposes. In fact laymen in modern American society are primarily aware of these uses of the psychedelics and most people find themselves taking a stand for or against them. The term "drug abuse" is frequently associated with thrill seeking and escapism; it connotes general disapproval of drug use, which is considered a danger to our "way of life" and harmful to individuals. There are several reasons for this view. First, psychedelic drugs in uncontrolled dosages may have dangerous physical and psychological side effects. Second, they may lead to psychological addiction and dependence, resulting in the users' withdrawal from other social activity. Third, they must be obtained through illegal sources, so that users may be influenced by "pushers'" other antisocial attitudes and become part of the criminal world.

Sale of psychedelic drugs is currently restricted by laws that provide punishment for convicted offenders. Black-market sources are the major suppliers, and doses are therefore poorly controlled; furthermore, the drugs are sold indiscriminately to anyone who can pay. Psychologists are interested in the social and psychological motives leading to drug abuse; but we shall take up that topic in Chapter 13.

PEYOTISM

The use of psychedelic drugs for religious or philosophical purposes also has a long history. Cactus and mushroom derivatives have been used in many cultures, especially those of the American Indians, for religious and ceremonial purposes. The Indians of Mexico used peyote to bring on experiences associated with divine intervention. The Spanish Inquisitors imposed strict bans on its use because according to their Christian beliefs, it was an invention of the devil. The tribes of northern Mexico, however, continued to use the drug, and it gradually spread through the southwestern Indian tribes of the United States and as far north as Saskatchewan in Canada.

Peyotism is considered the native religion of more than fifty American Indian tribes today. They have been legally incorporated as the Native American Church in order to prevent religious and political forces from stopping their use of peyote. Their rites are generally held in all-night sessions weekly and on special occasions. After ingesting the drug the participants sing and experience communion and revelation. Elements of Christian doctrine have been introduced into their ceremonies—the flesh of the cactus is considered the flesh of Christ. It has been suggested that the use of peyote has been of great value in furnishing the Indians with spiritual guidance and in rehabilitating Indian alcoholics (Masters and Houston, 1966).

THE PSYCHEDELIC-DRUG MOVEMENT

The current "psychedelic-drug movement" may be considered as based on philosophical use of these drugs. Thousands of people use them illegally on occasion and insist upon their value. They believe that the drugs bring about desirable changes in intrapersonal organization and interpersonal relations. Most of these people do not create social problems, and their drug-taking activities are generally not widely known. They are not completely enthralled with drug use and continue normal social life—in the "outer world." But intellectually they value inner experience and the understanding of other than overt actions and visible changes. In a sense they share a mystical doctrine, claiming to seek a greater meaning in the world than that of empirical reality. Generally they come from the better-educated segments of society; they include students, artists, clergymen, and scientists.

The fringes of this movement have become widely known through the publicity attracted by the "hippies," who have made drugs their major cause. Many of them have settled in cultish units, essentially rejecting the rest of society.

THERAPEUTIC USES

Another major use of the psychedelic drugs is as therapeutic agents. But recent legislation to restrict their use has reduced research possibilities considerably. The effects of L.S.D. have been studied most extensively and reports indicate that it has served as a useful adjunct to psychotherapy, resulting in significant improvement in alcoholics and criminals. Some studies have also suggested that L.S.D. reduces the period necessary to treat some neuroses. The therapist usually acts as a "director," or "guide," while the patient experiences the effects of the drug. Improvement is assumed to result from the patient's ability to perceive reality in new ways and to discover new aspects within himself that may lead to a more positive self-image and redefinition of goals. P. E. Masters and J. Houston have concluded:

> On the basis of a survey of a great mass of literature concerning the use of psychedelic drugs in psychotherapy, it seems safe to conclude that for certain kinds of patients, and also for certain kinds of therapists, these drugs have present value and an enormously greater potential value. However, not every therapist is able to use the psychedelics effectively or even without some danger to himself as well as to his patients. And while, for example, alcoholics, some sex deviates, and persons with anxiety problems often have been helped by LSD and similar drugs, the psychedelics are of little use with highly dependent individuals, persons of low intelligence, or in the treatment of compulsion neurosis. These drugs are regarded by some therapists as

specifically contraindicated in patients with deep depressions, with conversion or fixed neurosis, and in most all cases, with psychotics. (1966, pp. 55–56)

PSYCHEDELIC EXPERIENCES

The psychedelic experience is an individual matter. Its nature may be determined largely by the person's expectations and the guide's directions. There is no doubt that serious psychological difficulties may be caused by the experience, but such difficulties are more common after poorly controlled "trips." Psychological direction by a professional guide and proper dosage reduce the chances of "bad trips." Although each person's experiences with these drugs are unique, certain effects are frequently reported. F. Barron (1969) has aptly summarized them:

1. *Intensification of Esthetic Sensibility.* Colors become more vivid and glowing; the play of light on objects is enchanting; surface details become sharply defined; sensual harmonies, of sound, light, color become marked. There are beautiful synesthesias, in which patterns of association usually confined to a single sense modality may cross over to others: music is "heard" as colored light, for example.

In some cases, ugliness will become intensified. A garish light may seem horrible, an unmusical sound unbearable; a false tone in human voice may seem like a shriek; a false expression on a face may make it into a grotesque mask.

Both beauty and ugliness in objects thus are more than usually important and the esthetic qualities of the perceived world take on much greater value.

2. *Unusual Associational Patterns Are Much More Frequent.* Much as in the synectics technique when it works, the familiar can become quite strange. One may look at a familiar object as though seeing it for the first time. Perceptual habits drop away; hidden essences seem to reveal themselves. Analogical and symbolic properties of persons, events, and objects come into the foreground and combine to produce meaning and pattern where none was seen before.

3. *Intuition in Relation to Other People Is Increased.* Other people, whether they themselves are under the influence of the drug or not, are "seen through," though not necessarily in a negative sense. One subject wrote: "The faces of other people became clear and beautiful and open. . . . I could look at them without fear or shyness. . . . People looked naked, shed of a fog of dissimulations, anxieties, hypocrisies. Everyone was true to his own self and no one was ashamed."

Again, however, there can be a negative aspect to this. Intuition is a risky way of understanding others; it can result in brilliant successes or in almost incredible misapprehensions. It proceeds by seizing upon striking details at the expense of other details and making a sort of theory on very limited evidence on the basis simply of "fit." Fictional amateur detectives in the Sherlock Holmes tradition made intuition their stock in trade, and of course they were always right. But when the intuitive approach fails, it can be spectacularly wrong. So far as the hallucinogenic drugs are concerned, we can say with assurance that they increase the use of intuition and so increase one factor in creativity; but sober judgment is the final arbiter of the validity of the intuitive leap.

4. *Higher Purposes and the Motivation to Make One's Life Philosophically Meaningful Become Very Important.* Trivial motives, pretenses, social "games" are seen as distractions from the true business of life. One's own life and meaning may be meditated upon, and a new appraisal *sub specie aeternitatis* may be made. Thus, profound motivational change in the direction of dedicating one's life to a higher purpose may come about. The ordinary round of life will no longer do.

This too may have troublesome consequences, it need hardly be added. For one thing, it upsets other people, who can no longer count upon one's more mundane motives. Changes of this sort in motivational structure may result in ruptures in personal relations, work relations, financial arrangements, as well as general social behavior. If in this new cosmic scale of things one's life seems intolerably empty and too far gone to change, there may be impulses toward self-destruction or cessation of the known self.

5. *A Mystical Experience of Absolute Freedom May Occur.* This is perhaps not so frequent a phenomenon as to deserve to be called typical, but it occurs often enough in persons under the influence of hallucinogenic drugs to warrant remark; and as a source of motivational change it is by all odds the most powerful of all. In it, the personal ego seems utterly dissolved, and the individual has his existence in the grounds of being itself. The experience is of "the void"; that is, the "abyss" of which philosophers have spoken. Without entering into the metaphysics of the matter, we can say as psychologists that the individual who has had this experience emerges from it with a sense of inner freedom and power, although as usual there may be a negative as well as a positive aspect to this. (1969, pp. 151–154)

A more personal description of the mescaline experience has been given by A. Huxley:

Intensified light, intensified color and intensified significance do not exist in isolation. They inhere in objects. And here again the experiences of those who have taken a hallucinogen, while in a good state of mental and physical health, and with a proper degree of philosophical preparation, seem to follow a fairly regular pattern. When the eyes are closed, visionary experience begins with the appearance in the visual field of living, moving geometries. These abstract, three-dimensional forms are intensely illuminated and brilliantly colored. After a time they tend to take on the appearance of concrete objects, such as richly patterned carpets, or mosaics, or carvings. These in turn modulate into rich and elaborate buildings, set in landscapes of extraordinary beauty. Neither the buildings nor the landscapes remain static, but change continuously. In none of their metamorphoses do they resemble any particular building or landscape seen by the subject in his ordinary state and remembered from the near or distant past. These things are all new. The subject does not remember or invent; he discovers them, "out there," in the psychological equivalent of a hitherto unexplored geographical region (quoted in Cholden, 1956, p. 48).

We have mentioned that psychedelic experiences were originally believed to be similar to the symptoms of severe mental illness. It was hoped that study of these chemically induced experiences would lead to better understanding of mental illness. In fact, the initial enthusiasm of investigators led many

TABLE 4-1 SCHIZOPHRENIA AND DRUG-INDUCED "PSYCHOSES" [a]

	Schizophrenic Reactions	*Drug-Induced Psychoses*
Mood	Daydreaming and extreme withdrawal from personal contacts, ranging from sullen reluctance to talk to actual muteness	Dreaming, introspective state, but preference for discussing visions and ruminations with someone
Communication	Speech vague, ambiguous, difficult to follow; no concern about inability to communicate; past tense common	Speech rambling or incoherent but usually related to reality; subjects try to communicate thoughts; present tense used
Irrationality	Great preoccupation with bodily functions; illnesses attributed to unreasonable causes (the devil, "enemies")	Great interest in the vast array of new sensations being experienced; symptoms attributed to reasonable causes
Hallucinations	Frequent hallucinations, usually auditory and extremely threatening; hallucinations very real and attempts to rationalize them rejected	Hallucinations predominantly visual; the rare auditory hallucinations not so personal or threatening; subjects attempt to explain them rationally
Delusions	Delusions common, usually of paranoid or grandiose pattern	Delusions rare; when occur, probably due to individual personality conflicts
Mannerisms	Bizarre mannerisms, postures, and even waxy inflexibility manifested by certain patients	Strange and bizarre mannerisms rare

Source: Adapted by, Coleman from Hollister (1962) and Luby *et al.* (1962).

[a] The similarities between the symptoms of schizophrenia and those produced by the psychotomimetic drugs (most commonly LSD-25, mescaline, and psilocybin) have led many investigators to speculate that their biochemical bases may be the same. But schizophrenia and drug-induced symptoms differ significantly, not only in many particular respects, but most importantly, in overall pattern.

people to believe that those who experience L.S.D. in fact "go crazy." But the belief that L.S.D. experiences are the same as symptoms of mental illness has now largely been discarded. In Table 4-1 a number of differences between the drug-induced experiences and the thought disorders of schizophrenia are shown.

SUMMARY

In this chapter we have examined the perceptual processes. With the aid of an analogy—with the high-speed electronic computer—we have tried to simplify understanding of the complex process of sensing stimuli and converting them into meaningful percepts. At the input stage receptor organs act selectively to receive stimuli from the environment; the input is reorganized in the brain and given meaning; from meaning adaptive behavioral output results. In the processing of information attitudes, values, prejudices, and previous experience combine to determine the meaning to be assigned to input. Sometimes these factors promote adjustment, but sometimes they do not.

The experiences that arise when man is deprived of sensory input (sensory deprivation) are sometimes startling and often similar to those experiences of people classified as "disturbed." The effects of the experimental situations and subjects' resulting expectations must, however, be accounted for before the reported changes can be ascribed to reduced sensory input alone.

Parapsychology is the study of psi phenomena—extrasensory perception (E.S.P.) and psychokinesis (P.K.). In the former, individuals appear to perceive without sensory input—"reading" others' thoughts, becoming aware of events that occur far away, and predicting future events. Psychokinetic phenomena are colloquially called "mind over matter," the ability to affect objects by thought. This entire area is fascinating but in its infancy; few explanations of its phenomena are widely accepted.

Chemically induced perceptual changes include those from L.S.D. and peyote. The close association of these drugs with amoral behavior, religious doctrines, and social values has caused widespread public concern. Their use in treatment and the quality of the experiences that they produce have been overshadowed by public furor associated with "drug abuse." We have examined some of the more scientific findings about these drugs.

PART II

THEORETICAL
VIEWS
OF
MAN
AND
ASSOCIATED
TECHNIQUES

We use the term "theoretical views of man," rather than "theories of personality" because the term "personality" implies emphasis on the "inner working," the psychological "insides," of man. Indeed, some, though not all, theories focus almost entirely on what happens within the individual. Since our major purpose is to account for the totality of man's behavior and not just his insides, "theoretical views of man" seems a more appropriate term.

In this part we examine ways in which psychologists and psychiatrists explain man's behavior. In keeping with the basic purpose of the textbook, the therapeutic procedures associated with each view are described in connection with problems of personal adjustment.

Four general views of man are offered here. The description of classical psychoanalysis provides a historical background for the current emphasis in psychoanalysis, ego psychology. The other views reflect more recent trends: the humanism of Carl Rogers and the existentialists, the approaches of learning theorists and behavior therapists, and social-psychological perspectives.

In contrast to some traditional schools of psychology, theoretical views of man attempt to bring together his various functions—for example, perception, learning, emotion, and motivation—in single frameworks. The search for a complete understanding of man has been stimulated by observations in therapeutic settings. A psychotherapist cannot be content with understanding separate aspects of each client; he must see each person as a coherent whole. The theorist combines the findings of experimental psychology with clinical experience to develop a comprehensive picture of man's behavior. A useful theory organizes widely scattered findings as a guide to clinical application and generates further research hypotheses.

Views, or theories, vary in the stress on variables "within" the organism ("mentalistic" variables) or "outside" the organism (environmental variables). Psychoanalytic theories tend to stress the former and to postulate psychological dynamics as the primary causes of behavior. The humanistic orientation emphasizes the person's interaction with his environment. Currently humanistic psychologists are seeking their data through examination of their own overt and covert actions related to important life decisions. Social-psychological views are somewhat similar in this respect, but there is greater stress on the external world, especially as it is structured by social forces, than on individual perceptions. Learning theorists view man as object, sometimes even as a machine, emphasizing his reactions to environmental stimuli but not completely ignoring his "insides."

The treatment techniques associated with each of these views reflect its theoretical emphasis. Psychoanalysts and humanists stress psychotherapeutic techniques aimed at changing the internal functioning of the individual. Social psychologists often turn to environmental manipulation as the major instrument of change. Learning theorists stress the application of specific stimuli to eliminate "bad" habits and to create "good" ones.

The relation of therapeutic techniques to the particular theories and to empirical research also distinguishes the several views. Psychoanalytic theory, for example, grew from therapy—theorizing and research testing theoretical notions followed from clinical observation. At the opposite extreme learning therapists have based their therapeutic approaches almost entirely on experimental findings, therapies follow research, and theories of learning serve mainly to direct investigators toward discovering new therapeutic techniques. Existential psychotherapy is guided almost entirely by a philosophical view of man as more than either an object or a subject; research on this theory is sparse. Rogers' observations from his therapeutic practice form the basis of his theory, but client-centered therapy itself has developed hand in hand with research endeavors. Social psychologists rely on a combination of research and theory.

5

Classical Psychoanalysis and Ego Psychology

Introduction
I. CLASSICAL PSYCHO-
   ANALYTIC CONCEPTS
   A. Economic Concepts
      1. Psychic energy
      2. The instincts
   B. Topographical Concepts
      1. Levels of consciousness
      2. The dynamics of conscious-
         ness
   C. Structural Concepts
      1. The id
      2. The ego
      3. The superego
   D. Genetic Concepts
      1. Birth
      2. Stages of psychosexual
         development
   E. Psychoanalytic Concepts of
      Adjustment
      1. Anxiety
      2. Abnormal behavior
II. EGO PSYCHOLOGY
   A. Introduction
      1. Primary autonomy
      2. Secondary autonomy
      3. The synthesizing function
   B. Ego Defenses and Coping
      Mechanisms
      1. General characteristics
      2. Specific ego abilities and
         associated mechanisms
   C. Eight Stages of Man
      1. Basic trust versus basic
         mistrust
      2. Autonomy versus shame and
         doubt

      3. Initiative versus guilt
      4. Industry versus inferiority
      5. Identity versus role
         confusion
      6. Intimacy versus isolation
      7. "Generativity" versus
         stagnation
      8. Ego integrity versus despair
   D. Psychoanalysis as Treatment
      1. Characteristics
      2. Stages
      3. Professional considerations
      4. The case of Dora
Summary

INTRODUCTION

Sigmund Freud (1856–1939) is generally credited with having developed the first comprehensive theory of personality. His psychoanalytic theory and treatment of the neuroses have had a tremendous impact on the direction of psychology. Although modern psychology appears to be moving away from Freud's original ideas, many psychotherapists continue to apply his theory and techniques to adjustment problems. We shall describe his theory here in some detail, partly because many of his notions are still viable and partly because it has generated many current ideas.

Freud emphasized the biological nature of man and the inevitable conflict between the expression of biological needs and social constraints. He postulated levels of consciousness and psychic forces that direct behavior without the person's awareness. Mental processes (the id, the ego, the superego) and their interactions were postulated to account for individual differences in adjustment and to clarify the nature of psychological conflict. The adult personality was said to be largely determined by experiences during critical periods of development; consequently, understanding the patient's history can lead to accurate analysis of his present personality. More recently the ego psychologists, though following Freud's basic tenets, have stressed the adaptive capacities of man, whom they consider more an autonomous organism than a helpless pawn in the conflict between his biological drives and environmental constraints. The ego processes are emphasized because they are considered to be the adaptive capacities of man.

From the beginning and still today Freud's views have been the subject of controversy. C. Darwin's theory of evolution and Marx's economic theory are probably the only other bodies of thought to have stimulated so much popular interest. Most laymen's ideas of personality are popularized versions of Freud's ideas—including unconscious motives and conflicts, forgotten childhood traumas, slips of the tongue, dream meanings, and so on.

Freud's own training was strongly biological. He began with an interest in physiology and the laboratory study of neural processes. As a physician he specialized in neurology and the nervous disorders, which eventually led him to the new field of psychiatry. He always maintained a strong interest in philosophy but believed in the discipline of the natural sciences and their rigorous methods of investigation. He therefore resisted to a large degree the temptation to delve into the philosophical aspects of man. This combination of philosophical restraint and biological emphasis resulted in a highly deterministic theory. Freud argued that man's behavior is caused (determined) by preceding events, that he does not have free choice. It follows that an individual's early life is the primary source of data for understanding his later behavior.

Freud developed these notions from the results of his own self-analysis and the reports of his patients. Psychoanalytic theory is thus based almost entirely on clinical observation. Freud always considered his endeavors highly scientific, but we may wonder whether or not his laboratory background made him somewhat uneasy about the reliability of his clinical data.

Although it is difficult today to find many scientists who completely accept all Freud's original notions, psychoanalytic theory continues to have strong influence on psychology and psychiatry. Many other theories of behavior are now in open competition with it, however, and Freud's followers have also modified his original ideas as more data have become available.

CLASSICAL PSYCHOANALYTIC CONCEPTS

Psychoanalytic theory may be discussed under five arbitrary headings: "economic concepts," "topographical concepts," "structural concepts," "genetic concepts," and "concepts of adjustment." It is well to keep in mind that these factors interact to produce a continuously dynamic picture of personality (Baldwin, 1967; Blum, 1966; Monroe, 1955).

ECONOMIC CONCEPTS

PSYCHIC ENERGY

Energy is available for mental activity, and its primary function is to bring mental representations into awareness. For example, in reading these words we use energy to recognize the verbal symbols and to use them so that they serve their purpose. If a person were unable to control this energy he would be unable to understand what he had read. Freud believed that each individual has a limited amount of psychic energy; the way in which it is distributed consequently has important effects on behavior. If most of it is being used to read this page, for example, then little is available for other kinds of mental activity like daydreaming or keeping your thoughts on a TV program. Similarly, if energy is being used to *prevent* ideas from entering consciousness, it is not available for reading and so on.

THE INSTINCTS

The total amount of psychic energy arises from the tissue needs of the body. The mental representations of these needs Freud called the *instincts*. According to him, as a tissue need builds, energy is invested in the mental processes in the form of a *wish* to reduce the excitation created by the need. This wish is the instinct. (Freud used the term "instinct" in a way that might seem more appropriate to the term "drive," and these terms will be used interchangeably in our discussion.) Such instincts are present at birth and are considered an integral part of the biological system, but they do not have the same characteristics as do animal instincts. That is, they are not spontaneous, unlearned behavior that occurs in response to predetermined stimuli. Freud thought that all behavior results from tensions created by the instincts. His explanation of motivation is based entirely upon his conception of the energy aroused by tissue needs. Man acts because instinctual tension impels him to act, and his behavior can be understood as serving to reduce this tension.

FOUR CHARACTERISTICS

The *source* of an instinct is the tissue need from which it arises, whether it is a drive to maintain the biological integrity of the organism (for example, hunger or thirst) or one associated with reproduction of the organism. When energy from this source makes itself felt in tension and is recognized mentally, activities that have already been learned as means of reducing that tension are likely to occur. The *aim* of an instinct is always to reduce excitation. Freud postulates man as an organism that seeks homeostasis, that strives for quiescence by reducing excitation.

The amount of energy associated with an instinct is its *intensity*. The more intense the energy is, the more likely it is that the instinct will guide behavior. We can estimate the intensity of an instinct through observing the obstacles that a person will overcome in seeking a goal or the amount of time that he spends in specific goal-seeking behavior. For instance, when prisoners of war are subjected to starvation, their hunger instincts are judged very intense because so much of their behavior—even their fantasies—is directed toward obtaining and consuming food.

The activities that serve to reduce instinctual tensions are called the *objects* of the instincts. An object may be animate like a person or a kind of activity like eating, but generally it is a combination of the two. A hungry infant gratifies the hunger instinct by sucking (an activity) food (a substance). The entire process of sucking—grasping the breast and taking in the milk—is the object. But partial gratification can come from sucking alone or from sucking a substitute like a thumb. The object of an instinct is thus not fixed but is susceptible to change through the person's interaction with his environment. For example, as the child grows, his choice of food almost inevitably changes, as does his way of eating it. Even substitute objects may change; the thumb may be replaced by a pipe. Flexibility in the choice of objects is owing to *displacement*. The original object is displaced by another, whose selection is frequently determined by social training or other forms of cultural learning.

Ron, the young man whom we introduced in Chapter 1, was unable to deal with his own sexuality, partly because of his sexual instincts, which led to both pleasure and guilt. When tension was high he would masturbate. Masturbation (the object) reduced the tension (the aim) arising from tissue needs (the source), but he had learned that this object is unacceptable, and therefore he experienced guilt. When an instinct is directed toward an unacceptable object adjustment problems arise.

TYPES

Freud divided instincts into two basic kinds, life and death instincts. The former are those aimed at maintaining the organism's unity and survival. The energy associated with them is called *libido* or "libidinal energy." This category is further subdivided according to purpose. The *ego instincts* include the drives for self-preservation, for example, hunger, thirst, and the drive for oxygen. The *sexual instincts* are aimed at preservation of the species. Overt sexual activity is one expression of the latter drives, but many more general activities that enhance procreation also reflect the sexual instincts: activities associated with love, tenderness, child rearing, and so on.

Thanatos, the death instinct, is postulated as a need to complete the cycle of life and death. The generally unconscious *death wish* represents Thanatos in mental life. An important derivative is the drive to aggression. The life forces and other aspects of the personality tend to block the expression of the death instinct; consequently, tension is not released. But a substitute object, something besides oneself, can serve to dissipate tension. Aggression, turning one's self-destructive capacities outward, reduces tension. Aggression is not an inborn drive, but it is an expression of the death wish turned outward toward substitute objects.

INTERACTIONS

Instincts may work against one another, each struggling to reduce tension, or they may combine to generate activities that serve to reduce all the associated tensions. For example, eating may be considered a combination of aggression (an expression of the death instinct) and hunger (an expression of the ego instincts). Biting and chewing are aggressive activities, whereas consumption of food satisfies hunger. Freud also postulated that instincts can substitute for one another. Love, a derivative of the procreative instincts, may replace hate, a derivative of the death instincts, but it is not clear how this substitution takes place.

Psychoanalytic theory focuses on the expression of the sexual and aggressive instincts, the instincts whose expression is most often frustrated by social restrictions. The intensity of both is likely to be high, for tension mounts as expression is thwarted, and the organism must find release. Seeking acceptable ways to reduce sexual and aggressive tension is likely to create problems in adjustment. Ron, as we have noted, experienced much difficulty because of social restrictions on both his sexual and his aggressive instincts.

Freud has been criticized for holding too pessimistic a view of man. He postulated no inherent tendencies toward positive growth and development but considered man only as an organism with needs that must be met, living subject to social rules that restrict the expression of his animal nature. Man is thus, according to Freud, doomed to struggle between the expression of his instincts and the prohibitions of society.

TOPOGRAPHICAL CONCEPTS

Mental life may be conceptualized along a dimension of accessibility to awareness. Ideas, thoughts, feelings, and other mental material may be considered as residing at any one time at different levels of the psyche, forming a topographical map of the mind.

LEVELS OF CONSCIOUSNESS

Freud postulated three levels of consciousness: the conscious, the preconscious, and the unconscious.

THE CONSCIOUS LEVEL

Conscious awareness accounts for a relatively small part of mental life at any given time. It encompasses the continuous flow of thoughts and feelings. The main contents of our consciousness as we read this sentence are word symbols, though it is also possible that we may be thinking of a movie, an impending date, or other matters. At any rate, whatever we are aware of is *conscious*.

THE PRECONSCIOUS LEVEL

The *preconscious* level contains material not presently in the conscious but that can readily enter it if necessary; it is what we normally think of as available memory. An example of preconscious material is a person's birth date; as he turns his attention to it, he becomes aware of it, and it becomes available for such other cognitive activities as planning and remembering.

THE UNCONSCIOUS LEVEL

When ideas, feelings, and other mental material are not available to consciousness, even when attention is directed to them, they are said to be *unconscious*. The direct experience of many physiological processes—circulation of the blood, enzyme changes, and so on—never enters awareness. These processes are not important to psychoanalytic theory, however. The unconscious material that is important to the personality is in the *dynamic uncon-*

scious. It has the potential of moving into the preconscious, but for reasons that we shall discuss later it is not directly available to consciousness.

As Ron discussed his difficulties with his psychotherapist, he seemed to become aware of new reasons for some of his anxiety. He began to realize, for example, that his poor performance in sales (which he blamed on inadequate training by his father) resulted from his fear of relating to people. This knowledge was unconscious at the beginning of his therapy and became conscious as therapy progressed. Ron's original inability to recognize this idea had prevented him from taking positive steps to change himself and to seek a more appropriate occupation.

THE DYNAMICS OF CONSCIOUSNESS

The contents of consciousness generate behavior. The more intense a conscious idea is, the more likely it is that the person will guide his actions by it. The hungry prisoner of war, for example, has many conscious thoughts about food; because such thoughts in fact dominate his awareness, his behavior will be primarily directed at finding food. Behavior is both guided and limited by the contents of consciousness; it would be unusual for the starving prisoner to devote himself to artistic endeavors or social amenities.

DRIVE CATHEXIS

How do ideas become conscious? How does psychoanalytic theory explain the presence of one idea, rather than another, in consciousness? First, an idea must be supported by psychic energy if it is to make its way into awareness. If this energy comes from a drive it is called *drive cathexis*. Hunger contributes energy that carries into consciousness representations of objects associated with reducing hunger. As the intensity of hunger increases, consciousness receives an increasing number of elements associated with it. An object like securing money to bribe a guard for food is said to be "cathected" by the drive; that is, energy becomes associated with this idea so that it can become conscious and suggest behavior that will reduce the intensity of hunger.

COUNTERCATHEXIS

If drive cathexis were the only way in which psychic energy could be used, our behavior would be determined by each need as it arose. Obviously, it is not. Energy is also available to keep drives *out* of consciousness. *Countercathexis* is the term for such energy. The amount of countercathected energy available for a particular idea is determined by the pain or anxiety associated with the idea. Generally, we dislike pain and elements that cause it. Psychic energy is available to prevent pain, frustration, and activities that may result in negative feelings. For example, it is frustrating for a prisoner to think of food when none is available. If he allows food to be the primary content of his consciousness, he may be tempted to steal from the guards and risk severe punishment. There is thus a struggle between drive-cathected and counter-cathected energy, one trying to bring the idea into awareness, the other holding it back.

HYPERCATHEXIS

Freud also postulated a third source of energy, *hypercathexis*. Hypercathected energy is used in directing attention, in the active process of selecting a particular element for conscious use. In solving an arithmetic problem, for example, energy is available for the purposeful selection of elements from previous knowledge of numbers and arithmetical formulas. Thanks to hypercathected energy we attend to our studies, even though drive-cathected notions (connected with hunger, for example) compete for our attention.

There are thus three forces that determine whether or not an idea will enter consciousness. Drive cathexis pushes it toward consciousness, counter-cathexis pushes it away from consciousness, and hypercathexis serves as a conscious selector of objects for attention. When countercathexis is strong enough to prevent an idea from entering consciousness, even though it is supported by cathected and hypercathected energy, it is said to be *repressed*. A repressed idea is therefore unavailable to consciousness unless psychic energy is redistributed within the personality. As we shall see later, one aim of psychoanalytic treatment is to redistribute energy so that repressed ideas can be brought into awareness.

STRUCTURAL CONCEPTS

Freud also postulated different kinds of mental activities, each of which serves specific purposes in the personality. The terms for these activities—"id," "ego," and "superego"—are common parlance among many laymen and have become popular through mass media of communication. They are often called mental "structures," though in keeping with Freud's thought they should be understood as processes, rather than as specific "parts" of personality. Nevertheless, both laymen and psychologists tend to talk about these processes as if they were actual structures when they are not meant to be.

THE ID

All instincts are included in the id at birth and remain part of it throughout life. The infant's psychic energy is *free energy*; it can become attached to any mental element and bring it into consciousness rapidly with little or no countercathection. The infant reacts very impulsively: When he wants something he wants it immediately and acts upon his wish. Id processes reflect *primary-process thinking,* which is characterized by expectation of immediate gratification and inability to delay action. It is prelogical, infantile, and unguided by external reality. Freud conceptualized the id and primary-process thinking as operating on the *pleasure principle,* according to which the sole purpose of any activity is to avoid pain and to reduce instinctual tension to quiescence. Primary-process thinking is the only kind of mental activity available to the infant; other processes develop later to temper his actions.

The Ego

The child develops a different way of thinking once he has learned to experience the outside environment as separate from himself. The ego processes are responsible for maintaining the organism through evaluation of both its internal states and external environment. By most standards the functions of the ego can be called "adaptive." Its primary purpose is to see that instinctual gratification is brought about, but its aim is maximum, rather than immediate, gratification. Ego functioning is based on the *reality principle.* For example, when a three-year-old child spots an ice-cream truck across the street he is likely to dash toward it without hesitation. A five-year-old, however, is more likely to look in both directions before he runs across the street. The younger child's thinking is said to be "id dominated." The older child shows more ego development in his capacity to delay gratification in the light of external circumstances. The ability to delay gratification and to evaluate total circumstances is called *secondary-process thinking.*

In a sense the ego borrows energy originally associated with the instinct and uses it to countercathect that instinct temporarily until proper assessment of the situation can be made. The ego processes also control hypercathected energy, rendering logical trains of thought possible. Primary-process thinking permits the strongest drive to enter consciousness without regard for logic or realistic problem solving.

Ego development includes evolution of fairly stable ways of coping with energy that pushes ideas into consciousness. The use of ego energy gradually becomes more restricted to these ways and is said to be *bound* to them. The more that it is necessary for the ego to control id impulses, the less free energy is available for logical thinking and adaptive functioning. One of the primary purposes of psychoanalytic treatment is to free bound energy so that the ego can be more fully geared to adaptive functioning.

Ron, for example, though clearly intelligent, seemed "stupid" in much of his behavior. He was not able to evaluate his interactions with his father objectively, nor did he seem able to focus on ways of overcoming his inadequacies in relating to his peers. In psychoanalytic terms his ego functioning was drastically limited because a large proportion of energy was being used in countercathexis, that is, to prevent unacceptable thoughts from entering consciousness.

THE SUPEREGO

The superego represents the values, mores, and social restraints that a child learns from his culture. Whereas the ego and the id share the mutual aim of instinctual gratification, though through different means, the superego aims at the opposite. Its function is to prevent drive reduction by means that conflict with social standards. The superego does not necessarily represent the real values of society; the child's perceptions may have distorted them. A great deal of such distortion may accompany initial contact with social constraints—the "don'ts" may seem arbitrary, harsh, and uncompromising. The superego, as does the id, operates without reality testing. Its primary purpose is to enforce prohibitions as they exist in the individual's mental apparatus. If these prohibitions are distorted, the person's functioning may be unduly restricted. A child who has learned that sexuality is simply "bad," for example, may be unable to express his sexual desires in socially acceptable relationships later in life.

The ego is in the position of trying to satisfy, first, the prohibitions of the superego; second, the instinctual demands of the id; and, third, the demands of the environment. Consequently, the adequacy of ego functioning is directly related to successful psychological adjustment.

GENETIC CONCEPTS

Concepts relating to personality development and growth are called "genetic." Freud has postulated specific stages of personality development at each of which special adjustments must be made. The ways in which they are made determine characteristics of the adult personality.

Two processes of change accompany development. First, the ego grows and becomes differentiated, so that mental activity is increasingly based on the reality principle and secondary-process thinking. Second, the objects of instinctual gratification change as different regions of the body become major sources of libidinal pleasure and as social learning suggests substitutes.

Freud believed that developmental stages result from a maturation process common to the human species, that everyone is biologically programmed to pass through them. But he did recognize that the behavior of the people who interact with the child strongly influences personality development.

BIRTH

Birth is the individual's first conscious interaction with the environment and also generates his first experience of anxiety. The newborn infant typically shows the psychophysiological reactions that accompany fear and anxiety:

gasping, crying, wiggling, increased heart rate, and so forth. The infant's response to his passage from the protection of the mother's womb into a world in which he is bombarded by outside stimulation may serve as a prototype for his adaptation to anxiety later in life. For example, one way to reduce outside stimulation is to sleep; if it works well in his infancy the individual may continue to avoid anxiety by this means in later life.

One of Freud's early colleagues, O. Rank, emphasized the importance of the birth trauma, which, in his view, is a prototype of man's basic struggle between becoming independent and remaining dependent ("returning to the womb"). He developed a complete school of thought from this basic concept (Hall and Lindzey, 1957).

Stages of Psychosexual Development

Freud delineated stages of development based upon the body regions serving as primary sources of libidinal gratification during successive periods of growth. He suggested that the earliest gratification is obtained from the mouth, then from the anal, and finally from the genital region. Even though all three regions are always sources of some gratification one is dominant during any given phase of development.

As the primary source of gratification shifts from one region to another the objects of gratification also necessarily change. If these changes do not keep pace with overall development the individual is said to have invested excessive psychic energy in objects appropriate to an earlier stage. The energy is said to be *fixated* on the object. For example, a five-year-old who remains unusually attached to his bottle exhibits an oral fixation; energy has remained invested in an object appropriate to an earlier stage of development in which the mouth was the primary region of gratification. Normally psychic energy is redistributed at each stage, and object choices change. The normal adult finds his major libidinal satisfactions in heterosexual relationships. Fixations reveal poorly resolved problems in the developmental stage during which they occur. Traumatic experiences, conflicts, and frustrations are likely to result in excessive investment of energy in the objects associated with a particular stage.

Once again some of Ron's difficulties may be viewed in these terms. Because he continued to masturbate and could not relate to women sexually, we might say that masturbation represented a fixation at the phallic stage of development. The causes would be found by examining his history. At some point, presumably, he had suffered frustration or conflict—perhaps when his mother punished him for masturbating as a child—which resulted in a large investment of energy in masturbation.

Returning to an earlier method of gratification is called *regression* and is another sign of disturbed development. It is adaptive for an infant to be dependent, for instance, and to rely on others for his gratification. But a normal child gains autonomy as he develops, and dependence gives way to independence. In the adult dependence is a minor method of gratification, though it is never entirely absent. In periods of stress an adult may temporarily regress to dependence modes because later methods fail to bring gratification. He invests psychic energy in earlier object choices.

THE ORAL STAGE

The infant depends entirely upon others for survival; dependence is his primary mode of obtaining instinctual gratification. The body structure most frequently associated with drive reduction at this time is the mouth. He also receives pleasure from the kinesthetic feedback from closeness, cuddling, and the like, but objects associated with his mouth and entering it capture most of his psychic energey.

The first part of this stage is therefore called *oral-dependent*. The infant is unable to act in alleviating his own discomfort. He must wait passively for gratification. It is said that this stage is important in developing attitudes of optimism and pessimism. If the child suffers a great deal from neglect, illness, or other difficulties, he is likely to develop a pessimistic attitude, an expectation that relief from the environment will not be forthcoming. If his needs are met fairly consistently, however, an optimistic attitude is likely to develop.

The oral-dependent infant treats objects of gratification (love objects) in a characteristic way. As tension rises, he imagines (creates psychic representations of) objects that would lead to tension reduction. After suckling—incorporating the object—he becomes quiescent and the images disappear. The infant thus interacts with love objects by totally incorporating them into himself. Once his need is gone, the object disappears and has no more value. The egocentric infant loves his objects only while they are being consumed and reducing his tension.

Somewhere about the time that he is weaned the *oral-aggressive* phase begins. Aggression becomes more dominant, partly as a response to the frustration of weaning and partly because of teething, which leads to discomfort and anger. Biting becomes a source of pleasure: it reduces the pain accompanying the growth of teeth and also serves to express aggression toward the frustrating object. The object is destroyed as it is incorporated. Indeed, breast feeding may have to be discontinued because of the pain that the infant inflicts on his mother.

Freud postulated certain adult personality types resulting from disturbances at each stage of development which cause so much stress that much psychic energy remains associated with the objects of that phase. The *oral-passive personality* is likely to be dependent, optimistic, and generally act immature. He expects the world to provide him with nourishment, and he wants his parents or parent substitutes to continue to care for him. His general adjustment is characterized by passivity and the expectation that others will fulfill his needs. The *oral-sadistic personality* also wishes to receive from others, but he is suspicious and distrustful, often exhibiting sarcasm or bitterness and tending to attack others.

Fixations at the oral stage are likely to be reflected in adult love relationships. Such personalities want and take from others as long as their needs exist. Rejection and disinterest follow until their needs arise again; partners are valued only for what they give.

Development of the ego begins in the oral stage. It first appears in the recognition that the external environment is separate from the self. The child learns to recognize others and to react differently to specific people. Smiling and being playful brings him attention, which partially satisfies some of his needs. He is able to delay gratification somewhat, though the availability of substitute objects is helpful: He may suck his thumb or a "pacifier" until time for his regular feeding. The first steps toward autonomy are reflected in early language development. The infant associates objects with verbal symbols and learns to ask for what he wants.

THE ANAL STAGE

As oral satisfactions come increasingly under the child's control, the anal region becomes a focus of gratification. Distension associated with retention in the bowels and the stimulation of bowel movements become sources of libidinal pleasure. For most children this stage begins at one and a half to two years of age. The parents become interested in their child's control of his elimination and begin to focus on teaching him socially acceptable behavior. Setting limits on the child's anal pleasures (toilet training) may lead to frustration. As he learns the proper times and places for elimination he may come to look upon his feces as "gifts" to the parents—he pleases them when he delivers according to their instructions. Or he may find pleasure in withholding his feces and expelling them when his parents will be displeased, a show of rebellion against their control. As the child learns to obey rules and to follow commands, the stage is set for his autonomy. He learns to set limits on his own independent action. Learning the value of cleanliness is another feature of this period, and being clean is often associated with toilet training. Concern with cleanliness may become a central factor in the child's personality, depending upon the emphasis during the anal stage.

Love patterns change. In contrast to the oral stage, the objects of the anal stage do not lose their interest when they are no longer immediately necessary. Rather, objects may become cherished; love may be identified with giving or keeping. Adults with strong anal fixations often identify love with gifts. The loved person is looked upon as a valuable possession, rather than as an independent person.

Rudimentary development of the superego begins during the anal stage. The parents' prohibitions connected with toilet habits are learned as cultural values. If conflicts are severe the budding superego, the champion of the "shall nots," may become too strong. The ego also continues to develop and must deal with both internal pressures from the prohibitive superego and external demands of the environment. Less energy is available to the ego if excessive energy is invested in the superego, and the likelihood of realistic adjustment is less.

Adults reveal fixations at the anal stage through various traits. The *anal-obsessive character* values order, obstinacy, parsimony, even miserliness. The *anal-erotic type* seeks special attention from parents or other authority figures, especially valuing their praise because it has been associated with gratification during toilet training. Cleanliness is valued for its association with "goodness." Literal obedience, insistence on "going by the book" and "following the letter of the law," reflects a distortion of the real world that can be traced back to excessive emphasis on "minding" the parents. In his verbal behavior the anal character tends to make tiny distinctions, to "split hairs," and to stick obstinately to his points. He is unable to see "shades of gray" or to tolerate confusion and ambiguity. Early toilet training should result in a person who values possessions highly and takes good care of money, whereas later training should result in less concern for possessions and an ability to speculate freely. A psychoanalyst once commented that he wanted his banker to have been toilet-trained at thirteen months and his stockbroker at three years.

THE PHALLIC STAGE

At about age four a child's libidinal interests shift to his sex organs, as can be observed in his new interest in anatomical differences between the sexes, where babies come from, and the sexual activities of his parents. Mutual sex play is common among preschool children. Although their ideas of sexual relations are frequently inaccurate and not clearly formulated, their activities usually involve physical closeness, looking at the sex organs of others, and showing their own organs to others. Freud believed that most children understand sexual behavior more clearly than adults usually suspect. They have either observed their parents during intercourse (the *primal scene*), or they have built fantasies from clues in parental remarks or the comments of other children. Freud also believed that most children perceive the sexual act as an act of aggression against the mother by the father.

During this stage the resolution of the *oedipal conflict* is considered extremely important for later personality functioning.[1] The mother has been an important source of gratification for the child. Her interaction with him has generally been intimate, pleasurable, even sensual. For a boy she becomes the obvious source of genital gratification. Even though he has only a vague con-

---

[1] Freud modeled his description of this stage on the Greek myth of Oedipus, a prince who was separated from his family as an infant, only to return as a man to win the kingdom by unwittingly killing his father and marrying his mother. The ultimate revelation that his wife is also his mother drives him to blind himself and go wandering in exile.

ception of adult sexuality, he desires sexual intimacy with her. But his mother rarely allows him his wish. Her reactions vary from encouraging close contact to strongly discouraging it, depending upon her own needs and life situation. Strong rejection or strong acceptance is likely to increase the boy's drive level through frustration in the first instance and aroused expectations in the second.

Most of this activity occurs at an unconscious level, but the child vaguely perceives that to gratify his impulses he must replace his father, who thus becomes his rival, physically stronger and capable of destroying him. The boy's rivalry with his father results in fear that his father will hurt him; more specifically, he fears castration. Freud postulated that the penis is valued highly by both boys and girls during the phallic stage. The loss of this organ would therefore seem disastrous. *Castration anxiety* is the psychoanalytic term for the boy's fear of retaliation from his father.

The normal resolution of the oedipal conflict involves two processes. The boy's hostility toward his father and his sexual desire for his mother are repressed, and the boy *identifies* with his father, attempting to become like his father. His method is *introjection* of his father's traits, taking them as his own. Identification and repression serve to eliminate the threat of castration and also to allow vicarious gratification from the mother. As the boy is no longer his father's rival, he need not fear retaliation, and by introjecting aspects of his father into himself he draws gratification from his father's sexual activities with his mother. In the long run a normal resolution of the oedipal conflict results in development of "masculine" interests and values through identification.

A similar conflict is postulated for the girl, the *Electra complex,* also named from a Greek myth in which a daughter arranges to have her mother murdered because her mother and her mother's lover have murdered her father. Because of the high value that he believed is placed on the penis Freud argued that girls experience a "castration complex" at this stage. Because they do not have penises, they imagine that they have lost them. Girls may experience *penis envy* and tend to devalue femininity because of their "inadequate" genitals.

A girl's desire for her father is not unlike the boy's feeling for his mother, and she also perceives her mother as a rival. The ordinary resolution again includes repression of sexual desire for the father and identification with the mother. But the entire process is considered less important and less traumatic than it is for boys. Freud was not clear on this point, but he seemed to think that a girl, through identification with her mother, does come to accept female genitals as valuable because of their importance in producing babies. Some psychoanalysts believe that the birth of a woman's first child unconsciously represents to her the growth of a penis.

The superego develops rapidly during the phallic stage. As the child comes to take his parents' values as his own, his conscience becomes more clearly operative. He has inner controls that monitor his actions, and he is capable of suffering guilt. At this stage a potential difficulty in superego development arises: The ego may not be mature enough to evaluate parents' values accurately. The child may translate them too strictly, so that his superego becomes too rigid. The child's superego is quite concrete at first and depends upon specific instances: "Dividing things evenly is good"; "not hitting baby is good"; "not taking cookies without permission is good"; and so forth. As the child matures, however, the superego interprets prohibitions as reflections of general principles: fairness, tolerance, and honesty. If oedipal conflicts are very strong the child's concrete interpretation of social prohibitions may be repressed. The individual may then experience unrealistic guilt later in life and function less adaptively.

Adult *phallic types* show behavior typical of early adolescence, reflecting unresolved problems of the phallic stage. These people are usually exhibitionistic and very ambitious, narcissistic, and boastful. Freud suggested that the unsatisfactory resolution of conflicts during the phallic stage is the primary source of later neurotic difficulties. Repressed oedipal wishes require the expenditure of ego energy to keep them from consciousness; the result is that adaptive ego functions suffer.

LATENCY

A state of comparative sexual quiescence sets in between the time when a child enters school and the time when he reaches adolescence. As the phallic stage passes, the child's interest turns to learning skills and values. He learns to manipulate physical objects in his environment and to use language more adaptively, and his ego grows as he acquires new motor and cognitive skills. If development goes well, his superego acquires a more realistic system of values. People outside his family begin to influence his values, encouraging greater tolerance and different ideas. Latency is a period of libidinal quiescence and adaptive learning.

THE GENITAL STAGE

With the onset of puberty, latency ends and the genital stage begins. Physiological changes associated with sexual growth at this time result in increased sex drive. The conflicts temporarily resolved during the phallic stage are reawakened, and oedipal strivings return. The increase in sexual energy threatens to bring repressed sexual desire for the parent of the opposite sex into awareness; the child must take steps to avoid the associated anxiety.

One satisfactory resolution is to choose a partner of the opposite sex from among one's peers. Two important factors make adjustment at this time easier than at the phallic stage. First, the child is no longer as closely tied to his family; peers are available for sexual gratification. Second, an older child's love is less egocentric, and his immediate need for sexual gratification can thus be replaced by altruistic values. Ron's difficulties again demonstrate the relevance of Freudian theory to adjustment. In late adolescence he overheard his parents having sexual intercourse. It disturbed him so much that he decided to join the army and to leave home the next day. His closeness with his mother during his childhood suggests that his resolution of the oedipal conflict had been painful. Furthermore, because he perceived his father as a powerful figure but one not often present, he found it difficult to identify with him. His sexual attraction to his mother therefore had to be repressed with little aid from identification with his father. His awareness of overt intercourse between his parents during his adolescence (when sexual matters had again become important) threatened his defenses, and unconscious thoughts of having intercourse with his mother threatened to move into consciousness. He therefore fled the scene. Although his stated reason (conscious) was to have intercourse himself, his primary purpose (unconscious) was to avoid the recurrence of the disturbing incident so that his repressive defenses could be maintained.

Freud believed that the child goes through a "homosexual" period in early adolescence. His increased sexual energy is turned toward a person of the same sex in much the same way that identification helps to resolve the oedipal conflict. Overt homosexual behavior may not occur, but young adolescents may often become easily attached to adults of their own sex; boys "hero worship" males, and girls may have "crushes" on their female teachers. Usually the choice of object eventually shifts to a peer of the opposite sex, and courting begins. Adolescents typically experience varying degrees of emotional relationship with their partners; these experiences eventually culminate in the capacity to commit themselves emotionally, to love others in tender, as well as pleasure-seeking, ways.

In normal development the sex drive is directed at a substitute for the parent, and procreative purposes are fulfilled through marriage and raising a family. The *genital character* is one who has made a satisfactory object substitution and is able to enter a mutually rewarding love relationship.

Freud believed that the basic patterns of personality are established by the end of the phallic stage. The adult personality always includes a mixture of minor and major remnants from earlier developmental periods, but the ego of the ideal genital character is strong, and he uses his emotions, as well as his other adaptive mental functions, in realistic ways to promote positive adjustment. The degree to which remnants of earlier development remain in the adult personality indicates the amount of disturbance that has occurred during development.

PSYCHOANALYTIC CONCEPTS OF ADJUSTMENT

Anxiety

Although Freud postulated the life and death instincts as the primary motivating forces, fear and anxiety also contribute much to instigating behavior. The emotional response to danger is a warning for the ego to react in an adaptive way; "anxiety" is a signal of impending danger. Freud distinguished three kinds of anxiety, based on the sources of threats to the ego: the external environment, the id, and the superego.

OBJECTIVE ANXIETY

The emotional response to threats from the external environment is called *objective anxiety*. Adaptive behavior is usually possible: One can run away, attempt to master the circumstances, or simply do nothing while experiencing increased anxiety. Assuming that the individual is not destroyed by whatever threatens him before his anxiety reaches an unbearable level, he will ultimately regress to helplessness. Of course, in most instances responses are sufficiently adaptive to maintain integrity.

NEUROTIC ANXIETY

When the ego is threatened by the instinctual impulses of the id, the emotional response is called *neurotic anxiety*. Id impulses are threatening because they generate behavior that may result in harm. The threat that repressed impulses will become conscious causes a great deal of discomfort.[2] When the ego is successful in maintaining repression, the impulse does not reach awareness. The individual may, however, be unaware of the source of his discomfort; in seeking an explanation of his suffering, he may be tempted to blame external forces. Neurotic anxiety is common in psychological maladjustment.

MORAL ANXIETY

An emotional response to the threat of punishment from the superego is called *moral anxiety*. It can be reduced by following the dictates of conscience. It thus directs behavior into channels that are acceptable to the superego. It is not infrequent to find a great deal of moralizing among people who suffer poor psychological adjustment. A person is subject to irrational but compelling restrictions if his superego has not developed normally. Psychic energy invested in a strict superego deprives the ego, and the capacity for achieving realistic gratification is thus reduced. A poorly adjusted person often shows a strong need for impulse gratification but also has strong objections to suitable solutions.

ABNORMAL BEHAVIOR

Freud believed that the ego's failure to resolve realistically the frustration resulting from inability to express instinctual forces is the common element in all abnormal behavior. Resolving frustration in an "abnormal" manner indi-

---

[2] In neurotic anxiety the ego must find ways to maintain repression of the threatening impulses. The ego has various ways of bolstering repression, tactics that will be discussed later under the title "ego defenses."

cates that the ego has been ineffective in its conflict with either the id, the environment, or the superego.

In strong conflict between the ego and the id the ego may yield control to the superego, the suppressive forces. Then the original impulse is not gratified. The ego has compromised a realistic solution, by accepting substitute gratification in the form of one neurotic symptom for another. This symptom often has symbolic meaning that suggests the nature of the original conflict. For instance, an hysterical (without physiological explanation) paralysis of the hand may symbolize conflict over the desire to hit (kill) someone. Obsessive hand washing may symbolize conflict over "dirty" thoughts.

Strong conflicts between the ego and the environment may be resolved by transferring ego energy to the id, resulting in loss of contact with reality and bizarre behavior, including inappropriate sexual and aggressive activity, or expression of related impulses through psychotic hallucinations and delusions. The individual appears incapable of differentiating between fantasy and real events. His adaptive capacities may be reduced to the point at which he is dangerous to himself or to others. Society deals with these disturbances through external controls, usually hospitalizing the person until he changes.

Another kind of abnormal adjustment results from conflict between the ego and the superego. The ego seeks gratification for instinctual impulses, but the superego is too strict and condemning. Maladaptive behavior takes the form of self-destructive behavior and self-punishment, usually labeled "melancholia" or "depression."

The economics of psychic energy explain individual differences in responding to similar conflicts. If the ego is invested with a great deal of energy it will be able to resolve conflicts adaptively. A person with low ego strength will be susceptible to abnormal resolutions. An investigation of his life history is necessary to determine why his ego is inadequate.

EGO PSYCHOLOGY

INTRODUCTION

Several of Freud's early associates became disenchanted with his emphasis on sexuality and a view of man that explained behavior on the basis of life experiences alone. Some of them developed their own theories, stressing the view of man as a purposive organism, which seeks goals besides responding to its environment. C. G. Jung, A. Adler, and O. Rank (see Hall and Lindzey, 1957, for details on these theorists) were among these "early dissenters."

The neo-Freudians broke from the orthodox Freudian view somewhat later. They rejected Freud's total emphasis on biological (as opposed to social) factors as determinants of man's behavior. H. S. Sullivan, K. Horney, and E.

Fromm have all developed theoretical views stressing social forces (Hall and Lindzey, 1957).

Investigators who have remained "loyal" to psychoanalytic theory have increasingly stressed the role of ego functioning. Unlike the theorists who broke away from Freud, these *ego psychologists* continue to accept Freud's view of the instinctual drives as primary motivating forces. But they have developed new concepts that embody recognition of the importance of the ego. Freud supposed that ego functions develop from the conflict between instinctual gratification and the organism's need to maintain itself in the face of restrictions by reality. Essentially, he argued, the ego must "borrow" its energy from the id. Recently theorists have postulated that the ego has its own, autonomous source of energy. Their conception of man is therefore more positive, emphasizing individual striving rather than simply conflict resolution.

PRIMARY AUTONOMY

The functions of the ego, the *ego apparatuses,* are sensing, perceiving, memory, imagination and so on, processes that help the organism adjust to the world. Ego psychologists argue that these functions are hereditary and therefore have *primary autonomy*: They are independent of instinctual energy. Furthermore these functions are initially conflict-free, pleasurable in themselves and not controlled by any need to compromise instinctual drives with external reality. Ego psychologists do not deny that these apparatuses serve the instincts, but they believe that such service is not the ego's only purpose.

SECONDARY AUTONOMY

Another recent theoretical development is the concept of *secondary autonomy,* attributed to the patterns of behavior that develop from conflict. Although the ego may initially operate to meet the demands of drives in conflict with reality, the mechanisms that it thus develops do not necessarily remain limited to their original purposes. A child's habit of cleanliness may be connected with anal sexuality at first. But after toilet training it may develop more fully for several purposes, including mastering the social environment.

THE SYNTHESIZING FUNCTION

A third new concept is the *synthesizing function* of the ego. Ego apparatuses integrate different parts of the personality. Without using the term "self," ego psychologists have postulated the capacity of the ego to organize personality into a unitary whole. The resulting organized pattern is often subjectively experienced as "I" or "me."

EGO DEFENSES AND COPING MECHANISMS

Noting ego psychologists' emphasis on positive functioning, T. C. Kroeber (1963) has defined pairs of ego mechanisms for defense and coping (see also A. Freud, 1946).

GENERAL CHARACTERISTICS

There are characteristic differences between the defense and coping mechanisms. Defense mechanisms are rigid and involuntary. They help the individual to avoid the appearance of drives in its consciousness and allow impulse gratification only indirectly. Their primary goal is to eliminate disturbing feelings. Unacceptable thoughts must remain out of the individual's consciousness if he is not to experience anxiety. It is common, for example, both to like and to dislike one's parents. Some people, however, find it unacceptable to recognize their dislike, even at times their hatred, of a parent. To avoid conscious awareness of their feelings they may constantly praise him and defend him vehemently against any criticism—a *reaction formation*. But at the same time his insistence on his parent's perfect behavior is likely to cause others to challenge his claims and to express their negative opinions of his parent—the person's unconscious desire to hurt his parent is thus partially gratified.

In contrast, coping mechanisms are flexible, purposive, and selective. They operate to clarify situations. As they are based on secondary-process thinking, they may call for experiencing disturbing feelings if it seems helpful in the long run; gratification may also be delayed for greater future gains, even at the expense of some present discomfort. Impulse gratification is more direct, open, but tempered.

Ego mechanisms may be evaluated by means of observing an individual's behavior in the light of the criteria just described. The *strength* of the ego may be estimated from the frequency and effectiveness with which various mechanisms operate. The *autonomy* of the ego may be estimated from the relative reliance on coping and defense mechanisms. The more one uses coping behavior to resolve conflicts, the more likely it is that his psychic energy will be invested in the ego, which is consequently freer to operate on its own. The *quality* of the ego results from the hierarchy of preferences for various mechanisms. If an individual attempts to cope first and resorts to the less adaptive defense mechanisms only under great stress, he shows high-quality ego performance.

SPECIFIC EGO ABILITIES AND ASSOCIATED MECHANISMS

Specific kinds of defense and coping mechanisms are related to particular ego apparatuses (abilities). For each such apparatus there is a characteristic defense use and a characteristic means of coping.

DETACHMENT

The ability to speculate freely, to analyze, and to create without blocks from within or without is called "detachment."

INTELLECTUALIZATION is the defensive use of detachment. To intellectualize, one must retreat from any impulse or affect associated with mental symbols, separating feelings from ideas rather permanently. The intellectualizer lives in a world of words and abstractions; he views even personal events and conflicts in abstract terms. He is unable to bring appropriate affect together with ideas because he is threatened by breakthrough of his impulses. In therapy he can analyze his behavior on an intellectual plane but cannot respond more emotionally. He talks about himself as if he were an object to be observed.

INTELLECTUALITY is the coping mechanism related to detachment. It involves temporary separation of affect from mental symbolization for the purpose of impartial analysis. This separation is only in the service of the immediate situation, permitting effective problem solving even in heavily affect-laden circumstances. It is thus an adaptive use of detachment.

SYMBOLIZATION OF MEANS AND ENDS

The ability to use mental symbols for analyzing causal relationships, entertaining alternatives, and anticipating outcomes is called *symbolization of means and ends.*

RATIONALIZATION is the associated defense mechanism. It is the distortion of an actual chain of causal relations in order to defend oneself against perception of unacceptable feelings or needs. It severely limits a person's ability to evaluate alternatives. The man who loses one job after another because of poor performance but justifies his failures on the basis that his "bosses don't like him" is probably rationalizing in order to avoid low self-esteem. His rationalization provides an immediate gain in that he avoids the pain of recognizing his own incompetence. But his future in other job situations is in jeopardy because he cannot analyze accurately the causes for his having been fired before. He is likely to repeat the same behavior in his next job and be fired again.

LOGICAL ANALYSIS, the associated coping mechanism, is the capacity for careful analysis of a situation. Freedom of choice is then greater, and outcomes are more likely to be adaptive. If the man who was fired could see in what ways his performance has been inadequate, he could take steps to change his behavior and to hold his next job.

SELECTIVE AWARENESS

The ability to focus attention on specific aspects of a situation is called *selective awareness*.

DENIAL is its use to avoid painful thoughts or occurrences. The person who goes through life with "rose-colored glasses" necessarily denies much of what is really happening. His ability to test reality is distorted, his responses are frequently inappropriate, and he may be overwhelmed by the "badness" of things when environmental circumstances finally become too clear to deny.

CONCENTRATION, on the other hand, is adaptive focusing of attention. When disturbing or pleasant thoughts interfere with a task at hand the person who can temporarily shut them out has an advantage. For example, a student who can push aside his desire to go to the movie or his thoughts of vacation while studying for an examination is more likely to do well on the examination. Immediate gratification is surrendered in favor of completing a task that will bring long-term benefits.

SENSITIVITY

Sensitivity is the ability to comprehend the unexpressed feelings or ideas of others.

PROJECTION is the term for the defensive use of this ability, the ascription of one's own unacceptable feelings and ideas to others. For example, aggressive impulses may be unacceptable to a person because of his strict childhood training. When he feels aggressive toward his boss, he believes that his boss is angry at him! He projects his unacceptable feelings onto his boss. Furthermore, he then has an excuse to express his aggression by rationalizing that his boss "started it." He can thus absolve himself of blame, which permits him to recognize his otherwise unacceptable feelings. Projection is prevalent in paranoid disorders. When unacceptable impulses generate excessive frustration, a strong tendency to project them may result. Projected aggression can result in delusions like "People are trying to poison me," "The communists are trying to kill me," "My wife is trying to kill me." Sometimes the outcome of such thinking is an overt attack, an expression of the repressed impulse against those supposed to be plotting harm. Mass murders are generally attributed to such paranoid delusions.

EMPATHY is the related coping mechanism. It is the ability to put oneself in another's frame of reference in order to understand his feelings. Accurate understanding of another's feelings contributes to satisfactory relationships.

IMPULSE DIVERSION

Another aspect of ego functioning is the ability to modify the object of an impulse.

DISPLACEMENT, the defensive mechanism, involves temporary repression of the connection between the original object and the impulse; another object, usually one that is inappropriate, is then substituted. The man who is criticized by his employer becomes angry, but he represses his anger because of the danger involved in expressing it. When he goes home after work he uses a small incident as an excuse for a tirade directed at his wife and children; he does not recognize that they are simply substitutes for the expression of anger that is really aimed at his employer.

SUBLIMATION is the adaptive use of impulse diversion. To sublimate an impulse is to find socially acceptable alternative channels for its expression. In the previous example the man could have sublimated his anger by stopping at a gym and punching a bag. Some mental hospitals provide "mad rooms" where patients can hit, kick, yell, and so on until they have dissipated their hostility without infringing on others.

IMPULSE TRANSFORMATION

Impulse transformation is the ability to take energy from an impulse by disguising the impulse as its opposite.

REACTION FORMATION is the defense against expressing a very strong impulse that is strictly forbidden. The energy for this impulse is shifted to its opposite: to love from hate, to celibacy from carnality, and so forth. The person adopts the opposite course in a rather permanent and determined way, though the original impulse occasionally breaks through. For example, a man who is greatly threatened by homosexual impulses may crusade to "clean up" homosexual activities in his city; he may also actively seek out homosexuals to attack them physically or report them to the authorities.

SUBSTITUTION is the related coping mechanism. It involves secure transfer of energy to a temperate alternative. Homosexual impulses may be diverted to "manly" activities like body-contact sports, "stag nights," and so on.

IMPULSE RESTRAINT

Impulse restraint is the ability to inhibit the expression of an impulse.

REPRESSION is the associated defense mechanism which completely inhibits a feeling or an idea, which can then be revealed only unconsciously and symbolically in dreams, slips of the tongue, and so on. Freud suggested that repression is the primary defense mechanism in conflicts among impulses, reality, and social constraint—and that the other defense mechanisms all reinforce it. They provide what is essentially a second line of defense to prevent unacceptable impulses—impulses that have been repressed—from reaching consciousness. Repression is considered the primary defense mechanism in conversion hysteria. A repressed impulse may show itself as a physical symptom. A patient who wishes to stab his mother may, for instance, develop paralysis of the hand to ensure that the impulse will not be gratified. He focuses energy on his symptom to avoid the repressed wish.

suppression is the coping mechanism associated with impulse restraint. It is the capacity to hold back an impulse until it may be expressed in a socially acceptable way. For example, a sexual impulse may be kept from awareness until one is in a situation in which its expression is appropriate.

EIGHT STAGES OF MAN

E. H. Erikson (1963) has applied the ego psychologists' approach to the study of personality development. He has delineated developmental stages according to the ego qualities that emerge during each; the accomplishment of developmental tasks, he believes, results in ego identity, a feeling of self. To Erikson, the development of lasting adaptive qualities is more important than is the simple resolution of psychosexual conflicts. As a person grows he develops ego qualities that bring him into the structure of his society. Erikson has postulated eight developmental stages related to ego development and social values.

Basic Trust versus Basic Mistrust

During the oral stage described by Freud the infant has his first major social achievement: the ability to let his mother out of sight without anxiety or rage. He develops a rudimentary trust in the outside world, which remains part of his personality throughout development.

Intercourse between the infant and the environment becomes somewhat consistent, and expectations based on familiarity begin to evolve. The infant experiences awakening recognition of correlations between events that he remembers and sensations that he anticipates. Especially during the "biting stage," when he is in pain from teething and frustrated by weaning, he needs a sense of consistency in his environment. The quantities of food and love that he receives are not as important as is the quality of behavior toward him. Parents must communicate their reasons and meanings in what they do; showing that they trust in the practices they wish him to learn transmits a sense of trust to the child.

Disturbances during this period lead to mistrust and may generate serious emotional disorders. Children afflicted with infantile schizophrenia show high degrees of mistrust. They withdraw from others and remain in their private worlds; they appear to have little expectation of positive outcomes from interaction with the external environment. In adult psychoses, too, the predominant pattern seems to be an attempt to flee the external world. Recovery depends to a great extent upon establishing trust.

Erikson points out that the importance of trust is reflected in many social institutions. Religions, for example, share the importance placed upon trust in a higher power, an explicit recognition of human smallness and the need for trust in others. In many cultures and subcultures positive value is placed on trusting in a common faith; conversely, mistrusting is often considered evil. Thus, social institutions mirror and teach the worth of trust to the individual.

Autonomy versus Shame and Doubt

Muscular control becomes important in the anal stage. The child has some of his first experiences of "holding on" and "letting go," actions that may be reflected in his social interactions. Gaining a sense of control over his motor apparatus leads the child to feelings of autonomy and capacity for self-control. Along with autonomy come good will and pride, capacity for love and cooperation, and freedom of expression.

Shame is the response to undesired scrutiny from others. It is awareness of being "looked at" and an evaluation of oneself as dirty or evil. The focus of a child's experiences during toilet training is on what is behind him, on the functioning of his bowels. He may doubt what is behind him, whether he is behaving correctly or incorrectly, well or badly. Parents who are firm and reassuring during toilet training help the child to develop self-control and autonomy. He is protected against the potential anarchy of "holding on" or "letting go" indiscriminately, and thus from arbitrary shame and early doubts.

A poorly developed sense of autonomy may result in an overcontrolling conscience. In adult life it may be reflected in insistence on "following the book," rather than the spirit of regulations. In its extreme form, obsessive-compulsive neurosis, it is marked by an unrealistic need to repeat actions continually to ensure control. Power over even minute aspects of behavior is sought. This type of neurotic may, therefore, be unable to use or order things in a purposeful way so that it may be hard to arrive at realistic solutions.

Social institutions of law and order help to safeguard adults against shame and doubt. Rules delineate the proper order of things and reassure adults that this order will be maintained. Emphasis on substantive justice in economic and political life reflects early development of autonomy.

INITIATIVE VERSUS GUILT

During the phallic stage children experience pleasure in attack and conquest, activities that reflect initiative. Initiative is the active undertaking of a task. If the oedipal problem of this stage is successfully resolved the child retains his initiative and can use it in responsible performance of roles and tasks in society.

Excessive anxiety during the phallic stage results in an overdeveloped superego, which may generate conflicts in adult life. Hatred for the parent who was the original model may develop when he does not live up to the unrealistic values that the young child has introjected. Or the child may grow into an intolerant, self-righteous person who actually inhibits initiative. We have discussed other characteristic disturbances of this period under Freud's phallic type.

Social outlets are primarily through work, in which the initiative of the oedipal period is turned toward adult goals. The need to identify with a strong person during this stage is also reflected in adult society. "Ideal" adults are recognized by their uniforms, statuses, and role functions and provide models for others to follow.

INDUSTRY VERSUS INFERIORITY

During the latency period the child wins recognition by producing things. His preference for play is replaced by the desire to complete productive tasks. The fundamentals of his society's technology are learned during this stage; among literate peoples the development of language skills and other formal education is primary in opening later career possibilities. It is at this stage in his development that the child also learns a feeling of individual worth. If he encounters great difficulties, however, he may despair of his abilities and develop a sense of inferiority. His family life may have failed to prepare him for school, or school may not help him to realize his potentials. Feelings of inadequacy and hopelessness may dominate his attitude.

In later life, a person may compensate for feelings of inferiority by accepting work as the only criterion of his worth. Such an individual is likely to be a strict conformist, a slave to society's technologies, and an unwitting supporter of those who would use it to human detriment.

IDENTITY VERSUS ROLE CONFUSION

As the adolescent approaches adulthood he must establish an identity. His peer group is extremely important in providing feedback about "how he's doing" and "what he is." The adolescent needs confidence that the inner unity that he has developed earlier will be matched in others' perceptions of him. Emphasis on "in-groups" is a temporary way in which adolescents help one another have feelings of "doing okay." It is not uncommon for adolescents to identify too closely with their groups or to adopt heroes. Both serve to maintain a sense of their own cohesiveness.

Personal identity grows more secure as an adolescent establishes his modes of social functioning and directions for his career. Disruptions at this stage result in role confusion, uncertainty about oneself, a nebulous sense of dis-unity, and lack of direction. Delinquent behavior or short-term psychotic episodes may occur.

Ideologies and guides to social values are sought at this time. Youths must confront ideological issues and different systems of social rule. To be comfortable with their identities they must decide to take as their own the "best" values and follow those leaders who uphold them. If they cannot do so, if, for example, alternatives seem equally unattractive, they may become cynical and never relate to a system of values.

INTIMACY VERSUS ISOLATION

As the young adult emerges from his search for identity he must develop the ability to experience intimacy. He must commit himself to relationships and affiliations, and he must be strong enough to maintain them when significant compromises and sacrifices are necessary. This ability is possible only if he is not afraid that sharing with another will result in a loss to his ego. If intimacy threatens his identity, a deep isolation may result. He may become self-absorbed and unable to join with others in any satisfactory way.

Intimacy accompanies "genitality." Mature "genitality" involves more than just sexual capacity; it has larger social significance. Ideally it includes

1. Mutuality of orgasm
2. with a loved partner
3. of the other sex
4. with whom one is able and willing to share a mutual trust
5. and with whom one is willing and able to regulate the cycles of
   a. work
   b. procreation
   c. recreation
6. so as to secure to the offspring all the stages of a satisfactory develop-ment.
   (Erikson, 1963, p. 266)

Those who fail to develop a tolerance for intimacy tend to view others as dangerous when allowed to encroach on their own "territory." Prejudices reflecting the identity struggle of adolescence are likely to develop; in adoles-cence it is necessary to differentiate sharply between the familiar and the foreign in peer-group relations. Character problems may result from inability to commit oneself to intimate relationships. Self-centeredness, inability to enter social activities in typical ways, and frequent conflicts with social standards are telling signs that a person cannot be intimate with others. On the other hand, the development of an ability to experience intimacy leads to an "ethical sense," a sense of fairness with others' needs and desires, the mark of an adult.

"GENERATIVITY" VERSUS STAGNATION

The next stage of development occurs when one prepares to have a family of one's own. Generativity is a concern with establishing and guiding the next generation. It means taking on the task of teaching social living to those who will replace us. If a person fails in this development, he is likely to experience a sense of stagnation and personal impoverishment. He may become immersed in self-concern and perhaps even cease to function as a productive individual.

EGO INTEGRITY VERSUS DESPAIR

The final stage of development is acceptance of one's own life cycle, including acceptance of the necessity for leading, participating, and following at appropriate times. To gain ego integrity one must believe in defending his own life style and recognize it as a worthwhile endeavor within its larger cultural surroundings. To the person with ego integrity death is not frightening; he accepts it as the final step of the life cycle. Those who have failed to develop ego integrity, however, may despair. They recognize that time is short, that they have no chance to start other lives and no alternative roads to lead them to integrity. Remorse and disgust with life may mask despair, but both death and anguish are inescapable.

PSYCHOANALYSIS AS TREATMENT

Psychoanalysis served as a prototype for later developments in psychotherapy. Freud's techniques led to the popular stereotype of psychotherapy: a patient prone on a couch with the analyst sitting at his head taking notes. Laymen seeking the services of a psychiatrist or psychologist often expect to be psychoanalyzed, but most psychotherapists today do not practice psychoanalysis, nor are they trained in its specific techniques. Nevertheless, many therapists do continue to use orthodox Freudian methods (Fenichel, 1945; Fromm-Reichmann, 1950; Monroe, 1955).

CHARACTERISTICS

In Freud's early work with hysterics he used suggestive hypnosis to eliminate symptoms. After hypnotizing a patient he would suggest that the symptom (paralysis, blindness, and so on) was going to disappear when the patient awoke. Freud soon became dissatisfied with this technique. Sometimes the symptoms did not disappear or reappeared or were replaced by others. He saw that he was not bringing about real "cure." He began to experiment with *free association,* a technique destined to become one of his primary therapeutic tools. The *basic rule* agreed to by a patient who undertakes psychoanalysis is to say "everything" that comes into his consciousness.

The therapeutic environment is arranged in order to enhance free association. Typically the patient does recline on a couch, and the analyst does sit beyond his view. The patient's task is to express his thoughts and feelings, no matter what they are. The analyst's task is to "analyze" them and to interpret them in relation to what he knows of the patient's personality. *Interpretation* is the technique of communicating the analyst's understanding of the patient's free associations through restatements of their underlying meanings. The patient is thus led to understand his own conflicts. The goal is to eliminate repressions so that "bound" psychic energy can be released to the ego for adaptive use. Proper interpretation is a skill. Generally an interpretation is most effective when the material is already very close to consciousness. For example, an analyst would not interpret a patient's sexual desire for his mother (the repressed oedipal conflict) until very late in analysis when repression had weakened and the conflict had moved closer to awareness. In the early phase of analysis he would interpret derivations from this conflict: "You make frequent references to your mother." The analyst must recognize when the patient is ready to accept an interpretation; otherwise it may be wasted and resistance to analysis may increase.

In classical psychoanalysis the patient sees the analyst almost daily for a period of from one to several years. The ultimate aim is to restructure the patient's personality so that he can function adaptively. Freud postulated a poorly resolved oedipal complex as the basis of all neuroses, but successful analysis entails much more than recognition of this conflict. The patient has built up many defenses against recognizing his oedipal strivings, and they must be analyzed first. An apt analogy is an artichoke: To reach the center, each outer layer of leaves (defenses) must be removed. The analyst's job is to remove one layer at a time until the core of the conflict emerges. Successful analysis therefore takes a great deal of time and effort.

STAGES

Psychoanalysis is often considered to occur in stages, but it is actually a dynamic process, in which each stage overlaps with others. Although characteristics of all the stages may be present at once, as analysis progresses those of certain stages will successively dominate.

RESISTANCE

The first stage of psychoanalysis is dominated by the patient's unconscious attempts to impede the analysis. As analysis threatens to bring repressed conflicts into the open, the patient unconsciously defends himself against it: He resists. His conscious desire is to bring an end to his suffering, and he is not aware of his resistance; in that sense he is not responsible for impeding therapy. It is the analyst's task to make him aware of his resistance maneuvers; dealing with the latter is necessary before they can progress. Resistance shows itself in many ways. Typically it disrupts free association; the patient claims that his mind is blank, neglects to express some of his thoughts, goes through long silences, and so forth. It may also cause him to forget appointments, to arrive late, or to find excuses to miss sessions.

Resistance shows itself again from time to time during the course of analysis, particularly when recognition of an important conflict is impending. The analyst and the patient must be constantly alert to signs of resistance. Patients may actually stop analysis before its completion because of resistance.

TRANSFERENCE

When the patient ascribes characteristics to the analyst that are really characteristics of important people in his own past, he is said to be "transferring" them. As the analyst is out of sight most of the time and does not interact with the patient on a personal level, the patient knows very little about his characteristics. Almost no ascription of a characteristic to the analyst can be based on accurate knowledge. Indeed, part of the analyst's strategy is to remain "unknown" so that transference phenomena can occur. Transference may be positive, involving love of the analyst, strong positive feelings toward him as a helper, and so on. It may also be negative, expressed in anger and accusations. Transference may show itself in direct communication, free association, or the content of dreams.

At first, the analyst does not interpret the transference unless it is necessary to keep the patient in treatment. He allows it to develop until a *transference neurosis* has been established. He permits the patient to develop a number of unrealistic expectations and attitudes toward him. These expectations and attitudes then serve as a basis for interpreting early experiences. In essence the analyst creates a miniature neurosis in the therapeutic setting and uses it to show the patient how he interacts with important figures. Interpreting these interactions reveals the repressed childhood experiences behind them.

The analyst must be alert to the possibility of *countertransference*. That is, he may transfer feelings from his own past to the patient. As a result of the analyst's own distorted view of the patient, analysis may be impeded or even terminated. Most schools of long-term psychotherapy require their trainees to undergo analysis themselves as a safeguard against countertransference. The analyst's awareness of his own needs and conflicts makes it less likely that they will interfere with his treatment of others.

INSIGHT

The patient becomes aware of his defensive mechanisms and repressed conflicts through interpretations of the transference neurosis: He gains "insight" into his difficulties. At this stage the real source of his conflicts comes to light, and the transference neurosis is resolved.

WORKING THROUGH

During the final phase of analysis conflicts are "worked through" in the patient's everyday living. He has recognized his conflicts in the analytic setting, but their effects on his general behavior are not yet clear. He begins to apply the insights that he has gained in therapy to an expanded field of situations. Analysis is terminated by mutual agreement between analyst and patient that the working-through process is well along.

Professional Considerations

We have just described "classical" psychoanalysis. It has obvious limitations on general application. It is very expensive in both money and time, and many kinds of psychological problems do not yield to solution through psychoanalytic methods. Most psychoanalysts working within the Freudian frame of reference therefore prefer to practice short-term psychotherapy with more restricted goals; frequently the aim is to resolve specific adjustment problems. For instance, rather than eliminate defenses, the therapist may attempt to build a temporary defense to help a person through a particularly stressful period of his life. The patient rarely comes more than three times a week, and the total number of sessions usually ranges from ten to fifty, depending upon the problem.

The classical Freudian school has its own training institutes. The label "psychoanalyst" means that the therapist has undergone training in such an institute; it is neither an academic degree nor a legal title but simply indicates emphasis on psychoanalytic theory and technique. Several years of post-doctoral training are usually required before an institute will certify that a therapist is qualified. Beside knowing psychoanalytic theory the trainee is required to undergo his own analysis and to carry out analysis of at least one patient under the supervision of a qualified psychoanalyst.

Acceptance at psychoanalytic institutes is not dependent upon membership in any particular profession or holding any particular academic degree. In recent years there has been a strong preference for holders of medical degrees because of theoretical emphasis on biological factors as determinants of personality, but holders of Ph.D. degrees have been accepted as have others. Although Freud did not think that medical training is necessary, his followers, as part of an increasing institutionalization of psychoanalysis, have increasingly tended to restrict entry according to previous academic training.

THE CASE OF DORA

A brief examination of one of Freud's published cases shows how the interpretation of dreams is used in psychoanalysis. He has described the course of analysis in lucid detail, but his work has been drastically edited here. We have attempted to include only the high points, to give the reader some understanding of the psychodynamics involved.

Dora, an eighteen-year-old girl, was referred to Freud by her father. She had become dissatisfied with herself and her family and had eventually shown suicidal tendencies. She also complained of minor physical symptoms —difficulties with her throat, possible migraine headaches, and general loss of energy.

As a child, Dora had had a strange affection for her father and had rejected her mother. Like her father, a successful industrialist, she was very intelligent. He suffered from bouts of illness that drew Dora even closer to him. Dora's mother was very concerned with the concrete aspects of home-making, cleaning, and so on.

For many years there had been an unusual interplay among Dora, her father, and another couple, the "Ks". Dora's father and Mrs. K were having an affair, whereas Mr. K showed an active interest in Dora, which she had not reciprocated. Mrs. K had cared for Dora's father when he was ill. During that time Dora had liked her a great deal and had done nothing to prevent the relationship between her and her father. But her attitude had changed after Mr. K had made his intentions toward Dora clearer. He had attempted to embrace her while they had been walking in the forest near his house. Dora had responded to his advances with disgust and had begun to object strongly to her father's relationship with Mrs. K.

Freud analyzed her difficulties as the result of repressed oedipal conflicts. Incidents in her history, as he described them, fit his interpretation quite well. At this point we shall turn to excerpts from Freud's interpretation of a dream offered by Dora after she had been in treatment for some time.

Here is the dream as related by Dora: "A house was on fire." (In answer to an inquiry Dora told me that there had never really been a fire at their house.) "My father was standing beside my bed and woke me up. I dressed myself quickly. Mother wanted to stop and save her jewel-case; but Father said: 'I refuse to let myself and my two children be burnt for the sake of your jewel-case.' We hurried downstairs and as soon as I was outside I woke up."

As the dream was a recurrent one, I naturally asked her when she had first dreamt it. She told me she did not know. But she remembered having had the dream three nights in succession at L—— (the place on the lake where the scene with Herr K. had taken place), and it had now come back again a few nights earlier, here in Vienna. (The content of the dream makes it possible to establish that it in fact occurred for the first time at L——.) My expectations from the clearing-up of the dream were naturally heightened when I heard of its connection with the events at L——. But I wanted to discover first what had been the exciting cause of its recent recurrence, and I therefore asked Dora to take the dream bit by bit and tell me what occurred to her in connection with it. She had already had some training in dream interpretation from having previously analyzed a few minor specimens.

"Something occurs to me," she said, "but it cannot belong to the dream, for it is quite recent, whereas I have certainly had the dream before."

"That makes no difference," I replied. "Start away! It will simply turn out to be the most recent thing that fits in with the dream."

"Very well, then. Father has been having a dispute with Mother in the last few days, because she locks the dining-room door at night. My brother's room, you see, has no separate entrance, but can only be reached through the dining-room. Father does not want my brother to be locked in like that at night. He says it will not do: something might happen in the night so that it might be necessary to leave the room."

"And that made you think of the risk of fire?"

"Yes."

"Now, I should like you to pay close attention to the exact words you used. We may have to make use of them. You said that 'something might happen in the night so that it might be necessary to leave the room.' " (I laid stress upon these words because they took me aback. They seemed to have an ambiguous ring about them. Are not certain physical exigencies referred to in the same words? Now, in a line of associations ambiguous words [or, as we may call them, "switch-words"] act like points at a junction. If the points are switched across from the position in which they appear to lie in the dream, then we find ourselves upon another set of rails; and along this second track run the thoughts which we are in search of and which still lie concealed behind the dream.)

But Dora had now discovered the connecting link between the recent exciting cause of the dream and the original one, for she continued:

"When we arrived at L—— that time, Father and I, he openly said he was afraid of fire. We arrived in a violent thunderstorm, and saw the small wooden house without any lightning-conductor. So his anxiety was quite natural."

What I now had to do was to establish the relation between the events at L—— and the recurrent dreams which she had had there. I therefore said: "Did you have the dream during your first nights at L—— or during your last ones?" (I must explain that I knew that the scene had not occurred on the very first day, and that she had remained at L—— for a few days after it without giving any hint of the incident.)

Her first reply was that she did not know, but after a while she added: "Yes. I think it was after the scene."

So now I knew that the dream was a reaction to that experience. But why had it recurred there three times? I continued my questions: "How long did you stop on at L—— after the scene?"

"Four days more. On the fifth I went away with father."

"Now I am certain that the dream was an immediate effect of your experience with Herr K. It was at L—— that you dreamed it for the first time, and not before. You have only introduced this uncertainty in your memory so as to obliterate the connection in your mind. But the figures do not quite fit in to my satisfaction yet. If you stayed at L—— for four nights longer, the dream might have occurred four times over. Perhaps this was so?" . . . (Freud, 1950, pp. 78–80)

Much of the dream, however, still remained to be interpreted, and I proceeded with my questions: "What is this about the jewel-case that your mother wanted to save?"

"Mother is very fond of jewelry and had had a lot given her by father."

"And you?"

"I used to be very fond of jewelry too, once; but I have not worn any since my illness. —Once, four years ago," (a year before the dream) "Father and Mother had a great dispute about a piece of jewelry. Mother wanted to be given a particular thing—pearl drops to wear in her ears. But father does not like that kind of thing, and he brought her a bracelet instead of the drops. She was furious, and told him that as he had spent so much money on a present she did not like, he had better just give it to someone else."

"I daresay you thought to yourself you would accept it with pleasure."

"I don't know." (The regular formula with which she confessed to anything that had been repressed.) "I don't in the least know how Mother comes into the dream; she was not with us at L—— at the time." (This remark gave evidence of a complete misunderstanding of the rules of dream interpretation, though on other occasions Dora was perfectly familiar with them. This fact, coupled with the hesitancy and meagreness of her associations with the jewel-case, showed me that we were here dealing with material which had been very intensely repressed.)

" I will explain that to you later. Does nothing else occur to you in connection with the jewel-case? So far you have only talked about jewelry and have said nothing about a case."

"Yes, Herr K. had made me a present of an expensive jewel-case a little time before."

"Then a return-present would have been very appropriate. Perhaps you do not know that 'jewel-case' (*Schmuckkästchen*) is a favourite expression for the same thing that you alluded to not long ago by means of the reticule you were wearing—for the female genitals, I mean."

"I knew you would say that." (A very common way of putting aside a piece of knowledge that emerges from the repressed.)

"That is to say, you knew that it was so. —The meaning of the dream is now becoming even clearer. You said to yourself: 'This man is persecuting me; he wants to force his way into my room. My "jewel-case" is in danger, and if anything happens it will be Father's fault.' For that reason in the dream you chose a situation which expresses the opposite—a danger from which your father is saving you. In this part of the dream everything is turned into the opposite; you will soon discover why. As you say, the mystery turns upon your mother. You ask how she comes into the dream? She is, as you know, your former rival for your father's affections. In the incident of the bracelet, you would have been glad to accept what your mother had rejected. Now let us just put 'give' instead of 'accept' and 'withhold' instead of 'reject.' Then it means that you were ready to give your father what your mother withheld from him; and the thing in question was connected with jewelry." (We shall be able later on to interpret even the drops in a way which will fit in with the context.) "Now bring your mind back to the jewel-case which Herr K. gave you. You have there the starting-point for a parallel line of thoughts, in which Herr K. is to be put in the place of your father just as he was in the matter of standing beside your bed. He gave you a jewel-case; so you are to give him your jewel-case. That was why I spoke just now of a 'return present.' In this line of thoughts your mother must be replaced by Frau K. (You will not deny that she, at any rate, was present at the time.) So you are ready to give Herr K. what his wife withholds from him. That is the thought which has had to be repressed with so much energy, and which has made it necessary for every one of its elements to to be turned into its opposite. The dream confirms once more what I had already told you before you dreamed it—that you are summoning up your old love for your father in order to protect yourself against your love for Herr K. But what do all these efforts show? Not only that you are afraid of Herr K., but that you are still more afraid of yourself, and of the temptation you feel to yield to him. In short, these efforts prove once more how deeply you loved him." (I added: "Moreover, the re-appearance of the dream in the last few days forces me to the conclusion that you consider that the same situation has arisen once again, and that you have decided to give up the treatment—to which, after all, it is only your father who makes you come." The sequel showed how correct my guess had been. At this point my interpretation touches for a moment upon the subject of "transference"—a theme which is of the highest practical and theoretical importance, but into which I shall not have much further opportunity of entering in the present paper.)

Naturally Dora would not follow me in this part of the interpretation. I myself, however, had been able to arrive at a further step in the interpretation, which seemed to me indispensable both for the anamnesis of the case and for a theory of dreams. I promised to communicate this to Dora at the next sitting. (Freud, 1950, pp. 83–86)

Freud's theory of dreams incorporates and elaborates basic psychoanalytic concepts. Dreams to him fulfill wishes, but their actual meanings are often masked by symbolic representations. Dora's dream, according to Freud, actually represented her wish to have intercourse with her father. Some symbolic distortions were pointed out: jewel case for genitals, acceptance for giving. Repressed material is allowed expression in dreams but only in forms that are unrecognizable to the individual. In a sense dreams serve as "safe" gratification. Psychoanalysts use them to uncover unconscious conflicts.

Dora's case exemplifies the emphasis on sexual conflict in classical psychoanalytic theory. It also highlights the importance of sexual adjustment in adolescence, a topic already discussed in this chapter and to be discussed further in Chapters 11 and 12.

SUMMARY

In this chapter we have described the psychoanalytic theory of Sigmund Freud and some recent revisions by ego psychologists.

We focused first on the concepts of classical psychoanalysis. Economic concepts involve the sources and distribution of psychic energy, which Freud considered limited to a closed system. That is, no energy is lost or gained; it is simply redistributed among different mental functions. The instincts—mental representations (wishes) of tissue needs—are generated by psychic energy. Instincts have sources, aims, intensity, and objects. There are two major types of instincts. The instincts for life (libido) serve to maintain the organism's unity and survival; they include drives for self-preservation (ego instincts) and drives for species preservation (sexual instincts). The death instinct, Thanatos, has an important derivative in the aggressive drive. Freudians consider the conflicts of sexual and aggressive needs with social prohibitions the most important sources of maladjustment.

Topographical concepts are related to the degrees in which mental material is available to awareness. Three levels are postulated: conscious, preconscious, and unconscious. The most important material in personal difficulties is said to be in the dynamic unconscious. Thoughts or ideas must be imbued with psychic energy if they are to become conscious. When an idea derives energy from an instinct it is said to be "drive-cathected." Energy opposing drive cathexis—preventing an idea from entering consciousness—is called "countercathexis"; hypercathexis is energy used to direct attention to one idea or another. When an idea reaches consciousness overt behavior is likely to follow.

Structural concepts describe mental activities that serve specific purposes. The id consists mainly of inherited drives. Primary-process thinking, demands for immediate gratification and inability to delay action, characterize the id, which operates on the pleasure principle. The ego attempts to satisfy the instincts, but at the same time it seeks to maximize satisfaction, which may involve delay. It operates on the reality principle and is called "secondary-process thinking." The superego represents the values, mores, and social constraints taught by the culture. It functions to prevent socially unacceptable impulses from reaching awareness and being acted upon. As does the id, the superego operates on an unrealistic principle, rather than testing reality.

Genetic concepts relate personality development to stages of growth. In normal growth the ego is more differentiated than are the id or superego, and the primary sources of instinctual gratification shift from one body region to another. Psychosexual stages are named according to the body zones that predominate as sources of gratification: the oral stage, the anal stage, the phallic stage, latency, and the genital stage. At each stage of development specific conflicts are likely to arise, and when they are not satisfactorily resolved they will reveal themselves as character traits in the adult personality.

Anxiety and abnormal behavior are two psychoanalytic concepts related to adjustment. Freud postulated three types of anxiety, depending upon the source. Objective anxiety results from realistic threats from the external environment. Neurotic anxiety arises from the threat that repressed id impulses will enter consciousness. And moral anxiety results when the superego threatens punishment. Abnormal behavior is explained by the inappropriate ways in which the ego copes with the frustrations resulting from inability to satisfy instincts. If the ego yields control to the superego because of excessive id energy, instinctual expression is prevented and neurotic behavior will include substitute symptoms. When the ego relinquishes energy to the id, severe disturbances (psychotic disorders) occur, and the person loses contact with reality. When an over-strict superego is too strong to permit the ego to achieve more adaptive resolutions, the person suffers guilt, self-depreciation, and therefore depression.

In the second part of this chapter we focused on the ideas of modern ego psychologists. While accepting Freud's basic concepts they have placed more emphasis on the adaptive capacity of man and have suggested that the ego has its own source of psychic energy. The ego processes (abilities) may aid adjustment through either defense mechanisms that help to lock unacceptable thoughts within the unconscious or through coping mechanisms that contribute to realistic problem solving and reality testing. We have discussed a number of these ego abilities and their uses in both defense and coping. Defense mechanisms are only temporarily helpful and often hinder adjustment in the long run.

Erikson has divided man's development into eight stages. He stressed the development at each stage of specific ego qualities that serve to help man become integrated into his society.

Discussion of psychoanalysis as a method of treatment closed the chapter. Free association is the basic rule for the patient who participates in psychoanalysis. The analyst interprets the patient's associations in order to bring repressed material into consciousness. Psychoanalysis progresses through four stages: resistance, transference, insight, and working through. Psychoanalysts also practice short-term therapy. Freud's case of Dora served to exemplify the use of dreams in psychoanalysis and to demonstrate its relevance to adjustment.

6

The Humanistic View

I. EXISTENTIALISM
  A. Introduction and Background
    1. Society's constriction of man
    2. The existential problem
  B. Existential Concepts
    1. Dasein
    2. Being in the world
    3. Transcendence of the immediate situation
    4. Anxiety
    5. Guilt
  C. Existential Psychotherapy
    1. Techniques
    2. Presence
    3. Commitment
    4. The case of Eric
    5. Deflection
  D. Competence and Growth Groups
    1. Basis and cautions
    2. Techniques for expanding human awareness
  E. Existentialism in Practice
II. SELF THEORY AND CLIENT-CENTERED THERAPY
  A. Introduction
  B. Rogers' Theory of Man
    1. The phenomenal field
    2. Motivation
    3. The development of a self-concept
    4. The effects of the self-concept on behavior
    5. Revision and expansion of self
  C. Client-Centered Therapy
    1. The counselor's attitude
    2. Reflection of feelings
    3. Nondirective approach
  D. Process Research
    1. Process scales
    2. Results
  E. Recent Emphases
    1. The valuing process
    2. Learning to be free

Summary

The humanistic view of man is becoming increasingly popular in the United States. It is based on strong respect for man as an individual and emphasizes "phenomenological" understanding of him: To know him it is necessary to know how he perceives the world. Humanists also view man as a "being" with potentials whose positive attributes will be expressed unless restricted by neurotic characteristics. Man's interaction with his environment (especially human or social relationships) may distort his perceptions and cripple his attitudes, reducing his ability to fulfill his potential. Two specific views based on these assumptions will be discussed here: existentialism and self theory.

EXISTENTIALISM

INTRODUCTION AND BACKGROUND

Existentialism is not a theory of personality. It is a system of thought that offers a framework for approaching human problems; by itself existentialism does not provide answers nor does it furnish norms by which people can be judged. It stresses the roles each individual's unique potential and experiences play in shaping his own existence. A person's reality is considered to be defined almost entirely by the ways in which he perceives the world. Existentialists believe, however, that man can be understood accurately neither through study of only his subjective experience of the world nor through study of only his objectively observable actions and attributes. The reality of man is a structure underlying the experience of the individual as both subject and object. Although man can experience himself in both perspectives, he can also do more, he can take a detached view of himself. Reality, then, lies in the person who is capable of viewing himself as both subject and object. Neither process by itself represents what truly exists. From the existential point of view, man suffers from anxiety whenever he must view himself simply as subject responding to the outer world or as object to be observed and intellectualized about. Furthermore, as man has the capacity for both subjective and objective views of himself, at the same time he is aware that he is viewing himself in alternative ways: There is thus a third dimension of "self" or "I," a dimension that is uniquely human. The existential orientation is "centrally concerned with rediscovering the living person amid the compartmentalization of modern culture" (May *et al.*, 1958, p. 14). The primary need of life—and the fundamental human drive—is to fulfill potential. Every person has particular potentials, and developing them is his basic task.

The existential view grew out of the cultural crises associated with changing from medieval society to the Renaissance. Although existentialism does not view man as essentially a suffering being, its meaning and importance are nevertheless revealed with particular vividness during periods when people suffer from the spiritual and emotional upheavals associated with cultural change. In our time existentialism is most accepted among the vanguards in art, literature, and thought. Values once accepted no longer offer security; as they no longer serve man well in his daily life, they are questioned. To meet this challenge the individual has the alternatives of sinking into dogmatism and social conformity or of seeking new values by becoming more aware of his uniqueness and potential, more aware of his own existence. The existential view of man thus becomes sharper and clearer when old values are dying and the need for security is strong.

Because of the association of existentialism with human stress it is sometimes considered a basically pessimistic and unrewarding view of man, but this opinion represents a misunderstanding. Rather, existentialists consider that man is always *becoming*, that he always faces further possibilities for growth. These possibilities in turn generate crises, in that he must make choices in directing his own growth. But the crises, though representing a form of stress, do not necessarily indicate despair. They are positive, in that they open possibilities for further individual growth.

SOCIETY'S CONSTRICTION OF MAN

Since medieval times religion, industrialization, and working for concrete products have become increasingly important. The Industrial Revolution has served to separate man from his wholeness, forcing him to take a one-sided view of himself. To be successful in the modern industrial era man must often compartmentalize his life in social and economic roles that do not necessarily overlap, leaving him "disunited," separated from his total being. The accumulation of money as an indicator of success has further contributed to this separation. Man's rewards no longer consist of the actual products of his labors; rather, his reward is abstract, in the form of monetary value. Measuring his personal output in abstract or intangible value tends to "depersonalize him," and he becomes even further alienated. Repression, as Freudian psychologists have recognized, is parallel to division and specialization in industry. Freudians, who view man as object, are primarily interested in the person and his problems that lead to repression; existentialists are primarily interested in the man who must give up self-awareness to shield himself from reality. That is, they focus not on the particular content or social values that generate individual repression but on man as a being who has forsaken his potential for self-awareness. They believe that man has become his own problem.

The use of reason as a tool represents another difficulty connected with industrialization. Modern man tends to suspect his own emotional and "irrational" aspects; he limits the use of his reason to technical progress rather than to understanding further his own total existence. This limitation represents the enslavement of one aspect of man's potential to technical progress. According to existentialists, psychology, psychoanalysis, and other adjustment psychologies have fallen into this trap. Reason is used simply as a tool for understanding man as an object, yet using reason in this way may increase his alienation by providing a cultural sanction and standardization for it. By helping man adjust to an imperfect and stultifying society, rather than resolving man's basic dilemmas and bringing him back to wholeness of experience, psychoanalysis and psychotherapy can become part of the "neurosis of our time." They may act to continue those very forces that suppress potential.

Existential psychotherapy therefore defines neurosis as the destruction of man's capacity to fulfill his own being. Instead of studying the problems of the man, they study man as a being with problems.

THE EXISTENTIAL PROBLEM

Man must face one insoluble problem. He is subject to chance or accident in the time and place in which he exists; he is *thrown* into the world. In this sense he must question "why" he is where he is at this particular time. He must also face the question of "being-where." Man finds himself in an infinity of space and recognizes his lack of knowledge about it; he recognizes that he does not know where he is, that there is no satisfactory definition of his position. He also knows that our explanations of time and space are superficial. Our sciences may seem an inadequate refuge, self-aware men can see that what science truly understands can only offer superficial explanations for man's existence. Consequently, man experiences a deep anxiety arising from his awareness of the unknowable universe. This anxiety can be denied only through avoidance of questions.

EXISTENTIAL CONCEPTS

DASEIN

Dasein is derived from two German words, *sein* ("to be") and *da* ("there"). The distinctive character of human existence is the personal experience of being at a particular point in time and space, an experience that is the individual's alone.

Since man is conscious of his own existence, he is said to be responsible for it. His awareness distinguishes him from other beings. Other forms of life primarily respond to the environment, but man can choose his direction and can determine his existence to a much greater degree. Man is in the process of *becoming* what his potentials allow. One can understand another only as he moves toward the fulfillment of his potential, toward "becoming." To the existentialist the future tense is the most significant in understanding man. Ideally, man is responsible for himself and assumes the responsibility for becoming himself. Ron is an example of a person who was not "becoming" (see Chapter 1). His continuing growth as a person seemed blocked in many ways. He was unable to decide whether or not to stay in his father's business, to relate effectively to women, and to relate to his own sexuality. He was a young man whose potentials were hindered and constricted.

It is also necessary that man recognize that he will *not be* in the future, that at some time he will become a nonbeing (*nothingness*). Realizing nonexistence is a necessary condition for grasping fully the idea of being; nonbeing is inseparable from being. The ultimate nonbeing, of course, is death. Man may also, however, lose his being through crippling anxiety or the denial of his potential in conformity. Without recognition of the possibility of nonbeing existence is characterized by absence of concrete self-awareness and a sense of unreality in confronting oneself. When a person is unable to to accept his own anxiety, hostility, and aggression—unable to tolerate these signs of nonbeing without repression—his choices are restricted, and he is unable to realize his potential to the fullest.

To the existential therapist, a person must have undergone the *"I am" experience* in order to solve his problems. Although the experience is not in itself sufficient for solution, it is a necessary precondition. One becomes aware of his own aliveness, of being not simply cast in a social role, in a union with his own being. As Descartes has formulated it, "Cogito, ergo sum" ("I think, therefore I am"). The "I am" experience is considered beyond the ethical and social norms of evaluating experiences to a point at which one can judge independently what others demand of him or teach to him. One is capable of selecting his *own* place, his *own* position in response to external influences. One of the clearest signs of discomfort with one's own choice is rigid moralism, the strict clinging to social teachings through inability to evaluate one's own position. We have seen that Ron clung to early religious and moral teachings about sexuality and family position that restricted his expression of self and kept him from becoming what he wished to become and from fulfilling his potential.

BEING-IN-THE-WORLD

Another important existential concept is that of the *person-in-his-world*. The "world" is the structure of meaningful relationships in which each person functions, including the ways in which he participates in these relationships. All past and future possibilities are included.

The importance of this concept lies in its usefulness in helping us to understand the most acute problem of modern times—men who have lost-their-world. Such people have become alienated either from the "human" world (relations with others) or from the "natural" world (including their own biological drives and responses). Such disturbances in being-in-this-world reflect isolation and alienation from oneself. According to R. May and his colleagues, they result in

> . . . a man who is a stranger in his world, a stranger to other people to whom he speaks or pretends to love; he moves about in a state of homelessness, vagueness, and haze as though he has no direct connection with his world but were in a foreign country where he does not know the language and has no hope of learning it, and is always doomed to wander in quiet despair, incommunicado, homeless, a stranger. (1958, p. 57)

In A. Camus's novel *The Stranger* (1946), the main character is a young man who is isolated from many aspects of his world. He has formed relationships, but none has held deep meaning for him. People have criticized him secretly because he did not feel deep affection for his ailing mother, though he provided for her care as best he could. Even when he becomes involved in murder (almost by accident, as with much of his life) and is imprisoned awaiting the death penalty, he seems not to understand; he is a victim of his time and his experiences, simply watching his life pass by.

Existentialism defines three *modes of world*. All contribute simultaneously to one's being-in-the-world; focusing on only one can never give a complete picture of a person-in-his-being. The existentialists criticize other personality theories and psychotherapies because they tend to focus on single aspects of the world, thus failing to reveal man completely.

UMWELT

The mode of the world represented by nature and inorganic objects is called the *Umwelt*. Biological needs, drives, and instincts are included. If man were to exist without consciousness, the *Umwelt* would be the aspect of world that he would most frequently experience. It is "given," and we have little control over it. Each of us must adjust to it in some way. In existential terms it is the "thrown" world, aspects of the world over which we have no control, we have been thrown into it for no apparent reason.

To speak of adjustment and adaptation in the *Umwelt* is accurate because interaction between two objects, or between a person and an object, can occur. Disturbances in man's *Umwelt* take the form of alienation from nature, an alienation derived from several centuries of Western man's attempt to gain control over the natural world. Although he has largely succeeded in gaining such control, he has in the process become estranged from the world itself. He does not feel himself a part of nature or at one with his own body. Some aspects of young people's current emphasis on "back to nature" activities reflect their recognition of this estrangement from the natural world.

According to the existentialists, Freud emphasized man's interaction with the *Umwelt*, his biological drives, but in deemphasizing the other modes of world he failed to recognize the full reality of man as a being-in-the-world.

MITWELT

Another mode of the world is called *mitwelt*; it is the world of human relationships. "Relationship" is the most accurate term for man's being-in-the-*Mitwelt* because it emphasizes the mutual quality of encounters between people. When there is mutual awareness of each other's being-in-the-world, both are affected in some way. If, however, a person is too preoccupied or too anxious, so that his consciousness is extremely small, mutual awareness is not possible. Although "adjustment" describes man's interaction in the *Umwelt*, it is incorrect to view human relationships as between object and object or person and object. Mutual exchange results from human encounters.

The Neo-Freudians, because of their social orientation, stress the importance of the *Mitwelt*. Once again the existentialists see such theories as limiting, failing to portray man accurately in his total being. Social theorists frequently view the self simply as a reflection of social relationships, that is, of outside forces.

EIGENWELT

The last mode of world is the *Eigenwelt*, one's *own* world. The *Eigenwelt* is unique to human beings and reflects man's capacity for self-awareness and self-relatedness. Other schools of psychology have not taken it into account. Self-awareness and self-relatedness become tools for seeing the world in its true perspective, the basis for relating to its other aspects; they permit a grasp of what things in the world "mean to me."

The *Eigenwelt* is the basis, or the background, for the capacity to love, to accept another as a separate being-in-his-world and to value his uniqueness in relation to oneself. If one cannot understand himself as a separate being, he cannot relate to another as a separate being; complete acceptance of him as a being-in-his-world (love) is thus also not possible.

Modern man, especially in the Western cultures, has tended to ignore self-relatedness. As a result he appraises things as objects, including himself and others. Approaching oneself as an object has engendered arid intellectualism in thinking about oneself, with the consequence that one loses a sense of the reality of his own experience.

TRANSCENDENCE OF THE IMMEDIATE SITUATION

A unique characteristic of man is his ability to orient himself beyond the immediate limits of time and space. He is able to think of future possibilities and to evaluate the present in the light of past experiences. The ability to transcend the immediate situation allows man to learn from the past in order to guide his future. Transcendence is one basis of human freedom because it opens up a vast range of possibilities in any given situation. The range of possibilities depends upon the degree of self-awareness; a psychologically healthy person has a free imagination and can evaluate the past in order to choose his future behavior. The more alienated one is from his total being, the fewer alternatives are available; behavior therefore becomes increasingly stereotyped, conforming, and morally rigid.

Disturbing psychological experiences shake a person's sense of time. Anxiety and depression tend to blot out the future, so that capacity for evaluation and prediction is limited. On the other hand, repression blocks the past from the present, rendering experience unavailable for prediction and direction of future activities. The self-actualizing process (fulfilling one's potentials) is constricted and blocked by anxiety and neurotic rigidity.

Existentialists do not believe that man's behavior can be understood on the basis of his past alone. That is, childhood experiences are not sufficient by themselves to determine the future. The past consists of one's memories of being-in-the-world, which are partly shaped by the exigencies of present and future. People do not remember past events according to the frequency with which they occurred, for example, they remember those that are relevant to their interests in the present or the future. Recollections of going to school, an activity that occurred almost daily, may never enter awareness, yet a very special past event like the death of a loved one may emerge from memory when one seeks to change his future direction. In this sense, the future, "becoming," determines the past. A patient recalls his past when he has some commitment to the future; without such a commitment his past may seem drab, unproductive, almost useless for guiding choices in the present. Camus's "stranger," for example, has no goals or aspirations. He is content in a simple occupation that does not express his potential. His recollections of the past are vague and have little meaning in directing his life. He seems to float aimlessly as events happen to him.

ANXIETY

Existentialists define anxiety as experiencing the threat of imminent nonbeing, of losing oneself and one's world, of becoming nothing.

Anxiety has a positive aspect in that it indicates confrontation with an existing potential. It always involves conflict between an emerging potential and one's current state of being. Such conflict occurs because the emerging potential portends change, and man's need for security thus impels him to deny the potential; his denial of it conflicts with his desire to fulfill it. Ron, for instance, experienced conflict over his growing awareness that his work with his father was stifling his potential.

The less that one is able to relate to all modes of the world, the more likely he is to be overwhelmed by his emerging potentials. If he cannot relate to his being-in-the-world he is likely to experience crippling anxiety. Anxiety may overcome his awareness of existence, his sense of time may be distorted, his memory may be dulled, and his future may be erased. He is unable then even to conceive of existence without anxiety. That is, his sense of time is "bound" in his suffering, and he is unable to choose a different direction.

To existentialists fear and anxiety are not the same. Anxiety is a response to an attack on the concept of oneself, on one's experience as a being. Fear, on the other hand, is a response to the threat of pain or physical destruction. A person responds with fear when he comes unexpectedly upon a rattlesnake in the woods. His response may be quantitatively strong, but it is quickly forgotten when the situation changes. On the other hand, when a respected colleague criticizes one's work, the response is anxiety, which may continue for some time; it represents damage to the concept of self based on an important part of experience.

GUILT

Guilt is the reaction to having failed to fulfill one's potential through denial of the mental or physical aspects of existence. In this sense everyone experiences guilt, for no human being is able to evade all restrictions on his ability to live up to his potential. We can never completely fulfill our potential for knowing another person because such knowledge involves "being" that person. Our knowledge is always restricted because we must perceive others through our own eyes and our own being; we thus necessarily distort their beings. Recognizing our limitations is constructive, however, because it leads to humility. Humility helps us to become more sensitive in human relationships, and it then becomes possible to fulfill our potential more creatively.

Another source of unavoidable guilt is man's separation from nature. We can never completely fulfill our natural potential because to remain viable our social organizations must limit the expression of such potential. Guilt over unfulfilled biological possibilities does not directly reflect internalized social prohibitions, however; rather, it results from awareness that we have chosen not to explore all the possibilities. Certainly the particular content of this guilt varies from culture to culture, but all human beings experience it.

Neurotic guilt includes morbid features that lead to formation of symptoms. It results from avoiding inevitable guilt by restricting one's awareness of reality. Ron fought to rationalize his behavior and to prevent recognition of his own needs. Only slowly did he become aware of himself through psychotherapy. His guilt lessened as he saw the inevitability of the restrictions on his own potential that he had accepted.

Restricting awareness to avoid universal guilt tends to restrict further the ability to live up to one's own potential; consequently guilt continues to grow in a circular manner until it severely cripples functioning. Relating to oneself openly counteracts neurotic guilt.

EXISTENTIAL PSYCHOTHERAPY

It follows from the existential point of view that "knowing about" a person is not sufficient to "know him." Information about a person (from case records, test scores, and the like) is not necessarily inaccurate, but it is limited by the nature of the encounter in which it is gathered. When the therapist experiences "him" the patient becomes alive on a very different level from that reflected in the information "about him." The therapist's experience of "here's a new person" places the other information about the patient in its proper perspective. To encounter the patient and to understand him as a being-in-his-world, the therapist must be willing to love, to unite with him. If the therapist shuts off the relationship because of resentment or a need to avoid anxiety, his capacity to understand the patient is reduced, and the reality of the patient is distorted.

TECHNIQUES

Retreating into a technical view is a common way for the therapist to avoid the anxiety of an encounter; techniques must be subordinated to the "reality" of the person encountered. The therapist's primary task is to understand his patient as a being-in-his-world. Emphasis on technique is a sign that the therapist perceives him as an object, a reflection of the problem of modern man, who tends to impose techniques on objects. Techniques must follow from an understanding of *the* patient, rather than becoming standardized for patients in general. At any particular instant of therapy the therapist may use techniques characteristic of other therapeutic schools. But the total context of therapy will be distinct in focusing always on the patient's existence-in-his-world. A dream may be interpreted in a psychoanalytic sense if such an approach is appropriate to furthering understanding of the patient's world. For instance, when a patient's primary concern is his *Umwelt* (biological urges), then psychoanalytic theory, which emphasizes that mode of the world, is appropriate to understanding him. On the other hand, the patient is not to be viewed as an object exhibiting psychic dynamisms or psychic mechanisms; rather, he is to be viewed as a choosing, committing person, directing himself toward something at any moment of his being. Existentially oriented psychotherapists do in fact use a wide range of therapeutic techniques, varying from patient to patient and from one phase of treatment to another; the aim is always to illuminate the patient's being-in-his-world.

Existential analysts try to avoid placing their patients in theoretical categories. Aspects of any patient's behavior always draw their meaning from his existential situation. For example, a psychoanalyst would probably label a patient who interacts with him only on a superficial social level as "resistant" and would interpret the resistance as a means by which to maintain repression. To an existential analyst this aspect of the encounter would indicate the patient's absorption with the *Mitwelt,* the world of social relationships. He would likely interpret it as the patient's attempt to renounce his unique potential by merging himself in the anonymous mass. Such attempts to conform generally represent resistance to other aspects of the world. Furthermore, the classical psychoanalytic interpretation of transference is that the patient's feelings toward the therapist are a neurotic projection of earlier feelings toward important people in his life. The existentialist sees this means of relating as a restriction of the patient's potential in that developmental experiences have limited the means available to him for interaction with others; only "immature" methods have been developed, and the resulting behavior appears fixed and rigid.

PRESENCE

Existentialists emphasize the need for *presence* in the therapeutic relationship. That is, the therapist strives to make his relationship with the patient "real," as opposed to technical. The value of presence is that it helps the patient to experience his own existence as real. If the therapist were to take a technical stance he would forfeit some "realness" in the relationship; by not doing so he makes it more likely that the patient will experience what "he himself is doing" in the relationship. Realization of his own existence sets the stage for the patient to use his knowledge of why he does what he does; such knowledge is not helpful if he is unaware of his unique existence.

Most patients who are classically labeled "neurotic" are usually concerned with their biological world (*Umwelt*). They need to experience the world of self-relatedness (*Eigenwelt*). It is the therapist's task to bring the patient's self-relatedness into awareness, and it is the patient's task to "live it." Patients may rid themselves of some anxiety and symptoms by adjusting to their culture, but existential analysts do not find this solution satisfactory; it is simply another way of evading existence. One must become self-related, must recognize the different modes of world, and must make decisions based on full understanding of being-in-the-world.

COMMITMENT

Existential therapists emphasize *commitment*. "The patient cannot permit himself to get insight or knowledge until he is ready to decide, takes a decisive orientation to life, and has made the preliminary decisions along the way" (May *et al.*, 1958, p. 87). The patient must thus be ready to make decisions; it is the therapist's task to help him to avoid indecisiveness. To this end, he must help the patient seek all the possibilities of his existence, including the possibility of nonbeing; only then is the patient able to make realistic decisions and to move forward fulfilling his potential.

THE CASE OF ERIC

Eric participated in a therapeutic experiment on the "nondiseased" person (Burton, 1967). A. Burton believes that psychotherapy is more than simply a kind of treatment; it is a "joint discovery of creativity." Even when an individual shows no signs of serious disturbance, psychotherapy may still serve him as a positive impetus to growth. A number of subjects were asked to take part in the experiment. They all met the criteria of "nondisease," that is, they had never been treated by a psychiatrist, psychologist, or social worker, and they were functioning satisfactorily in their personal, social, and occupational endeavors. Once selected, each was asked to engage in twenty-five hours of psychotherapy.

Eric almost fit the classical stereotype of the white, middle-class college student. He denied having adjustment problems. His home life was happy, he was making good grades in school, he was a leader in his fraternity, and he had many other achievements to his credit. Traditionally he would have been considered a well-adjusted young man in no need of psychotherapy. One of his dreams indicated his mode of being-in-the-world at the time of the experiment:

> I was tied upside down from the ceiling of a hall, helpless. Someone pushing me, making me swing, then laughing about the control which he was exercising over me. It seemed that it was not he who tied me, but some large organization. The next thing I knew, this man was also tied, but not upside down.
>
> I found that I could wriggle free from my bonds, and was soon free. My first response was to somehow tease the man (who was still tied), or otherwise show him that now I had the upper hand. Instead, I untied him. I was glad, because now we were both together in our illegal attempt at escape from the "organization." As we hopefully crouched on the floor, about to plan our escape, I saw two large shadows on the floor in front of us. My heart sank. I turned around to see two men in uniforms, smiling. They had known all the time that I never had a chance. (Burton, 1967, pp. 388–389)*

A tape-recorded interview from the twelfth session shows something of how Eric saw his life situation. It gives some idea of why he, with his apparently good adjustment, should wish to remain in psychotherapy for twenty-five hours.

> *Dr. B:*   Eric, would you say that your problem is one of a gap between practice and an ideal rather than a neurotic situation? If you were willing to settle for less then there would be no problem?
> *Eric.*   Right.

*This and the following case reprinted by permission of the editor and publisher from A. Burton, "The Psychotherapy of a Non-Diseased Person," in *Modern Psychotherapeutic Practice*, A. Burton (Ed.), Science and Behavior Books, Inc., Palo Alto, California, 1965.

Dr. B: Well, what do you think about this business?

Eric: Well, really, you see, I don't know that much about what constitutes a neurotic—I haven't ever thought of myself that way.

Dr. B: You haven't.

Eric: Well, this has always been what I thought has been my problem—that I do have an ideal—that I do look at my capabilities and say, "Well, I can do this," and yet I don't do it. And I do see, you know, I would like to—even with girls—I figure, well, heck, you know they're really going to like me because of the kind of guy I am, and yet I'm still kind of afraid with them. Sure, I'd like to be a great lover. You know, I was thinking of something else today that, well, I don't really want to be a conformist. The fact that I used to smoke Pall Malls—and everybody smokes Pall Malls, so I changed to Philip Morris. Then I tried these Old Golds which I don't like, just so I could be smoking something different from somebody else. I like the idea that I'm smarter than other people, that I can think things out for myself where they can't, that I can come to a better decision than they can, and yet, I don't allow myself to use this ability in a self-situation. I'll just retreat or give a kind of all-knowing glance, you know, like "Well, I know what's going on here," but I'm not going to fight it—there's nothing I can do about it but go ahead and act stupid.

Dr. B: H'mm.

Eric: I was wholly avoiding your question. But I'm not in a constant state of —how I conceive of a neurotic is in a constant state of agitation about everything—because when I do think things out of a hole, that's the kind of hole it is—where I realize that I'm different from these guys. I have different ideas, and yet, I'll let them go on as they are. Even though I don't feel this is right, that's what I do because I don't want to get hurt. So, I just let it go and I don't feel terribly bad about it all the time, but there are times when I do. And I can go along for months just perfectly happy in my little cubbyhole, but the more I'm in this the more I realize that it is a cubbyhole. I'm kind of, as you can see, wrapped up in this cyclical kind of thinking. Do you have any thoughts from an outsider that might lend something to the situation? Do you think I'm neurotic?

Dr. B: I'm indifferent to that question. I do think you have a discrepancy between your functioning and your ideals—that some people ignore it, or can ignore it, and others can't or don't want to.

Eric: I've always had hope for myself. I've always considered that I'll do well. I always when I go into a test figure that I'll get an A on it. I consider that I will do well in my life work—I figure that I will get a girl that is right for me— that has all the qualities that I like. I see these things in the future, and yet I'm getting more and more disgusted with evidence coming through that I'm not doing anything now to help myself toward that.

Dr. B: Do you sometimes feel like it is no problem at all?

Eric: Not if I think about it. A lot of times I don't think about it. If I think about it, I'll realize that there is a problem.

Dr. B: Well, why don't you make the decision, then, to live a more authentic life?

Eric: Because I have things—some of them which have been brought out here—they are my needs, they are irrational, they are the cause of fears but they are still there, and maybe if I could bring them out I could see them, maybe I can do something about them. Maybe I can't. Maybe they will just prey on my mind all the more. Or maybe I'll give in to them more and more when I realize what they are.

Dr. B: You feel that it isn't in your power to be more authentic because of these irrationalities?

Eric: Well I certainly have—somewhere there is a desire to be more authentic.

I don't know if it is in my power or not, and I don't even know what authentic is, yet. And I don't completely give in. I'll often retreat instead of fighting a battle that I don't feel is good, that would do any good. I couldn't convince those guys to be any different during Hell Week. I've worked on them a little bit—guys that I feel could understand. I kind of slip my views in, you know. But I'm not going to face up to them—I'm not going to make them my enemies. And sometimes—you're right—sometimes I don't give a damn! Just too much effort—is what I feel most of the time. But then when I come to the point— sometimes I come to the point and it just depresses me when I see the way that things are, and I feel that I should exert the effort but I don't. Whether it is in my power or not, I don't know. Whether it would be advantageous or not —I don't know. Whether I would lead a richer life. You see, I'm still looking for the things like sex and drinking and being one of the boys, that I didn't really have until I got in college, that I missed, you know, and I wanted to try it. And now that I'm starting to, you know, try these things. You know, I read a little more and get a little more sophisticated and they become less important to me and I have to start looking further ahead, which doesn't answer the question in your mind. I'll have to start answering pretty soon as far as my profession goes, I suppose. (Burton, 1967, pp. 389–392)

Eric's difficulties were not medical, nor did they fit the model of mental illness. Yet they were characteristic of man's struggle as conceived by the existential school; Eric was seeking greater self-actualization and authenticity as a person. When he came to the experiment he did not appear aware of his struggle; a number of personality defenses had permitted him to avoid facing his conflicts over actualization and authenticity. We can only guess how things would have turned out had he not undertaken the experimental sessions.

According to Burton, Eric's problems can be conceptualized along several existential continuums. First, he had difficulty in "being-with." Although his interpersonal relationships appeared quite adequate to outside observers, Eric felt that he could never actually meet the other person "at his heart"; he always just missed the mark, not quite reaching a feeling of true relatedness. He had protected himself with many subtle mechanisms from feelings of basic alienation. His very strong interest in poker kept him from more intimate contacts. He so much wanted to be fair, honest, and open that he was actually closed from others; he approached women in a conquering way, and this "Don Juan" attitude really permitted him to avoid intimacy.

A second difficulty was "being in the hole." Eric recognized that he saw himself as alienated, in a hole, different from others, and that it served a protective function by helping him to avoid hurt. His approach toward women showed how his actions kept him in the hole and away from authentic relationships. He categorized women in two groups: "pigs" and "good girls." The "pigs" served for one or two sexual encounters, short-term relationships; consequently, a girl who was sexually open caused him to maintain an emotional separation and to reject her. On the other hand, the good girls were not to be touched at all. But Eric then found himself separated from them (in the hole) and felt guilty because he could not give the affection necessary for an authentic relationship. Although he made vigorous attempts to have "good" girls fall in love with him, he dropped them when he was expected to give in turn. His concept of a "good girl" ruled out overt sexual behavior, but he was not satisfied to go without sexuality, even when the girl was. Consequently, he would break up with her on the rationalization that both of them were being denied a mature growth experience, which might result in a bad marriage. By his actions he defended his alienated position in-the-hole. No woman was allowed intimacy because *he* could not express it; by establishing his rules for women, he avoided recognizing his own unfulfilled potential.

Another of his conflicts involved "being-in-love." Eric gave into peer pressures by seeking to attain sexual "notches in his holster," but he also recognized and admired a kind of transcendent love that he was unable either to define or to experience. Holding back his own potential for love left him with feelings of guilt. He recognized that love can add the deepest and most fundamental meaning to human relationships, yet he was unable to interact with another person with tenderness and mutual understanding.

Other material from therapy showed that Eric's "being-in-time-and-space" was disturbed. When he was able to experience tenderness, time opened for him and he found freedom to be and to grow; yet the experience of tenderness was seldom available to him, and his world became constricted. Eric tended to calculate time, rather than to live it—he valued acts by the time that they took. Acts of tenderness may be experienced as "living in time," rather than as "passing time." But, as tenderness was difficult for Eric, his "being" was compressed in space; he felt the need to travel, to be on the move.

Burton thought that Eric had made gains during the course of the experiment.

> Eric is by self-report and observation much more of a person, happier, and much readier to help people as a future psychologist and man. Not that Eric has overcome all of his felt deficiencies. He still has some trouble with girls. It is rather that he now understands that these are existential deficiencies and knows how to go about altering them. He has made the choice to be authentic, but it will require years of living before we will really know how effective our work was. (Burton, 1967, p. 398)

DEREFLECTION

V. E. Frankl (1963) has developed what he calls "logotherapy." Its aim is to provide meaning (*logos* is Greek for a "meaning" or "reason") to man's existential being, uniqueness, and responsibility for self-actualization. Frankl has developed several specific therapeutic techniques. He uses *dereflection* to shift the patient's focus from his illness and symptoms to giving positive direction to his life.

The following excerpts from a therapeutic interview exemplify the use of this technique. The patient was a nineteen-year-old female art student, who had displayed symptoms of latent schizophrenia.

THE CASE OF THE ART STUDENT

At the outset the patient complains of apathy, then she refers to her "being confused" and asks me for help. So I start dereflecting her:

F: You are in a crises. You should not concern yourself with any specific diagnosis; let me just say that it is a crisis. Strange thoughts and feelings beset you, I know; but we have made an attempt to tranquilize the rough sea of emotion. Through the quieting effects of modern drug treatment we have tried to have you slowly regain your emotional balance. Now you are in a stage where reconstruction of your life is the task awaiting you! But one cannot reconstruct one's life without a life goal, without anything challenging him.

P: I understand what you mean, Doctor; but what intrigues me is the question: What is going on within me?

F: Don't brood over yourself. Don't inquire into the source of your trouble. Leave this to us doctors. We will steer and pilot you through the crisis. Well, isn't there a goal beckoning you—say, an artistic assignment? Are there not many things fermenting in you—say, unformed artistic works, undrawn drawings which wait for their creation, as it were, waiting to be produced by you? Think about these things.

P: But this inner turmoil. . . .

F: Don't watch your inner turmoil, but turn your gaze to what is waiting for you. What counts is not what lurks in the depths, but what waits in the future, waits to be be actualized by you. I know, there is some nervous crisis which troubles you; but let us pour oil on the troubled waters. That is our job as doctors. Leave the problem to the psychiatrists. Anyway, don't watch yourself; don't ask what is going on within yourself, but rather ask what is waiting to be achieved by you. So let's not argue about what we have to deal with in your case: an anxiety neurosis or neurotic obsessions; whatever it may be, let's think of the fact that you are Anna, for whom something is in wait. Don't think of yourself, but give yourself to that unborn work which you have to create. And only after you have created it will you come to know what you are like. Anna will be identified as the artist who had accomplished this work. Identity doesn't result from centering on oneself, but rather from dedication and devotion to some cause, from finding oneself through the fulfillment of one's specific assignment. If I am not mistaken, it was Hölderlin who once wrote: "What we are is nothing; what matters is where we are going." We could say as well: "Meaning is more than being."

P: But what is the origin of my trouble?

F: Don't focus on questions like this. Whatever the pathological process underlying your psychological affliction may be, we will cure you. Therefore, don't be concerned with the strange feelings haunting you. Ignore them until we make you get rid of them. Don't watch them. Don't fight them.

(Rather than reinforcing the patient's schizophrenic tendency to autism through plunging into psychodynamic interpretations I try to elicit her will to meaning, as it is called in logotherapy.)

F: Imagine, there are about a dozen great things, works which wait to be created by Anna, and there is no one who could achieve and accomplish it but Anna. No one can replace her in this assignment. They will be your creations, and if you don't create them, however, even the devil will be powerless to annihilate them. Then you have rescued them by bringing them to reality. And even if your works were smashed to pieces, in the museum of the past, as I should like to call it, they will remain forever. From this museum, nothing can be stolen since nothing we have done in the past can be undone.

P: Doctor, I believe in what you say. It is a message which makes me happy. (And with a bright expression on her face, she gets up from the couch and leaves my office.)

Within a few weeks the patient was free from schizophrenic symptomatology to the extent that she could resume her work and study. (Burton, 1967, pp. 368–370)

Frankl disregarded the patient's concern with her illness and turned her attention to positive goals, goals that she had to strive for if she was to become an actualized person.

COMPETENCE AND GROWTH GROUPS

The growth of institutions and techniques whose primary purpose is to develop human potential in general has been fairly recent. They aim to help normal people to function better. "Better functioning" may, however, be defined in many ways, ranging from increases in executives' problem-solving capacity to development of the "authentic self," a person who has relinquished psychological defenses in order to experience the fullness and richness of life.

BASIS AND CAUTIONS

A number of psychologists have been interested in utilizing the influencing properties of groups for purposes other than psychotherapy. The earliest of these groups were fairly structured. Individuals were brought together for training in group problem solving. The leader's function was to enhance the members' skills in working with other people so that the group as a whole could function more effectively. Recently, however, the director has increasingly focused on interpersonal relatedness and the capacity of participants to become sensitive to their own and others' behavior. The aim is to create personal competencies in living, a more general aim than group problem solving. Supporters of the humanistic schools of psychology have been very active in this movement. These groups purport to counteract some of the loss in human potential resulting from the constriction of the society.

The spread of growth groups has been great, and their momentum appears still to be gathering force. Industry has frequently incorporated group techniques into personnel practices; higher-level personnel management may be excused from normal duties for a week of sensitivity training, or consultants may be hired to conduct weekly group meetings in the work setting. Several large institutes advertise both personal experiences for the public and courses for professionals interested in leading such groups.

As is common with new counseling and psychotherapy techniques, applications of growth groups have far outrun their evaluation. Instead of objective evaluators we find proselytizers on one hand and vehement opponents on the other. The dangers of participating in such groups are not really known nor are their positive effects, however; as with other procedures it is always advisable to determine the competence of the leader before embarking on such an experience. Schostrom (1969) has tried to clarify some of the dangers involved in poorly led groups. He has suggested some "fairly strict no's" to consider before entering a group.

1. Do not respond to newspaper advertising or cheap mimeographed flyers promising all sorts of marvels, especially erotic ones. The ethical standards of trained professionals prevent them from advertising except through modest notices to professionals in relevant disciplines. Referral by a reputable counselor is one of the best guarantees of a group's appropriateness.

2. As a rule of thumb, avoid groups with fewer than six members or more than ten. In smaller groups scapegoating and vicious ganging up develop too easily, whereas in larger ones it is almost impossible for the leader to monitor all the participants effectively.

3. Do not enter a group if you feel that your psychological balance is tenuous; do not join on impulse. The group experience can be most upsetting at times, and an encounter group may be quite disturbing to someone with weak controls.

4. Do not enter groups with people who are close associates or with whom you have competitive social relationships. The group is a special environment, and communications within it are to be considered privileged. Although openness and candor can enrich experience, it should be clear that outside the group they must be monitored by the setting.

5. Beware of a group that seems to strive for a single aim with missionary zeal, that has an ax to grind. If the group seems likely to insist that you have certain interests and attitudes to participate, then it cannot meet your individual needs.

6. Do not enter a group that is not associated with a reputable professional. The group leader or his professional adviser should be licensed to practice counseling in your state. His reputation may be checked through

professional associations, which are normally listed in the yellow pages of the local telephone book. If an encounter group uses words like "psychologist," "psychiatrist," "psychotherapy," and "therapy," it is usually subject to regulation by state law. The recent deemphasis on therapy has, however, led to many encounter groups that concentrate on "growth," "fulfillment of potential," "honesty," "awareness," and so on. Be wary of such a group until you have been able to check out the backgrounds of its leaders.

Although these cautions should be kept in mind, groups may offer much in the way of emotional and interpersonal education. If the prospective participant uses common sense, as he would in seeking any professional service, he will probably find participation beneficial to his adjustment. Perhaps a quote from the prologue to *Joy* (Schutz, 1967) best expresses the aims of encounter groups.

> I suppose it all started when Ethan was born. The idea of writing about joy had been rummaging around for some time, but he crystallized the feelings behind the rummaging. He emerged via natural childbirth, Lamaze method, and I was there. I saw him enter the world, get turned upside down, cry a little and then stop, get cleaned off, wrapped up, and put into my arms.
>
> As I looked at him, he was very quiet and very curious. He lay quite still, concentrating on the "blooming, buzzing confusion," apparently entranced. For an hour we held him, and he was warm and close and peaceful. I even found myself trying to explain what he was getting into—and he listened carefully. I kept thinking that this might be the most important hour of his life. What a way to begin, by giving joy to parents!
>
> The joy continues. When Ethan smiles, every cell of his body smiles, including his turned-up toes. When he is unhappy, he is thoroughly unhappy, all over. When he is interested in a new object, only he and the object exists. He touches it, tastes it, smells it, puts it in things, puts things in it, gives it to people, takes it from people, looks at it from far and from near. The total absorption is beautiful to watch.
>
> And his pleasure now, during his first fifteen months, is mainly physical —being thrown up in the air, sliding off the refrigerator into his father's arms, being tickled and hugged, having his cheeks chewed, his behind munched, his face caressed, rubbing his cheek against another's cheek. And he touches. It's hard to match the feeling of his little finger exploring my teeth way inside my mouth while his face has that curious, intent look.
>
> And on it goes. He is joyful and he gives joy. He wakes up each morning eager for new adventure. Maybe today it will be a piece of string, or the toilet plunger, or the telephone, or pots and pans, or—more rarely—a new toy.
>
> Ethan is joy. He enjoys each aspect of his life with his whole being. He gives joy to those near him. His joy is contagious.
>
> But will something happen to Ethan as it does to us all? Where will his joy go? In most of us it becomes depleted, distorted, contorted. Guilt and fear begin to defile it. Somehow the joy of Ethan goes, never to fully return.

Perhaps we can recapture some joy, regain some of the body-pleasures, share again the joy with other people that once was possible. (Schutz, 1967, pp. 9–10)

Types of Groups

T-GROUPS

Most of the early small groups were called "training groups" (T-groups). At this point in time, however, the name of a group may no longer precisely reflect what happens; the "encounter group," the "sensitivity group," the "growth group," and so on may have quite similar characteristics and goals.

C. Argyris (1968) has stressed use of the T-group as a reeducational tool for increasing interpersonal competence. He thinks that such groups will eventually become the primary resources in programs for mental health, functioning to increase adaptive capacities of the population as a whole and thus reducing the need for therapeutic assistance.

Groups differ in type of setting, number of sessions, and so forth. They may meet in circumscribed environments outside the stream of normal living. Mountain camps are not uncommon. The participants may live there as long as a week, spending several hours or more a day in group encounters. Or, groups may meet as infrequently as once a week in other settings, and the participants may go about their daily routines between sessions.

MARATHON GROUPS

A fairly recent development is the *marathon group* (Bach, 1966; Mintz, 1967). The leader applies the same techniques as in other encounter groups; the main difference is that interaction is continuous over a single time span. The participants meet for an extended period of time, perhaps fifteen to forty hours, without interruption. Proponents of marathons claim that the intensiveness of the encounters wears down normal defenses, making rapid (in terms of calendar time, not session time) change possible. The combination of physical strain and uninterrupted interpersonal encounter tends to demolish the façades that participants can rebuild between shorter sessions.

Marathon groups are also used for therapeutic purposes. One author has described them:

> In theory, anyway, a marathon group moves from mistrust to trust, from polite acceptance to genuine critique, from peeping-tomism to participation, from dependency to autonomy, from autocracy to democracy. During this trial by intimacy, one's roles, masks and pretenses tend to peel away layer by layer, revealing a more authentic self. (Bindrim, 1969, p. 26)

P. Bindrim has added a new dimension to marathon groups by holding them in the nude. On the hypothesis that nude encounters between men and women, in which body contact is encouraged but sexual expression prohibited, can lead more quickly to emotional intimacy and strong personal identities, they hasten two of the primary goals of all marathons.

He has reported on a group that met in a nudist camp from 9:00 P.M. Friday until 3:00 P.M. Sunday, sleeping six hours each night. The participants removed their clothing if they wished; none refused after all had first shared their anxieties about nudity. They went to a large bath, where they disrobed and saw one another nude. Next they went to the main meeting room, where colored lights were flashed on their bodies as one by one they stood in front of the group (participation was completely voluntary). They were able to view themselves before a full-length mirror while others sat watching quietly.

Saturday morning opened with a discussion of Friday evening's activities. Pleasure at the freedom to look at others' bodies and to be looked at in return was frequently expressed, as were exhilaration, inhibition of the desire to touch, feelings of group closeness, shame about their own bodies, and relief among the men that they had not had erections. Two more bathing periods followed, with more spontaneous body contact and an hour of movement and sensory awareness led by a dance therapist.

Sunday included meditation sessions with "sensory saturation." Members of opposite sexes sat close together looking directly into each other's eyes. They then selected partners to sit with while listening to classical music with eyes closed. During this time they would touch, taste, and smell items that they had been asked to bring with them, things that they enjoyed. One member, for instance, touched velvet, ate chocolate, and smelled a rose. This exercise was meant to bring about a peak state, or "high," and each participant was asked to remember the best moments of his life. After recalling these moments vividly the participants were asked to touch fingertips and to gaze quietly into one another's eyes. Following the exercise they again formed a circle to share their experiences.

Bindrim's initial nude marathon, as evaluated in reports by the participants during the sessions, immediately after it, and several weeks later, was quite effective. He believes that nudity brings about self-acceptance and identity more fully and more quickly than is possible in regular marathons. He has postulated that physical contact, which is generally inhibited in our society except between mates, may have therapeutic value in itself. It seems to allow "genuine mental and emotional exposure and acceptance" to flower more naturally and more beautifully. He has also argued that self-acceptance is often associated with one's body image. Exposure to the nude group may help to correct imaginary distortions of one's body image and consequently to increase psychological strength. The experience of sensual contact may also ease the difficulties of those who cannot express sexuality freely.

Bindrim is aware of the ethical requirements and social restraints associated with using nudity. To his credit, he has taken definite steps to comply with these demands by meeting in secluded spots under voluntary conditions and he is attempting to evaluate objectively the effectiveness of his innovation.

Techniques for Expanding Human Awareness

Schutz (1967) has described a number of techniques that encounter groups use to expand awareness and to fulfill individual potential: "Fulfillment brings to an individual a feeling that he can cope with his environment; the sense of confidence in himself as a significant, competent, lovable person who is capable of handling situations as they arise, able to use fully his own capacities, and free to express his feelings" (Schutz, 1967, p. 15).

The techniques are organized according to specific aims: increasing personal functioning, facilitating interpersonal relations, and heightening the effectiveness of organizations.

INCREASING PERSONAL FUNCTIONING

Being "closed" appears to be the primary difficulty among people who do not fulfill their potential. Being "closed" restricts the outputs and inputs available to the individual, and opportunities for change and expansion are thus reduced. The "job of helping a person become more open and enriched" has three aspects: The individual must be helped, first, to remove emotional blocks; second, to develop an awareness of himself and his feelings; and third, to develop sensitivity to other people and to the world around him.

The *fantasy game* is one method of helping a person become aware of his own feelings and thoughts. When a conflict or specific situation is encountered in the group, the members are asked to imagine the experience and then to report what it was like for them. For example, the leader may ask for volunteers to give an opinion in front of the group. To help them understand their own conflict over volunteering, the leader asks each member to imagine two people inside him, one taking a positive position, the other negative. He is to imagine these people trying to convince each other until one wins out; then, the two fantasized persons are to meet each other and interact by expressing themselves nonverbally. The members are then asked to report their fantasies, including how the people looked and sounded, how large they were, what they said, their physical positions, who won, and so on. The differences in individual fantasies are, of course, generally great. The point of the exercise is to help the members become more aware of their inner struggles and their characteristic ways of dealing with conflict.

ENHANCING INTERPERSONAL RELATIONS

Schutz thinks that one of the most widespread human problems is making contact with others. Methods have been developed to facilitate such contact. In *feeling space* members of the group are asked to gather close together, close their eyes, stretch out their hands, and feel the space all around them—in front, behind, below, and above. A discussion of their experiences follows: Were they comfortable or uncomfortable when intruding on others' space? Did they seek and enjoy the contacts? Was one person inviting, another forbidding, and so on? This exercise leads to exploration of personal feelings about contact and aloneness.

Bumping is another contact exercise. One person is placed inside a circle formed by the other members. He bumps their shoulders with his own, and they bump him back. Forcible physical contact is easy, and, of course, it is not allowed to proceed to the point of actual physical harm. After one bumping experience one member felt greater camaraderie toward the others. He felt that he had met them on a "real" level; the experience had been good, solid, releasing:

> I took my seat again beside the fellow I had tried to communicate with. I no longer really cared what he thought of me, or whether or not he wanted to pursue what I was trying to say to him. I chuckled and told him he could go to hell. I was half kidding. But I felt ten times stronger and more a part of things. I had established a deeper relationship with the group; it was one more stem in my growing freedom and ability to relate with other people at a deeper level of mutual interaction. (Schutz, 1967, p. 126.)

Other difficulties in interpersonal relations revolve around control—whether a person is too submissive or constantly taking charge. Either extreme may be quite damaging to adjustment. *Breaking out* is for constricted people, who are generally controlled by others and unable to break through their own inhibitions. The group forms a tight circle around the subject, arms interlocked, while he tries to break out in any way that he can. As the activity may become quite vigorous, there should be ample space for movement. People with heart conditions or other limiting physical conditions should not participate. Here is one example of breaking out.

THE CASE OF NANCY

Nancy, a twenty-four-year-old girl, was trying to deal with her problem of being too tight and constricted. She spoke in a low and controlled voice, and was always very logical and organized. Her face was usually expressionless, her movements were stiff and graceless, and her relations with people lacked spontaneity and vitality. She had had an earlier fantasy in which she entered her body and found her father fastening down all the organs of her body with steel straps. This, together with her recollection of early childhood, pointed to the central role of her father in her constriction. These considerations led to a psychodrama in which she confronted her father, portrayed by another group member. Here she tried to express to him the feelings that she had never been able to articulate to him directly. When she attempted to declare her independence of him she weakened, her voice faltered, and she reverted to infantile behavior. At this point something was required to give her the additional strength and confidence necessary for her psychodramatic confrontation with her father. She was transferred from the psychodrama to the breaking-out situation. Her frustration led her to start out furiously, pounding fiercely at the people in the circle, but the group held fast and she fell to the floor exhausted and, characteristically, gave up. But the group wouldn't let her. They simply reminded her that she hadn't yet broken out, and they stood their ground around her. This unexpected reaction sparked her to get up and try again. Following a lengthy and combative exchange, she finally smashed through.

After catching her breath she was asked to return to the psychodrama. Immediately on her return she grabbed the group member enacting her father, put him down, placed her knee on his chest, and told him that he was never going to hold her back again, in a very articulate and forceful statement.

She felt elated directly after the experience and her behavior changed markedly thereafter. She was lighter and gayer, became much more feminine, her face brightened, and her relations became more informal. . . . (Schutz, 1967, pp. 170–171)

The physical experience was a new one for Nancy, raising her confidence when she finally broke out. She related the experience to the source of her original constriction and was then able to respond differently in the psychodrama involving her father. Her typical behavior of making one try and giving up did not work; she was forced to try a new approach. In so doing, she recognized her capacities as being greater than she had expected.

PROMOTING ORGANIZATIONAL RELATIONS

To promote the functioning of organizations and thus to maximize the development of individuals within those organizations, Schutz has suggested three main techniques.

The first is the use of the encounter group or T-group, as explained earlier. The group may take any of several forms, depending upon the needs of the organization. The most common procedure is to send company personnel at similar levels (line supervisors, for instance) for a week of encounter-group training. None of the participants works directly with the others, but they will "seed" the company with individuals who are perhaps more sensitive to the needs of other workers. Another possibility is for a leader to meet with functional groups: a supervisor and those responsible to him or a school principal and his teachers.

In a second approach behavioral scientists are used as consultants. Such a consultant starts from the organization's chief complaint and attempts to discover the mechanisms underlying the difficulties. He then recommends or applies the techniques that seem most appropriate to resolving the problem.

A third approach is to conduct research within an organization. The results are used as feedback in meetings with personnel from different departments. The personnel review the findings, compare them with their own experiences, and perhaps ask for further research. Using research findings in this way requires that personnel become active participants and helps to forge them into a team.

EXISTENTIALISM IN PRACTICE

Existentialism has not been highly productive of research. It is not difficult to understand the reasons when we reflect on the basic philosophy of existential therapy. First, research science as we know it today stresses objectivity; in the existential sense it thus dehumanizes man. Indeed, one primary objection to modern society is that this emphasis on technology and objectivity has been carried to the point at which man has lost his ability to experience his own totality. Furthermore, the aspects of man that existentialists want to emphasize are extremely difficult to define objectively, and therefore their ideas are not readily amenable to empirical research. On the other hand, the existentialists do not deny rational and scientific approaches to the study of man; they simply think that current methods and techniques are inadequate to measure his most important characteristics.

Existentialism can be considered a way of viewing man, rather than an organized theory of personality. Existential therapists come from various psychological backgrounds, but many have been trained in psychoanalysis and thus view psychotherapy as a long-term process. They frequently use therapeutic techniques characteristic of psychoanalysis but shift their emphasis to understanding the "wholeness" of man.

The existential view is spreading rapidly among American psychologists and psychotherapists and now represents one of the main currents in psychotherapy.[1] But it has long been popular among European psychotherapists. Its immediate roots can be traced to late nineteenth-century and early twentieth-century European philosophers. When we consider the pragmatic and materialistic orientations current in the United States, it is not surprising that the more idealistic existential view has been slow to gain acceptance among our professionals. Now, however, the existential view, though it may not be labeled as such, seems an integral part of youth's "rebellion" against the "establishment." Complaints of isolation and "nonhumanness" are clearly to be heard among the protests of the young against the currently prevailing way of life in the United States.

SELF THEORY AND CLIENT-CENTERED THERAPY

INTRODUCTION

C. Rogers has formulated a theory of personality based on his observations in psychotherapy. He has argued that, if scientists are to understand man, they must investigate his subjective world, the world as he experiences it. Research and theory represent disciplined efforts to make sense of the phenomena of subjective experience (Rogers, 1959). Scientists can never be completely objective, but the best way to avoid self-deception is through the

[1] Another currently popular movement, behavior therapy, reflects a philosophical position almost diametrically opposite to that of the existentialists. Man is considered primarily an object, which can be changed through the application of specific procedures. The background and techniques of behavior therapy will be discussed in Chapter 7.

use of experimental methods and concepts. Rogers and his coworkers have followed a program of research that they hope will lead ultimately to a more complete understanding of man's experience of himself.

Because the science of psychology is in its early stages of development Rogers thinks that crude observation and inaccurate theorizing are unavoidable and even necessary. A high level of specification and quantification is not in itself a satisfactory measure of achievement; rather, advancement of knowledge can occur through the application of whatever approach one prefers in understanding man. Forward movement, regardless of the approach, is the main goal of science.

Rogers has taken a definitive stand on theory, which he considers a network of concepts intended to incorporate solid information and to lead to further understanding; it serves primarily as a stimulus for further creative thinking. Theory should never be taken as dogma, nor should an investigator invest so much in any one theory that he closes his mind to other possibilities. It is also important to recognize that, as we turn away from the particular data on which a theory has been based, its weaknesses become more apparent. We must therefore continue to broaden our research if we are to develop a theory of personality with general validity.

On the basis of these views, Rogers and his colleagues have subjected their theoretical notions to an extensive program of research and have thus generated a great many data on the therapeutic process and notions of the self. It is to Rogers' credit that he has stimulated so much research in psychotherapy. His emphasis on the combination of theory and research has been instrumental in furthering our understanding of man.

ROGERS' THEORY OF MAN

Rogers has stated his theory in the form of nineteen propositions, partly for the sake of clarity but primarily so that each can generate experimental hypotheses (Rogers, 1951). We shall present them here in five groups that exemplify his views of personality.

THE PHENOMENAL FIELD

THE PRIVATE WORLD OF EXPERIENCE

Basic to an understanding of man is recognition that he exists in a world of private experience. The individual is the center of a continuously changing world that includes all sources of experience for the organism, though probably only a small portion is consciously experienced at any one time. Yet a large portion of this world is available to consciousness; particular sensations can be brought into awareness when they are related to the satisfaction of specific needs.

REALITY

A person's phenomenal world can be known, in a genuine sense, only by him. Although we can attempt to measure his experience, only he can encompass its actuality; his experience is indeed private. It follows that the phenomenal field is "reality" for the individual and that he reacts to it in accordance with his perceptions and experiences. Similar stimulus inputs will mean different things to different people, and they will react in different ways. For example, a person who is sympathetic to Black Power may react to a speech by an advocate with praise and applause, ascribing "goodness" and "strength" to the speaker and even contributing money to the cause. An individual who opposes Black Power will, however, probably perceive the speaker as "unintelligent," "savage," perhaps even "criminal"; he may react to *his* reality by jeering, walking out, even attacking the speaker.

Man continually checks his perceptions against one another in order to test hypotheses about his reality. In our example the anti-Black Power listener checks his auditory input (militant speech) with his visual input (black, beard, and so on); both confirm his perception of the speaker as a Black Power militant. Seeing a different person saying the same thing—for example, white skin, business suit, television studio, a different visual input—would lead to a different hypothesis about reality, the incongruence of the visual and auditory inputs in this case may lead this person to conclude that the speaker is a white comedian. Checking perceptions and confirming hypotheses lead to a sense of security in our perception of reality. As we shall see later, distorting inputs can serve to maintain desired perceptions of the self.

THE PERSON AS A WHOLE

Rogers has suggested that a person reacts as an organized whole to his perception of reality; his behavior cannot be explained by specific stimulus-response pairs. Basic to an understanding of man is recognition that specific kinds of behavior reflect total, organized, and goal-directed responses; the underlying purpose of a particular type of behavior is to achieve a goal. If the organism is blocked in one avenue of approach, it will organize its total capacities to find another. "The outstanding fact that must be taken into deep theoretical account is that the organism is at all times a total organized system, in which alteration in any part phenomena must start from the central fact of consistent, goal-directed organization" (Rogers, 1951, p. 487).

From these notions it follows that the best understanding of an individual is obtained through observation of his internal frame of reference. We must try to see another person's experience as nearly as possible through his eyes. Evaluating him from our own general frame of reference, perhaps dismissing his talk as "delusions" or "abnormal behavior," prevents us from actually understanding his behavior and its purpose for him.

MOTIVATION

SELF-ACTUALIZATION

Rogers has also argued that behavior results from the organism's basic tendency to actualize, maintain, and enhance itself. Man's primary motive is to mature and to maintain himself as a viable organism. Self-actualization is not a smooth process; it involves struggle and pain. Rogers has compared the process to a child's learning to walk:

> The first steps involve struggle, and usually pain. Often it is true that the immediate reward involved in taking a few steps is in no way commensurate with the pain of falls and bumps. The child may, because of the pain, revert to crawling for a time, yet, in the overwhelming majority of individuals, the forward direction of growth is more powerful than the satisfactions of remaining infantile. The child will actualize himself, in spite of the painful experiences in so doing. In the same way, he will become independent, responsible, self-governing, socialized in spite of the pain which is often involved in these steps. (Rogers, 1951, p. 490)

GOAL-DIRECTED BEHAVIOR

Behavior is defined as goal-directed attempts by the organism to satisfy its needs within the phenomenological field that it perceives. Needs take the form of physiological tensions, and behavior represents attempts to reduce these tensions. Understanding reactions to the field *as it is perceived* is important in explaining why an individual behaves as he does. For example, a man may struggle to accumulate wealth because on some level he believes that it will bring him emotional security when, in fact, it will not satisfy this need. Nevertheless, because of his perception, he continues to strive for wealth. Rogers has further remarked that behavior is caused by present needs, rather than by what has happened in the past. A person responds to needs and tensions, behaving in ways that will reduce them as they are experienced in the present. Rogers has recognized that past experiences influence the meanings of present experiences, though behavior is always determined by present need.

EMOTION

Goal-directed behavior is facilitated by emotion. Unpleasant or excited feelings generally accompany goal seeking; calm or satisfied feelings are associated with the consummatory response and need satisfaction. Behavior perceived as crucial to the organism's maintenance is often accompanied by intense emotion, whereas less crucial behavior arouses less affect. A soldier leaping into a foxhole to avoid machine-gun bullets for instance, experiences a high level of emotion and perceives his own behavior as vital to self-preservation. On the other hand, a low level of emotion is experienced when he stands Sunday inspection; this behavior he considers less critical to self-maintenance.

THE DEVELOPMENT OF A SELF-CONCEPT

The concept of self is central to Rogers' theory of personality. As an infant develops, he gradually distinguishes a portion of his total perceptual field as his self. The self is that portion of the private world that comes to be recognized as "me," "I," "myself." "Self" does not refer to the total organism, it is the awareness of being and functioning.

Whether an article, a part of one's own body, or some other event is recognized as part of the self depends upon whether or not it is perceived as under the control of the self. Rogers uses the example of the "foot going to sleep" from lack of circulation. When we lose control over a foot, it seems an object to us, and we are not likely to consider it part of ourselves at the moment.

INTERACTIONS WITH ENVIRONMENT

The self is shaped by interaction with the environment, especially with other people. As it grows it becomes "an organized, fluid, but consistent conceptual pattern of perceptions of characteristics and relationships of the 'I' or the 'Me,' together with values attached to these concepts" (Rogers, 1951, p. 498). Evaluating experiences is comparatively simple for the very young infant once he has become aware of himself as a separate being, as an "I." He distinguishes experiences according to whether or not he likes them, whether they are pleasing or displeasing to him, and so on.

Such evaluations result from his responses to direct experiences. In some instances, however, values can be drawn indirectly from other people though distorted to the point at which they seem to have been taken from direct experience. Such distortions often occur in the child's interactions with his parents. The child experiences evaluations of the self by others (most frequently by parents) at an early age; remarks like "That's a good boy" and "You're a bad boy" constitute a large and significant part of his perceptual field. A young child may perceive himself as lovable to his parents, yet at the same time he may have positive feelings about hitting his baby brother. But his parents are likely to tell him that hitting his brother is bad and that they do not love him when he acts this way. When he is thus confronted by a major threat to his self structure, the incongruity of his perceptions must somehow be resolved. A characteristic way out of this dilemma is to take the parents' view as if it had come from his own experience rather than theirs. An accurate understanding would be "My parents perceive my behavior as unsatisfying," but to preserve the concept of himself as lovable he is likely to distort it to "I perceive my behavior as unsatisfying." The child has in fact enjoyed his aggressive behavior toward his younger brother, but he must now deny it and act as if it has been unpleasant. By means of this process the child *introjects* the values of his parents and of others, perceiving them, however, as the results of his own sensory experience.

KINDS OF EXPERIENCE

The structure of self grows from direct and introjected evaluation of experience. It becomes an organized configuration of perceptions that are admissible to awareness. Continuing experiences in life are dealt with in different ways, depending upon the development of the self. Some experiences are considered irrelevant to the self and are mainly ignored. They occur near the periphery of the phenomenal field and are not perceived as related to the needs of the self.

Experiences perceived as relevant to self structure are more important. Some are received into consciousness because they are consistent with the self structure and reinforce its organization. To demonstrate this process, Rogers has cited the example of a client who perceived herself as "unable to take a place in society like others." She incorporated experiences that reinforced her self-concept: "I fail when attempting things," "I don't react normally," "I don't learn well from my school work," and so on. Other experiences are organized into consciousness because they are related to *needs* of the self: "I am hungry; therefore, I notice a restaurant sign," "When it is time to buy a new car I notice the ads and changes in style," and so on.

Another important group of sensory experiences is prevented from entering awareness because they are incongruent with the perception of one's self. Some incongruent experiences may be consciously denied. For instance, the young woman who saw herself as not fitting into society was unable to accept positive comments from others; she therefore continually deprecated them— "They don't really think I'm intelligent," "They can't judge intelligence," and so on—actively denying such comments in her awareness.

A more important type of incongruent experience is one that achieves conscious symbolization only in very distorted form because a true representation would be highly inconsistent with the self-concept. Rogers has offered the example of an adolescent boy who has been raised in an oversolicitous home, developing a concept of himself as grateful to his parents. Their continual attempts to control him, however, may have aroused intense anger toward them. Conscious symbolization of these experiences ("I hate my parents") would, however, be quite inconsistent with his self-concept; therefore they could not be allowed into consciousness. To resolve this problem he might have denied access to consciousness completely, or he might have symbolized experiences in a distorted way consistent with his self structure: His organic sensations of anger might have been perceived as a bad headache.

Experiences that are not allowed conscious symbolization are not necessarily negative. They have simply been denied symbolization because they contradict the self. The young woman who could not accept positive remarks demonstrated denial of positive experiences contradictory to the self-image.

The Effects of the Self-Concept on Behavior

BEHAVIOR CONSISTENT WITH SELF

Most of the ways in which a person seeks to enhance himself are determined by his self-concept. A person who sees himself as nonaggressive cannot, or generally does not, use aggressive behavior to attain his goals; he resorts to other modes that lead to the same end. Most neurotic behavior results from distortion of incongruent experiences in order to maintain consistency within the self; the distortions also serve to fulfill the unacceptable needs. When a pilot who sees himself as "brave in the face of danger" is assigned to a particularly dangerous mission, he feels fear, but he denies it consciousness. If he chooses to yield to his fear and halt the mission, he may have to distort other perceptions; for example, his engine may seem to be running poorly, his stomach may be upset, and so on.

There are times when unsymbolized experiences and needs cause us to behave in ways that are inconsistent with the self. Such behavior is, however, frequently denied by individuals, as reflected in statements like "I didn't know what I was doing" and "I really wasn't myself." Under great stress or threats, an individual may act uncharacteristically; a generally timid man may, for example, strike out and inflict serious injury on an attacker. In accounting for his behavior, he is likely to say, "I don't know what happened; I wasn't myself!"

The same sort of behavior may occur when a very strong organically experienced need is refused conscious symbolization. Rogers has told the story of a boy who had been raised to have a conception of himself as "pure and free from base, sexual impulses." The boy was arrested for lifting the skirts of two little girls and examining their genital areas, which he denied having done. He was confronted with witnesses, and then he insisted, "I was not myself." He had eventually given in to behavior that would satisfy his strong need, though the behavioral expression of his need and his self-concept remained separate.

PSYCHOLOGICAL TENSION AND ANXIETY

Psychological *tension*, and therefore the potential for maladjustment, is present when a person denies awareness to significant experiences so that they cannot be organized into an overall picture of his self. Such tension arises from difficulties in maintaining conscious control over behavior that would satisfy unacceptable needs. The individual, aware of his tension, feels *anxious*; he experiences a feeling of disunity, lack of integration, and unsureness of direction. Psychological adjustment is reflected in his ability to incorporate the symbolic representations of his sensory and visceral experiences into his self-concept; they are not necessarily in his consciousness, but they are available to conscious symbolization. When one's self-concept approximately reflects all experiences, a person can be free of inner tension. An individual whose experiences are thus integrated is able to grow and to move in healthy directions.

EXPERIENCES INCONSISTENT WITH THE SELF

Experiences inconsistent with the self-concept are perceived as threatening. The more frequently they occur, the more likely it is that the structure of the self will become rigid in order to maintain itself. Disintegration and psychological breakdown result when the self is inadequate to defend against threats.

Rogers has illustrated these points in the example of a woman who sees herself as a "good mother," though an outside observer would perceive her as rejecting. Feelings of aggression and hostility toward her child are unacceptable to her self-concept; she must therefore justify fulfillment behavior by perceiving her child's behavior as bad, bad for him, and deserving of punishment. Aggressive acts toward him are thus in keeping with her self-concept of good mother. Because she has denied her need for aggression, she experiences tension in her relationship with her child. If she were able to allow her hostile feelings into consciousness, she could conceive of herself as a good mother who feels affection for her child but also dislikes him at times. When confronted with her behavior by an outside observer (a therapist or friend), she is likely to become quite rigid. She will attempt to eliminate any experiences that may threaten her concept of herself as a good mother; that is, she may scorn the observer's training, criticize his method of observation, scoff at his claims to understanding of the mother-child relationship, and so on.

Figure 6-1 shows diagrammatically the personality in tension and in harmony, serving to clarify the preceding discussion. The two circles represent all the experiences through the individual's sense modalities at a particular

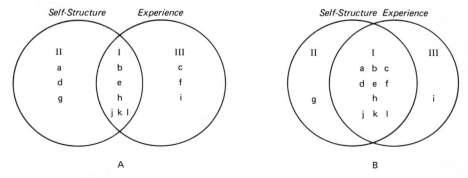

Figure 6-1 Schematic representation of psychological tension. From C. R. Rogers, *Client-Centered Therapy*. Reproduced by permission of Houghton Mifflin Co., copyright © 1951, pp. 526–527.

time. The self structure is available to awareness and comprises the individual's perceptions and evaluations of his characteristics and relationships. Area I represents the part of the phenomenal field in which the concept of self is congruent with evidence from sensory and visceral experience. Area II represents that portion of the phenomenal field containing distorted experiences: the values and concepts that have been introjected from other people in the environment but are perceived as the product of one's own sensory experiences. Area III represents experiences that are denied awareness because they are inconsistent with the self-concept.

Material from one of Rogers' clients (Rogers, 1951, p. 525) lends concrete meaning to Figure 6-1A. The small letters *a*, *b*, and *c* represent a young woman's attitudes and experiences related to her father. The letter *a* stands for a value introjected from her mother; it means that "she feels nothing but hatred toward him and that she is morally correct in doing so." Her mother has criticized her father frequently because he deserted them when the client was small. The letter *b* represents experiences congruent with introjected feelings of hatred toward the father, experiences caused by earlier unpleasant contacts with him. They are congruent with the woman's self structure and have been assimilated into consciousness. The letter *c* represents experiences that engendered positive feelings toward her father that are not congruent with her self structure. Such experiences are either denied to awareness or admitted only in distorted ways (for example, "I am like my father in several ways, and this is shameful"). The inconsistencies represented by the various attitudes and experiences create psychological tension.

Figure 6-1B is a schematic representation of this client's personality after successful psychotherapy. The *a*, *b*, and *c* elements have been integrated into a consistent picture. They may be expressed somewhat as follows: (a) "I recognize that my mother has reason to hate my father and that my mother would also like me to agree with her feelings"; (b) "In some ways and for some of his actions I dislike my father"; (c) "There are things that I like about my father, and it is acceptable for me both to like and to dislike him." Experiences and attitudes are thus perceived realistically, rather than distorted. The woman's self structure has been extended to include previously inconsistent characteristics, and she no longer experiences psychological tension.

REVISION AND EXPANSION OF SELF

CONDITIONS FOR CHANGE

Rogers has argued that experiences inconsistent with the self-concept can be perceived and examined and that the self structure can be revised to assimilate them. This process may occur when a person is completely free from threats to his self structure; one of the primary aims of client-centered therapy is to create such a situation. Gradually, as the client realizes that nothing is threatening his self-concept, he is able to examine experiences that he previously denied. He can then perceive them as what they are and can change and broaden his self-concept so that tension becomes unnecessary. Therapy is a process of learning about oneself. The counselor's acceptance of the client allows self-exploration (at a safe rate of speed) and learning.

DEVELOPING AN INTEGRATED SELF

An individual who develops a more consistent and integrated picture of himself also becomes more understanding of others and is better able to accept them as separate individuals. Rogers has postulated the following steps:

> The person who denies some experiences must continually defend himself against the symbolization of those experiences.
> As a consequence, all experiences are viewed defensively as potential threats, rather than for what they really are.
> Thus in interpersonal relationships, words or behaviors are experienced and perceived as threatening, which were not so intended.
> Also, words and behaviors in others are attacked because they represent or resemble the feared experiences.
> There is then no real understanding of the other as a separate person, since he is perceived mostly in terms of threat or nonthreat to the self.
> But when all experiences are available to consciousness and are integrated, then defensiveness is minimized. When there is no need to defend, there is no need to attack.
> When there is no need to attack, the other person is perceived for what he really is, a separate individual, operating in terms of his own meaning, based on his own perceptual field. (Rogers, 1951, pp. 520–521)

NEW VALUES

As perceiving and accepting experiences proceed, the client finds that his value system is changing. His original system was determined largely by symbolically distorted introjected values. When he is able to reevaluate his own experiences and to develop his own values based upon his own needs, the ideal outcome "is the emergence of value systems which are unique and personal for each individual, and which are changed by the changing evidence of organic experience, yet which are at the same time deeply socialized, possessing a high degree of similarity in their essentials" (Rogers, 1951, p. 524).

CLIENT-CENTERED THERAPY

THE COUNSELOR'S ATTITUDE

Rogers has emphasized the importance of the counselor's attitude, rather than specific techniques in psychotherapy. Strong positive regard for the client's ability to deal constructively with all aspects of his life is necessary, for the client—regardless of his choice of action, even suicide—can direct his life without help from the therapist. There is no intention on the part of the "doctor" to take charge of the patient's "crippled" life, for there is no presumption that the client is incapable of managing his own life.

If the counselor approaches a client with this attitude, the client's tendencies to maintain and to actualize himself will emerge to further positive growth.

> It is the counselor's function to assume, in so far as he is able, the internal frame of reference of the client, to perceive the world as the client sees it, to perceive the client himself as he is seen by himself, to lay aside all perceptions from the external frame of reference while doing so, and to communicate something of this emphatic understanding to the client. (Rogers, 1951, p. 29)

Rogers has presented the following statement by a client to permit the reader to examine the attitude that he takes toward clients:

> *Client:* I don't feel very normal, but I don't want to feel that way. . . . . I thought I'd have something to talk about—then it all goes around in circles. I was trying to think what I was going to say. Then coming here, it doesn't work out. . . . I tell you, I just can't make a decision; I don't know what I want. I've tried to figure out which things are important for me. I thought that there are maybe two things a man might do; he might get married and raise a family. But, if he was just a bachelor, just making a living—that isn't very good. I find myself and my thoughts getting back to the days when I was a kid and I cry very easily. The dam would break through. I've been in the army four and a half years. I had no problems then, no hopes, no wishes. My only thought was to get out when peace would come. My problems, now that I am out, are as ever. I tell you, they go back to a long time before I was in the army. . . . I love children. When I was in the Philippines —I tell you, when I was young I swore I would never forget my unhappy childhood—so when I saw these children in the Philippines, I treated them very nicely. I used to give them ice cream cones and movies. It was just a period—I'd revert back—and that awakened some emotions in me I thought I had long buried. (A pause. He seems very near tears.) (Rogers, 1951, pp. 32–33)

Rogers has demonstrated the kinds of thoughts that one would have if he were evaluating the client entirely as an object, rather than attempting to experience his phenomenal field:

> I wonder if I should help get him started talking.
> Is this inability to get underway a type of dependence?
> Why this indecisiveness? What could be its cause?
> He's a veteran. Could he have been a psychiatric case?
> What is his interest in children? Identification? Vague homosexuality?

On the other hand, when the counselor is successful in penetrating the inner world of the client, the following thoughts might occur:

You're wanting to struggle toward normality, aren't you?
It's really hard for you to get started.
Decision just seems impossible to you. To you the army represented stagnation.
Being very nice to children has somehow had meaning for you.

Rogers firmly believes in the therapeutic utility of this second attitude. The more willing the counselor is to rely upon the strength and potentials of his client, the more likely he is to discover such strength and potentials. In Rogers' view, if the client is to experience his full capacity for self-direction and growth, the therapist must be completely willing to allow him to choose any outcome or direction. "It is as he is willing for death to be the choice, that life is chosen; when neuroticism is to be the choice, that a healthy personality is chosen. The more completely he acts upon his central hypothesis, the more convincing is the evidence that the hypothesis is correct" (Rogers, 1951, p. 49).

REFLECTION OF FEELINGS

Although Rogers does not stress technique, *reflection of feelings* is the most frequent way in which a client-centered therapist communicates his understanding of the client's world. As many as 60–80 percent of a client-centered therapist's responses may be classified as reflections of feelings. In "saying back" to the client what the therapist has understood him to have expressed, the therapist acts as a "mirror" for the client. The client can then evaluate his own thoughts and feelings with less distortion. When he has difficulties in expressing what he feels, the therapist must be able to experience the difficulties too. At such times the client is likely to perceive the therapist as a companion in the search for meaning; the therapist and the client are a team working toward the goal of understanding. The therapeutic relationship, as well as the reflected feelings, offers potentials for growth within the client.

The following excerpt demonstrates a counselor's attempts to reflect a client's feelings.

> S: It seems—I don't know—it probably goes all the way back into my childhood. I've—for some reason I've—my mother told me that I was the pet of my father. Although I never realized it—I mean, they never treated me as a pet at all. And other people always seemed to think I was sort of a privileged one in the family. But I never had any reason to think so. And as far as I can see looking back on it now, it's just that the family let the other kids get away with more than

they usually did me. And it seems for some reason to have held me to a more rigid standard than they did the other children.

C: You're not so sure you were a pet in any sense, but more that the family situation seemed to hold you to pretty high standards.

S: M-hmm. That's just what has occurred to me; and that the other people could sorta make mistakes, or do things as children that were naughty, or "that was just a boyish prank," or "that was just what you might expect," but Alice wasn't supposed to do those things.

C: M-hm. With somebody else it would just be just—oh, be a little naughtiness; but as far as you were concerned, it shouldn't be done.

S: That's really the idea I've had. I think the whole business of my standards, or my values, is one that I need to think about rather carefully, since I've been doubting for a long time whether I even have any sincere ones.

C: M-hm. Not sure whether you really have any deep values which you are sure of.

S: M-hm. M-hm.

C: You've been doubting that for some time.

S: Well, I've experienced that before. Thought one thing, when I make decisions I don't have—I don't think—it seems that some people have —have quite steady values that they can weigh things against when they want to make a decision. Well, I don't, and I haven't had, and I guess I'm an opportunist (laughing). I do what seems to be the best thing to do at the moment, and let it go at that.

C: You have no certain measuring rods that you can use. (Rogers, 1951, p. 152)

Even in very trying situations, the client-centered therapist attempts to maintain his open attitude and to convey his understanding of the client's experience:

S: (Silent for two minutes. Then begins to talk in hard flat voice, quite unlike her usual tone. Does not look at counselor. There was much repetition but the following excerpts give the major thoughts.) You feel I want to come, but I don't! I'm not coming any more. It doesn't do any good. I don't like you. I hate you! I wish you never were born.

C: You just hate me very bitterly.

S: I think I'll throw you in the lake. I'll cut you up! You think people like you, but they don't. . . . I wish you were dead.

C: You detest me and you'd really like to get rid of me.

S: You think my father did bad things with me, but he didn't! You think he wasn't a good man, but he was. You think I want intercourse, but I don't.

C: You feel I absolutely misrepresent all your thoughts.

S: . . . You think you can get people to come in and tell you every-thing, and they'll think they're being helped, but they're not! You just like to make 'em suffer. You think you can hypnotize them, but you

can't! You think you're good, but you ain't. I hate you, I hate you, I
hate you!

C: You feel I really like to make 'em suffer, but that I don't help them.

S: You think I haven't been straight, but I have. I hate you. All I've
had is pain, pain, pain. You think I can't direct my own life, but I can.
You think I can't get well, but I can. You think I had hallucinations, but
I didn't. I hate you. (Long pause. Leans on desk in strained exhausted
pose.) You think I'm crazy, but I'm not.

C: You're sure I think you're crazy.

S: (Pause.) I'm tied, and I just can't get loose! (Despairing tone of
voice, and tears. Pause.) I had a hallucination and I've got to get it
out!. (Goes on about her deep conflicts and tells of the hallucination
she has experienced with terrific tension in her voice, but with an
attitude very different from that at the beginning of interview.) . . .
(Later in interview)

S: I knew at the office I had to get rid of this somewhere. I felt I could
come down and tell you. I knew you'd understand. I couldn't say I
hated myself. That's true but I couldn't say it. So I just thought of all
the ugly things I could say to you instead.

C: The things you felt about yourself you couldn't say, but you could
say them about me.

S: I know we're getting to rock bottom. . . . (Rogers, 1951, pp. 211–
213)

NONDIRECTIVE APPROACH

A *nondirective* approach follows from the client-centered therapist's attitude; that is, he does not make the client's decisions for him. As he respects the
client's ability to grow and recognizes that only the client understands his
own private world accurately, he permits the client to make his own decisions.
The therapist's main job is to provide an environment in which the client
can free himself from tension-producing perceptual distortions so that he can
make decisions in his own best interests.

PROCESS RESEARCH

Rogers has long emphasized a continuous research program and has made
many notable empirical contributions. One of them has been greater understanding of the therapeutic process (Rogers and Dymond, 1954).

PROCESS SCALES

Rogers and his coworkers have developed several scales on which to measure the verbalizations of therapists and clients. These verbalizations are classified from a sampling of the contents of tape-recorded sessions, in order to

determine what kinds of responses lead to other kinds of responses and to relate particular types of responses to the outcome of therapy.

CLIENT SCALES

Three scales have been developed for classifying clients' responses.

On the *problem-expression scale* the client's statements are rated according to recognition and concern with the personal aspects of his problems. A low rating means that he shows no recognition of personal responsibility for his problems; a high rating means that he continually resolves his problems on the basis of his own experience.

On the *interpersonal-exploration scale* the client's statements are rated according to self-exploration. At the low end personally relevant material is completely absent from his statements, whereas at the high end there is evidence of profound exploration into himself.

On the *manner-of-relating scale* the client's personal acceptance of the therapeutic relationship is measured. Comments indicating rejection of the therapist are rated low and warm personal exchanges are rated high.

THERAPIST SCALES

The therapist's statements are also rated on three scales.

The *congruence scale* measures the degree to which his statements reflect awareness of the experience between the client and himself. At the low end his comments reflect aloofness, distance, and insincerity; at the high end they reflect openness, spontaneity, and genuineness.

On the *accurate-empathy scale* the degree to which the therapist is aware of the client's feelings is measured.

Finally, on the *positive-regard scale* the therapist's caring for his client is measured; inattention, disinterest, and aloofness are rated low, whereas perceptible deep caring and warmth are rated high.

RESULTS

Outcome and process research in psychotherapy has generally supported Rogers' theoretical postulates. A. E. Bergin, after reviewing outcome research in psychotherapy, declared, "To date, the only school of interview-oriented psychotherapy which has consistently yielded positive outcomes in research studies is the client-centered approach" (1966, p. 241). He went on to explain, however, that mere identification with the Rogerian school does not necessarily guarantee a "good" therapist. It is the variables (congruence, accurate empathy, and positive regard) measured in the three scales that are actually related to positive outcome. Practitioners with other theoretical orientations may score equally high on these scales, even though they do not accept Rogers' theory.

Several general findings in psychotherapy are related to process variables and their effects. F. van der Veen studied the relations of the scales to the outcomes of psychotherapy:

> It may be tentatively concluded that a sequence such as the following is likely to occur: when the therapist is perceived by both patient and therapist as genuine, empathic, and accepting, then both behave in ways that foster the patient's personal exploration of problems, which in turn leads to successful therapeutic outcome. Though these results were clearly exploratory, their coherence is encouraging. An urgent question implicit in the findings is how to provide conditions conducive to personality change for patients whose process levels and perception of positive interpersonal attitudes are very low. These and other studies suggest that these patients are not likely to be helped through psychotherapy. (1967, p. 302)

Although this statement suggests that some patients do not benefit from psychotherapy, regardless of how the therapist behaves, we also note the positive aspect of such findings: They may reveal directions for overcoming such difficulties. The association of process variables with outcomes may thus lead to more successful applications.

RECENT EMPHASES

As Rogers and his coworkers have attempted to expand his theoretical concepts and therapeutic approach to a wider variety of people—including chronic schizophrenics and groups of "normals"—their focus and terminology have increasingly reflected emphasis on the existential concept of "becoming" (Rogers, 1961, 1969; Rogers and Stevens, 1967; Rogers, *et al.*, 1967).

In the early 1970s Rogers was a resident fellow at the Western Behavioral Sciences Institute in La Jolla, California, where the emphasis is on the practical use of group methods in business, education, and other human enterprises. Rogers' focus remains on individual change guided by humanistic values, but his aim is to spread this orientation through social groups so that it can be reflected in organizational functioning. We shall examine two of Rogers' more recent theoretical contributions, his concepts of values and of learning to be free.

The Valuing Process

As we noted earlier, the infant evaluates events according to his own responses; they are "good" or "bad" according to whether or not they enhance his self-actualization. Furthermore, this valuing process is flexible. Sometimes the infant values security and rest, but at others he rejects both in favor of new experiences. (For a vivid description of the infant's openness to experience see the excerpts from Schutz's introduction to *Joy*, 1967, earlier in this chapter.) Rogers has called this valuing an "organismic valuing process . . .

in which each element, each moment of what he is experiencing is somehow weighed, and selected or rejected, depending on whether, at this moment, it tends to actualize the organism or not" (Rogers and Stevens, 1967, p. 15). The source of this process is within the infant himself. The infant knows what he likes and dislikes; he suffers no doubt and does not vacillate.

Before long, however, the valuing process becomes more inflexible in most people, and individuals learn to apply external criteria in determining likes and dislikes. Rogers has described a boy who decides that he wants to be a physician. He notices (perhaps unconsciously) that when he talks of being a doctor his parents seem more pleased with him than when he talks of being an artist. Eventually, through such differential reinforcement, he "decides" that what he wants to be more than anything else is a doctor. He has introjected his parents' value; that is, he has used their views as a reference point in deciding his own value, but his choice, once made, seems inflexible. This child is beginning to lose touch with his own ability to evaluate in the light of his own needs for self-actualization, and he is likely to end up as have many adults who take others' values as their own. To Rogers, this problem is a major human dilemma: "This fundamental discrepancy between the individual's concepts and what he is actually experiencing, between the intellectual structure of his values and the valuing process going on unrecognized within him—this is a part of the fundamental estrangement of modern man from himself" (Rogers and Stevens, 1967, p. 20).

The "mature" person is, according to Rogers, in some ways quite similar in his valuing process to the infant. The process is fluid and flexible, based on personal experiences that enhance immediate self-actualization.

> The process is complex, the choices often very perplexing and difficult, and there is no guarantee that the choice which is made will in fact prove to be self-actualizing. But because whatever evidence exists is available to the individual, and because he is open to his experiencing, errors are correctable. If a chosen course of action is not self-enhancing this will be sensed and he can make an adjustment or revision. He thrives on a maximum feedback interchange, and thus, like the gyroscopic compass on a ship, can continually correct his course toward becoming more of himself. (Rogers and Stevens, 1967, p. 32)

The suggestion that the "mature" evaluation process is similar to that of an infant may seem rather "hedonistic." Rogers has, however, offered clinical evidence of a "deep and underlying thread of communality" in men who are free to make their own choice; they generally adopt some values that are social and altruistic, as well as some that are hedonistic.

> I dare to believe that when the human being is inwardly free to choose whatever he deeply values, he tends to value those objects, experiences, and goals which make for his own survival, growth, and development, and for the survival and development of others. I hypothesize that it is characteristic of the human organism to prefer such actualizing and socialized goals when

> he is exposed to a growth-promoting climate. (Rogers and Stevens, 1967,
> p. 26)

The "growth-promoting climate" of which he speaks is based on his notions
of the therapeutic attitude in client-centered therapy (whether individual
or group therapy) that we have reported.

Rogers has suggested a new resolution to the issue of values posited as
good for everyone, a "universality of values." To replace values imposed from
"out there" (by groups, rulers, and the like), he sees the possibility of values
deriving "from the experiencing of the human organism."

> The suggestion is that though modern man no longer trusts religion or science
> or philosophy nor any system of beliefs to "give" him his values, he may
> find an organismic valuing base within himself which, if he can learn again
> to be in touch with it, will prove to be an organized, adaptive and social
> approach to the perplexing value issues which face all of us. (Rogers and
> Stevens, 1967, p. 27)

LEARNING TO BE FREE

Rogers has spoken of freedom as an "inner thing . . . quite aside from
any of the outward choice of alternatives which we so often think of as con-
stituting freedom" (Rogers and Stevens, 1967, p. 52). It is subjective freedom,
a sense of choosing one's own way: "I can live myself, here and now, by my
own choice." Rogers has admitted that human culture restricts human freedom, that man is partly the product of social forces, and that his early conditioning (learning) affects the choices that he makes. Yet this conception of
freedom is meant to complement scientific stress on the "psychological universe of cause and effect," the view of man as a product of his conditioning,
which Rogers has called "rigid determinism."

> We are speaking then, of a freedom which exists in the subjective person, a
> freedom which he courageously uses to live his potentialities. We are speak-
> ing of a freedom in which the individual chooses to fulfill himself by playing
> a responsible and voluntary part in bringing about the destined events of his
> world. This experience of freedom is for my clients a most meaningful de-
> velopment, one which assists them in becoming human, in relating to others,
> in being a person. (Rogers and Stevens, 1967, p. 53)

We need not become involved in argument over whether or not man's
behavior is entirely determined by his biological makeup and his past experiences (so that he can never be entirely free); we shall simply note that freedom of choice occurs by degrees. If freedom of choice were complete, Rogers'
hypothesis of naturally occurring forces toward self-actualization would be
irrelevant. If man were indeed to possess this "drive" toward self-actualization
he would be ipso facto a victim of it and therefore not free. The main point

is that Rogers has credited man with the ability to expand his own range of choices through his ability to relate to himself as a person free of the perceptual distortions that can result from interaction with his environment.

Inner freedom, according to Rogers, develops as the person "learns to listen to himself," to attend to his organismic experiences as valid sources of information for directing his self-actualization. He evaluates his feelings less and learns to attend to them more accurately. "I can, through accepting my individuality, my 'isness,' become more of my uniqueness, more of my potentiality." Certain conditions are, however, necessary for the development of this inner freedom; they include those related to the therapeutic attitude that we discussed earlier.

Rogers has related all these notions to "student-centered" teaching. Without denying the importance of learning course content he has sought to complement it with the development of "freedom." That is, the teacher (or institution) is to provide conditions that encourage the development of inner freedom while at the same time conveying formal course content. First, Rogers believes that education that is relevant to life's problems and adjustments facilitates learning but that "in our culture we tend to try to insulate the student from any and all of the real problems of life . . ." Yet we also want students to learn to face life, to be free and responsible.

As we might expect from the material presented earlier, certain attributes of teachers are necessary for these conditions to occur. They must trust the human organism to develop its own potential once it has been permitted to choose its own way. The teacher does not therefore decide what is to be learned but allows each student to determine for himself what he wishes to learn within a general topic area. Furthermore, the teacher must be "real": sincere and without an artificial façade, "not a sterile tube through which knowledge is passed from one generation to the next." He must not only accept his students as imperfect human beings with many feelings and many potentials; he must also prize their feelings and opinions. Acceptance is the reflection of a teacher's trust in his students. The "student-centered" teacher further shows understanding of the process of learning in the student: He is empathic in all his interactions. The teacher also provides resources, concentrating on "all kinds of relevant raw material for use by the students, together with clearly indicated channels by which the student can avail himself of (them)." His personal competences are clear, and he is available upon request to assist students as he can.

Rogers has reported from empirical investigations (though limited ones) that student-centered programs have furthered psychological maturity (inner freedom) while maintaining the usual standards for content. The indications are that these classes have generated more independent extracurricular learning, greater creativity, and increased responsibility. The content learning appears to be "roughly equal to that achieved in conventional classes."

SUMMARY

Existentialism offers a framework for understanding man, rather than a formalized theory of personality. Man is viewed as a "being" who can experience himself as both subject and object; should he be limited to experiencing one or the other he will miss his own reality as a being-in-the-world. Culture is critical in determining whether or not man will fulfill his potential. Our modern industrial societies—because of their materialistic emphasis on production—have tended to cast man as object. Modern man thus suffers alienation from himself and often from others. To reach fulfillment it is necessary to recognize one's own "being," one's own personal existence in time and space, and a future time in which one will also "not be." Three modes of world are always present and must be experienced; they are the natural world, the world of human relationships, and the world of oneself. Neurotic behavior blocks man's relatedness to his own being and consequently the fulfillment of his own potential. All men suffer existential guilt because they cannot completely realize their potentials, and all men suffer anxiety because they must face the threat of losing the world. It is man's nature to take responsibility for himself. In contrast to other animals, he has greater freedom of choice, and must use it if he is to fulfill himself. Existential therapists also emphasize understanding of the "patient-in-his-world"; specific techniques are secondary. They are applied according to their usefulness in providing increased understanding of each patient's existence. In several examples we have demonstrated existential psychotherapy and the functioning of growth groups.

Rogers has developed a theory of man based on his therapeutic observations. He and his coworkers have combined research with theory and practice in order to understand man's subjective field more fully. According to Rogers, it is necessary to know as fully as possible how an individual perceives the world in order to understand him. Man develops an image of himself through his experiences with the environment, and the "self" plays a major role in determining his behavior. Distorted perceptions of the world result when a child's needs are threatened; distortions cripple his self-actualization by making some experiences unavailable for evaluation. Rogers' client-centered therapy reflects his optimistic view of man. The therapist has positive regard for the clients' ability to care for themselves. His approach is nondirective, aimed at eliminating distorted perceptions so that each client's "self" can be free to make choices in its own best interests. Research on psychotherapy has been another of Rogers' primary contributions. He and his colleagues have stimulated many studies, beside having developed experimental methods for attacking this difficult task. More recently Rogers has emphasized man's value formation and orientation and the meaning of freedom, especially to be a choosing organism.

7

A. Introduction
B. Basic Assumptions
  1. Neurotic behavior as maladaptive habits
  2. Determinism of behavior
  3. The therapist's responsibility for treatment
  4. Moral and religious values
C. Behavior-Modification Techniques from Classical Conditioning
  1. Concepts from classical conditioning
  2. Counterconditioning techniques
  3. Aversive conditioning
  4. Extinction techniques
D. Behavior-Modification Techniques from Operant Conditioning
  1. Concepts from operant conditioning
  2. Behavior therapy and operant conditioning
  3. Recapitulation
E. The Learning Theory of Personality
  1. Hypothetical constructs
  2. Interpretation of psychological conflict
F. Conclusions
G. Summary

Learning,
Behavior
Modification,
and
Personality

INTRODUCTION

Learning theorists focus primarily on each person's responses to his external environment and the habits that he develops through interaction with it. Personality is synonymous with the total of learned behavior. What a person has been like, what he is like, and what he will be like are determined by the response patterns that he has learned. In the frame of reference of learning theory the external environment is (through the stimulus situation) the central determinant of personality. Some learning theorists have suggested, as have the previous personality theorists whom we have studied, internal mechanisms to account for behavior, mechanisms that are of minor interest compared to stimulus-response patterns that are more directly observable. The stimulus situation, rather than the inner characteristics of the individual, is central to learning theory.

Therapies based on learning theory and research offer the clearest example of the interaction between empirical findings in psychology and their application. The study of learning began, not with interest in personality, but with study of the basic processes involved in learning. As investigation of the learning process is one of the oldest areas in psychology, a number of learning principles have already been confirmed through well-controlled studies and are currently accepted as scientifically valid. Psychologists interested in the study of personality have brought together the various findings from learning research and have applied them to understanding the whole person. As principles established in the laboratory have been applied to human situations, further knowledge of learning has been gained.

The contributions of research to the basic understanding of learning and to techniques for furthering it furnish a nice example of how applied and "pure" research interact to build a body of knowledge. Compared to the other theories that we have examined, learning theory can be said to have a firmer experimental foundation and to be more closely tied to objective data. Because of the intimate connection between applied learning theory and laboratory experimentation, the language of learning theorists is generally geared to empirical testing. New empirical observations lead to theoretical modifications, and these modifications lead to further research. This close relationship is also reflected in applied scientists' interest in testing the validity of their techniques. Increased confidence has followed positive research findings, and behavior therapists have felt free to modify their concepts and techniques in keeping with objective results.

In this chapter we shall examine some "behavior modification" techniques that have grown from knowledge of the learning process. As with other views of man, learning theory offers a framework for understanding

172

attempts to relate to the world, that is, to adjust. Although much of our basic knowledge of learning has been gained from experimentation with animals, generalization to human behavior has proved valid in many instances. Two learning paradigms—classical conditioning and operant conditioning—have provided the basic conceptual grounds for the practical techniques of behavior modification currently used to aid adjustment. In order to furnish the student a clearer understanding of these applications, we shall provide a brief survey of experiments and related theoretical concepts before investigating behavioral techniques. First, however, we shall see how behavior therapists define their approach to behavior change.

BASIC ASSUMPTIONS

The techniques following from classical conditioning and operant conditioning are not separated in practice; the therapist applies whatever technique seems most appropriate to his client's problem. Several basic assumptions characterize and direct behavior therapy (Wolpe and Lazarus, 1966).

NEUROTIC BEHAVIOR AS MALADAPTIVE HABITS

Neurotic behavior is interpreted as consisting of habit patterns that cause the patient to suffer; neurosis is not viewed as an illness. Neurotic habits are said to have been learned under specific conditions, in which fear, or anxiety, have played a central role; they are maladaptive and quite resistant to extinction. The aim of behavior therapy is to eliminate such habits.

The essence of neurotic behavior is a learned connection between negative emotional responses (anxiety) and particular classes of stimuli. For example, an individual has learned to experience fear in high places. Although some patients seem to experience general uneasiness and suffering, it is frequently possible on closer inspection to isolate specific patterns of stimuli that account for "generalized" anxiety. Behavior therapists recognize fear as a highly adaptive warning signal. It often becomes associated with inappropriate situations, however.

DETERMINISM OF BEHAVIOR

Behavior therapists have a deterministic view of neurotic behavior; that is, they think that all learning occurs through the patient's interaction with his environment. What he is and what he will become have been so determined. As the patient has had no choice in what he has become, moralizing and blame are inappropriate; it is not the patient's fault that he finds himself unhappy. The patient's suffering cannot be attributed to his unwillingness to become well or to a lack of moral fiber in overcoming his difficulties. The behavior therapist does his utmost to reassure the patient that he need not feel guilty over his disturbance. The therapist attempts to relieve the guilt and the sense of unworthiness that are often associated with emotional suffering and mental illness.

The Therapist's Responsibility for Treatment

Behavior therapists take explicit responsibility for the accurate analysis of the patient's problems so that proper techniques can be applied to correct his unhappy situation and to eliminate maladaptive habits that cause suffering. The only requirements for the patient are that he enter the therapeutic situation conscientiously and perform the specific remedial tasks assigned to him. As long as he fulfills these expectations, the burden of direction lies with the therapist. It is the therapist's job to select the appropriate techniques in any given instance; if no improvement occurs, it is the fault of the therapist, not of the patient.

Evidence of positive change in a patient is the only justification for continuing to use a specific technique. The therapist is never justified in continuing a technique because he is certain it is the right one and that it will work if only the patient will allow it to. As long as the patient cooperates, attributing therapeutic failure to his unconscious resistance and so forth is unacceptable. Furthermore, the behavior therapist is responsible for informing his patient when he does not know a technique that is likely to help. He continues to support the patient and to provide encouragement that new techniques are being developed, but frank admission of defeat is sometimes required.

Moral and Religious Values

The behavior therapist takes a positive line of action that may bring him into direct conflict with moral and religious values. If religious beliefs or moral values are interfering with a patient's ability to function free of undue suffering, the therapist does not avoid attacking these beliefs on rational grounds. In taking this stand he assumes responsibility for distinguishing among technical decisions, his own moral code, and the needs of the patient. It is vital that the therapist does not confuse the different aspects. He must have the skill to distinguish technical decisions from moral ones, and the tenets of his own moral code must be kept separate from the moral requirements of the patient's situation. That is, the therapist must be careful not to impose his personal beliefs on his patients. He attacks only beliefs that cause them suffering.

We shall turn now to closer examination of behavior-modification techniques and their theoretical background.

BEHAVIOR MODIFICATION TECHNIQUES
FROM CLASSICAL CONDITIONING

CONCEPTS FROM CLASSICAL CONDITIONING

CONDITIONED RESPONSE

I. Pavlov, a Russian physiologist, conducted some of the earliest investigations of learning (Pavlov, 1927, 1928). The *conditioned response* and its characteristics were discovered in experimentation with animals. Figure 7-1

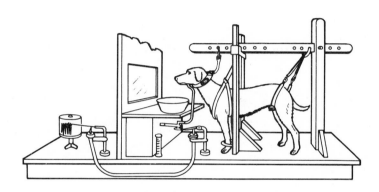

Figure 7-1 Arrangements used by Pavlov in classical salivary conditioning. From R. M. Yerkes and S. Morgulis, The method of Pavlov in animal psychology. *Psychological Bulletin*, 1909, **6**, 257–273.

shows Pavlov's experimental setup with a dog. The animal is placed in the harness, and meat powder is placed in his mouth to cause salivation; the amount of saliva secreted is measured by the flow of liquid through a tube inserted in the salivary duct. Pavlov discovered that stimuli associated with presentation of the meat powder bring about salivation when presented alone. For example, after a buzzer had been in close association with the presentation of meat powder a number of times, the sound of the buzzer alone would cause salivation; the dog had "learned" to salivate to the buzzer. The salivary response without the meat was called a *conditioned response* (CR), a learned response to a new stimulus. In this example, the meat powder was the *unconditioned stimulus* (UCS), a stimulus that calls forth a natural response. Salivation, the natural response, is called the *unconditioned response* (UCR).

A *conditioned stimulus* (CS) is any stimulus that has been associated with an unconditioned stimulus and has become the cue for a response similar to the unconditioned response. The unconditioned stimulus for Pavlov's animal was the sound of the buzzer associated with the introduction of the meat powder. The buzzer became a conditioned stimulus when it elicited the salivary response by itself.

The conditioned response is similar to the unconditioned response but it is associated with a stimulus different from the original unconditioned stimulus. In our example the conditioned response is salivation at the sound of the buzzer alone. It varies somewhat in quality and quantity from the original unconditioned salivary response; the animal salivates less to the buzzer than he did to the meat powder.

Pavlov's isolation of these four concepts (UCS, UCR, CS, CR) established the basis of many learning situations. The process of classical conditioning may be diagramed:

First-Order Conditioning

1. Original response situation   UCS $\longrightarrow$ UCR
                 (meat powder)   (salivation)

2. Pairing of conditioned stimulus with uncondi-   CS
tioned stimulus   (buzzer) UCS $\longrightarrow$ UCR

3. Unconditioned stimulus alone   CS $\longrightarrow$ CR
                              (salivation)

An example of this process that is more directly related to adjustment is that of an individual who has learned to respond with fear (anxiety) in social interactions. He feels constricted and ill at ease. Looking back at Ron in Chapter 1, we see that some of his difficulties were of this nature. At any rate, from the individual's conditioning history we would find that being around people, probably unfamiliar people, had been associated with fear. As a child, for example, he may have been attacked by other children (UCS) and responded with fright (UCR). The presence of other children (CS) became associated with the fright response until at some point it came to elicit fright by itself (CR). Consequently, the child, and later the adult, experienced fear in social gatherings. A behavior therapist would apply one or more techniques to overcome such difficulties.

HIGHER-ORDER CONDITIONING

Conditioning does not cease at the level of the primary CR; *higher-order conditioning* may occur in a manner similar to that of first-order conditioning. For example, second-order conditioning involves the pairing of a new stimulus (CS′) with the conditioned stimulus until the new stimulus results in a response when presented alone. Pavlov found that, after his dogs had learned a conditioned response to the buzzer, pairing a light with the buzzer led to a response to the light alone. The light stimulus was two times removed from the original unconditioned stimulus (meat powder); hence the term "second-order conditioning." If still another stimulus were paired with the light, one would obtain third-order conditioning. Second-order conditioning can be diagramed as follows:

Second-Order Conditioning

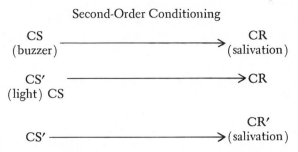

Again the second-order response (CR′) differs slightly in quantity and quality from the first-order response. As the stimulus is further removed from the unconditioned stimulus, this response is increasingly different from the unconditioned response, usually of less magnitude; at some point far enough removed from the initial unconditioned stimulus, response to a new stimulus will be too small to measure.

The relevance of higher-order conditioning to human learning is quite apparent. For example, a child's first experience of candy causes him to salivate. The shape, color, and other properties of the candy are closely associated with his response, and he is soon likely to salivate when he simply sees the candy (CR). If the candy is kept in Grandma's "candy jar" the constant association between jar and candy may soon result in salivation at sight of the bowl (second-order conditioning); a characteristic sound associated with opening the jar may eventually elicit the response even when the child is in another room (third-order conditioning) and so on.

REINFORCEMENT

The association of the conditioned stimulus with the unconditioned stimulus is called *reinforcement*; repeated reinforcement increases the strength of the conditioned response. A child who experiences many frightening situations with peers, for example, is more likely to show fear of social interactions as an adult. Conversely, when the conditioned stimulus is presented but is not accompanied by the unconditioned stimulus, reinforcement does not occur; consequently, the conditioned response becomes weaker.

EXTINCTION

Experimental extinction is the eventual elimination of the conditioned response through repeated presentation of the conditioned stimulus without reinforcement. If the child has been frightened only once and subsequently his interactions have all been positive, his fear response will soon disappear.

SPONTANEOUS RECOVERY

Another characteristic of the conditioned response is *spontaneous recovery*. This term refers to the reappearance of a conditioned response after it has been extinguished. For example, after a dog shows a conditioned salivary response to a buzzer, the buzzer can be presented frequently without the meat powder (without reinforcement). Eventually he stops salivating at the sound of the buzzer, and experimental extinction is said to have taken place. When the animal is brought back to the laboratory after a rest period, however, he may make the conditioned response to the buzzer, even without prior reinforcement.

GENERALIZATION

Once a conditioned response to a particular stimulus has been learned, other stimuli similar to the original tend to call forth the conditioned response. The more the new stimulus resembles the original stimulus, the more likely it is to elicit the conditioned response. When a tone is paired with the meat powder, a conditioned response is eventually associated with the tone. After the response has been conditioned, tones that closely approximate the original one will also bring forth conditioned responses. And, the more closely the new tone resembles the original one, the more likely it is that the conditioned response will follow.

In this way new conditioned stimuli are learned without reinforcement (pairing with the unconditioned stimulus). Eventually, however, as the tone is changed more and more from the original, the conditioned response becomes weaker until a very dissimilar tone calls forth no response at all. The rate at which the conditioned response weakens as the stimulus becomes less similar to the original is called the *gradient of generalization*. The discovery of generalization explains how learning can occur without reinforcement of each stimulus situation and how several similar stimuli may result in similar responses simply because of their similarities. As the child learns to respond to particular kinds of candy, perhaps lemon drops, it is likely that he will most easily respond to other candy with similar characteristics (orange drops) even though it is not directly associated with the lemon drops. Without the concept of *generalization*, it would be very difficult to adopt the hypothesis that most human behavior is learned, for each person would have to be exposed to all possible stimuli in the environment before he could learn responses to them.

DISCRIMINATION

The reverse of generalization is *discrimination*, the reinforcement of a particular class of stimuli and the failure to reinforce other, similar stimuli. If the original tone in our earlier example is consistently reinforced and a similar tone is not reinforced, the animal will eventually respond only to the original tone and will eliminate his response to the similar tone. The animal's ability to discriminate even closer tones will be limited by his physical abilities to tell them apart. That is, when the animal's hearing cannot distinguish one tone from the other, he will not be able to learn the difference in their reinforcement values. Our candy-eating child may confuse moth balls and lemon drops at first, but he soon learns to discriminate between the two because of the differences in associated reinforcement.

As can be extrapolated from the examples already cited, classical conditioning may play an important part in adjustment. Especially the pairing of fear (anxiety) with different circumstances may result in maladaptive habits that reduce a person's ability to relate to others or to himself.

We shall turn now to the examination of applied techniques that have grown out of experimental work and the theory of classical conditioning. Because of the strong emphasis on the organism's behavior, rather than on the interior processes of the organism, the techniques described in this chapter are called *behavior therapies*, or "behavior-modification techniques."

Counterconditioning Techniques

The association of anxiety with particular patterns of stimuli results in maladaptive (neurotic) behavior. The purpose of counterconditioning is to weaken the bond between the stimuli and the anxiety responses; the responses are inhibited. To condition inhibition of anxiety one introduces a competing response in the presence of the stimuli originally associated with anxiety. Replacing anxiety with a competing response is called *reciprocal inhibition*. It is defined as follows: "If a response inhibitory of anxiety can be made to occur in the presence of anxiety-evoking stimuli, it will weaken the bond between these stimuli and the anxiety" (Wolpe, 1969, p. 15).

A number of responses will inhibit anxiety; they include a relaxation response, an assertive response, and a sexual response. In the following discussion we shall examine techniques based on each of these responses.

SYSTEMATIC DESENSITIZATION AND THE RELAXATION RESPONSE

The technique of systematic desensitization uses deep relaxation. Several studies have shown that relaxation is accompanied by responses of the autonomic nervous system (that is, physiological responses associated with the subjective experience of anxiety) diametrically opposed to the autonomic responses connected with anxiety (Jacobsen, 1964; Clark, 1963; Wolpe, 1958, 1969). When a patient is completely relaxed, it is virtually impossible for him to experience anxiety. As long as the stimulus situation does not arouse anxiety to the point at which relaxation is impossible, the relaxation response will become associated with the stimuli.

Studies of experimental neuroses in cats have provided the basic information used in developing systematic desensitization (Wolpe, 1958). The cats received high-voltage, low-amperage shocks while confined to small cages, which caused withdrawal and fear responses associated with the cage. The "neurotic" responses were not overcome simply by placing the cats in the cages without the original fear-producing stimulus (shock); that is, extinction of their behavior through nonreinforcement was almost impossible. An effective procedure for reducing the animals' fear was to feed them in settings progressively similar to the original cage; eventually the animals could eat in the cage, and their "neurotic" fears were eliminated.

These studies led to the idea of eliminating anxiety by gradually approaching the anxiety-arousing stimuli in the presence of a response that competes with anxiety. In early work patients were taught relaxation and requested to approach real-life situations that aroused fear gradually. Real stimuli proved very difficult to manage, however, because the patients had to seek appropriate experiences outside therapy—experiences over which the therapist had little control.

The next step in developing systematic desensitization was to use fantasied stimulus situations instead of actual ones. Hypnosis was used at first to facilitate both relaxation and imagination. It was necessary to develop a series of fantasy situations graded according to the anxiety associated with them—and to present them under relaxed conditions. The technique that is currently in use works as follows: After the therapist has determined that systematic desensitization is the technique of choice, he begins to teach the patient to relax and how to construct appropriate hierarchies, lists of situations associated with increasing degrees of fear. Several sessions may be necessary before the patient reaches the desired level of relaxation and learns to construct suitable hierarchies.

By clenching his fists and then relaxing them, for instance, the patient learns to feel the difference between tense and relaxed muscles. All parts of his body are tensed, then relaxed, in this fashion until he understands the process of relaxing. He is instructed to practice relaxation techniques between therapeutic sessions. Relaxation training may or may not include hypnosis.

Approximately half of each session is devoted to relaxation training and half to gathering the information necessary to establish hierarchies. The therapist and the patient must first identify specific sources of neurotic fears before hierarchies can be developed. For example, it may be rather simple to develop a list of fear-arousing situations for a person whose primary fear is of heights. The least anxiety-arousing situation may be one in which the patient imagines climbing a flight of five steps; a moderate situation may be one in which he is atop a one-story building, and so on. Being on a high mountain or a high building may arouse a great deal of anxiety. Most hierarchies comprise approximately ten levels, but patients frequently have more than one hierarchy. A single patient may, for instance, have fears associated with high altitudes, closed places, and groups of people; each of these anxiety situations may produce a separate hierarchy of fantasies.

Once the anxiety hierarchies are understood and relaxation training has been accomplished, systematic desensitization begins. The patient is instructed to fantasize the lowest-level situation in a hierarchy while he is deeply relaxed. The anxiety response is thus inhibited, and its association with the stimulus is weakened. The patient receives instructions to raise his finger if he begins to experience anxiety; if he signals the therapist suggests a situation that arouses less anxiety. The use of such a signal prevents further strengthening of the bond between anxiety and the stimulus. When the treatment is successful a patient progresses up his hierarchy until he is able to fantasize the most anxiety-arousing situation while remaining relaxed. The transfer of the responses to real stimuli outside the therapeutic setting occurs through stimulus generalization. The following example has been described by Wolpe.

THE CASE OF MISS C.

Miss C. was a 24 year old art student who came for treatment because marked anxiety at examinations had resulted in repeated failures. Investigation revealed additional phobic areas. The hierarchies are given below. All of them involve people, and none belong to the classical phobias. (Freedom from anxiety to the highest items of each of these hierarchies was achieved in seventeen desensitization sessions, with complete transfer to the corresponding situations in actuality. Four months later, she passed her examinations without anxiety.)

Hierarchies
   A. Examination Series
      1. On the way to the university on the day of an examination.
      2. In the process of answering an examination paper.
      3. Waiting before the unopened doors of the examination room.
      4. Awaiting the distribution of examination papers.
      5. The examination paper lies face down before her.
      6. The night before an examination.
      7. On the day before an examination.
      8. Two days before an examination.
      9. Three days before an examination.
      10. Four days before an examination.
      11. Five days before an examination.
      12. A week before an examination.
      13. Two weeks before an examination.
      14. A month before an examination.
   B. Scrutiny Series
      1. Being watched working (especially drawing) by ten people.
      2. Being watched working by six people.

3. Being watched working by three people.
4. Being watched working by one expert in the field. (Anxiety begins when the observer is ten feet away and increases as he draws closer.)
5. Being watched working by a non-expert. (Anxiety begins at a distance of 4 feet.)

C. Devaluation Series
1. An argument she raises in a discussion is ignored by the group.
2. She is not recognized by a person she has recently met three times.
3. Her mother says she is selfish because she is not helping in the house (studying instead).
4. She is not recognized by a person she has briefly met twice.
5. Her mother calls her lazy.
6. She is not recognized by a person she has briefly met once.

D. Discord between Other People
1. Her mother shouts at a servant.
2. Her young sister whines to her mother.
3. Her sister engages in a dispute with her father.
4. Her mother shouts at her sister.
5. She sees two strangers quarrel.

(Wolpe, 1969, pp. 117–118)

After relaxation training and the establishment of these hierarchies the first desensitization session proceeded:

> I am now going to ask you to imagine a number of scenes. You will imagine them clearly and they will generally interfere little, if at all, with your state of relaxation. If, however, at any time you feel disturbed or worried and want to draw my attention, you will be able to do so by raising your left index finger. First I want you to imagine you are standing at a familiar street corner on a pleasant morning watching the traffic go by. You see cars, motorcycles, trucks, bicycles, people and traffic lights; and you can hear the sounds associated with all these things. (Pause of about 15 sec.) Now stop imagining that scene and give all your attention once again to relaxing. If the scene you imagine disturbed you even in the slightest degree I want you to raise your left index finger now. (Patient does not raise finger) Now imagine that you are home studying in the evening. It is the 20th of May, exactly a month before your examination. (Pause of 5 sec.) Now stop imagining the scene. (Pause of 10 sec.) Now imagine the same scene again—a month before your examination. (Pause of 5 sec.) Stop imagining the scene and just think of your muscles. Let go, and enjoy your state of calm. (Pause of 15 sec.) Now again imagine that you are studying at home a month before your examination. (Pause of 5 sec.) Stop the scene, and now think of nothing but your own body. (Pause of 5 sec.) If you felt any disturbance whatsoever to the last scene raise your left index finger now. (Patient raises finger) If the amount of disturbance decreased from the first presentation to the third do nothing, otherwise again raise your finger. (Patient does not raise finger) Just keep on relaxing. (Pause of 15 sec.) Imagine that you are sitting on a bench at a bus stop and across the road are two strange men whose voices are raised in argument. (Pause of 10 sec.) Stop imagining the scene and just relax. . . . Now I am going to count up to 5 and you will open your eyes feeling very calm and refreshed. (Wolpe, 1969, pp. 126–127)

Miss C.'s behavior was reported as commonplace, the kind that does not indicate future difficulties. Her visualization was clear, and there was evidence that her anxiety was decreasing with the repetition of each scene. The therapist predicted that they would be able to continue through all the hierarchies with little difficulty, as indeed they did.

Spontaneous recovery may occur in later sessions; the patient may experience anxiety in response to fantasies that he has already been able to experience without anxiety. The procedure then is to return to lower levels in the hierarchy before again attempting to ascend the scale. Spontaneous recovery may be eliminated, or reduced a great deal, by "overlearning" at earlier levels; that is, by fantasizing a scene several times after it has ceased to arouse anxiety.

Desensitization may not proceed according to the therapist's expectations, however; the patient may experience no decrease in anxiety over imagined scenes, or he may report no reduction in anxiety outside the therapeutic setting. Three major reasons for such failures should be explored: He may be having difficulty relaxing; the hierarchies may be misleading or irrelevant; his imaginative abilities may be poor. Special effort, including application of other techniques, can then be made to overcome the difficulties.

ASSERTIVE TRAINING

Assertive training is often appropriate for people who suffer a great deal of anxiety in interpersonal relations, which inhibits more appropriate responses and blocks necessary adaptation. Patients who are likely to benefit from assertive training often appear ingratiating at first and too concerned about "proper" behavior, or they may be undemonstrative and may regard emotional expression as childish and inappropriate. The aim of assertive training is to enable the patient to adapt to situations in which his effectiveness is normally reduced by anxiety. The therapist's interventions are aimed at augmenting every impulse toward eliciting these inhibited responses. The expectation is that each time they are enacted there will be, through reciprocal inhibition, an inhibiting of the anxiety, that leads to some degree of weakening of the anxiety-response habit.

Assertive behavior is defined quite broadly, to cover any socially acceptable behavior that demonstrates a person's rights as an individual. The expression of anger and resentment is common among such responses, though many others—for example, a polite "no" to an unreasonable demand—are also effective. The therapist encourages the patient to exhibit such responses in situations associated with anxiety, on the assumption that they will serve as counterconditioning agents. Assertive actions are often followed by rewards (reaching a goal, a change in an antagonist's behavior, and so on), and therefore such training frequently develops adaptive social habits, beside diminishing socially determined anxiety.

The therapist discovers what situations are associated with anxiety and encourages the patient to assert himself in those situations. As in systematic desensitization it is valuable to determine the degrees of anxiety associated with specific stimuli and to start with the easier assignments. For example, a patient who shows anxiety in many interpersonal interactions may first be given the task of asserting himself in situations with good friends. As training progresses, he will assert himself in settings that are increasingly difficult. Increasing self-assurance should thus develop until he is able to assert himself whenever appropriate.

The patient is instructed to take notes of his own interpersonal interactions and to discuss them in detail with the therapist. It is important to analyze difficult situations until they are clearly understood and plans can be made to overcome them. *Behavior rehearsal* is a frequent adjunct technique in assertive training. For example, a patient describes a situation in which he feels unable to assert himself and as a consequence has always performed ineffectively; the therapist then sets up roles for each of them, similar to those described by the patient. The patient reenacts the conflicted relationship with the therapist in the role of the other person. This approach affords the therapist the opportunity to evaluate the patient's behavior and to make suggestions for methods of assertion. The two continue to practice until the patient learns to behave adaptively under the actual circumstances.

A journalist gave his reactions to the therapeutic use of assertive responses in the following words:

> I have been given the assignment of winning emotional victories in daily life. To win them involves a new attitude on my part to people. It means that I no longer regard them as being more important than myself. It means that I am no longer over-anxious to please them just because they are other people. Public opinion? I represent it just as much as any one person. This is the important discovery I made—and it is a satisfying one emotionally. Other peoples' opinions and feelings count—*but so do mine.*
>
> This does not mean that I have become aggressive, unpleasant, or inconsiderate to other people. That would merely be putting myself in a false position. Emotionally I would gain nothing—unless, of course, it was a situation in which aggression was required. This new method of coping with interpersonal situations simply boils down to doing the things which, if you were an onlooker watching the situation, would seem fair and fitting. (Wolpe, 1958, p. 118)

THE CASE OF MISS G.

Miss G., a very attractive woman of 28, came for help in acute distress at her lover's growing coolness toward her—following the pattern of numerous previous love affairs. Having gained a man's interest, she would at once abandon herself to him and adopt an attitude of extreme dependence and submission. He would become increasingly contemptuous and after a time reject her completely.

She had spent her childhood in an unstable, uneasy atmosphere with a younger sister and brother. Her father was an amateur philosopher who preached peace and brotherhood but gave vent to frequent unreasonable fits of violent temper sometimes with physical brutality toward his son. Her mother was very possessive and jealous, and nagged and shouted a great deal. Miss G. had always been at the top of her class at school, which she had greatly enjoyed and felt to be a haven from home. Financial difficulties had forced her to leave at 15 to become a shorthand typist.

In general she lacked assurance, was very dependent, and practically never free from feelings of tension and anxiety. Her Willoughby score was 45, reflecting very considerable neuroticism. Her Bernreuter self-sufficiency score was 34 percent—distinctly on the low side. A year previously she had terminated a two-year course of psychoanalysis, which had benefited her somewhat. She came to me only because her analyst was not available, and during the first few interviews she repeatedly expressed doubt regarding the value of my nonanalytic treatment.

At her fifth interview she stated that she "felt very good" for a few hours after each interview and then became very anxious, feeling that she had "no ability to take any kind of initiative." At this interview the unadaptiveness of her anxieties and the rationale of the reciprocal inhibition principle were explained to her, and she left feeling optimistic. At the next interview she was told how to behave with firmness and take independent courses of action with her lover. She was also shown how to counterattack her nagging mother and to deal with her boss and other people who easily upset her. Through appropriate action she gradually developed a feeling of mastery, both at home and at work.

Although her lover was obviously not genuinely interested in her, Miss G.'s emotional involvement with him was so great that it was difficult for her at first to behave toward him consistently according to prescription. Each failure upset her. The turning point came after the ninth interview when he approached her to lend him 10£ ($28). *She refused without explanation and without permitting discussion,* and was left with a profound feeling of triumph. Within a week she was able to terminate the association finally—with dignity and satisfaction.

In the meantime, another beau had commenced to pursue her. She made an effort to be firm and to be guided by her own wishes, but one evening she permitted herself to be seduced although clearly aware that she was motivated by a fear of not pleasing. Recounting this at the eleventh interview, she expressed some disappointment, but I praised her for the measure of her success after so short a time under therapy.

During the week that followed, she did better. When she went out with her previous week's seducer, she did not let him make love to her at all and noted with surprise that this made him more keen on her. She also went out with a divorcé who took her to his apartment "to play music"—in vain! Taking her home, he apologized for treating her as "cheap"—also to her surprise. She was no longer upset by the tantrums and nagging of her mother, which had been greatly reduced in response to Miss G.'s assertiveness. However, she felt ill at ease when she had to spend "too many evenings" at home.

At her thirteenth interview she reported a further gain of control over minor sexual situations. She said that she was making more rapid progress than ever—felt increasingly constructive and decreasingly anxious. After this interview she went on holiday and returned six weeks later to say that she had made continued efforts to control interpersonal situations and was feeling much more stable emotionally. She was much better poised and had been a social success for the first time in her life. She no longer felt, as in the past, that it was important to go out a lot. On holiday she had met a man who attracted her, and now her feelings had an adult, independent character. After handling many difficulties admirably, she married him three months later. Her Willoughby score had dropped to 17. She had 14 interviews in all, and two and a half years later was reported to be a happily married mother. (Wolpe, 1958, pp. 127–128)

The case of Miss G. indicates how assertive training can be applied in practice. Assertive trainees generally follow a similar pattern of development in the course of treatment. At first there is an increased awareness of their own nonassertiveness and the negative repercussions that result. An intellectual understanding of the positive effects of assertive behavior follows, along with an increasing distaste for their own ineffectiveness. Resentment develops toward the circumstances that maintain their nonassertiveness and tentative, often clumsy, attempts at self-assertive responses are tried. When positive effects follow, the probability of the person engaging in more assertive responses increases. In some cases, previously timid and dominated patients tend to overassert themselves as they derive increasing emotional satisfaction from their behavior. However, the combination of negative environmental feedback and the therapist's monitoring is usually sufficient to tone down these responses. The drilling of assertion for assertion's sake that may be required in the early part of the treatment gives way to a more discriminating use of assertion. The patient learns to stand up for his own rights without being dominating. Finally, as the patient is aware of his growing mastery in interpersonal relations, he often develops a reasonable indifference to minor slights and other insignificant irritations of everyday interactions.

USING THE SEXUAL RESPONSE

Difficulties in sexual behavior often result from anxiety associated with sexually arousing stimuli. If sexual arousal has not been completely inhibited, it may serve as a competing response for anxiety. Of course, when sexual arousal does not occur in such situations, other techniques must be used to reduce the patient's anxiety.

The most common kinds of sexual difficulties encountered in males range from almost no sexual arousal at all to moderate lack of pleasure in coitus, especially ejaculation without sensation. In females the constellation of frigidity ranges from women who become panic-stricken in any sexual encounter to those who find intercourse mildly unpleasant. The conditioning of these disturbances varies a great deal. There may be a rather simple history of trauma associated with sexual intercourse. For example, one man suffered the trauma of a coronary attack during intercourse and after that responded with anxiety and partial impotence in his sexual relationships. At the other extreme there are detailed histories of negative training in sexual activities because of parents' poor sexual attitudes.

The physiology of the sexual response is such that anxiety tends to inhibit erection and to promote ejaculation in the male. When anxiety accompanies sexual activity, he may therefore be unable to have an erection or he may have a premature ejaculation—in either instance his partner is left unsatisfied. The aim of treatment is to reduce anxiety by reciprocally inhibiting it with the sexual response.

Using the sexual response is the same, in principle, as systematic desensitization with relaxation and assertive training. It is first necessary to establish clearly what the anxiety-arousing situations are and then to approach them in steps so that the sexual response remains dominant and counterconditioning can take place. By gradually approaching the desirable behavior, usually extended coitus, the patient maintains arousal and anxiety is displaced.

Sexual inadequacy is often accompanied by shame or guilt over not satisfying one's partner. The therapist attempts to eliminate such reactions by teaching other methods to bring about satisfaction of the partner, frequently through manual stimulation to orgasm.

When the difficulty is premature ejaculation, a technique of controlled stimulation of the man's penis by his partner leads to progressively longer periods of stimulation before ejaculation.

> If fatigue is present in either partner, he or she should sleep for a brief period of time. After this, love play is begun and progresses to mutual stimulation of the penis and clitoris. Each is instructed to inform the other of the stage of sexual excitement being experienced. When the husband feels a sensation which is, for him, premonitory to ejaculation, he informs his wife and removes her hand until the sensation disappears. Stimulation is begun again and interrupted by the husband when the premonitory sensation returns. By continuing the technique described above ejaculation can eventually be postponed indefinitely. Both husband and wife are advised that if erection subsides more than temporarily, a brief sleep or postponement of further stimulation is to be preferred to continuing their efforts at that time. Next, each is told separately, and later together, that ejaculation occurs more rapidly with the penis wet than dry. It is necessary, therefore, to use a bland cream or other means to lubricate the penis while the procedure is repeated. (Wolpe 1969, pp. 75–76)

When the focus of difficulty is on coitus, the partners are instructed to approach final consummation gradually. The patient is told to do nothing that he cannot do without anxiety. The therapist must determine through interviews at what point anxiety begins and at what point sexual arousal is possible.

Difficulties may arise in treatment when the partner refuses to cooperate. Sometimes partners may not be available for single patients; at other times marriages may have been damaged to the point at which the partners do not care. In any event, behavior therapists do not hesitate to suggest extramarital activity, whether with interested partners or with prostitutes.

> Perhaps there will someday be "a pool" of accredited women who will sell their services to men with sexual problems. At present there seems to be no other recourse than to seek out a regular prostitute—and it is usually no easy matter to find one who is both personally appealing and able to muster enough sympathetic interest to participate in the therapeutic program. One patient with a 16 year history of impotence tried about ten prostitutes before he found a warm-hearted and considerate one with whose help his sexual anxiety was overcome and his potency restored. (Wolpe, 1969, pp. 77–78)

This case offers an example of how the sexual response can be used to inhibit anxiety in sexual behavior.

THE CASE OF MR. I.

Mr. I., a 36-year-old realtor, had suffered from premature ejaculation ever since the beginning of his coital life at the age of 16. Ejaculation generally occurred within 15 seconds of intromission. He had married at 24. His wife, though deriving some satisfaction from digital orgasms, had become increasingly conscious of her incomplete fulfillment, and had in the past two years been showing interest in other men. About 18 months previously, Mr. I. had had about 25 consultations with a "dynamic" psychiatrist. Though he had found the probing type of approach irritating, his general confidence had been improved by the treatment; but his sexual performance had remained unchanged. In three short-lived extramarital affairs, his sexual performance had been no better than with his wife. He usually felt that he was doing the "chasing," and was being accepted to some extent on sufferance.

Mr. I.'s Willoughby score was 30, with highest loadings for humiliation, stage fright, and being hurt. He lacked assertiveness in relation to people close to him, but not at all in business affairs. A program of assertive training was seen as a secondary but very relevant therapeutic requirement.

Mrs. I., briefly interviewed, expressed great willingness to take part in a behavior therapy program. She stated that digital orgasm satisfied her physically but not emotionally. She felt that even a relatively small degree of prolongation of intromission would enable her to have coital orgasms. She regarded her marriage as very satisfactory in all other respects. Therapy of the sexual inadequacy based upon use of sexual responses made combined use of two lines of approach: (1) graded penile stimulation by the technic of Semans (see above); and (2) gradual advances toward coitus. Mr. I. kept a detailed record of his performances, which he timed as accurately as possible with a bedside clock. The data of the early and middle stages of his record are reproduced below. Each figure refers to the *number of minutes of manual stimulation of the penis by his wife that brought him just short of ejaculation* for each successive sequence of stimulation.

First occasion (Saturday) 8, 6, 6, 6, and 3 minutes.

Second occasion (Saturday) 11, 7, 3, 4, and 4 minutes. . . .

Fourth occasion (Sunday) 17 minutes. . . .

Twelfth occasion (Friday) partial insertion (glans penis) for 20 minutes during which Mrs. I. alone moved and in this way gradually manipulated the penis deeper. At the end of the period Mr. I. withdrew as he felt ejaculation imminent. . . .

Nineteenth occasion Orgasm after 29 minutes of small movements. Mrs. I. said that she too had been on the point of orgasm.

Further sexual occasions enabled gradually increasing excursions of movement, and finally a major breakthrough occurred after the thirteenth therapeutic interview. While Mr. I. retained his erection, Mrs. I. had four orgasms, and he ejaculated during the last of them. From this time onward there was mutually satisfactory sexual performance that gradually improved. There were 14 therapeutic interviews in all, over 5 weeks. (Wolpe, 1969, pp. 78–81)

AVERSIVE CONDITIONING

Anxiety-arousing stimuli can be associated with undesirable, obsessive, or compulsive habits to develop avoidance responses. The aim of aversive conditioning is the opposite of that of relaxation, assertion, and sexual-arousal techniques; it is to *create* an anxiety response to particular stimuli. The result is conditioned inhibition of an undesirable habit. Any stimulus that is displeasing or noxious to the patient will serve to inhibit a response. A very small electric shock is usually preferable because it can be easily manipulated, and accurate timing of its introduction with undesirable stimuli is comparatively simple.

Electrodes are attached to the patient's arm so that shock—at a level distinctly unpleasant to the patient but that he can withstand for a short period of time—can be administered at the therapist's discretion. The patient is then instructed to look at the undesirable stimulus, and shock is administered. For example, an alcoholic looks at a glass of liquor while shock is administered; as soon as he exhibits an avoidance response, like turning his head from the glass, shock ceases. The avoidance response is thus rewarded with reduction of shock (reinforced), and the undesirable response is associated with anxiety; the rationale is that conditioned inhibition of the approach response strengthens the avoidance response. Imaginary stimulus situations may be used in aversive conditioning when the real stimuli are not readily available.

Male homosexuality has also been treated through aversive conditioning. A picture of an attractive male is presented in conjunction with a painful shock. As the shock ceases, a picture of a female is flashed on the screen. This procedure combines two types of learning: learning an avoidance response to one stimulus and learning an approach response to another stimulus. Successful treatment results in association of anxiety with homosexual stimuli and association of anxiety relief with heterosexual stimuli.

EXTINCTION TECHNIQUES

Other techniques are classified under experimental extinction, a concept discussed earlier in this chapter. When a response receives no reinforcement, the probability that it will be repeated is less; that is, habits become increasingly weaker if they are not reinforced. The application of this principle thus weakens undesirable habits that go unreinforced over a period of time. Two techniques of extinction will be described here.

NEGATIVE PRACTICE

As long ago as 1932 K. Dunlap adopted the term "negative practice" for a technique of eliminating undesirable habits. Tics (involuntary muscle jerks) and stammering (stuttering) are the two most common habits treated by means of negative practice. The therapist and patient carefully analyze the motor movements involved in the habit; the patient's task is to repeat those movements to the point of exhaustion. Theoretically, continued evocation of the response without reinforcement will result in extinction. In order to speed the process, patients are instructed to "practice" their habit outside the therapy sessions. Sometimes they are instructed to perform the motor components in front of a mirror. The purpose of the mirror is to ensure that the behavior is reproduced accurately, so that the process of extinction can be more specific and therefore more rapid.

Wolpe and Lazarus (1966, p. 136) have reported the cure of a twenty-six-year-old female suffering from chronic and severe grinding of her teeth (bruxism). She was told to grind her teeth for one minute without stopping, to rest for a minute, and then to repeat the procedure five times in a row. She performed this task six times a day for approximately two and a half weeks. At the end of that time her husband reported that involuntary gnashing of her teeth had ceased. A followup almost a year later showed that her improvement had remained.

ANXIETY FLOODING

Strong anxiety responses may also be treated by experimental extinction. The procedure is to present imaginary stimuli that arouse maximum anxiety and to continue doing so until the anxiety response no longer occurs. Theoretically, the anxiety response becomes extinct because it is not reinforced when present; that is, no actual harm or aversive stimulus occurs in the therapy situation. Although this technique has produced improvement in a number of instances, J. Wolpe and A. A. Lazarus have suggested extreme caution in its use because they fear the establishment of even stronger anxiety responses and increasing resistance to other methods of treatment. There has been growing interest in this approach, however, under the title "implosive therapy" (Stampfl and Levis, 1967). The proponents of this method claim a rather high success rate in comparatively little therapeutic time.

The following are several examples of anxiety flooding.

THE CASE OF DR. E.

Imaginal stimuli were employed with Dr. E., a dentist who had had an extraordinarily severe and widespread neurosis, that had in most respects responded very well to varied sometimes prolonged application of the commoner behavior therapy techniques, such as assertive training and systematic desensitization. But two disabling neurotic constellations remained—an inability to give dental injections because of a fear of the patient dying in the chair, and an extravagant fear of ridicule. Since attempts to desensitize Dr. E. to these were making insufferably slow progress, I decided to try flooding. Under light hypnosis he was asked to imagine giving a patient a mandibular block, then withdrawing the syringe, standing back and seeing the patient slump forward dead. Dr. E. became profoundly disturbed, sweating, weeping and wringing his hands. After a minute or so, I terminated the scene and told him to relax. Two or three minutes later, the same scene, presented again, evoked a similar but weaker reaction. The sequence was given three more times, at the last of which no further reaction was observed. Dr. E. said that he felt he had been through a wringer—exhausted, but at ease. At the next session, the fear of ridicule was introduced. Dr. E. imagined that ·he was walking down the middle of a brilliantly lighted ballroom with people on both sides pointing their fingers at him and laughing derisively. At the fifth flooding session, it was clear that nothing remained to be treated. Four years later, at an interview with Dr. E., it was evident that his recovery had been fully maintained.

THE CASE OF MRS. C.

In vivo [in real life] flooding is exemplified by the case of Mrs. C., a woman with agoraphobia so severe that she was unable to go on her own more than two blocks by car without anxiety. Attempts at systematic desensitization had failed apparently because she was unable to imagine scenes realistically. After other measures had also proved ineffective, I decided to persuade her to expose herself to flooding, which had to be *in vivo* because of the demonstrated inadequacy of her imagination. After resisting strenuously for some weeks, she agreed to take the plunge. Plans were made for her husband to place her, unaccompanied, on a commercial aircraft one hour's flight away from the airport at which I was to wait to meet her. When Mrs. C. in due course alighted from the plane, she walked towards me smiling. She had felt increasing anxiety for the first fifteen minutes of the flight, and then gradual subsidence of it. During the second half of the journey she had been perfectly comfortable. This single experience resulted in a great increase in her range of comfortable situations away from home. She was now able, without anxiety, to drive her car alone three or four miles from home and to make unaccompanied trips by plane without any anxiety. Plans to build upon this improvement by further flooding were foiled by problems of distance.

THE CASE OF DR. K.

The following is one of several patients made worse by attempts to "flood" them. Dr. K. was a physician who, following a horrifying encounter with a mental hospital patient that need not be detailed here, had developed a severe phobia for insane people and insane behavior. He was in military service, and soon after he began to consult me was offered a transfer to a psychiatric hospital. I encouraged this, in the hope that the phobia might be overcome by flooding. Following my advice, he exposed himself continuously to the presence of schizophrenic patients, sometimes for hours at a stretch. Far from decreasing, his reactions to such patients grew progressively worse, and, in addition, he was assailed by a rising level of pervasive anxiety. By the end of the second day he was so extremely anxious that he had to be relocated to a general hospital. He had become much more sensitive than ever before to "insane stimuli." He was now a far more difficult case than when I had first seen him; and far more effort was needed to overcome his neurosis by desensitization. (Wolpe, 1969, pp. 190–192)

BEHAVIOR-MODIFICATION TECHNIQUES FROM OPERANT CONDITIONING

CONCEPTS FROM OPERANT CONDITIONING

B. F. Skinner (1938) investigated another kind of learning situation, which he called "operant conditioning." His early contributions came from studying animals in an apparatus that has become known as the *Skinner box*. An animal, usually a rat or a pigeon, is placed in a soundproof box. It is required to perform certain actions before food is released into the food dispenser through an opening in one end of the box. Rats must usually press a bar to obtain food; pigeons must usually peck at a disk placed on the wall. Operant conditioning differs from classical conditioning in two ways:

First, there are differences in the types of response. In operant conditioning the response (bar pressing) that is learned is different from the response (eating) normally associated with the unconditioned stimulus (food). In classical conditioning the animal associates the original response (salivation) with new stimuli, whereas in operant conditioning the original stimulus (food) produces different responses.

Second, in operant conditioning the animal controls the presentation of food (the UCS in classical conditioning), and reinforcement is dependent upon its own behavior; if it presses the bar or pecks the disk it receives food. In classical conditioning the appearance of the unconditioned stimulus is entirely under the control of the experimenter. After the buzzer is sounded, the meat powder will be placed in the dog's mouth whether or not the dog responds to the buzzer.

There are two ways to measure the strength of an *operant*, that is, a response that the organism brings about by itself. One way is to record how frequently it occurs; the number of times that a rat presses the bar in a given time, for example, determines the operant rate of bar pressing. When the rate of response increases, the probability that the response will be repeated also increases; the higher the rate, the stronger the operant is. Another way to measure operant strength is to determine the total number of responses necessary in the absence of reinforcement before the animal returns to his preconditioned level of response. That is, the number of responses necessary for extinction indicates the strength of the operant.

SCHEDULES OF REINFORCEMENT

The way in which an operant is reinforced makes a difference in operant strength and also in the animal's behavior during learning. C. B. Ferster and B. F. Skinner (1957) discovered that some changes in learning depend upon how reinforcement is scheduled.

FIXED-INTERVAL REINFORCEMENT   On a fixed-interval schedule the animal is reinforced at specific intervals as long as it performs the operant at least once during the time period. For example, the experimenter may decide that he is going to reinforce the animal every minute, as long as it presses the bar once during that interval. It does not matter whether the animal presses the bar once or fifty times during the interval; the first response after the interval begins is sufficient to obtain total reinforcement. Under these conditions the response rate (the rate of bar pressing) will vary proportionally with the length of the interval between reinforcements. If the reinforcement interval is short, the animal will respond more often within it than if it were long. The behavior of the animal suggests that it adapts to the schedule and learns that reinforcement will occur after a given period of time. Typically it responds very little immediately after reinforcement but increases its response rate as time for the next reinforcement approaches. After reinforcement the pigeon walks around the box, pecks once in a while, and appears generally uninterested in the disk; as the end of the minute approaches, however, it becomes more interested in the disk and pecks rapidly just before the food is dropped into the box. After receiving the food, it again performs little work until the end of the interval is near. Fixed-schedule reinforcement can be likened to a salary, as opposed to a piece rate. The individual knows that a certain amount of work is required to earn his pay, but he can relax during the early part of the pay period and finish the required work with a burst of energy as pay day approaches.

On a schedule of fixed-interval reinforcement the operant is comparatively weak; the response rate is not very high, nor does it take many unreinforced trials to reach extinction. Motivation (drive) is held constant by withholding food from the animal, so that its body weight is maintained at a selected percentage below its normal weight on a free diet. The results are not the same when drive is significantly lowered. For example, an animal that is sated (has a low drive level) will not necessarily behave the same as if it were hungry. A person who has all the money that he needs is analogous to a sated rat; we do not expect high output when the reinforcement is more money. Although it is comparatively simple to control animal drive in an experimental environment, it is not simple to control the drives of human beings in "natural" environments. We shall see later that finding effective reinforcers is crucial to the successful application of operant-conditioning techniques to human problems.

FIXED-RATIO REINFORCEMENT   In fixed-ratio conditions the animal receives food only after it has made a predetermined number of responses. The experimenter may decide to reinforce the pigeon after it has pecked the disk ten times and only then. A great range of reinforcement ratios is possible, from reinforcement after each peck to reinforcement after a very large number of pecks. If the experimenter decides on a reasonable number of responses, the pigeon on a fixed-ratio schedule will show a steady and high pecking rate. Operant strength is greater than that on a fixed-interval schedule. The pigeon responds steadily and does not slow down as much after each reinforcement as does the pigeon on a fixed-interval schedule. More unreinforced trials are required for extinction. The analogy between piece rates and salaries is again appropriate. Fixed-ratio reinforcement is similar to piece-work pay rates, for which an employee works steadily to produce pay units.

VARIABLE-RATIO REINFORCEMENT   On a variable-ratio schedule the animal is reinforced for an average number of responses, perhaps every ten pecks, but it may receive reinforcement after two pecks one time, after twenty pecks another time, after five pecks the next time, and so on. Although the average reinforcement is consistent over a long series of responses, a consistent number of responses is not associated with each reinforcement. A rather remarkable change in behavior can be observed on a schedule of variable-ratio reinforcement. The animal responds at a very high rate, sometimes as rapidly as five times a second, a rate corresponding to the ticking of a watch, and it continues to respond a long while after reinforcement ceases. One minute of training may result in an operant strength that requires hours of extinction trials and thousands of unreinforced responses. Variable-ratio reinforcement results in greater operant strength than does either the fixed-interval or the fixed-ratio schedule.

Human habits of a compulsive type are analogous to habits learned under variable-ratio schedules. For instance, gambling may be highly resistant to extinction because one never knows when it will be reinforced; each throw of the dice and each pull of the "one-armed bandit" may bring reinforcement. Habits learned under such conditions, often called "inconsistent reinforcement," engender behavior patterns that are very difficult to eliminate.

REINFORCERS

Skinner has defined reinforcers by their effects instead of by their pleasantness or unpleasantness. *Any stimulus that increases the probability of a response is a reinforcer.* There are two types of reinforcing stimuli.

POSITIVE REINFORCERS A *positive reinforcer* is a stimulus that tends, *when added* to the learning situation, to increase the probability of a response. Food, water, and other stimuli that we generally associate with pleasantness or drive reduction are examples of positive reinforcers.

NEGATIVE REINFORCERS Any stimulus that tends to increase the probability of a response *when it is taken away* is a *negative reinforcer.* Generally, we think of negative reinforcers as obnoxious to the organism. Electric shock is a common negative reinforcer for animals. An animal will tend to repeat whatever behavior he is performing, like pressing a bar, if it is associated with cessation of electric shock. Conditioning to a negative reinforcer is called *avoidance learning.* The animal learns a response to avoid obnoxious stimuli.

PUNISHMENT

It is easy to confuse negative reinforcement with punishment, but they are not the same. Punishment is, for example, the administration of shock to an animal when it makes an *undesirable* response; ending the shock when it makes the *desired* response is negative reinforcement. Human beings often use punishment to train children (or adults, as in law enforcement). After a child performs an undesired behavior—eating with his fingers, for example—he is scolded or spanked. Negative reinforcers are not as commonly used. An example is forcing a child to stay in the corner until he apologizes for a misdeed. The most characteristic alternative in human training is the application of positive reinforcers; when a child eats with his fork he is praised.

Findings on the use of punishment indicate that a response cannot be eliminated any more rapidly through punishment than when it is not used. Only unreinforced trials (extinction) result in permanent weakening of a response. Punishment suppresses a response so that it is not available for un-reinforced trials; consequently extinction cannot take place. Emotional arousal frequently accompanies punishment and tends to suppress other responses beside the one for which the individual is being punished; this result is not desirable if new responses are to be learned. Punishment may, however, be helpful in practical situations. We can use the period of response suppression after punishment to reinforce responses that are more desirable, or we can hold a certain response at low strength by continuing punishment indefinitely. In the latter instance occasional punishment is as effective as is frequent punishment.

SECONDARY REINFORCEMENT

According to the concept of *secondary reinforcement*, a stimulus that was not originally reinforcing may gain reinforcement value when it is associated with a stimulus that is reinforcing. For example, if, while a rat is learning to press a bar for food, a light comes on in the food bin whenever food is introduced, the presence of the light alone will become reinforcing after a certain time. The reinforcing properties of the light may be demonstrated by extinguishing the bar-pressing response in darkness and then presenting the light alone when the rat presses the bar. Increased bar pressing will follow reintroduction of the light, demonstrating that the light has taken on reinforcing characteristics. Many different stimuli may become reinforcing in similar fashion.

Money is an example of a secondary reinforcer in human behavior. It can be called a *generalized reinforcer* because it has gained secondary reinforcing characteristics from association with many primary reinforcers. A young child probably first learns the reinforcing value of money in association with something like candy. As he moves through life, he experiences many other reinforcing situations that are also associated with money. Money eventually becomes reinforcing in itself. Many kinds of behavior are performed in order to obtain money, even though it has no intrinsic reinforcement value.

STIMULUS DISCRIMINATION

Organisms learn specific kinds of behavior under specific stimulus conditions. Learning the appropriate conditions for a specific operant response is called "discrimination learning." Once a pigeon has learned to peck a disk in a Skinner box for reinforcement, the experimenter may choose to change the color of the disk from white to black. He may also decide that the pigeon is to be reinforced only when it pecks the white disk. The pigeon soon learns to peck only when the disk is white. The pecking response to white is reinforced and gains operant strength, whereas the pecking response to black is not reinforced and becomes extinct.

Stimulus discrimination can be readily observed in everyday life. A person approaching an electrically operated cigarette machine does not put his money in it if the lights are out, for putting his coins in the machine will not result in reinforcement. From previous experience he has learned to respond when the stimulus conditions indicate that reinforcement is available, that is, when the lights are on.

RESPONSE DIFFERENTIATION

Animals can also be taught to distinguish between responses in order to receive reinforcement, through a process called *behavior shaping*. For instance, the experimenter may decide that he wants the rat to press a bar and then to turn in a complete circle to the right before receiving reinforcement. To teach the animal this behavioral series he reinforces each step as it approximates the final complex act. At first he may reinforce the animal when it looks toward the bar (reinforcement is accomplished by pressing a manual switch to the feed box); next he reinforces the animal when it moves toward the bar, then when it touches the bar, then when it presses the bar, and so on until the rat has performed the entire series before receiving reinforcement. The experimenter has thus "shaped" the rat's behavior. We shall examine the application of behavior shaping to human problems shortly.

Behavior Therapy and Operant Conditioning

Operant techniques are particularly useful in instilling new habits (Bandura, 1969; Krasner and Ullman, 1965; Ullman and Krasner, 1965). The primary aim is to develop adaptive habits, rather than to eliminate undesirable ones, but the latter may be extinguished in the process through lack of reinforcement. S. H. Lovibond (1963) has discussed positive conditioning to eliminate nocturnal enuresis (bed wetting). A bell connected to a special blanket rings when the first drop of urine causes an electric circuit to close. The patient is awakened by the bell, so that repeated pairings of bladder distention and awakening occur; eventually, the child awakens when his bladder is distended, and he is able to go to the bathroom.

BEHAVIOR SHAPING

Behavior shaping has already been discussed in connection with the learning of response differentiation in animals. The same principles have been applied to developing adaptive response patterns in human beings. Most of this work is being done with children who show severe behavioral disturbances like autism and mental retardation. For some time educators have been intuitively "shaping" behavior by reinforcing progressive steps in the learning of complex tasks, but recently behaviorally oriented therapists have refined the method so that it is more effective and more widely applicable. Some of the most important refinements have resulted from clearer understanding of the importance of, first, speedy rewards; second, proper timing of rewards for small segments of behavior that approximate the desired goal; third, consistency and accuracy in rewards; and, fourth, rewarding desired behavior and not rewarding undesired behavior. Behavior therapists have studied patterns of behavior very carefully and have analyzed them into sequences that contribute to the final pattern. The knowledge of each behavioral step ensures that the child will not be given too difficult a task; consequently his learning experience will be consistently associated with positive reinforcement, and learning will acquire generally positive meanings.

An example of work with mentally retarded children (Ball, 1966) will serve to clarify the technique of behavior shaping. The children were of school age but lacked most of the adaptive skills that we normally associate with children that age. Most were not toilet-trained, had minimal if any capability of speech, could not follow verbal directions, could not dress or undress themselves, and frequently offered serious behavior problems. Although specific tasks can be taught to such children more often the results are a general "habit of success" and more positive attitudes toward attacking new problems. The general approach consists of several steps but the basic principle of consistent reinforcement is always in force.

STEP ONE   The first goal is to teach the child that the attendant (therapist) is a source of reinforcement, that he has "good things." This step is analogous to the rat's learning that food (reinforcement) is available in the Skinner box.

The child is brought into the room, where the attendant meets him with a variety of rewards (like candy and toys). Rewards are given without accompanying demands until the child clearly recognizes the therapist as a source of such rewards. Verbal signals like "Good boy," always accompany concrete rewards, in order to establish secondary-reinforcement value for such verbal cues. Associating words with primary reinforcement lends reinforcing characteristics to the words. Eventually they can be used alone as the reinforcing agent.

STEP TWO   Next the child learns that he must do something in order to receive reinforcement. He is given commands that the therapist knows he can follow, and he is reinforced if he carries them out. For instance, the therapist may say, "Come to me." If the child moves at all in the therapist's direction he is reinforced. At the end of this stage the child is generally aware that he must comply with requests before he will be reinforced.

This step also has a clear parallel in animal experiments. Animals that have been used frequently in behavior-shaping experiments quickly learn that when they are placed in the Skinner box they must do something to receive food. In hopes of receiving food, they will immediately begin random movements or behavior that they have learned previously.

STEP THREE   It is necessary to teach disturbed children to pay attention. The therapist must have the child's full attention when he teaches more complex tasks in later stages of training. To build attention he may flash a light beam on the wall and say, "Look," reinforcing the child when he gazes at the light. The child is instructed to attend to a series of objects in the room until he pays consistent attention to the therapist's directions.

STEP FOUR Toilet behavior is frequently one of the last kinds of behavior taught to the mentally retarded child. He must first be taught to sit down and to remain seated for a period of time. Teaching appropriate responses to the requests "Sit down" and "Stay there" is the primary goal in the fourth stage. Clear nonverbal signals are used along with verbal commands. For instance, the therapist holds the palm of his hand facing the child and says, "Stay there." Or he shakes his head "no" if the child starts to rise. The therapist may mildly restrain the child who starts to stand up, but the main emphasis is on extending the time that the child remains seated by reinforcing him initially for sitting several seconds and expecting him to stay for increasingly longer periods before each subsequent reinforcement.

STEP FIVE The goal of step five is to teach the child to undress himself. A large T-shirt is used because it is easier for the child to take off. The therapist may begin by placing only one arm in the shirt and telling the child, "Take off your shirt." If the child is only partially successful in removing his arm, he is rewarded, and the trial starts again. Rewards are withheld in subsequent trials until he progresses farther toward removing his shirt. Through successive steps the therapist thus works to the point at which the child can remove his shirt completely in response to a verbal command. The task is considered to have been mastered when the child will take off his shirt in other locations beside the training room. That is, the behavior must be generalized to other stimulus situations.

STEP SIX More complex behavior becomes the focus of training: complete undressing, dressing, toilet behavior, and so on. The only limitations on shaping further skills are those that result from the child's limited physical or mental capacity. For example, a child whose motor coordination is too poor to permit him to lace his shoes is not expected to learn that skill; a child who is unable to grasp the concept of numbers is not expected to learn subtraction.

The behavior that we have discussed requires a very low level of competence and perhaps such training does not appear to be a great therapeutic breakthrough. Yet, compared to the original abilities of these children, who had for a long time been considered hopelessly committed to custodial care, there was a vast improvement; their lives within the institution were enhanced, and it was also possible to save considerable staff time. It is even possible that children with somewhat greater capacities can learn sufficient skills to make placement in foster homes and more satisfying lives feasible.

REINFORCEMENT PROGRAMS

Group programs based on operant conditioning have been developed (Ayllon and Azrin, 1968). Early results suggest that they may be widely applicable. We shall examine two such programs: one in an adult mental hospital, the other for educationally handicapped children.

THE MENTAL HOSPITAL EXPERIMENT A program based on operant conditioning principles for mental-hospital patients who had not responded to normal treatment and consequently had very low expectations for improvement was established (Schaefer, 1966; Schaefer and Martin, 1969).

Experimental findings about chimpanzees served as the basis for choosing reinforcers in the hospital. It had been demonstrated with the animals that "tokens" can acquire secondary reinforcing value if they are first associated with primary reinforcers. The chimps could receive tokens for performing prescribed acts; the tokens could in turn be used in food-vending machines, where bananas and other fruit were available. Not only did the chimpanzees learn to work for tokens; it was also not long before they learned to hoard tokens when they were not hungry and to "live on their savings" later. The similarity between their behavior with tokens and man's behavior with money is striking and has led to the term "token economies."

In the mental hospital, it was assumed that most patients would generalize their money habits to tokens—or at least that they would quickly learn the secondary-reinforcing characteristics of tokens. The initial aims of the program were to promote living habits necessary for hospital life: bathing, taking medicine, making beds, household chores, and so on. The ultimate aim was socialization that would enable the patients to return to their communities.

Before the program began the nursing staff underwent training in operant conditioning, the difficulties associated with establishing appropriate rewards, the problems in analyzing behavior, and so on. The general goals for all patients, as well as specific goals for individual patients, were discussed.

The program was launched one morning at 8:00, when the patients were expected to arise. Nurses passed through the ward depositing one token on each empty bed and returned five minutes later to deposit a token on each bed that was made. When the patients arrived for breakfast they were admitted to the dining room for the price of one token; those without tokens were turned away, and the doors were closed to those who were more than a half-hour late. As the investigators expected, most patients had done something to earn tokens by lunch time.

The general plan was to build adaptive behavior through reinforcement and to extinguish bizarre ("crazy") behavior through nonreinforcement. A variety of reinforcers beside food was used. If the patients wished to sleep on comfortable beds with sheets, rather than on minimum-standard army cots, they were required to pay rental fees in tokens. In part of the dining room there were tables with tablecloths and china; the rest had tin plates and no coverings for the table. Extra tokens were required for placement at the better-furnished tables. Shopping privileges and other rewards were also available for tokens.

In setting up the program the investigators found that terms frequently used by the hospital staff—for instance, "good personal hygiene"—meant different things to different people and were not sufficient to indicate the precise kinds of behaviors that they wished to elicit. To make a term like "good personal hygiene" more meaningful, they had to be quite specific: no dirt on the insteps or heels, no dirt on legs and knees, no body odor, no residue in the navel or under fingernails, neat and recent shaves for men, nicely combed hair, clean underwear daily, and so on.

Individual problems were also dealt with in the program. Hallucinations were a problem with some of the patients. The staff found that the contents of the hallucinations were largely determined by the other people present and the feedback that patients received from them. It therefore seemed wise to let the patient hallucinate in the presence of different people so that consistent patterns of hallucinations would not be established. The problem was approached by inviting the patient to hallucinate in front of a staff member and paying him one token for every minute that he hallucinated. Thereafter he was told that he could pay for the privilege of hallucinating elsewhere at the price of three tokens a minute. Encouragement of hallucinations was gradually diminished, and the cost of hallucinating elsewhere was constantly increased. Finally the patient was told that his discharge would depend upon the absence of hallucinations outside a specified period. In the final stages of his hospitalization he was told that everyone has odd thoughts and sensations at times but that he should not describe them to random audiences on random occasions. The patient learned that there are appropriate people to whom to report unusual sensations—professionals. By reporting his sensations only to a therapist he could reduce the chances that his abnormal functioning would be disruptive outside the hospital.

The case of Mr. G. furnishes an example of such treatment of individual difficulties.

THE CASE OF MR. G.

Mr. G. had been at Patton [the hospital] for five years before he came to the program. He was a seclusive, anti-social, evasive, sarcastic person, but in good contact with reality. He didn't have any friends, either among patients or employees, because as the staff put it, "his tongue was too bitter." One of his verbal idiosyncracies was to reflect back every question asked of him with a new question. He also began every verbal response with a proposition and made deductions. His sentences were often complex and he lost his listeners in a tangled web. He was put on a schedule in which he could earn money only by pronouncing sentences which could be understood by the listener. He was also reinforced for starting conversations with other patients or staff members. Once these behaviors were established, they became self-reinforcing. The patient had previously refused to go to any recreational activities in the hospital, but now frequently goes to movies and dances. He also visits his parents as often as possible. He now can communicate with his fellow man and is being considered for discharge. (Schaefer, 1966, pp. 35–36)

THE ENGINEERED CLASSROOM   Another reinforcement program has been established for children with learning difficulties resulting from low intelligence, emotional disturbance, or specific perceptual deficiencies. Classrooms for these children are typically small, usually with fifteen or fewer students for each teacher and teacher's aide. The classroom is divided into two basic areas: one for tasks and one for reinforcement. The aim of the program is to establish work habits in the task area by reinforcing appropriate behavior; the children go to the reinforcement area after they have performed satisfactorily in the task area (Hewett, 1968; Hewett *et al.*, 1970).

Establishing suitable reinforcers for all the children was a major problem. It is critical that reinforcers be available for each child; limiting them to toys, candy, and other food has been found to be unnecessary in such programs. Reinforcers can be selected after observing children's spontaneous activities and recording those that are most frequent. Such activities are assumed to be reinforcing. For instance, if children prefer talking together, reading picture books, and coloring, the teacher places these activities on a "reinforcement menu" from which the child may select his reinforcement when he has performed satisfactorily in the task area. The "reinforcement menu" is always subject to change, according to which activities are selected most often. Activities that are rarely selected are replaced by high-frequency activities.

The task area has work desks and materials for different school tasks. Each child has an individual program, depending upon his level of competence. As long as he fulfills the teacher's expectations, which may be simply that he sit still for a short time or solve arithmetic problems, he will be reinforced at the end of each work period. Work periods are generally short, usually fifteen minutes or less; it is easier to keep the child's attention and motivation high during short periods in the task area.

The pupil's reinforcement is contingent upon his performance of tasks; this kind of program is sometimes called *contingency management*. The teacher, or contingent manager, performs several specific functions in directing the child's educational progress. One is evaluating the behavioral difficulties of each child: short attention span, aggressive behavior, and so on. He eliminates these difficulties by progressively building up opposing behavior through positive reinforcement. It is also the teacher's job to evaluate the child's achievement and to ensure that his tasks are geared to guarantee success and consequent reinforcement. Educational materials programmed to direct progress in small steps are available. The teacher's other primary function is to maintain a viable reinforcement menu through the procedures already described.

When a child does not perform adequately in the task area it is the teacher's responsibility to find out why. The task may be too difficult, the proper reinforcer may not be available, or the child may temporarily dislike a particular task at that time. In classes of emotionally disturbed children or those with many behavioral difficulties there is an established procedure for intervening in disruptive behavior. A child who is unable to work in the task area will be approached by the teacher in the following way:

1. Evaluate the level of work being asked of him. If inappropriate move to a lower level so that he may succeed.
2. If he is still unable to work, change the task.
3. If he is still unable to work, place him in an isolation booth partitioned off from the rest of the class so that he is not distracted. Provide a task in that area.
4. If he still cannot work, ask him to leave the room briefly until he feels he is able to work.
5. Send him to the principal's office if he is unable to work after returning to the room.
6. If he is still unable to work, ask him to go home for the remainder of the day and to return the next day when he is able to work.

The overall aims of this kind of program, beside teaching specific educational tasks, is to develop a positive attitude toward school work and the classroom situation. In a program of contingency management all learning is associated with positive reinforcement. The teacher takes full responsibility for a child's inability to learn; the child is never blamed for failure. Failure is considered to result from either improper reinforcement or choice of a task that is inappropriate or too difficult. The teacher should always have a clear idea of his goals for each child.

TEACHING MACHINES

A natural development from Skinner's work on operant conditioning is the use of machines to provide optimal learning environments. In fact, Skinner's work has stimulated the development of teaching machines constructed on the principles of operant conditioning. Two advantages are claimed for teaching machines: First, they offer individualized instruction that consistently follows the principles of good learning, and, second, they provide more time for the teacher to work with individual students. Part of the class can work with the machines while he works with the rest of the class.

Machines are constructed to provide immediate feedback and reinforcement of correct responses. Although the specified designs of machine vary, the basic procedures are the same. The student responds, answering a review question, for example, and his immediate reinforcement is being allowed to move on to the next question; if he is incorrect feedback is immediate. Academic material is presented in such a way as to maximize learning, in ordered levels of difficulty. Arranging the material in this fashion is called *programming*. Learning specialists write programs for arithmetic, English, spelling, and so on. The teacher selects a program for a particular student and starts him at a level at which he can succeed; then he moves in logical steps toward higher levels of achievement. The programs also incorporate generalization, interference, and the need for spaced review. Typically the child studies a short block of material and then systematically reviews what he has studied. Review usually takes the form of questions and answers and reinforcement and feedback are provided. The student progresses only when he has learned the previous material, and blank spots in his knowledge therefore do not occur.

Individuals can use teaching machines to fulfill their own needs or interests. A person who wishes to learn a subject may select the proper program and proceed on his own without entering a formal educational setting. Variants of teaching machines are increasingly being introduced, as part of self-improvement courses, into mental hospitals, vocational counseling, and homes. Any subject matter can be programmed, from the simplest reading to calculus, foreign languages, and the like.

RECAPITULATION

Skinner's laboratory work led to discovery of the principles of operant conditioning, which in turn led to techniques of behavior modification that have applications in education, mental health, and human adjustment generally. These approaches are producing results far beyond those produced by classical therapeutic methods applied to similar problems. Judging by the material that we have reviewed we believe that operant techniques hold definite promise for helping man to relate to himself and to others.

Not so clear, however, are the applications of operant conditioning to entire cultures and to man's relation to his culture. Skinner has described his vision of a utopian society in *Walden Two* (1948), speculating on the creation of certain humanistic values through the technology of operant conditioning.

At this point we shall turn from objective findings of learning research to the attempt to account for personality through learning theory.

THE LEARNING THEORY OF PERSONALITY

J. L. Dollard and N. E. Miller (1950) have used C. L. Hull's comprehensive theory of learning (1943) in interpreting personality concepts; more specifically they have tried to show how psychoanalytic concepts can be understood in terms of learning theory. Earlier in this chapter we examined constructs based on objective observation, constructs that are widely agreed upon by learning theorists. But learning theorists do not readily agree on what goes on *inside* the organism. Dollard and Miller's conceptualizations are only one example of the constructs offered to explain unobservable behavior. E. Hilgard (1956) has examined those of other learning theorists.

HYPOTHETICAL CONSTRUCTS

It is necessary to introduce some additional concepts from Hull's theory in order to understand Dollard and Miller's interpretation of personality.

MOTIVES

Human beings are born with primary drives like hunger, thirst, reactions to pain and cold, needs for oxygen and sex, and the need for a relatively constant temperature. The arousal of primary drives motivates the organism to action, and activities that reduce drive levels are reinforced. A basic tenet of Hull's theory is that drive reduction is necessary before learning can occur. Events associated with the reduction of primary drives may themselves assume the power of drives. Other people are almost always associated with reducing an infant's primary drives, and in the absence of people his need for food or warmth may be unfulfilled. The nearness of people (affiliation) thus becomes associated with drive reduction. Later in life a need for people, "need for affiliation," is seen. A child whose primary needs have been infrequently met in infancy may develop a very strong need for people because he has learned under conditions of high drive arousal. In later life his behavior will reflect this strong need, though the expression of it may be determined by other learning patterns. One person may behave in a fawning, helpless way, whereas another may become proficient in social skills like politeness, garrulity, and so on. Both show high needs for affiliation, but they have distinctly different personalities. Such learned (secondary) drives become increasingly frequent as the child grows older and begins to direct a larger portion of his own behavior.

Other social motives are learned from associations with either primary- or secondary-drive reduction. Although the reduction of primary drives is the basis for learning, behavior that satisfies secondary motives may account for many of the complex personality patterns observed in adults. These motives become reinforcing in themselves so that learning occurs when they are reinforced; that is, they become autonomous drives capable of directing behavior, even though the original primary drive with which they were associated is not reduced in the process.

THE THOUGHT PROCESSES

Thinking, reasoning, judgment, and conceptualization are internal responses that occur between presentation of stimuli and observable responses. These internal responses (thinking, etc.) have a great deal to do with human behavior and are the main basis for man's most adaptive capacities. Although some observed responses appear to be almost automatic, without thought intervening, they are often not the most adaptive responses. Many automatic responses result from "overlearning"; they are practiced until the internal responses (thinking) no longer reach awareness. Motor skills, for example, often become automatic through practice; the beginning typist thinks about where the fingers are placed on the keyboard and which one to move to the proper key, but when he becomes accomplished his fingers move automatically, and he is no longer aware of intervening thoughts. Although automatic responses are important in our lives, other behavior is most crucial to adaptation: specifically our abilities to plan and to predict future events.

Language helps to strengthen our thinking processes. Its symbols increase our power to generalize and free us from the immediate stimulus circumstances. If we are interviewing job applicants about whom we already have some knowledge from other people, for instance, our responses to the immediately observable stimuli are already partly determined. If a previous employer has called one of our applicants "lazy," we shall probably be less impressed by his vibrant social behavior or his remarks about how hard he works. The verbal symbol "lazy" allows us some independence of the immediate stimuli.

Verbal labels also enhance our ability to discriminate. Because we have verbal concepts for numbers we can distinguish between different monetary denominations, even though they are very similar in objective stimulus characteristics. A five-dollar bill and a one-dollar bill look quite similar, and a child may not be able to differentiate them. Once he learns number concepts, however, he has a tool to use and can discriminate easily between the two. No concrete stimuli are necessary, such as five separate bills, for us to differentiate many highly similar objects or events.

From this discussion it should be clear that language symbols can serve as cues for action, usually intervening between the stimulus and the observable response. Dollard and Miller apply the same principles of learning to thought processes as to learning on a simpler level.

ANTICIPATORY RESPONSES

Responses closely associated with the point of reinforcement tend to occur before they are actually stimulated; that is, they anticipate reinforcement. It is common, for example, to salivate before a juicy steak actually enters the mouth.

In order to increase our chances of positive outcomes we respond in ways that will prepare us for future possibilities. Much of our training as children involves anticipatory responses; dangerous situations, in particular, require them if we are to avoid painful or humiliating consequences. When driving a car we produce frequent small movements in the steering wheel to anticipate and prevent veering off to one side in oncoming traffic. We do not wait until the car actually veers before we make the response. In social situations we respond in anticipation of embarrassing or aggressive encounters. We may recognize a boisterous person who has over-imbibed and move to the other side of the room to avoid his potential insults.

PERSONALITY CHARACTERISTICS

Learning theorists have not developed new concepts to explain personality. Rather, they have applied established learning concepts to show how various personality characteristics may be learned. Human behavior (personality) is explained almost entirely on the basis of what one learns from interaction with the environment. The importance of the biological characteristics of the organism is not denied, but it is considered less in the development of personality.

AN INTERPRETATION OF PSYCHOLOGICAL CONFLICT

We shall now turn to examination of some psychoanalytic concepts that Dollard and Miller have explained in terms of learning theory.

FEAR AND AVOIDANCE LEARNING

The emotion of fear or its less well-defined psychological counterpart anxiety is of central importance in learning neurotic behavior patterns. Learning to avoid situations that arouse fear or anxiety often results in apparently irrational behavior, characteristic of neurosis. According to Freud, two features are the basis of neurotic patterns: unconscious material and psychological conflict. Dollard and Miller have attempted to explain both aspects in terms of learning theory. First, we shall examine the process by which material may become unconscious—in learning-theory terms, the process by which verbal labels become unavailable.

THE UNCONSCIOUS

There may be no verbal labels available for some stimuli. Before a child develops verbal ability he cannot label conflict situations, and therefore they remain unconscious. Similarly, an individual whose verbal facility is very limited will be unable to label many cues.

Verbal labels may also be missing because some experiences are not included in our language. Some drives, cues, and responses are, therefore, unconscious simply because verbal labels are not available for them at the time they are experienced. A young child may observe his parents quarreling angrily or even fighting yet have insufficient language facility to label what he sees. His observations are nevertheless likely to arouse a great deal of fear and avoidance behavior. Avoidance responses may later be generalized to other interpersonal relationships and may constitute a neurotic pattern.

Because he lacks verbal labels for such situations, he can not use the adaptive and discriminative properties of language, therefore he may not differentiate his parents' behavior from other people's behavior. His behavior may thus be over-generalized.

Even when verbal labels are available, material may become unconscious through *repression*. In psychoanalytic terms repression is a defense mechanism of the ego that prevents unacceptable impulses from entering consciousness. Dollard and Miller have explained it as an avoidance response negatively reinforced by the removal of anxiety. According to them, repression is active avoidance learning. Because of social training or frightening past experiences certain types of thoughts (conscious verbal symbols) may arouse anxiety. In our society, for instance, incest is frowned upon. If a child has incestuous thoughts he is likely to experience anxiety, which can be relieved when he stops thinking them. "Not thinking" is thus reinforced. The initial "not thinking" phase of repression is called *suppression*. A person actively "tells himself" to stop thinking certain things. When he stops his anxiety is dissipated, and he experiences relief. Most of us actively suppress some thoughts without harmful consequences, but suppression carried too far can develop into repression.

The next step in the process of repression is the development of anticipatory responses to dreaded thoughts. Such an anticipatory avoidance response may be called forth by cues related to the forbidden thoughts themselves. Stimuli associated with a boy's mother may draw forth an anticipatory response of "not thinking" about sex relations with her; as anxiety is then avoided, the anticipatory response is reinforced. The avoidance response becomes established so that incestuous thoughts do not enter the lad's awareness.

PSYCHOLOGICAL CONFLICTS

When drives oppose each other conflict exists. Primary drives may be pitted against each other; for example, hunger and pain may exist at the same time. A person in such conflict must achieve some sort of resolution: to eat and suffer pain or to avoid pain and not eat. It is quite likely that anxiety will result from such conflict. Primary and secondary drives may also conflict. The boy with incestuous thoughts, for example, has a primary sex drive, but he has learned that a family member is not an acceptable sexual partner, a secondary drive to avoid disapproval. Very strong anxiety may result from this sort of conflict, and strong demands may be made on the individual's capacity for adjustment. Two secondary drives may also be in conflict. A soldier facing an attacking enemy, for instance, may want to flee, but the learned drive to avoid "cowardice in the face of the enemy" is very strong and motivates him to hold fast (a conflict between a primary and learned drive). But the alternative of killing the enemy soldier may conflict with another learned drive based on the principle that "killing is a sin." Even though he resolved the first conflict he still finds himself in a situation of great anxiety that is very difficult to resolve.

Conflict situations in childhood are considered especially important for later psychological adjustment. In the first place, children have less verbal facility than do adults so that conflict is more likely to be unconscious (unlabeled). Children are quite dependent upon their parents and often cannot change their environments, so that conflicts in patterns of child rearing are often forced upon them. Further, children have not yet developed many skills for handling conflicts and are more likely to try solutions that are inadequate and do not resolve the conflict. Many parents do not recognize the demanding nature of a child's drives, which are more compelling because he has not yet learned the means of controlling them. A child may thus frequently be in conflict because unreasonable demands are made upon his impulse controls.

Dollard and Miller have listed childhood conflicts that arise during socialization. They have reinterpreted in terms of learning theory critical learning tasks first postulated in Freud's psychosexual stages of development.

Early childhood (Freud's oral stage) is a period of total dependence upon others for survival, a crucial period for acquiring secondary drives related to sociability and love. The association of people with primary drive reduction—feeding, warmth, comfort and so on—results in learned attitudes toward people in later life. The child may become pessimistic about others and may develop fears of being alone or anxiety about aspects of his dependence. At this early stage the child is also quite susceptible to unconscious conflicts because he is still nonverbal.

In the next developmental stage (the anal stage in psychoanalysis) training in cleanliness and the management of elimination are emphasized. Strong emotions are often aroused when parents impose their wishes on the child. As a consequence his attitudes toward authority, neatness, conformity, and resistance may become firmly established at this stage.

In a similar way the child learns sexual values at the next stage of development (the phallic stage). Conflicts between learned social values (conscience) and the sex drive can arouse emotions and lead to repression of the conflict; the repressed material may affect later sexual functioning. This phase is made even more difficult by the facts that many sexual activities are poorly labeled, especially by children, and that talking about them is frequently forbidden. Sexual conflicts are thus more likely to be repressed and therefore to disrupt later adjustment.

NEUROTIC BEHAVIOR

Dollard and Miller have explained neurotic behavior as the learning of avoidance responses to emotionally arousing situations. Avoidance responses turn the neurotic from goals stimulated by normal drives, so that alternative behavior does not occur and cannot be reinforced. The neurotic has difficulty in learning new approaches to situations. Though he often makes tentative attempts at resolution, he almost inevitably retreats to an old but ineffective method. He may appear "stupid" because repression results in inability to use his thought processes to solve problems effectively. He is less able to distinguish one situation from another, and extinction of unrealistic fears is thus very difficult. A vicious cycle of inadequate responses followed by anxiety increases his unrealistic fears. Because he is prevented from finding satisfactory solutions he often behaves in maladaptive ways that further heighten his drive level—and his misery. Although psychological defense mechanisms (see Chapter 5) can partially reduce fear, they cannot eliminate it; they themselves are extremely difficult to replace in the neurotic because they prevent attempts at other more effective responses, which cannot therefore be learned.

The neurotic find himself in a trap: He is dissatisfied with his behavior, yet he cannot change it. Instead, his fear rises and more unrealistic behavior complicates the total pattern.

CONCLUSIONS

Probably the clearest thing that can be said about learning therapy is that it is based on a large body of empirical research. Adding to our confidence in the conclusions from this research is the fact that many observations have been verified and are readily repeatable. On the other hand, though we have not gone into detail here, learning theorists do not agree upon which hypothetical internal factors account for learning. This disagreement raises problems for those who apply research results. Two of the techniques that we have examined—anxiety flooding and systematic desensitization—appear to operate on exactly opposite principles, yet the success of both is explained by learning concepts. Anxiety flooding is interpreted as extinction and systematic desensitization as counterconditioning; the one technique is designed to arouse maximum anxiety, the other to reduce it. Clearly, more research is necessary to explain why such very different approaches are both so effective.

Behavior therapists have been very willing, even eager, to base their techniques on methodologically rigorous research. Because the results have been encouraging, the acceptance of behavior techniques has been widening, and they are being applied to many adjustment problems. Behavior therapies claim much higher percentages of "cures" than do adherents of more orthodox techniques of psychotherapy, but it remains to be demonstrated that these initial gains can be maintained through continued use of the techniques. Also the specific effects of these techniques remain to be separated from the effects of other factors. For example, is it the juxtaposition of heirarchies with relaxation that makes the difference, or is it relaxation itself, focusing on the problem, or what? Research on this problem is being carried out at present, and studies are being designed to separate the non-specific effects from the effects of therapeutic techniques.

Learning theory is not a theory of personality, but the application of learning concepts can help to explain how people become what they are. New constructs have not been proposed to help describe the person as an organized whole. This heavy emphasis on learning is objectionable to theorists who think that the uniform unfolding of biological processes contributes greatly to the development of personality. Other psychologists criticize the notion that secondary drives are learned through association with reduction of primary drives. Much research suggests that many of the so-called "secondary" drives may themselves be innate. Curiosity, problem solving, competence, and so on may not have to be learned; only the specific forms that they take may result from learning.

SUMMARY

The primary focus of this chapter has been on techniques of behavior modification that have been derived from learning concepts and related research. These techniques are comparatively new and appear to be major advances in dealing with problems of personal adjustment.

We first examined the basic assumptions of behavior therapists: that neurosis is a set of maladaptive habits, rather than a sickness; that the individual's behavior is determined by past experiences and that, as he is not to blame for his responses, guilt and shame are inappropriate; that as long as the patient cooperates the responsibility for change lies with the therapist; and that the behavior therapist attacks beliefs and values that cause the individual suffering.

Behavior-modification techniques have been developed from the concepts of classical conditioning. Pavlov's experimental findings provide the background for these techniques. The association of fear (or anxiety) with particular kinds of stimuli engenders the major adjustment difficulty for most people. Counterconditioning techniques are one way of reducing fear responses; they represent an attempt to weaken the bonds between anxiety and the stimuli that produce it by encouraging substitute responses like relaxation, assertion, and sexual arousal.

Aversive techniques are used primarily to break undesirable habits like alcoholism and homosexuality. An aversive stimulus (shock) is administered in association with the stimulus (alcohol or a picture of a nude male) in order to condition an anxiety response to that stimulus—a procedure exactly the reverse of counterconditioning.

Extinction techniques are based on the principle that a response will be weakened if it is not reinforced. Negative practice is a procedure through which an undesirable habit (stuttering, for example) is purposely encouraged but not reinforced and therefore extinguished. Anxiety flooding, or implosive therapy, evokes maximum anxiety without reinforcing it, which should lead to extinction of the response.

Another group of behavior-modification techniques has been developed from Skinner's work on operant conditioning. The basic premise of such conditioning is that a reinforced response is more likely to recur, and one that is not reinforced is less likely to recur. In behavior shaping, operant conditioning is applied to seriously disturbed (mentally retarded or autistic) children. The desired behavior is approached step by step; each nearer approximation to it is reinforced until the entire behavior complex is learned. Operant procedures are also applied as reinforcement programs, or token economies, in group settings. One important application of operant techniques is the teaching machine. Educational material is programmed to take advantage of principles of reinforcement, rapid feed back, and so forth to provide individual instruction and to free the teacher for more attention to individual pupils.

Dollard and Miller have applied learning concepts to the understanding of personality, reinterpreting Freud's psychoanalytic concepts in learning terms and thus bridging the gap between learning and dynamic theories. Their interpretation of psychological conflict and neurotic behavior is the portion of their work most relevant to problems of adjustment.

I. ROLE THEORY
   A. Introduction
   B. Concepts in Role Theory
      1. Role
      2. Role enactment
      3. Variables important to role enactment
      4. Uses of role theory
   C. Cognitive Strain as a Substitute for Anxiety
      1. The mythic nature of anxiety
      2. A model of cognitive strain
      3. Application of the model to schizophrenic thinking
      4. An eclectic approach to treatment
   D. Concluding Remarks
II. EXPERIMENTAL SOCIAL INNOVATIONS
   A. Introduction
   B. A Model
      1. Definition
      2. Naturalism
      3. Innovation
      4. Comparison
      5. Context
      6. Evaluation
      7. Responsibility
      8. Cross-disciplinary approach
   C. Phases
      1. Planning
      2. Action
      3. Evaluation
      4. Dissemination
   D. An Innovative Program in a Mental Hospital
      1. The alternative program
      2. Experimental problems
      3. Results
      4. New hypotheses

Summary

8

The Social-Psychological View

SARBIN'S ROLE THEORY

INTRODUCTION

According to role theory, adjustment is a function of the individual's attempts to understand his environment, a cognitive activity, and his ability to behave according to his social statuses. How well he enacts the roles of student, boyfriend, football player, and son, for instance, and his success in establishing a social identity through the performance of these roles largely determine the effectiveness of his adjustment. If an individual deviates significantly from the role behavior expected of him, he is likely to be evaluated negatively by those around him. Depending upon the setting and the degree of his deviation, negative sanctions may follow. For example, a college freshman who has come from a rural area to a sophisticated urban university may on his first date in the city pick up baked chicken in his fingers and devour it in his customary way. If his date has been raised in the city and learned that it is impolite to eat baked chicken with the fingers, she may refuse to go out with him again.

More serious consequences may be incurred by a person who violates accepted norms for communication. The individual who communicates that he is in direct contact with God and hears His voice telling him to carry out certain acts is likely to cause shock and disbelief in everyday settings. But he may receive praise and reinforcement in certain religious circles. In the everyday setting it is likely that he will be directed to mental health workers and possibly be committed to a mental hospital. In the religious setting he may become a leader or gain status. T. R. Sarbin's analysis of such behavior does not rely upon "mentalistic" explanations (involving id, ego, and superego) or on explanations in terms of mental illness (schizophrenia, paranoia, and so on). Instead, he has argued that a valid understanding of behavior must be based on "naturalistic" concepts with observable empirical referents and on careful analysis of the total circumstances in which behavior occurs.

According to role theory, stress is a cognitive reaction to perceptions that diverge from beliefs, expectations, and the like. The divergence results in cognitive strain, which in turn leads to behavior aimed at its reduction. Although such behavior is adaptive in the sense that it reduces "strain," it may be considered deviant by others; when exaggerated it is often considered symptomatic of mental illness in our society. To analyze this aspect of human behavior Sarbin has offered a cognitive-strain model with which deviant acts that are otherwise accounted for by ephemeral agents within the individual (mental illness, psychic entities) can be examined.

Role theory bridges the gap between the constructs of sociology and of psychology. The interaction of the individual with his environment is the primary focus; the isolated study of the individual per se has no place in role theory. A person's conduct can always be at least partly understood through the effects created by other people—either through direct interaction, previous teaching, or imagined presence. The social environment must thus always be taken into account in efforts to understand behavior. On the other hand, role theory does not deny those aspects of the individual that cannot be readily observed: thinking, problem solving, emotions, and so on. The terms used to describe these phenomena are, however, anchored in observable behavior (reports, questionnaires, adjective check lists, ratings, and so on) (Sarbin & Allen, 1968).

CONCEPTS IN ROLE THEORY

The metaphors of role theory have been borrowed from the drama. A person is said to act "as if" certain conditions are present. For example, the person on the stage acts as if he were Hamlet. The word "role" is intended to denote the conduct associated with certain "parts" or social positions, rather than with the particular players who read or recite the "parts." The focus is on the parts taken by real people as they attempt to adjust to their imperfect societies. Investigation must therefore encompass the entire scope of a role: social requirements, other people involved, and the person enacting the role.

As with any metaphor there is always a danger of "reification," that is, of dropping the "as if" and treating the term literally. To "reify" the terms of role theory would involve assuming that role theorists find people insincere in their behavior, believe them simply to be "playing" roles in the same sense as do the actors on a stage. This implication is certainly not the one that role theorists wish to convey. The professional football player, for example, usually enacts his role very seriously. He expends a great deal of physical and emotional energy in fulfilling expectations of his performance. Although role conduct is usually in earnest, it is also true that the degree of sincerity associated with different performances varies.

ROLE

The central concept *role* is defined as a group of behaviors agreed upon by a collectivity of individuals as appropriate to a particular position or status in society. For example, the role of student may entail attending class, taking lecture notes, studying, taking examinations, and so on. Furthermore, qualities and attitudes like "seriousness," "brightness," and "questioning" are also imputed to the student role. Their presence is deduced from behavior.

The role theorist emphasizes performances—"enactments"—and examines the factors contributing to their appropriateness and conviction.

Individuals are constantly shifting roles in their daily activities; according to the setting and time, some roles are more important than are others. In its simplest form determining what role to enact involves evaluation of external and internal stimuli through cognitive activity. The individual attempts to understand the significance of such stimuli, which leads him to decide upon the most appropriate role. Once the decision to enact a particular role has been made, various kinds of skill and knowledge are brought into play for the performance. The effectiveness of enactment depends upon many variables, including the individual's understanding of the required role behavior, his ability to exhibit it, others' responses to his conduct, and so on. Sarbin has investigated specific roles by positing, in understandable and measurable terms, variables that may affect role enactment.

ROLE ENACTMENT

The overt behavior and the attitudes associated with a specific role are called "role enactment." After a person has evaluated his setting and determined which role he will enact, he performs those activities that he thinks are appropriate to the role. It is at this point that other people judge the appropriateness and conviction of his performance. In keeping with the empirical orientation of role theory, role enactment is usually taken as the dependent variable in experimental study. That is, the quality of role enactment is studied in relation to other variables that modify it. For instance, an investigator might try to determine the effects of intelligence (a role skill) on enactment of the role of college student. Students with varying levels of intelligence could be compared on the basis of their grade-point averages.

In everyday life the effectiveness or appropriateness of role enactment is commonly assessed through global judgments. For instance, an instructor is likely to judge those students whose behavior most closely matches his ideas of "good student" as "good students." His total impression of their motor and verbal behavior determines his judgment of the quality of their role enactment. In a global assessment the judge (or audience) is not neutral but assesses performance in terms of his own expectations of the role.

Role enactment may also be assessed by codifying the behavior and attitudes that define appropriateness. For the student role a list of qualities and attitudes like "interest," "questioning," "brightness," and so on and a list of behavior, like classroom test scores, intelligence test scores, term-paper grades, and so on might be selected as appropriate by a faculty body. To determine the effectiveness of an individual's role enactment, a judge (or judges) evaluates the degree to which these attitudes, qualities and behaviors are present in his role enactment. The judge is to take a neutral stance in observing and reporting the degree to which the performances match the criteria agreed upon.

VARIABLES IMPORTANT TO ROLE ENACTMENT

Several variables influence the accuracy of role performance; each of them may be important to personal satisfaction. These variables are not necessarily independent, and they often overlap in certain roles. One variable may be more important in one role than in another, depending upon the types of behavior expected and the environmental conditions for enactment.

These variables will be discussed here in the order in which they generally come into play from the time that a person assumes a role until he has completed his enactment. The role of "college student" serves to exemplify the effects that each variable may have on the convincingness and effectiveness of role enactment.

ROLE LOCATION

The act of locating oneself in the role system, of determining which role (pattern of conduct) is appropriate, is an important determiner of successful social behavior. Role location is a cognitive activity, the success of which is dependent upon the individual's attention to external and internal cues. Cues from the environment and cues from cognitive (thought) and physiological processes help to locate the roles of the other (or others) and in turn, roles for oneself. Role-location cues include posture, complex overt activities, physical appearance and manner, gait, utterances, and so on. The individual's degree of sensitivity and accuracy in recognizing what cues belong to what roles others take largely determine how effective he is in determining what role is appropriate for him to enact in response.

In the process of role location the person seeks answers to the questions "Who is he?" "Who are you?" "Who am I?" and "What is expected of me?" In Chapter 4 we noted that patients labeled "schizophrenic" showed little ability to label accurately stick figures meant to convey internal dispositions. As a consequence we speculated that these individuals had difficulty in establishing proper reciprocal roles during social interaction. Their behavior was therefore judged inappropriate or "crazy."

College students constantly scan their environment for role-location cues. Before the instructor enters the classroom a student may be engaged in conversation with a friend, but when the instructor appears in the front of the room a role shift from "friend" to "student" occurs. The person's behavior changes accordingly, and he is more likely to enact the student role convincingly. Those who fail to make this shift are judged by the instructor to be poor or disinterested students; if effective enactment of the student role is related to their personal goals, their adjustment may be threatened as a result.

SELF-ROLE CONGRUENCE

In role theory the self is defined as the referent for the pronouns "I" and "me," the sum of the characteristics that a person attributes to himself. It is determined by the residue from past and present interactions with objects and events. Characteristics of the self may be measured by common personality inventories, which usually take the form of "I" statements (to be answered "true or false"): "I am a happy person," "I like strange and unusual things," and so on. Or the self can be defined operationally, from the results of an adjective list on which the subject checks off those adjectives that he thinks describe him.

Once an individual has established the role that he is to enact on the basis of another's behavior, role location, his own characteristics partly determine whether or not he will enact the role and how well. If he finds the role unsuited to most of the characteristics he considers to be himself, he is likely to reject it and to search for a substitute. For instance, the student who believes that all relationships should be on an intimate personal basis may reject the role of "obedient student" expected by a professor who believes in respect for authority, age, knowledge, and so on. He will then seek an alternative role more in keeping with his own characteristics: "rebel" or "dropout," for example.

If a person's characteristics match the requirements of a particular role he will probably be motivated to perform that role. Self-role congruence is the motivational variable in role theory; when a person's description of himself matches the characteristics of a given role, he is said to have a liking for, a propensity toward, or a preference for the role. And, other factors being equal, a more convincing role enactment results when role requirements are in harmony with personal characteristics.

The student role requires certain kinds of general behavior: studying, attending lectures, taking notes, expressing interest in new topics, and so on. A person who describes himself as studious, attentive, interested in new things, and so on will probably reveal high self-role congruence in the student role. His liking for the role will probably lead to more effective enactment of it.

ROLE EXPECTATIONS

During the socialization process the individual learns what kinds of behavior are expected of people in various social positions. Role expectations are collections of cognitions—beliefs, subjective assessments of probabilities, and bits of knowledge—that specify the appropriate conduct for those occupying particular positions. In the enactment of specific roles certain kinds of behavior are omitted, others inhibited, and others included. Social groups, as well as individuals, have fairly clear behavioral expectations of given roles. The young man who ate his baked chicken with his fingers would have benefited from fuller knowledge of role expectations associated with city table manners.

Although most roles are accompanied by expectations in a given culture, many idiosyncratic expectations modify general roles. The individual or the person judging his conduct may have specific expectations. The professor who expects students to be "obedient" as well as interested, etc., for instance, further refines the ways in which one must enact the student role if he is to receive positive evaluations from that professor. The student whose expectations are similar to those of his professor is more likely to be judged a good student than a student who has different expectations.

The observer may make his expectations clear through verbalizations, or he may communicate them through nonverbal gestures: facial grimaces, posturing, and so on. In a seminar, for instance, the instructor may state clearly that he expects students to enter into discussion and to offer their own ideas on the topics to be presented. By silence and questioning glances around the group, he can also communicate the expectation that they, rather than only he, will take an active part.

Role expectations come into play as role location is being completed. Role behavior is determined partly by the individual's belief about the appropriate actions for the chosen role.

ROLE SKILLS

An individual who enacts a role has the task of fulfilling related expectations in the best way that he can. The effectiveness of his performance depends upon the relevant skills at his disposal. When other variables are held constant, the effectiveness of role enactment can be accounted for by differences in role skills. Role skills, like other skills, are combinations of native endowment and learning. They may be either cognitive (knowing) or motor skills, and they may have either wide applications in many roles or very specific application in certain roles.

GENERAL ROLE SKILLS   are useful in many social interactions. The individual who is sensitive to the behavior of others is more accurate in role location and thus more effective in choosing appropriate reciprocal roles. Individuals also vary in the general motor skills that they use in assuming appropriate postures, facial expressions, and so on for specific roles. With a higher level of general skills the individual can perform a wider variety of roles flexibly and effectively. The unfortunate individual who suffers from cerebral palsy has obvious difficulties in carrying out many social roles effectively.

MANY ROLES ALSO REQUIRE SPECIFIC COGNITIVE AND MOTOR SKILLS,   varying from manual dexterity in the typist to verbal dexterity in the poet. The enactment of a specific role is more effective when the actor has a command of the specific role skills required.

The college student who takes comprehensive notes, develops effective study habits, can concentrate on his work, has facility with manipulating verbal symbols, and so on is more likely to enact the student role successfully because he has developed role-specific skills. General role skills—pleasing the professor, relating well to other students, coordinating the student role with such other important roles as son, employee, and boyfriend—may also be helpful in the student role.

Role skills come into play after the individual has located himself in the role system, decided that the role is sufficiently congruent with his own characteristics, and brought forth his expectations for that role. The effectiveness with which he fulfills role expectations is determined partly by the level and appropriateness of the skills at his command.

ROLE DEMANDS

When the person has correctly located the status of another, has established the role that he is to enact, and has developed a set of role expectations to facilitate interaction, the choices open to him have been reduced from near infinity to a small number. Additional features of the situation may further limit them and must be taken into account. They are called "role demands" and are usually implicit. Even so, they may be more important than other more obvious factors in modifying ongoing behavior. In other contexts they have been called "recognition of social values or mores" and "propriety norms." In fact, the silent operation of these demands may dictate a role choice contrary to the one that would have been made otherwise. Norms for modesty, communication, control of aggression, face saving, and so forth nearly always have some effects on role enactment. Violation of these norms usually leads to negative reinforcement; a person therefore usually enacts a role in accordance with the norms. In psychological experiments, for instance, it has been shown that subjects tend to confirm investigators' hypotheses as they perceive them. They respond to the silent demand for "cooperative experimental subject" (see Chapter 4) in hopes of furthering the aims of science. But what happens in fact is misinterpretation of the results. The investigator believes that his experimental manipulations have caused the results when in reality the subjects' responses to implicit expectations were the determining factors.

In enacting the student role an individual may not speak up in class even though the professor has encouraged this behavior. Role enactment is modified by a norm implicit among peers: "Exhibiting one's knowledge in class is a form of showing off." The professor may interpret the silence as evidence of disinterest, apathy, hostility, or the like, and as a consequence he may eliminate class discussion or punish students.

Role demands come into play during role enactment. Their effects upon a specific role vary with the setting and the cultural norms invoked. For instance, a student may not ask a professor to clarify a point during class because he does not want to embarrass the professor (or perhaps himself), yet after class he may embellish the student role by requesting clarification.

THE REINFORCING PROPERTIES OF THE AUDIENCE

In role theory the term "audience" is not limited to other people whose function is only to listen or observe; rather, it implies that role enactment is the object of the attention of one or more other people whose presence may be either objective or imagined, contemporary or remote. An audience is therefore always present either in the flesh or in imagination.

The audience serves several functions. First, it furnishes cues to the actor about his actual performance. Changes in facial expression and posture provide cues that may cause the actor to change the quality or direction of his enactment. The audience may also serve as a source of social reinforcement by providing positive or negative feedback through gestures and vocalizations. The therapist who listens to his patient intently, for example, is encouraging further enactment of the same behavior. Another function of the audience is to maintain behavior over a period of time. That is, an individual performs his roles in ways that meet the expectations of his audience. The delinquent who has developed specific role behavior but wishes to change it, may find that changing is extremely difficult in his customary environment because of the expectations of others. It may be necessary for him to change neighborhoods to avoid these pressures. "Going along with the gang" is an example of the audience's effects on behavior.

The audience effect on the student role is often all too clear. The professor's responses to student's utterances and test performances modify his behavior, depending upon their nature. Parents and others also furnish expectations in the form of feedback that modifies role enactment. The influence of peers is no less noticeable, as every student knows.

The effects of the audience come into play after role enactment has begun. They not only include modifications of role enactment but may also provide cues for role shifts of a magnitude sufficient to elicit entirely different roles.

Uses of Role Theory

These concepts can be applied to the analysis of a single role. It should be obvious by now that role theorists do not perceive human behavior as simply the result of inner forces. Rather, they take into account many influences, including cultural mores, other people, and the individual's conception of himself.

To understand an individual's adjustment we must investigate the complexities of the roles that he enacts. Some roles are obviously more important at different times than are others, and some roles of course will never be enacted by all of us. The effectiveness of adjustment depends upon proficiency in enacting relevant roles.

Role theory in its present form is helpful in understanding and directing research on specific roles related to adjustment (mental patient, delinquent, and so on). The findings lead to general corrective measures, but it should be noted that all the variables that we have discussed have potential for drastically modifying or completely inhibiting a specific role enactment for any individual. The inhibiting effect of self-role congruence we have already indicated, and the other variables can operate in the same way. A severe verbal reprimand, for instance, may overshadow all the other variables contributing to a child's role enactment: The influence of the audience in this instance is of prime importance in understanding his behavior. Consequently, in dealing with individuals we must still go through the process of gathering clinical information about each of these variables. A determination of how they are applicable to a particular person in his setting is necessary before he can participate effectively in programs of behavior change.

The usefulness and importance of role theory in personal adjustment lie in its broad conceptions of behavior. It directs attention to important aspects of the environment that are frequently neglected by theories emphasizing the psychological functioning of the individual.

COGNITIVE STRAIN AS A SUBSTITUTE FOR ANXIETY

Anxiety is a central concept in many psychological theories, and most people take for granted that we understand what it means. Closer inspection reveals, however, that anxiety engenders different kinds of behavior, depending upon one's theoretical point of view. Some theorists (and laymen) mean only overt behavior like trembling, stuttering, and coughing; others have in mind more complex conduct like defensive denial and avoidance; still others define it by antecedent events like aversive stimuli and memories of derogatory comments; some people mean only physiological responses; and some mean states of mind, psychic states, or affects and feelings. The experimental literature is no less confusing. There are more than 100 different procedures for measuring anxiety, including questionnaires, projective tests, physiological measures, and ratings of overt behavior. In general, anxiety is not clearly defined.

The views of man that we have described in Chapters 5, 6, and 7 all include specific definitions of anxiety. The Freudians and existentialists have in mind a psychic state inferred from subjective reports of discomfort or distress. Behavior therapists apply the term "anxiety" to observed avoidance of particular classes of stimuli. Aside from this question of multiple referents, Sarbin (1964, 1968) objects to the term because it tends to direct attention inward, toward mental apparatuses, to the neglect of external events. As an alternative he has offered "cognitive strain," which carries fewer connotations. He has also proposed a model for direct investigation of the antecedents of cognitive strain and explanation of why individuals choose some kinds of behavior over others to reduce the effects of stress.

THE MYTHIC NATURE OF ANXIETY

METAPHOR TO MYTH

Sarbin (1964, 1968) has argued that anxiety has lost its initial metaphorical meaning and has been redefined as an actual "state of mind" or "psychic state." In the history of language, when no term is available to describe an occurrence, it is natural to use metaphor, an "as if" statement that helps to communicate our observation. In ordinary speech we say that A is like B or that it is "as if" A were B. An event for which there is no readily available name, will thus be named first for similarities to known events; it may even be labeled with the same word. With the passage of time, however, the implied "as if" may be dropped, and the metaphor may become reified. The event is now considered identical with the literal referent of the initial metaphor. Instead of saying that A is like B or that it is as if A were B, a person may say A *is* B. When this occurs, the metaphor turns to myth and people act as though A in fact is B; that A was at one time simply a helpful metaphor is forgotten. It is Sarbin's claim that "anxiety" has undergone such a transformation.

ANGUISSE

His analysis begins with a tracing of the word "anxiety" back to the old French *anguisse*, a term for a painful choking sensation in the throat. With the rise of the medieval Church many terms denoting activities of inner entities that were believed to cause suffering and other strange behavior came into use. *Anguisse* developed into "anguish," meaning mental or spiritual suffering and the direct antecedent of "anxiety." Sarbin has suggested that the term "anguish" developed as follows:

> A choking sensation in the throat, produced, let us say, by swallowing a chicken bone, is denoted by the term anguisse or anguish. The death of a loved one, a misfortune, recognition of sin, and similar events often lead to a similar proximal event—a globus in the throat. Here are two proximal events that share one property, namely, the discomfort or pain in the throat. To complete the analogy, their symbols are also shared; the term denoting one is employed to denote the other—ignoring the weighty fact that their antecedents are in different modalities, different idioms. (1964, pp. 633–634)

LOCUS IN "MENTAL STATES"

It remains to explain how "anxiety" came to be considered a cause of such uncomfortable occurrences. There are two types of sensory inputs associated with pain and emotion. One is connected with an outside event, like the sensation of skinning your knee in a fall. The second occurs in the absence of recognizable external events; it includes headaches and toothaches. As no external source for these inputs could be located, the causal locus had to be established "inside" the body. Without adequate knowledge of anatomy medieval priests, preachers, and philosophers ascribed these unexplained events to an invisible, immaterial spirit (soul) residing in the otherwise empty spaces of the body. After Freud had published his work with its emphasis on internal, "mentalistic" metaphors, "anxiety" became a common term for a mental state, as if there actually were a "mind" (or "psyche" or "spirit") like other bodily organs, and that it were capable of experiencing separate "states." Investigators who think of anxiety in these terms are naturally led to examine the "inner" workings of the individual in order to explain why he avoids certain external events and circumstances.

A MODEL OF COGNITIVE STRAIN

Sarbin (1962) introduced his model with an examination of a case of hypochondriasis, somatic complaints without physiological basis. A person may complain of backaches, stomach cramps, or other malfunctioning, but no physical reasons can be located. Hypochondriasis has been treated as a disease by psychiatrists—it has an identifiable symptom picture and a supposed internal cause—but such diagnostic labeling has not led to specific treatment as it usually does in the physical illnesses. To say that a person has hypochondriasis or is a hypochondriac is to say essentially nothing; it does not tell us why he has chosen the "sick role" instead of the "well role," nor does it suggest specific forms of intervention that will alter his choice of roles. According to Sarbin, the individual hits upon this particular role by trial and error in his efforts to reduce tension, to neutralize the strain developed through attempts to solve apparently insoluble personal problems. As other roles become fixed through the effects of the audience, so does the sick role. "Cognitive strain" is the term that Sarbin has applied to the source of stress. The person's active efforts to reduce cognitive strain (the strain of knowing) lead to behavior that may later become fixed in the sick role.

Figure 8-1 represents the model of cognitive strain. It indicates that the inputs to an organism are matched against its cognitive organization (storehouse of knowledge) in attempts to make sense of them, to categorize them, to "instantiate" them, which means to understand them as an instance of some class. When instantiation does not occur cognitive strain results, and the organism undertakes activities to reduce it. This "adaptive" conduct is subject to social reinforcement and may develop into rather stable role enactments. We shall discuss each component of the model.

Component I, the distal ecologies, comprises specific aspects of the environment to which an individual attends. "Environment" is a very broad term, and "ecologies" implies that there are several aspects of the outside world most crucial to man's survival, aspects of reality to which we especially direct our attention. At least four conceptually different aspects of the environment are attended to by the individual.

The aspects of the environment connected with physical survival constitute the *self-maintenance ecology*. Ordinarily, however, it is of minor psychological importance to civilized man because his social institutions perform many of the functions most intimately connected with it. The primary function still remaining to him is establishing whether or not inputs signal potentially hostile objects or people. When a person attends to these inputs he tries to answer questions like "What is that?" or "What is next?" simultaneously,

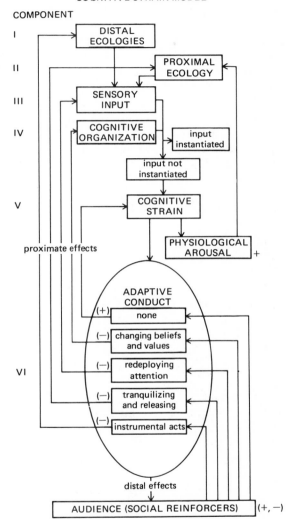

COGNITIVE STRAIN MODEL

Figure 8-1 Cognitive strain model. From T. R. Sarbin, Schizophrenic thought: A role theoretical interpretation. *Journal of Personality*, 1969.

he answers the question "What am I in relation to this occurrence?" "Am I in danger?" for example. Although most people establish themselves satisfactorily in relation to the self-maintenance ecology, dysfunctional conduct can have disastrous consequences. The classical phobias offer an example: The person is afraid of apparently benign objects or circumstances (like elevators or other closed in places) and his resulting conduct has far-reaching effects on his adjustment (he may be unable to drive his car or work in an office building).

The *social ecology* provides cues to one's position in the role system. A person almost constantly receives inputs from this aspect of the environment during his daily activities. We attempt to answer the question "Who am I?" by first answering the question "Who are you?" We try to establish our roles in the social ecology and the total of all such answers may be called our "social identity." To establish a social identity an individual must receive approval of his performances from the relevant audiences. When he fails to orient himself correctly in the social ecology, his conduct will not satisfy the expectations of others, and the feedback will not support his conception of his social identity. For example, a black man who thinks "I am a free American" but is refused service at a restaurant does not receive feedback verifying his notion of his social identity.

In orienting ourselves to the *normative ecology* we ask "How well am I doing"? or "Am I meeting the standards of my culture?" The answers to these questions lead to evaluations of oneself as good or bad, depending upon the cues. Guilt or shame is likely to accompany failure to meet prescribed norms. The impact of the normative ecology may, however, be modified. For instance, the student who fails an exam may attribute his failure to insufficient studying, a reason which increases his guilt, or he may blame it on the unfairness of the exam, a reason which reduces his guilt. His interpretation will, of course, determine the nature of his subsequent behavior. In the first instance he may study more; in the latter he may turn to other activities.

The *transcendental ecology* is related to the self-maintenance ecology, though it differs in comprising abstractions rather than concrete objects and occurrences. The questions asked are "What is my relation to God, the universe, mankind, justice, and so on?" Failure to find satisfactory answers may lead to chronic doubt, obsession, and other problems that interfere with adjustment.

Component II is the *proximal ecology*, comprising stimuli arising from physiological processes and received through proprioceptive receptors. We normally pay only minimal attention to the proximal ecology, though it is necessary to recognize cycles of hunger or thirst. But the stimuli accompanying emotional arousal usually demand attention and lead to changes in conduct.

Components III and IV can be discussed together. *Sensory inputs* are the stimuli received by the sense organs and transmitted to the brain. They are exposed to *cognitive organization*—expectations, bits of knowledge, beliefs, and so on—which assigns meaning to them. The individual attempts to relate an input to a known class of objects or events; the input is said to be "instantiated" (to become an instance of some class) when its class has been determined. If, however, the input cannot be classified *cognitive strain* (component V) results. Cognitive strain leads to physiological arousal (emotional responses), which in turn provides more input through the proximal ecology. An individual experiencing cognitive strain is thus quite likely to experience bodily responses that increase the inputs requiring classification.

In component VI several types of conduct meant to reduce cognitive strain are indicated. Those that reduce it are noted in the diagram by small minus signs. When *adaptive conduct* is not taken, or when it does not succeed, cognitive strain remains or increases. It should be noted that "adaptive" means reduction of cognitive strain in this context and not necessarily adaptive social behavior. Four kinds of adaptive conduct are included in the diagram.

One way to reduce cognitive strain is to *change beliefs or values* related to events and objects. The subsequent change in cognitive organization may permit the problematic input to be classified satisfactorily. An individual who wants to buy a new car in order to appear to be his neighbor's financial equal, for instance, may, in fact, not have enough money. His social identity includes the role of "family provider" equal to that of his neighbor. The inputs from the social ecology (his neighbor's new car) cannot be instantiated in the light of his current belief, and cognitive strain results. If he changes his belief to "material objects are not a good indicator of ability as provider," then the input will fit a category.

When more important beliefs are contradicted by reality, cognitive strain may be greater. The more difficult it is to change a belief, the less likely it is that this sort of adaptive conduct will occur. Of course, there is no necessary limit on adaptive conduct, and two or more types may appear concurrently.

When a distal ecology cannot be changed we sometimes reduce cognitive strain by limiting sensory input. The most obvious way is to turn away from unpleasant sights or to plug our ears against unpleasant sounds. The husband who fails to hear his nagging wife has *redeployed attention* to some other input like a newspaper, a book, television, or fantasy. The pollyanna limits his attention to the pleasant aspects of life and ignores others. Redeployment of attention limits the sensory inputs that must be classified.

To reduce cognitive strain an individual may take drugs or engage in activities that change the nature of proximal inputs. *Tranquillizing* drugs, alcohol, narcotics, and sleep are common examples of such agents; dancing, laughing, crying, sexual activity, and physical sports are common examples of *releasing* techniques. All these agents and activities modify proximal inputs and therefore may reduce the need to classify other inputs. The phobic person may, for instance, receive inputs from the distal ecology that he perceived as threatening, but reducing emotional feedback through drugs helps to prevent further inputs that would intensify the problem of instantiation. Consequently, fear may not build to an intolerable level at which functioning would be drastically reduced.

A person may adopt *instrumental activities* to change the inputs from the distal ecologies so that they can be satisfactorily instantiated. A straightforward example of such an activity is running away from a dangerous situation, which changes the inputs from the self-maintenance ecology so that the new inputs can be adequately categorized. Phobic people commonly employ instrumental activities to avoid situations that arouse fear.

Component VII is the effect of the audience on the maintenance or disruption of particular forms of adaptive conduct. If conduct receives positive responses it is likely to continue and to be used again to reduce cognitive strain. On the other hand, if it receives negative responses it is less likely to become characteristic.

To recapitulate, sensory inputs are received from both the proximal ecology and the distal ecologies. The information is examined in the light of the existing cognitive organization. If it can be satisfactorily classified (instantiated) cognitive strain does not occur, but if not, cognitive strain follows. Cognitive strain leads to conduct designed to be adaptive, whether by changing the distal ecologies through instrumental activities, the proximal ecology through tranquillizing and releasing activities, the sensory input by redeploying attention, or the cognitive organization by altering beliefs and values. The audience serves as a social reinforcer helping to determine whether or not a particular kind of conduct will be continued in other instances of cognitive strain. The way in which a person arrives at a characteristic mode of adaptation is by trial and error.

We can now examine the antecedent conditions of hypochondriasis that lead an individual to choose the "sick role." We may assume that as a young child our patient complained of stomach aches (probably caused by emotional arousal) when he was in conflict with members of his family. His mother probably responded with sympathy, put him to bed, perhaps called the doctor, gave him nice things to eat, and so on. The cognitive strain associated with the conflict was unintentionally reduced by the shift of attention to his physical functioning. That is, simply by accident (trial and error) he hit upon a form of conduct that would reduce cognitive strain and that particular conduct was reinforced. Perhaps a week or so later, while being scolded by his teacher, he again experienced pain in his abdomen. When he told her about it she may have sent him home, where he again received attention from his mother. At this point we see the "sick role" beginning to consolidate. As the child developed he hit upon various modifications like headaches, sore muscles, and so on, becoming increasingly subtle in his ways of dealing with cognitive strain and management of other people. In general, he has learned that taking the "sick role" relieves stress. As an adult he continues the same conduct in the expectation of being reinforced by his wife, friends, doctors, and so on. It may not be long, however, before those close to him stop reinforcing his behavior, driving him to seek other stimuli to maintain this mode of handling people. In American culture mass communications can be most helpful in this respect. The media abound with advertisements for products contributing to health and fitness: preventives for indigestion, antidotes for tired blood, examinations for signs of cancer, and so on. He selects those that contribute best to his redeployment of attention to his body functioning; he tries different medications and goes from one physician to the next in search of a cure for his imagined difficulties. At some point during this process he will be labeled "hypochondriac."

APPLICATION OF THE COGNITIVE STRAIN MODEL TO SCHIZOPHRENIC THINKING

Schizophrenia has commonly been classified as a mental disorder, a disease of the mind. The implication is that something inside the individual's mental apparatus is wrong, leading to certain kinds of behavior called "symptoms." One of the primary "symptoms" of schizophrenia is thinking described as "scattered," "illogical," and so on. Without examining the model of deviant behavior in detail we can note that labeling as a disease is the common way of accounting for observations of "schizophrenic thinking."

BECOMING A STABILIZED PATIENT

Sarbin has demonstrated an alternative way of looking at the language and thought called "schizophrenic": "In brief, many of the language and thought defects noted in hospitalized schizophrenics are *products, resultants,* or *outcomes* of certain describable social events associated with labeling a person as mentally ill and with the unintended instrumental acts and rituals carried out by medical, legal, and other professional personnel" (1969, p. 192). Studies that have claimed to show differences between schizophrenic and normal thought patterns have falsely attributed such differences to a disease process. They have failed to take into account the settings of the experiments and the social and psychological effects of becoming a mental patient. An alternative analysis of the interactions associated with becoming a mental patient must be performed. Sarbin has outlined the following sequential steps in becoming a patient:

Sequence 1. remote ecological events, postulated genetic and constitutional events
Sequence 2. prepatient role
Sequence 3. unsettled patient role
Sequence 4. stabilized patient role

It is at sequence 4 that most research studies have examined the thought processes of schizophrenics. These subjects have already acquired the roles of "cooperative," dependent inmates. Investigators who conceptualize schizophrenia as an illness tend to attribute the differences in the thinking of these patients from that of normal people to events in sequence 1, usually events that have occurred early in the patient's life: an unbalanced mother, the early death of a parent, genetic or constitutional events, even body type. Although Sarbin has not denied the importance of such events, he argues that events during sequences 2 and 3 may more appropriately explain observations during sequence 4.

Sarbin has declared that people who are classified as schizophrenic and ultimately hospitalized have adopted redeployment of attention as their major adaptive technique. Inputs from their social ecologies are very often not instantiable and lead to cognitive strain. To reduce this strain they turn their attention to matters that may be thought of as inappropriate by friends, family, or neighbors. This technique is often called "withdrawal" because the individual may turn his attention to fantasies that can be instantiated within his knowledge structure. It is common to hear professionals say that schizophrenics live in fantasy worlds much of the time, implying that such behavior is caused by illness. Sarbin, however, views this behavior as attempts to redeploy attention and to reduce cognitive strain.

The person whose attention is directed to fantasies much of the time does not move into a prepatient role until the relevant audience has evaluated his behavior negatively. When his redeployment of attention results in role enactments inappropriate to his age, sex, occupation, family, and other roles the audience labels his behavior "deviant." Members of his family and other close acquaintances are not prepared to deal with it, and the functioning of the group is thus threatened. They must turn to social institutions with authority to deal with such deviant people—the police or mental health personnel. The person's unusual behavior nearly always leads to his being excused from fulfilling many of his social roles, and he is therefore referred to the institutional resource for sickness, the physician. The physician upon finding no signs of "real" illness diagnoses the behavior as symptomatic of "mental" illness. In the prepatient sequence, then, the significant people in the individual's environment begin to look upon him and act toward him as if he were able to enact only roles carrying minimal obligations. Roles demanding more responsibility may be quietly, sometimes stealthily, taken from him as his family conspires to have him properly "treated" with minimum fuss. Reducing the number of his roles also reduces the size and complexity of his social ecology, forcing him to depend even more heavily on inputs from his private world. His claims to identity are challenged, and he is subtly stripped of it as he is assigned the position of "sick person," with its minimal requirements.

The usual signs of illness, like pain or body dysfunctions, are not present, and the person may therefore have difficulty in accepting others' judgments that he is ill. He has essentially two choices at this point. On one hand, he can accept what others tell him: that he is mentally ill and that whatever is being offered to him is for his own good. On the other, he can reject it. Accepting others' views places him in the role of a trusting child with no capacity for critical appraisal. Resisting may, however, simply reinforce others' convictions that he is mentally ill; in fact, he is likely to find himself in a locked ward at the mental hospital.

Sequence 3 involves further stripping of his usual roles from him. He may be locked in a psychopathic ward for observation, his civil rights are taken away through commitment procedures, sometimes his personal clothing is taken away and replaced by hospital attire, and other hospital entrance ceremonies further degrade him. As fewer and fewer environmental supports are available to support a valid social identity, redeployment of attention becomes even more attractive. As instrumental activities to change the social ecology (violence, argument, pleading) are negatively reinforced by the hospital staff, about the only means of reducing cognitive strain is to produce his own fantasy inputs.

It is, of course, possible that interested relatives, other patients, or professional personnel may try to help him find other ways to deal with the outside world (some form of therapy). The patient may then search for, and in fact learn, other adaptive techniques that will enable him to again function in the community in a relatively short time.

If such positive assistance is not available, however, the patient enters sequence 4. Hospital housekeeping and medical routines further shape him into a stabilized patient. This role ("chronic," in medical terms) includes only minimal rights, responsibilities, obligations, and duties. In essence the patient becomes a "nonperson," which further encourages his attention to fantasy.

EFFECTS ON COGNITION

Private cognitive activity is characterized by short cuts. When it is unnecessary to describe one's reasoning in public, it is quite acceptable to skip logical steps, but, in conversation with others skipping steps may lead to confusion. The speaker must be ready to make explicit any tacit or hidden premises that have led to his conclusions. For instance, if he says, "Socrates is a man; therefore Socrates is mortal," a listener may legitimately ask how he has arrived at such a conclusion. The speaker is then obligated to complete his reasoning by providing the major premise: "All men are mortal; Socrates is a man; therefore Socrates is mortal."

In sequences 2, 3, and 4 the so-called "schizophrenic" increasingly skips logical steps in speech, for he attends primarily to his thoughts and neglects communication with others. Investigators generally compare his speech in this sequence with that of subjects who have not undergone the desocialization of earlier sequences. Sarbin has suggested that the social effects of institutionalization, including loss of social identity, account for the "symptoms" of thought disorder observed by investigators of schizophrenia. The differences in communication can as easily be attributed to the cognitive effects of social withdrawal and desocialization as to some underlying disease process.

This interpretation has implications for treatment. Rather than trying to treat a disease entity inside the patient, therapists can adopt a social-systems orientation to discover what aspects of the patient's environment have created cognitive strain and take steps to change them.

An Eclectic Approach to Treatment

Sarbin (1967) has taken his cognitive-strain model as a point of departure in formulating four types of conduct change (treatment): behavior therapy (see Chapter 7), psychodynamic theory (see Chapter 5), the humanistic-existential view (see Chapter 6), and community psychology. Each of these therapeutic systems seems to him to be related to one of the four distal ecologies.

Behavior therapy, based on learning theory, has its greatest success in changing habits. Although changes in attitudes and beliefs have also been reported, the "strict behavior therapist is unconcerned with possible changes in self evaluation, and identity transformation, or alterations in other abstract properties." The major focus is on discrimination between threatening and benign stimuli and on responding correctly. Behavior therapy appears to be the preferable treatment of dysfunctional conduct resulting from unsatisfactory orientation in the self-maintenance ecology. The phobias, for instance, have had major importance to behavior therapists, and they appear to be the type of maladaptive conduct most amenable to learning techniques.

Psychodynamic theories, with their emphasis on the psyche, or mind, and on patients' self-evaluations, are aimed at disturbances resulting from misplacement in the normative ecology. The primary therapeutic tool is the subject's verbal report about his inner workings, and the goal is rearrangement of his beliefs about himself. When a person has difficulty answering the question "How well am I doing?" a therapy directed at discovering more satisfying evaluations is probably the appropriate choice. The troubled individual must be able to express his beliefs and perceptions through detailed talk, so that interpretations based on some dynamic theoretical framework can lead to understanding of his position in the normative ecology.

The humanistic-existential perspective, rooted in humanistic philosophy and theology, emphasizes man's relations to cosmological entities, as well as the more abstract relations between man and man and man and nature. It attempts to resolve the kinds of questions presented by the transcendental ecology: "What is my relation to God?" "What is my relation to my own being?" and so on. In an age of continuing existential threats, questions related to the transcendental ecology are not easy to answer and may result in a great deal of cognitive strain. To the extent that a culture reflects these threats the existential orientation is a useful form of intervention. Obviously it is limited to clients who are nearly always well educated, abstractly intelligent, and from the middle class. "It is an open question whether one's relations to transcendental figures and entities are as salient to miseducated, unassimilated lower class members of racial minorities whose existential problems stem primarily from their efforts to locate self in the social ecology."

Community psychology focuses on organizations of people whose conduct is dysfunctional because of misplacement or "nonplacement" in the social ecology. (Sarbin does not recognize the expansion of the "mental illness" model into the community as representative of this view.) Therapy is directed at those individuals who have been misplaced in the system of roles, at individuals as members of collectivities, interacting with others in a continuous search for answers to the question "Who am I?"

Many patients in mental hospitals and mental health clinics come from lower-income groups. Their problems are intensified by unemployment, lack of skill, few material goods, and other stresses related to the ways in which they have to live. The source of their difficulties is in the circumstances of their lives, which prevent them from filling roles that depend upon achievement and contribute to positive social identity (like "productive member of the community"). Social-action programs designed to change the environment offer the most effective measures for dealing with this kind of situation; treatment is directed not at isolated "patients" but at the settings (including other relevant figures and negative social factors) in which roles are enacted. Interventions are not limited to one-to-one verbal contacts, although the latter may be included in the total approach; rather, they are designed to change aspects of the environment that impede development of positive social identity.

Research is aimed at discovering groups (as well as individuals) who live in conditions in which development of positive social identity is extremely difficult if not at times impossible. A social-systems approach then shapes the individual's circumstances to make such development possible. As social circumstances are changed, cognitive strain is reduced, and the "adaptive" behavior labeled "deviant" or "symptomatic of illness" is frequently no longer necessary.

CONCLUDING REMARKS

Sarbin has redefined and changed the focus of the psychology of adjustment. His is a broader view of man than those that we reviewed earlier, as is especially apparent in his emphasis on the influence of forces emanating from social systems. His theory and analysis of specific problems alert the reader to the human condition: to man's attempts to cope with influences that are often beyond his control and of which he is essentially a victim.

Although individual therapy may sometimes be effective, for the great majority of people labeled "mentally ill"—especially those being treated at government expense in mental hospitals and clinics—changing the environment is the most effective way to change behavior and to reduce stress.

"Anxiety" is only one of several terms that Sarbin has effectively shown to be at least useless, if not actually detrimental, to research and practice. His ideas are vigorously opposed to theories that man's behavior is motivated and to be understood primarily in terms of mental structures or processes.

He recognizes the importance of cognition, but it is the individual's use of his cognitive abilities in response to external and internal events that explains why he behaves as he does.

In the following section we shall explore the influence of Sarbin's views, and views similar to his, in applications of social-psychological concepts to major social problems.

EXPERIMENTAL SOCIAL INNOVATIONS

INTRODUCTION

A new breed of scientists is growing up around the social psychological view, scientists who seek to apply their problem-solving methods to social issues. Historically social-science research and social scientists themselves have proceeded in relative independence of cultural innovations. Social programs have largely been introduced through political channels, with little or no previous evidence that the changes would produce the desired effects. Such programs have been carried out almost entirely on faith alone and in most instances without incorporated procedures for evaluation. In contrast, the physical sciences have long concentrated on the importance of continual evaluation and the application of the best research methods available. The space program is a current example. It would be unthinkable to proceed on the faith that "this seems the right thing to do" without obtaining solid data to evaluate effectiveness. But social programs have proceeded as if rhetoric and conviction were sufficient criteria. The new breed of social scientists is directing its efforts to correcting this error at last.

Why has this state of affairs existed? Social problems are certainly as important as are technological problems, yet social scientists have nevertheless effectively isolated themselves from participating in social change. Fairweather (1967b) has attributed this isolation to three historical traditions: attempts to emulate the physical sciences, characteristics of academic institutions, and absence of organized ways to induce social change.

He has argued that social scientists have sought to become accepted as "real" scientists by concentrating on certain superficial similarities to the physical sciences: precision of measuring devices, complex experimental designs, and laboratory controls. Although these techniques are important, social scientists have failed to recognize sufficiently another important aspect of the physical sciences: careful observation in the field. They have therefore found themselves ignoring features of "natural" settings, including pertinent social problems.

Academic institutions are also traditionally isolated from the conflicts that affect other institutions of society (industrial, political, and so on). Academic scientists have tended to define their role as "pure"; as their sole purpose is to find "truth," they have been unconcerned about the social significance or application of their findings. Social scientists have generally studied established systems in the community; they have been reluctant to join with politicians and legislators in innovating. In a sense, a myth that "pure" research is more important than "applied" research has been created. Pure research has therefore offered more "payoff" in terms of status and promotion to the academic scientist.

Academic institutions have also emphasized the separation of disciplines. Each has come to function administratively as a discrete entity with little or nothing in common with the others. This superficial separation makes it difficult to integrate the subject matter of different disciplines, yet in dealing with complex social issues it is necessary to coordinate many kinds of knowledge.

Academic institutions have, furthermore, emphasized the quantity, rather than the quality, of research. That is, academic scientists who have published a great deal usually have higher status than do those who have not. Short-term research is thus encouraged, even though it may yield only minor contributions to the understanding of social problems. A study must often be carried out over a long period of time in order to evaluate a social program effectively.

A third historical tradition is the absence of procedures for inducing social change in our society. No government organization functions to anticipate necessary social reforms. When changes do occur, they are nearly always direct responses to political crises. That is, new social programs are usually implemented to correct, rather than to forestall, bad situations. Social change is consequently very rapid when social pressures are at a peak. At such times social scientists suddenly become "experts." Even though they have had little or no direct experience with the problems in question, they find themselves giving opinions to national committees on possible courses of action. Their testimony is often rather naïvely taken as if it were based on experimental findings, when in fact it generally consists of "best guesses" based on whatever theoretical notions are current. In these instances social scientists make statements that they would never make in the scientific realm without experimental evidence. But society demands experts in times of stress, and such "experts" help those in power to institute some types of change. The recent clamor over drug abuse is a good example of diverse "expert" testimony based almost entirely upon conjectures and hunches. The simple fact is that experimental evidence on drug abuse is insufficient to offer definitive answers.

Social scientists and legislators are becoming more aware of the blocks to social innovation. The clinical psychologist's attitude toward the social contexts in which his patients' problems arise must change; the analysis of individual personality can be only a part—often a minor part—of clarifying difficulties and directing change. The social psychologist investigates possible changes in those aspects of the environment that create stress and perpetuate untenable living situations, for environmental manipulation is the basic method of social innovation.

A MODEL

The general aim of social innovation is to discover programs that can contribute to solving, or at least containing social problems. Fairweather (1967b) has named eight conditions that he considers necessary for experimental social innovation. Together they may be considered a model of social innovation.

DEFINITION

It is necessary, first, that the problem be defined, an obvious starting point for any method. It is especially important in social innovation, however, because it may be critical in determining possibilities for carrying out the program. To receive support from the community and the pertinent political resources—support that is critical to implementing a program—the problem must be defined as relevant and important. The definition must include a clear description of the individuals affected and the circumstances surrounding their difficulties.

NATURALISM

The experimental social innovator must make observations in the settings where problems occur. He cannot simply view situations remotely from his laboratory, desk, or office. It is necessary to move into the setting and to observe the factors that shape the problem. If an investigator is interested in change in slum areas, for example, he must expose himself to slum conditions, personally observing such conditions as unemployment and delinquency.

INNOVATION

A new social subsystem must be established on the basis of the investigator's ideas for overcoming specific difficulties. The service approach (in which help is provided, as in Head Start, mental-health clinics, and so on) also establishes new subsystems in the form of projects, but it does not provide for the critical evaluation associated with experimental social innovation. A program for job training might, for example, be implemented in a slum area in order to evaluate its effects.

COMPARISON

An experiment must be designed to compare the effectiveness of the new subsystem with that of the old one. Simply establishing a new subsystem like Synanon or the Job Corps is not sufficient. A control subsystem incorporating previous social practice must be used for comparison: Treatment for drug addicts at a county hospital could, for example, be compared to the Synanon program. This aspect is the crux of experimental social innovation. The new subsystem is evaluated according to its effectiveness relative to previously existing subsystems. Criteria for improvement (relevant to the sponsors of the study) must, of course, be decided upon and clearly stated; a city-sponsored program may, for instance, be geared to finding out whether or not drug recidivism can be reduced, thus lowering tax expenditures.

CONTEXT

The innovative subsystems must be established in social settings so that their effectiveness in the natural habitat can be evaluated. The subsystem cannot, for instance, be tried in a laboratory setting or in a social setting different from that in which the problem exists. It must be tested under conditions like those in which it will have to operate if it is ultimately adopted. If job training were to be provided in slum areas, for example, the trial program could not be established in some other part of the city and trainees bused there. It would have to be in the slums.

EVALUATION

Adequate evaluation of new programs must be longitudinal. That is, it must be conducted over a considerable period of time, months or even years. Immediate gains that do not endure are insufficient justification for continuing most programs.

RESPONSIBILITY

The researchers and social innovators must take responsibility for the lives and welfare of participants in the program. They are actively involved with these people and cannot simply isolate themselves as observers. They fill the same roles as do the personnel who will administer nonexperimental programs in the future—but with the added responsibility of research evaluation.

Cross-Disciplinary Approach

Depending upon the specific social problem, various appropriate sciences must be represented. Dealing with ghettos, for example, may require the services of economics, political science, psychology, and sociology. Social innovation can almost never be limited to one discipline.

Other methods of social investigation have been used in the past, but none has met all eight of these criteria. The method that has come closest is the "service approach," but it has fallen short on the "comparison" criterion; control groups are usually not established to provide data on comparative effectiveness of old and new programs.

PHASES

Fairweather has constructed a method of experimental social innovation, involving four phases: planning, action, evaluation, and dissemination.

Planning

Planning is crucial in determining the ultimate usefulness of a program. One of the first steps is to choose the problem that will be the initial focus of investigation. This step in itself requires a great deal of time and work. Several sources of information must be used to define the scope and character of the problem. Observations in the field are one such source, as are a review of the scientific literature from all relevant disciplines and discussion with other scientists and experienced people. This information provides the background and allows the investigator to begin isolating the variables that appear most important. At this point he must be strongly influenced by his own interests, for several relevant problems will probably reveal themselves; as experimental social innovation usually requires years, it is important that the investigator choose a problem that will hold his attention. A psychologist interested in unemployment in the ghetto may be led by his reading, observations, and discussions to suspect several important causal variables: lack of occupational skills, low motivation to achieve, poor health, and high competition for jobs in the immediate vicinity. If his training has been in clinical psychology he is likely to prefer a program to raise the level of motivation, one that incorporates group processes and personal counseling.

There are some difficult practical steps during the planning phase, not the least of which is obtaining administrative commitments from those currently in positions of power. In the mental hospital, for example, it is necessary to obtain the cooperation of the director and other administrative personnel responsible for the patient population. The investigator must also evaluate the feasibility of carrying out a long-term project in the subsystem in question. He must estimate the effects that his results may have on the operation of the institution and what possibilities they may offer for practical change.

It is important that the mutual commitments of the researcher and the administrator be spelled out clearly before the project begins. As most past research efforts have been carried out in settings other than that where the direct services are being offered (for example, evaluating a new therapy in an attached unit instead of the regular hospital), this kind of research will be new to administrators. Beside requirements for personnel, space, and so on, the administration will have to delegate responsibilities to the research director that would not normally be required. Innovative social research does not consist simply of examining subjects or administering questionnaires within the institution. Rather, a complete service complex must be organized in conjunction with the research, which generally extends beyond the normal boundaries of established institutions and community agencies. It is therefore most important to the success of the experiment that all these groups be well coordinated and that their roles be clearly established before the program is initiated. In a mental hospital, for example, the research team will establish another service section, staffed by nurses, psychiatrists, and so on. It will not simply come into an existing program, take measurements, and leave. The researchers' experimental subjects, *their* patients, will also be in contact with other community agencies: welfare, vocational-rehabilitation, employment services and so on. The experimental service must therefore be coordinated with them, and respective roles must be precisely defined before the program begins.

Planning also involves research design, selection and measurement of variables, and so on; these details are very important in carrying out a controlled experiment in a "natural" setting. The two (or more) subsystems under study must be approximately equal in their participating populations; they must be matched on significant variables, and all possible steps must be taken to increase the likelihood that differences between the two groups will result from the innovative subsystem and not from initial differences in the populations. Experimental hypotheses must be established, and a plan of operation must be formulated before implementation can begin.

Action

If planning has been careful the program should operate quite smoothly. In the action phase the experimental subsystem is established, experimental measurement is begun there and in the control subsystem, and the participating service and research personnel begin to carry out their roles.

Naturally these programs are not as neatly conceived or performed as are experiments in laboratory settings. Changes must be made as unexpected problems arise. Adjustments are often necessary at first so that the experimental subsystem can fulfill its goals. For example, a contract for medical services may be initially signed with a hospital some distance from "motivational centers" for the unemployed, but once the program has actually begun it may become clear that most of the participants do not have transportation to the free medical services. "Pickup services" may be added, or a small clinic may be set up nearby. The problem is recorded for the aid of future administrators of similar programs, and the experiment continues. The initial establishment and operation of the program require flexibility to permit changes in the research plan. Such changes must be recorded, so that their effects can be evaluated in the light of the total study.

After the program has been initiated some forces may threaten to alter it so much that the initial experimental conditions are destroyed. For instance, other investigators may become interested in the project and ask to observe its operation or even to incorporate some of their own interests in the study. Such interference may change the program significantly by creating new social demands within the experimental subsystem. It is important to maintain the new program in as "natural" a condition as possible. If it is opened to other investigators their influence may not only affect the results but may also create conditions that will not be duplicated in future programs.

Staff turnover and personnel changes are potential sources of interference. It is important to establish procedures for handling them. Methods of training new personnel should be ready, in order to minimize distortions associated with arrivals and departures from the program.

Publicity can also interfere by introducing elements in the experimental program that will not be encountered in later programs of less interest to the public. The participants may also be affected, depending upon the nature of the publicity. The research team must guard against placebo effects, changes caused by the expectation of success because it is a new program. The "newness" and interest will not be present in later programs.

The length of the experimental period must also be planned beforehand to ensure smoothness. Ultimately the research personnel may turn over the administration of the program to private sources or service organizations while the participants continue in the program. In some instances programs may simply be completed, the participants transferred to other programs, and the personnel assigned to nonexperimental work. The experimenters' responsibility ends with the completion of the action phase; the responsibility for continuing the program is shifted to community members with those skills. Collection of data does not, however, cease at this point; there are nearly always followup data to be gathered.

EVALUATION

The evaluation phase involves mainly statistical computations and the ordering of research data. Much of this work has been planned, but the nature of the data may require changes in analytical methods. Once statistical analysis has been completed the researcher draws inferences from his own experiences in the program and his understanding of the overall social problem. He is then in a position to report on the outcome of the experiment, as well as to suggest new ideas for future investigation.

DISSEMINATION

The last step is to make the results available to other investigators and to people in the community who are interested in the program. Most important is the comparison of the new subsystem with the previous one, which involves evaluation of the outcomes to determine whether or not the experimental program produced greater benefits. If improvement occurred, it is up to the investigator to determine to what extent it can be generalized to similar social problems. He examines the representativeness of his sample as an indicator of how closely the natural groupings in society have been replicated, the social context of the innovation to determine how typical it is of settings for similar problems, and the outcome in relation to society's consensus on improvement. He then makes recommendations to those interested in the research.

It is incumbent upon the investigator to pass on more than simply his experimental results. Most publications are not sufficiently detailed for accurate replication of procedures. When new programs are to be established as a result of an experiment, their leaders need guidance either through direct contact with the investigators or through written descriptions that are clear enough to be followed precisely.

AN INNOVATIVE PROGRAM IN A MENTAL HOSPITAL

The conceptual basis of social innovation will become clearer as we examine a concrete example and the kinds of goals that it accomplished. Fairweather was the senior investigator in a study (1964) of chronic mental-hospital patients. His point of departure in defining the problem was the difficulty that such patients experience in filling acceptable community roles after discharge. Relevant research has shown that the scope of the problem is quite large; regardless of the kind of treatment, around 70 percent of the patients return to the hospital within eighteen months. Some never leave at all. These statistics suggest that treatment that helps patients adjust to the hospital has little effect upon their subsequent adjustment to the community. Changes do not carry over into community life, though the same patients, again adjust to their hospital roles when they return. This situation is clearly an important social problem, in terms of both the financial burdens and the lack of personal fulfillment for patients. A new approach that will help patients to bridge their roles in hospital and community life is called for.

One possibility is to form patient groups in the hospital and later to move them as units into the community. Role behavior in the hospital will then overlap with demands under normal social conditions. Each patient will thus belong to a group that provides a secure frame of reference while he learns or relearns skills of community participation. In order to carry out an overall plan of this nature it is necessary first to show that typical mental-hospital patients are capable of forming self-sufficient groups that are in turn capable of moving into the community. Fairweather's study examined the feasibility of this first step in the more ambitious program.

THE ALTERNATIVE PROGRAM

Several studies have demonstrated the progressive influence of group membership on an individual over time, and it thus seemed logical to expect that patients who could be organized into cohesive problem-solving groups in the hospital would have better chances of working out role requirements in the community. The group could function as a residential unit, a source of problem-solving strength, and a point of departure toward readjustment. But if such groups were to be established the hospital program had to be changed. The hypotheses can be formulated in two sets of questions: First, can small problem-solving groups be established? And if so how will the program differ from the traditional hospital program? Second, presuming such groups are established, what processes best facilitate their development and operation? The necessary experimental design requires that both the outcome and the process of the small-groups program be compared to the traditional hospital program.

Means of implementing and developing autonomous problem-solving groups in the hospital setting were studied. The task was to determine what requirements were necessary to enable such groups to function on their own, to handle their own difficulties, and to make almost all their own decisions.

Patients were assigned to task groups upon entering the experimental ward. A group had the responsibility of orienting a new patient to the ward and explaining the program. Each group met daily to discuss difficulties, progress, and so forth without staff intervention. The staff communicated with them through a note system, participating as consultants in group meetings only when requested to do so. The group discussions led to recommendations that were then transmitted to the staff in writing. The staff examined the recommendations, approved or disapproved them, and rewarded the group when its procedures and recommendations indicated that it was learning to deal with difficulties realistically. By contrast, the traditional program was more staff-centered; the professionals made the decisions, and the patients depended upon them for direction and guidance. Although patient meetings were held, there were no autonomous work groups.

Concrete reinforcement was given for individual and group behavior—primarily in the form of increased spending money and more frequent passes from the hospital. Reinforcement was associated with the successful completion of four steps. First, the patient had to show responsibility for his personal care, being punctual in his assignments, and orienting new group members. After meeting such requirements he received $10 a week to spend and a one-day pass each week. In the second step he had to perform his job assignment acceptably in addition to the tasks of step one. He was then allowed $15 a week and an overnight pass every other week. In step three the patient received $20 a week and three overnight passes in each four weekends. He was expected to be responsible for recommending money and passes for other members of his group, as well as continuing to meet all the requirements for steps one and two. In the fourth step he was expected to be responsible for planning his hospital departure in addition to all the earlier tasks. At this point he was given unlimited passes and free access to his money. (Most patients had some income of their own that the hospital managed.)

Four out of five days the task groups met on their own. Early in the program it was found that when staff members sat in on the meetings the patients would turn to them for advice, which weakened the group autonomy that the program was designed to build. Patients evaluated one another's performances and prepared recommendations to present to the staff in a joint meeting on the fifth day. The staff listened to the recommendations but could not suggest courses of action; its primary role was to approve or disapprove the recommendations, to reinforce realistic problem solving, and to provide any information that the group might need to arrive at reasonable decisions.

During the week communication between staff and group was accomplished by notes in a designated box. The staff would comment on the behavior of group members that should be worked on in the group sessions. For instance, if one member did not shave or show up for his work assignment, the staff would write a note to that effect and put it in the group box. Staff members were not to interfere with the individual directly; it was up to the group to solve the problem.

The following is a sample of the interaction of the staff and a group during one week.

1. Notes Given the Task Group during the Week:
   Sunday: "Mr. Edwards did not get up in time to shave."
   Monday: None.
   Tuesday: None.
   Wednesday: None.
   Thursday: None.
   Friday: None.
   Saturday: None.
2. Task Group's Verbatim Log:
   Monday: The group spent considerable time discussing Mr. Watson since he has become something of a problem to the group. In the design of the group to help Mr. Watson as much as possible, it was decided to defer any action until Mr. Watson had conferred with Dr. Jones. Mr. Watson was given permission of the group to consult Dr. Jones. The group would like to know

whether there is any medical or mental reason that Mr. Watson cannot take a more active part in the group discussion.

Action on Mr. Edwards. Mr. Edwards received a note stating that he did not get up in time to shave. It was noted by the group that Mr. Edwards had not shaved for the second day since receiving the note. Since this is negligence on the part of Mr. Edwards, the group decided that he be reduced in step from step 3 to step 2. The vote was as follows: unanimous with the exception of Mr. Watson, that Mr. Edwards be reduced to step 2. A change in the pass list for that week was made by the group secretary.

Tuesday: By unanimous vote Mr. Watson was reduced to step 1 without privileges. It was noted by the group that Mr. Watson was unable to obtain help from his interview with Dr. Jones, and the group felt that his lack of response in the group business left no other alternative.

Mr. Thompson had been given permission of the group to be absent in order to obtain an interview with the Social Security representative.

Wednesday: It was decided by the group that Mr. Jacobs would submit plans in preparation for entering step 4. Mr. Jacobs submitted a plan for family care, but this plan was rejected by the group for its lack of long-range planning during home care and after.

Mr. Williams was also under discussion but action is deferred until after the next report on his IT (hospital job) assignment. Mr. Williams has decided that he will try to obtain employment with Brewster Aviation after his ME (patient employment) has expired. The plan met with the approval of the group.

Thursday: It was decided by the group that a card would be purchased and sent to the Salvation Army. The suggestion was made by Mr. Scheerer. It was also decided that a card would be sent to each member discharged to show the discharged patient that he had the well wishes of the group. Money for the cards is donated by members of the group.

Mr. Parsons left on 90 day TV (trial visit). Mr. Parsons will be missed by the group to whom he gave his every service. Mr. Martin was unanimously elected to fill his post as secretary.

Friday: Group advancements as follows: Mr. Jacobs to remain in step 3 until he has forwarded a better detailed plan for the future (by majority vote). Mr. Greybeal to remain in step 3 until he has advanced plans for his future action. Mr. MacConnell, Lyons, Maddox, Thompson, Scheerer, Rollins, to be advanced to step 3. Unanimous vote. Mr. Watson to remain in step 1. Unanimous vote. Mr. Martin and Mr. Williams to remain in step 4, there being no change in future plans and their plans meeting the approval of group and staff. Mr. Edwards reduced to step 2.

By unanimous vote of group, Mr. Thompson and Mr. Lyons were voted to committee men. (This group had appointed its own steering committee.) Mr. Watson was removed from committee until further notice by unanimous vote.
3. Staff's Evaluation of Task Group Recommendations:

The staff continues to be pleased with your high morale and group spirit. We feel problems and recommendations were handled appropriately. Keep up the good work!

Step 4—Mr. Martin and Mr. Williams.

Step 3—Mr. Jacobs, Graybeal, MacConnell, Lyons, Maddox, Thompson, Scheerer and Rollins.
Step 2—Mr. Edwards.
Step 1—Mr. Watson. (Fairweather, 1964, pp. 184–186)

EXPERIMENTAL PROBLEMS

To evaluate the effects of the small-group program adequately it was necessary to keep all other variables as nearly constant as possible. Previous research had suggested at least five requirements for experimental design, each of which included control conditions to broaden applicability of the findings.

MATCHING THE TREATMENT PROGRAMS

To make the innovative program exactly like the traditional program, except for its innovative aspects, it was necessary to plan identical daily schedules, except for the hours when the task groups met. During those hours patients in the traditional program were assigned to individual work assignments or recreation. In a twenty-four-hour period only two hours were differently structured in the two programs.

Another difference was intake procedure. In the traditional program orientation to the hospital and its routines was primarily the responsibility of the staff. The task group performed this function in the experimental ward. In the traditional ward a patient's privileges and decisions were between him and his psychiatrist, whereas on the experimental unit they were between him and his task group.

THE EXPERIMENTAL UNIT

Because of the nature of the problem to be studied, the appropriate social unit was a mental hospital ward. Previously existing wards that were physically similar were chosen for the experiment. Special units were not set up because the results were to be applicable to "natural" subsystems, that is, mental-hospital wards.

MATCHING THE STAFFS

It was necessary to eliminate some differences between the personnel on the traditional and small-group wards. Obviously each ward had to have the same number of staff members; it was less easy to match the two staffs on variables like proficiency, interest, and the like. It would have been desirable to examine several different staffs in order to strengthen generalization to other settings, but this step was not feasible. To control the difference between ward staffs, halfway through the experimental period the staffs were switched.

SAMPLING PROCEDURES

Two aspects of the sample were important. The first was matching on certain characteristics: diagnosis, age, and length of hospitalization. The purpose was to eliminate the possibility that pre-existing differences in the populations could account for differences observed later. All the patients were interviewed at the start of the program, and they were assigned to the wards to ensure maximum similarity between the populations. Patients who arrived after the program had begun were assigned to wards and their characteristics were tabulated for comparison at the end of the program. Final tabulation showed that the two wards had indeed been quite similar in these variables.

It was also desirable to have a representative sampling of mental hospital patients. Because long-term hospitalization had been such an important variable in previous studies, it was especially important that the patients vary widely in lengths of their previous stays. Furthermore, the samples were selected to represent the diagnostic categories commonly found in mental hospitals. These steps ensured that the results of the study would be more applicable to different settings and would support the feasability of similar programs in other hospitals.

ASSESSMENT DEVICES

It is not necessary to describe in detail the various measuring devices used in the study; they were selected or designed to measure the outcome of the program, as well as the processes during its operation. Measures of the patients' social interactions in structured and unstructured situations, interpersonal variables, patients' perceptions of the treatment program, and their attitudes toward various aspects of hospitalization were evaluated. Different group characteristics like leadership and cohesiveness were measured, staff attitudes and opinions about the program were evaluated, and several indicators of success in adjusting to the community were obtained.

A total of 195 patients participated in the experiment over a period of twenty-seven weeks. Followup data were gathered twenty-six weeks after the program had been completed.

RESULTS

As in any program of social innovation several results had to be evaluated. Some led to further hypotheses and some offered information about the success of the program in question. It was found that the patients who had participated in the task-oriented program differed from those in the traditional program in several ways.

BEHAVIOR IN UNSTRUCTURED SITUATIONS

Observations during recreational hours were considered to have furnished samples of patient behavior in unstructured settings, for recreation time was theirs to do with as they pleased. The overall effect on the task group was to stimulate ward activities. The members were physically more active and showed greater participation in two- and three-person groups, whereas patients in traditional treatment spent a great deal of time in solitary activities. The members of the experimental ward became adept at forming spontaneous groups of five to seven patients for various purposes, and their levels of verbal behavior were much higher than were those of the control patients. The experimental patients, when left to themselves, thus exhibited levels of physical activity and sociability that would prove helpful outside the hospital.

BEHAVIOR IN STRUCTURED SITUATIONS

Observations at large group meetings (between ward patients and staff) provided information on behavior in structured settings. Again behavior and attitudes were very different in the two groups. The task-group patients showed greater interest in themselves and their fellows, attempted to use the suggestions of other members in solving problems, established norms of behavior that were useful and problem oriented, and in general demonstrated to the staff that they had earned freedom and decision-making powers. In contrast, the traditional ward meetings were stereotyped, and the patients were rigid and dependent upon staff intervention, rather than upon their own control.

INTERPERSONAL CHOICE

A measure of the amount and intensity of interpersonal choice among patients (whom they liked and so on) was also taken, and the results again revealed an increase in social activity on the experimental ward. Task-group patients generally showed more and deeper interest in other ward members. As a group they were more closely knit and cohesive. Also the task group apparently functioned to promote close alliances among its members and enhanced the social acceptability of each member to the other members of his group.

PATIENTS' EVALUATIONS OF THEIR TREATMENT

In general, the patients on the small-group ward were more involved both positively and negatively in their program. They saw it as potentially helpful but as requiring a more difficult adjustment than the traditional program did. Upon arrival in the experimental ward the new patient was likely to be anxious over the pressures and responsibilities that confronted him. More positive attitudes tended, however, to replace his initial negative attitudes as he adjusted to the ward.

Task-group patients much more frequently thought that they had been helped by others and that other patients had been the most helpful. In direct contrast, the traditional ward was dominated by the belief that only staff members—or no one at all—had helped. It appears that under certain conditions patients act therapeutically toward other patients.

GENERAL ATTITUDES TOWARD MENTAL ILLNESS

The patients' attitudes toward mental illness and the structure of the mental hospital, including staff status and ward regulations, did not change in either group. The task-group experience did, however, make a difference in other more specific attitudes. These attitudes were found to be generally accepted in the group. The patients in the small-group program were optimistic about the future and anticipated advances in employment. They also anticipated spending more time with other people after their discharges; even their expectations of marriage were more positive. Attitudes thus did not seem to have been affected unless they were specifically related to the attitudes that developed in the groups.

VARIABLES RELEVANT TO THE HOSPITAL

Several variables of importance to the hospital administration were also examined: the total time each patient spent in the treatment program, the amount of medication required, the use of passes, the number of visitors, the use of recreation facilities, and the transfer of patients from the ward. The two groups studied differed on only one of these variables—the length of time spent in the treatment program. The small-group patients stayed on the ward an average of forty days less than did the patients in the traditional program.

FOLLOWUP: COMMUNITY ADJUSTMENT

Even though small-group treatment reduced the length of hospitalization, resulted in higher employment after discharge, and encouraged more active involvement with others, the basic problem of recidivism was not significantly changed. Approximately half the chronic patients returned within six months. Apparently the gains through the small-group program could not be maintained when the individual faced the stresses of readjusting to his community.

OTHER RESULTS

Several process variables were also studied: leadership, communications systems, rewards, group cohesiveness, group norms, and composition of small groups. The findings are relevant indicators of the types of groups that develop the highest degrees of cohesiveness and problem-solving behavior. Although it is beyond our scope to explore these findings in detail, it is important to note that the investigation of such variables in any program of social innovation leads to fuller understanding of other results and provides information to professionals who want to establish programs along similar lines.

The impact of this study on the hospital and the hospital personnel was also examined. Evaluation of staff attitudes and the responses of administrative personnel shed light on the kinds of disagreements, problems, and gains to be expected from similar programs. Again this information may be very important in the establishment of similar programs in other settings. It allows the investigator to anticipate personnel difficulties and to take steps to minimize them.

The interrelations of the various measures were also examined. Measures of posthospital adjustment were not significantly correlated with most of the measures taken in the hospital setting. The patients who remained out of the hospital longest were those in supportive living situations in the community, were in communication with other people, and were employed in low-status jobs. The less time the patient had stayed in the hospital, the more likely he was not to return. But the only hospital measure that was significantly related to staying out of the hospital was being "a cooperative task-group member"—incurring few penalties from the task group.

Because of the low correlation between measures in the hospital and followup measures, future investigators are warned of the importance of relating the two kinds of measures before concluding that their programs have been successful. It is not enough to be satisfied with improvement in the hospital alone.

New Hypotheses

As we noted earlier the results of an experimental social innovation should furnish additional hypotheses and narrow the range of possible approaches to solving the initial problem. In this study it seemed clear that shorter hospitalization and several variables like patients' social activity and staff morale were positively associated with the model program. The approach thus appeared to offer definite advantages, though recidivism was not significantly reduced. The question of what can be done to reduce this high rate of return to the hospital, especially among chronic patients, remains.

Followup data showed that the variables most closely associated with remaining out of the hospital were related to the patients' environment (living situations and jobs). We can formulate the hypothesis that the treatment program should be located in the community itself, the hospital serving as only one aspect of the overall setting. What is learned in the hospital must be transferred directly into community practice; implementing such a program necessitates a design requiring minimal professional participation. Otherwise the demand for professionals would be so heavy that the program would not be practical.

From this reasoning the investigators presented several hypotheses for future testing. Small groups are to be formed in the hospital initially, then transferred into the community, where they will continue to solve their own difficulties with minimum professional assistance. The task group is to be more than simply a supportive body, though support will be an important function; it is to operate a business that provides jobs for its members. A general type of business—gardening or janitorial services and the like—is most appropriate because it requires different levels of abilities in its organization and functioning. Some members can fill administrative positions, others laboring positions, and so forth.

The investigators have in fact put these ideas into operation on a small scale. Initial evaluations are promising, and it is hoped that the final results will contribute to overcoming the problem of the chronic mental patient.

SUMMARY

In this chapter we have examined man in relation to his internal and external environment, especially emphasizing social forces that determine his behavior. Although a number of points of view can be found in social psychology, Sarbin's role theory, offering a comprehensive view of man from a social-psychological perspective, is particularly relevant. This theory has served us as a vehicle for the introduction of the complex interaction between man's cognition and his social environment. "Role" indicates a group of behaviors associated with particular social statuses and positions (father, lawyer, student, mental patient, and the like). The study of man's enactment of his social roles has supplied the data to support this view. Sarbin has postulated six variables that can be measured and related to the effectiveness of role enactment: knowing what role the other person is enacting (role location); the similarity of role requirements and the person's conception of himself (self-role congruence); knowing what actions are required by a given role (role expectations); abilities and attributes necessary to carrying out general and specific conduct (role skills); modifying tendencies derived from social mores, values, and standards (role demands); and audience influence on behavior (reinforcing properties).

Sarbin has objected to the use of terms that were once understood as metaphors but have come to be taken literally. "Anxiety" is one such term. As a less misleading alternative to it Sarbin has introduced "cognitive strain," which clearly reflects his emphasis on combining social and psychological variables to understand human behavior. Cognitive strain, a condition portending action, occurs when inputs from the environment cannot be satisfactorily classified according to the cognitive system (beliefs, values, and so on). As cognitive strain is uncomfortable an individual takes action to reduce it; repetition of this adaptive behavior depends upon others' responses to it. Some behavior is adaptive in reducing cognitive strain but not in meeting social expectations. For instance, a person who has learned to believe in his own worth but continually receives inputs (from prejudice and so on) indicating the contrary may reduce cognitive strain by shifting his attention to other inputs. If the alternative inputs lead to evaluation of himself as a worthwhile person cognitive strain is reduced, but others may consider him preoccupied with fantasies of self-aggrandizement or suffering from delusions of grandeur.

Sarbin has applied the cognitive-strain model to a reinterpretation of the medical view of "schizophrenic thinking," focusing on antecedent and concurrent social variables as a person becomes a stabilized mental patient. He has argued that the depersonalizing effects of hospitalization increase cognitive strain and encourage redeployment of attention. Differences between stabilized mental patients' (schizophrenic) thinking and that of people who are not hospitalized can thus be explained on the basis of social changes leading to the patient role, rather than of a disease process.

According to Sarbin, psychoanalysis, behavior therapy, existential therapy, and community psychology are appropriate to problems arising from different aspects of the environment. No one approach in itself is sufficient for all human problems; each has its applications and limitations

Fairweather typifies a "new breed" of social scientist willing to become directly involved in social issues and innovation. It is not enough, however, for the scientist to be simply interested in social change but he must also apply his knowledge and techniques in the creation of new social subsystems to help overcome existing problems. The preferred model of social innovation includes comparative evaluation of new and old programs. Logic provides insufficient assurance that proposed programs will work; only empirical validation provides acceptable criteria of effectiveness.

Experimental social innovations are not abstract; they are planned and carried out in definite phases. Each phase, from initial planning through final dissemination of results, has requirements different from those of ordinary experimental approaches. The direct connection of the program with existing social subsystems creates difficulties that are infrequent in laboratory and contrived settings. Investigators who wish to pursue social innovations must therefore be ready to face these problems.

We closed this chapter with a description of an experiment in social innovation aimed at helping chronic mental patients stay out of the hospital. This problem is a formidable one for our society because of the enormous loss in financial resources and personal satisfactions that it represents. Although these patients seem capable of adjusting to hospital life, their ability to remain in the community after discharge is very poor.

Fairweather and his associates viewed the problem as one of failure to bridge the role requirements of hospital life and of the community. As a first step toward change, they initiated almost entirely autonomous patient task groups in one mental hospital. Evaluation of the patients in these groups showed positive gains compared to the performance of patients in the traditional hospital program. Many of them nevertheless returned to the hospital within a short time after their discharges. But the results nevertheless were sufficiently encouraging to suggest the feasibility of the next step: the transfer to the community of task groups established in the hospital.

PART III

ADJUSTMENT: ACCOMPLISHING TASKS IN THE LIFE CYCLE

The six chapters in this part break human adjustment down into developmental tasks. Although many tasks persist throughout life, they are usually more critical at certain stages. Motor coordination, for example, is a critical task for the preschool child. Once mastered, however, it is usually incidental to other challenges. In this part we examine the process of human development, focusing on its relevance to adjustment.

In Chapters 9 and 10 we summarize the development of the individual from conception until early adolescence. In subsequent chapters we follow him through adolescence and adulthood. Even before birth a person must cope with demands that threaten to retard his personal growth. Of course, he has little if any control at this stage. One of the important characteristics of adjustment, however, is increasing ability to deal independently with imposed demands. As an individual grows he expands his range of activities; consequently he constantly meets new challenges—challenges that call for adjustment. He moves from complete concern with self to deep personal attachments and a wide variety of social commitments. He changes from a relatively undifferentiated infant to an adult with an integrated personal identity. In reaching these various developmental goals a person meets challenges all along the way. The specific tasks differ with the stage of his progress.

In these chapters, then, we introduce the student to most of the important adjustment tasks in life, providing a background against which he can evaluate his own adjustment.

9

Adjustment in Childhood

I. THE PRESCHOOL YEARS
  A. Introduction
  B. Prenatal Development
    1. Stages
    2. Effects of prenatal experience
  C. Birth
    1. The birth process
    2. Complications at birth
  D. Adjustment Tasks of the Preschool Child
    1. Physical development
    2. Weaning and solid foods
    3. Toilet training
    4. Speech and language
    5. Beginning self-awareness
    6. Early socialization
II. THE SCHOOL CHILD AND THE PREADOLESCENT
  A. Introduction
  B. The Concept of Time in Development
    1. Developmental time
    2. Confusion of chronological and developmental time
  C. Developmental Tasks
    1. Peer-group interaction
    2. Sex-role development
    3. Mastering culturally relevant skills
  D. Processes of Change
    1. Piaget's theory of cognitive development
    2. Learning and identification
Summary

THE PRESCHOOL YEARS

INTRODUCTION

The preschool years are important in determining the course of later development and adult functioning. Some of the effects of genetically determined characteristics have already been discussed in Chapter 2. The developing embryo and the infant are subject to a large number of other influences as well. The child and parents may have no control over some of these influences, but for the most part they have a great deal to do with the shaping of personality.

In the prenatal period and early infancy, human beings are largely at the mercy of environmental forces and completely dependent upon adults. The first adjustments after birth are the responses of the infant's life systems to the demands of the extrauterine environment. Each system must accommodate the exchange of gases, nutrients, and waste materials formerly accomplished automatically in the fluid environment of the mother's uterus.

Psychological and sociological factors become increasingly important as the infant gains physiological independence. The degree to which early experiences determine later personality traits is not precisely known, but many psychologists believe that these early years are the formative ones for adult character.

The preschool period is one of parental adjustment as well. Parents find that they must modify their own behavior, learn new patterns, and in general adjust to the changing roles of mother and father. The interaction of their adjustments with those of the child, plus the physical and social settings in which growth occurs, all add to the complexity of the developing child's life and largely determine the kinds of stress or support that greet his attempts to cope with an imperfectly organized world.

PRENATAL DEVELOPMENT

Many people do not think of the period before birth as a time of "real" life. Indeed state laws vary in the requirements for length of pregnancy before an abortive death is recorded. The biological growth of new cell tissue is continuous, but the beginning of legal life is arbitrary. Most people do not consider life "real" until the unborn infant at least resembles a human being and has developed some characteristically human physiological processes. Yet prenatal experiences are extremely important in shaping the yet unborn individual's future.[1]

[1] See J. Pikunas (1969) for more detailed information on early development.

STAGES

Pregnancy has been divided into three periods. Specific growth tasks are accomplished during each, as long as serious obstacles and dangers do not disrupt it.

THE ZYGOTE

The first major developments occur during the two weeks following fertilization, or conception, when a sperm cell penetrates the ovum (or egg). Chemical changes immediately begin to produce a membrane around the ovum to prevent further penetration of sperm. If the developing infant is to survive, the fertilized cell must make its way from the upper tract of the fallopian tube into the uterus. On its journey the fertilized egg (zygote) is sustained by nourishment from the egg yolk. Once the zygote has implanted itself in the uterine wall it obtains nourishment from the mother's life systems. The zygote period is considered to have ended when implantation occurs. But cells have already begun to differentiate themselves into outer and inner layers of tissue, and a small globule of protoplasmic material exists in each.

If nourishment from the yolk is insufficient or the zygote implants itself somewhere outside the uterus, death will almost certainly result. "Pregnancy of the tubes," for example, involves implantation in the fallopian tube itself instead of in the uterus. Even when the embryo is successfully implanted in the uterine wall it can be dislodged, and miscarriage follows.

THE EMBRYO

The embryonic period lasts until about the end of the eighth week of pregnancy and is characterized chiefly by rapid growth. Development progresses to the point at which the embryo is recognizably human. The most important change is the differentiation of cell tissue into specific body structures. These structures are not yet functional, but all of the major organs and body systems have appeared by the end of this stage.

Embryonic development is sequential, as each organ and organ system emerge in a particular order. Disturbances during this period may critically damage an emerging system. Maternal illnesses and accidents are especially dangerous; later on they may have relatively little effects on the developing infant. It has been estimated that 72 percent of all miscarriages occur before the end of the third month of pregnancy. The causes vary from falls and injuries through malnutrition, hormonal imbalances, and other factors. At any rate, the embryonic period is clearly critical for normal development.

THE FETUS

The fetal period completes pregnancy and ends in birth. The organ systems developed during the embryonic stage are further refined and perfected until they are capable of sustaining the infant's life. The fetus receives its nourishment through the placenta, the tissue connecting it with the mother. There is only indirect exchange of nutrients and oxygen between mother and fetus; direct exchange of blood does not occur.

It is during the fetal period that the child's heart begins to circulate blood, and probably all the nerve cells have been formed before the end of the fifth month. Nerve cells continue to grow in size for some time after birth.

Normally all the organs and activities necessary for survival after birth are functional at about the end of the seventh month. Children born much before then have a very small chance of survival; chances of survival increase as the normal nine month term approaches.

The fetus also develops a wide variety of reflexes and general movements in preparation for its life after birth. Although babies vary a great deal in the amount that they move during pregnancy—some are active as much as 75 percent of the time, whereas others hardly move at all—nearly every expectant mother experiences some fetal movement.

EFFECTS OF PRENATAL EXPERIENCE

Three factors control development during the prenatal period: heredity, the egg and its composition, and the prenatal environment produced by the mother. Any change in one of these factors may modify the child's development. A great deal more is known about harmful effects than about minor effects that may be beneficial.

It has been estimated that probably one-fifth or more of all human pregnancies do not reach final term. It is also highly probable that many eggs die before the women know that they are pregnant. The great majority of these zygotes would, however, likely produce defective children if they lived until term.

The negative effects of disturbances (accidents, diseases, and so on) during pregnancy depend a great deal upon the developmental stage of the unborn child. As the first two or three months of pregnancy is the time when organ systems are developing most rapidly, it is also the most critical period for developmental problems. In general, effects at this time are quite severe and cause abortion of the embryo or fetus. Infection, a toxic condition from the ingestion of chemicals, heavy smoking or drinking, or severe emotional strain in the mother may affect her metabolism or oxygen supply, which may in turn interfere with fetal development. There may be rather dramatic organ effects; for example, infants whose mothers have received the tranquillizing drug thalidomide during pregnancy are frequently born without arms or legs.

DISEASES

German measles (caused by the rubella virus) in the mother has long been recognized dangerous to fetal development. The worst time for an expectant mother to contract the disease is during the first three months of pregnancy, when rapid embryonic growth occurs. The virus (it is small enough to pass easily through the placenta) attacks the growing cells, and numerous malformations may occur: heart defects, congenital cataracts, deafness, and the like. The recent development of what appears to be an effective vaccine should bring about a large reduction in births of deformed babies from this cause.

Other diseases, especially venereal infections and the viruses of measles and mumps, can also affect prenatal growth. The seriousness of the effects depends a great deal upon the severity and duration of the harmful disease, the stage of fetal development, and the vigor of the fetus and of the mother.

EMOTIONAL UPSETS

The expectant mother's emotional state and the occurrence of emotional upsets have caused concern for some time. Actually there is no direct evidence to indicate that "nervous" or upset women produce emotionally unstable or poorly adjusted children. Strong emotional reactions in the mother are, however, irritating to the fetus, as is usually indicated by large increases in fetal activity at such times. Some animal studies have shown that when expectant mothers are fearful and nervous their offspring are more fearful and nervous than are the offspring of control mothers. Nevertheless, we can say only that there is a possibility that the babies of highly emotional mothers will be more active than are those of calmer mothers. Considering the character of our society it is questionable whether it is more adaptive to be a somewhat anxious and nervous individual or one who is extremely calm (Scott, 1968).

DIET

There are many old wives' tales about the eating habits of expectant mothers, probably because pregnant mothers are subject to unusual cravings. One of the oldest tales is that the mother must eat for two. On the contrary, overeating is often one of the greatest causes of difficulty during pregnancy. Excess weight gain can cause difficulties at birth and endanger the health of both mother and child.

Marked dietary deficiencies, either in general nutrition or in specific minerals and vitamins, will, of course, affect fetal growth. The fetus does, however, have priority over nutrient intake; the mother is the first to suffer from nutritional deficiencies.

OXYGEN DEFICIENCIES

When the fetus is gaining weight rapidly during the last stages of pregnancy, it is quite important that adequate oxygen be available to him. Normally oxygen is no problem, except at high altitudes. For instance, babies born at high altitudes, especially above 10,000 feet, are more likely to be premature. Consequently, there is a greater risk of neonatal death (Grahn and Kratchman, 1963).

BIRTH

Birth is the point that most people consider the beginning of life. It usually occurs about 266 days—approximately nine calendar months—after conception. The birth itself and the first days of extrauterine life may be especially important in later adjustment.

THE BIRTH PROCESS

The fetus descends into the lower abdominal cavity approximately t o weeks before birth. The mother may experience a "lightening" effect and be able to breathe more easily because the pressure in her upper abdomen has been relieved.

A period of labor immediately precedes birth. Its beginning is generally signaled by at least one of the following: a blood-tinged discharge from the vagina, the rupture of the membrane containing the fetus and a resulting discharge of "water" (amniotic fluid), and "false labor pains" from intermittent and irregular contractions of the uterus.

COMPLICATIONS AT BIRTH

Premature birth (usually defined as the birth of a child weighing less than five pounds, eight ounces or after a period of pregnancy of less than thirty-seven weeks) carries added danger for the infant. The delivery is often prolonged and difficult. The fetus may be fragile and not completely ready for birth; its lungs and digestive system may not be sufficiently developed to perform their functions. The premature baby is more susceptible to infections of various kinds, and therefore the possibility of secondary infections and illness may be a threat for several months after birth. The chances that a premature infant will survive are directly proportional to his birth weight. The heavier he is, the more likely he is to be fully developed and consequently able to cope with the extrauterine environment.

Mechanical damage is another possible source of future difficulties. The use of surgical instruments in the delivery or severe pressure from contractions and a narrow birth canal can injure brain tissue. A long, difficult birth increases the chances that the neonate will suffer lack of oxygen, which may in turn cause destruction of brain cells. The loss of brain tissue may, of course, reduce intellectual potential and result in later behavioral difficulties.

Excessive sedation of the mother during birth can also cause lack of oxygen and result in damage to the sensitive nervous tissue of the infant's brain. Sedatives and chemical analgesics (pain killers) depress the infant's respiration so much that it may be extremely difficult to start his breathing after delivery. The physician must be very skillful and cautious in using these drugs because individuals differ in their capacities to benefit from them.

If the mother is a narcotics addict the baby will also be addicted and will suffer withdrawal symptoms shortly after birth. A mother who keeps her addiction a secret runs a serious risk that her infant will die from those withdrawal reactions. In general, the severity of the child's withdrawal depends upon the extent of the mother's habit, including the amount and timing of the last dose before delivery. The chances of survival are much greater if the physician is alerted beforehand. With proper treatment the baby can be eased through withdrawal and cured of his addiction.

ADJUSTMENT TASKS OF THE PRESCHOOL CHILD

Personal adjustment may be conceptualized as the organism's ability to master developmental tasks, including its trials and successes in growing from an extremely dependent infant to an adaptive and independent adult. At each age specific developmental changes must occur in order for growth and adjustment to continue in reasonable fashion. Some developmental tasks continue over a long span of time, but many have their greatest importance in specific periods.

PHYSICAL DEVELOPMENT

Learning to coordinate motor and perceptual activities is a necessary step toward independence. Without such coordination many skills necessary for coping with the world cannot develop. Coordination of the eyes with body movements is one of the first tasks for the infant. Its accomplishment appears to depend a great deal on the "maturation" of the nervous system. As nervous tissue develops, a protective myelin sheath is laid down around each cell. This sheath allows the nerve cell to function appropriately. If maturation has not progressed sufficiently, it is impossible for the child to learn visual-motor skills.

At first the infant's only responses to perceptual stimuli are physiological, an increase in respiratory or pulse rate, for example. He next develops the ability to fix his eyes on an object and to separate it from its background. Fixation is possible because his coordination has developed to the point at which the eye muscles can be guided in response to perceptual activity. In the next phase the baby begins to incorporate general motor activity with fixation: He follows the stimulus with his eyes, his head, and sometimes his entire body. Eventually his arms, then his whole body, move toward the stimulus in an attempt to grasp it—he has performed his first "true" action. His movements become increasingly stronger and more decisive as his eyes become better coordinated with muscular control. Accomplishing this comparatively simple task of coordination equips the child to learn a great deal more about his environment.

Other important motor functions also develop systematically. For instance, from studying films of young children A. Gesell (1943) distinguished fourteen stages in learning to walk and ten in learning to grasp. Figure 9-1 shows the progressive stages in learning to walk. The child's world broadens, and his ability to learn is greatly enhanced when he has mastered locomotives skills.

Aside from this mastery of specific tasks, development also follows general directions. The first is from head to "tail" (cephalocaudal development). The movements of the head, the eyes, the shoulders, the arms, and so forth develop in that order, from the head region toward the "tail" region. A child gains strength in his arms before he is able to stand on his legs. Development also moves in a proximal-distal direction, from the center of the body toward the extremities. In learning to reach for an object, for example, the baby is able to use his shoulders and elbows before he can use his wrists and fingers. The gross movements of the central regions are developed before the finer movements in the extremities.

The dramatic change from helpless infant to energetic toddler scurrying about his neighborhood clearly reflects the important relationship between motor development and independence. By the time that a child reaches four or five years of age he has learned many perceptual-motor skills that help him to explore his surroundings and, when necessary, to perform a great deal of survival activity.

WEANING AND SOLID FOOD

The infant's early development is primarily concentrated in improving the efficiency of his physiological systems. At birth his only source of nourishment is liquid, either from the mother's breast or from a bottle. Within the first few months, however, he is generally able to take some solid food. The length of time that the child is allowed to nurse depends a great deal upon his culture; no physiological norm appears to be involved. Some tribal cultures, for instance, allow suckling until the onset of adolescence, whereas others are quite restrictive and use early and abrupt weaning techniques. Differences among modern industrial cultures also exist, but they are usually not as great. The technique and timing of weaning vary with the mother's, or the family's, ideas of child rearing.

In general, the more permissive one's child-rearing beliefs are, the less likely it is that the infant will experience stress during weaning. The child naturally gives up suckling for more desirable sources of nourishment if weaning is permissive. He is usually weaned before the end of the first year in any event, and from that time on he begins to develop preferences for other types of foods, preferences that are likely to stay with him for the rest of his life. As

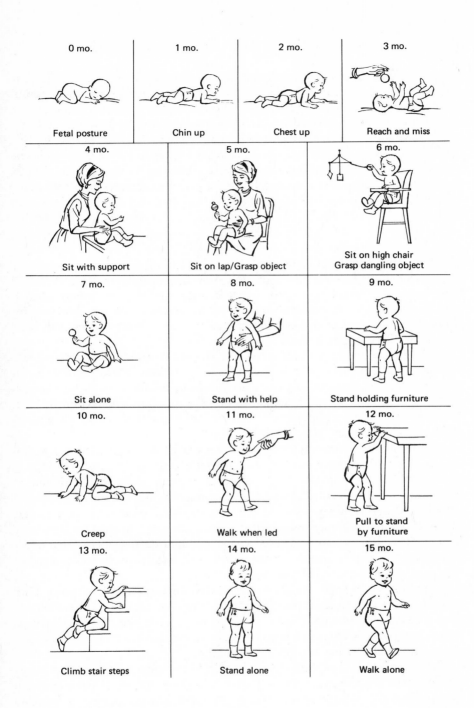

0 mo.	1 mo.	2 mo.	3 mo.
Fetal posture	Chin up	Chest up	Reach and miss

4 mo.	5 mo.	6 mo.
Sit with support	Sit on lap/Grasp object	Sit on high chair Grasp dangling object

7 mo.	8 mo.	9 mo.
Sit alone	Stand with help	Stand holding furniture

10 mo.	11 mo.	12 mo.
Creep	Walk when led	Pull to stand by furniture

13 mo.	14 mo.	15 mo.
Climb stair steps	Stand alone	Walk alone

Figure 9-1   Stages in learning to walk. From Mary M. Shirley, *The first two years: A study of 25 babies. Child Welfare Monograph,* 1933, no. 7. By permission of the University of Minnesota Press.

we all know it is very common for children to have a "sweet tooth." The proportion of sweet receptors in the tongue is higher in children than in adults. Consequently, though children may show a strong preference for sweets, when they reach adulthood this preference for sweets is usually reduced.

Probably the only advice currently agreed upon by experts is that feeding should be accompanied by love and trust. During either breast or bottle feeding the mother's emotional tone will be reflected in her tension. Quietly talking to the baby and handling him slowly and deliberately are considered helpful in avoiding feeding problems.

Toilet Training

The young child takes a significant step toward socialization when he learns to control his urination and defecation in socially acceptable ways. He has not only learned to impose his will upon himself, an important step toward meeting social expectations, but he has also opened new horizons for himself. He can attend social functions in new environments from which he had previously been barred.

Toilet training is a double task for the child. First, he must institute voluntary control over an act that is basically reflexive. Such control is, of course, necessary if the child's elimination is to be regulated in socially acceptable ways. Second, he must relinquish or delay personal satisfaction in favor of social control; the spontaneous relief of bladder or bowels, though pleasurable, must be delayed.

In most modern societies much stock is placed on cleanliness and health habits. Most Western cultures do not tolerate haphazard disposal of human excrement. Many parents are therefore anxious to train their children in cleanliness and frequently attach excessive rewards or punishments to toilet training. When training is started too early, perhaps around one year of age, many children are simply not physically mature enough to exercise the necessary control. By age two, however, many children are capable of voluntary control. The spontaneous development of toilet habits can be encouraged at this age by moderate social pressures.

Parents vary a great deal in the ways that they teach toilet habits. Ultimately, however, the child must give in to them in order to receive their approval. They will not compromise on this issue, even though some may be much less severe in their demands than are others. Every child is expected to learn the social customs related to elimination.

Accomplishing this task successfully should engender feelings of autonomy in the child. For the first time he has seriously opposed social demands with his own desires. He was able to relegate his desires to a secondary position and, in the process, he learned that pleasure comes from giving (or giving in to others) as well as from receiving. His ability to control and divert himself —his autonomy—has truly begun. Once the child has been toilet-trained he is ready to turn to other tasks that further his independence.

It may be difficult for some children to complete toilet training, or they may return to earlier habits under emotional stress. If a child frequently wets the bed (nocturnal enuresis) after the age of three he may require professional attention. A rather high percentage of children, however, show intermittent enuresis for some time, even into the early school years. "Accidents" are especially common among boys through age five or six. If they continue to persist past that age, however, a child may begin to feel ashamed, and his self-image may suffer. It is a good idea for the parents (perhaps with the help of a professional) to help the child work out a program to gain control.

Several kinds of therapy have been tried with enuretic children, including surgery, drugs, and mechanical devices. Many parents have resorted to severe punishment and shame in attempting to overcome the problem, but these methods may create more severe problems and disrupt the relationships between child and parents. The main difficulty is usually that the child has not properly learned the cues associated with impending urination. Several techniques can help him to learn them and build bladder control (Kessler, 1966; Verville, 1967).

SPEECH AND LANGUAGE

Learning verbal communication is extremely important. Not only are the child's horizons a great deal expanded, but his future learning capacity also largely depends upon his skill in understanding and manipulating verbal symbols. It is man's highly developed verbal ability that makes him unique among biological organisms; it is his most adaptive skill. Verbal and written communication frees him from the necessity of learning everything through direct experience. The exact pattern of speech and language development is not completely understood. It appears, however, to occur in steps as do other developmental tasks (Brown, 1965).

The child begins by producing various sounds with no specific reference to objects or categories. At first, his crying is undirected, yet it is effective because it alerts adults to his needs. Parents seem to learn differences in a baby's cries as well: whether they indicate hunger, pain, or other irritations. Although some communication thus occurs, it is not the same as reciprocal language. Only when he produces sounds purposefully is the child beginning to use language.

Before the child is one year old he is capable of producing all the sounds used by adults, plus many more. During this first year, however, sounds associated with the parents' language are apparently distinguished, and others begin to disappear because the sounds that adults use are strongly reinforced, whereas others are not. The unreinforced sounds seem to be extinguished (through lack of reinforcement).

The child's first understanding is passive. Some sounds and phrases appear to have acquired meaning for him, probably as a function of the setting and tone of voice. He does not, however, repeat the words for his own purposes.

A major step in language development is the child's first utterance of a word—usually between nine months and one and a half years. Sounds that have been randomly emitted are at last combined to indicate a particular object or group of objects, for instance, "pa" may refer to any adult. It is still not clear how first words are chosen, however. Sharply contrasting sounds seem to be important. They make it easy for the child to differentiate them and to put them together into a word. The child then builds his vocabulary, adding words that refer to concrete events in his immediate environment.

The next step is the first sentence. A sentence is probably best defined as using a series of words for a purpose other than simple labeling—a new function. Rather than simply denoting an object, the child wants to say more about it: where it is, its relation to him, and so on. The adult sentence "There's a dog" becomes "There dog" in child language. The child means both to label the dog *and* to tell where it is. Sentences take such simple forms for some time as the child tries out different words within the structure.

In the next step the child begins to include more elements in his sentence structure. Instead of saying "Dog run," for example, he may say "That dog run." He gradually incorporates more auxiliary words and verb tenses to broaden the scope of his communications.

From two or two and a half years on, the child progresses rapidly to the use of more parts of speech. His vocabulary increases rapidly, almost tripling each year. Refinement of language becomes quite important at this point, and the influence of adult models can be very strong. The children of parents who are interested in verbal development and provide a great deal of verbal stimulation are more competent in their use of language.

Parents may become distracted by the amount of verbalization that their child produces around the age of three. He may constantly ask questions either to obtain valid information or simply to attract attention. Language development is most rapid at this age. The child is extremely interested in language and is curious about almost everything. Being able to communicate verbally is highly gratifying to him.

BEGINNING SELF-AWARENESS

The meaning of the term "self" varies with different theories of personality, but each of us recognizes something that he commonly calls "I" or "me." Most of us also recognize that the idea of self is extremely important in our lives and behavior. Development of the self begins in the preschool child and continues throughout his life.

The young infant does not seem to differentiate external objects and parts of his own body. He treats his own extremities, for example, as if they were not part of him. Even at ten months he does not seem to have integrated his sensations with his physical image: He cries when he pinches himself and laughs when he tickles himself. At a year and a half his behavior still seems centered on himself, and his relations to surrounding objects are poorly defined.

The combination of his parent's showing him love and calling him by name with the beginning of his resistance to their control appears to be primary in the beginning of his development of self. Learning his name provides him with a stable referent in relation to other people or other objects; he can separate the symbol for himself from symbols representing other things. His resistance to control of his behavior by others leads him to begin to do things "by himself" and "for himself." This stage may seem "negativistic" to parents, but it reflects the child's discovery of his own will.

The next step seems to be development of roles in relation to other children, to his peers. At around two and a half years he passes from relating to peers only through toys and other objects over which they may quarrel to true social interaction. He begins to take parts which will later become social roles that contribute further attributes he considers part of himself. Gradually more and more things become identified as parts of himself—not only his name, habits, characteristics, and so on but also things associated with his parents and family. The five-year-old, for instance, has taken over his entire body. Every part of it seems integral to himself, and the concepts associated with his name and the first-person singular pronoun have formed a unity.

EARLY SOCIALIZATION

Examination of "critical periods" may help us to understand the early development of social behavior. J. P. Scott (1968) has suggested that critical periods can be defined as periods in which rapid growth of internal processes occurs. At such a time the rapidly growing attribute is most susceptible to external influences. The nature of the resulting organization can be directed more easily at this point than at any other. Furthermore, changes during one of these periods may become relatively fixed features of later organization. We mentioned the concept of critical periods in our discussion of rapid growth during the first two or three months of pregnancy.

Primary socialization also seems to be a critical period. In the human being a smiling response to faces begins at around six weeks and presumably marks the beginning of socialization. At six months the child is capable of distinguishing familiar faces from strange ones. The first social relationships, usually between parents and infant, take place between the ages of six weeks and six months.

EFFECTS OF ISOLATION AND SEPARATION

Complete isolation of human infants is encounterd only rarely in clinical cases and has never been used experimentally for obvious reasons. There have been children who have been locked away from the outside world or abandoned when very young to fend for themselves in wilderness areas. In the instances that have been reported the children have generally exhibited marked social and intellectual deficiencies. But it is impossible to know whether these children were abandoned because of their abnormalities or their abnormalities resulted from their experience of isolation.

More detailed and reliable results are available on the effects of periods of partial isolation. Most children show an immediate response to being left alone. They cry. Their response seems quite adaptive for infants, who would not survive if left alone for long, because it brings attention.

Separating an infant from his customary surroundings or breaking a social relationship with him may cause him great stress. L. J. Yarrow (1964) studied infants who had been transferred to foster mothers during their first year of life. A high percentage of those transferred when they were six months old showed serious emotional disturbances, whereas all those over seven months had reactions severe enough to be called "emotional trauma." Other studies have revealed emotional reactions to separation in the second half of the first year. As the child becomes older, however, he also becomes capable of managing longer periods of separation.

Most parents have observed the difficulties associated with leaving their children with baby-sitters for an evening and especially with leaving their children with a stranger for a weekend. A good baby-sitter will distract children and keep them amused, so that they do not focus on their upset and depression. Parents may notice a partial withdrawal and coldness after returning from a longer separation. Some psychologists argue that the child's withdrawal indicates his reluctance to enter close relationships and again run the risk of the pain associated with separation. Even casual observation suggests that breaking a relationship is important to a child; it seems that it should be kept to a minimum, especially when children are very young. It is questionable, however, that complete avoidance of separation is any more adaptive. As the child must grow up in a world in which separation is inevitable, early learning seems likely to be profitable up to a point.

The question of adoption naturally arises from this discussion. Early adoption appears desirable. There is no reason why the child adopted as an infant should not react to his adoptive parents just as he would to his real ones. The period between five weeks and seven months is critical to the initial formation of relationships; the earlier such formation begins, the more likely it is to be successful. Once the child has begun to show fear of unfamiliar people, the chances of establishing good relationships with adoptive parents is less.

Children adopted later in life tend to be less well adjusted. It is still an open question whether the important factor is the emotional damage from the timing of adoption or the parents' response to a child who may initially be afraid and cry a great deal. At any rate, when a child is past seven months of age at adoption it is well to remember that he will be slower to form new relationships and may be afraid of unfamiliar environments. To ease this change the prospective parents can visit the child in familiar surroundings for a few hours at a time, over a period of days, then bring him to his new home for short periods until he grows used to it. The point is to help the child by maintaining continuity between his familiar environment and the new one.

AUTISM

As yet no definite cause of autism in children is known. In fact, there are no clear criteria for labeling a child "autistic." It is generally believed, however, that autistic children behave as if they had become socialized to themselves alone. They seem to live in their own world and to be interested primarily in their own bodies and actions. An autistic child will play alone for hours and reject all attempts to interrupt him; he seems entirely content with inanimate objects.

It is quite difficult to separate the autistic child from the retarded, deaf, or neurologically impaired child. One of the best indicators is inconsistency in performance; that is, the autistic child will occasionally behave normally before returning to his autistic preoccupations.

In the past it was supposed that the autistic child would require exceptionally long treatment in psychiatric hospitals. Even then the chances for improvement seemed small. In a sense such treatment reflected acceptance of the child's own solution to his problems, in which he restricted stimulus input in order to cope with his environment. Newer programs have incorporated efforts to break through the child's resistance to interpersonal contacts. The behavior-shaping programs discussed in Chapter 7 have been helpful in building social and verbal skills in autistic children. Other programs are geared to work with each child individually, accepting his leads at first but gradually imposing structure and limitations upon his activities. As he begins to respond to the limits, he is moved into a regular nursery with normal children. The treatments that appear most successful so far are structured, less permissive, and more educationally oriented than "feeling" oriented.

EARLY MORAL CONCEPTS

From approximately two years on, the child begins visibly to conform to the rules of his society. Conforming to social restrictions apparently contributes to what has been called "conscience," an internal response to the "rights" and "wrongs" defined by one's culture. Nearly all investigators agree that conscience is acquired, rather than innate.

Observations suggest that moral learning is at first quite concrete. A child's earliest moral code stresses obedience and punishment; the seriousness of a transgression is related to the objective harm or damage that follows. The child's rules are likely to be absolute, rigid, and arbitrary, though he may break them whenever he thinks that he will not be caught. In general, as his thinking becomes more flexible, his moral code becomes more subtle. His sense of wrongdoing is increasingly internalized; that is, morality becomes a matter of internal, rather than external, restrictions. If the early rigid morality does not soften into a more flexible one, the individual is likely to find himself in serious conflict with his changing society and its changing value systems. On the other hand, if conscience fails to develop at all, he will find himself in conflict with society and perhaps involved in delinquent activities.

As moral concepts develop the child first recognizes the "no no's"; as his ability to verbalize and conceptualize expands, his moral behavior shows signs of increasing flexibility and internal control. Moral development is necessary in relations with others and with culture. The child who does not develop adequate moral patterns is likely to experience social difficulties later if not earlier.

THE SCHOOL CHILD AND THE PREADOLESCENT

INTRODUCTION

The grammar-school years seem to include fewer critical periods than do the preschool and early adolescent years. Learning and adjustment continue along with physiological and intellectual development. The emphasis in adjustment switches from physiological stability to the building of culturally relevant skills, peer relationships, and prevocational learning. These years are important for consolidating the beginning of a self-image, or identity. The primary developmental tasks include acquisition of skills to be applied later in adult social and vocational roles. Adults other than family members now teach many of the most important skills. In this sense the school is an important agent of development; the central position of the family has weakened.

THE CONCEPT OF TIME IN DEVELOPMENT

To most of us "time" is synonymous with calendar time. The earth's rotation and its revolution around the sun provide consistently recurring experiences that permit man to keep track of events by years, months, days, hours, minutes, and so on and thus to measure chronological age (C.A.). The time units in the development of individual organisms are, however, rarely that precise.

DEVELOPMENTAL TIME

Psychological and physiological development is individual, and no two people experience it at exactly the same rate. Nor does any stage of development occur at exactly the same chronological age in two different people. Data from the Berkeley Growth Study (Bayley, 1956) can serve to illustrate. Patterns of development in individual children were quite striking, each reflecting a unique growth. The subjects were observed periodically from infancy to over twenty years of age. Their growth in height, weight, head circumference, skeletal maturity, motor skills, and intelligence were plotted. Figure 9-2 shows how individual subjects differed in their rates of development. The intersections of the curves show that even the rates of individual boys differed at different times. Figure 9-3 represents one girl's rate of development on all six variables, compared to those of the other girls in the study. By examining the figure in detail we can see that this girl was small and slender, with a small head, who matured slowly and grew into a tall slender adult. Though consistently superior in intelligence, she was relatively higher at some ages than others. Scores in motor tests varied between superior and average. When her intelligence score was highest (one year old), her motor scores appeared to be almost at their lowest.

That expecting certain levels of development from a given child at any specific chronological age is a mistake should be obvious. One way to gauge developmental age is to measure the particular developmental process in question. It is not so simple, however, to find adequate measures.

Normative studies provide data that make it possible to compute average levels of development at different chronological ages. The I.Q., for example, is actually a summary of a child's test score relative to those of children

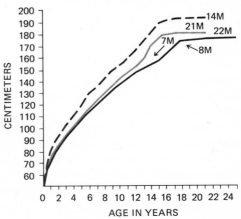

INDIVIDUAL CURVES OF GROWTH IN STATURE
Berkeley Growth Study

Figure 9-2 Curves of stature by age for five boys in the Berkeley Growth Study. From Nancy Bayley, Individual patterns of development. *Child Development*, 1956, **27**, 55. By permission of the Society for Research in Child Development, Inc.

CURVES OF STANDARD SCORES BY AGE FOR SIX VARIABLES

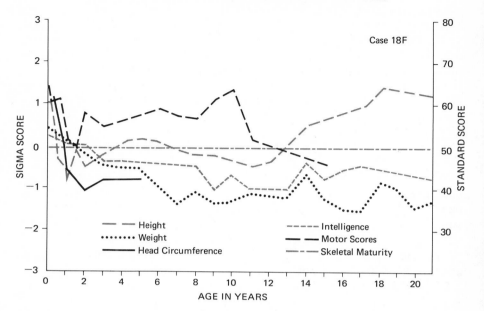

Figure 9-3   Curves of standard scores by age for six variables, for Case 18F. From Nancy Bayley, Individual patterns of development. *Child Development*, 1956, **27**, 53. By permission of the Society for Research in Child Development, Inc.

approximately his own chronological age; it is a deviation score, showing how much he has scored above or below the mean for his age peers. For example, a child who scores 115 on the Wechsler Intelligence Scale for Children has scored one standard deviation (a statistical concept indicating the variability in a set of scores) above the mean for his age group. The psychologist can judge approximately where the child stands in relation to his peers. In this instance he has scored as high or higher than have approximately 83 percent of his age peers.

   Because growth rates vary within children, as well as among children, the same child may score nearer the mean at one age than he does at another. If this developmental rate is quite rapid when he is young, his I.Q. is probably a great deal above the mean; if it slows as he grows older, his score probably will fall closer to the group mean. There is nothing final about any I.Q. score, though it does become more stable with age. Except for those who score at the extremes the I.Q. measure is not stable enough to justify precise or irreversible judgments of intellectual ability and achievement.

   The common measure of intellectual development is "mental age" (M.A.). A twelve-year-old child with an I.Q. of 60 (in the retarded range) has an M.A. of around five years. The I.Q. tells us that he has scored in the lowest 2 percent of his age group, and the M.A. tells us that he performs at about the mean for a five-year-old child. The M.A. is thus a measure of intellectual development, providing information on the kinds of intellectual tasks that the child is capable of performing. From the I.Q. score alone we know only that he has done poorly in comparison with other children his age.

Intellectual and physical growth is not the only process that reflects individual rates; behavioral and emotional control does so as well. As we noted earlier (see Chapter 2) some children appear to be inherently more active than are others, but there are also individual differences in the rapidity with which they gain control over their impulses and social behavior. Measures of the maturity of these attributes can be most helpful in working with young school children.

CONFUSION OF CHRONOLOGICAL AND DEVELOPMENTAL TIME

Some obvious problems—and some less obvious ones—result from confusing calendar time and developmental time.

RESEARCH

Research findings may be distorted if the two kinds of time are equated. For example, if we were to examine the effects of a preschool program on later intellectual development, using subjects chosen on the basis of chronological age alone, our results would be misleading. A group of four-years-olds, though equal in calendar age, is not necessarily equal in intellectual age. At best, the measure would provide a gross indication of the utility of the program. Although we might be able to determine that in general these children showed higher school achievement than did children not in the program, it would be impossible to determine at what point in intellectual development preschool stimulation is most beneficial. To make such fine determinations we must measure intellectual levels like mental age. We can then make qualifications, for example, that four-year-olds who are advanced intellectually more than two years do not benefit from the program. The financial savings owing to such fine determinations are obvious. The possible advantages to children are less easily detected but even more important; the bright youngster may be spared many boring hours, the slow child may not be embarrassed by having to compete with those who are advanced, and so on.

SCHOOL PLACEMENT

Complex and heated conflicts often arise over the age at which a child should start school. Educators are becoming more aware of the problems that arise when all children at a given chronological age are taught the same things and treated the same way. The similarity in intellectual development within a given age group is usually great enough so that most children are able to handle the same intellectual tasks, but there are always children who are not yet ready for specific tasks and others who are already beyond them. Whether behind or ahead, exceptional children may suffer from school programs based on chronological-age placement. The slow developers consistently experience unrewarding feedback. Repeated exposure to negative conditions often sows the seeds of general dislike and fear of school—attitudes that can drastically interfere with later achievement. The advanced child, on the other hand, may find the work monotonous and boring. He too is likely to develop undesirable attitudes and behavior patterns.

Most modern educational systems are developing programs that emphasize developmental age and individual differences. There is no reason to believe that five calendar years mark the magic age at which formal education should begin. The child's developmental level is a more accurate indicator of readiness for school. The more individualized school programs generally test children before or shortly after school begins, in order to determine their levels of intellectual, emotional, and behavioral development. Some children are not yet behaviorally or emotionally ready to cooperate successfully in groups; consequently the school may recommend waiting a year before starting formal education. Classrooms in these schools are formed according to developmental age; the academic material and behavioral expectations are then geared to each group. One first-grade class may, for instance, have only very short periods of concentrated work and more periods of active play. Another may confront tasks generally considered "kindergarten level," whereas still another will do work commonly considered appropriate to second or even third grade.

Special education programs are now widely available for children with specific learning difficulties and those at the developmental extremes. Classes are provided for retarded children, gifted children, and children suffering from neurological or emotional disturbances. This increase in special classes probably offers a preview of education in the future. Educators are becoming more aware of the importance of programs tailored to each child's developmental level and capacity. It is not impossible that the comparatively recent advent of "ungraded" classrooms will lead to "ungraded" schools. Teachers will concentrate on their particular areas of competence and interest, and students' programs will be geared to their interests and abilities. Programmed instruction (see Chapter 7), which allows each child to progress at his own rate, will probably also play an increasingly important part in education.

ADULT EXPECTATIONS

Parents and other adults may make the mistake of substituting chronological age for developmental age in their expectations of a child. Too often they have only fuzzy ideas of the appropriate behavior for any given chronological age. A child who is psychologically advanced or retarded is therefore likely to cause adults a great deal of unnecessary frustration. The retarded child is not ready for certain tasks, and the advanced child quickly becomes bored with them. Adults must be aware of the wide variation in developmental rates, especially in young children, in order to avoid unnecessarily disruptive interaction. Many adults are implicitly aware of this variation and intuitively treat children as individuals. Others are less skillful. Their unrealistic expectations usually create great difficulty for themselves and their children.

DEVELOPMENTAL TASKS

The elementary-school child must accomplish several adjustments. How he approaches them has important effects later. As he meets the challenges of this period his behavior may cause consternation to his parents. Nevertheless, from the time that he starts school until he reaches early adolescence, major changes in his behavior patterns, his attitudes toward other people, and his beliefs and values will occur.

PEER-GROUP INTERACTION

Before entering school most children are able to play cooperatively with other children at least to a limited extent. Learning to communicate with peers is a gradual process that continues during the school years. In the first years of school the ability to interact with other children is necessary. Each child must learn to conform to group requirements, to follow various rules, and to curb many of his impulses in favor of the demands of either the peer group or the teacher. If he cannot do so, he is very unlikely to succeed in school, and he will have to suffer the consequences of failure. Some behavior that has served him during his dependent early years must be put aside if he is to cooperate with his equals or to obey the instructions of an adult.

Investigators generally agree on certain aspects of social development (for example, Mussen *et al.*, 1969; Muller, 1969). In the early stages of social interaction children try to attract attention and to win the popularity of their peers. At first they do not seem to discriminate one child from another; any child who leaves them or fails to provide the desired attention may be the object of their special efforts. Progressively they show less need to please everyone. By the age of eight years or so most have begun to select a few children as friends. How their chosen friends react to them becomes important at this time and, of course, continues to be important later.

It is also common for children to become highly critical of one another and especially of children who are not "popular." Group attacks on one child are not unusual and a child may be severely humiliated, by adult standards, for being "fat," "stupid," "dirty," and so on. Many children, on the other hand, will respond to adults who try to correct this behavior. They are likely to reverse their attitudes toward the child who is being berated, especially when other children do the same.

Friends begin to replace parents as companions and fashion setters in the fourth or fifth grade. The peer group becomes a model and a source of feedback for the child; peer opinion increases in importance relative to parental wishes. Peer groups often develop their own rules and insist that they must be followed. Both organized clubs and spontaneously formed groups are common at this age. In the United States, for instance, preadolescent youngsters are often members of football and baseball teams, conservation organizations, young farmers' organizations, and so on. Many youngsters between ten and twelve have already participated in groups whose activities are quite similar to those of groups to which they will belong in late adolescence and adulthood; parliamentary procedure, leadership positions, group decision processes, and so on are already familiar. The interpersonal skills that children develop in these settings may serve them in the future in dealing with problems related to others.

One of the more serious adjustment problems in the early school years is the *school phobia* (Verville, 1967; Kessler, 1966). The difficulty reveals itself in varying degrees, from initial hesitancy to start school to unreasonable fear of school. This fear may appear dramatically. Suddenly a child whose attachment to school has seemed established pleads to stay home; he cries, he trembles, and he insists that he does not know why he is afraid. In fact, he frequently does not know why he is afraid, and forcing him to give a reason will contribute little to clarifying the problem. It is not uncommon for some specific event to precipitate the reaction, especially in children who are already somewhat hesitant and unsure of themselves in the school environment. An accident, an illness, the birth of a new baby with whom he must compete, or a specific school event that frightens or displeases him may trigger his fear.

Although children with school phobias often appear timid and frightened at school, they are sometimes quite the opposite at home. Frequently they have been able to dominate their overprotective mothers, and their fathers have been permissive or inactive in their upbringing. Several investigators believe that the basis for many school phobias is the children's fear of separation from their mothers, the threat of losing comfort and nurture. The school comes to represent a frightening stimulus complex, in which failure, hurt, and neglect are possible.

The more instruction that the child has missed, the more likely he is to be embarrassed before his classmates when he returns to school. It has therefore often been useful to send the child back to school as soon as possible, even though he need not rejoin his class. Instead he can complete his assignments in the office of the principal, the nurse, or the counselor. Usually he regains his courage in a few days and is able to return to his regular class. The teacher can help by organizing class exercises so that the child interacts with different children. In this way he comes to know more of them better and thus the total environment may become more comfortable.

SEX-ROLE DEVELOPMENT

Controversy over "natural" sex roles still exists. Do men and women act differently because of inherited differences? Although there is no definitive answer yet, a great deal of evidence suggests that cultural expectations mainly determine how each sex behaves in a given society. Cultural anthropologists

have shown clearly that cultures vary widely in the behavior that they prescribe for the sexes. In one primitive society, for instance, the male takes a
role that many members of our society would consider feminine: He gossips,
cares for children, takes care of the home, and so on, whereas the female
tends the gardens, gathers herbs and fruits, and the like.

In American society the imposition of sex roles sometimes begins at
birth: Baby clothes are usually blue for boys and pink for girls. It is not long
before cultural expectations are reflected in the infant's toys. Girls are given
miniature homemaking implements and boys miniature tools and vehicles.

Usually before a child enters school his parents have already suggested
sex-appropriate behavior, but they have usually not made a big issue of it.
It is during the school years themselves that more pressure is placed on the
child to recognize and exhibit appropriate sex-role behavior. This pressure
can be quite annoying or upsetting, depending upon the child's interests.
For example, the little boy may have copied his mother's sewing or knitting
under the tolerant smiles of his parents. Once he is of school age, however,
he finds himself called "sissy." His peers tease him, his parents subtly try
to turn him in other directions, and relatives and friends pressure his parents
to change him. Girls seem to have less difficulty being "tomboys" than boys
have being "sissies." Nevertheless the aggressive little girl must control her
temper and avoid physical assaults; if her interest in sports is not channeled
away from direct competition with boys she must tolerate subtle—and not
so subtle—comments about her lack of femininity.

A clearer division of sex roles reveals itself around nine or ten years of
age. Each sex comes to depend more upon companions of the same sex than
it did earlier. The boys group together, and the girls group together. Activities
with the opposite sex are avoided, except on the pretense of interrupting its
play. Girls and boys become very critical of each other, less from direct
antagonism than to strengthen their own sex identifications. Flirtatious behavior characteristically takes the form of mild or moderate aggression toward
the opposite sex. The most popular girl in the class may also have the largest
number of bruises on her arm from her admirers' blows.

Although adult sex roles are becoming less distinct in our society, the
cultural expectations are still fairly clear. Boys are expected to demonstrate
strength, skill, daring, and dominance; not to need comfort; and not to cry
when abused or frightened. Each failure to live up to this strong masculine
image is a sign that the boy is not filling his role adequately. In our culture
boys generally have more difficulty in finding adult models than do girls because much of their time is spent under the supervision of women both at
school and at home. Their task is therefore more difficult.

It is easier for a girl to fill her role because it is not drastically different
from that of dependent child. She is allowed greater freedom of emotional
expression than a boy is, and she is not expected to face up to challenges or
danger, regardless of the consequences. Her biggest adjustment is to curb

her aggressiveness and tendencies to dominate, which may mean stifling her intellectual or physical potential.

The development of sex-role behavior does not cease with the school years but continues important in adolescence and adulthood. Being male or female influences almost any activity.

That male and female role expectations are gradually becoming more alike in most industrial countries is a matter of everyday observation. Men and women may now enter many of the same professions—a rarity in the not-so-distant past. It is still true, nevertheless, that women are discriminated against (usually covertly) in the vocational marketplace. They are likely to find it more difficult than men do to obtain both education and employment in some vocations. Family roles are also changing. The father now shares many of the child-care activities that were traditionally the mother's sole responsibility, and it is not uncommon for both parents to work. Men's saloons (in which women are not allowed) are almost a thing of the past; only a few remain as landmarks in the history of sex-role changes. Many men's clubs have female auxiliaries. The "secrets" of the lodge in many instances are no longer limited to the "man of the house."

These changes have implications for personal adjustment. One's identity as man or woman is complicated when cultural expectations clash with personal preferences. Interpersonal relations are also affected, depending upon the congruence of a couple's views. The man who expects his wife to be entirely oriented toward the home will usually find his relationship with a career-oriented wife fraught with tension. Changing sex roles may also create conflict between parents and children. The young are more likely to accept them, indeed to create them—their elders often cannot.

MASTERING CULTURALLY RELEVANT SKILLS

An important part of the school child's development is learning skills that will enhance his effective performance as an adult. These skills are both cognitive and behavioral and are related to future social and vocational roles.

PHYSICAL SKILLS

The mastery of physical skills often plays a part in the development of a positive self-image. Elementary-school boys, for example, often place a great deal of emphasis on athletic prowess. Physical coordination develops first in the gross motor activities that are important in skills like running. The development of the more difficult perceptual-motor coordination required for organized sports occurs later and continues into adolescence.

Physical skills are also important in social interaction. Children learn the appropriate cultural expressions for different emotional states; they learn table manners, male-female etiquette, and nonverbal gestures that enrich communication. A child who avoids or withdraws from group activities and peer interaction may be handicapped by failure to learn the physical skills that enliven interaction. An early hesitancy may snow-ball and the child may become increasingly inept. The school child who enters into peer activities is, on the other hand, likely to use his body to communicate in accordance with cultural expectations. His interactions are generally more successful, he is more self-confident, and he is more adept in group activities as an adolescent and an adult.

INTELLECTUAL SKILLS

Most people think of school as a place where practical intellectual skills are developed. Indeed, teaching such skills is one of the school's major functions in modern cultures. Learning such skills as reading, arithmetic, and the expression of ideas in writing is highly adaptive. It was not long ago that most Americans did not complete their formal education. A significant proportion of the population was illiterate in even the most advanced Western cultures. In modern industrial societies, however, occupational requirements demand more and more academic skills. Fifty years ago only a small proportion of adults were college graduates. Now, however, many jobs require skills taught at the graduate level; bachelor's degree is often only a starting point.

Reading is probably the most basic and important of all educational subjects. Learning in any content area basically depends upon the ability to read. Learning to read is thus an extremely important step toward a successful future. As with other attainments, children of the same chronological age show wide variation in their capacity to learn reading. Not only is general intelligence important but also specific visual-motor ability is required. Motivation, which is often determined by the child's background, may be an important factor. Children from lower socioeconomic levels, for instance, may not have been taught that achievement at school is important. They may not expend a great deal of energy in overcoming some of the frustration associated with learning to read. Other children may not have achieved sufficient social maturity to take advantage of the teacher's assistance or to attend to instructions that facilitate learning.

In the days before the typewriter, when almost all written communication was in longhand, penmanship, neatness, and style were more important than they are now. There is little need to stress these topics today, for it is necessary only to write legibly enough for others to read. Nevertheless, some teachers continue to emphasize penmanship. Because of inordinate insistence on "neatness" such teachers may create emotional disturbances in otherwise normal children.

Writing, in the sense of expressing ideas ("composition") is, however, becoming increasingly important in many modern occupations. But today's schools do not seem to teach composition and creative writing with much success. A great deal of time is spent on drill and rote memorization to increase vocabulary and punctuation skills. The task of translating ideas into written form is usually not approached systematically until the high-school years, and then it is often elective. It is not unusual for high-school graduates to be unable to write a clear, expressive personal letter. To a large extent American schools (including colleges and universities) reinforce achievement through memorization of facts. It is much easier, of course, to use objective criteria to judge a student's grasp of content and to grade short-answer exams than it is to grade or evaluate ideas presented in free-flowing composition. Almost any college professor will attest to the difficulties that he encounters in reading essay examinations; clarity of expression, even in graduate students, nearly always falls short of what is desirable.

Arithmetic is another important academic skill. Whether or not it is important in one's vocation, it is obviously helpful in everyday living. Upon entering school, children are usually less well prepared to deal with number concepts than with language concepts. Frequently they have done little more than count objects, if even that. In recent years teaching arithmetic has changed from methods based primarily on memorizing to methods based on understanding the operations from which calculations are derived. The fourth- or fifth-grade child will, for example, bring home "new math" assignments that completely confuse his parents who have been taught by the old methods. The new approach is an attempt to develop the child's understanding of the concepts underlying numerical systems. Once they are understood, he will be better able to deal with circumstances that may not fit exactly the operations previously taught by memory. As a result, many numerical concepts are now introduced in the elementary years.

PROCESSES OF CHANGE

Development does not take place at random. If it is not interrupted it progresses in orderly fashion. Theoretical explanations to account for the gradual process of developmental change have been offered. Two of these explanations will be examined in this section: J. Piaget's theory of cognitive development and the theory of identification.

PIAGET'S THEORY OF COGNITIVE DEVELOPMENT

Piaget has been a leading theorist on child development throughout this century. Through semicontrolled observations he has attempted to account for the course of intellectual development in children (Baldwin, 1967; Inhelder and Piaget, 1958; Piaget, 1952, 1954, 1959).

BASIC CONCEPTS

The notion of *schema* is basic to Piaget's theory. The biological concept of "structure" is the parallel functional unit. Schemata may vary a great deal in their complexity—from reliable, simple responses to a given stimulus (like the knee-jerk reflex) to very complex response chains including cognitive representations (thoughts), intermediate actions, and consummatory actions (as when a child thinks about a candy bar, goes about obtaining one, and then eats it). Schemata may be very simple, almost unitary, or as complex as biological systems (the digestive system, for instance); they may also be highly differentiated and widely distributed throughout the body. A schema is defined by the function that it serves. Piaget's schemata usually include a multiple of activities, rather than simple unitary responses to specific stimuli.

According to Piaget, development progresses as it does because the person is building more complex schemata. A "natural drive" leads the child to build complex skills from simple ones; the outcome is the attainment of complex functions (schemata).

Schemata show increasing *mobility* with age; that is, scope of their application broadens. For instance, the child's ability to reach out and grasp an object is generalized to more objects. At first he may be able to grasp only larger objects that fit into the palm of his hand, but eventually he learns to pick up smaller ones and thus becomes adept in dealing with his environment.

There is another aspect to mobility as well: In the early development of a schema it may be an end in itself. Grasping, for instance, is apparently first done for its own sake. As the skill becomes more mobile, however, it becomes more instrumental: The child will grasp something in order to bring it close for visual inspection. As the child's schemata become increasingly mobile he is better equipped to manipulate his environment for his own ends.

Adaptation is another important concept. Piaget does not use the term in a general sense; he refers only to changes in schemata that permit them to become more useful to the child. Adaptation is the process through which individual skills and competences (schemata) grow and develop into the complex activities common among adults.

Adaptation of schemata occurs through a combination of *assimilation* and *accommodation*. The use of an existing schema to bring novel stimuli under effective control is assimilation. The environment challenges a child by presenting new objects—a new rattle, for example—and he uses his already existing grasping ability to bring them closer and to learn more about them. His grasping schema, though it has not changed in itself, has broadened his knowledge and increased his effectiveness in dealing with his environment. He has assimilated new objects through his skill. When the existing schemata are not sufficient to meet a new environmental challenge, he must change or broaden them: He must accommodate his schemata to the stimuli. If a safety pin, for example, were presented to him and his grasping schema had been applied only to larger objects, he would have to learn finer coordination before he could deal with it effectively. As he accommodates, of course, a whole new range of stimuli become available for assimilation. As a child alternately assimilates and accommodates, his schemata become more effective in dealing with the environment: They become more adaptive.

Equilibration is the combined process of assimilation and accommodation. To Piaget, the occurrence of events or objects in the child's environment stimulates him and serves to motivate assimilation. That is, the child is motivated to adapt to new circumstances as long as they represent a challenge but not so great a challenge that success is nearly impossible; he would not, for instance, attempt to pick up an automobile. Such stimulus situations are called *aliments*. They may be partially assimilated but may also require some accommodation.

Mastering new aliments is equilibration, and greater mobility of sensory-motor and cognitive schemata result. Sensory-motor schemata include overt activity like grasping, whereas cognitive schema include thinking activities like counting, logical deduction, and so forth.

Development, then, according to Piaget, is the progressive transformation of simple schemata into more complex schemata. The motive force behind this process depends upon aliments and their equilibration. When the environment furnishes a realistic challenge the child is motivated to test his schemata, to modify them, and thus increases his adaptiveness. From birth onward the child's schemata become more complex and more adaptive, building to the higher cognitive processes observed in adults.

DEVELOPMENTAL PERIODS

Piaget has postulated four developmental stages, each characterized by particular changes in the child's thinking:

Sensory-motor period: birth to two years
Preoperational period: two years to seven years
Period of concrete operations: seven years to eleven years
Period of formal operations: eleven years on

Clinical observation in a standardized setting has been Piaget's primary method of study. His hypotheses have been derived from observations of children handling toys and dealing with other objects in their natural environment, as well as working on tasks devised especially for his purposes.

THE SENSORY-MOTOR PERIOD The major development in the *sensory-motor period* is the acquisition of internally controlled, mobile, primarily motor and sensory schemata. Only at the very end of this period does evidence of cognitive and representational schemata appear.

The child learns to coordinate information from his senses and to organize information about the same object from different sources. He reaches the point at which he can both look at and listen to what he manipulates. By coordinating all these modalities he gains a great deal more information about the object than he would have earlier.

An infant begins by grasping something that is pressed in his hand. He cannot do much with it except open and close his fingers, and he often drops it as he moves about. When he develops the ability to guide his grasp and to hold an object where he can examine it with his eyes, he gains more information. By the end of the sensory-motor period several internal schemata have been well developed. Learning to coordinate the sense organs with motor activity increases the child's effectiveness greatly. The use of cognitive representations in long-range planning and in decisions among alternative modes of action are, however, not yet in operation.

Another major development during this period is the concept of reality. The infant learns, or acts as if he has learned, that the external world has a permanence. That is, at first he treats objects as if they exist only when he can see them. Later, however, he acts as if he knows that they exist even when he cannot directly sense them. He has apparently learned the concept of "permanence." To demonstrate permanence the observer can take a familiar object from an infant, place it surreptitiously under the pillow, and bring his hand out empty for the child to examine. In the earliest phase of development the child acts as if the object has disappeared; he does not look for it in the person's hand. Later, however, he looks in the observer's hand with determination and perhaps even acts as if he thinks the object may have been left behind his pillow. Finally, the child recognizes the possibility that it has been left under the pillow, a response that suggests that he has begun to use symbolic representations of objects functionally. The object now has a quality of permanence through his cognitive mediators; it need not be directly observable to affect his behavior.

A final phase of the sensory-motor period is the development of purposive behavior. The child can now put several actions together in order to reach a goal. This advance marks the beginning of experimentation with new objects and testing of schemata that are already in operation. It is as if the child were purposely trying to learn what effects he can have on his environment. He varies his behavior intentionally and learns to solve problems through systematic trial and error.

To demonstrate purposive behavior we can place a desirable object on a pillow beyond the child's reach. In his struggle to reach the object, he may accidentally hit the pillow and cause the object to move. If his behavior has become purposive, he will then begin to move the pillow deliberately while watching the object. It is as if he were exploring the effects of this new way of moving the object. The child soon discovers that by pulling the pillow toward him he can reach the object. His initial discovery of "moving the pillow moves the object" has been accidental; nevertheless, he is now capable of taking deliberate action toward a solution. At the end of this stage the child is performing clearly purposive problem solving in this way.

THE PREOPERATIONAL PERIOD The *preoperational period* is mainly transitional and marked by expansion of the child's internal picture of the external world, its laws, and its relationships. His conceptual schemata are at first simply internal copies of sensory-motor patterns and behavioral schemata. Cognitive schemata nevertheless become organized as interrelated systems. They become "operational," useful in affecting the environment.

The child develops internal representations and gains facility in using them adaptively, but their use is still unstable and inconsistent. At this point the child may contradict himself quite easily and be unaware of it. For example, when two identical glasses are filled to the same height the preschool child will agree that there is an equal amount of liquid in each. But, when the liquid from one container is poured into a taller and narrower container as the child watches, he may not believe that it is still the same amount. He agrees that none has been added and none taken away, but he remains convinced that the taller container holds more. Piaget explains that the child's cognitive schemata are not yet integrated in a way that allows rule-following, one observation affecting the next in a logical way. The child has failed to integrate events separated in time and has not used evidence from the original situation to understand the one that followed. Preoperational children often inspect the containers to determine whether or not the answer lies in the immediate situation. To the older person, of course, the relevant datum is the original equality of the amounts. The child's schemata at this stage also lack reversibility: He does not realize that the liquid can be poured back into its original container and again be the same. The child seems capable of dealing with width or height by themselves, but combining the two confuses him.

THE STAGE OF CONCRETE OPERATIONS   The *stage of concrete operations* is characterized by two major kinds of logical rules: class inclusion and serial ordering.

In the preoperational stage the child is unable to think about parts and wholes independently. When, for example, preoperational children are shown a box of wooden beads, eighteen brown and two white, they will agree that all are wooden beads and that some are brown and some are white. But when they are asked if there are more brown beads than wooden beads, they reply that there are more brown beads: They are unable to deal simultaneously with the two separate concepts of part (brown beads) and whole (wooden beads). The child in the stage of concrete operations is, however, able to distinguish part and whole in his thinking. He understands that objects may be classified in two ways at the same time. The capacity for higher levels of classification has been developed, and a brown bead can be recognized as part of the larger class, wooden beads.

Capacity for serial ordering also develops, in relation to many dimensions —height, weight, length, width, amount of money, and so on. In this stage the child is able to apply the operations of class inclusion and serial ordering to concrete objects, but he has difficulty with objects that are present only in imagination.

THE STAGE OF FORMAL OPERATIONS   The major change at early adolescence, *the stage of formal operations,* is the growing use of cognitive operations without the need for concrete stimuli. The child begins to reason deductively and to think about problems whose ingredients are all contained in his own thoughts. He is also capable of evaluating the logic and quality of his own thinking: He has become more aware of his own thoughts and is able to reflect upon them as a younger child cannot. He now has the ability to construct theories, to deduce, and to arrive at hypotheses; in general he has developed what is known as "scientific" thinking.

"Combinatorial" thinking has also developed; that is he can appreciate the differences among all the possible combinations for arriving at a solution and can systematically eliminate them in reaching an answer. Piaget presents his subjects with the task of discovering the function of unknown liquids. Each subject is given five bottles of colorless liquid; four of the bottles are identical, the fifth is smaller. The liquid from the smaller bottle can be added to the other liquids to change the colors, for each liquid contains chemicals that produce colors when mixed with the agent in the small bottle. The child is asked to discover how to produce a particular color using any or all of the five flasks. He is also required to describe the function of each liquid in the process of creating the color. For example, liquids 1 and 3 may have to be mixed with the agent to produce the color yellow; adding liquid 2 may have no effect one way or the other; liquid 4 may bleach the yellow color created by the mixture of liquids 1 and 3. The point of the problem is to present the subject with a situation in which all possible combinations of the elements (liquids) must be tried; there is no way to solve the problem certainly without observing all possible combinations. The way the subject goes about discovering all of the possible combinations and their systematic elimination shows the degree of "combinatorial" thinking he has attained. A child in the previous stage of concrete operations is unlikely to recognize the possibility of combining more than one liquid with another.

Piaget has thus classified intellectual development in four stages. Minimal symbolic activity is involved in the first stage, in which the child learns that certain activities have specific effects upon his environment. In the next stage he learns words for objects and events, but his thinking remains intuitive and inconsistent. In the third stage logical rules are applied to concrete objects but not to abstract ones, nor can the child reflect upon his own thinking. In early adolescence the child begins to reason deductively, to think about his own thinking, and to approach problems in a "scientific" way by systematically eliminating all possibilities. He is able to use silent trial and error in evaluating the suitability of specific cognitive operations under given circumstances.

LEARNING AND IDENTIFICATION

By what means does a child change from an "animal" into a member of a society? How does he become socialized? In this section we shall examine hypothetical processes that are considered important in socialization. Much of this material follows P. Mussen's views rather closely (Mussen, 1967).

Several basic dimensions will become apparent as we examine socialization. First, there are the *kinds* of behavior that become socialized. Research on this dimension usually focuses on systems of behavior—groups of behavior centered around a given drive like sexual expression, curiosity, achievement, and so on—rather than on specific responses. The individuals and groups who influence a child's socialization—the *agents* of socialization—constitute another important dimension. They may vary a great deal from culture to culture, but the family is always important. In most modern societies there are many other agents as well: teachers, doctors, ministers, colleagues, and peer groups. All may have significant effects on socialization. A third dimension encompasses the various *techniques and practices* of socializing children; they too differ a great deal among cultures and subcultures. Investigations of this dimension focus on child-rearing practices like weaning, instilling conscience, toilet-training, controlling aggression, and so on.

All three of these dimensions may be examined with the aid of two concepts: learning and identification. The remainder of this section is devoted to such an examination.

LEARNING

Learning has been discussed in more detail in Chapter 7. Its characteristics have been studied extensively in psychological laboratories and now constitute a large body of scientific knowledge. For the present, however, its definition is limited to the acquisition of habits through reinforcement. As learning is related to socialization it may be defined as the modification of behavior through practice, practice which is usually associated with reward and punishment. Socializing agents, whether individuals or groups, reinforce responses that they consider desirable and punish behavior that they consider undesirable. Through this process children learn culturally acceptable conduct. Those kinds of behavior that are reinforced developed into habits; those that are punished or not reinforced are eventually eliminated.

The developmental tasks of the preschool child largely involve shaping the expression of basic drives. Learning to eat "properly," toilet behavior, and sexual expression are shaped according to culturally accepted standards. To a large extent learning accounts for the specific forms that these habits take. Proper social responses are taught during the early years of childhood. Eating habits (table manners), how to interact with adults, how to interact with other children, and other behavior is reinforced or punished by parents or parent surrogates. Learning, in the sense of purposeful reinforcement and punishment, therefore accounts for many of the kinds of behavior that a child acquires.

Children also, however, learn a great deal that is not deliberately taught to them. The agent and the child may in fact be unaware that significant social learning is taking place. The establishment of trust in an infant, for example, appears to be dependent upon the nature of the early interactions between mother and child. The infant whose needs are inadequately met finds his first social interactions uncomfortable. If his mother handles him roughly or brings tension to his feeding, he is likely to develop mistrust of her and later of others in general.

"Generalization" is an important learning concept. Similar stimuli, which are not present when learning occurs, will arouse responses similar to those that greeted the original stimulus. In our example the child's initial mistrust of his mother will be generalized to other people, and he will develop pervasive mistrust in human relationships. Many other aspects of the child's personality are also inadvertently learned through reinforcement, including methods of child rearing, parental attitudes, and family interactions. Some of these topics are discussed in more detail in Chapter 10.

IDENTIFICATION

Another subtler process appears to facilitate socialization: identification. In general terms, identification reflects the desire of children to be like their fathers and mothers. Learning through identification does not result directly from reinforcement, at least not from reinforcement that can be explicitly outlined and identified. The child seems spontaneously to acquire complex reactions and response patterns, that is, patterns that no one intends specifically to teach and the child does not specifically intend to learn.

A theoretical question that is still to be satisfactorily answered is whether or not identification can be explained by learning theory. Learning theorists view identification as a drive that is acquired because of the association of reinforcement with imitating what the parent (model) does. If such behavior is regularly rewarded, then, in the language of learning theory, imitation acquires secondary-drive characteristics.

A. Bandura and R. H. Walters (1963) have argued that "identification" is not a useful term. They would like to substitute "imitation" because it is clearer and more economical. They have also suggested that "observational learning" is what accounts for a child's tendency to take on the characteristics of parental models. Their investigations of imitative behavior have provided rather convincing evidence in support of their notions. Primarily because of their work, Mussen (1967) was led to restrict his definition of "identification" to certain very significant kinds of imitative behavior.

> Identification, then, may be defined as a hypothesized process, accounting for the child's imitation of a model's complex, integrated patterns of behavior—rather than discrete reactions or simple responses—emitted spontaneously without specific training or direct reward for emulation. Two further characteristics of major importance differentiate identification from imitation. Identification responses generally are assumed to be relatively stable and enduring rather than transient. Moreover, while a child may imitate the behavior of a model with whom he has only the most casual

relationship, identification rests upon intimate, personal attachment to the model. (Mussen, 1967, p. 81)

We are led, then, to examine a process that appears to be quite important in socialization, though its nature is still not clearly understood. Several theories have been offered to account for this type of behavior.

THEORIES OF IDENTIFICATION

DEFENSIVE IDENTIFICATION: The earliest theory of identification, put forward by S. Freud (see Chapter 5), is that a child emulates his parent because he envies his powers and capabilities. In this Freudian version the boy identifies with his father because he envies him his mother's love. By being like his father he receives vicarious gratification from his mother. More recent investigators have broadened this concept. The child is said to emulate adults because he envies their enjoyment of activities that he values but is not allowed to share. When a child sees that his parents have more freedom than he does and are able to obtain desirable objects seemingly as they wish, he is motivated to act as they do in hopes of obtaining similar gratification.

The other aspect of the classical Freudian theory is that the boy sees his father as an aggressor. His desires for his mother arouse fear that his father will retaliate by castrating him. In order to defend himself against this possibility, he becomes more like his father. According to the Freudian view, this *defensive identification* occurs between the approximate ages of four and six, the oedipal period, and is associated with fear of castration. The little boy replaces jealousy, hostility, and rivalry with the idea "If I am like him, he will not hurt me."

The available evidence, however, does not offer much support for the notion that identification is a defensive process for warding off anxiety. Most of the support comes from case histories. A. Freud (1946) has reported several cases that illustrate defensive identification. She has described, for instance, an elementary-school boy who would respond to his teacher's reproaches by making faces. The faces seemed silly and out of place, and the class would burst out laughing. Close observation of teacher and pupil revealed, however, that the boy's "faces" were caricatures of the teacher's angry expressions. His behavior was thus attributed to his efforts to identify with the aggressor and to reduce his own anxiety.

B. Bettelheim (1943) has described how prisoners in a Nazi concentration camp modeled their behavior on that of their oppressive guards. The final stage of adjustment to camp life was to accept the Gestapo's values as one's own. The prisoners not only emulated their captors' aggressive behavior but also went so far as to try to obtain old pieces of their uniforms and to dress as did the guards. This behavior, of course, supports the notion that identification is a defensive process that serves to reduce anxiety.

Although such reports are striking and appear to offer some evidence for a theory of defensive identification, clinical reports cannot substitute for well-controlled research findings. At best they offer good examples of what is meant by "defensive identification."

Systematic empirical studies have furnished little substantial support for the hypothesis. W. Mischel and J. E. Grusec (1966) found exactly the opposite results from what would be expected from defensive identification. The "model" (experimenter) in this study interacted initially with half a preschool sample in a warm, affectionate, rewarding, and nurturing way. With the other half she was much less responsive and more distant. Following the initial interaction, each child went with the model into an experimental room, where they played a game with a toy cash register. During their play the model exhibited some behavior not directly relevant to the game: marching around the room, repeating irrelevant sounds, and so on. She also showed some distinctly aversive reactions to the child, criticizing him and delaying rewards. At the end of the session the child was left alone to play with the cash register while he was observed through a one-way mirror. He was then taken back to the playroom and told that he was to be given a treat: He could show someone else how to play the cash-register game. The degree to which each child imitated the model was measured by the number of times that he performed the model's neutral or aversive behavior when in her presence, when alone, and when showing the game to another child. Both neutral and aversive behavior was imitated more often by the children who had first experienced warm relations with the model. In fact, the findings support the predictions that one would make from another theory of identification, the "developmental" hypothesis.

DEVELOPMENTAL IDENTIFICATION: Some theorists believe that identification occurs because of love, affection, and respect for the model. Freud had a somewhat similar explanation for a girl's tendency to identify with her mother. As she does not have a penis, she obviously cannot fear castration, but she can resent her mother for creating her without a penis. Because of this resentment she may turn to her father as her primary love object. The possibility that she may lose her mother's love is, however, threatening, and she does identify with her mother, putting herself in her mother's place and competing for her father's affection. In general, the *developmental identification* hypothesis is that a child attempts to emulate a model so that he can reward himself in a manner similar to that in which his parents have rewarded him. Imitating his parent is a substitute for the direct affection that he no longer receives as he grows older and moves toward independence.

The evidence for the developmental hypothesis is much more compelling than is that for the defensive hypothesis. Studies like the one just reported have demonstrated that children who are exposed to warm, nurturing models are more likely to imitate the models' behavior than are children who are exposed to neutral or punitive models. Studies of nurture in parent-child interactions have also given support to the developmental hypothesis. Nurturing mothers are more likely to be imitated by their children.

Because identification supposedly results in the development of conscience, studies of the relation between children's and parents' values should throw some light on the process. In general such studies have supported the developmental interpretation. The children of very warm and accepting mothers are more likely to develop strong consciences.

IDENTIFICATION AS ROLE PLAYING   A third way to account for identification has been suggested chiefly by sociologists and social psychologists. They consider *identification as role playing*. Their explanation incorporates some of the features of both the defensive and developmental hypotheses. The strength of identification is said to be determined by the frequency and intensity of the child's interaction with the model and by the model's power over him. A child identifies with his father, for example, because he is warm and nurturing and also because he is potentially threatening. The main point is that in the child's eyes he has the power to control the administration of *both* rewards and punishment. It is thus predicted that children will both overtly and covertly practice the behavior of adult models who have the most control over them.

The role-playing theory has not been tested extensively, though Mussen and L. Distler (1959) and Mussen and E. Rutherford (1963) have conducted experiments designed to test all three theories. They attempted to find out how boys with strong "masculine" interests, boys who presumably identified strongly with their fathers, perceived their fathers. The three hypotheses would predict respectively that the boys would perceive their fathers as punitive and threatening (defensive identification), that they would perceive their fathers as nurturing and rewarding (developmental), and that they would perceive their fathers as powerful agents of both reward and punishment (role playing).

Very "masculine" boys' perceptions of parents, compared to those of a group of less "masculine" boys, offered some support for all three theories. The mothers of these children were not, however, perceived differently by the two groups. Their perceptions of their fathers differed primarily in that the "masculine" boys saw their fathers as more nurturing, which tends to support the developmental hypothesis. They also saw them as more punitive (though this finding was not quite statistically significant), which would support the defensive hypothesis, and more powerful in distributing rewards and punishments, which would support the role-playing hypothesis. The evidence is most convincing for the developmental view, however.

CONCLUSIONS   Obviously, the nature of identification is still open to investigation. Indeed, it is still debatable whether or not it should be considered separate from learning, though Mussen has separated the two. He has conceded, however, that learning theorists may eventually be able to account for identification completely.

It seems that the available evidence nevertheless allows comparatively reliable conclusions about the kinds of parental behavior that encourage imitation. Warm and nurturing parents appear to inspire the most imitation in children and are probably therefore most successful in passing on social values and attitudes.

SUMMARY

In this chapter we have examined the development and adjustment challenges of childhood, which begin with the union of sperm and egg.

The organism faces many challenges even before birth. The developing fetus is for the most part a passive recipient of his intrauterine environment during the prenatal period, but systematic development from conception prepares it to sustain life after birth. Trauma, harmful microorganisms, oxygen deficiency, and other mishaps may harm the organism; the seriousness of the damage is partially determined by the stage of development. Generally the most critical period is the early part of pregnancy, when the major life systems are still being formed. The success of the organism in meeting prenatal demands is best ensured through proper care of the expectant mother.

Unusual stresses may be associated with birth, and again the neonate has little control over his environment. Adequate medical care at this point may be critical to later adjustment. Expectant mothers are not helpless, however; they can take positive measures to reduce the possibility of birth complications.

Of the important developmental tasks in the preschool years physical development looms large and contributes significantly to the formation of adaptive motor skills. During these years the child changes from helpless infant to mobile, coordinated individual. Learning to ingest solid foods further increases his capacities for adjustment by making him less directly dependent upon his mother as the only source of food. Toilet training frees him for social activities in which important learning occurs. The development of speech expands his horizons even farther and enables him to participate in the human community. As his entrance to school approaches, the beginnings of self-awareness become apparent. The child comes to recognize himself as a unique person who can relate to his environment in various ways. Furthermore, the foundations of the socialization process are laid during the preschool years.

All these developments may be retarded or blocked by stresses from various sources. Failure to accomplish these tasks, of course, reduces the possibility of normal adjustment. But again positive action can be taken to lessen the chances of abnormal development.

One of the important concepts in understanding children is "developmental time." A child's age in calendar time is only a very crude, often inaccurate measure of his developmental progress. Children vary in the rates at which they develop physically and psychologically; all five-year-olds do not have the same physical, intellectual, and social abilities, though they may end up quite similar as adults. The concept of developmental age permits special evaluation of individual abilities, which in turn serves as bases for realistic expectations, rather than the sometimes unrealistic ones associated with chronological age. In some communities special education is provided for children who are very advanced or retarded in development compared to their age group. It appears, however, that the ideal form of education provides individual instruction for all children, instruction in which each child's academic tasks are geared to his developmental level.

School children face several important developmental tasks. They must learn to interact with other children and to become integral members of human groups; some children find this step most difficult and come to exhibit "school phobia." Another important task is to learn the expectations and conduct deemed appropriate to one's sex. Boys learn that their behavior should be different from that of girls and the reverse. Learning sex-role expectations does not, of course, cease with this period; it continues to be important in adolescent adjustment. The school child must also master culturally relevant skills that will contribute to his self-image and future adjustment.

Piaget has developed a theory of cognitive development to explain how and why children develop intellectual abilities. He has formulated and demonstrated his notions through observation of children as they develop new intellectual skills and increase their mastery over the environment. He has postulated several developmental periods, based on the child's increasing ability to use cognitive stimuli (bits of knowledge) in problem-solving situations. Two other processes that have also been postulated to explain development are learning and identification. Their comparative importance in understanding children's development must be examined in the light of research evidence.

10

Influences on Childhood Development

A. Introduction

B. Physical Determinants
1. Environmental effects on learning capacities
2. Sensory stimulation and development of sensory capacities
3. Stimulation and motor development

C. Cultural and Social Determinants
1. Geographical conditions
2. Sociocultural groups and social roles
3. Personal relations

D. Family Determinants
1. Family atmosphere
2. Maternal types
3. Consistency, discipline, and guidance
4. Maternal expectations
5. Birth order
6. Conclusions about the family
7. The Case of Robert

E. Therapy: A Corrective Influence
1. Play therapy
2. Family therapy
3. The Case of Dick

F. Summary

INTRODUCTION

In this chapter we shall examine several determinants of development. Theoretically development proceeds at a uniform pace that follows from such processes of growth as physical and cognitive maturation. Understanding the systematic growth processes is, of course, important in understanding personal adjustment; other factors are equally important, however, because they determine a person's specific (as opposed to his general) characteristics. Although development occurs within the organism, the variables in which we are interested here occur in the external environment and affect the quality of personal adaptation. Internal processes must interact with these external variables. The results may be very important to the individual. For convenience and clarity we shall examine these variables under four major headings: physical determinants, cultural and social determinants, family determinants, and therapeutic determinants.

PHYSICAL DETERMINANTS

Although a child's relationships have long been considered the most important factors in his development, recent research has shown that purely physical stimulation and stimuli have much greater impact on later behavior than was previously suspected. From the time that the infant is born—and even before his birth—he is in constant contact with physical stimuli of one kind or another. Usually he is well protected from danger by his parents and his own physiological safeguards. Nevertheless, physical stimulation, even though it is not extreme or easily recognizable by the casual observer, may have telling effects on the child's development and adjustment.

J. P. Scott (1968) has organized the evidence on this topic quite well. Much of the discussion that follows has been adapted from his work.

ENVIRONMENTAL EFFECTS ON LEARNING CAPACITIES

Environmental stimulation may affect the development of learning capacities and thus influence adjustment. Academic learning has become especially important in vocational achievement in modern society. If a large proportion of our child population lives now in conditions that offer less than optimal physical stimulation, we shall indeed have a major social problem on our hands in the future.

People in lower socioeconomic and occupational groups usually score lower on measures of intelligence. Furthermore, their children tend to remain at the lower socioeconomic levels because their environments hinder development of whatever potential they may have. In comparison to the physical environments of middle- and upper-class homes those of lower-class are generally less stimulating. The middle- and upper-class child thus benefits from an "enriched" environment that enhances his capabilities, and he is more likely to be able to provide the same or better surroundings for his own offspring. Children raised in less stimulating environments, on the other hand, are less likely to develop their abilities and therefore tend to raise their children under circumstances similar to their own. In this sense they are "trapped" by their culture; a way out is required.

In recent years government Head Start programs have been initiated for this specific purpose. These programs attempt to provide enriching experiences for early preschool children from lower socioeconomic environments. The children are exposed to a variety of physical stimuli and training in interpersonal skills before entering the formal school system. It is hoped that these programs will supplement the natural environment and encourage optimal intellectual growth. Although this goal seems reasonable in the light of our current knowledge (based primarily on animal studies), relevant large-scale research on the effectiveness of enriching the environment has not yet been carried out with human beings. It is informative, though, to examine some of the research that led up to these programs.

D. Hebb (1947) carried out the first work in this direction. He suspected that the behavior of his laboratory-raised rats showed the effects of a monotonous environment. He took some of his animals home to be reared as pets, then later tested them in a learning maze against rats in the laboratory. The pet rats' performance was much superior to that of the others.

Experimenters have since become interested in the concept of enriched environment. Animals raised in standard "enriched" cages containing various objects and playthings are compared with those raised in ordinary cages. Even though the artificially enriched environments are more restricted than are wild environments, great differences between the groups occur.

Other research has shown that an enriched environment has its greatest effects during certain phases of development. The most crucial period for rats is shortly after weaning; less impressive results occur when they are younger or older. This discovery raised the question of why effects should be so strong at this particular time. Two factors seem to be involved. First, this period is the one in which exploratory behavior first appears in rats; they have been weaned and are mature enough to leave the nest. If they learn to explore, the habit will remain with them in later life; if not, they will be less adaptive. Second, weaning seems to coincide with the animal's development of confidence to explore, which seems to lead to a general trait of confidence. The earlier in life it learns confidence, the greater the chances are that it will be confident in new circumstances. The animal will then be more likely to enter new settings in which new learning is possible, and the chances that it will develop its intellectual capacity more fully are therefore increased.

Another team of investigators compared the brain sizes of rats raised under enriched and sterile conditions; the former group of rats had larger brains, especially in parts of the cerebral cortex (Bennett *et al.*, 1964). The period of enlargement was not, however, related to the critical period right after weaning. It occurred whether the rats were placed in enriched conditions before or after weaning. These findings illustrate the effects of stimulation on the growth of nervous tissue, but the effects are apparently not associated with increased learning capacity.

Scott (1968) has suggested that these experiments have implications for human beings. There are two stages in human development that may correspond to the critical periods in animals. The first is the period at about two years of age, when the child makes significant strides toward independence; he begins to walk and learns to chew food with his new teeth. At this age the child is also ready to learn language, an extremely important skill in later life. It is a period analogous to that in which the newly weaned rat begins its explorations. As the results of Head Start programs have not been especially encouraging so far (children generally make immediate gains but lose them within a year or so), it seems worthwhile to experiment with programs for much younger children.

The second possibly critical period in human beings comes at around seven to eight years of age. Children become physically independent at this time. They can run swiftly and can quickly learn complex motor actions. Scott suggests that this period probably corresponds to the period at which prehistoric children were able to leave their original social groups and still survive.

SENSORY STIMULATION AND DEVELOPMENT OF SENSORY CAPACITIES

Experiments have also demonstrated that early physical stimulation is necessary for the development of normal sensory capacities and consequently for the adaptability of the organism. Most of these experiments have examined the visual and tactile modalities.

Work with chimpanzees reared in various degrees of light and dark has revealed definite effects on the ganglion cells of the retina, including biochemical changes in the tissue. The length of time that animals were kept in the dark influenced their ability to recover from visual deprivation. One chimpanzee that was reared in darkness for a year suffered extensive and permanent loss of retinal nerve cells. The conclusion to be drawn from studies of this sort is that normal development of nervous tissue requires physical stimulation. The eye is not completely functional at an early age, but its final form is probably affected by its use or disuse. Although deprivation studies with human beings have not been conducted for obvious reasons, it seems likely that our sense organs would also suffer from lack of stimulation.

Other studies have suggested that tactile stimulation is necessary to the development of young animals and humans. It has been consistently found, for example, that young rats, stimulated in some way (by handling, electric shock, shaking, cold temperatures, and so on) grow faster, live longer, and endure physical stress better than do animals that have been left undisturbed and unstimulated (Scott, 1968).

Human infants are normally handled a great deal. Studies conducted in settings where they are not, however, have produced interesting results. Observation of babies reared in orphanages or hospitals, where they receive minimal handling (though their other physical needs are met), have revealed high incidences of depression and physical illness, as well as retarded intellectual, emotional, and social development (Bowlby, 1951). Although these findings have generally been explained by the inadequate emotional climate (the absence of maternal love), the evidence from animal studies suggests that the absence of physical stimulation may be more important. Some of these children were placed in more stimulating environments and made rather dramatic gains in intelligence scores and social behavior.

STIMULATION AND MOTOR DEVELOPMENT

Retarding of motor development has been demonstrated in studies in which animals have been raised in impoverished environments. Puppies reared in a large field, for instance, were extremely agile and skillful, compared to those of the same age who had been raised in a small room with a flat floor. When placed outside, the "room" pups were unable to jump into a house where they could eat and sleep, even though it was only a couple of feet off the ground. They were unable even to climb a ramp provided to make it easier for them. Animal species vary, however, in the severity of their responses to such experiences; some can learn motor skills even in maturity (Scott, 1968).

In general the findings about motor learning indicate that there are crucial times for learning specific skills, but these times have not yet been established for human beings. The best time to learn motor skills is probably when capacities have matured to the point at which learning is quick and easy. As individuals vary in the ages at which they reach this point, it is impossible to make specific recommendations applicable to all children. A reasonable alternative, however, is to provide children with environments that permit a great deal of physical freedom in which they can test their growing capacities and develop them when they are ready. Contact with various physical objects that can be manipulated or climbed helps to ensure that the necessary stimuli for most motor skills are available at crucial times. Head Start programs have included many physical objects for this purpose, but many gross motor skills have already been developed by the time children reach the age when they are eligible for these programs.

Trying to teach motor skills before a child is ready does not produce the results that most parents desire. A child who is trained before he is ready does not perform significantly better than does a peer who learns spontaneously when he is ready. Most children are unable to perform activities requiring fine coordination of the whole body before they are seven or eight. An early introduction to such skills usually results in unskillful performance or failure, with the added danger that the child will develop a negative set toward the skill and lose interest.

CULTURAL AND SOCIAL DETERMINANTS

A child's development is determined to a large extent by his cultural milieu, including geographical conditions, social expectations, and personal relationships. The family obviously cannot be realistically separated from these factors, but, because of its importance, we shall discuss it separately later.

Children are to a large extent captives of their cultural surroundings. They are not independent, and they are forced to develop and adjust within the specific cultural framework in which their parents live. Migrations from one country to another or from one part of the world to another indicate that some cultures may be more stressful than others. The degree to which a culture provides the resources for individual growth, for example, affects a person's development. Each culture also has its own expectations of appropriate and inappropriate behavior in various social positions. In addition, there is wide variation among cultures in the degree of economic mobility possible for their members. Modern Western cultures, for instance, allow quite a lot of upward mobility in social status, whereas some cultures still maintain rather rigid caste systems. Personal relations also vary in importance with the culture's social system.

GEOGRAPHICAL CONDITIONS

The physical characteristics of a child's environment are largely beyond his control. People live in various climates, on varied terrain, and with a different access to natural resources. Geography may impose limits on the health and wealth of a population. For instance, whether a child is raised in a nomadic tribe that spends most of its energy obtaining enough to eat or in an American middle-class home in which necessities are taken for granted is crucial. The effects of disease on a child in a rural area where medical attention is scarce may be much more severe than are those on a city child, who may have access to adequate medical treatment even without money.

Although there have been no systematic studies of the ways in which climate and terrain affect psychological development, several suppositions have been put forward. People in warmer climates, for example, seem less energetic than do people in colder ones, presumably because the cold climate requires more hard work and energy for survival. Nor is it difficult to imagine that climatic conditions encourage certain personality characteristics (Mussen, Conger, and Kagan, 1969).

A firmer line of investigation suggests that people living in unfavorable climates or terrains tend to adapt physiologically to those conditions. Native workers in the high mountains of Bolivia average more red corpuscles than do Americans. They are therefore able to make better use of the rarefied atmosphere, with its low oxygen content. Their average lung capacity is also about twice as large as is that of Americans.

Even without systematic research it is not difficult to predict some social effects of the environment. It is not surprising, for instance, that children raised on the southern California coast are likely to enjoy the ocean and activities associated with it. Nor would we be surprised to find that more of them grow up to work in the fishing industry than do children raised in the Midwest.

A relatively new field of study, *environmental psychology*, has taken up such problems. Investigators attempt to relate characteristics of the environment to psychological and characterological trends. For example, H. Barry and his colleagues (1959) have classified primitive societies according to whether or not they store food supplies, then have related each society's emphasis on this collective economic endeavor to its educational practices. They have found that societies that characteristically store food also educate their children to obedience and responsibility. The other societies emphasize individual accomplishment, self-confidence, and autonomy. This correlation was almost high enough to allow perfect prediction of educational attitudes from this economic custom.

Other investigators are interested in how the sizes and shapes of houses, organization of neighborhoods, and so on are related to personality characteristics and interpersonal functioning in different cultures. Of course, it is difficult to establish what causes what. The personality characteristics of a group may determine how it constructs its homes, or the reverse, cultural practices may modify personal characteristics. It is possible, nevertheless, to carry out controlled research in some settings. New housing projects, for instance, are often constructed for various subcultural groups. By taking personality measures before and after the building, it is possible to evaluate changes in the people who have changed physical surroundings.

The effects of architecture and methods of construction on the traits of a population are still a matter of conjecture. Many psychologists believe that they are important, though they have largely been ignored in the past. The manmade environment has generally been considered a product; it is new to view it as a modifying influence on those responsible for it. Common sense suggests, however, that spacious rooms with pleasant views of the sea can encourage calm and feelings of well-being. It is thus not difficult to imagine that the general living conditions of a population can also influence its predominant personality characteristics.

SOCIOCULTURAL GROUPS AND SOCIAL ROLES

A child's attitudes and characteristics are partly determined by the general expectations of his culture, which vary according to customs, values, aesthetics, and other cultural constructs. At the highest conceptual level we may differentiate the Western world and the Eastern world. Such gross classifications undoubtedly do reflect actual differences in general beliefs and values, but are clearly limited in what they contribute to an understanding of the individual.

BASIC PERSONALITY

It is more common, however, to think along national or tribal boundaries. At this level investigators speak of "basic personality" types: constellations of very general characteristics that distinguish one group from another.

There are, of course, wide individual variations within any one population. Anthropological studies have shown some rather marked personality differences within tribal cultures. M. Mead (1949), for example, has studied two New Guinea tribes living in the same general region. The Mundungumor are a warlike, aggressive, competitive, and vengeful people. They are generally jealous and suspicious of one another. The Arapesh tend to be peaceful, cooperative, kindly, and nonaggressive. They view human nature as essentially good. The basic personality differences between these two tribes are so striking that it seems hardly possible that they can be accounted for by climate and physical setting. As they have developed in approximately similar physical environments, it seems very likely that these traits have been passed down through the centuries. It is impossible, however, to know the exact ways in which they were first adopted. Mead's observations furnish a rather dramatic example of the effects that tribal values, beliefs, and attitudes can have on personality development. It is highly improbable that a child will completely escape personality traits encouraged by his cultural background unless he is a complete social outcast.

SOCIOECONOMIC STATUS AND SOCIAL CLASS

Social class, or socioeconomic status, is another factor that influences development. Americans tend to believe that few class differences exist in their society, but many studies have revealed rather clear social-class stratification, though it varies somewhat from community to community and from region to region. For research purposes socioeconomic status is determined by the educational and occupational levels of the head of the household, the family's residential area, and sometimes its level of income. The importance of class membership for development lies in different values and attitudes associated with class and their implications for behavior. These differences are, of course, transmitted from parents to child. Viewing American society at three social levels—upper, middle, and lower class—reveals differences in attitudes and expectations among them. For our purposes we can think of the upper class as wealthy, long-established families and professionals with high incomes; the middle class is by and large skilled and semiprofessional; and the lower class consists of the unskilled, relatively uneducated groups.

In education, for instance, the upper class emphasizes quality and prestige of the school. Its members are more concerned about sending their children to schools known for excellence than in having them learn a great deal in order to establish a vocation that will increase their personal income. They emphasize training in higher-level administration, rather than the acquisition of specific skills. The children often "take over" established sources of high income. The middle class places comparatively greater emphasis upon grades and achievement and is quite concerned about the possibility of failure. Education represents prestige, in the sense that it is the road to advancement or security. The middle class emphasizes academic training (in skills and professions) that can be exchanged for financial reward. Lower-class families, on the other hand, often consider the child's education secondary to other needs of the family. The child may, for example, be encouraged to leave school and go to work in order to contribute to the family's immediate financial support. School is not usually considered a pleasant or even very useful place. Little stress is placed on high academic achievement.

Sexual attitudes also vary with social-class membership. The upper class tends to inhibit sexual behavior in the early years, but considerable freedom is acceptable in late adolescence. The middle class severely inhibits sexual behavior in the early years and also creates anxiety over sexual impulses. Middle-class adolescents' sexual activities are usually limited to petting and masturbation. The pattern in the lower classes is somewhat different. Sexual behavior is accepted as a matter of course, and children tend to have early sexual experiences. Lower-class boys are more likely to regard sexual intercourse as proof of their masculinity, than are upper- and middle-class males whereas petting and masturbation may be considered forms of perversion (Mussen *et al.*, 1969).

Other differences in attitudes among social classes exist. The two examples that we have cited are, however, sufficient to demonstrate the possible effects of social class on development. As education is so important to adaptation in a modern society, the lower-class child may be handicapped from the beginning. His family's values and attitudes, which he probably learns almost unconsciously, do not motivate him toward educational goals. It is not surprising that schools attended by students mainly from the lower class are characterized by difficulties in discipline and low achievement.

The sexual attitudes of the middle class increase the likelihood that both children and parents will experience more difficulties in heterosexual relationships because of anxiety. When a child from one class interacts with a child from another difficulties are likely to arise because of their different attitudes toward sexual activity. Value differences may set off aggressive or rejecting behavior in personal relationships, even though there is no valid reason to claim that one set of values is more "correct" than is another.

Once again it is necessary to recall that these observations about differences in attitudes are generalizations; there are wide individual variations. It would be unfair to conclude that all lower-class people see little value in education. This kind of generalization can too easily justify bigoted people in their efforts to limit educational opportunities for lower socioeconomic groups.

SOCIAL STATUS AND ROLES

In every society there are designated statuses and roles that influence a child's development. A social status is a position in society that carries certain privileges and responsibilities. In general, the more responsibilities that are associated with a given status, the more privileges accompany it too.

Others' status expectations usually exert pressure on the child. A father who wants his son to become President of the United States or to achieve some other high position is likely to make harsh demands. The child is likely to please such a father rarely, and praise will be withheld except for really exceptional achievement. How the boy responds will vary with circumstances, but one of two directions is most probable: He may become highly achievement oriented, especially if he meets with a frequent early success, or he may give up trying because nothing that he does seems to be enough.

Societies prescribe social roles, defined as the behavior deemed appropriate to specific statuses. A detailed discussion of "role theory" has been presented in Chapter 8, and we shall not recapitulate it here. It is sufficient to point out that a person's roles and how well he performs them will to a great extent determine how successful he considers his own adjustment.

In American society almost everyone must fulfill a variety of roles. The child, for instance, is expected to act as a son or daughter, a student, a friend, and so on. Roles become increasingly numerous and complex as the child grows older and becomes more involved in society, and it is not unusual for the demands of one role to conflict with those of another. His attempts to mediate role conflicts—as between the roles of student and boyfriend on the night before exams—often cause stress.

It is important to emphasize that, although different cultures and social classes teach attitudes and values that may be at variance, each isolated group often feels or strongly believes that it is following the dictates of common sense and that other groups are "wrong." Rarely is an individual aware that his values are acceptable to him only because he has learned them from his culture and that other people have undergone a similar learning process with their own values. It is only as people become aware that different groups have approached the basic problems of life and solved them in different ways that they can gain a perspective allowing mutual respect and open exchange across cultural boundaries.

PERSONAL RELATIONS

Family relations will be discussed in the next section, and peer relations have already been discussed. These relations are significant to personal adjustment, but peer contacts are generally less important in the early years than during adolescence. Their effects on adjustment will be examined in more detail in connection with adolescent development.

Because teachers are assigned the role of transmitting cultural values and skills in our society, the teacher-child relationship is likely to have a strong influence on the direction of development. Many of us have been deeply influenced or know others who have been deeply influenced by relationships with teachers. Sometimes a child's educational and vocational goals may change drastically through such a relationship. A child does not simply enter school and continue the same behavior that he has learned at home; his teacher may become an important model for conduct that is otherwise unrelated to school. A child who has been rejected by his parents may, for instance, learn trust through his relationship with a warm, understanding teacher. On the other hand, a negative, hostile teacher may set the stage for maladaptive patterns.

TEACHER CHARACTERISTICS

Studies have generally shown that student behavior depends largely upon teacher behavior. Teachers who adopt a democratic approach in their classes, for example, tend to foster the same type of behavior in their pupils. The children are also more interested and show more personal initiative.

H. H. Anderson and G. L. Anderson (1954) have carried out a series of studies of the group atmosphere established by the teacher and its effects on pupil behavior. More specifically, they examined whether democratic and authoritarian teachers fostered similar behavior in the children whom they taught. Teacher-pupil interaction provided measures of democratic or authoritarian approaches. The "authoritarian" teachers used force, commands, threats, shame, and blame and insisted strongly on children following the teachers' rules. The more "democratic" teachers tended to show approval, to ask questions about the children's interests, to be sympathetic, to encourage mutual participation with children, and to invite interest in activities. The children under these democratic conditions more often reflected spontaneity, initiative, and constructive social attitudes in their behavior; those under authoritarian conditions tended to be resistant, nonconformist, inattentive to their work, and easily distracted.

Studies of children's preferences in teacher behavior have revealed similar trends. In the United States children of all ages tend to prefer teachers who possess more democratic characteristics. They like their teachers to be kind, cheerful, natural, and even-tempered; fair, consistent, impartial, and respected; well-groomed with nice voices and generally attractive; helpful, democratic, interesting, and enthusiastic. In general, research does not support the adage "Spare the rod and spoil the child." On the contrary, teachers who provide stimulating classrooms, support and encourage their pupils, and treat children as peers to some degree have greater success in promoting the type of classroom atmosphere that most teachers and adults prefer.

SELF-FULFILLING PROPHECIES

The teacher-student relationship may have far-reaching effects on a child's educational success. The child who is branded a "troublemaker" early in his school career is likely, for instance, to be expected to fulfill that role later. Teachers' written or verbal comments may be passed on and may help to determine how the child behaves.

Educators and psychologists have long been aware that previous achievement records and other test results, whether accurate or not, may follow a child through school and partly determine his success. More recently research has shown the specific impact that teachers' expectations may have on a child's future (Rosenthal, 1968; Rosenthal and Jacobson, 1968).

Rosenthal and Jacobson (1968) examined the effects of teacher expectations on academic behavior in a large school system. Specifically, they tested whether or not children seemed "brighter" when their teachers expected them to be so. To create the teachers' expectations a test supposedly developed to predict "intellectual bloomers" was administered to all the children in an elementary school. The teachers were led to believe that the test would predict which children would begin to accelerate intellectually in the near future. About 20 percent of the children in each classroom were randomly selected as the experimental group, that is, as children who should "bloom." The teachers were given their names and told that they had scored high on the test and that they should show large gains in intellectual development during the next eight months. But the only real difference between these children and the rest of the children was the teachers' expectations.

At the end of the school year the designated "bloomers" showed an average gain of four I.Q. points more than did other students. Nor were the effects limited to students at lower levels of achievement; children at higher levels were affected equally. Furthermore, the teachers described these children as being more interesting, more curious, and happier than were the others, as well as more appealing, better adjusted, more affectionate, and requiring less social approval.

Those children who showed improvement but had not been designated as "bloomers," that is, those children who showed unexpected improvement, especially those with low ability, were considered less well adjusted, less interesting, and less affectionate. This finding suggests that in the eyes of teachers unpredicted intellectual growth may be hazardous.

One of the same investigators (Rosenthal, 1968) replicated these findings, with some variations, in several other school districts; the effect certainly does not appear to be isolated. In one of these studies it was shown that the teachers' altered their approach, gearing it more toward pupils who they believed would respond favorably. Apparently teachers' expectations are not only translated into subtle vocal and other cues that probably encourage the child inadvertently but also cause significant alterations in teaching styles.

The implications of these studies for school psychologists and others who submit material for student files should be obvious. Test scores and other information indicating that a child may have difficulty in school may influence his teacher to fulfill these expectations. It seems imperative that teachers and other educational personnel recognize—and take steps to minimize—the difficulties associated with self-fulfilling prophecies.

In the same vein the school psychologist's work can be much more effective when he takes into account the teacher-child interaction in helping a child. Although it is commonly said that mothers and children tend to blame teachers for children's shortcomings, it should also be recognized that teachers are human too—that, in fact, they do get along better with some children than with others. The nature of a teacher's interaction with a child may encourage the kind of behavior that leads to referral to the school psychologist.

Evaluation by a school psychologist is generally requested for one of two reasons: The child has become a behavior problem in the classroom, or he is not achieving satisfactorily. The psychologist's usual approach is to administer a battery of tests in order to pinpoint the difficulty and then to make recommendations. This approach is not, however, always the most effective, especially when the child's classroom conduct is the major complaint. This behavior is in itself an important source of information, and his teacher's way of working with him may be crucial.

Suggesting to a teacher the possibility that his behavior is part of the child's problem is difficult; because of threatening implications, the psychologist's recommendations may be rejected. To handle this sensitive issue the psychologist may observe the child in the classroom under the pretense of obtaining a better sampling of his behavior. In reality, however, he observes the interaction between the teacher and the child: how often the teacher rewards the child, how often he punishes him, the child's behavior preceding the teacher's responses, and so on. From these data he can better evaluate the seriousness of the child's behavior; more important, he can make recommendations for changing teacher-pupil interaction. Furthermore, his recommendations may be presented in a way that does not suggest that the teacher has been contributing to the problem. For instance, recommending that the teacher reinforce certain kinds of behavior and ignore others does not imply that he is at fault; but, it can lead to significant changes in the way that he interacts with his pupil.

FAMILY DETERMINANTS

Few would deny that the family is the single most important socializing agent. Family influence is important in shaping attitudes, values, and behavior patterns. Nevertheless, it is well to keep in mind that other sources can modify the effects of the family. Especially as the child grows older his age mates, his teachers, and other adults become increasingly important in his life.

Research findings, coupled with clinical observations, indicate patterns of family interaction that appear to influence child development in specific ways. But it is also important to understand that no one-to-one relationship between modes of child rearing and the ways in which children's personalities develop exists. The effects of any particular parent-child relationship or family interaction pattern will vary considerably, depending upon the constitution of the child, the concepts of himself that he has already developed, and the other circumstances of his life. Although one child may become inhibited and anxious because of an overprotective mother, another may become aggressive, self-centered, and "spoiled"; still another may seem not to be affected in the least.

Family Atmosphere

Several dimensions of parental behavior have been studied in order to determine their influence on children's behavior and personality development. Are the parents' warmth, permissiveness, and open affection, for example, related to their children's behavior? In a general sense, the results of these studies indicate that the home atmosphere provides opportunities for the child to learn specific patterns of conduct that will be reinforced and to identify with the general attitudes of his parents.

PARENTAL ATTITUDES

The Fels Institute in Ohio and the Institute of Human Development in California have sponsored extended research on home atmosphere and child behavior. At the Fels Institute nursery-school children were rated on a number of personality characteristics by teachers and trained observers (Baldwin, 1949). Their homes were visited by an observer who evaluated parent-child interactions (family atmosphere) and rated the home on thirty carefully defined scales. A statistical analysis of the results showed several clusters of parental behavior, two of which seemed important: "democratic," and "controlling." The basic findings reflected the differences between democratic and controlling atmospheres. Democratic parents characteristically accepted their children's self-expression, frequently discussed family decisions and rules, and encouraged children's curiosity. Controlling parents did not encourage freedom, adopted clear-cut rules and restrictions, and seldom discussed disciplinary procedures with their children.

Children from the democratic homes were outgoing, active, competitive, original, curious, foresighted, self-assertive, and aggressive. They were enthusiastic, tended to be leaders, and were able to express themselves freely. Children from the controlled homes presented an almost opposite picture. They generally did what they were told without question, and they were socially unaggressive, well behaved, and quiet. They appeared to lack curiosity and originality and were inhibited in self-expression. These results confirmed expectations based on learning theory. It appears that the children had learned the conduct that their parents reinforced and had dropped that which was unacceptable. The hypothesis that children tend to identify with their parents was also supported: They not only learned to follow rules, for example, but also imitated their parents by accepting those rules.

The California studies (Schaefer and Bayley, 1963) were aimed directly at discovering the effects of home atmosphere. The results were obtained by observing mother-child behavior through approximately twenty testing sessions. Each mother's behavior was evaluated on such global aspects as expression of affection, emotional involvement, fostering dependence, irritability, and so on. The child was rated on a series of scales that were combined to yield four major scores: friendliness, cooperativeness, attentiveness, and facility in test performance.

A consistent correlation between the maternal dimension of love-hostility and child behavior was found. Mothers who expressed affection, were relatively equalitarian in their relations with their children, and continually evaluated their children positively were likely to have friendly, cooperative, and attentive children. These mothers played a great deal with their children, talked with them on their own level, and praised and rewarded them liberally. Mothers who were rated higher on hostility ignored their children, punished them, and were irritable. They appeared not to understand or to respond to their children's needs, nor were they tolerant and patient. Their children were not rewarded for being friendly and cooperative at home; in fact, they were likely to be rejected or punished when they produced these responses. Consequently they were rated as unfriendly, uncooperative, inattentive, and easily distracted. Again the results support the notion that the home environment is directly reflected in child behavior through the processes of learning and identification.

A study in which questionnaires and interviews were administered to mothers of 379 five-year-olds established the importance of maternal warmth and the negative effects of punishment and permissiveness (Sears *et al.*, 1957). Children with mothers who were punitive and "cold" were more likely to have problems with feeding, bed wetting, aggressiveness, toilet training, and development of conscience. Punishment thus appeared to have the opposite effect from that intended. If toilet accidents were severely punished the child ended up a bed wetter; if dependence was punished the child became more dependent; if aggressiveness was punished the child became more aggressive; and so on. These findings again confirm that child behavior results from reinforcement and the conduct of parental models.

FAMILY INTERACTION

The ways in which families interact have been studied less than have the overall home atmosphere and the child-rearing attitudes of the parents. Recent studies, however, suggest that the modes of family interaction may be very important in child adjustment and development. A series of studies in which families have been observed in structured problem-solving conditions (see, for instance, the family Rorschach studies of Singer and Wynn, 1965) have indicated that families with emotionally disturbed children also reach decisions in ways different from those followed by "normal" families. The "abnormal" families did not appear capable of communicating in ways that lead to effective problem solving. These findings support the hypothesis that ineffective communication is an important factor in emotional disturbance.

A study by Coe and his colleagues (1969) has shown that families of psychiatric patients tend not to admit to having problems within the family, whereas a control sample of "normal" families rather freely admitted disagreement on many aspects of family functioning. There were no apparent significant differences between the kinds of activities that the families engaged in or in which members held the most power. The "psychiatric families," however, suppressed disagreement.

The above studies suggest that members of disturbed families are unable or unwilling to express themselves openly and clearly, especially about their differences. It seems likely that tensions build within such families until one or more members find release, perhaps in deviant conduct that results in diagnosis of mental illness. In any event, members of these families are more likely to be under stress, thus increasing the chances that their adjustment will be adversely affected.

Maternal Types

More specific types of maternal behavior have long been discussed in clinical circles; recent empirical research has sometimes supported older notions and sometimes not. Because much of this evidence comes from clinical reports, the conclusions may be biased. That is, the subjects (the children sampled) all showed some sort of abnormal behavior. Specific types of maternal behavior are therefore more likely to be associated with abnormal child behavior. When random samples of children and mothers are investigated, the same type of maternal behavior may occur in mothers of undisturbed as well as of disturbed children. Recognizing that conclusions so far reached may be somewhat inaccurate, we may still find it worthwhile to examine work done on maternal types. Much of the following information has been adapted from J. W. Kessler's work (1966).

THE REJECTING MOTHER

Because of the social values attached to motherhood, the rejecting mother is likely to be noticed most quickly. She has certainly been more often the topic of clinicians' analyses than has any other type. Maternal rejection is not as easy to define as we might imagine. It may range from overt hostility and disinterest in the child to inability to interact warmly because of a rigid and isolated character structure. The concept has more recently been included under the general heading of deprivation, which we have already discussed in connection with the influence of physical environment on the child. If a fully developed mother-child relationship is absent the child is deprived of conditions important to his growth.

Rejection may thus lead to the same problems in social relationships, including conduct classified as serious mental disorder, as do other kinds of deprivation. "Rejection," however, is probably too broad and unspecific a term to be useful to the clinician. He usually attempts to investigate the child-parent relationship in more detail, establishing the points at which the mother rejects her child, how she does it, how the child responds, and so on. It is well to recognize that no parent always acts lovingly toward his child and that his behavior may change with the child's level of development. Some parents, for instance, like totally dependent infants, whereas others are deeply threatened by their helplessness. Some parents may become upset when their children begin to strive for independence and may respond by rejecting them. The effects of rejection, then, cannot be stated in general terms. It is a complex response that requires explicit, individual evaluation.

THE OVERPROTECTIVE MOTHER

Some mothers appear to be exactly the opposite of rejecting mothers; they spend most of their time caring for their children. Many clinicians believe, however, that the motivational pattern of an overprotective mother is quite similar to, if not the same as, that of a rejecting mother. They suggest that an overprotective mother is compensating for her desire to reject her child. At any rate, her behavior often has adverse affects on children, often more adverse than the effects of punitive parental attitudes.

Overprotection may be characterized by either domination or indulgence. In either instance there is a great deal of contact between mother and child, resulting in prolonged infancy and retardation of independent behavior. The child who is dominated is, however, more likely to develop traits like passivity and dependence, whereas the indulged child is more likely to become "spoiled" —demanding, disobedient, and given to tantrums.

Although the evidence is certainly not firm, clinicians have associated a mother's inability to let her child go with most of the difficulties of childhood. She tends to retard her child's development in many ways. It is quite likely, for example, that her child will show low motivation to achieve. He is typically not rewarded for independent behavior and is usually restricted from activities that will take him out of sight of his mother's watchful eye. On the other hand, the mother who expects early self-reliance and independent behavior and rewards her child for them is more likely to have a child with high motivation to achieve.

CONSISTENCY, DISCIPLINE, AND GUIDANCE

Consistency—or inconsistency—in parental behavior is not completely understood. Most investigators, however, agree that children prefer to know where they stand. The more inconsistent a parent's behavior is, the more likely it is that the child will suffer from conflict and frustration.

Various inconsistencies occur in the family. Among the most common are those reflecting parental disagreement on child-rearing practices. This disagreement may or may not be based on real differences in beliefs. It may serve as a comparatively safe way to express more serious mutual dissatisfaction that cannot be expressed directly. The child, of course, ends up in the middle and is used as a vehicle for the expression of anger between his parents. Daddy says "yes," Mommy says "no," and the rhubarb ensues. A child may learn to use such a pattern to his advantage, playing one parent against the other to obtain his ends. But the child's personality development is affected nevertheless. When he is the vehicle of marital strife he is likely to become withdrawn and anxious and later will avoid close relationships. If he learns to play off his parents against each other he may follow a similar pattern of manipulation in other relationships.

Parents may also be inconsistent in their responses to the same behavior at different times. Personal problems, for example, may make them less tolerant at one time than at another. Children find themselves having difficulties knowing what behavior is accepted when on one occasion Daddy laughs and on the next he "blows his stack." Such vacillation occurs to some degree in most families, and all of us learn to judge others' moods, but when vacillation is extreme and entirely unpredictable the child may become anxious and uncertain of his ability to predict anyone's reactions. New situations and new people will thus threaten him and his social adjustment will suffer.

Parents are often inconsistent because they have different standards for themselves than for their children: The old problem of "It's okay for Mommy and Daddy to do it, but not for you." Obviously, some of these standards are clearly upheld by culture and are generally accepted by children and adults. One must reach a certain age before he can legally drive a car, purchase alcohol, and so on. Other inconsistencies, however, reflect less clear standards. Sometimes they are quite amusing to outside observers who can recognize them when parents do not: for example, the mother who screams at her child, "Don't yell!" or the child who is spanked to teach him that he should not hit other children (only big people can hit little people!). Sometimes these inconsistencies can be worked out once the parent becomes aware of them. He then says something like, "I know I do this, but you'd be better off if you didn't." The child may understand, especially if his parents are sincere, that they are really trying to help him rather than to take advantage of him because he is smaller.

There is fair agreement among psychologists and students of child development that consistency and structure are important in shaping a child's development. Placing clear limits on a child's behavior makes it easier for him to understand approved goals, procedures, and standards of conduct. The children's roles in the family should be adequately defined, so that they know what is expected of themselves and their siblings.

Parental roles should also be defined, and the methods of encouraging certain behavior and discouraging misbehavior should be clear. The emphasis should be on reinforcing positive behavior and minimizing punishment. Each child differs in his response to punishment, and therefore the same types of punishment are not equally appropriate to all children. A swat on the behind may be helpful in controlling one child, but in another it may produce an extreme emotional response that makes him less secure.

Beside structure and consistency, parental guidance is also important. Children need and seek guidance, though they do not want it forced upon them at all times. They need to know that they are trusted to act independently in various situations, yet they also need criticism from adults at times. It is the parents' responsibility to be aware that their child will face certain developmental tasks during particular periods of his growth. There is no need to be extremely directive, but a parent can arrange circumstances so that it is easier for his child to recognize his tasks and to find ways to master them. There are times, as the child approaches critical periods in his development, that guidance and understanding are crucial. Starting school, reaching puberty, and experiencing failure, for example, all place excessive demands on the child.

MATERNAL EXPECTATIONS

Mothers' expectations of their children may significantly modify the ways that they treat them. For example, the mother who expects her child to become very famous (for reasons usually unknown to her) is more likely to over-respond to her child's behavior, even though she is generally loving, than is a mother who accepts her child simply as a person who will be what he wants to be.

B. Merrill (1946) has studied the effects of maternal expectations on the behavior of young children. Thirty mothers and their young children were first observed in single half-hour sessions. Half the mothers were then told that their children had not "realized their capabilities"; the other half were given no specific information about their children's performances. In the ensuing sessions the mothers who had been led to expect more of their children interfered more and were more critical than were the other mothers.

Merrill's study has revealed not only the effects of mothers' expectations but also the effects of presumably expert advice. The professional (teacher, psychologist, nurse, physician) who tells a mother that her child is under-achieving may create expectations that will drastically alter her behavior toward the child. Considering the profusion of professional advice available to most modern mothers (via books, television and specialists), it seems unfair to blame them for their behavior without knowing the conditions that have led up to it.

BIRTH ORDER

Nearly everyone has some understanding that a child's position in his family is important to his personality development. The most common stereotype is that of the "only child"—who has been given almost everything he wants and is a spoiled brat. Psychologists have also taken seriously the influence that birth order may have upon personality development. It seems obvious, for example, that the conditions of social learning for a firstborn child are different from those of a third child. The parents may be relatively inexperienced when dealing with their first and may exhibit greater concern about his behavior than when their third arrives. The firstborn is also an "only child" who must subsequently adjust to losing this status.

The youngest child in the family is likely to receive a great deal of attention and to be treated as "the baby," which indeed he is. He may, however, continue to be treated this way—even after he reaches adulthood. All his attempts to break out of this role may be futile. He is also likely to be taken advantage of by his older and stronger siblings, especially if they resent his having taken some of their parents' affection.

On the surface it appears that the ordinal position of a child does indeed have an important influence on his development. But, regardless of how tempting it is to simplify matters in this way, the experimental evidence is not nearly as clear as we might expect. There appears to be a complex network of relations among the number of children in a family, their sexes, and the differences in their ages. Birth order by itself is therefore an inadequate criterion for defining special atmospheres for social learning.

Some constancies have nevertheless evolved from research in this area. H. L. Koch (1956) has studied 384 children from two-child families. Sibling combinations varied in sex: Older boy-younger girl, older girl-younger boy, sisters, and brothers were classified by the gaps in their ages. The children were rated on various personality traits that were then related to birth order. Although the findings are not perfectly clear, some general statements can be made. All children with brothers showed more "masculine" traits. "Tomboyishness" was greater among girls with older brothers. All girls with brothers were more aggressive and scored higher intellectually than did girls with sisters. Boys with older brothers were more aggressive and daring than were boys with older sisters. From the point of view of identification theory these findings would be expected. That is, the older sibling becomes a model for younger siblings, probably because he seems stronger and more confident. The masculine characteristics of older brothers were imitated, regardless of the sex of the younger siblings.

There was also a difference between first- and second-born children. First-born children were more responsible, less aggressive, and more intellectually curious; they also tended to have stronger consciences than did the second-born children. These characteristics, however, were very dependent upon the sexes of the siblings and the number of years between them. If two siblings were of the same sex and close together (less than two years) in age few differences existed between them; siblings of the opposite sexes and more years apart exhibited marked behavioral differences.

These findings suggest that the critical point lies between two and four years of sibling separation. The three-year-old child is, for example, apparently more threatened and more anxious over the arrival of a new child than is a one-year-old or a four-year-old child. It is possible that the one-year-old child's world is not well enough differentiated for him to notice the effects of a new sibling, whereas the older child may be more independent of his parents and less threatened by a new arrival. The older child is also more likely to become a model for his younger sibling, probably because he seems more adaptive and more powerful than would a sibling closer in age.

Although these generalities are helpful in understanding development, the interaction of other factors may modify the effects of ordinal position. Postulating an "only child" syndrome or any other such specific categorization is not justified on the basis of current knowledge.

Conclusions about the Family

The research cited here strongly indicates that parents' behavior and attitudes toward their children will show themselves directly in the children's behavior. Children learn parental behavior through reinforcement and also through the process of identification. There are also some indications that certain types of parental behavior and certain patterns of family interaction create stress leading to disruptive behavior in children.

More precise research is being conducted on the complexity of family life, and the interaction of independent variables are increasingly being recognized. Future findings should therefore permit firmer statements about the effects of specific parental behavior on child development.

GENERAL GUIDELINES

Parents and future parents are rightly concerned about what psychologists think are the most effective ways to raise children. The only realistic response, however, is that there are no certain answers at present. Few students of child behavior would disagree with the general statement that each child is an individual and must be treated accordingly. Each child differs in the quality and quantity of his needs and resources; particular responses may have different effects on different children.

Another generalization on which most investigators would probably agree is that rigid teaching of parental values is not in itself sufficient to prepare the child to meet the world in which he is to live as an adult. Especially today the world changes so rapidly that it is foolish to guess which particular values will be adaptive when a child becomes an adult. There is always the risk of preparing the adults of tomorrow for the world of yesterday. Recommendations are thus probably best geared to encouraging psychological flexibility. To equip a child to meet change with maximum confidence in his own judgment, it is best to aim for freedom of investigation, flexible behavior, and independent thinking. It no longer seems possible to rely on any particular value system over an extended period of time.

THE "AUTHENTIC" CHILD

A. D. Button has presented a view of child rearing (1969) that reflects this preference for encouraging independence and flexibility. Button has used a humanistic framework (see Chapter 6) to interpret interactions between children and parents. He has not told "how to do it"; instead he has attempted to communicate a general attitude toward life, which he has called "authenticity."

The "authentic" child, according to Button, is a product of authentic parents; for that reason, much of his study has been directed toward parent-child communication. Authentic parents respect the uniqueness of their child; they find fulfillment in living with him. Authenticity is "the condition of realness and full functioning, of expanding sensitivity and awareness, of absorbed involvement in issues and work and people, of joy, and of love—" (Button, 1969, p. 11). Furthermore, the authentic person considers himself unique; he chooses his own directions, and he allows others the same independence in his relations with them. He has a firm respect for their uniqueness. "It is this model that I have adopted as exemplary of the kind of parent-child relationship most conducive to the freedom of development of both child and parent and therefore most productive of healthy and secure persons" (1969, p. 11).

The authentic parent, according to Button, is highly aware and appreciative of his child's complexities and the contradictions in his behavior. He observes with humor and grace as the child's individuality unfolds. The parent experiences a feeling of richness as he watches and interacts with his children and derives a great deal of pleasure from knowing that he will never leave them, though he will allow them to leave him when it is time. As a consequence his children become authentic. In terms of learning theory (not Button's orientation), the children identify with and learn from parents who hold and express certain values. They become flexible, open adults, who tend to encourage and stimulate democratic values and ideals.

Button believes that the children of inauthentic parents suffer from behavioral disorders, are extremely competitive, achieve much, are polite and good. They are the children who to him develop most of the undesirable characteristics that the emphasis on materialism and financial success in our modern society encourages.

It is instructive to examine one of Button's cases, which demonstrates the flavor of his orientation and serves as an example of one approach to child psychotherapy.

THE CASE OF ROBERT

Consider Robert, a "spoiled" child, according to the unanimous testimony of his grandparents, teachers, neighbors, and father. His mother is more inclined to diagnose Robert as "misunderstood," and she has, faithful to her diagnosis, alienated Robert's teachers, neighbors, her parents, and her husband. They, in turn, lose no time in labeling her a neurotic mother, which justifies their irritation with her. Her husband has long since stopped talking to her on any level but that of immediate practicalities. She senses easily the barely disguised groans and eyes rolled heavenward every time she goes to Robert's school. The principal, self-righteous in his weary knowledge of her neuroticism, automatically discounts anything she says, which she well knows, and he has officially told Robert's teacher to do the same. Robert's mother feels increasingly that she is in a smoky Kafka-esque void, her weakening cries that her son be given attention yielding only discordant echoes. She continues crying, though, and her martyrdom is becoming almost sensually gratifying to her as she fights the heroic fight against the unbeatable foe for the sake of her son.

Robert is eleven and obese. He is a bully, and he is loud and unpleasant. Once in an unguarded moment, he said his only wish was that all the kids at school consider him their best friend. His behavior, however, in complete opposition to his fantasy, is unendingly designed to bug, to torture, to alienate all the kids at school. His laugh is raucous and cruel. His hands are forever poking and pinching, hurtfully and obscenely, the other children. He greets adults with a shattering blow to their shoulders. Nobody (including his mother) likes him.

Robert's therapist (who doesn't like him, either), massaging his aching shoulder, dictates, following a session with the boy: "The closer I get to verbalizing with Robert his feeling of despair and loneliness, the stronger his resistance becomes, the more deafening his laugh, designed to drown out my words, the more assaultive his physical relationship with me. His scorn at the 'sissy' and 'baby' toys and games in the playroom, his ear-shattering scrambling techniques at any attempts at verbal communication seem virtually impenetrable. Robert is not the only one in the playroom who despairs."

Robert's strength and ferocity, his unpleasant forcefulness that subdues and drowns out all opposition, have created a world of perfect freedom for him, over which he reigns by terror, a lonely tyrant, striking out at the enemies on his borders. His mother and his therapist are simply spies, filtering through the borders, infringing upon his dreadful freedom. But Robert is not truly free. He is trapped, by his cumulative rejections, within his bristling fortress and he cannot get out any more than others can get in.

Robert can get out if he chooses to, but he can choose only if he is truly free. As long as he must fortify himself against rejection, and as long as he must fight fire with fire (and he sees fire even when, rarely, it does not exist), he is still in bondage, and his behavior will eventuate in expulsion from school and from his family and, not unbelievably, in ultimate membership in the Hell's Angels.

Robert got out of his fortified prison with the help of a college boy whom the therapist, claiming failure on his own part, finally recommended to Robert's mother. This young man, a football player, had been like Robert when he was younger, but had had the good fortune of having an involved father, a farmer, who refused to see his boy destroy himself, and who took his rehabilitation firmly in hand. The student met Robert three afternoons a week (at $1.50 an hour, compared with the therapist's $30) nominally for tutelage and companionship, actually for liberation. Unthreatened by Robert's violence, unrepulsed by his personality, this young man met Robert's challenge head-on. If Robert wanted to fight, they fought—and Robert lost. If Robert wanted to taunt or to laugh, he was nondefensively, even amusedly, taunted back and outlaughed by the undevious, sincere, and merry young man. Withal, out of the depths of his own security and calm knowledge of his own likability, the college boy never once stopped liking Robert. He got furious at him, he pounded both of Robert's shoulders black and blue, he railed at him, sometimes for an hour at a time. But Robert sensed the boy's regard for him. At first appeared a hero-worshiping reaction that the athletic young man instantly inspired in all preadolescent boys; later, when Robert had begun to drop some of his defenses, he sensed directly both the boy's warmth and imperturbability. Still later, Robert's positive feelings for the boy were greatly increased by the beginning of a process of identifying with him. He stopped wolfing down food in the gargantuan manner he had long been enjoying, as stuffing for his emotional void; and in an attempt to emulate his companion in his muscular physique he lost weight rapidly. There was no coercion, no shaming, no diet. Robert wanted to look like his hero, and he decided the best way to do it was to lose weight and then to exercise; and so he did freely.

Robert made another decision, equally freely, after a month of the college boy's companionship. He said that he'd like to invite his father on one of their outings. The father, shocked out of his withdrawal by his son's spontaneous invitation, accepted with real gratitude. The three of them thoroughly enjoyed an afternoon baseball game and a dinner out. Robert, in his ecstasy, was almost too well behaved. The father, feeling more and more affection for his son brimming up in him through the day and frankly enjoying the respectful yet light-hearted manner of the likable young man, experienced a new sense of freedom himself. And *he* thereupon began to make decisions, one of which was to take an active part on Robert's side against the smothering ministrations of his wife. Robert's mother, incidentally, reacted to this change in her husband with undisguised relief and delight. For one thing, it showed her, finally, that someone else did understand Robert and, for another, that someone was reacting to her, even negatively. The mother and father began to talk to each other again. (Button, 1969, pp. 80–85)

This discussion of Robert reveals that diagnosis, history, and background were interesting mainly in showing how he became what he was. The important aspect of treatment, however, was the athletic student's authentic attitude, his ability to see the child as he was at that moment, and to allow him freedom to grow. The existential child therapist emphasizes the authenticity of the relationship rather than specific techniques or professional knowledge.

PARENTAL PARADOXES

Button has outlined what he calls "blocks" in the unauthentic parent's perception of his child. They prevent him from seeing the child as he exists here and now and thus keep him from allowing his child to develop in freedom.

Three of these blocks are described as paradoxes. The first is based on a contradiction between the way that parents see themselves and the way that they see their children. They see themselves as complex but others as simple. Button has described a wife who was upset when her husband was late for dinner because he had stopped and had a drink with friends on the way home from work. She put his meal in the oven and privately decided that they would not have sex that night. But when her four-year-old son complained that his older brother was playing with his favorite toy she responded, "Honestly, Petey, you're so selfish." Her own selfishness she largely ignored; she sees her life as complex but Petey's as simple.

The second paradox involves a subject-object split. It shows as a lack of empathy, assuming that oneself is capable of understanding the forces that act upon him and others and being able to respond appropriately, but that others (especially one's children) cannot. Button's example is a father who told his son not to do a particular thing. His son replied that his father had done the same thing when he was young. The father retorted, "That was different." His reply showed lack of empathy and blocked a good relationship. This father treated his child as if he were an object, a dupe or sucker, someone unable to deal with the intricacies of living. Such assumptions may generate resentment and drive his son from him.

The third paradox involves inflicting pain on children through unawareness that they have the same feelings that adults have. The little boy who has been soundly spanked, for instance, tells his mother that he will run away; she replies, "Okay, I'll help you pack." His search for compassion has been defeated. Something begins to harden inside him, and his own ability to feel compassion starts to die. This same mother may be quite sensitive to rejection from her own peers yet can systematically inflict pain and rejection on her child.

THERAPY: A CORRECTIVE INFLUENCE

The four sources of influence on adjustment that we have described so far may be considered "natural," circumstances and conditions that are unavoidable in one form or another in everyone's life. In modern society, however, there is another possibility, which has grown from our understanding of development and the problems of adjusting to various kinds of stress: psychotherapy. To be sure, not many children experience psychotherapy, but with the proliferation of mental health clinics and their increasing emphasis on child development, more and more "problem children" (or children with problems) are subjected to professional attempts to modify their behavior. Two approaches to therapy with children will be examined in this section: play therapy and family therapy.

Play Therapy

Play therapy is a method of modifying the behavior of children who are judged emotionally disturbed. We shall focus on therapy with the individual child, but it should be understood that he is rarely the only member of a family to participate in counseling, guidance, or psychotherapy. It is quite rare for parents or other people close to the child to be excluded from a complete therapeutic program.

Play is useful in treating children for several reasons. First, it is a natural way in which younger children express themselves. They have yet to develop verbal skills or to adapt language to working out problems, especially problems of a personal and disturbing nature. In play a child is free not to complete a task as he would in work, and he is also freed from the rivalry involved in rule-following games. He may act out his fantasies and be "unsensible." He can therefore express his needs, drives, and conflicts in nonthreatening ways. Play also serves as a channel for discharging excess energy—expressing impulses and relieving emotional tensions. It serves, too, as a means of practicing skills. Under the direction of a therapist, a child may thus learn more adaptive ways of coping with life.

For all these reasons, play seems a natural process to put to therapeutic use. It affords a means of direct interaction with a child in a situation that is not unfamiliar to him. As it is quite unlikely that a young child can have an intellectual understanding of his psychological difficulties, he is not likely to perceive play therapy as "treatment." Throughout its course he may never realize that he is being "helped" by a professional, at least in the same sense that other doctors have "helped."

OBJECTIVE CHARACTERISTICS

Play therapy usually occurs in the playroom of a private practitioner's office or in a room specifically designed for this purpose in a clinic or institution. The setting is not always limited to a playroom, however. Depending upon the child's individual needs, interests, and so on, play may occur out of doors; even hikes through parks or wooded areas, fishing, and other activities may be considered appropriate. Although there are no strict limits on the type of setting, some of these outdoor activities require a great deal more professional time and probably for that reason are used less often. There is no reason to believe, however, that they are less effective.

Play materials are not limited to specific toys or games. A wide variety of materials should be available, many chosen for specific purposes. For younger children a doll's house with a variety of rooms, movable furnishings, and different dolls (father, mother, children of different ages, pets, and so on) is nearly always appropriate. Materials for artistic expression—fingerpaints and colors for brush painting, modeling clay, and building sets—are also usually available. A wide assortment of dolls, sometimes including dolls with sex organs, is also common. For older children various games like checkers, cards, and so on are provided. Aggressive toys (dart guns, darts, toy guns, and so on) are also commonly provided to allow the opportunity for expressing pent-up anger or resentment.

Aside from a general array of age-appropriate toys and toys amenable to the expression of specific drives, the therapist may provide materials to match the requirements of therapy with a particular child. A rather amusing example has been described by a therapist who was working with an aggressive nine-year-old boy. After the first few sessions he found it necessary to purchase shin guards like those worn by baseball catchers in order to protect himself from the boy's kicks. In this particular instance the boy began with physical assaults on the therapist, using aggressive and destructive toys and wreaking havoc in the playroom, even though attempts were made to control him. He progressed to playing checkers with the therapist and talking about his conflicts with his recently divorced mother. It is not unusual to observe that, as a child acquires skills in relating to himself and to others, he progresses from "younger" toys and activities to more age-appropriate behavior.

Play therapy is usually based on a one-to-one relationship between therapist and child. Group play therapy, or "activity therapy," has, however, been recommended by some therapists (for instance, Slavson, 1952). Sometimes three to five preschool children are treated at the same time; the same techniques and materials used for individual therapy are used for the group. Another approach is to form something like a club, the purpose of which is to provide a setting in which to practice for real social life. This sort of group is most suitable for children who are almost ready for social participation but still unable to deal with the competition and greater social pressures of real life.

Another kind of group is frequent in day centers for autistic children. Essentially, the children are "in school," though their tasks are not academic ones. The autistic child, it will be remembered, is withdrawn and turned inward upon himself. In these groups several children with aggressive behavioral disturbances may serve as "catalysts" for the autistic children. If an autistic child is sitting by himself in a corner, for example, immersed in his own movements and apparently unaware of the rest of the world, such a "catalyst" is likely to intrude aggressively, forcing the withdrawn child out of his autistic preoccupation into interpersonal contact. Thus, the type of children making up the group may in itself achieve some beneficial effects.

TYPES OF PLAY THERAPY

Throughout this book different theoretical approaches to psychotherapy have been presented. Therapists work somewhat differently, depending upon their theoretical views; play therapists are no exception. Some aspects are consistent, regardless of orientation, however. A close relationship between the child and the therapist is considered important by all. And, as therapy is basically a learning process, the specific techniques and the therapeutic setting are designed to provide maximum opportunity for the child to learn new and more adaptive attitudes and behavior.

In general it is quite difficult to differentiate adherents of one point of view from those of others by observing their activities. Most therapists respond sensitively to children's needs as they perceive them. The greatest actual practical difference is probably that between behavior therapists (Chapter 7) and all others. The former usually follow more specific procedures and techniques than do the latter. Even though therapists are alike in many ways, it is still fruitful to examine several approaches.

NONDIRECTIVE THERAPY   V. M. Axline (1947) has favored an approach first worked out by C. Rogers (see Chapter 6). The child is free to do or say anything that he wishes, within certain limits, while he is in the playroom. The therapist remains friendly and interested but offers no direct suggestions or guidance. He is alert to the child's expressions during conversation and play, and he attempts to provide an accepting and understanding atmosphere. As follows from Rogers' theory, an atmosphere of warm regard should afford an opportunity for the child to play out his tensions, frustrations, insecurities, and so on.

Treating anything that the child says with dignity and respect builds a sense of complete acceptance. The child is provided with a unique experience, in which an adult offers no suggestions, directions, restraints, criticisms, disapproval, or other intrusion upon the child's activities. As a result of complete acceptance and permission to be himself, he will, it is hoped, gain the courage to become a more mature and independent individual.

According to Axline, this relationship between therapist and child is the deciding factor in the success or failure of therapy. The child's feelings must be "reflected back" so that he can gain insight into his own behavior and recognize that the therapist understands and accepts him completely. If a child is using a mother doll to scold a child doll (presumably a symbolic substitute for the child), the therapist might say, "Mommy is mad for what he has done, but he is mad too." The therapist accepts anger that the child may be unable to express directly and therefore makes it easier for him to accept his own anger toward his mother. The therapist shows that he respects the child's ability to solve his own problems; the child is always the leader. In this example the therapist does not intervene in the child's play but simply supports whatever attempts the child may make to resolve the anger between mother and child. As in the Rogerian approach generally, the freeing of the child's growth potential through an accepting relationship is considered the curative force.

CONTROLLED APPROACHES In controlled approaches the theoretical background may be psychoanalytic, but in contrast to the psychoanalyst, the therapist uses standardized situations. He selects the materials and sometimes the plots in which the child engages.

Release therapy is a method for relieving severe anxiety; it has been recommended by D. M. Levy (1939). Fear reactions and night terrors resulting from such specific traumatic experiences as accidents, divorces, and operations are especially likely to be treated with this approach. The specific circumstances believed to have caused the difficulty are reenacted so that the emotions previously associated with them are released.

One four-year-old boy was referred for treatment because of night terrors, a very negative attitude, and sibling rivalry that had lasted three weeks. Acting out sibling rivalry and losing a fight with a companion had been associated with negative behavior changes in the child earlier. The child came daily for a total of six sessions in which sibling-rivalry situations were acted out. He showed a quick release of primitive hostility against the mother doll, the baby doll, and the dolls' breast. His night terrors stopped after the second session, and followup interviews for as long as four years after treatment indicated a marked reduction in sibling rivalry.

FINAL REMARKS ABOUT PLAY THERAPY   P. H. Mussen and his colleagues have pointed out (1963) that therapy sessions may be most economically explained in terms of learning theory. A child may acquire new responses, attitudes, and feelings in the context of a relationship in which his experience is continually rewarding. Inhibited and oversensitive children, for example, may change because many of their independent responses receive approval from the therapist instead of the punishment that they have received at home. Shy and withdrawn children may develop more outgoing and sociable responses through reinforcement in their favorable relationships with the therapist.

In controlled play settings, especially those normally associated with fear, repeated presentations may provide reciprocal inhibition, thus reducing anxiety. A child is also reinforced when he produces more adaptive reactions to conflicting circumstances. As he tries out new and more effective responses the therapist reinforces them, and they become habitual. These new reactions may then become generalized to the more important settings of real life.

Many other play-therapy techniques have been reported; each is claimed to be effective for specific kinds of difficulties. Child analysis, for example, is deemed most appropriate for children who have repressed unrealistic anxiety stimulated either by their parents' attitudes or their own fantasies. Children who have developed behavior problems because of poor training and children who are in very poor touch with reality are not considered good candidates (A. Freud, 1946). Levy has recommended "release therapy" for children whose maladaptive behavior results from specific traumatic incidents.

An attempt has been made throughout this book to emphasize that no single therapeutic approach seems best for all circumstances. Our knowledge of the processes and effectiveness of psychotherapy, though growing, is still too limited.

Family Therapy

Along with increasing acceptance of a psychosocial view of disordered behavior, there has been increasing emphasis on family therapy. Although the family has long been considered an important source of stress, as well as of comfort, therapy aimed at the family unit, rather than at the individual patient, is a comparatively recent development. The emotional closeness among family members and the frequency of their interactions lend obvious psychological importance to the family unit. Most of us know from personal experience that family interaction can be extremely stressful; most family members have the ability to hurt one another. On the other hand, this same emotional closeness can be extremely fulfilling and a great aid in coping with other stresses of life. Because of these potentials investigators have come to recognize the impact of disrupted family relationships and also the therapeutic possibilities of helping families to interact in ways that stimulate growth. Methods of direct intervention with the family group have developed as a means to attack major behavioral difficulties at their roots.

Family therapy has taken many forms. Some therapists prefer to see family members separately and to combine the data for subsequent individual use. The general trend, however, has been away from individual interviews; some combinations of family members are currently preferred by most practitioners. They may include all members, selected pairs and trios, or combinations of both. Two approaches to family therapy will be presented here: conjoint family therapy and an operant learning approach.

CONJOINT FAMILY THERAPY

Psychologists at the Behavioral Research Institute of Palo Alto, California, have particularly emphasized the role of communication in family disorders (see Satir, 1967). Much family disharmony can be traced to members' inability to communicate their needs, wishes, and desires clearly. Unnecessary conflicts arise, inevitable misunderstandings disrupt family life, and children may easily become intermediaries and substitute objects in family strife.

Some characteristics of a dysfunctional communicator (one who is not able to send a clear message) are relevant. For one thing, he may confuse characteristics that *he* attributes to things or people with the actual things or persons. For instance, he may say, "That picture is ugly," as if his opinion of the picture's aesthetic qualities is actually part of it. He does not separate his opinion from external reality. When speaking to a functional receiver, however, he will be forced to clarify and qualify his message. A functional receiver might say, "What do you mean when you say that picture is ugly?" The communicator may then be forced to clarify his statement: "Well, let me try to state it another way. It seems ugly to me, I don't like it." If he is quite dysfunctional, however, his response may not clarify his statement at all.

A functional communicator sends clear messages from the start; he might have said, "I don't like that kind of picture; to me it's ugly." The receiver would then have known what he meant, and the possibility of misunderstanding and possibly acting upon a mistaken supposition about the communicator's beliefs would have been minimal. A functional communicator is thus able to state his points firmly and clearly. He can ask for feedback, and he is receptive to it when it comes.

In therapy it is common to find dysfunctional communicators sending no messages at all but acting as if they had. The following interchange between a wife (W), a therapist (Th), and a husband (H) is an example.

W: We had no bread for dinner. You forgot it.
Th: You mean your husband?
W: Yes.

Th: (To husband) Did you know that you were out of bread in the house?
H: No, heck no I didn't.
Th: Do you remember her telling you?
H: No. No, she never told me. If I had known, I would have picked some up on the way home.
Th: Do you remember telling him that you were out of bread and asking him to pick some up?
W: Well, maybe I didn't. No, maybe I didn't. But you'd think he'd know. (Satir, 1967, p. 72) *

The wife's failure to tell her husband that they were out of bread and her expectation that he would know are fairly clear signs that communications between this couple promote disharmony. Usually when a communicator acts as she did he is expressing an internal wish that he can never put into words. Here, for example, the wife was most likely saying that she wished that her husband paid more attention to her. Her comment "You'd think he'd know" suggests that she thought he did not pay enough attention to his home life.

It is impossible to achieve completely clear communication because communication is by its very nature incomplete. A functional communicator tries, however, to make his desires, feelings, and thoughts clear. He does not leave the other person guessing about what he said. The receiver does not have to rely on assumptions from his own internal experience.

LEVELS OF COMMUNICATION   Communicating is not a simple matter; the receiver must assess all the ways in which another person communicates, as well as being aware of how he himself receives. The likelihood of distortion is always present, and the result may be quite disruptive. To complicate matters further communications are sent on at least two levels: the *denotative level* (the literal content of the words) and the *metacommunicative level* (the sender's feeling about them). A metacommunication is a message about a message. It conveys the sender's attitude toward the message, toward himself, toward the receiver, or a combination of the three.

Metacommunication may be verbal or nonverbal. If it is verbal the sender modifies his initial words with others, in order to clarify his meaning. For example, a message followed by the statement "It was a joke" tells the receiver how the message was meant, and how to respond (laugh at it). Or one might say why he sent it: "You hit me. So I'll hit you back." And so on.

Other metacommunications are expressed nonverbally. The message may be qualified by frowning, grimacing, smiling, stiffening, slumping, drawing back, and the like. Each of these actions qualifies what is being said and leaves the receiver to interpret the message in different ways.

Satir has demonstrated the process of attempting to understand a communication.

*Satir, V. *Conjoint Family Therapy*. Rev. ed. Palo Alto, California: Science and Behavior Books, 1967.

A husband says, in an irritable tone, "The dog is on the couch." The wife, in this relationship, may go through the following process:

A. He is telling me where the dog is.

B. But he is doing more than that. He sounds irritated.

C. Why is he telling me about his irritation? Is he criticizing me for the fact that the dog is on the couch?

D. If he is not criticizing me, what does he want me to do? Just listen to him? Sympathize with his irritation? Take the dog off the couch? Or what?

E. I wanted a dog. He didn't. I went ahead and got one without his agreement. Now, when he shows his irritation at the dog, he is complaining about what I did. He is criticizing me for disobeying him. He undoubtedly wants me to take the dog off the couch, but does he also want me to get rid of the dog and apologize to him for going against his wishes? (1967, p. 80)

The husband's communication forces the wife to guess what he is really trying to communicate. If she acts upon her best guess she may be wrong. In fact, an unhappy incident between them may result. Had his communication been clear she might not have liked what he said, but she would have been in no doubt about what it was. Had he said: "Take the dog off the couch, and get rid of him. You should never have bought a dog. I told you I didn't want one," she would have had little trouble in assessing his message. From that point they might have been able to work out their disagreement; of course, they might also have simply continued to disagree.

CONGRUENCE   The different levels of communication may or may not be congruent. In the previous example, in which the husband said irritably that the dog was on the couch, his communication was congruent. His tone of voice told his wife that he was irritated, and his words told her why, because the dog was on the couch. Had he said cheerfully that the dog was on the couch, with his wife knowing that he hated dogs, his messages would have been incongruent.

Investigators have dubbed any message that seemingly demands one response on the face of things but another on the metacommunicative level a *double bind*. For example, a mother might say to her child, "Come love your mommy" while at the same time pulling away from him or becoming tense. The message presents contradictory demands at the two levels, and the child does not know which he should obey. If he approaches his mother he is likely to be received coolly or brushed aside; on the other hand, if he does not come to her she is likely to accuse him of not loving her. The regular occurrences of such messages creates a great deal of stress for the child. In fact, studies attempting to associate double-bind communications with mothers of disturbed children have often shown positive results.

THERAPY   The difficulties just described exemplify the kinds of communication problems that the conjoint family therapist looks for. He seeks to discover these disruptive patterns, to point them out, and to help the family to overcome them. He is best viewed as a resource, a person who remains neutral as an "official observer" within the family framework and gains members' trust. He must therefore try to function as a "model communicator" himself, besides helping to clarify the family's interactions.

The following example demonstrates the kinds of interaction that occur in conjoint family therapy when clarification of communication is the primary tool for change.

Th: (to husband) I notice your brow is wrinkled, Ralph. Does that mean you are angry at this moment?

H: I did not know that my brow was wrinkled.

Th: Sometimes a person looks or sounds in a way of which he is not aware. As far as you can tell, what were you thinking and feeling just now?

H: I was thinking over what she said (his wife).

Th: What thing that she said were you thinking about?

H: When she said that when she was talking so loud, she wished I would tell her.

Th: What were you thinking about that?

H: I never thought about telling her. I thought she would get mad.

Th: Ah, then maybe that wrinkle meant you were puzzled because your wife was hoping you would do something and you did not know she had this hope. Do you suppose that by your wrinkled brow you were signaling that you were puzzled?

H: Yeh, I guess so.

Th: As far as you know, have you ever been in that same spot before, that is, where you were puzzled by something Alice said or did?

H: Hell, yes, lots of times.

Th: Have you ever told Alice you were puzzled when you were?

W: He never says anything.

Th: (smiling, to Alice) Just a minute, Alice, let me hear what Ralph's idea is of what he does. Ralph, how do you think you have let Alice know when you are puzzled?

H: I think she knows.

Th: Well, let's see. Suppose you ask Alice if she knows.

H: This is silly.

Th: (smiling) I suppose it might seem so in this situation, because Alice is right here and certainly has heard what your question is. She knows what it is. I have the suspicion, though, that neither you nor Alice are very sure about what the other expects, and I think you have not developed ways to find out. Alice, let's go back to when I commented on Ralph's wrinkled brow. Did you happen to notice it, too?

W: (complaining) Yes, he always looks like that.

Th: What kind of message did you get from that wrinkled brow?

W: He don't want to be here. He don't care. He never talks. Just looks at television or he isn't home. (Satir, 1967, pp. 97–99)

This excerpt shows how the therapist goes about clarifying communications at both the verbal and nonverbal levels and the possibilities that the technique suggests to the couple for trying to communicate outside the therapy sessions.

FAMILY OPERANT CONDITIONING

As an example of family operant conditioning I shall present one of my own experiences as a clinical psychologist in private practice (Coe, 1970a; 1970b, in press). I am often faced with the difficult task of working with children seven to thirteen years old who exhibit behavior problems at home or in school. Verbal psychotherapy is usually ineffective because their normal mode of expression involves action, rather than words; few have developed the ability to examine their own motivations as a means of control. Play therapy is also usually ineffective because they have passed the play stage though they have not yet reached a sound alternative mode of expression through verbal means. The most effective approach for me in the past had been to work with their families, attempting to discover and resolve intrafamily conflicts. Frequently, however, little progress resulted, and the parents felt guilty because of the implication that the children's difficulties were their fault. Because the more classical approaches seemed ineffective, I became interested in a psychosocial emphasis and began to develop a technique incorporating "common sense," work with the family, and a point system.

By the time that a child has been referred to me the family has usually become quite upset, school authorities have intervened, and home life has generally been disrupted. The child's self-image has already been degraded, his responses to such feelings have been intensified, his parents have become increasingly short-tempered, and reactions and counterreactions are snowballing. Second, and this point should not be underestimated, private therapy is expensive. Long-drawn-out treatment can *increase* difficulties because of financial stress and conflict over paying for treatment as "good" parents should. In my practice I rarely see people for whom money is not a difficulty. Incomes are generally too high to justify the substantial fee reductions available at government clinics and too low to pay private fees comfortably.

It seemed realistic and a matter of common sense to use the resources of the home itself to establish a "point" system based on the principles of operant conditioning (see Chapter 7). The following case study demonstrates my ideas in application.

THE CASE OF DICK

Dick and his family were referred by a school psychologist because of Dick's behavioral difficulties in school and at home and his parents' upset over them. I requested that Dick's mother and father accompany him to our first meeting. I talked with them alone briefly, talked with Dick briefly, then talked with all of them together. From these short interviews I obtained the following information.

Dick was twelve years old. His motor coordination and learning abilities were reduced because of a neurological handicap, apparently from a birth defect. Dick had become increasingly difficult to manage as he approached adolescence. He frequently quarreled with his mother, refused to do what she asked, and had prolonged temper tantrums involving cursing, yelling, running away from home, and even threats of physical attack with a knife. These tantrums were the major complaint. At school he was difficult to manage, did not get along with the other children, refused to do his lessons, and was frequently truant. The school had reached the point of limiting his attendance to two hours a day of special classes and one hour a week in a recreational program. As the school psychologist said, "He is really a tough one."

The "hassle" at home had grown to major proportions. His parents wanted to ship him off to an institution, and he would have been willing to leave at a moment's notice if there had been any place to go. In my talk with Dick, however, it became apparent that he was not an "animal," that he was not beyond control, but that he had a very low opinion of himself and that his negative behavior only reinforced it.

Dick's parents were surprisingly reasonable people (something that I had not been led to expect) but obviously at their "wits' end." Both vacillated between anger at his behavior and guilt over his neurological handicap. It was also clear that they had reached the point of total helplessness and hopelessness. While they were talking with me I could see "here we go again" written all over their faces. They had already run the professional gamut—psychiatrists, neurologists, pediatricians, child-guidance clinics—but nothing had done much good. Dick's mother had benefited temporarily from individual therapy aimed at helping her to cope with the difficulties involved in raising him. Drug therapy for Dick had been tried; in fact, it was still being used. But, except when the dose was large enough to sedate him, it had had little effect. The parents also thought that the school had pushed them from one alternative to another with no results. I am certain that to them I seemed just another therapist who would talk to them and make everything seem okay or just another doctor who was going to tell them that they had to expect this behavior from a "brain-damaged" child. In general, they felt confused, alienated, guilty, and hopeless in coping with their difficulties.

I saw all three together for the last half of the first session. Their interactions reflected the distrust and alienation that had grown from their difficulties. When Dick said that he was going to try to improve, his parents only looked at him knowingly and remarked that they had "heard that before." Rather than allowing them to continue to bicker, I intervened quite directly and began to explain the "point program."

First, I told them that what I thought was happening had little to do with Dick's actual neurological difficulties. They had worked themselves into a "circular hangup" that was making the situation extremely difficult for all of them.

"In order to stop this, and to make everybody more comfortable, we're going to let Dick do essentially what he wants to do, which is, by the way, to behave properly. And you, his parents, are not going to have to punish him or continually ride him to have him do what you want."

Needless to say, the eyebrows of all three went up following this proclamation. Dick gave me a knowing smile, indicating that he now "had it made," and his parents began to protest that he could not be left to his own choices. Again I interrupted, saying that they should at least listen to my plan and explanation before making judgments. I went on to say that Dick was to be treated as an adult now and given the responsibility for determining his own actions.

"To help him do this, we are *all* going to agree on Dick's desirable behavior and on his undesirable behavior. Then we will establish a reason for *everybody* wanting to see them come about. (I always stressed total family participation.) For the next week you are going to have to continue dealing with your difficulty as you see fit; however, before seeing me again the *three of you* are to agree on a list of behaviors that are satisfactory to all of you. One list will be the things that *all* of you want Dick to do but that he has difficulty carrying out. Another list will be the behaviors that *all* of you do not want Dick to do. And the third list will be those things that Dick values the most at present."

At that point we stopped to find some examples of each of these behavior groups. Dick's mother made the first comment: "I want him to be good." My reply was: "I'm sure all of us want Dick to be good, but that's too vague an idea to be very useful. One of the important parts of this program is to be sure that everyone knows *exactly* what behavior we're talking about so there is no conflict about whether or not he performs it. He has a right to know *exactly* what's expected of him as well as you have the right to know *exactly* what to expect from him. Therefore, we'll have to look for more specific things."

At that point Dick said that he did not want to have temper tantrums. Everybody agreed heartily, and we had our first agreed upon example of behavior. We put it in the category of negative behavior. His mother then said, "I'd like him to go to school willingly." My answer was that going to school was adequate for our purposes, but it is impossible to be certain whether a person is "willing" or not. They all agreed that Dick should go to school, which we placed in the positive behavior category. The things that Dick liked to do were a little easier to define; for example, he liked to watch television and to eat popcorn. These activities were included in the list of "reinforcing" behavior.

I closed the session by explaining that Dick would be paid in points for all the positive behavior that they decided upon; for example, if he went to school he would be paid perhaps ten points. On the other hand, he would have to pay for any of his negative behavior. A temper tantrum, for example, would cost him one point a minute. The third stipulation was that Dick would also pay for the things that he liked. Popcorn might be worth five points a bowl. They were also instructed to establish the numbers of points that Dick could earn for positive behavior and the costs for negative and reinforcing behavior before the next session. I explained that, although this system might seem a little strange at first it is exactly the way that most adults conduct their lives except that they use different currency. They are paid for certain things, and they pay for other things. Dick's response was positive, though his parents still seemed doubtful.

At the second meeting a week later they presented me with three lists of behavior, some of which required further clarification. For instance, one kind of reinforcing behavior was staying up past 9:00. It was necessary to be more explicit: The costs would include a time factor, ten points for the first half hour, thirty points for the next half hour, and so forth, in order to prevent him from staying up all night. At any rate, at the second session a trial system was established and was to be implemented immediately. Any difficulties were to be noted, and if they could not be resolved by the family they would be discussed at our next meeting.

At the third meeting I was quite gratified by the progress made. Dick literally bounced into my office saying, "Doctor Coe, I'm worth 400 points!" I suspect that it was the first time in some years that he had felt anything but a misfit, a neurologically handicapped child. His parents followed, smiling and shaking their heads in disbelief. Dick had not had a temper tantrum all week (they had been almost daily occurrences before), and he had been exhibiting all the specified positive behavior. In fact, he had refused to spend all but a few of his points for reinforcing behavior, choosing to accumulate them instead. Obviously, the points themselves held great significance for Dick at that time. I anticipated, however, that they would soon lose their attractiveness and discussed the possibility of a conversion program for excess points. Rather than simply using his points to purchase things that he liked he could trade them in for money or special activities, depending upon what the *family* thought was appropriate. All agreed that it was a good idea, and I suggested that we terminate the sessions. They could call me if something went wrong, and we could meet to discuss it. Without thinking I added, "There is no sense running up the bill." Their spontaneous look of gratitude caught me off guard and made me realize the importance of financial stress on such a family. Dick picked up this statement, and subsequently, when a problem had been resolved, he would say, "Well, that's that, no sense running up the bill!"

Two weeks later I received a call from Dick's mother. She was quite upset because Dick had had a temper tantrum. I made an appointment for them to come in and discuss the matter, but in the meantime she had had his medication increased to the point at which he had been almost immobilized. As it turned out, the source of his temper tantrum had been a failure on her part to follow their program. Dick had asked to stay up late and had been willing to pay the points required, but she had responded, "Dick, I'd rather you didn't stay up tonight." He had become insistent and upset and had eventually thrown a "humdinger" of a temper tantrum. His mother recognized what had happened, but Dick had "bankrupted" himself through his tantrum. Consequently, she thought that the point system was finished, Dick was discouraged, and the situation appeared irremediable. Quite frankly I was somewhat baffled myself. Dick was dejected, his mother was dejected, and mournful silence filled the room. After a few moments I said: "Okay, what happens to an adult when he faces bankruptcy? Well, he can either declare bankruptcy and be relieved of any further indebtedness, or he can pay off his debts in some reasonable way."

We dismissed the idea of declaring bankruptcy because that would mean that Dick could have a tantrum whenever he wanted and that the point system would thus lose its effectiveness. We decided that he could work out his debts, but in order not to deprive him of all reinforcement he would be paid double points for his positive behavior; 80 percent of his earnings would go to paying off his debt, and the remainder to buying reinforcements. Satisfied with the resolution of the crisis, they again left with instructions to call me if necessary.

A few other instances occurred, but our meetings became shorter and farther apart. Dick's parents began to figure out unique and creative ways to adapt the point system to their particular circumstances; in fact, they seemed quite confident that they could deal alone with the problem.

Dick's behavior was generalized to his school work; in fact, a step in our program had been to enlist the cooperation of school personnel, Dick's teacher in particular. Dick received points from his teacher for academic achievement and positive classroom behavior. It was also the first summer that the family had been able to enjoy a vacation with Dick, and he was off the point system on vacation.

At my last meeting with Dick he asked to be "let off" the point system. Even though he was building up a small "bank account" with excess points, he wanted to show that he could do it "on his own," that he did not need outside restrictions of any kind. He "blew" his first week off the system, and we all agreed that it was better to proceed at a slower pace. Our plans are to accomplish the change progressively, allowing him to be off the point system for increasing periods of time, depending upon his behavior.

Obviously, several factors beside the point system were instrumental in treating Dick. First, his family found a positive focus around which it could consolidate its efforts to overcome the disruption of its functioning. In itself this gain reduced the stress of guilt, fear, and so on. The family began to operate as a unit toward positive goals. Dick and his parents recognized that he could control his own behavior; his brain had not been damaged to the point at which he could not conduct himself as a socialized person.

I recognize that the report on Dick lacks scientific rigor. I am not entirely certain exactly what happened, but I am convinced that it was worthwhile. I am also more firmly convinced from my experience with Dick that the psychosocial view is going to open up many new avenues that will revolutionize our understanding and handling of disordered conduct.

SUMMARY

In this chapter we have dealt with some of the important human relationships and environmental factors that influence child development. It is becoming increasingly apparent that the physical environment has an important impact on development and consequently on adjustment. It is now known that sensory, learning, and motor capacities can be severely limited solely through inadequate physical stimulation in the environment. The Head Start program for disadvantaged children is one practical result of this research.

Other important determinants of development are related to the cultural and social mileu. The climate, the general productivity of a cultural group, and the common domestic enterprises of a culture impose limits on development. Being raised in an agricultural society, for example, decreases the child's opportunities to enter certain service professions. Recent investigators (especially environmental psychologists) have postulated that many of the concrete characteristics of a culture (like architecture and city organization) are important in personality development. Socioeconomic status, social class, and social roles are other factors that impose limits on development. Every child learns particular attitudes and values associated with his parents' social position, and his behavior is affected by parental expectations that arise from their particular place in the social order.

Specific personal relationships are also important to a child. In our society relations with teachers are obviously important. Teacher-pupil interactions can have far-reaching and often permanent effects on a child's unspoken attitudes, as well as on his overt behavior. For that reason, it is important to explore the kinds of teacher behavior that seem to promote positive development.

The influence of a child's family is probably as important in his development as is any other single factor. It is generally true that children acquire many of their attitudes and behavior patterns from models who live with them. Certain ways in which mothers interact with their children (for example, rejection and overprotection) also shape children. Furthermore, the position of a child in his family—as first, second, or third child—appears to have some general effects on development, though they cannot be simply described.

Therapeutic play and family therapy may serve to influence development of children with emotional and behavioral problems. All versions of play therapy are aimed at eliminating maladaptive patterns and instilling more adaptive responses to the environment. Two family approaches have been presented. One emphasizes clarifying communications, and the other applies learning theory to modifying family patterns.

11

A. Introduction
   1. Criteria of adolescence
   2. A flexible definition of
      adolescence
B. Effects of Physical Changes at
   Puberty
   1. Changes in primary sex
      characteristics
   2. Secondary sex changes
C. Psychological Adjustment to
   Physical Change
   1. Male adjustment
   2. Female adjustment
   3. Effects of developmental rate
   4. Sexual arousal and expression
   5. Body image
D. Interpersonal Adjustment
   1. The beginning of independence
   2. The peer group
   3. Boy-girl relationships
   4. Cognitive change
   5. Summing up early adolescence
E. Summary

Adjustment in Early Adolescence

INTRODUCTION

CRITERIA OF ADOLESCENCE

Before turning to the substance of this chapter it is well to attempt a definition of adolescence. The term "adolescence" literally means becoming an adult, as "obsolescence" means becoming obsolete. It seems that almost everyone takes for granted the existence of an adolescent period. On closer investigation, however, it is clear that widely differing criteria are used to define it. Most students of development and most laymen nevertheless agree that adolescence is a time of transition from childhood to adulthood. This general definition is suitable to casual conversation, though even then there are problems in defining adult and child. Cultural influences blur the lines even more. The length of the transition from childhood to adulthood varies greatly in different cultures, aside from cultural differences in definitions of adulthood. In some native tribes, for example, children who have reached puberty are initiated into the rites of adulthood within a single day or week. In that short span most of the rights, privileges, and responsibilities of adults are granted to the young people. In our own society we are familiar with Christian confirmation and the Jewish bar mitzvah, which indicates that a child is becoming an adult. He is awarded some of the privileges and responsibilities related to his religion, but it may be as long as ten years or more before he receives all the other privileges and responsibilities associated with adulthood.

Another fairly common assumption about, or perhaps a criterion of adolescence, is that it is a period of psychological stress and strife. Again this assumption depends largely upon culture, rather than on characteristics of adolescence itself. In societies in which sexual behavior is encouraged, accepted, and enjoyed; in which social roles are well defined; and in which training for adulthood is clear, there is little reason to believe that adolescence is anything but enjoyable and comfortable. Cultures and subcultures vary in the restraint, structure, encouragement, and so forth applied to their children. The stress and demands for adjustment during the adolescent transition thus also vary. In modern Western societies adolescence is generally prolonged, but it need not be extremely stressful. Regardless of our tendency to focus on the stresses and problems of youth, many children progress through adolescence in a very smooth and fulfilling way.

A closer examination of some criteria commonly used to define adolescence will be instructive.

334

THE BIOLOGICAL CRITERION

A classical criterion of the beginning of adolescence is the physical changes associated with sexual maturity, or puberty. During puberty the child experiences changes in drive level, especially in relation to the sexual drive, that require some adjustments. These physiological changes affect the child and present him with challenges and crises. The biological criterion by itself, however, is inadequate. Children reach puberty at vastly different ages, sometimes as early as nine or ten years old, sometimes not until fifteen or sixteen. It is inadequate, if not incorrect, to say that a fifteen-year-old high-school boy is not an adolescent solely because he has not developed physically. Obviously, even though puberty is still to come, changes in his peer relationships and adult expectations are already forcing him to make adjustments characteristic of the transition to adulthood.

OBJECTIVE SOCIAL STATUS

Every modern society establishes certain chronological age limits for some of its adult privileges. The legal voting age, for instance, is eighteen years old in the United States; it represents explicit recognition that at this age a person is responsible enough to take part in choosing his government. Other privileges and responsibilities are granted at different ages: marrying without parental consent, purchasing tobacco and alcoholic beverages, driving a motor vehicle, conscription into the armed services, and trial of offenses in adult criminal courts.

All these "landmarks" are determined by chronological age, but we know from earlier discussions that chronological age is often a quite arbitrary, inaccurate measure of developmental level. Many very intelligent sixteen-year-olds would probably be more responsible voters than are many older people. Or perhaps an eighteen-year-old boy whose social and emotional development is similar to that of most twelve- or thirteen-year-olds should be tried in juvenile court, whereas certain seventeen-year-old offenders may have the stable antisocial personalities appropriate to adult courts. Although the privileges attending certain chronological ages are usually very important to adolescents—most cannot wait to drive cars for instance—they are not much help in providing a meaningful definition of adolescence.

SOCIAL ROLE EXPECTATIONS

There comes a time when peers, as well as adults, begin to expect a child to fill certain new roles. As he approaches adulthood, these demands become more apparent and more stringent, and he is increasingly pressured to meet them. In pluralistic American society it is quite difficult to define adolescence, or adulthood for that matter, on the basis of such expectations alone, however. In a tribal society, in which the child passes through initiation rites in one or two days and role expectations change drastically in a very short period, they may be used to define adulthood—or the passing of childhood—rather precisely. But in modern societies changes in roles are less apparent and less clear. A college student may, for example, be married and raising children before he fills an occupational role in which he is financially independent. His parents may still consider him a child who needs guidance, understanding, and sometimes supervision. Although role expectations are extremely important in American society, they do not lend themselves to a clear definition of adolescence.

SELF-EVALUATION

If we could measure self-evaluation accurately it might represent a valid criterion for defining adolescence. There are frequent instances, in our society, however, when it becomes painfully clear that young people evaluate themselves as adult before important adults agree. A fifteen-year-old girl may feel that she is ready for dating, but her parents may insist that she not date at all, or at least not without a chaperon, until she is seventeen or eighteen. The nineteen-year-old boy soldier who considers himself financially independent may find himself in error: That is, his financial resources actually are sufficient only to allow him to leave his post housing and dining facilities periodically.

The sense of having found one's "own plot of ground," of "making it on one's own," indicates to an individual that he has reached adulthood. These feelings may occur in a twelve-year-old boy who has had to "grow up fast" and provide a major financial contribution to his family. By the time he is fifteen his self-evaluation is in many ways quite correctly that of an adult, even though his body is still not developed and society does not allow him the privileges of twenty-one-year-olds. On the other hand, a sixty-year-old man may still be supported at home by his sister or mother. Although he may rationalize his circumstances, his true self-evaluation is likely to be that of a child, not of an adult. In either instance it would be difficult to use self-evaluation as the only criterion of adulthood or childhood.

A Flexible Definition of Adolescence

It appears that no one of the criteria we have described is sufficient in itself to define adolescence. Our preference here is to combine them into a definition that relates more closely to personal adjustment. Thus the onset of adolescence may be described as the time at which changes in the child's environment present clear challenges to his current modes of functioning. It is a time when forces require him to change his behavior if he is to continue his growth successfully. These challenges may come from changes associated with physical growth, social status, role expectations, or self-evaluations; one, or all, may mark the introduction of adolescence. By this definition a pre-pubescent boy whose friends are beginning to date girls, for example, is considered adolescent. He must adjust to his changing peer roles and to the expectations attached to them whether or not he has begun to develop mature sexual characteristics or date himself. On the other hand, the boy who reaches puberty early while his friends still act as if they do not care about girls begins adolescence by adjusting to his increased sex drive and changes in his body image.

Adolescence ends when the child has successfully met the above challenges. He will be an integrated member of the adult society, physically developed, filling roles assigned to adults, and evaluating himself as an adult. Adolescence does not end on the basis of vocational and social skills alone; an independent self-image is also required. For example, a man who continues to live with his mother, rather than establishing a separate life of his own, even though his skills would allow him to live independently, is by this definition still adolescent. His self-evaluation does not allow him to function independently. On the other hand, a fifteen-year-old boy who marries, holds down a job, and feels himself capable of caring for himself and his family may have completed adolescence.

Several developmental steps are associated with early adolescence. They arise from the demands associated with physiological growth, as well as with social and cultural expectations.

Increases in sex drive and sexual potency change the adolescent's life. Not only does he experience a greater need for sexual outlet, but he has also reached the point at which sexual activities can result in significant social changes—marriage because of pregnancy, for example. Changes in body size and proportion also occur, and changes in facial features, height, and strength necessitate a new physical image that will most likely last most of the adolescent's life.

Important changes are also occurring in his relations with others. Peer interactions begin to take on new meaning, and adults begin to reciprocate by adopting new roles. He must acquire new social and interpersonal skills to meet these changes effectively.

The young adolescent's intellectual ability is also changing, and he must begin to channel it to fit his own pattern of needs. His interests will broaden a great deal from those of childhood, and he will face questions of social, religious, and political values.

The end of early adolescence is necessarily defined arbitrarily. Each child varies in the chronological age at which he reaches it. Usually, however, there is a time late in high school or early in college when adult attitudes toward the child begin to reflect less indulgence of his experimentation, greater expectation of consistent patterns of behavior, and demands that he "get with it," that he start working seriously to fulfill the adult roles.

EFFECTS OF PHYSICAL CHANGES AT PUBERTY

The early adolescent must come to grips with the changes in his body and the increased energy frequently associated with them. He must recognize that these changes will be permanent. On another front, he must compromise his increased sex drive with the restrictions set forth by his society.

Rapid changes at puberty are stimulated by an increase of gonadotropic hormones, chemicals released by the anterior pituitary gland, the "master gland," whose secretions control hormone balance throughout the body by governing the hormonal secretions from the other ductless glands. Gonadotropic hormones stimulate the activity of the sex glands, which in turn produce sex hormones. Male and female hormones are secreted in both sexes, but the male gonads secrete a higher percentage of testosterone than of estrogen, whereas the ovaries produce according to an opposite ratio. It is the comparative secretion of testosterone and estrogen that differentiates males from females chemically (Committee on Adolescence, 1968).

CHANGES IN PRIMARY SEX CHARACTERISTICS

"Primary sex characteristics" are those of the reproductive organs.

THE MALE

The time at which puberty begins in males normally varies between ages ten and fifteen. The growth of the testes and scrotum (the sac containing the testes) is the first noticeable sign of puberty. Pubic hair follow shortly after, appearing first at the base of the penis. The penis soon begins to grow rapidly. Approximately one year after the appearance of pubic hair the boy is likely to have his first ejaculation through nocturnal emission, masturbation, or some other means. The penis, testes, scrotum, and internal tubes that direct the sperm from the testes to the penis also continue to grow.

Although the ability to ejaculate indicates to the boy that he is capable of reproduction, it is not necessarily true that he is. There is evidence to suggest that boys remain sterile for considerable periods after the development of pubic hair. This information is not especially clear, however, because of the obvious difficulties in testing fertility accurately.

A boy's first ejaculation may cause concern, depending upon how he attains it and his prior knowledge and attitudes about sexuality. Many boys are relatively sophisticated about sex at this age. Not infrequently they have engaged in mutual inspection with others and have masturbated. The first ejaculation may then be taken as a sign of masculinity, something of which a boy can be proud. On the other hand, boys who are, for one reason or another, anxious about sexual matters may react with surprise or shock. The erotic dreams that often accompany nocturnal emissions may intensify the uninformed boy's shame and guilt. As a rule, however, boys are not very concerned about nocturnal emissions probably because they talk freely with their friends about such matters (Committee on Adolescence, 1968; Mussen *et al.*, 1969; Pikunas, 1969).

THE FEMALE

Development of the breasts is the first external sign that a girl is entering puberty. The ovaries, fallopian tubes, uterus, and vagina begin to grow at the same time that the first pubic hair is noticeable along the labia. Again, there is wide variability in the ages at which puberty begins in girls. Pubescence may begin anywhere from eleven to fourteen years of age, though most girls reach menarche (begin menstruation) between eleven and fifteen years; the extremes are as early as nine and as late as twenty.

The most notable change for a girl is the beginning of menstruation. The discharge of bloody material from her vagina is a clear sign that she is reaching sexual maturity. It is the hallmark of adult femininity, and circumstances associated with early menstruation may determine a girl's eventual adjustment to her femininity. It is important, therefore, that her initial experiences be as free from strain as possible.

Girls who are more informed about sex are likely to accept menstruation easily and to take pride in it. In our society, however, many "old wives' tales" and puritanical notions about menstruation may engender shame or fear. Some adolescent girls, though probably not a large percentage of the total, are extremely upset by the onset of menstruation. Their shame may be strong enough to cause them to hide the fact even from their parents.

Girls are more likely to react to the menarche maladaptively if they have been exposed to negative attitudes. Hearing complaints about the physical discomfort associated with menstruation, for example, may cause them to anticipate discomfort. A girl who hears adults speaking of menstruation negatively—calling it the "curse," the female "plight," or "being unwell"— may adopt similar attitudes.

The best method for easing adjustment to menstruation is to explain the naturalness of the process and to emphasize pride and pleasure in greater maturity. A girl's mother can be especially helpful by counseling her daughter wisely. A girl's entire sexual future, as well as the way in which she accepts her adult role, may be affected by attitudes toward her first objective sign of adult sexuality (Committee on Adolescence, 1968; Douvan and Kaye, 1957).

Secondary Sex Changes

Secondary sex characteristics are those that occur during puberty but do not directly involve the reproductive organs (see Table 10-1). There is a "growth spurt" during puberty. Boys usually experience sudden increases in height and weight between the years of thirteen and fifteen. They may grow four to twelve inches and gain fifteen to sixty-five pounds during these years. Girls begin about two years earlier than boys do, but they do not grow as much. Increases in height and weight practically cease within three years after the growth spurt (Committee on Adolescence, 1968; Mussen *et al.*, 1969).

Female breasts are, of course, a prominent secondary sex characteristic. First, the papilla (nipple) is elevated to form a small mound, and the areola (the colored area around the nipple) increases in size. The formation of a secondary mound, composed of areola and papilla, above the general level of the breast is next. At maturity, however, the areola recedes leaving the papilla projecting. Development of milk glands does not occur until pregnancy.

The male's breast also changes but to a lesser degree than does that of the female. The areola usually doubles in diameter, and about one out of three males also experience some mammary development with projection of the areola.

TABLE 10-1.   USUAL SEQUENCE OF PUBERTAL DEVELOPMENT *

Male	*Female*
1. Growth in testes begins, enlargement and reddening of scrotal skin	1. Initial breast enlargement, elevation of papillae (nipples), and increase in diameter of areola
2. Appearance of straight, pigmented pubic hair at base of penis	2. Appearance of straight, pigmented pubic hair along the labia
3. Penis begins to enlarge, mainly length	3. Period of maximum physical growth
4. First voice changes, including deepening and "squeaking"	4. Appearance of kinky pubic hair
5. First ejaculation	5. First menstruation, usually after full growth is attained
6. Appearance of kinky pubic hair	6. Growth of axillary hair under arms and on limbs
7. Maximum physical growth	7. Reproduction becomes possible, usually one to two years after menstruation
8. Growth of axillary hair under arms, on face (upper lip), and on limbs	
9. Marked deepening of voice	
10. Growth of facial hair (beard)	

* Once development of primary or secondary sex characteristics begins in either sex, it continues until adulthood is reached.

The deepening of the male voice during puberty is often striking. The larynx enlarges at about the same that penis growth takes place, and as penis development approaches completion the boy's voice usually deepens perceptibly. Voice changes may be very embarrassing, though often amusing. Some boys lose their voices almost completely with little warning, only to recover them shortly with entirely new, deep tones. Others go through periods of uncertainty, never knowing whether their voices will come out high or low. Sometimes the voice may change right in the middle of a sentence. Many boys, however, experience only gradual deepening of tone that may go almost unnoticed until others begin to recognize that they are speaking in men's voices.

Growth of hair is also a significant part of the pubertal development. Pubic hair immediately adjacent to the sex organs is one of the first signs of puberty. It may continue to grow into the middle twenties or longer.

Axillary hair, not directly associated with the sex organs, usually appears about two years after the appearance of pubic hair. It typically occurs under the arms in both sexes. Males usually also develop hair on their chests and stomachs and especially on their faces. A boy often takes the appearance of a "beard" as a sign that he is "really" becoming a man.

The sebaceous and sweat glands also develop. At about the time that axillary hair begins to grow the sweat glands become enlarged, and the typical odor of adult perspiration becomes noticeable. The sebaceous glands (glands secreting fluid that gives luster to hair) also become enlarged and more active; ducts, however, do not enlarge as rapidly as does their capacity for secretion, so that they can easily become plugged and infected. The result is, of course, acne, a common skin condition among adolescents. Even mild acne can be a very serious concern. Physical appearance is extremely important to adolescents, and those who develop severe acne may be deeply ashamed of their appearances. The rest of their lives they may reflect the personal and social insecurity that they develop in adolescence.

The blood vessels grow more slowly than does the heart during puberty. Blood pressure thus often creates a strain on the heart and associated tension and tiredness. The energy level and general health of the young adolescent may thus be quite unpredictable. He may often feel ill or suffer from headaches, stomach pains, and other discomforts. At times he has little energy or is completely exhausted, whereas at other times he is exuberant and overexerts himself. Regardless of this variability, however, he should not be "babied." Severe illnesses are not specific to this stage, and except for accidents children do not usually perish from "adolescent" illnesses.

PSYCHOLOGICAL ADJUSTMENT TO PHYSICAL CHANGE

Considering the rather dramatic changes in the young adolescent's physical appearance, it is not surprising that many adjustment problems arise. The importance of puberty in most societies tends to focus adult attention on the child, making him even more aware of his physical changes and new social expectations. His physical characteristics become permanent and will partly determine the ways that others will react to him throughout his life. How he reacts to these changes will be important in formation of his self-concept.

MALE ADJUSTMENT

As a rule boys are more concerned about the development of their primary sex characteristics than are girls. The reason is not clear, but it is probably because the penis and scrotum are external and easily observed. It is commonly believed in many cultures, without objective basis, that large male genitals are signs of virility and potency. Adult males do show wide variations in genital size. During adolescence, however, the size of a male's sex organs reflects his stage in physical development rather than his adult status. Most adolescent boys have ample opportunity to observe one another in locker rooms and communal showers, and they are likely to make covert comparisons between themselves and their peers. They may feel inferior if their genitals are smaller or embarrassed if they seem overdeveloped (Committe on Adolescence, 1968). For Ron (see Chapter 1) genital growth was both a source of shame and embarrassment and a source of pleasure. He preferred not to recognize his sexuality because it encouraged masturbation, but his physical growth made ignoring it all but impossible.

Secondary sex characteristics are as important to adolescent boys as is genital development. In many ways they are more important because they are the main sources of sexual attraction between the sexes; obviously, they are more easily observable. Our cultural standards of male desirability leads boys to be concerned about their height, the breadth of their chests and shoulders, muscular development, and facial and body hair. A study in which junior-high-school students were asked what they did not like about themselves has revealed the importance of physical characteristics in early adolescence (Jersild, 1952). Physical characteristics were mentioned more often than were either intellectual or social traits. This trend was, however, much less marked in high school.

Specific body characteristics are usually the basis for a boy's feelings about whether or not he is attractive to girls. Although there is no rational basis for associating specific characteristics with his capacity for "romance," there is nevertheless little doubt that attractiveness is fairly well defined in his culture. The ideal of the attractive male as defined in questionnaire responses by adolescents is six feet tall with well-developed muscles, body and facial hair, broad shoulders, and a deep voice. Boys who do not meet these standards are likely to perceive their bodies as inadequate; negative self-evaluations and disturbances in interpersonal relations may follow.

Female Adjustment

Primary sex characteristics are of much less concern to girls than to boys. Girls are more likely to become preoccupied with menstruation. Other physical features, especially breast size and facial characteristics, are quite important to girls. Hair, facial features, and "shape" are primary. Girls use many cosmetics and spend hours arranging their hair in accepted ways. What is "in" varies from one adolescent group to the next, but it is always important. Girls may spend unusual amounts of time in front of the mirror examining minuscule facial features (Committee on Adolescence, 1968).

A "good shape" is another typical concern. Current American society places emphasis on well formed breasts, small waist, and substantial—but not too substantial—hips. Many girls carefully observe and literally measure the growth of their breasts and the broadening of their hips. The stereotype of the ideal female generally stresses smallness and delicacy (though there is wide variation in its acceptance); a tall girl is likely to feel out of place and unattractive to boys.

The stereotypes of attractiveness for both males and females change from one generation to the next. Currently, for example, longer hair for boys is accepted as a sign of masculinity. The middle-aged generation thought of short-clipped hair—the crew cut—as masculine, probably because of its currency among service men during World War II. It also appears that muscular development and athletic prowess are losing ground, whereas a thinner, slimmer male physique is becoming popular in the current generation. The ideal female today also appears to be changing to a slenderer and taller woman, with less emphasis on the breasts. Female hair styles change so rapidly that it is almost impossible to designate current preferences with any accuracy.

EFFECTS OF DEVELOPMENTAL RATE

Several studies have demonstrated the effects of unusually early and late development on adolescent adjustment (Mussen *et al.*, 1969).

Maturing late is usually disturbing to a boy. He is embarrassed to seem to his peers a boy among men. He not only lacks the secondary sex characteristics that make them attractive, but he is also weaker and less likely to be successful in athletics. Research findings suggest that late-maturing boys develop a need to compensate for their physical disadvantages, often by engaging in attention-getting behavior. Their peers judge them as restless, talkative, and bossy; they are less popular, more concerned with themselves, and less likely to be leaders. The early-maturing boy, on the other hand, is treated more as an adult by adults and peers and is therefore more likely to gain self-confidence. Early maturers are more likely to be student-body leaders in high school, to be considered matter of fact and unaffected in their attitudes, and to show relatively little need to strive for status.

John, a seventeen-year-old boy whom I treated in psychotherapy, was a late maturer. He was only beginning to develop secondary sex characteristics. His behavior was not only "immature" (giggling, teasing, little contact with girls), but his interests were also definitely not the same as those of his peers. He was quite content, for instance, to stay with his parents and to let them tell him what to do and to care for him. Although he was large, he was not strong, and he was singularly unsuccessful in any kind of athletic endeavor. He had a great deal of difficulty relating to others. Boys and girls both made fun of him; he became the clown of the school but was nevertheless "picked on" for almost any reason, including his overweight. Even though he was as large as many of his classmates, he continued to behave in ways more appropriate to junior high school than to high school. Therapy consisted mainly of helping him to learn new ways of interacting, of bringing his behavior up to a level that was acceptable to his peers.

Although rate of development may be important in a child's adjustment, it does not necessarily supersede other characteristics. Many late maturers, for instance, compensate through intellectual endeavor, pleasant social manners, and other positive attributes. Even the advantages gained through early maturity can be neutralized by acne or increased drive levels that set a boy apart from his peers.

The effects of developmental rate on girls' adjustment are not as great. Early-maturing girls are more likely to experience difficulties with their body images than are late maturers. They suddenly find themselves larger than most of the boys their own age and may be embarrassed by growth of breasts or body hair; they seem to "stick out like a sore thumb." The very late-maturing girl, of course, may experience difficulties similar to those of the late-maturing boy, though usually to lesser degrees. Her friends are all dating and interested in boys, whereas her interests may remain at the elementary- or junior-high-school level; she is therefore likely to feel left out. It is well to emphasize, however, that there are wide age ranges for normal maturity. The children at the extremes are those most likely to encounter problems, but even then other factors may compensate adequately.

Sexual Arousal and Expression

Sexual arousal and sexual satisfaction are no small problem for the young adolescent. Although the sex drive has not yet reached its peak, unfamiliarity causes the child more concern about sexual functioning than he will experience later. His sensations associated with sexual arousal are new and of compelling interest. But in most cultures sexuality is almost always closely hedged by taboos and social mores. How and at what price does the early adolescent achieve sexual satisfaction and explore his budding sexuality?

Most early adolescents are unwilling to reveal their most private thoughts about sex even to their closest friends. It is not uncommon for boys and girls to discuss sex with friends, but to reveal personal fantasies, especially as they may seem quite bizarre, is rare. Many children consequently think that they are the only ones who experience such thoughts and sensations associated with sexual arousal. To the extent that they feel unique and that their sexual morality is rigid, they will suffer guilt and anxiety.

We may again think back to Ron and his problems with sex. Although he was quite interested in it and masturbated for pleasure, his past training caused him to feel a high level of guilt. Relating to his own sexuality had been quite distressing during early adolescence and had remained so into adulthood.

The physical characteristics associated with sexual arousal are usually not understood by early adolescents; they may imagine all sorts of things. A boy often experiences an erection for no apparent reason. He may suffer varying degrees of embarrassment, depending upon where it occurs. He wonders if others have noticed the bulge in his pants or if his parents noticed it while he was in bed. The lubricating fluid that most males secrete with an erection may cause alarm or further embarrassment. The fluids secreted by the sexually aroused female may also be misunderstood and cause concern to her. A boy or a girl may imagine that something is wrong with his or her sex organs or may feel uncomfortable around other people because of the possibility that the physical signs of arousal associated with private sexual fantasies will be detected.

Masturbation and self-exploration are the most common ways in which young adolescents learn about their sexuality and obtain sexual discharge. A high percentage of boys and a moderate percentage of girls engage in masturbation. Although there are many "old wives' tales" about masturbation, it is an essentially normal response to increased sex drive. In many ways it serves to engender comfort with sexuality and to permit more complete understanding of one's own sexual functioning. It has the obvious advantage of relieving sexual tensions in a comparatively safe way. Masturbation does not cause psychological disorders, though excessive masturbation or complete abstinence may be signs of difficulty in sexual development. It is not uncommon for adolescent boys to masturbate daily; the frequency decreases as they become older and heterosexual opportunities become more readily available.

Adolescents usually do not simply masturbate to orgasm; they experiment. They learn that erection (of the penis or clitoris) and arousal can be initiated through fantasy or direct stimulation, that the orgasm can be controlled by the ways in which they masturbate, and that sexual tensions will quickly subside following orgasm. In this way, masturbation can increase their sense of mastery over sex drives and reassure them about their sexual capacities. In boys especially the ability to maintain erection and experience forcible ejaculation can increase the sense of developing masculinity (Committee on Adolescence, 1968).

Even though masturbation may contribute positively to the child's development, it is much more common in our society for a child to experience various anxieties and guilts over his behavior. These negative responses are not restricted to boys; girls may feel equally guilty and, probably because social taboos are more stringent about female sex behavior, girls are more secretive about masturbation than boys are. It is not uncommon, for example, for a group of young adolescent boys to experiment with group masturbation. They may compare their penises, manipulate one another, observe ejaculation, and even race to see who can ejaculate first—the "circle jerk" of adolescent boys. It is rare, however, for girls to engage in similar group activities, probably because our cultural values stress male sexuality and virility and underplay sexual expression in females. The boy is essentially showing off to his friends, but there is no similar reinforcement for the girl. Postpubescent girls nevertheless may engage in various types of masturbatory activity with friends.

The psychological conflicts around masturbation are many. The major source arises from rumors about the harmful effects of masturbation, supported by parents who show disapproving or prohibitive attitudes toward sex. Ron's mother, for example, was very punitive of masturbation but offered no reasons except that it was "bad" and "dirty."

Children may also develop their own fears and false ideas about masturbation. A boy, for instance, may worry that the leakage from his penis is a sign of disease, and girls may regard the vaginal discharge associated with sexual arousal as proof that they have harmed themselves. Ejaculation may frighten a boy into thinking that he is draining himself of virility. He may have notions that handling his sex organs will increase or decrease their size. Adolescents also worry that their secret sex behavior will be revealed to the world through physical signs like acne, spontaneous erections, shifty eyes, staying in the bathroom too long, and so on. All these thoughts, of course, have no basis in reality. They can nevertheless significantly distress the young adolescent.

The young adolescent rarely has an opportunity for heterosexual intercourse. He is not in close contact with members of the opposite sex; boys and girls are usually just beginning to interact in reasonable ways. Although fantasies of intercourse and sexual contact are often associated with masturbation, children at this age are still sufficiently interested in their own developing sexuality and new experiences to be satisfied with postponing heterosexual relationships. We do not claim that young adolescents have no heterosexual experiences, but in American culture those that do are more likely to experience them with older members of the opposite sex. Early-developing girls, for instance, may date older boys and become sexually involved with them. Young boys, on the other hand, may have experiences either in groups or individually with older girls or young women.

Early adolescence may also be the period in which incest is most common. In some subcultures, in fact, for the male of the family to have sex relations with the female children is not exceptional. Incest is, however, illegal, and by middle-class standards deviant, and entirely unacceptable.

"Homosexual" contacts are not uncommon in early adolescence. There is usually no reason that they should be especially damaging to the child. Shifting from homosexual to heterosexual experiences normally occurs as the dating age is reached. Homosexual incidents are sometimes erroneously considered signs of depravity. While they may precede adult homosexuality they are more properly viewed as normal responses to early sexual development. It is only later, when social expectations strongly encourage heterosexual relationships, that homosexual behavior can become a serious problem for the individual.

Body Image

Most of what we have said about sexuality so far is relevant to young adolescents' perceptions of their bodies. The evaluation of an adolescent's physical characteristics by himself and by his peers and the degree to which it corresponds with his ideal of attractiveness contribute to his developing image of his body. He must also face the realization that "this is it," essentially the way that he is going to look for most of his life. It is true that during puberty the child can only begin to develop a stable body image, but his first impressions can weigh heavily in determining the final outcome.

The young adolescent's heightened awareness of his physical attributes probably contributes much to what is generally accepted as "awkwardness." Although the awkwardness of early adolescence has often been accounted for by poor coordination resulting from uneven growth rates of the muscles and the bones, examinations of skeletal and muscular growth at this period do not indicate great disparities or irregularities. From a purely physical point of view, then, awkwardness may be accounted for by rapid changes in physical dimensions. A child reaches for a glass, for example, but opens his fingers just an instant too late and knocks the glass to the floor. His arm is slightly longer than he anticipated because it has grown in a comparatively short time. The rapidly growing child may simply not have had time to adjust to his new dimensions.

Changes in the body make the adolescent feel "not himself"; his dimensions are no longer in accord with those that were comfortable earlier. The development of primary and secondary sex characteristics especially may heighten his self-consciousness. It may be that adolescents adopt awkward postures and gestures because of self-consciousness. A girl who is embarrassed by the emergence of her breasts, for example, may walk in a stoop or some other awkward position in an attempt to hide her maturity. It is a period of getting used to a "new" body.

Awkwardness can also be partly accounted for by the changing social demands placed on adolescents. They are expected to behave more maturely and more responsibly. Young adolescents nevertheless have little experience. By and large they have not behaved in such ways before, nor have they been allowed to participate in many adult social situations. It should not be surprising then that they feel self-conscious and inadequate in these new roles. Their uncertainty may in turn be reflected in strange postures, increased restlessness, and generally inappropriate responses. As adolescents acquire more stable body images, usually by early adulthood, they are less likely to appear self-conscious and awkward.

INTERPERSONAL ADJUSTMENTS

Although physical changes dominate the adjustment patterns of early adolescence, the beginnings of important interpersonal changes also occur. The pressures of new social roles accompanying changes in school status and extracurricular activities create major changes in the ways in which a child relates to his peers, his family, and other adults.

THE BEGINNING OF INDEPENDENCE

Becoming independent is rather difficult for adolescents in the United States because of conflicting sets of values. On the one hand, adults emphasize freedom of individual choice, opportunities for social mobility, finding oneself, and selecting suitable roles. But on the other, they expose the adolescent to demands for conformity and dependence. Considerable emphasis is placed, for example, on "fitting in," on not being too different. Furthermore, the adolescent has been taught earlier that he should depend upon his parents for direction.

These contradictory demands are, of course, not limited to early adolescence; adults face them as well. Nevertheless, they represent a particularly formidable task for the child who must turn from the dependence of childhood to conduct considered independent, self-directed, and responsible.

RELATIONS WITH PARENTS

One of the obvious changes related to becoming independent is a break in the emotional attachment to and dependence upon parents. The parents become the primary focus of the adolescent's bid for independence. In the fairly recent past parents were less important in this sense. Families were close across several generations, and people rarely moved great distances from their original homes. The children therefore had many close relationships with family members. Now, however, it is much more common for the parents to be the only close contacts and therefore the ones most likely to feel the entire force of their child's striving for independence.

The relationship between a child and his parents may become conflicted in many ways. He still needs support, and up to this point his parents have been the major sources of it; now he feels that he must become independent of them. A fairly common reaction is rejection, or at least questioning, of parental judgments of other people. They are no longer taken for granted as they were earlier. The child may strike up relationships with people of whom his parents disapprove and thus test what he previously accepted without question. It is not unusual for parents and their adolescent children to be in conflict over the children's choice of friends. In extreme instances, for example, children may insist on their right to associate with whatever extreme adolescent clique is in vogue: hippies, perhaps, or the like. Other children may abide by their parents' restrictions on the surface but sneak in a few encounters with people whom they know would meet with parental disapproval. Even for the rebellious child the important point is to decide according to his own experience. He may eventually reject "far out" peers after finding that he is not really comfortable with them, or he may decide that some of their values are acceptable whereas others are not. Through these small (or large) forms of defiance the adolescent learns to make his own decisions and to break the ties of dependence upon parents (Committee on Adolescence, 1968).

The adolescent may also completely reject what his parents do or say, treating them as simply unworthy of serious consideration. This possibility has been graphically illustrated by a cartoon strip. In the first scene a small boy is looking up at his very large father; in the second, as an adolescent, he is looking down on his very small father; and in the third, as a young adult, he is once again looking up at his very large father. A fitting caption for this cartoon series might well have been taken from Mark Twain, who remarked that when he was fourteen years old he thought that his father was the most stupid man alive but that at twenty-one he had been surprised to find out how much the old man had learned.

EMOTIONAL CONFLICTS

Withdrawal from parents does not occur without emotional difficulties. The child, whether he admits it to himself or not, is usually in conflict over breaking his emotional ties with his family. He often appears very "moody." He experiences periods of isolation and loneliness, as if there were no one to whom he could turn. At such times he is likely to feel a strong need for gratification, perhaps in the form of masturbation or excessive eating, after which, depending upon his values, he is likely to be filled with self-condemnation and greater despair. Finding a new friend, male or female, can change his mood to elation and exaltation.

Adolescent mood swings are often directly related to making or breaking relationships, sometimes in fantasy, sometimes in fact; but the importance of such relationships becomes paramount. The adolescent "crush" is a common phenomenon. Adulation of adults or older adolescents who are considered "with it"—perhaps a teacher, a coach, a camp counselor—serves to replace partially the loss of his parents. Adolescents are also quick to find heroes and to have violent crushes on them. Singers, musicians, sports figures, and movie actors or actresses are his most common fantasy objects. He identifies with these people and may even imitate their behavior, attitudes, and values. Each trial of this sort helps him to discover more about the kinds of conduct that suit him best and those that feel alien.

Conflicts between adolescents and their parents often arise from doubt on both sides over just what developmental stage the former are in. Both have contradictory feelings about the children's growing up; they may be at war not only with each other but also within themselves. The parents are ambivalent because they want their children to become adults but are also keenly aware of their weaknesses. Because they do not want the children to fail they may try to provide too much protection and guidance. They may not understand that the only way to overcome weaknesses is to cope with real problems.

Probably a more basic reason why parents slow their children's progress toward adulthood is their recognition of how the years have slipped away—a recognition that they themselves are aging. A child's growth can make parents very aware of middle age. The pleasures of being very young are past, never to be recaptured. For parents whose primary identity revolves around being mother and father, bids for adulthood may be perceived as the end of their own usefulness. From now on their lives will lose much of their meaning, will become empty and less worthwhile.

Parents may also simply resist relinquishing the control that they have had over their children. Life is much simpler when they can say what to do without having to answer questions. Adolescents, however, do not usually see things this way. Even when they appear to be complying, they often do what they want in secret.

The child is also ambivalent about growing up. It is one thing to say that he wants independence and its privileges but another to carry the associated responsibilities. Each time that the adolescent reaches for adulthood he faces the possibility of failure. Although to most adolescents failure is unthinkable, its specter repeatedly arises as they face the tasks of adulthood. Parents are often put in an untenable position by their adolescent's mixed feelings about independence. If they intervene in his decisions they are snoopy and domineering. If they do not they are unfeeling and uncaring. They are "damned if they do and damned if they don't." Adolescents nevertheless usually respect parental control, even though they claim to dislike it. Often the knowledge that their parents will help to limit their behavior offers relief and bolsters their own controls.

Conflicts may arise between an adolescent and his parents over almost any subject. As we noted earlier, it is not uncommon for disagreements to arise over his choice of friends, male or female. Dress and grooming, long hair versus short hair, makeup versus no makeup are also common topics of controversy. His responsibilities and privileges—domestic chores, table manners, use of the family car, allowance, dating, use of the telephone, and so on—usually provide constant fuel for the fire. The adolescent nearly always seeks more freedom. During early adolescence his parents are more likely to exert controls in the same ways that they have done in the past, telling him what the limits are and expecting him to observe them. As he gains more freedom (dating, driving the car, going on trips with peers), however, a reciprocity between his privileges and responsibilities becomes more noticeable. The responsibilities associated with the privileges become restricting in themselves. If he wants a car, for example, he may have to take a part-time job to finance it.

DEGREES OF CONFLICT

E. Douvan and J. Adelson (1966) have noted that much of what has been written about adolescent adjustment has been based on information from two extreme samples: delinquents and sensitive, articulate, middle-class children. Both represent exceptional rather than usual solutions to adjustment. These two groups are alike in several ways: They are unusually independent of their families, they are very discontented with the social order, and they adopt radical solutions to help them form their identities. Although these groups are worth studying, it is a mistake to assume that their modes of adjustment are common to all adolescents. These extreme samples reflect great stress and are not typical of most American adolescents. Douvan and Adelson investigated a fairly random sample of thousands of adolescents. Interviews with these children led them to conclude that adolescence is not generally a time of extreme strife between parents and children. On the contrary, their results suggest that most adolescents tend to avoid overt conflicts with their families. The conflicts that do occur often represent a sort of "war game" in which the ammunition is not "real," no one is hurt, and the issues— like personal taste in dress and grooming—are really trivial. It appears that parents and children have agreed to disagree on small issues only, on the "teen" issues, and to avoid genuine conflict on important issues. Essentially the findings indicate that the average middle-class adolescent—who constitutes the great majority of adolescents in the United States—is not seeking or gaining much independence except in the realm of superficial behavior. Most often he clings quite closely to the attitudes and beliefs of his parents.

Douvan and Adelson have further concluded that the peer group (we shall turn to peer relations in more detail in the next section) does not function at all in the way it has been supposed to behave by most students of adolescent behavior. It has been described as an arena for confrontation of the self, for testing and trying new identities, and for developing new values. Although some adolescents seem to use their peer groups in this way, many nevertheless use them primarily for learning social skills and sociability. "The peer culture is all too often a kind of playpen, designed to keep the children out of harm's way and out of the parents' hair. The peer group, with its artificial amusements and excitements, more often acts to hinder differentiation and growth" (Douvan and Adelson, 1966, p. 353).

On the whole, Douvan and Adelson's conclusions imply that American adolescents are not deeply involved in ideology nor are they prepared to do much individual thinking on large value issues. The investigators have accounted for their findings by means of an analysis of present-day cultural demands. Many vocations in American society require long periods of preparation. The parents and child must therefore endure long years of dependence. A decisive testing of wills over when the child is ready to leave the home is rare, compared with its frequency in the past. Today, for example, a sixteen-year-old boy rarely states, "Today I am a man!" packs his bags, and sets out to make his fortune. Nor do parents, especially in the middle classes, any longer impose heavy restrictions on their children. A great deal of freedom is available to the child, and he is often free to leave at a very young age if he wants. But it seems that the adolescent and his parents are captives to the knowledge that he must depend upon them for some time if his future success is to be ensured. In a sense, then, true adolescence, the mobilization of capacities and strengths for genuine autonomy, is given up in favor of becoming a "teenager." "He keeps the peace by muting his natural rebelliousness through transforming it into structured and refined techniques for getting on people's nerves. The passions, the restlessness, the vivacity of adolescence are partly strangled, and partly drained off in the mixed childishness and false adulthood of the adolescent teen culture" (Douvan and Adelson, 1966, p. 354).

THE PEER GROUP

Other children are important to the prepubescent child, but at no other time in his life are peers as important as they are during adolescence. The adolescent's striving for independence and the associated need to break family ties leave him without trustworthy judges of his conduct. He turns to his peers for this vital judgment. Assuredly, he does not completely ignore his parents and other adults, but by and large feedback from peers is considered more reliable. His friends' actions, and less often their direct comments, let him know whether or not his behavior is meeting the standards of his society, that is, the peer society. The striking conformity typical of teenage behavior patterns reflects the need for positive feedback (Committee on Adolescence, 1968; Douvan and Adelson, 1966; Muller, 1969).

GROUP SUPPORT

The teenage group serves an important function by giving support in numbers to a member who is trying to decide what behavior is appropriate. The group is very supportive, for example, when adolescents are beginning to interact with the opposite sex. Being thrown together alone with no previous experience of this kind of relating can be distressing. Group activities and "chance" meetings of boys and girls, on the other hand, offer comparatively safe means of establishing these first relationships.

There is also "safety in numbers" when adolescents wish to promote causes or activities that are not completely acceptable to the adult community. An extreme example is the behavior of adolescents attending outdoor "rock festivals." At these gatherings, which thousands of adolescents attend, vast numbers have performed illegally, taking drugs, appearing nude in public, and engaging in public sexual activities, without suffering legal sanctions. Adolescent protest mobs have destroyed property and injured people with little restraint. Undoubtedly, were individuals or small groups to violate the same social norms, ordinary law enforcement would be swift.

More intellectually inclined adolescents may become completely immersed in groups proposing ideal ways of living and different philosophical values. They may try communal living or "back to the earth" movements. Younger adolescents are less likely to be drawn to such groups because their activities and interests are still more closely associated with school and immediate personal needs rather than ideals. An early adolescent may, of course, try one of these groups, but it is much more difficult for him because he usually must go against his parents' authority and the resistance of the older adolescents and because his own mobility is limited by legal age restrictions.

Peer-group functions have varying meanings for different people. Peer-group interaction dominates all the behavior of some children. "Gangs" of lower-class juvenile delinquents, for example, become the centers of their members' lives, controlling their behavior almost completely. Even though gang activities are antisocial they may serve very realistic ends for a poor child, providing material advantages that he must otherwise do without and a source of protection from the members of other gangs. Adolescents from higher-income families may, however, also form delinquent groups. Their antisocial behavior is more likely to be motivated by the desire for "kicks" than for materialistic gain. Their activities unify these groups, which in turn offer feelings of belonging and identity.

SOCIAL LEARNING

As noted earlier, Douvan and Adelson (1966) have proposed that the peer group does not have the dramatic effects on the majority of middle-class youngsters that are often assumed. Rather, it functions primarily as a natural laboratory for social learning. For the young adolescent social skills are the most important. He learns the acceptable "manners" and the expectations related to various social circumstances that he will face "for real" only a few years later.

CONFORMITY AND POPULARITY

The feedback function of the group is clearly reflected in the adolescent's conformity to peer-group standards and values. In early adolescence most of these values take a very tangible form: styles of dress, speech, habits, hair styles, and cosmetics. Because adolescents are striving for independence it is not surprising that their codes are different from those of the adult culture and that some are nearly always deviant enough to cause surprise and indignation among conservative adults. Nowhere can independence be more openly asserted than in adolescent dress and grooming. And, as Douvan and Adelson have put it, these issues are not very important to society at large. Serious changes in religious, social, or political beliefs are rare except among small groups of older adolescents and young adults.

"Being popular" often means fitting the stereotype of a particular peer culture. Largely thanks to modern transportation and communications an "adolescent culture" with its own language, customs, social institutions, modes of solving problems, and philosophies has developed. Each town or section of a city may vary the general theme, but dress, hair style, and other characteristics are widely accepted across geographical and political boundaries.

In contrast to the older adolescent or adult, the postpubescent youth still lacks a strong, stable self-image, and it is very difficult for him to be satisfied with himself unless his behavior arouses positive feedback from his peers. The louder that they acclaim him, the "better" he feels he is; he is not alert to subtle reinforcements and praise. Without appreciative feedback doubts and insecurity tend to arise. Peer feedback is often given in order to elicit approval in return. The young adolescent especially is often naïvely unaware of his companions' motivations and feelings. He still thinks that he is the only person in the world who has the needs and thoughts that constantly plague him. It is therefore often very difficult for him to see that other youngsters are also looking for support and that they too are uneasy and feel out of step. In fact, the occasional adolescent who is not concerned with popularity and goes his own way may find to his surprise that he is the center of attention. The security that allows him to act independently is recognized as a sign of strength by his less secure peers.

COMMON VEHICLES FOR PEER INTERACTION

Of the various media of interaction during early adolescence the telephone and dancing stand out. Both offer means of expressing heterosexual interest while maintaining a comfortable distance.

Communications of all sorts may, of course, be sent over the telephone. Communications between a boy and girl, however, can take on an erotic quality when enhanced by the safety of physical distance. A voice in one's ear and an "ear at one's lips" can seem quite intimate, yet at the same time there is no danger that sexual feelings will be overtly expressed. Adolescents also find privacy from their families through the telephone, even in their own homes. In fact, one of the more subtle status symbols today is the adolescent's private telephone with a separate listing in the directory. The child with his own telephone has an independent means of interacting with the outside world plus physical, public proof in the community telephone book of his individuality.

Dancing is an essential part of many cultures, serving the needs of adults, as well as of adolescents. But for adolescents dancing can also be of major help in their development. In the first place, the social rituals associated with it offer a rich opportunity for learning interpersonal and social skills. Probably more important, however, is the opportunity for mutual physical expression with members of the opposite sex. The movements and the accompanying discharge of tensions in themselves serve to relax the child. (The young adolescent who is just beginning to dance may not agree that tension is reduced; heaven help him if he does the wrong step! But once the initial hurdles are past he usually enjoys the release of energy.) Sexual and aggressive urges are easily and acceptably expressed through dance, and the first step in heterosexual foreplay often occurs then.

Many of the body movements of modern adolescent dances are overtly sexual, though it is unusual for the partners to touch. Dancing, however, obviously does not provide a complete discharge of sexual tensions, and probably for that reason new forms are constantly replacing old ones. At the same time adolescents want to have their "own thing," dances included. New dance styles add to a generation's sense of independence and help to separate it from adults.

The sexual component of dancing is obviously important, but probably even more important to the young adolescent is the opportunity to learn skills of interaction, especially with the opposite sex. Teenage dances often offer the first opportunities through which an adolescent can learn appropriate ways of making contact with members of the opposite sex. Of course, the precise ways in which to interact vary with each generation. At one time, for instance, a boy was taught to bow politely and say, "May I have this dance?" More recently the thing to do is to catch the girl's attention and nod toward the dance floor.

Dancing and the telephone are only two examples of a multitude of activities that serve as vehicles for meeting the developmental challenges of early adolescence. Nearly all adolescent activities share the important goals of establishing unique, age-specific patterns separating them from adults and presenting important opportunities for cultural and social learning.

Boy-Girl Relationships

Although boys and girls are obviously peers, the changes in their relations at adolescence are great enough to be considered separately. In the late junior-high-school and early high-school years many new expectations about heterosexual contacts arise. The typical "standoffishness" of prepuberty gradually gives way to interaction based on mutual respect and interest. The transition period is nevertheless fraught with uncertainty and doubt, as the child tries to fill his new roles and evaluate his success.

Girls usually become interested in boys first, probably because their physical development is earlier and because their identities depend more upon interpersonal skills than do boys' identities. During the pubescent period there is thus often a striking contrast between "little boys" and "young ladies" in the same classrooms. The early-maturing male is therefore likely to have an advantage in boy-girl relations. Like many of the girls, he is also physically developed, and his interests are beginning to change in the same direction as are theirs.

As a rule girls tend to give up their female peer groups more readily than boys give up their male groups. Of course, relations with other girls are maintained and some are very intimate; but many others are tenuous and easily destroyed by rivalry over a boy or other concerns. A boy, on the other hand, is much less distracted from his male relationships by problems with girls. These sex differences in early adolescence spring from genuine differences in developmental goals. Boys find security and personal identity through the mastery of cultural skills and consideration of potential vocational aims, whereas the identities of most girls will depend upon their mates' accomplishments. Boys are not unconcerned about their acceptability to girls; on the contrary, it is extremely important to them though less related to ultimate personal success (Douvan and Kaye, 1957).

There is little doubt that most children become extremely interested in sex during puberty. Most adolescents actively seek information through discussions with peers, reading, or both. Adults are generally shut out of this aspect of the adolescent's life because sex has not been—and still is not, despite some claims to the contrary—a topic open for discussion. Even in the most "liberal" families there is more talk about being open about sex than there is talk about sex.

Adolescents, boys more than girls, are generally preoccupied with heterosexual daydreams and masturbation fantasies. Their thoughts are likely to be highly romanticized but sparse in concrete details. Most adolescents become very interested in books, magazines, and other sources of information about sex and sexual activity, though they often hide them from adults. It is no problem today for an American adolescent, or anyone, to obtain magazines picturing nude men and women in sexual activities of all sorts. Most of these publications are produced and sold for purely erotic purposes. They disseminate highly distorted information or present sex as a "super" emotional experience. Although sexually arousing they may lead an adolescent to feel cheated when he actually engages in sexual activities. Although some of the information from these sources is valid, it is extremely difficult for a young adolescent to distinguish between what is meant to be simply arousing, an aid to sexual fantasies, and what is valid information about the role of sexual activity in life (Committee on Adolescence, 1968).

As we mentioned earlier, most children's first sexual activities are likely to be homosexual or masturbatory. Early sexual interests are, however, ultimately expressed in relationships with the opposite sex. The first heterosexual contacts are usually similar to those characterizing prepuberty, involving aggression as an excuse for touching but on an expanded scale. Heterosexual interchanges are likely to have a teasing quality or even to involve open insult and degradation when closeness becomes too threatening. Body contact usually takes the form of games or roughhousing, perhaps disguised to the adolescent but usually obvious to an adult. It is more likely that girls will not be completely aware of the sexual quality of these contacts, but boys are often clearly aware of their aims even though they may not openly admit them. Because of their semi-concealed nature such "roughhouse" contacts are even common among adolescent siblings. On the surface they say that they cannot stand each other. Arguments often arise when their physical contacts result in pain, and their constant bickering may become very disconcerting to their parents. As adolescents move through this stage, more formal types of boy-girl interaction replace the aggressive interchanges.

It is well to note that there are wide individual differences in the ways that young adolescents express boy-girl interests. Some do not appear to express them at all; they stifle sexual feelings and especially thoughts of overt sexuality. Ron, we remember, shied away from girls almost completely in this phase. Others seem quite comfortable with their sexual interests. A girl may be called "boy crazy" simply because she accepts her sexuality and makes no bones about it. Other young adolescents may continue to act "immature" and to evade intimate contact with the opposite sex. Nevertheless, whether shortly after puberty or a few years later, nearly all adolescents eventually enter into the more formal, adult kind of heterosexual interaction. Sexual expression and gratification generally shift from self-interest and homosexual activities to heterosexual lovemaking and intercourse.

COGNITIVE CHANGE

The adolescent's interactions with others change because of his intellectual growth. As he develops the ability to think in abstract, scientific ways, he can no longer easily accept others' ideas. He begins to look for causal and logical relations between events and objects. Simple, factual statements no longer satisfy him. By about the fifteenth year most adolescents have begun to think abstractly. They are able to evaluate the logic of their own thoughts, and reflection and cognitive reorganization are available for solving problems (see Chapter 9).

Adolescents begin to question parental values partly because abstract thinking is a novelty and partly because they are trying to separate themselves from their parents. Some parents become very upset when their children question the values that they have taken as absolute for years. In fact, parents may be hard-pressed to find logical support for their moral and social codes, especially those that interfere with their child's striving for independence. Parent-child and adult-child relations often begin to change from "child as accepter" to "adolescent as challenger." This change is not easy for some parents and children, especially in strongly authoritarian homes. It is usually quite difficult for authoritarian parents to entertain alternative ideas about cherished values.

Even though many young adolescents are capable of abstract thinking, they are at first unlikely to evaluate values and mores. On the contrary, they are usually so concerned with themselves that they make few intellectual contributions to the outside world. They are more likely to use their new abilities to rationalize their own behavior. They will use these abilities in their school work and turn their interests to larger social purposes only after most of the conflicts arising from puberty have been resolved (Committee on Adolescence, 1968; Mussen *et al.*, 1969).

Summing Up Early Adolescence

Adolescence has been divided into early and late phases somewhat arbitrarily. The main social and psychological changes discussed here, however, seem connected with the body changes of sexual maturation. The child's primary task in this early phase is to come to grips with his new self, especially the concept of his body and his sexual needs.

At the same time he must begin to break from his parents. Almost frantically he learns the rules of his "teenage culture" so that he will "fit." His dawning independence from his parents is more likely to be reflected in verbal disagreements at first. But it is expressed in action as he gains more mobility with age. Some young adolescents go through a period of open rebellion that severely disrupts family functioning. Usually, however, such rebellion is less drastic, causing only some parental concern and recognition of change in their children. In this period the child needs guidance more than ever, but at the same time he must break from his parents—the people who have been his major source of guidance.

The peer group serves several vital functions for the young adolescent. It offers support as he breaks his bonds of dependence upon parents; it serves as a mirror permitting him to evaluate the effectiveness of his behavior and a setting in which he learns the skills necessary for successful contacts with the opposite sex. Skills that will eventually lead to overt heterosexual behavior are learned largely through interaction with peers.

As the child partially accomplishes these tasks, the time when he is expected to begin acting as an adult draws near. He is expected to learn what is necessary to function in adult society. This next period, late adolescence, is the topic of Chapter 12.

SUMMARY

In this chapter we began by exploring definitions of adolescence. Four criteria have been suggested: biological change associated with puberty and rapid physical growth; such changes in objective social status as eligibility for a driver's license, marriage without parental consent, voting, and so on; new social role expectations, including prevocational learning, heterosexual interactions, mature conduct in social gatherings; and evaluation of the self. We have chosen to define adolescence in terms of changes in personal adjustment: Adolescence begins when new forces challenge his characteristic ways of behaving. The forces may arise initially from either physical or social changes; the earliest pressures, regardless of their source, indicate the beginning of adolescence. The end comes when the individual has acquired the skills necessary for independent functioning and feels confident of being able to care for himself. For some people it may never end.

The effects of the physical changes associated with puberty, especially changes in the sex organs (primary sex characteristics), require adjustments from both boys and girls. A boy's erotic dreams and first ejaculation may be stressful. The beginning of menstruation can be psychologically disturbing to a girl. Changes in secondary sex characteristics—growth of axillary hair, breast development, alterations of facial features, and so on—also demand adjustment.

Boys appear more concerned about the characteristics of their genitals than do girls, probably because they are external. The boy's physique is often an important factor in his conception of his own attractiveness. Girls are more concerned with the secondary sex characteristics associated with "beauty" than with their sex organs. A "good shape," a "correct" hair style, and so on become the focus for many young adolescent girls. Developmental rate can also affect an adolescent's adjustment. Early-maturing boys often become leaders because of their greater physical prowess. Late-maturing boys may suffer rebuffs from peers and may compensate with nonphysical activities to bolster positive self-images. The early-maturing girl may experience difficulties because she is bigger than her peers.

The increased sex drive associated with puberty also calls for adjustment. Boys may be embarrassed by spontaneous erections and erotic fantasies. Cultural taboos are nearly always woven around sex and may engender guilt or shame as the young adolescent experiences sexual arousal. Masturbation is a common sexual outlet at this age, especially in boys, and it may cause guilt when it contradicts moral teachings. On the other hand it can serve as a useful learning experience by allowing the adolescent to become comfortable with his new sexuality.

The "body image" also changes with physical growth. A person's evaluation of his physical appearance is likely to be consolidated during early adolescence. Physical awkwardness seems characteristic at this stage, but changing social roles may contribute to this phenomenon as much as or more than physical growth and lack of coordination does.

Finally, we examined the more important interpersonal adjustments associated with early adolescence. The child experiences the beginnings of independence, with conflict between demands for more freedom and for continuing dependence. Conflict with parents is not uncommon as the adolescent adopts the standards of his peers and seems to reject the authority of his parents. Age-related activities like dating are not easily agreed upon by many parents and their adolescent children. Both parents and child are often ambivalent about independence. Some investigators have questioned the degree of upheaval normally assumed to characterize this period. Some findings suggest that the vast majority of adolescents do not rebel against traditional values and conduct but rather disagree on superficial issues like hair style, dress, and so on. They thus avoid genuine encounters over more important matters.

The peer group serves several important functions for the adolescent who is striving for independence. It is a source of group support that allows the individual to participate in conduct that would otherwise be too threatening: for example, boy-girl encounters. Peers also serve as resources for social learning. The peer group is a comparatively safe place in which to test and practice skills appropriate to adults. It is further a force for conformity and a source of popularity. In developing a stable, positive self-image it is important to "fit in" and to be "popular." Two major media of peer interaction are the telephone and dancing, which permit the young adolescent to interact with his peers in ways that move him toward adulthood.

Boy-girl interactions have a new importance in adolescence. Girls generally become romantically interested in boys before boys become interested in girls. Early adolescents are extremely interested in sex, but they are still preoccupied with themselves, and heterosexual contacts do not generally characterize their relationships.

Intellectual abilities also grow in adolescence and further determine the nature of interpersonal contacts. The development of abstract thinking leads to questioning of others' ideas, especially those of parents. Adolescents are, however, still more concerned with themselves than with the more abstract values and mores of society. They are more likely to use their new intellectual powers for personal goals and school work.

12

A. Introduction
   1. Factors that retard growth
   2. The struggle against conformity
   3. Evaluation of future goals
   4. Personal identity
B. Choice of Future Vocation
   1. The importance of vocation in identity
   2. The characteristics of work
   3. Factors in vocational choice
   4. Vocational counseling
C. Heterosexual Relationships
   1. Male-female differences
   2. Dating
   3. Premarital sex relations
D. Summary

Adjustment in Late Adolescence: Vocations and Sexuality

INTRODUCTION

Late adolescence is a time of mutual evaluation between "child" and adult. Physiological functioning has become stabilized with age, growth rate has decreased, and adolescents find themselves more closely involved in the larger society than ever before. They begin to encounter people other than their peers and on levels different from those of childhood. They begin to hold jobs and to frequent places of adult entertainment; their physical and intellectual behavior may now appear threatening to adults, and if they break the law they are treated as adult offenders instead of as misbehaving children. People able to control an adolescent's ultimate goals evaluate his conduct critically, and in turn he begins to evaluate theirs.

FACTORS THAT RETARD GROWTH

There are several factors that work to slow, as well as to encourage, adolescent growth. Laws establish the minimum chronological ages at which adolescents are permitted to share in the privileges and responsibilities of their society. For example, in some states they must be sixteen years old to drive cars, girls must be eighteen, and boys twenty-one, to marry without parental consent, they must be twenty-one years old before signing legal contracts, and so on. Most of these laws are double-edged, defining the ages at which some adolescents are not eligible for specific statuses and at the same time declaring to others that they are responsible enough for such statuses. These rules often appear arbitrary to adolescents. Indeed, in terms of developmental ages they may well be. A fourteen-year-old boy may, for example, be more qualified to drive a car than are some thirty-year-old men. Adolescents may therefore find society more rigid than they had anticipated, though not infrequently the rigidity is exaggerated in their fantasies and some genuine flexibility goes unrecognized.

Society tends to react strongly to nonconforming adolescents, often to a degree suggesting that adolescents' rational powers and ideas do not warrant respect. Quick adult retaliation for conduct deemed inappropriate by the established community may occur. Such encounters often occur first in the schools; children are told to conform or be suspended. Parents frequently convey the same message, enforcing their disapproval of friends or dress by reducing an allowance or "grounding" the child. Young people are likely to have the impression that they are little more than puppets and that their individuality is unimportant as long as they do as they are told. Their efforts to establish independence and individuality seem arbitrarily obstructed by pressures to conform.

362

The Struggle Against Conformity

Adolescent responses to pressures to conform are, of course, varied. Some band together to attack conventional standards. They may establish a society within the larger society, one that emphasizes their own needs, rather than those of adults. The recent advent of hippy living groups is an example. Others may come to feel alienated. They view themselves as on the outside looking in, of no interest or use to adults. Their responses frequently take the form of simply being "against" things, without any accompanying preference "for" other things.

It is true that our society tends to suppress individuality. Complex industrial organization demands greater conformity and adherence to rules than does an economy in which people live farther apart and depend less upon one another for fulfillment of economic needs. An adolescent who is willing to accept what he is offered may find conformity very comforting. It is comparatively easy for many people to follow the unwritten rules and to incorporate compliance with these rules into their self-images. It is never easy, however, for very creative or intelligent people to do so. They nearly always have strong needs to express themselves in unique ways. Some will never find personal satisfaction or be able to contribute to the larger society, but most will become innovators of the future.

For example, the bright young person who enters college with enthusiasm for expanding his knowledge about life may encounter classes in which memorization of facts is encouraged, test scores are emphasized, and new ideas and discussion are discouraged. He may strike out personally or through group action to change the "system." The resulting conflict with adult authorities may end in his dismissal from school, a bitter sense of personal defeat, and withdrawal from the mainstream of modern society. At the other extreme, another young person may be stimulated by the same experience to more effective action through partial acceptance of the demands of adult authority; from this framework he may make contributions that in fact do start changes in the system. Encouraged by his success, he may continue on in positions of leadership that eventuate in his becoming part of the adult authority of the next generation. From this position he may continue to exert influence on society.

What is "right" or "wrong" is not the question here. The question is how is the personal growth of a particular individual affected? Each adolescent reacts in his own way, from complete comfort with structured expectations to extreme discomfort with any blocks to or controls on individuality.

Evaluation of Future Goals

In evaluating their future goals and activities some adolescents still seem very much like children in their sense of time: They are impatient and look for immediate results (Committee on Adolescence, 1968). In a sense, many adolescents are still "playing" at life, rather as they did when they were children, though now the consequences of their actions begin to be more lasting and serious. Many adolescents still feel that what they do really does not count, that their behavior will be overlooked, that they are not completely grown up. But in fact their performance records are becoming more crucial, and their futures may be determined by evaluations of what they have done in the past. It is rare, for example, that anybody cares about, or even looks at, a grammar-school record, but high-school records become important sources of infomation for those who make decisions affecting the adolescent's future. Criminal offenses are now truly "criminal." Rights and privileges may be rescinded, and a "record" can have drastic effects on future success. Indeed, adults are often amazed and chagrined at what seems the adolescent's idiotic concern about the possible consequences of his actions. It is almost unbelievable to many adults that a child can drop out of school with no more reason than that he wants to; that a young girl will risk unwanted pregnancy simply to have fun; that an adolescent will take whatever drug happens along simply for the "experience." Some adolescents do these things and suffer the consequences, but the vast majority manage to develop their abilities and to assume the responsibilities of adulthood.

PERSONAL IDENTITY

All the points covered so far may be consolidated under what many think is the major developmental task of late adolescence—establishment of *personal identity*. The individual comes to grips, with more awareness than ever before and perhaps ever again, with the following questions: "Who am I?" "Where am I going?" "Why are things as they are?" It is answering these questions, partly or completely, that leads to adulthood.

The concept of identity is much too universal to be passed off easily as if we all knew what it meant. The rest of this chapter and all of the next one will be devoted to the examination of adjustment tasks that define individual identity. The older adolescent is involved in at least three major adjustments simultaneously: deciding vocational plans, expressing heterosexuality, and developing a system of beliefs and values. Each plays a major part in shaping his identity, and each must somehow be dealt with before the child emerges into adulthood.

The end of adolescence, though it is never sharply defined, requires separation and independence from the parents, followed by relations with them based on an equality similar to that found in relationships with peers; commitment to work and recognition of one's abilities and how they contribute to society; establishment of a comparatively firm sexual identity within one's culture and the capacity for tenderness, as well as for sexual love, with members of the opposite sex; and a system of personal values and beliefs that need not be strict and rigid and may in fact change throughout life but nevertheless serves as a foundation for approaching important issues (Committee on Adolescence, 1968).

CHOICE OF FUTURE VOCATION

The selection of a vocation is crucial. But many adolescents do not "select" in the usual sense of the word. Ask any migrant worker, prostitute, or day laborer at what point he or she "selected" a vocation, for example. Nevertheless, awareness of future goals leads to definite planning and preparation and may largely determine the kind of life that an individual will lead.

In many ways work is one of the most "human" of all activities, one that transforms the environment to serve man. In this sense man's work has become increasingly productive, and probably accounts in large part for his successful adaptation. Work also has important social characteristics; the efforts of different workers are mutually interdependent. Division of labor largely accounts for the development of modern cultures. It has freed men from complete concern with their most basic needs, food and shelter. Becoming part of the working community signifies to the adolescent that he is entering adulthood.

The need to choose an occupation does not, of course, fall upon the late adolescent "out of the blue." Nearly everyone has contemplated since early childhood the kinds of work that he might do. Fantasies are influenced by contacts with adults and the communications media. Young children are likely to be quite unrealistic about vocational goals. They prefer the active and exciting occupations portrayed in stories, movies, and television. It is not surprising that many young boys want to be cowboys, firemen, astronauts, and detectives. As children grow older, however, they are more likely to become interested in occupations that have prestige in the adult community. Nevertheless they still have a marked disregard for realistic evaluation of vocational requirements and their own personal abilities. Not infrequently they want to become famous scientists, lawyers, physicians, politicians, and the like. But, as adulthood approaches, most begin to appraise their preferences and capabilities more realistically. Vocational interests are likely to be consolidated during this process until at about age twenty-five they are usually firmly established (Muller, 1969; Mussen *et al.*, 1969).

THE IMPORTANCE OF VOCATION IN IDENTITY

Having an occupation and participating in certain kinds of work have many implications for personal identity. Successful performance in most jobs in itself ensures at least economic freedom from parents and thus a significant gain in independence. In American society, in which career preparation may last into the middle or late twenties, economic freedom is often the last kind to be won. It may indeed be the final sign of adulthood.

When a person starts to work he joins one of the largest communities of man. Even casual observation reveals the importance of work in adult identity. It is an important source of feelings of worth, and it also partly determines how one is treated by others. An unemployed person, for example, or the individual who is unable to perform any kind of job has lost an important part of his identity. Failure to meet vocational demands carries negative sanctions in most cultures. On the other hand, certain vocations greatly enhance social prestige and consequently identity.

Although some adolescents choose to rebel against the established social system by refusing to enter traditional occupations, preferring to "bum" around the country, society does not tolerate their choice for long. Nor do most adolescents tolerate the same behavior in older people. To many people it is one thing to be a rebellious twenty-year-old striving for ideals but apparently quite another to be a forty-year-old "bum" who refuses to work.

Work also gives adolescents an opportunity to satisfy many desires. Economic rewards allow them to purchase material goods, and families of their own become feasible. Other desires may be met indirectly through substitute gratifications. The need for social recognition, for instance, though often not acceptably expressed through direct action, may be fulfilled by high occupational performance. Dominance and aggression may also be partially accepted in some occupations.

Vocational choice is generally more important for men than for women, largely because of the historical associations with masculinity in Western cultures. For the male adolescent vocational choice may be of the utmost concern for his identity. The male role requires financial independence and personal autonomy, both of which are highly related to vocational achievement.

For the male, achieving autonomy is a primary task in late adolescence (Douvan and Adelson, 1966), and he may face serious emotional crises in the process. The female's identity, on the other hand, stresses interpersonal success and the development of social skills; it is much less dependent upon autonomy, including occupational endeavors. In describing this sex difference we do not mean to deny the importance of vocational success for many women; rather we simply point out that the core tasks of development for males and females have traditionally differed. Vocational adjustment is thus usually less stressful for females than for males. The recent women's liberation movement in the United States, if it is effective in changing sex-role expectations, should modify these observations. Vocational achievement will come to play a larger part in feminine identity.

THE CHARACTERISTICS OF WORK

Work has changed the nature of human history, but the nature of work has also been changed by the societies that it has helped to develop. Work is increasingly characterized by finer divisions of labor (more specialization) and shifts in the relative importance of various jobs.

THE HISTORICAL TREND TOWARD SERVICE PROFESSIONS

Earliest man spent almost all his time obtaining raw materials for human consumption, work that is currently part of agriculture and mining. As social organization increased some people took on the task of "manufacturing." They ground corn and other grains or fashioned implements from stone and later from metals. A third occupational level accompanied the introduction of service and administrative personnel, people whose jobs were to distribute goods, provide organization and control, and offer special service skills. By 1800, for instance, agriculture overwhelmingly dominated the vocations. There were a small class of craftsmen portending the beginning of industry and only a very small service class. Today, however, relatively few people work in agriculture (though production per acre has greatly increased); the industrial occupations have grown tremendously but are now stagnating and perhaps declining because of automation; the service and administrative vocations are growing rapidly. Modern cultures are increasingly dominated by those in service professions (teachers, lawyers, physicians, entertainers, and so on) in combination with large automated industrial complexes that need less human labor to maintain production levels (Muller, 1969; Pikunas, 1969).

THE NEED FOR EDUCATION

The changes in society's vocational needs are very important for adolescents. The kinds of positions most needed in modern society require increasing levels of education and training. The vast number of jobs previously available to unskilled and semiskilled workers is rapidly declining; the openings left require varying degrees of formal education and vocational training. The near panic of many parents as they try to impress their children with the importance of education is not idle. Within a brief period of time the requirements for even being considered for a job may rise rapidly, and increasingly, a "ticket," often in the form of a high-school or college diploma is necessary even for an employment interview.

The demand for education is even more pressing in the United States than it is in other countries. Forty percent of the college-age population is enrolled in institutions of higher learning, whereas the percentage in modern European countries ranges from 7 to 15 percent. It is not difficult to imagine the competition that a young American faces in the "education market." A factor intensifying competition in the job market is that many of the most intelligent high-school graduates do not obtain college degrees. Thus, many take jobs below their potentials, and these jobs are then unavailable to other, less able young people who could handle them satisfactorily. Technological development is a third factor that has made education almost a necessity for the young. The poorly educated are increasingly competing with machines that can produce on a level equivalent to that associated with a high-school diploma. Without a college degree the certainty of obtaining desirable employment becomes less and less.

It is also noteworthy, that, according to the 1963 census figures, the high school dropout earns only 12% more than the eighth grade graduate, while the high school graduate earns 15% more than the high school dropout. The college graduate earns 42% more than the high school graduate and 83% more than the eighth grade graduate. Since the American picture of success is related to both education and earnings, school and college are the major stepping stones for rising above the earlier status. Investments in education will continue paying big dividends. (Pikunas, 1969, p. 302)

FACTORS IN VOCATIONAL CHOICE

At least two general factors affect an individual's vocational choice: his socioeconomic level and his sex. They may also be important determinants of his subsequent vocational success and satisfaction.

SOCIOECONOMIC STATUS

Certain jobs seem clearly associated with certain socioeconomic levels. Generally, occupations considered "below" one's socioeconomic level will be disapproved of by relatives and peers. Vocational choice is therefore often limited by social class, especially in the upper and middle classes. A boy from an upper-middle-class family whose father is a physician would be unlikely to decide to become a factory worker or laborer. Unless he were handicapped in some way that limited him to these occupations, such a choice would be considered completely rebellious if not downright stupid. As a child a preference for manual labor would make little difference, but an adolescent's choice is of paramount importance to his parents and his peers.

Parents, especially when their child chooses a lower-level occupation, may fear social disapproval both for him and for themselves. They may also be concerned that his choice will not provide him with the financial rewards required to continue their "way of life" or that he will not continue associating with the same "class" of people.

Choosing to pursue occupations associated with higher socioeconomic levels is less likely to meet with overt disapproval, and in many instances it is encouraged. There may nevertheless be pressures on an individual to remain in his own social class. Older members of various subcultures especially may feel that their children are "stepping out of their position." Other motives, like envy and jealousy, may cause peers to apply both overt and covert pressures to keep adolescents "in their places."

Socioeconomic level may also limit vocational goals by limiting awareness of various occupations. A child from a laboring family, for instance, is not likely to meet many people in the professions and is unlikely to have much first-hand information about the occupations associated with higher socioeconomic status. The same is true in reverse, but the pressures in our culture to remain at higher levels are usually great enough so that lack of exposure to lower-level occupations is less important.

Some very practical factors associated with social class may affect vocational choice. A boy from a poorer home may find it financially impossible to continue his education, even though he wants to and his parents want him to. He must find ways to help himself or seek financial help from other sources. Poorer parents sometimes do not encourage their children (not always consciously) because of the financial hardships that they cannot meet. Even when parents do encourage him, the child is less likely to choose medicine, for example, when he realizes the expense of long years of study and training. In families that place little value on education and more value on financial rewards the child may be encouraged to go to work as soon as he is old enough. He is not likely to spend a great deal of time contemplating higher-level occupations.

People from different social levels often exhibit typical patterns of dress, speech, and social behavior. These characteristics may reduce or increase their chances of being hired for particular jobs, whether or not they are otherwise qualified. Employers, whether or not they openly acknowledge it, are often biased against people from other social classes, especially lower ones. They claim to select on the basis of competence or "personality," but in fact they select according to traits associated with social class. The sales manager of an automobile firm, for example, is expected to look and behave in different ways from those in which a mechanic in the same building looks and behaves. An individual who has not had the opportunity to learn certain class-related modes of dress and speech is unlikely to be hired for the sales position.

SEX DIFFERENCES

Although vocational choice and success are not as important to most females as they are to males, many women are intensely interested in vocational success. Furthermore, many women work for at least short periods before marriage, even though their primary goals are not vocational. For these reasons they are frequently more willing to settle for jobs less appropriate to their abilities than are boys. To them jobs may seem vehicles for independence before they marry and sources of additional income after they marry. It is also commonly believed that premarital work experience provides a form of economic security in the event that they are widowed or divorced.

Because certain occupations become culturally stereotyped as appropriate to particular sexes they are unavailable to members of the other sexes who are not willing to suffer personal and social abuse. Our society, often apparently arbitrarily, has assigned certain vocations to men and certain ones to women. The female business executive, for instance, often causes raised eyebrows if not outright nasty comments about her femininity from both men and women. She may be subtly shunned or overtly insulted in terms like "castrating bitch," "lesbian," and so on. The reason is not that women inherently lack ability to fill such positions but that executive jobs have characteristically belonged to men in our culture. It is interesting to note that considerably more than half the physicians in Russia are women, whereas in the United States women constitute only a small percentage of the medical profession. Similarly, some vocations are socially out of bounds for males. The male nurse, for example, may encounter problems similar to those of the female executive. Men who pursue these occupations are open to the same kinds of personal abuse as are women in characteristically male jobs.

Women run into further conflicts when they find their jobs more rewarding and interesting than their homemaking duties. Conflict often arises between these two sets of duties, making it difficult for them to pursue their vocations. When they are first hired they may find themselves working below their abilities, especially in the professions, because they often work only part time or their permanence is in doubt because their husbands may decide to move. Pikunas (1969) has suggested that this conflict between homemaker and other vocational roles may reflect a problem in our educational system. The importance of vocational skills is often emphasized in school, whereas those related to establishing and maintaining a successful home are not. He has suggested that the roles of homemaker and mother, especially their creative qualities, should be emphasized considerably more.

Vocational Counseling

In view of the importance of vocational choice in personal adjustment, it should be based on potential satisfaction and personal abilities. An appropriate occupation not only contributes to personal fulfillment but also determines one's contribution to his society. We have seen how important this choice was in Ron's adjustment (Chapter 1).

NEED FOR COUNSELING

In our comparatively free society, family traditions or pressures alone too often direct an adolescent's vocational goals without proper consideration for his personal needs and abilities. A young person should take it upon himself (and those close to him should encourage him) to appraise his vocational future realistically. Simply following family preferences is potentially disastrous.

As the range of possible vocations has become increasingly complex special consultants have emerged to help individuals with vocational guidance and planning. Employment specialists first did little more than disseminate information about opportunities for vocational training in their particular districts. Now, however, vocational specialists actually counsel.

Most adolescents do not yet have firm vocational interest patterns. Many aptitudes and abilities may, however, be predicted quite accurately. Counselors usually try to help people to discover the broad vocational areas that seem appropriate; specific jobs are rarely suggested. Vocational counseling is especially useful for adolescents because they rarely have clear ideas of their own abilities and interests or the requirements of various occupations.

Vocational counseling and guidance are, of course, not limited to adolescents. Problems of living for adults may be partly or totally caused by the stress of inappropriate vocational roles. Ron, for example, found himself unfulfilled, disgusted, and generally dissatisfied with his life. Vocational counseling is a potential aid to adjustment for such people. Others may experience drastic changes in their lives that make vocational counseling useful. The housewife who has never been employed but has been widowed prematurely, for example, needs to find ways to become self-supporting.

The U. S. Employment Service, most colleges and universities, and many high schools make vocational counseling services available. Even a young person who feels certain about his occupational future may find it useful to examine his plans with a specialist. There is always the chance that his motivations and interests are not as clear as they seem.

THE COUNSELING PROCESS

We may justly ask how psychologists evaluate the appropriateness of a person's vocational choice. In the first place, the aim of such guidance is to maximize the client's chances for vocational success and personal satisfaction. It is therefore necessary to develop a rather complete picture of the individual: his strengths, his weaknesses, his likes, his dislikes, and so on. Once these characteristics are known they can be matched with various vocational requirements. The counselor can suggest ways to overcome weaknesses that might otherwise prevent the client from entering certain jobs. An intelligent person with only a high-school education and strong interest in the biological sciences, for example, can not qualify for medical training without further education. The outcome of counseling may therefore be plans to attend college. By overcoming this educational handicap, the client can become eligible for a vocation commensurate with his interests and abilities. A more complex counseling problem arises when a change in the client's personality is necessary. A man who fears interpersonal relationships, for example, but who shows otherwise strong potential as a salesman might undertake psychotherapy to overcome his fears.

The counselor, then, must evaluate several areas of his client's functioning. In order to arrive at reasonable conclusions, he must know his client's interests, his skills, his aptitudes, and his personal characteristics. He gathers this information primarily through interviewing and psychological testing.

THE INTERVIEW Vocational counseling nearly always begins with a personal interview, which provides various kinds of information. One function is to determine the need for and appropriateness of counseling itself. The counselor decides whether or not the person's difficulties are primarily vocational. One woman whose husband had died unexpectedly exemplifies a situation in which other measures are more appropriate. During the first interview it was found that she had been employed for a number of years as a salesclerk. In fact, she had only recently become a full-time housewife. As the interview progressed, it became increasingly obvious that she was very depressed about her husband's death. A friend had advised her to seek vocational counseling because she thought that it would "do her good to get out of the house." The client's immediate need was not for vocational guidance but for short-term psychotherapy. She had been satisfied in her previous job, and had performed it adequately; there seemed little reason for her to change it. Consequently, she was referred to a psychotherapist.

The counselor must thus first decide why a client has sought his services. If his services are not appropriate, he is ethically obligated to make a proper referral. Once the need for vocational counseling has been established, however, he begins to gather information. Usually the client's own statements of vocational interest weigh heavily. The kinds of jobs that he has liked in the past, his hobbies and pastimes, his favorite school subjects, and his reading preferences suggest other possibilities. The pattern of interests revealed in the interview can be compared later with patterns obtained from tests. If they are compatible, the counselor can be more certain that he has a reliable understanding of his client's interests. When discrepancies occur, he can seek further clarification.

The interview also suggests an estimate of occupational skills and abilities. The client's job history will reveal the skills that he has already learned. His educational level and academic achievement records are sources of information about intellectual capacity and educational potential. A person with only a high-school education is, for example, immediately eliminated from consideration for many jobs. But examination of his academic records may indicate the wisdom of continuing in higher education.

The client's personal characteristics are assessed directly during the interview and indirectly from his personal history. Motivation to achieve may be at least partially gauged by comparing his potentials with his achievements in previous jobs or academic work. The kinds of jobs that he has sought in the past may indicate how he perceives his personality strengths and weaknesses. If jobs involving interpersonal skills were common, for example, it is likely that he feels confident in dealing with people.

The interview thus furnishes specific data and many leads. Neither interviewing nor testing alone is sufficient however. Maximum knowledge of the client results from combining both sources of data.

PSYCHOLOGICAL TESTS *Vocational-interest tests* are constructed in different ways, but their function in counseling is to provide an additional source of information about the client's likes and dislikes.

The most commonly used interest test for college students and intelligent high-school students is the Strong Vocational Interest Blank (S.V.I.B.) (Strong, 1943). Its developer began by asking people in different occupational fields about their activities, jobs, hobbies, traits, and preferences. By comparing the responses of one vocational group with others, scoring keys were derived that optimally separated the groups. As a result, each occupation has a separate scale. The S.V.I.B. does not measure ability or personality characteristics appropriate to specific positions; it can simply show the degree of similarity between a client's interests and those of people successfully working in those positions. Long-term validation studies have supported the notion that people who choose vocations indicated by their S.V.I.B. scores tend to be satisfied and successful in their jobs.

Other tests measure broader areas of interest: artistic, scientific, service, and so on. Scores on these scales suggest broad spectrums of occupations that clients may find appealing.

Scores on vocational-interest tests should usually not be taken as signs that specific occupations are most appropriate. Rather, they indicate general occupational areas that clients should examine. A person may, for instance, score high in interests related to helping and biological professions, but within these general areas there are many specific jobs at different levels and with different requirements. The test results help the counselor and the client to focus their discussion on appropriate general areas.

Among the most common types of tests are *ability and aptitude tests*, especially those designed to evaluate general intelligence. The vocational counselor wants an I.Q. measure so that he can estimate his client's learning potential. This score also often determines at what occupational level his client can succeed. A person with an average I.Q., interested in the biological sciences, may, for example, perform quite adequately as a laboratory technician but would almost certainly fail as a research scientist. General intelligence is also a fairly good predictor of a person's potential for academic achievement, and for that reason test scores may be an important source of information for deciding about further education.

Academic-achievement tests help to estimate the client's level of achievement in specific academic skills: arithmetic, language, reading, and so on. They measure his retention of such skills and indicate the grade level at which he performs. Educational deficiencies and strengths may be evaluated, and practical recommendations for increasing them can be offered before a client tackles a particular kind of job. A woman who wants to work as a clerk, for example, may first undertake a night course in business arithmetic.

Some tests permit estimation of specific aptitudes and abilities. Clerical skills, for example, may be measured by the client's speed and accuracy in matching numbers or names with other symbols. Tests can also measure mechanical skills, manual dexterity, artistic appreciation, and so on. These tests are usually not administered until after the counselor and client have agreed upon general vocational goals. When their search has become focused on more specific occupations these tests can make significant contributions.

Personality tests are another important source of information on the client's characteristic ways of functioning. Some personality traits are more suitable to certain vocations than to others. A picture of the client's personality helps to specify those vocations to which he is best suited. Inappropriate traits may be discovered and sometimes overcome through methods like psychotherapy.

FINAL STEPS   After gathering the necessary information the counselor must help the client to formulate an appropriate vocational goal. In order to do so effectively, he must be familiar with the requirements of a broad variety of occupations. The client's strengths and weaknesses must be matched to occupational requirements.

In the final interview the actual program is launched. Sometimes prevocational plans like obtaining more education are put into action. At other times reasonable goals are agreed on, and the client then directs his efforts toward obtaining the desired employment. Sometimes the results do not indicate a clear direction. It may then be necessary for the client to try several vocations, and the relationship with the counselor may continue intermittently until his goals can be consolidated.

HETEROSEXUAL RELATIONSHIPS

In early adolescence the child incorporated sexuality into his identity, but it largely took the form of self-interest and learning about his body. In late adolescence, however, sexuality becomes a mode of relating to members of the opposite sex. Purely physical sexuality is not unimportant or necessarily even secondary, but our emphasis will be on its part in the kinds of social relations that ultimately result in marriage.

Late adolescence is the time for "falling in love," for experiencing intense feelings for another person. Whether or not the first love lasts long, the partner is of paramount importance—quite a change from the almost complete self-interest of earlier periods. Sexual feelings are now moderated by feelings of affection and tenderness, and sexual experience becomes something to be shared.

Although love is one of psychologists' favorite topics, they actually know very little about it. It is very difficult to measure or to observe. Muller has described its very personal qualities:

> It is a shattering discovery for everyone. Whether it happens in a friendship or in first love, it tears down in a moment the whole network of habit and conformity and reveals new scales of values, and from that moment life is transformed, carried forward by a new impetus, taking its rhythm from the absence and presence of one person whom one is perpetually astonished to find so necessary. (Muller, 1969, p. 230) . . . Those who do not know how things have a way of caving-in beneath one's feet in the presence of the loved person, and of being drained of all meaning when that person is absent or far away, are the poorer for the lack of a formative human experience. (p. 232)

As the science of psychology has thus achieved little objective understanding of this overwhelming human experience, we must examine other aspects of heterosexuality in more concrete terms. We do not intend to denigrate the experience of love; we simply recognize that to science this highly important human phenomenon is inadequately known.

MALE-FEMALE DIFFERENCES

It is again important to note the major differences between boys and girls in adolescent development. The studies by Douvan and Adelson (1966) show striking differences between them: The boy's major concerns are with "achievement, autonomy, and authority"; girls are preoccupied with "friendship, dating, popularity, and the understanding and management of interpersonal crisis."

Girls are more likely to explore the nature of their sexuality in relation to other people's feelings toward them. They seem to have greater need for intimate friendships with other girls as a way of understanding relationships in general. Boys are more challenged by independence and autonomy and are likely to view sexuality in this light, rather than in that of interpersonal relations.

In view of these differences, Douvan and Adelson (1966) think that the time at which sexuality is incorporated into identity differs for boys and girls. A girl defines her identity only after she has attained a relatively satisfactory integration of sexuality with relationships. Boys, on the other hand, develop their identities before experiencing intimacy. If they do not already have fairly firm images of themselves as autonomous, it is unlikely that they will be able to share intimate relations with girls.

OVERT SEXUAL EXPRESSION

Boys and girls differ in their expression of sexuality. A. Kinsey and his colleagues have provided the major available information on sexual conduct, especially in the American middle class (1948, 1953). More recent studies have confirmed the same basic findings, with the exception that minor increases in overt sexual expression appear to be taking place. Freedom to talk about sex on the other hand has increased greatly.

THE MALE Nearly all boys (95 percent) have experienced their first orgasm by age fifteen. Most first orgasms (approximately 67 percent) are experienced during masturbation; the rest come from heterosexual intercourse (about 13 percent) and homosexual activity (about 5 percent).

More than 90 percent of all adolescent boys masturbate. For most young adolescents masturbation is the major source of sexual release. Heterosexual intercourse begins to replace masturbation after age sixteen. Between the ages of sixteen and twenty masturbation accounts for approximately 38 percent of total sexual outlet, whereas intercourse accounts for 42 percent. The other sources of sexual outlet between sixteen and twenty years are homosexual behavior (8 percent), nocturnal emissions (7 percent), and petting to climax (2.5 percent).

The male reaches the peak of his sexuality, measured by frequency of orgasms, between sixteen and seventeen years of age, averaging 3.4 orgasms a week. The frequency remains essentially the same until about thirty, after which there is a gradual reduction.

By the late teens, almost 75 percent of American males have engaged in premarital intercourse, but the frequency of premarital intercourse is related to social class. Lower-class adolescents generally have more experiences of coitus than do their middle-class counterparts at this age. Fewer than half the college men, for instance, had had intercourse during adolescence, compared to more than 75 percent of men the same age who had not finished elementary school. Social class seems to imply different implicit standards of conduct for boys. Upper and middle-class boys, for example, generally consider masturbation and petting to climax more acceptable than coitus. Lower-class boys, on the other hand, are likely to consider the former practices abnormal and intercourse acceptable. Mussen and his colleagues (1969) have concluded that lower-class boys view sexual experience as an index of masculinity; they do not overlook the possibility that upper-class boys take the same view. Sexual behavior is sometimes related less to the desire for sexual gratification as such than to establishing adult status as defined by the immediate culture.

THE FEMALE In view of the double standard of sexual behavior in American culture, it is not surprising that females report less sexual activity than do males. On the other hand, the average adolescent girl is not the picture of pure virginity and virtue that some believe. These double standards are slowly disappearing, though we are probably still far from allowing women the same prerogatives that we allow men.

Compared to boys, many fewer adolescent girls have experienced orgasm. It is not until around age thirty-five that they catch up with the 90 percent figure of the adolescent males. At age twenty slightly more than half have achieved orgasm. Only 37 percent of women achieve their first orgasms through masturbation, 30 percent through intercourse, and 18 percent through petting to climax. Girls are much less likely than are males to experience intercourse before age twenty: 40 percent, compared to 71 percent. The frequency of masturbation is less than half that of males.

Girls are also less sexually active generally than are boys, reaching maximum frequency of orgasm (1.83 orgasms a week on the average) between ages twenty-six and thirty. Furthermore, only 30 percent of women have experienced orgasm before marriage, whereas almost 100 percent of men have done so.

These figures suggest that girls in our society have been more restricted in their attitudes toward sexual behavior than are boys. E. A. Douvan and

C. Kaye (1957) have found that girls are much more likely to condemn their peers for open displays of sexual interest. They seem to believe that a girl's "reputation" depends upon chastity, or at least upon discretion.

Although socioeconomic status does not seem to be related to differences in female sexuality, religion appears very influential in both adolescence and later life. Inactive members of the Protestant, Jewish, and Catholic faiths are more active sexually before and after marriage than are active church members. Female members who attend church frequently are less sexually active than are any of the other groups.

SOME EXPLANATIONS Two explanations of the rather striking differences between male and female have been formulated. One is based primarily on physical differences. Most females of other species are sexually active only during estrus (heat), whereas the males can be continually active. Some scientists have postulated a similar but much less pronounced difference in the human species. Second, the anatomy of the sex organs suggests that the baby girl's genitals are less likely to be manipulated so that, if masturbation is not socially recognized or taught, girls are less likely to discover it through trial and error.

There may be some validity in such explanations, but most sex differences are probably caused by normative standards. Western cultures tend to be more restrictive of the sexual behavior of females than they are of that of males. Girls thus risk much greater social disapproval when they engage in premarital sexual behavior.

ATTRACTION BETWEEN THE SEXES

Before examining some general concepts of sexual attractiveness among adolescents, we should emphasize the individuality of most such judgments. Each adolescent's attitude toward the opposite sex and thus his perception of attractiveness are influenced by his early heterosexual experiences. A boy who has been exploited or dominated by his mother is likely to anticipate the same traits in other women. He may, of course, develop a negative conception of women, which may reduce their "attractiveness" in general. The same process occurs with specific attributes. A child may have been very attached to an older person with red hair, for example, and may afterward always be attracted to redheads.

How individuals respond to the roles assigned to members of the opposite sex can also affect their attitudes. In our culture, for example, girls may feel a general antagonism toward boys because boys often have more privileges and freedom. An adolescent girl may reject most boys or find attractive those whom she can dominate. Of course, many other motives may contribute to the same behavior. On the other hand, some boys find girls who dominate unattractive. Even though they recognize unfairness in sex roles, they may seek girls who accept socially imposed double standards.

Studies of adolescent preferences suggest the traits and personal characteristics that are generally admired. Girls prefer traits related to getting along with people. They like boys who can get on well with all kinds of people, who are good conversationalists and good listeners. Boys place more emphasis on physical appearance but prefer girls to to be considerate, to be good conversationalists, to be feminine and also friendly, and to be versatile, especially in outdoor sports. In high school both sexes admire intelligence and a good sense of humor. Girls also list "good physique" as desirable, but it appears to be less important than are other traits.

Evidence from college samples indicates that men prefer intelligent women. In the 1800s girls were supposed to "play dumb," a rule for some girls even at present, but studies now suggest that such behavior is not likely to be successful, especially with college men (Pikunas, 1969).

DATING

If there is any one important cultural activity that stimulates and encourages heterosexual relationships more than others do, it is dating. Dating experiences are distinctly different. There is no one dating pattern; rather it varies from individual to individual. Dating patterns also vary sharply at different stages of adolescence and among social classes (Mussen *et al.*, 1969).

Nor can the function of dating be described simply: It serves several functions simultaneously. The most general one is as a device for selecting a mate. When young people date they learn to know each other, fall in love, and ultimately marry.

Nevertheless, most adolescents, especially younger ones, do not consider marriage the primary goal in dating, nor does it serve this function alone. It also provides settings in which to learn social graces and culturally accepted behavior. Privacy offers opportunities for sexual experimentation and discovery. Dating also frequently serves as a vehicle for exhibiting popularity. The "popular" girl has many dates and is constantly in demand. Being seen at functions that require dates may be more fulfilling than the dating relationships themselves.

In preadolescent dating neither partner is deeply involved emotionally. Frequently adults "set up" dates to teach their children social skills. Dating in early adolescence may, however, involve a great deal of anxiety and concern. It is only after this anxiety subsides in late adolescence that true relationships begin to develop and superficiality gives way to serious emotional depth. It seems that understanding, sensitivity, and feeling can be established only after a child has become comfortable in his interactions with the opposite sex.

A PROTOTYPE FOR ADULT RELATIONSHIPS

Douvan and Adelson (1966) think that American dating is dangerous to later relationships. Because of the anxiety and insecurity surrounding adolescent dating, implicit behavioral prescriptions meant to keep relationships casual, superficial, and emotionally free may instill harmful habits. Superficiality helps to protect the child from hurt and danger while at the same time providing controlled exposure to a potentially dangerous situation. Ultimately, this control should result in satisfactory relations with the opposite sex, but these "rules" actually create problems. The difficulty lies in what is considered a "good date."

In general, though the pattern varies with age, social status, and other subcultural variables, a "good date" is able to keep his impulses and emotions under control in circumstances that tend to stimulate them. He or she is able to "keep things going," to be verbally facile and amiable. Any extreme behavior—like overt aggression or sensuality—is considered out of place. It is all right to be gay but not frivolous, to be bright but not serious or "intellectual," to offer comments but without vehemence, to offer variety but not deviance. The girls must usually be amused by the boys' efforts. Regardless of how a girl actually feels about a boy or what they are doing, she is supposed to build his image in a positive way. Because dating is quite important to most youngsters these implicit prescriptions are easily learned. Furthermore, they may acquire positive value of their own because of their adaptiveness at this time of life, with the consequence that the "dating personality" may be continued into adulthood.

One reason that Douvan and Adelson find the present dating system damaging to character formation in the United States is the early age at which it begins. The American adolescent, even the preadolescent, is often on his own in hetereosexual interaction. In elementary schools there are coeducational dances and parties. Parents worry that their children will not be popular because they do not develop early interest in the opposite sex. The "microsexy" ten-year-old girl decked out in air-filled bras, eye makeup, and other adult beauty accessories reflects the pressures on American children to become prematurely heterosexual. Our vast clothing and cosmetic industries do much to support this pressure through mass advertising, and no doubt American business profits by it.

Why should the heterosexual precocity necessarily be a negative thing? Douvan and Adelson have answered that adolescents' outward display of self-assurance and erotic dexterity is usually simply a facade. The more central problems of development, of relating to one's own sexuality and to others, have not been confronted. They see social maturity as preceding psychosexual maturity, indeed, as influencing its direction. The dating process only reinforces emphasis on "social face," retreat from sincerity, and the conflict-free aspects of personality. Although it may seem good for children to learn early to present positive images to the outside world, this "empty" life orientation is poor equipment for dealing with more intense relationships like those of marriage and family life.

Another objection to the dating system is the kind of sexuality that it promotes. Petting patterns involve stimulation without discharge or at best a conflicted drift toward either mutual masturbation or intercourse. In most instances impulses must be checked or avoided, especially by girls, and even complete surrender may arouse fear and guilt. The adolescent is likely to learn that sexuality must be restrained, and in marriage he may be unable to correct his attitude. Fantasies of perfect sexuality, to be found in marriage, are thus encouraged, and reality may seem very disappointing, especially for a couple that has learned sexual restraint.

THE AMERICAN DATING GAME

F. D. Cox (1968) has also recognized the trend toward early sexual sophistication of American children. He views it as resulting from pressure for early transition to adulthood, especially in the expression of sexuality. Because dating provides the opportunity for young people to be alone, it is the primary vehicle of early "adulthoodization." The advent of the automobile, a "mobile bedroom," has made sexual activities much more a reality for modern youth.

Cox has offered his interpretation of the "American dating game," a general pattern in the middle-class guided by unwritten rules and carrying psychological implications for its players. As an example he has introduced a young American couple, a pair of nice, well-brought-up, clean-cut adolescents. Their conduct is socially acceptable, and in no way is their story intended to indicate a "bad" or promiscuous relationship.

The boy has reached legal driving age and has permission to use the family car for his date. He has known the young girl superficially for some time but only recently has he worked up the courage to ask her to a movie. Movies are safe for first dates because little interaction is required.

When he arrives at the girl's home he finds that she is "not quite ready." Actually she has been ready for some time, but making him wait serves two purposes. First, she does not appear overeager; her mother has already told her that she should play "hard to get." Furthermore, her parents can have a few moments to look the boy over and to discuss the rules with him. When the first part of this ritual has been completed the couple departs.

The darkened theater actually becomes the location of the first confrontation. The young man strongly feels the pressure of his friends, and the anonymous larger group of peers loosely defined as "the boys." According to the mores, enough of the double standard remains so that it is he who must take the initiative. And, indeed, to feel masculine and proud among "the boys," the young man is obliged to at least try some type of physical contact with the girl. Thus, as he sits watching the movie, the first of many conflicts concerning sexuality begins to take form. He notices that her hands are lying one inch in his direction upon her lap. Perhaps this is a clue. Should he attempt to hold her hand? If she vigorously rejects this advance everyone in the row might notice and his embarrassment will be acute. If, on the other hand, she accepts, how will he be able to withdraw his hand from hers when it becomes sweaty and begins to cramp without her taking it as some kind of rejection? This game is obviously at a very early and naïve level.

The fascinating and unique characteristic of the American dating game is what one may term "escalation." In other words, dissolution of this first level minor conflict does not end the problem. If the girl accepts this first advance, then the pressure he feels to prove himself to "the boys" actually increases since the whole procedure is designed to test just how far he can go toward overt sexuality with the girl. Granted, much of this pressure may be unconscious for the boy, yet he feels the need to prove himself. Naturally, the further the boy moves, the more pride he will feel when bragging to his friends of his prowess with the girls. Thus, once he has taken her hand, he must now look to the slightly greater problem of attempting to place his arm around her. The rewards are obviously greater but so are the risks. If she vigorously rejects his attempt, the whole movie house will notice (at least it will seem this way to him). If she accepts, there is always the ensuing cramped shoulder to look forward to as well as the necessity of facing the new escalation level and all of its ensuing conflicts and insecurities. The girl is having conflicts too because she does not want to lose her reputation and yet at the same time she does like the boy and thus does not want him to think her a prude in which case he may not ask her for another date.

The American dating game evolves into a game of offense versus defense, and in the course of history a defense has never won a war. With each step toward sexual intercourse taken by the boy, the girl will have to retreat and reintegrate her new behavior into her value system. Since her value system will in all probability already be vague and nebulous because of the swift changing and pragmatic character of the American society, the continuing pressure upon her will cause great confusion and insecurity. (One of the most susceptible periods for the girl insofar as premarital sex is concerned is after she and her steady boyfriend have broken up over sexual problems and then go back together again. Her fear of losing him makes her acquiesce to his demands as a way of holding him.) By this age, it will be the peer group that yields the greatest influence and both she and the boy will be highly susceptible to the argument that everyone else engages in such behavior. Her own insecurity will be her worst enemy. (Cox, 1968, pp. 25–26)

If the two continue to date, especially if they go steady and date frequently, escalation is likely to take the following line: "necking, petting, petting to orgasm, and finally to intercourse." The girl usually makes the rules in this strange game. Her responsiveness and the degree of intimacy that she will tolerate depend upon how sexual activities are classified in her value system. If petting to orgasm, for instance, is classified as "not sex," then she can engage in it without guilt. The boy, on the other hand, finds his masculinity threatened when his advances are not accepted.

The problem, as Cox has formulated it, is that the psychological dynamics described tend to focus dating on sex. Emphasizing sex reduces the amount of interpersonal learning possible; furthermore, placing a high value on sexuality may lead to choice of a marital partner on that basis alone and may almost entirely determine modes of interaction with members of the opposite sex. Adolescents in cultures that are more accepting of early sexual experimentation are not so preoccupied with the "sexual game." Sex has a more natural place among the many possible interactions between a man and a woman, more specifically in the long-term relationship between a man and his wife. In this way the American dating game tends to limit adolescent growth.

GOING STEADY

As early as junior high school boys and girls may pair off and limit their interactions solely to each other. There may be little emotional meaning in these early pairings, which perhaps reflect "the thing to do" more than any serious groping toward heterosexual relationships. In high school and college, however, the tendency is for boys and girls to make increasing commitments to each other. The chance of premarital intercourse is much greater in couples who are frequently together and who come to know and care a great deal about each other. The question arises, however, whether adolescent growth is promoted or hindered by "going steady."

There are certainly advantages to going steady. It is especially reassuring to know that one will have a date for whatever social events come up. The risk of being rejected by a new person is also reduced to nil. And, on a very practical level, it may simply cost less to take out someone who has learned not to expect "grand treatment."

There are, on the other hand, several disadvantages. Limited experience with members of the opposite sex is important in itself, and obligations to the steady partner tend to restrict even further the variety of experiences open to an individual.

Cox (1968) believes that many young marriages that go "sour" because mates "have changed" after marriage are those of couples who have gone steady most of their dating lives. They may not necessarily have gone steady with each other but failure to "play the field" has resulted in limited understanding of the opposite sex. The frame of reference for evaluating a partner is narrow. When they must live in very close proximity they begin to discover behavior that they had not so easily noticed before; they are bewildered and may feel that their mates have "tricked them" by changing after marriage.

Clearly, there is no certain answer to the question whether or not going steady is "good." It depends upon the particular peer culture and the meaning that "going steady" has in it. The primary danger appears to lie in the limitations imposed on an adolescent's experiences with members of the opposite sex and the consequent inflexibility that he may show in later adjustments.

PREMARITAL SEX RELATIONS

The question whether or not an individual should have premarital sexual relations is important and difficult in our society. Although almost everyone recognizes taboos against premarital intercourse, it is clear that they are violated on a large scale. Studies indicate, for example, that approximately 50 percent of American women have had intercourse before marriage and that 85 percent or more of men have (Cox, 1968).

THE QUESTION OF SEXUAL REVOLUTION

Currently there is a great deal of discussion about the "sexual revolution" in the United States. What actually seems to be happening, however, is less a great increase in sexual activity than the assumption by young people of responsibility for establishing standards of sexual behavior. They are more independent in this as in other areas, and their parents' influence is thus declining. They openly question sexual mores and talk about sex more than has ever been possible in this country before.

It is naïve to assume, however, that strong attitudes against premarital intercourse do not exist. Perhaps they are undergoing modification, but there is still pressure to limit, or completely to avoid, premarital sex. Prohibitions left over from our Puritan heritage have not changed greatly, even though they seem much less appropriate today than they were in the seventeenth century. Originally these prohibitions appear to have been based on fear of venereal disease, of the destructive impact of illegitimate births on family titles and property rights, of rivalry within the family, and perhaps of desire to control the younger generation. Obviously, some of these reasons have disappeared or been modified. Nevertheless, existing value systems continue to prevail, whether or not they have a rational basis. The more important question, however, is what are the potential effects of premarital sexual activities on personal development?

There are in the United States opposing views on premarital intercourse. One is permissive and based on the argument that our sexual mores are outdated because unwanted pregnancies can now be prevented or aborted and venereal diseases can easily be treated. As teenagers are physically capable of sexual intercourse, they should be permitted experiences that help to consolidate their identities and interpersonal relationships. Furthermore, this vital aspect of marriage and adult pleasure deserves practice. The choice of a marital partner may be more realistic when physical sexuality is allowed to assume its proper perspective, whereas other aspects of life are more likely to be effectively evaluated. Society should thus provide as a matter of course, protection against pregnancy and venereal disease. Older adolescents acting responsibly should be free to seek sexual experience with a variety of partners. The pleasure-seeking aspect of sex is acceptable, but learning and growth are even more important and should be emphasized.

The other view is in sharp contrast. Coitus is considered not simply another form of pleasure but an adult activity requiring more emotional maturity than most adolescents have gained. Sensation-seeking in the guise of encouraging growth may simply fixate an individual's sexuality at a pleasure-seeking level. Furthermore, most adolescents have already internalized cultural prohibitions against sexuality, so that premarital relationships will inevitably lead to guilt and psychological upset.

FACTORS TO CONSIDER

These views are extreme, but they nevertheless represent the range of attitudes (aside from the "hellfire and brimstone" preference for eliminating premarital sexual intercourse completely) of Americans. Each person, of course, ultimately decides on his own sexual behavior. It is therefore instructive to examine some of the important considerations that guide an adolescent in his decisions. These questions can be classified as arising from personal principles, general social principles, religious principles, and psychological principles (Cox, 1968).

In the first category an adolescent must decide how premarital sex fits his personal values. Will it contribute to his performance as spouse or parent? Will he or his partner be physically or psychologically harmed? What will be the general result of his conduct for him and his partner?

In regard to social principles he must think about what conduct is best for future society. To the degree that established social mores are broken, there is pressure for these mores to change. That is, the adolescent who decides upon premarital intercourse contributes to the future relaxation of codes. He must ask himself what kind of behavior he wishes to predominate in his society and whether or not he is willing to contribute through his own behavior.

The importance of religious principles varies with the individual's beliefs. He must decide what sexual conduct is approved by his religion, whether or not his church and society are in conflict about such conduct, and to what extent he is willing to let religion guide his behavior.

Decisions in these three areas are all inappropriate for psychology to attempt to influence. They reflect individual preferences because no scientific principles have been established to answer value questions. Nevertheless, a thoughtful adolescent should recognize their importance.

Psychological principles can be discussed more directly, even though a great deal more knowledge remains to be discovered. Most adolescents know that premarital intercourse is often "winked at," especially for men, but many people have been taught since early childhood that it is wrong. Whether or not they actually believe that it is wrong, their ingrained attitudes are not easy to overcome. Christianity especially has restricted sexuality. Furthermore, its primary means of controlling behavior has been to instill guilt. An adolescent may thus experience an emotional response that he does not expect after engaging in intercourse. He must ask himself how well he can handle the guilt that is almost certain to arise.

Foreseeing the possibility of guilt in itself should help to reduce its impact. Of course, a frank discussion between partners about the meaning of intercourse for each is a realistic way to approach a decision. Such discussion is not, however, characteristic of adolescents unless both have grown quite secure with their identities. More likely than not, intercourse will result from the escalation of the "dating game."

Guilt over premarital relations can also affect later marital adjustment. A man especially may not be able to tolerate the idea that his wife has had sexual relations with other men. Discovery of the fact can be a serious blow to his masculine identity and cause him to reject her whether or not he really loves her. Neither spouse, of course, has any right to believe that his partner's behavior should have been geared to his values before they became intimate.

A spouse who feels guilty about premarital relations and has not confessed them to his or her partner may live in fear of discovery. The marriage usually suffers under these conditions. The guilty person is likely to suspect his partner, whether justly or not, in order to reduce his own guilt. Such circles of suspicion can be quite disruptive. The best solution seems to be frank discussion between prospective spouses. Their previous relationships can be openly acknowledged, accepted, or rejected, and then they can start marriage on a realistic basis. Past experiences, of course, need not affect the happiness of a marriage. As long as both partners have accepted their pasts and love each other, there is no reason that they cannot live together in harmony.

Another psychological effect of premarital intercourse may show itself in the quality of marital coitus. The problem is that negative premarital experiences may damage a couple's chances for a satisfying marital relationship. Premarital coitus often occurs under anxiety-arousing conditions. Because of double standards girls are much more susceptible to these influences, so that sex may become associated with tension, anxiety, and guilt. Also the common notion that boys show their masculinity by putting "notches in their belts" sets the stage for expectations that sex is an aggressive, manipulative activity.

Adolescents who do not experience sexual intercourse before marriage, are not necessarily free from the negative influences of social taboos, however. Approximately one-third of American wives have trouble achieving sexual climax. It is unlikely that physical problems account for this frequency; rather, most of these women are victims of social values. They have been taught that sex is essentially unpleasant, or that only "bad girls" really enjoy it. Guilt, of course, is probably the major factor in restricting their ability to derive pleasure from sex. Even when they recognize that sex is entirely permissible after marriage—that the taboo is lifted—their ingrained guilt frequently remains. Realistic sex education in the schools and more open, honest discussions about sexual behavior should help to reduce this kind of stress on future generations.

Other factors also contribute to a girl's negative attitude toward intercourse. First, a great amount of misinformation about the female climax is current. It is often described as comparable to the male orgasm, an intense muscular response lasting a brief interval and followed by a dramatic release of tension. Actually female orgasms are more variable and not likely to be comparable to those of men. Some women do experience muscular contractions in the vagina and a release quite similar to that of a male. Others, however, respond in a milder way, which is equally normal, but they are likely to berate themselves for not experiencing what they believe to be "true orgasm."

Another reason for negative attitudes toward sex is the ignorance of the American male. Most men respond to stimulation more rapidly and completely than do women. A man who is ignorant of such matters is likely to assume that the woman responds in much the same way that he does and that physical stimulation leads to quick sexual arousal. Most females, however, require attention to the psychological side of sex as well. Whether this difference is innate or the result of cultural learning is not completely clear. Nevertheless, it seems to be rather prevalent among American women. It is well for a boy to remember, even though he may not need tenderness and soft feelings himself, that a girl wants to experience them in conjunction with physical arousal. The old adage about being tender and caring—"candlelight and sweet nothings"—may go a long way in helping a girl find sexual satisfaction. But the adolescent boy is unfortunately usually too preoccupied with himself or too embarrassed to meet his partner's psychological needs.

Although we have described some potential problems of premarital intercourse, we do not believe that unmarried couples cannot experience the fullness of mature sexuality. Especially when the partners are willing to examine their values openly and to arrange for a pleasant, relaxing setting there is no reason why they cannot find emotional fulfillment. The primary deterrents to successful premarital sex are cultural pressures. Awareness of these forces may be useful in avoiding pitfalls.

PROS AND CONS

Many arguments for and against premarital intercourse have been offered by a variety of people. It is well to look at some of these categories; they may be especially useful for stimulating discussion.

SOME PROS One reason advanced in favor of premarital intercourse is its function as a sexual outlet. Many adolescents must wait a long time after puberty before marrying. They feel a need for, and some people believe that they should have, sexual release with partners of the opposite sex. It is claimed that the individual will function more effectively in other areas, when his physiological needs have been met, provided that he feels no guilt. Furthermore, heterosexual experiences are considered more adaptive to later life than are the solitary sexual activities most frequent otherwise.

Another argument is that learning about sex is a positive, if not necessary, growth experience. Knowledge of the opposite sex and of sexuality is necessary before committing oneself to a mate. Individuals have opportunities to learn emotional adjustments that may be important in marriage, especially physical techniques that may increase the satisfactions of marital sex.

Other reasons have also been offered. Physical and emotional adjustments, for instance, are more easily made when people are young than when they are older and their patterns have become more stable. The failure of a premarital relationship is socially less disastrous than is the failure of a marriage; there is usually less stress, and children are rarely involved. Early heterosexual experience may also prevent the development of homosexuality and other practices considered deviant in our society.

SOME CONS Several arguments against premarital intercourse have also been offered. The most frequent are the dangers of unwanted pregnancy and the threat of venereal disease. These ancient problems have recently been reduced in theory, if not in fact. Quite effective contraceptive devices are now available, abortion laws allowing competent medical care are becoming more frequent, and venereal diseases can be treated quite successfully. Nevertheless, illegitimate births have increased over the last few decades, and venereal disease is once again becoming a major problem among the young. Although the challenges to these arguments seem rational, there is no solid evidence yet that in fact the arguments are invalid.

Other reasons have already been mentioned. Guilt reactions among many young people and detrimental effects on later sexual functioning are both reasons for avoiding premarital coitus. The necessity for unwanted marriages because of pregnancy or a sense of emotional obligation is also frequently cited. It is also claimed that premarital coitus may be so satisfying that an individual will delay marriage for a long time or forever. Furthermore, habits of premarital sex are thought by some to lead to extramarital infidelity that may destroy an otherwise satisfactory marriage. There are objections based on moral and religious values as well: Premarital coitus is simply considered wrong. Practical consequences of doing wrong include guilt, rejection of females by men who want to marry virgins, and possibly punishment for sinning.

There are no simple answers to these arguments. The youth of today must determine what direction it wishes to take. The more information it has, the more effective its decisions will be. Young people who have more freedom of sexual expression must decide how they want to incorporate sexuality with other principles and values.

SUMMARY

In this chapter we have focused on two adjustment tasks of late adolescence: choosing a vocation and expressing sexuality.

The adolescent finds that society offers him opportunities for both growth and stagnation. Laws first restrict him, then tell him that he is "old enough." For all the talk of individual freedom, the adolescent finds that adult society often responds negatively to nonconformity. There is pressure to live up to the predominant system of social values and beliefs. To complicate things further adolescents frequently look upon their future goals as "not yet real." Adults may respond with surprise and disbelief at some of the resulting impetuous behavior. The combination of all these and other factors leads to the conception of adolescence as a time for developing "identity," a vague term that is concretely defined only by the roles and skills that the adolescent achieves through performing tasks of adjustment.

The selection of a vocation is crucial. It represents an adolescent's entry into one of the largest social communities of man: the community of shared labor. His vocation becomes an integral part of his identity. It offers financial independence, proof of maturity, and many other satisfactions. For men it represents the achievement of autonomy and is perhaps at the core of identity; it is generally less important in female identity.

The nature of work has changed through history, becoming more specialized. Emphasis has shifted from jobs that provide raw materials (as in agriculture and mining) to those in manufacturing, to those in service professions. The major implication for today's adolescent is that he must acquire higher levels of skills, especially academic skills, in order to find satisfying work. Educational demands are even more pressing in the United States than in other countries.

Vocational choice may be affected by factors not directly related to personal preference. Socioeconomic class may limit choice: The individual is unlikely to choose a vocation below his station (or in some instances above it); limited familiarity with a wide variety of occupations restricts choice; practical considerations, especially financial ones, may prevent advanced training; class characteristics like speech, dress, and manners may help or hinder entry into some jobs. Sex also restricts vocational choice. Some jobs are considered appropriate to men and some to women for purely traditional reasons. Women who achieve high status and men in "feminine" occupations may have to endure unpleasant reactions from others.

Vocational counseling has developed with the expansion of vocational possibilities. It is now available to many young people. Its purpose is to help the individual to match his skills to an occupation that he will find interesting and in which he may succeed. The counselor must therefore understand his client's interests, skills and aptitudes, and personal characteristics. Two primary tools for gathering information on them are interviews and psychological tests.

In late adolescence there is also a change from sexual self-interest to deeper sexual relationships with members of the opposite sex. One is likely to "fall in love" during these years. Differences between boys and girls in sexual expression can probably be explained by different kinds of stress in the formation of their identities. Boys are concerned primarily with achievement, autonomy, and authority, whereas girls place more emphasis on interpersonal skills. For this and probably other cultural reasons, girls are less active sexually than are boys.

Sexual attractiveness appears to follow fairly stable patterns. Girls generally admire traits associated with successful interpersonal contacts: amiability and good conversation. Boys are more interested in physical appearance but also admire friendly personal traits. Attractiveness is nevertheless still a matter of individual taste, partly determined by past experience.

Dating is a primary vehicle for establishing heterosexual relationships. The "good dating personality"—in control of emotions, verbally facile, amiable—has been criticized by some investigators as a prototype that leads to superficiality in adults. They have further objected to the quality of sex relations encouraged by the American dating system. In most instances impulses must be checked and a fantasy of "ideal sexuality" is encouraged; later sexual behavior may thus seem disappointing. Cox (1968) has offered an analysis of the "American dating game," which he views as a process of escalation in which the male must make increasing sexual advances as the female accepts one after the other. Pressures on both sexes lead them from initial hand holding to sexual intercourse.

The question of premarital sex relations has aroused extreme partisanship in our society. Many traditional arguments against it—for example, the risks of venereal disease and pregnancy—have been undermined by medical advances. There are, however, several factors that the adolescent still must consider: personal, social, religious, and psychological principles. Scientific conclusions are appropriate only to psychological principles; the other areas belong to the realms of personal belief and philosophy. Adolescents should consider that premarital intercourse may create guilt because of past training; that subsequent marital adjustment may be affected by guilt, fear of discovery, and suspicion; and that negative premarital experiences may lead to negative marital sex. There is no reason, however, that premarital sex cannot be positive and growth-producing if the negative factors are understood and properly dealt with.

13

A. Introduction
  1. The adolescent's interest in
     values
B. Factors in Choosing Values
  1. Limits on Personal Philosophies
  2. Sources of conflict
C. The Question of Religion
  1. The functions of religion
  2. Religion and social values
  3. The question "Is God dead?"
D. The Generation Gap
  1. Introduction
  2. The question of higher
     education
  3. The student drug culture
E. Summary

Adjustment in Late Adolescence: Choosing Values

INTRODUCTION

THE ADOLESCENT'S INTEREST IN VALUES

Adolescent values related to sexual behavior and vocational choice were discussed in Chapter 12. Now we turn to discussion of the older adolescent's more general task of choosing a broad system of values. This task usually begins late in high school and continues through the early twenties. If accomplishing any one developmental task completes personal identity, the task is this one. A person must bring the many facets of his life together and must decide on a system of values for making it meaningful.

The social importance of this process cannot be denied. In all the major social and economic revolutions the young have played important parts. Their struggles to discover what is good for mankind are often executed with the zeal and vigor necessary to accomplish significant social change.

Why do values begin to play such an important part in late adolescence? What makes young people question or support current ethical systems? The answers to these questions are not simple, nor can they be put forth with any certainty. But several interrelated factors that at least partly account for the adolescent's new interest in values can be identified.

First, the older adolescent is more involved in society and thus more likely to meet people who are themselves interested in social values and religious beliefs. They may stimulate his interest in these matters. He also has developed the intellectual abilities necessary for dealing with abstract concepts —the raw material of discussions of values and ethics. The older adolescent thus is equipped to deal with abstractions and has access to environments in which they are important. Finally, he has reached the point in his development at which he must consolidate his unique identity, besides fitting into society. He must therefore find a system of beliefs that will lend meaning to his life within a larger context that includes other men, as well as himself. One motive force, then, is the need for beliefs and values that will help him to organize his behavior in the present and in the future. His values provide guidelines and direction for his behavior and anchor it to purposeful goals.

IDEALISM

The idealism of adolescents is legendary. Idealistic zeal is especially characteristic of those who choose values different from the ones that predominate in their society or in their parents' generation. These young people often seem to vacillate between deep cynicism and hopelessness when they discover the discrepancy between word and deed in the adult generation. As the inconsistencies and contradictions that exist in all societies become apparent for the first time, these adolescents are likely to espouse hopeful programs designed to eliminate the evils of society and to bring about a "perfect" world. Even youngsters who generally accept existing value systems may be shocked by the hypocrisies with which many adults have become comfortable. And they may find it hard not to sympathize with their more idealistic peers who actively challenge these inconsistencies.

Adolescent commitment to an ideal does not reflect simply lack of experience with reality, though inexperience is frequently also an element; having causes and believing strongly in values help to fill a void in adolescents' lives as they leave childhood to become independent adults. Not that their ideals are without merit; but they also serve psychological needs in this phase of development. Idealism often provides a kind of group support. Young idealists usually establish a group identity that in itself lends purpose to their lives. They may also find within the group social roles with which they can identify and have experiences of being useful.

It is also true that many young idealists become the conservatives of the next generation. As they move into other social roles, especially those related to family and vocation, they drop their single-minded striving for perfection in favor of some acceptance of the world as it is. Others, however, continue as staunch social critics, always seeking change and perpetually dissatisfied with the weaknesses that they perceive in society.

We turn now to some more specific aspects of choosing values in late adolescence.

FACTORS IN CHOOSING VALUES

Although each generation must deal with the specific issues of belief and values of its time, some general characteristics seem to recur. We have already described patterns of growth in adolescence. Other factors also tend to limit the range and variety of the value systems from which an adolescent can choose. Although these factors are not necessarily immutable, they seem stable enough to be considered by themselves.

LIMITS ON PERSONAL PHILOSOPHIES

As the adolescent approaches his decision on a system of values that will direct his life, he is necessarily limited to thoughts and ideas that have been set down by men throughout the ages. It is a rare adolescent indeed who develops his own original system of values.

Science, of course, has no special knowledge of rightness or wrongness of a personal philosophy. The individual's choice of a particular set of values depends upon his personal preferences as determined by early experiences and current influences.

A wide range of values and philosophies is current in contemporary societies. Many are contradictory and even opposed on their most basic premises. But many societies are quite tolerant, allowing different beliefs to exist side by side; only a very few societies are still organized around one set of values alone. The adolescent therefore has a choice to make, a choice that may be restricted because of his childhood training and therefore fraught with possibilities of guilt and discomfort.

P. Muller (1969) has outlined six main philosophical orientations in Western culture from which most adolescents make their basic choices. A brief description of each may be helpful.

THE JUDEO-CHRISTIAN TRADITION

The Judeo-Christian tradition predominates in the Western world and undoubtedly constitutes the most comprehensive single value system. The common belief of all the associated religions is in one God who has created all things, including man. Man has, however, been set apart, created in God's image, but unlike God he is fallible. He has sinned against his Creator and has therefore been sent into the world. The only path to redemption is through complete submission to the divine will as revealed in the religious books of the specific sects or through belief in God's appearance on earth in human form. Judaism and Christianity differ, of course, in certain aspects of their beliefs; the most basic difference is in beliefs about the Savior, whether he is Jesus Christ or the Messiah still to come. Among Christian faiths there are also many doctrinal differences.

THE HELLENIC TRADITION

The ancient Greeks also believed that man is set apart from other creatures, but they believed that it was his ability to reason that has put him in his special position. He is thus able, through seeking wisdom, to control his environment and to direct its course to some extent. Although it is not necessary to believe in God to accept this view, some faith in man's unique power to direct the order of things is required.

THE TRADITION OF MAN AS TOOLMAKER

Another view stresses man's adaptive capacities, especially his technological abilities. Man is considered not a special organism but an animal among other animals, but one with greater advantages in the struggle for survival. His ability to make tools that increase his power over the rest of the animal world is most significant.

Man's drives and desires are considered the same as those of other animals, but theorists differ in the importance that they place on specific ones. For example, one will consider the sex drive as the core of human motivation, whereas others will emphasize aggression, love for power, materialism, and so on.

THE TRADITION OF MAN AS FALLEN ANIMAL

The antithesis of viewing man as dependent upon his technological capacities for his mastery of nature is the pessimistic view of man's technical skills as the source of trouble. By emphasizing them man actually threatens the entire animal kingdom. The development of nuclear weapons is a striking example of man's potential to destroy himself and the rest of the world. His other technological developments are increasingly restrictive of life, a response to the suppression of animal drives in societies that have been created primarily through intellectual effort.

The adherents of this view strive for man's return to unity with the cosmos, to "live by the images of his dreams, by poetic creation, by the irrational joys of which sexual ecstasy is one form, and the effect of which is each time to punch him back into a cosmic unity which he too often forgets" (Muller, 1969, p. 241).

THE TRADITION OF MAN AS RESPONSIBLE

Another existential view is more optimistic: Man is considered responsible for the world and able to choose how it will be. He is capable of overcoming the restrictions imposed by his own technology. Things in the world have meaning only when man decides to take responsibility for them and to use them toward the goal of a "human world."

THE TRADITION OF MAN AS CITIZEN

The conception of man as a citizen

> is less extreme than the last two. It starts from man's animal inheritance, but does not reduce him to his biological impulses. It endows him with a certain responsibility, but not for the whole of the universe—simply and imperatively for the creation of an integrative society. It is through his efforts to dominate his environment and establish mutual bonds of non-violence and reason between men that man has a history, that this history has a direction and a goal, and that the moral judgments that emerge from it are more than just a reflection of education or the particular social culture. (Muller, 1969, pp. 241–242)

None of these six views has any more scientific validity than any other. Each person must decide for himself which elements are most compatible with his own experience and way of life. Clergymen, philosophers, scientists, and educators can offer only information and sources of information to help him reach a decision.

SOURCES OF CONFLICT

It is a rare adolescent who does not experience some sort of conflict over values. It is almost certain that at some point the values that he has chosen or learned will be rudely jolted. The result is psychological conflict. P. H. Mussen and his colleagues (1969) have described several important causes of such conflict.

CONSCIENCE

Conscience lies at the core of all value conflicts. By adolescence most young people have learned "rights" and "wrongs" from their parents, their peers, and other important adults. Conscience means that one can no longer act comfortably simply on the basis of expedience. He now behaves in a certain way not solely because he will benefit but also because he can thus prevent guilt and anxiety. Feelings of guilt are the signal that his conduct is unacceptable.

Adolescents often have conflicting motives, which arouse anxiety and guilt. The developmental tasks of late adolescence frequently bring them into conflict with what they learned earlier and therefore with their consciences. Increased sex drive, for example, often tempts adolescents to behave in ways that they have been taught are wrong and for which they will suffer guilt and anxiety. Striving for independence may also place them in situations that they were warned earlier to avoid (Mussen *et al.*, 1969). As a child a person may have been told that "children are seen and not heard," but as an adolescent he is expected and may desire to enter into conversations with visitors. When he does, however, his new position is likely to raise conflicts. If he speaks, guilt or anxiousness may follow even though it is now perfectly acceptable for him to speak. His past training is not so easily overcome.

PEER GROUP VERSUS PARENTS

The necessity for choosing between peer-group values and parental values is a common source of conflict. Many parents lose touch with changing social customs and do not recognize what their youngster and his friends consider entirely appropriate. How girls and boys interact, their dress, the acceptability of smoking, and many other issues can cause conflict for an adolescent who is trying to impress his peers favorably and at the same time to please his parents. This conflict is reflected in the common plaint, "Ah, Mom, all the kids do it."

Larger values associated with religion and general morality do, of course, cause conflict between peer and parental values, but less often. Children tend to associate with peers of the same social class whose parents have similar values, and these values are generally learned and adhered to by adolescents.

A source of more serious conflict between peer and parental values arises when parents and peers are of different classes or racial background. A high-school athletic star from a first generation immigrant Mexican-American background, for example, is likely to find that the values of his peers at school are at odds with those of his family. His parents may not believe in unescorted dating and he must deceive them to go with the group. He may then experience guilt for going against his parents or have open difficulties with them.

SHIFTING STANDARDS

Conflict also arises when an adolescent must replace old responses with quite different ones appropriate to his growth from childhood to adulthood. As a child he is expected to believe one thing and as an adult another. For example, a girl is taught that sex before marriage is to be avoided; but when she marries, the standard shifts quite suddenly and she is expected to be sexually open, free, and loving. Such radical shifts are difficult to make. A child is expected to be obedient and to do as he is told, yet as an adult he is expected to be independent.

Shifting standards also create conflicts in values. Perhaps for this reason adolescent moral standards become more flexible and more expedient than they were in childhood. Superstitions begin to disappear, and adolescents are less likely to criticize their peers even when they feel that they are wrong. They accept a greater variety of behavior than they did as children. Their new flexibility, their hesitance to criticize, and their tendency to evade moral conflicts help to protect them from many potentially troublesome circumstances.

THE QUESTION OF RELIGION

An examination of value systems would be incomplete without consideration of religion. Organized religions are among man's most extensive value systems. There is probably no ethnic, geographical, or cultural group that does not have some sort of religious beliefs. As societies become more complex their religions follow suit. Primitive religion is likely to be more concrete, involving worship of idols and other tangible objects. More advanced cultures have turned to abstract gods and worship through symbols; in Christian communion, for instance, blessing the wafer and wine symbolizes their transformation into the body and blood of Christ.

A characteristic of all religions is that their accepted and institutionalized values are extremely resistant to change. Although great changes in religious doctrine have occurred—the Protestant Reformation for example—much time and often extreme measures are usually necessary to bring them about. The Soviet Union offers an example of massive government intervention to turn people away from religion, yet it has been only partially successful. Many people think, however, that religion in the United States is undergoing significant change at this time, a notion to which we shall return.

Our purpose here is not to evaluate the truth or accuracy of specific religious beliefs. In fact, it is inappropriate to suggest that science has or ever will produce answers in this realm. Social scientists have nevertheless been interested in objective investigations of religion and the attitudes and values of those who practice various faiths. Some of their data do shed light on the relation of religion to personal adjustment. Other information has been drawn from observation and is consequently more liable to subjective interpretation. We shall examine some data and some interpretations that seem relevant to understanding religion and personal adjustment.

THE FUNCTIONS OF RELIGION

R. L. Wrenn and R. A. Ruiz (1970) have viewed religion as serving three distinct functions: the personal, the divine, and the social.

PERSONAL

The personal function of religion is perhaps the oldest: It is to fulfill man's desire to believe in aid and comfort from an unknown power greater than he. Christians express this desire in the prayer "Give us this day our daily bread." In our complex society organized religion may offer various other personal advantages. The simple survival needs of primitive man are less important than the more complex needs associated with the search for personal meaning or success in financial and social endeavors. We shall see later that people who stress the personal function of religion are also likely to hold other values, like racial prejudice, that help them to feel more secure.

Probably every religious person has some practical personal motives for holding his beliefs. He may pray that he will be able to live the right kind of life, or as a soldier he may promise God to be "good" if he is spared from death. Probably many also derive financial gain and social prestige from their religious associations. For some these gains are the main goal; for others they are simply side effects accompanying other satisfactions. Whether we approve or disapprove of the personal use of religion, it does exist, and it is the sole motivation for some religious adherents.

DIVINE

The divine function of religion is to help man to comprehend the nature of the cosmos. Faith in a supreme being can settle some doubts. Religious doctrine usually centers on accounting for creation and death, providing understanding and comfort. Belief in life after death—and whatever it holds for the individual—is generally an important part of religious belief.

SOCIAL

Religions teach man how to prepare for entrance into the "other world." Nearly all religions have evolved ethical codes to help him to live as a social being. Limits on the kinds of behavior to be tolerated are set, and they help to balance individual freedom and social responsibility. Religions base their particular ethical codes on spiritual values. The Ten Commandments of Judeo-Christian belief are an example of such a code serving both the divine and social functions of religion.

Religions and individuals vary in their stress on these three functions. The functions are likely to be in conflict and consequently to create conflict within a religious person. For example, the religious person is taught that he should love his neighbor, but he may find himself in business competition with him. Young people in our affluent society, in which the positive value of striving for monetary rewards is losing strength, may find especially the personal use of religion extremely hypocritical. They may therefore consider religious faith irrelevant to current social issues that they consider important.

RELIGION AND SOCIAL VALUES

M. Rokeach (1965, 1970) has been a leader in studying attitudes and values of religious people. In general, his and other work has indicated that the average churchgoer and the self-professed religious person are generally more prejudiced than are people who do not attend church and nonbelievers, a rather surprising finding in light of most religious doctrine. Furthermore, the results seem fairly consistent across the three major religions in the United States—Roman Catholic, Jewish, and Protestant.

On one hand, religion supposedly teaches love and acceptance, but, on the other, religious people are more intolerant of racial and ethnic groups (except their own) than are nonbelievers, including communists. Nonbelievers are not necessarily more tolerant in all respects; they are often intolerant of those who disagree with them.

Rokeach (1970) has reported results from a large sample of Americans, ranging in age from twenty-one to eighty and drawn from different religious groups. His data were obtained in a value survey scored in two parts. One part indicates the individual's goals in life, which supposedly direct his behavior. The other measures the means that he uses to reach his goals. For example, a person's goal might be "a comfortable life," and his means might be "honesty." Subjects were also asked about their feelings about the assassination of Martin Luther King, Jr., choosing among "anger," "sadness," "shame," "fear," and "he brought it upon himself." It was believed that the last two responses indicated less compassion than did the first three.

Among all groups some goals were generally favored: A "world at peace," "family security," and "freedom" were most important, and "an exciting life," "pleasure," "social recognition," and a "world of beauty" were least important. Each group also agreed that the most important way to reach these goals is to be "honest," "ambitious," and "responsible"; all placed less value on being "imaginative," "intellectual," "logical," and "obedient."

Jews placed relatively greater value on such goals as "equality," "pleasure," "family security," "inner harmony," and "wisdom" and on means that emphasized personal competence: being "capable," "independent," "intellectual," and "logical." The answers of nonbelievers were similar to those of Jews in many ways. Both Jews and nonbelievers placed less emphasis on social traits like "clean," "obedient," and "polite" than did Christians.

Although members of Christian sects differed somewhat, they agreed on two main values: the goal of "salvation" and the importance of "forgiving." Jews and nonbelievers ranked "salvation" last and "forgiving" low. Christians who attended church frequently ranked "salvation" and "forgiving" higher than did those who attended less frequently. Although Christians often saw themselves as loving and helpful they valued these qualities no higher than did Jews and nonbelievers.

Comparison of these claimed values with subjects' reactions to the assassination of King and their sympathy with the racially oppressed, the poor, and student protesters showed that those who valued "salvation" most highly were less compassionate. Those who cherished "forgiving" were no more and no less sympathetic than were those who valued it less.

> In general, a negative relationship between religious values and social compassion was strongest for the Protestant groups, especially the Baptists. But the results for Catholics were somewhat less disturbing: for them there was no relationship rather than a negative relationship, suggesting that for Catholics, at least, religious values are more or less irrelevant as guides to a compassionate social outlet. (Rokeach, 1970, p. 37)

Rokeach's findings led him to conclude that there may be deeply embedded inconsistencies in the Christian religion. Those who value "salvation" highly are anxious to maintain the social status quo; they are generally unsympathetic to the black, the poor, and student protesters, and they do not want their churches to become involved in social and political issues.

Rokeach believes that the Christian institution stresses "thou shalt not"s rather than "thou shall"s. As a consequence, "religious values serve more as standards for condemning others or as standards to rationalize one's own self-pursuits than as standards to judge oneself by or to guide one's own conduct" (Rokeach, 1970, p. 58). He suggests that, to change this state of affairs, a shift of focus to the idea that "salvation" and "happiness" are rewards for "doing good," rather than for "not doing bad," would be effective.

> Such a simple shift of focus, however, will probably require a profound reorganization of the total structure of organized Christianity. And if this reorganization does not come about, the data presented here lead me to propose that men will get along better with their fellow men if they can forget, or unlearn, or ignore what organized religion has taught them about values and what values are for. (Rokeach, 1970, p. 58)

Apparently, however, Rokeach has not told the entire story. Christians are not necessarily bigoted and without compassion. Other research has suggested that there are different types of religious believers and that their social values differ. R. C. Brannon (1970) has suggested that there are two basic types of religious involvement, similar to those that other investigators have postulated but labeled slightly differently. One type stresses "instrumental" involvement in religion. The instrumentally religious person seeks selfish goals and uses religion as a means, rather than as an experience in itself. He therefore accepts no obligations of his religion that are not absolutely necessary. As for prejudice, the instrumentally involved person may also use it to satisfy his own needs for feelings of worth and for status. Attendance at the "right church" can enhance his status and reduce his insecurity about death. Prejudice reassures him that there are groups of people who have lower status than he does, thus bolstering his own insecurity and self-esteem. The relationship between religion and bigotry, then, may simply reflect prior attitudes of individuals drawn to both these modes of adaptation.

On the other hand, there appears to be a group of church-goers with a "devotional" orientation toward religion. They value religious experience as an end in itself; their beliefs become integral parts of their lives and direct their activities. They are more likely to be open-minded and tolerant of cultural and religious differences.

Brannon's research led him to conclude that type of religious involvement is related to racial prejudice. People who use religion for selfish purposes are also likely to use other means, including racial prejudice, for the same purposes.

> More research must be done before we can understand this relationship clearly, but it is not too early to consider some of its implications. We cannot rely on organized religion in and of itself to apply the social doctrine of the New Testament. Only a small minority of church-goers, those with a strong devotional commitment to a religion, have heeded the parable of the good Samaritan. (Brannon, 1970, p. 44)

The Question "Is God Dead?"

Wrenn and Ruiz (1970) have framed the question whether or not God is dead in a less absolute way. They have argued that man's ideas about God are changing and that changes are bound to generate controversy. One change that they see is a shift in emphasis from the divine to the social function of religion. Modern man, according to them, is more concerned with ethics than with the specific worship of a powerful and vengeful deity. He may be experiencing a rebirth of religious interest in a form so altered that it is not yet widely recognized. As examples Wrenn and Ruiz have cited the activities of many young people: hippy philosophy, flower power, and the love movement, all of which have focused on social functions like those of religion. This major cultural shift will, of course, be resisted as are other changes in deep-seated beliefs. We shall turn now to some findings that may help us to understand better the causes of this shift and the part that organized religion has played in it.

SOCIAL RELEVANCE

Americans live in a time of rapid social change, upheaval, and conflict. To the extent that organized religion has something to offer toward resolution of social issues people are inclined to consider it relevant. Churches, with their huge memberships and potential moral authority, could be a potent social force.

R. Stark and his colleagues (1970) have analyzed sermons delivered by Protestant ministers in California, on the assumption that sermons are one of the primary sources from which church members learn Christian values. But, as we noted earlier, members do not seem to internalize these values. According to Stark and his colleagues: "It turns out that whether or not people listen, there is not much to hear. Most sermons rarely touch on controversial moral and ethical issues" (Stark *et al.*, 1970, p. 38). In general, their data revealed that more than one-third of the 1,500 ministers in their survey had never taken a stand on a political issue from the pulpit. In fact, only 25 percent had given at least five sermons on controversial topics within the previous year.

The investigators also examined the relation between religious conviction and speaking out on pertinent issues. Each minister was asked to what degree he believed in five traditional doctrines: "The existence of a personal God, the divinity of Jesus, life beyond death, the literal existence of the devil, and the necessity to believe in Jesus in order to be saved."

The ministers were categorized according to the number of these doctrines that they professed to believe; a small minority (the "modernists") rejected all of them, whereas the majority (the "traditionalists") accepted all of them. Ninety-three percent of the modernists and 42 percent of the traditionalists had taken public stands on political issues; 92 percent of the total sample, however, believed that their congregations would not approve of their taking stands in the pulpit on political issues. The modernists, however, thought that their colleagues in the clergy would approve of such sermons, whereas traditionalists did not think so. But the difference between these groups has still to be explained. The traditionalists did not strongly oppose the use of the pulpit for such purposes. They believed that social ills will take care of themselves when enough men have turned to Christ and that preaching the basic doctrine of the world to come will bring about this conversion.

The results are also disappointing to those who may have looked to the modernist minority to bring about reform. Only 14 percent of the modernists said that they would enter the clergy if they had it to do over, whereas 75 percent of the traditionalists said that they definitely would. Defection from the ministry is high, and recruitment is declining. Furthermore, it is the modernist ministers who seem more likely to drop out. The authors have concluded, "So far as we can tell, Sunday mornings will remain the same, with America's silent majority sitting in the churches, listening to silent sermons" (Stark *et al.*, 1970, p. 61).

THE SEARCH FOR IMMEDIATE EXPERIENCE

Another factor seems to contribute to many people's dissatisfaction with organized religion. Harvey Cox, author and theologian, while being interviewed by G. T. Harris (1970) remarked that religion has lost its quality of immediate experience, of fantasy and festivity; more and more a church is simply an administrative body focusing on the theological past. The church, following the general bureaucratic and instrumental development of society, has become oriented to production and efficiency, to the detriment of "experiencing the non-rational dimensions of existence." Cox's impression was that many people are searching for modes of immediate experience and for activities involving fantasy and festivity because organized religion offers only second-hand experience. People can experience religion only through careful study of those who experienced it long ago. In Cox's words, "I suspect that we have inherited a perverted form of Christianity, deodorized and afraid of smell" (Harris, 1970, p. 66).

As an alternative he has suggested that postindustrial man rediscover festivity. Church meetings need not be somber, quiet, restrictive services, as they nearly always are today. "You know, there is always a John Wesley around to wonder why the Devil should have all the good things. Judson Memorial in New York and a few other churches have had 'revelations,' the nude dancers and psychedelic lights at the altar" (Harris, 1970, p. 66).

Cox thinks that some form of institutionalized religion will survive, though he predicts that denominational Christianity, with its headquarters in urban skyscrapers and branch offices in the suburbs, is fated for rapid extinction. Christ will begin to appear as the

> personification of celebration and fantasy in an age that has lost both. It is a truer sense of Christ than the saccharine, bloodless face that we see painted so often. He was part Yippie and part revolutionary, and part something else. On his day of earthly triumph, Palm Sunday, he rode to town on a jackass. One of the earliest representations of Jesus in religious art depicts a crucified figure with the head of an ass. A weak, even ridiculous church somehow peculiarly at odds with the ruling assumption of its day can once again appreciate the harlequinesque Christ. (Harris, 1970, p. 67)

THE GENERATION GAP

GENERAL OBSERVATIONS

Much has been said recently about the differences between the values of young and old: the generation gap. There is still, however, little objective research to enlighten us about the ensuing difficulties. Wrenn and Ruiz

(1970) have pointed out that the problem is not new. Hieroglyphics from ancient Egypt indicate that the Egyptians attributed their gradual loss of political power to lack of respect among the young for the wisdom of their elders and to the tendency not to honor and obey old laws. Specific issues change from one historical period to another, but the conflict over perceptions of society's needs by the old and new appears to be constant. It is true that sometimes it is more pronounced. Periods of relative quiescence are interspersed with more traumatic periods. Many people (for instance, Wyzanski, 1969) view our current problems as indicative of more profound change than those in some other periods of history. At any rate, the young think that older people do not or will not understand them, that they are unresponsive to new social problems; older people stand by their own ways and view the young as disrespectful or delinquent, without the wisdom that can be gained only through experience of life.

THE PROBLEM

Typical complaints today are aimed at the inconsistencies in the ethics of adults, especially in those relating to sex, religion, race prejudice, and striving for material gain. In our society the material goals of the generation of the 1930s have in many ways been achieved. Young people have been raised to expect material success and the freedom that comes with having money. They have also been raised in a more permissive atmosphere. Correctly or incorrectly, the material goals so common among their parents seem to many young people to have either already been reached, or to be superficially important compared to the human condition generally. Increasing numbers of them are searching for other areas of achievement, areas that have to do with human fulfillment and the experience of direct relationships with themselves and others. We noted some of these new directions in our discussion of religion. In many ways they exemplify the shifting emphasis from material and personal goals to social values and problems.

THE "PRIVATISM" ETHIC

Many young people, of course, do not fit the rebellious and critical adolescent stereotype that is so often presented in the mass media. J. K. Hadden (1969) found empirical support for this observation in a survey of college seniors from every type of campus. His subjects were asked more than 200 questions on various issues. His conclusion was that "the overall student body did not fit into either the liberal scheme of reality or the radical one, but it was also clear that they did not fit into any conservative's dream either" (Hadden, 1969, p. 32). The most striking feature was the growth of a personal orientation, which he has called *privatism*. Apparently the young are developing an ideology of withdrawal from institutions and turning inward upon the self. "This generation rejects meaning or authority outside of the self" (Hadden, 1969, p. 32). It rejects the legitimacy of established institutions and is thus in direct conflict with the "organization slave" philosophy, the dedication to a business establishment that has become so prevalent with the growth of large corporations emphasizing material production.

Hadden has also concluded that students are idealistic and socially aware, perhaps more so than any generation before them, and that their idealism often inspires contempt for the inconsistencies that they observe between the words and deeds of older generations. Adults have been unable to break the institutional restraints that they have imposed upon themselves and to act upon their stated ideals. The young do not, however, completely reject all existing institutions, and their rejection is generally less extreme than the mass media suggest. Furthermore, they appear to lack a realistic sense of what public and social action their ideals imply. It is true that they profess altruistic aims, but their commitment to these aims is less clear, especially when it may conflict with privatism. Privatism is self-centered, anti-institutional, and ambiguous. It posits acute sensitivity to others and a determination to contribute personally to an ideal society.

> The prospects are both ominous and promising. If turning inward to discover the self is but a step toward becoming a sensitive and honest person, our society's unfettered faith in youth may turn out to be justified. However, privatism's present mood and form seem unbridled by any social norm or tradition and almost void of notions for exercise of responsibility toward others. On campus, as in their outside world judgments, students react to any threat to the private preserves of their existence. (Hadden, 1969, p. 33)

C. E. Wyzanski, Jr. (1968), a Federal court judge, has recognized that hypocrisies of the older generation are undesirable and that the young should be heard on the subject of social change. He has also observed, however, that, though it is youth's right to seek change, merely seeking it is not enough; those who bring about change must also take responsibility for its consequences. This sense of responsibility does not seem to him widespread among youth today. The young will build the next "establishment," and it is their very real task to decide what kind of establishment they will have. Recognition of problems is only one step; responsibility for directing solutions cannot be shrugged off.

THE "PREMORAL" GENERATION

Another view of the current generation has been put forth by R. Zoellner (1968). He has focused on morals and ethics in an admittedly subjective view. He believes that the generations under thirty and over thirty have basically different moral attitudes. The older person is morally bound; the younger person is still deciding on "rights" and "wrongs." This difference reflects differences in early training. Zoellner, who was himself approaching fifty when he wrote, views most of his generation as "inheritors of a sick, moribund morality." Younger people have not been subjected to the same training. The ideas of the young are not immoral or amoral; rather, he calls them "premoral." That is, the young are morally concerned and morally aware without necessarily being committed to particular codes. They are therefore more likely to be interested in the actual effects of conduct than in abstract "rights" and "wrongs." An older person, for example, is likely to have an automatic negative response to the idea of premarital sex or smoking pot. But the young person is more likely to examine the probable consequences of each act before concluding whether or not it is wrong. If Zoellner's hypothesis of premorality in the young is accurate, we can more easily understand the discomfort of the older generation. The young may or may not eventually agree with older moral values, but the tension between the generations will grow as the young test out behavior before making such decisions.

We turn now to two current social issues: the nature of education and the use of drugs. Each reflects some of the differences between the younger and older generations in American society today.

THE QUESTION OF HIGHER EDUCATION

Probably the "generation gap" has been more apparent in the protests and riots at colleges and universities than in any other setting. It is common to hear members of the older generation say, "If they don't like their education throw them out; let others take their place who appreciate the opportunity that is offered." Such statements evade the questions about education that are being raised by thoughtful students. When educational institutions that older people have worked so hard to guide are challenged or rejected, their own efforts appear to be held in contempt by the young— the very people for whom the institutions were ostensibly designed. The reaction may be fear or anger, leading to heated remarks. But there may be some justice in complaints about irresponsibility among the young. Those who demand change must also recognize the difficulties and apply their abilities to achieving it responsibly.

THREE PERSONAL VIEWS

CLARK KERR (1967), former President of the University of California, believes that students are seeking two major changes in education. One is greater relevance of course work (especially in the social sciences and humanities) to their lives. To achieve this goal Kerr has proposed less sharp separation of disciplines and a fruitful integration of knowledge that can contribute to the understanding of people and community. Some changes in this direction are already apparent. Interdepartmental courses are being organized. At the University of California at Santa Cruz, for instance, an undergraduate seminar on "aggression" has been conducted by a psychologist, a biologist, and an anthropologist, each sharing special knowledge on the topic.

Students also seem to want to break down the impersonality of large campuses and to develop a sense of community. This desire reflects the humanistic swing away from the corporate image and the quantitative goals of modern Western societies. Kerr has suggested that large campuses be replaced by smaller colleges, each with its own specialty and identity, in which students and professors all know one another. As books have tended to favor centralization around the library, the new technology of programmed learning will favor decentralization. The sense of community can thus be achieved without loss of the intellectual and cultural advantages of the university.

> It could be enormously exciting and incredibly personal. You might have a central campus core and there have the people who prepare the programs for the computers, the big library, laboratories, and graduate students—but no undergraduate students. And then you might set up, maybe ten miles away and maybe up to fifty miles away, little colonies of students with some senior people who are not necessarily expert in anything except helping to lead discussions and perhaps to give some personal guidance and help people along over the rough spots. The small campus is tied in with the central computer for limitless, precise knowledge. The individual student can work in his own room with a computer teaching machine. He can get his information, be corrected, and be graded, too. (Kerr, 1967, p. 29)

RICHARD FARSON (1967) has presented a view not dissimilar from that of Kerr. As a psychologist he has spoken from a humanistic vantage point (see Chapter 6), emphasizing the reaction against industrialized society in which man is a victim of his own institutions, having lost his capacities for love, creativity, joy, sensory and aesthetic appreciation, and interpersonal relations. Cognitive and intellectual skills are most emphasized in education at present; "humanness" must be added. According to Farson, innovation in education will come about as does innovation in any field: through invasion from without and rebellion from within.

The impact of new educational hardware is already being felt. The use of machines is changing the teacher's role, freeing him from burdensome detail to interact on a more human basis with his students. Farson has predicted that the greatest resistance to technical innovation will nevertheless come from teachers, for, even though the machines free them in many ways, they may also fear replacement by the machines. He has also recognized a subtler type of anxiety, aroused by mixed feelings about interacting with students without the protective barriers of record keeping and evaluation.

New social techniques are another outside source of change. They can lead to social systems that are freer, more flexible, and more responsive to the needs and goals of their members. Among these techniques is the intensive use of small groups (see Chapter 6) within an organization to promote individual growth and organizational effectiveness. "Systems engineering," based on analysis of large and complex organizations like educational institutions, forces them to clarify their goals. The aim is to bring about changes that will release the forces of growth within education and thus lead to change.

The "educational game" is a third method. Simulation, or role-playing, exercises can be used in studying important subjects like international relations, national politics, community leadership, business decision making, and home management. Beside the classical academic skills, decision making, communicating, influencing, resisting, and so on can thus be taught, so that the subject matter is integrated in a more realistic and relevant way.

The student revolts that have so shocked the "establishment" are examples of rebellion from within. According to Farson, young people are attempting to create a new kind of society to fulfill a new set of demands; they seek the "right to be fully human, to be honest, to be themselves, to create their own experiences, to discover new experiences, and to control their own lives" (Farson, 1967, p. 35). They are demanding more voice in decisions about what and how they will learn than students did in the past. A few professors, teachers, parents, counselors, and administrators are also experimenting with letting students determine their own educational needs by offering permissive, acceptant conditions where growth may occur.

Farson, nevertheless, has recognized that there are barriers to such change in our culture. In the first place, there is a prevalent notion that education should be drudgery. If it is exciting, fun, or easy, it does not seem "really" educational. There is also an "allegiance to the accustomed." Even though new ideas may seem to be accepted, they are cast into old forms that compromise their advantages. Further, the content of education tends to remain the same as before and the new may be rejected. New areas of learning, including recognizing feelings and emotions, expanding aesthetic sensitivity, acquiring taste and judgment, and developing skills in human relations are not considered "appropriate" according to the old model. Another kind of resistance to teaching interpersonal skills arises from the widespread belief that only certain kinds of professionals (psychologists, psychiatrists) are qualified to deal with emotional or interpersonal relationships, that it is dangerous for individuals not so trained to engage a person on these levels. Such myths were propagated by early psychiatrists. It is therefore understandable that teachers are hesitant, if not openly afraid, to deal with students on an emotional level. Furthermore, our society has an elaborate set of social devices for promoting distance, for keeping emotion and intimacy out of most working relationships. There is a general fear that the machinery of social organization, in the schools, for example, would not function well if people became concerned with one another instead of tending to business.

Farson has concluded his essay with a prediction of what education will be like in the twenty-first century:

> a life-long, richly rewarding experience engaged in because it is fun, joyful, deeply involving. It will be designed to expand and enrich all aspects of human experience—sensory, emotional, and aesthetic, as well as intellectual —and to liberate creativity in all these realms.
>
> And people will be declaring, as they are today, that education isn't nearly as good as it could be, and that something will have to be done about it. (Farson, 1967, p. 35)

Social scientist and social philosopher DAVID RIESMAN (1969) has taken a somewhat less optimistic view of recent student revolts. He has directly questioned some of the values that students have proposed. One of his major theses is that, as adult authority disintegrates, the young become increasingly captive of one another, with a resulting loss of communication between adults and young people. The increasing "separatism" of teen-age culture and the massing of numbers of young people in high schools and colleges partly account for a social condition leading to a new atmosphere that questions the legitimacy of adult authority. As a result adherents of the extreme and simplistic political views of the far right and the far left are exploiting the universities and their students. Riesman has also remarked that some faculty members have gone too far in sympathy with students because that is where the power is. In some instances they are even using student protests for the "settling of scores of their own personal grievances with administrators" (1969, p. 30). Riesman has further questioned the notion of student organization represented by the more militant groups: "Many protests are more like a traffic jam than anything else. They are serious things that build up from smaller ones, and then people search for causes" (1969, p. 30).

Although Riesman has conceded that student dissent may have short-run payoffs, he fears a "backlash" from the outside adult community that will harm university education in the long run. Many adults, especially those in the working class who are less educated and continue to strive for mainly material goals, may be driven to a political position opposing education so that it will be slowed or stopped whether or not such action is necessary.

Riesman has questioned one of the main student beliefs: that feelings in themselves are all important, that learning and wisdom are a hindrance. Those who "proclaim loudest, who wear the biggest hearts on the biggest sleeves" seem to him the ones who matter (1969, p. 64). He believes instead that what matters is how feeling is used and integrated with reason. He also views the "cult of intimacy," the effort to dissolve curriculums in favor of tiny groups "doing their own things" as a danger to the universities' major functions: the preservation of cultural heritage, research and scholarship, and the dissemination of knowledge.

THE ACTIVISTS

The views of Kerr the educator, Farson the psychologist, and Riesman the sociologist are subjective, based largely upon their personal experiences with students and the educational system. Nevertheless, because each is deeply involved in education and highly respected in his discipline, his views should not be taken lightly.

We shall complete our discussion with an examination of an empirical study by R. Flacks (1967).

Flacks was interested in a minority of the student population, the activists in student movements, for he believed that their activities were especially significant. Partly this significance lies in the failure of social scientists to predict the student movement. The social scientists of the 1950s had described the young of their time as uninvolved and almost completely receptive to American middle-class achievement values. Another factor that interested Flacks was the widespread though passive acceptance of the movement's ideals among the total student body.

The findings suggest that student activitists may not have been in revolt. Flacks has concluded that activism has usually been a *result* of parental guidance and value systems, not a challenge to them. From interviews with students and their parents he found that they shared beliefs different from conventional religious, political, and social attitudes. Many activists came from middle- and upper-class families in which both mothers and fathers were well educated, politically liberal, and permissive and democratic in their child-rearing practices.

The activist students and their parents adhered strongly to humanistic values, whereas other students and their parents shared dominant middle-class values: occupational achievement, conformity to peer opinion, and self-control. The humanistic orientation, on the other hand, stresses the development of self-expression and spontaneous responses to the world. Free expression of emotions is believed essential to development of the individual. Activists were raised largely free of restraints, free to experiment and to express themselves spontaneously. They were more interested in aesthetic and intellectual capacities and concerned about the social conditions of others. This humanitarian outlook tended to make their parents politically and socially aware, and they shared their views with their children. When the children arrived at school and discovered that they were expected to pursue goals unacceptable to them, they began to perceive school as regimented and threatening to self-expression and self-direction.

One of the basic value differences between the parents of activists and of nonactivists involved self-expression and self-control. The activists' parents and their offspring believed strongly in the value of self-expression and were very sensitive to beauty and emotion. They also valued intellectual activity and read extensively, especially in philosophy, the humanities, and the social sciences. Finally, they were acutely aware of hypocrisy and revealed "a wish for self knowledge and understanding, concern that one's own personal potentialities—as well as those of others—be realized, rejection of imposed standards of behavior and acceptance of situational ethics" (Flacks, 1967, p. 22).

Activists and their parents disagreed, however, on the value of material wealth and status. The students rejected materialism and status emphatically, whereas their parents did not. It is on this issue that activists' parents were most likely to be surprised by their children's conduct.

Even though students and their parents shared many of the same values, the intensity of student involvement also depended upon other factors besides family background: teachers' influences, the particular colleges that they attended, and the groups that they joined in their first college year.

Flacks' results also suggest that the activists have had some impact on other students to whom protest was new. "Fascinatingly or alarmingly, depending upon one's viewpoint, recent recruits more closely resemble the general student population. They come from widely diverse backgrounds, even from conservative and conventional parents. Protests appeal to an increasingly broadened spectrum of students. The movement is spreading to the dominant culture" (Flacks, 1967, p. 61).

THE STUDENT DRUG CULTURE

For many adults probably one of the most alarming aspects of the current generation has been its acceptance and heavy use of various drugs, which are taken for their psychological effects. The current controversy over these drugs ranges from complete rejection and demands for severe criminal sanctions to complete acceptance as the basis for a way of life. Nearly all our social institutions—schools, churches, mental health agencies, courts, and so on—have been involved in the problem of drug use. Programs of education, treatment, and prevention have been established. Drug use has even become a problem at the grammar-school level in some instances, and there is probably not a high school in the United States in which at least some students do not use drugs illegally. The younger the people who use and abuse drugs, of course, the more shocking and alarming the problem seems to the adult population. Our task here is not to review the entire drug scene but to examine a small group of drug users among college students.

MOTIVES FOR DRUG USE

Probably the most common question that adults ask is why do young people use such potentially dangerous substances? The extremists on either side of the issue offer simplistic answers, but for any one person there may be several reasons why he uses drugs. Blanket explanations of the motives of drug users are inaccurate.

MOTIVES COMMON TO ADOLESCENCE   In the first category we find the familiar adolescent motives of seeking approval from peers and testing new experiences. Drugs of one sort or another (probably whatever is available at the time) are likely to be tried by adolescents who want to "go along with the gang." As we noted earlier there is a rather strong need in adolescence for peer support and approval. The possibility of being called "square" for refusing to try marihuana or some other drug may be sufficiently threatening to cause some adolescents to indulge. The possibility of punishment seems relatively inconsequential.

It is also characteristic for adolescents to seek out new experiences and to try them. Listening and reading help to broaden their world view, but direct experience is frequently much more satisfying. The adolescent may then compare his feelings and perceptions with those of his peers, which may be reinforcing by serving as a basis for social contact and shared experience. Drug use is, of course, not the only type of activity that adolescents try; they seek many kinds of thrills. Fast driving, for instance, is another obviously dangerous but common adolescent activity, as the high percentage of automobile accidents among young drivers attests.

Another characteristic motive for many adolescents is the quest for cosmological or religious experience. The propaganda of the drug culture insists that drugs, especially the psychedelic drugs like L.S.D., will lead to greater understanding of the universe and the meaning of life. Some adolescents try them with corresponding expectations.

MOTIVES INDICATING DISTURBANCE   Other reasons for using drugs arise from personal and social conflict. Many adults also use drugs for their tranquillizing and energizing effects. Some drugs reduce anxiety, and others combat depression. Some people fall into the routine of regulating their emotional levels with drugs, alternating tranquillizers and energizers. The feeling of well-being following drug ingestion can be highly reinforcing to drug use.

Some people appear to take drugs as a form of self-punishment, consciously or unconsciously. A person who feels guilty, for example, may think himself so worthless that he does not deserve a rewarding life. He therefore sets about destroying himself through alcoholism or drug abuse.

Conflict between the adolescent and his family may also be a motive for drug use. Sometimes the child literally sets out to punish his parents for the way that they treat him: When he is arrested his parents will suffer shame.

Some young people use drugs as a means of rebelling against the existing social order and adult authority. They believe man should turn from concentration on material affluence to developing his other capacities. They question other middle-class values, particularly noting the existence of war, racism, divorce, and emotional isolation. Sexual behavior, business ethics, and love are other issues cited as evidence of adult inconsistency. And they question why alcohol is legal as long as marihuana use is severely punished, for the ravages of alcoholism in the United States have been clearly established, whereas there is very little evidence that marihuana creates similar, or as serious, problems.

Furthermore, there is a growing "cult of experience" among the youth of today. Young people seek experience for its own sake and often turn to the mind-altering, or psychedelic, drugs in search of a beautiful world, a nirvana in which immediate experience is more valued than is the future. They recognize the isolation from self and others common in industrial society and seek to break down the barriers through drugs.

THE COLLEGE SCENE

K. Keniston (1967) has analyzed the use of drugs, especially L.S.D., on college campuses, seeking the reasons why some students have turned toward it. Although drug-taking students are a minority, he has argued that they are closely related to the nonusers in that both seem to search for meaning through intense personal experience. His analysis has led him to suggest two particular sources of stress for students. One he has called *cognitive professionalism*, the other *stimulus flooding*.

COGNITIVE PROFESSIONALISM has several aspects. First, there is increasing pressure on young people to attend college if they wish to be successful. Admission standards have thus become more stringent and competition much greater; adolescents are under considerable pressure to perform well academically even before they enter college. Much of their time, effort, and emotional investment go into school work. And more and more schooling is required for future success. Four years of college is often not enough; two to six years of professional or graduate work are now required for many goals. The pressure to achieve academically therefore continues over a long period of time and causes students to become increasingly serious. They have less and less time for fun and experiences that develop other aspects of their personalities. Enthusiasm for the typical pastimes of earlier college generations—sports, fraternities, panty raids, and the like—has declined among the current student population.

Furthermore, the rewards for academic achievement are largely impersonal: either quantitative (grades) or abstract (future expectations). The entire system of higher education requires delaying emotional gratification and leaves students with little outlet other than work. Feelings, moral responsibility, artistic and aesthetic endeavors, and interpersonal growth are neglected.

STIMULUS FLOODING is another phenomenon that Keniston believes a source of stress for students. They are bombarded with excessive stimulation from all sides. They daily encounter objects of all kinds, people of all kinds, and theories of all kinds. There are simply enormous numbers of stimuli that can be received, and it is impossible to attend to all of them. As a defense, students tend to shut many of them out. They select only what they can deal with at any given time and what is most important to their goals. They thus build protective shells around themselves, armor that numbs them to the impact of excessive stimulation. In Keniston's terms they experience *psychological numbing*, which is, of course, adaptive in that it enables the individual to discriminate important stimuli from others. But it may become too pervasive, and then the student begins to feel trapped and unable to make contact with others. He finds that he cannot let in *enough* stimuli to permit satisfactory relations with others.

The combination of stimulus flooding and cognitive professionalism leads to a personality that is almost totally impersonal, concentrated on the quantitative, oriented to the future, and unemotional. But many students wish to search for meaning in other than the professional areas of their lives and to pursue experience for its own sake. Because they have shut themselves off from many experiences they feel a greater need for them. The drug culture may offer a quick way to break through their armor and to obtain the experiences that they seek.

THE DISAFFILIATES   Keniston has suggested that the students most likely to become drug users are the "disaffiliates." Most students have reasons for not using drugs. They may believe that they should reach their goals without the help of chemicals, or they may refuse to use them illegally. They may have strong religious beliefs to deter them; some are afraid of the effects of drugs, and others simply may not have access to them. Disaffiliates, however, have strong motives for using drugs and few for not using them. They generally reject the prevalent American value system in favor of more aesthetic, cultural, and humanistic values; they consider the prevalent system as ugly, cheap, commercial, and dehumanizing. Their resentment is reflected in titles of popular songs ("Nowhere," "Little Boxes," "The Eve of Destruction") and on some popular buttons (the slogan "I am a human being—do not spindle, mutilate, or fold" or Adolf Eichmann's picture labeled "I was only doing my job").

Disaffiliates also feel an intense estrangement from their own experience. They are very aware of the facades and armor that they have built. They seek to destroy these aspects of themselves and others, and drugs offer a means by which to do so. Their estrangement often engenders fantasies of mystical oneness with nature, a coming together of their experience and the world. In drug propaganda, of course, such experiences are said to be commonplace, especially after the use of psychedelic drugs. Standard moral arguments against drug use have little meaning to people estranged from such values. In fact, they may strengthen rebellion and encourage defiant drug use.

THE SEARCH FOR ANSWERS

Assuming that drug use, or at least drug abuse, is personally damaging and has negative effects on personal and social adjustment, what approaches will be most effective in reducing it? The answers are not simple or easy, but some ideas have been offered.

First, it should be clearly recognized that the values and goals of many drug users are not in themselves invalid. Some people may think that they are sought through inappropriate means, but the search itself and the goal may be quite legitimate.

It should also be recognized that drug use reflects a dilemma faced by an entire generation; it is not simply an individual problem. The drug culture is a commentary on our entire educational system and our entire social system, and perhaps it is in these directions that we should take a hard look. What kinds of change will help to meet the needs so clearly expressed by the young? Education, for example, can be made more lively, more creative, and less bound by the values of the American middle class. In the same way other social institutions can be analyzed, questioned, and turned from narrow goals to fulfillment of a broader spectrum of human needs. It is possible that we may thus "cure" our society along with individual members.

In individual counseling it should be acknowledged that drug use is not simply a medical issue: It involves existential, philosophical, and ethical problems, as well. The use of medical findings to scare drug users is generally ineffective. Most of them are quite aware of the physical consequences of drug abuse; in fact, they often know more than their counselors do. But as many legal "drugs" can also cause grave physical harm to users, singling out illegal ones begs the question and convinces adolescents of adult hypocrisy. Their awareness of the legal and medical risks involved in drug use suggests that they have made their choice on the basis of other considerations, probably existential notions. Frequently the most help that a counselor can offer is to lead the user to confront the fact that his use of drugs is a statement about how he wishes to live his life. Once this point is clear the counselor may be able to serve as an example of alternative routes to the goals that the client desires.

SUMMARY

In this chapter we have focused on the late adolescent's choice of a personal system of beliefs and values. Accomplishing this task brings together the various aspects of the individual into an organized identity. Adolescents become interested in values because they are more involved in adult society; because growing independence requires individuality, as well as the ability to "fit in"; and because an independent individual needs a system of beliefs to guide his behavior toward desired goals. Idealism is characteristic of adolescence. The discovery of inconsistencies in adult society leads to vacillation between cynicism and demands for a "perfect world."

Several factors affect the adolescent's choice of values. One is the limitation imposed by the values current in a given culture; few people develop value systems for themselves. In modern cultures six main traditions have been identified: the Judeo-Christian, Hellenic, and existential traditions and the traditions of man as toolmaker, fallen animal, and citizen.

Conflicts also influence the choice of values. Conscience arouses guilt when personal motives like those based on sexual needs and moral goals conflict. The choice between accepting peer-group values and accepting parental values is often another source of conflict. A third is the shift from childhood to adult values, which are frequently quite dissimilar.

Religions account for many of the value systems current in modern societies, but they resist change. Three functions are served by religion. The personal function is to provide aid to the living through belief in a power greater than they, and more concrete financial and social gains are made through church associations. The divine function is to reduce man's incomprehension of the cosmos. The social function is to provide ethical codes that facilitate men's living together. Current dissatisfaction with religion appears to arise from its relative lack of emphasis on the social function. Rokeach (1965, 1970) has studied religious people and has discovered that they tend to be less tolerant of racial and ethnic minorities than are the less religious and the unreligious, which is a paradox in view of Christian teachings. Other research, however, has suggested that there are different types of religious persons. A majority of people seem to use both religion and prejudice selfishly, whereas a minority is committed to the altruistic values taught by the church.

The question "Is God dead?" cannot be answered simply. There appears to be a contemporary shift in emphasis toward the social function of religion, toward religion as a source of guiding principles for social interaction. One survey has revealed that most ministers questioned avoided preaching on social issues. Cox (Harris, 1970) has offered the notion that religion must become more oriented to immediate experience, rather than to the past. Postindustrial man is rediscovering festivity and is no longer satisfied with experiencing religion vicariously through teachings about early Christian figures.

Central to value choice is the generation gap. It is not a new phenomenon and appears in every generation. Its intensity, as well as the particular question and methods of resolution on which it hinges, varies from one historical period to the next, however. Hadden (1969) has noted that "privatism" appears to be gaining prominence among the present generation of young people. They tend to reject outside authority, and their actions are sometimes inconsistent with their professed values. Nor is their recognition of the responsibilities associated with change nearly as apparent as is their fervor in pointing out current problems. Zoellner (1968) has argued that the young are basically "premoral," willing to evaluate the actual consequences of certain conduct like premarital sex and smoking pot before judging it "good" or "bad."

One current issue between the generations is the form that higher education should take. Kerr (1967) believes that students want education to be more relevant to their lives and a sense of community. He has envisioned smaller campuses and integration of currently separated academic disciplines. Farson (1967) has emphasized the necessity for education to expand into personally relevant areas like love, creativity, aesthetic appreciation, and interpersonal contacts. He has recognized blocks and aids associated with this goal. Riesman (1969) has expressed trepidation about student revolts, fearing an adult "backlash" that could retard innovations whether or not they are necessary. He has also questioned some of the dominant values in student dissent.

Empirical research on student activists and their parents has suggested that these students are not in revolt against parental values and guidance but are encouraged by them. That is, activists and their parents share many of the same humanistic beliefs and values. New student recruits to protest movements, however, are coming from homes with dominant middle-class values.

The student drug culture is another example of generational conflict. Several motives enter into drug use (or abuse) among the young. Some are common to adolescents generally: desire for peer approval and for new experiences. Others are more indicative of personal or social problems: the need for tranquillizing and energizing effects, self-punishment, punishment of the family, rebellion against current beliefs and institutions, and participation in a "cult of experience."

Keniston (1967) has explored drug use among college students and has recognized an overemphasis on academic achievement ("cognitive professionalism") and "stimulus flooding" as two sources of stress on the current student generation. The combination may lead a person to focus on the rational and nonemotional aspects of himself to the neglect of interpersonal and affective components. The "disaffiliate" also has a value system opposed to the predominant cultural one. He is led to drugs, especially psychedelic drugs, in his search for solutions to personal and existential problems.

There are no simple solutions to the problem of drug abuse. A realistic assessment of current social institutions and their failure to fulfill human needs is important. Changing our society may be more effective than concentrating on curing individual drug users.

14

Adjustment in Adulthood

A. Introduction
B. Marriage
   1. Reasons for marrying
   2. The young marriage
   3. General indicators of marital happiness
   4. Sexual adjustment
   5. Parenthood
C. Adjustment to Increasing Age
   1. Vocational tasks
   2. Social functioning
   3. Physical deterioration
   4. Self-concept and personality development
D. Summary

INTRODUCTION

Adulthood may be considered the time when previous learning and physiological development culminate in an integrated personality, a personality that accommodates to the adult roles of society. The individual's basic intellectual, emotional, and social skills have been developed. They are ready for further refinement through the tasks of achieving larger goals and integration with society. The purpose of this chapter is to present some of the most important adjustment tasks encountered by adults.

Many investigators have taken adulthood to be synonymous with maturity. Like the concept of normality presented in Chapter 1 maturity is frequently defined as an ideal that is rarely completely attained by anyone. There is a further implication that satisfying the criteria for maturity ipso facto ensures satisfactory adjustment. J. Pikunas has attempted to weld various views of maturity into one conception:

> A mature person structures his environment and is able to perceive himself and others correctly. He has acquired a personal identity and integration of his total personality. In the process of living he attains the developmental tasks for his level of life and develops an ever increasing number of abilities and skills for coping with the present and future. (1969, p. 323)

These criteria suggest a person who is flexible in developing and applying his skills and in forming open and meaningful relationships, one who is guided by a unified system of beliefs and values that help him to fulfill his own design for living. He is able to delay gratification of his own needs in favor of longer-term goals, and he respects the needs of others. The mature individual is thus a contributing member of his community both personally and vocationally. It is plain that only a few individuals, if any, reach high levels in all these areas. Some balanced middle position is more common. Nevertheless, these criteria do furnish crude guidelines permitting the individual to evaluate his own and others' levels of maturity.

We turn now to some of the important tasks that the adult faces as he progresses through life. Again we shall emphasize how accomplishing these tasks affects the ability to adjust.

MARRIAGE

One of the first and most important adjustment tasks that many adults face is marriage. Of all one's personal relationships in a lifetime the marital one will probably have the greatest effects. It can determine whether he judges his life "beautiful" or "ugly." Marriage is also a prerequisite for other important roles: parent, grandparent, in-law, and so on.

Reasons for Marrying

It would be encouraging if most people decided on marriage partners after objectively evaluating their characteristics and interests, attributes that are important in developing mutual respect and long-lasting bonds. Even casual observation reveals, however, that most people do not. Varying degrees of rationality and irrationality are commingled in most such decisions. At one extreme there is the couple who experiences "love at first sight" and marries with almost no mutual knowledge. The relationship may continue to grow, or it may not. At the other extreme there are couples who have long engagements and marry, only to find that they are incompatible.

At our present stage of knowledge we simply cannot accurately predict the success of marriages, except on very gross levels. Commercial enterprises claiming to match couples effectively are nevertheless springing up. Their basic function is to bring together adults who have similar interests and preferences and may therefore be compatible. It is an open question whether their success (assuming that their claims are valid) is simply the result of introducing people who are seeking mates or of their procedures for matching personalities and interests.

Motives for early marriage

Marriages contracted in the middle and late teen years are more likely to end in divorce than are those that begin later. Examination of the reasons why people marry young suggests that external circumstances are often important in their decisions. Premarital pregnancy is a common reason. Other alternatives may or may not be discussed, depending upon the value systems of the people involved, but many decide on marriage, even though they recognize that the circumstances are not ideal. Obvious problems may arise in such a marriage from the start. Both partners feel that they have been forced into the situation. Other difficulties may be exaggerated by this awareness so that realistic solutions are more difficult.

A couple that has already planned to marry before pregnancy is discovered is less likely to have these difficulties. The partners probably have deep feelings for each other and have already assessed their compatibility to some extent. When their first child arrives in less than nine months parents, grandparents, and friends are likely to wink. There is at least tacit recognition that most engaged couples indulge in premarital intercourse and that "slips" are likely to occur.

Another unrealistic reason for marrying young is one partner's (usually the girl's) desire to "get away from home." Even though there may not be overt strife within the family, the child feels pressure to cast off parental restrictions and to become "independent." Marriage often seems the only way to do so. The girl may convince herself that, even though she does not really love her prospective spouse, she will come to love him in time. Marriage provides an avenue of escape from the family, but then the young couple is faced with the difficult adjustments of marriage. It is not uncommon that the partners are disappointed. The freedom that they sought has still not been achieved: The husband (and possibly the wife too) must work hard to make ends meet, there is not enough money to do many of the things that they had hoped to do, and they have little time to enjoy their "freedom." The love that was supposed to grow often does not materialize.

One young woman came to therapy after seven years of marriage; she was seriously contemplating divorce. She had wished to attend college after high school but her family's finances would not allow it. She had little choice but to live at home and take a job that was not particularly meaningful to her. To make matters worse, her parents were quite restrictive. She therefore married a man whom she found acceptable: He was established in his vocation, well mannered, and nice looking. Her basic motive for marriage, however, had been to leave her family. She believed that, because of his positive attributes, she would grow to love him and that their marriage would succeed. But as time passed, she began to realize that as a wife and mother she could not develop her creative and intellectual capacities as she had wanted to. She had kept her dissatisfaction from her husband for years. They had worked on their home together and had taken a great deal of interest in raising their children. To other people they had appeared to be the "ideal couple." Yet all that time she had never loved him and had not gained the kind of freedom that she had wanted initially. When she finally revealed her needs and desires, they had come as a shock to her husband. Quite understandably he could not fathom what seemed to him her rapid change in attitude. The final outcome was a divorce over his protestations.

MOTIVES WITH PROBLEM POTENTIAL

The popular comment "love is blind" suggests another common reason why people marry. As we have already remarked, love is something that science is not yet able to explain adequately, but the reality of the experience can be attested to by nearly everyone. Somehow an extremely positive attraction between two individuals, one that overshadows all other considerations, occurs. Some couples marry solely on the basis of such attraction. They may or may not find their subsequent lives together satisfying, though attraction generally helps. It is not uncommon, however, for one or both partners to "snap out of it" under conditions of adversity and subsequently to wonder why they married in the first place.

Premarital idealism about love as proof against all problems, no matter how difficult, does not always hold up under life's actual stresses. For example, a man and a woman who are deeply attracted may think that they have adequately discussed the problems associated with their different religious beliefs or educational backgrounds before they marry. But after their initial attraction begins to weaken, they may increasingly be driven apart by such differences, and the couple that was so much in love finds itself on the verge of divorce. Although love is compelling, it is still usually wise to evaluate potential sources of conflict in a fairly extended engagement. The couple is then more likely to experience the reality of conflicts and have the opportunity to test its ability to resolve them.

Other people may marry because "it is time." For most people there comes a day when they feel the pressure to marry and to begin families. The pressure itself may come from various sources and may be indirect—perhaps a sense of being left out as friends marry one by one—but the immediate motive is a sense that one should marry *now*. Then an individual is likely to convince himself that his current dating partner or the next person whom he meets is *the* person for him. Although data on the frequency of this motive are not available, probably many people marry at least partly for this reason. Again the typical pattern is to dismiss consideration of potential problems as much as possible and to exaggerate the positive characteristics of the partner. After marriage, however, the initial motive loses strength, and a more realistic appraisal is likely. Newly discovered incompatibilities may then be exaggerated because they are unexpected. Marriage counselors are not unfamiliar with this problem. The client often states it clearly: "He just happened to come along at a time when I was ready to get married. Now it seems a mistake."

THE YOUNG MARRIAGE

Several studies (for example, Cox, 1968) have shown that the age at marriage is inversely related to the success of the marriage. That is, marriages that occur when the couples are young are more likely to break up. The reasons are not entirely clear, but many investigators seem agreed on a number of contributing factors. First, the young couple often finds that its freedom to explore, adventure, and test life is drastically curtailed, which may cause a sense of unfulfillment in one or both partners. Second, one partner may simply outgrow his spouse, so that the relationship is no longer satisfying to him. Third, problems with money are also more frequent among young couples, for young husbands have rarely attained positions high enough to provide substantial incomes. The tensions resulting from the struggle to make ends meet often lead to marital conflict. And, often when a couple does finally reach a satisfactory income level, the partners may already be so disillusioned by the hostilities developed during their period of hardship that it may be too late to repair the marriage. Fourth, the partners are usually not mature enough to fulfill responsibilities, make decisions, and compromise disagreements. The birth of children may intensify these difficulties, and especially in marriages brought on by premarital pregnancy this complication occurs during the critical first year. Children also, of course, add to the financial burdens of a young couple.

All these difficulties have led one author to conclude that "marriage should be postponed until at least the middle twenties for the male and that marriage before the completion of education should be discouraged" (Cox, 1968). It is instructive to examine Cox's view of two types of marriage that are becoming more common: the college marriage and the "independent child" marriage.

THE COLLEGE MARRIAGE

After World War II many returning veterans chose to continue their education, but understandably they did not want to delay marriage. Their lives had already been interrupted by several years of war, and they were ready to settle down to civilian life. Partial financial aid was available through the G.I. bill, and many were mature enough to accept the responsibilities of attending school while starting families. The large increase in married college students in the late 1940s represented a new phenomenon. The typical image of the college student changed as these more serious young men settled down to achieve their educational goals and their wives worked to supplement family incomes. The stability of these couples and the husbands' academic achievements changed the popular notion that marriage and college are incompatible.

Since the 1940s it has become increasingly common for college students to marry and to continue their education. At first, it seemed logical that the wife delay her schooling for a few years to help support her husband, even at the sacrifice of some traditional advantages of marriage. What Cox has called the "altruistic wife syndrome" became common, but the reasoning behind it, however rational it may have seemed, was often not borne out by reality. Two major differences between college marriages after World War II and later ones probably account for the limited success of the latter. Young men today rarely have the extra support of the G.I. bill. Although the money was not much, it could be counted on, and it did help to supplement the wife's earnings. Perhaps more important, college couples today are generally younger and less mature. They do not have much experience with other people or with the necessities of independent living that might help them to handle the tensions arising from their circumstances.

Usually the young wife, probably untrained, must take a fairly low job as file clerk, salesgirl, waitress, or the like. She works most of the day and returns home to face the household chores while her husband settles down to study. Especially if she is intelligent, she may become both tired and bored with her job. The partners' differing schedules permit them to see each other very little. The husband usually becomes interested in his school work, about which the wife is ill informed. Some wives try frantically to work, keep house, and learn as much as their husbands but usually end up simply exhausting themselves. The husband begins to outgrow his wife intellectually, and his campus acquaintances are often more stimulating than she is. Arguments usually become more frequent as she becomes aware of her own stagnation. She is likely to become jealous of her husband's growth, as well as of the girls with whom he associates on campus. The husband may feel inadequate because he is financially dependent upon his wife (in contradiction to the traditional male role); he may feel that his wife is restricting his freedom and suspect her of using her financial support as a weapon of blackmail (which may be true). As Cox has so succinctly put it, "upon graduation day, the wife often receives her own diploma, a divorce subpoena" (1968, p. 50).

This case exemplifies most of the difficulties encountered in college marriages.

The girl was eighteen, and the boy nineteen when they decided to marry. He had entered military service quite young, before he had finished high school. Their romance had been a "whirlwind affair" ending in marriage over the protests of the girl's parents. She was intelligent and hard-working, believed that her husband had great potential, and wanted the best for him. Mainly through her own doing (for he had at first no special achievement goals) she arranged for him to obtain his high-school diploma after an examination, and to be accepted in a four-year college. During the four years that he studied for a degree in pharmacy she worked and borrowed money from her parents. Everything seemed to be going well. Encouraged by his success in undergraduate work, they decided (again mainly at her behest) that he should apply to medical school, and he was accepted. She continued to support them as he became increasingly involved in his medical studies. As he matured intellectually and began to feel the pressure of his dependence upon his wife, however, tensions began to appear. Apparently without her awareness she became more and more domineering, as if to compensate for her own sense of unimportance next to her husband's growth. She became pregnant twice during his first two years of medical school, miscarried both times, and complications required a hysterectomy, which eliminated the possibility of children of their own in the future. He began to spend more and more time with his fellow students and his studies, and she became less and less secure in her position. The marriage finally ended in his third year of medical school. He became involved with a nurse, and she became pregnant. After his divorce he completed medical school, married the nurse, and started a successful career in medicine. After many years the first wife, though she had married twice more, had still not recovered from the humiliation and loss that she had experienced in her first marriage.

Not enough is known to permit prediction that all college marriages will be unsuccessful. If both partners are mature enough to cope with unforeseen difficulties, they will probably be able to grow together or even become closer through facing adversity as a team. Nevertheless, it is important to consider the costs and the present and future rewards of early marriage. Although a young couple can enjoy the companionship and sexual activities of marriage several years before its peers do, it may also miss many interesting opportunities that are part of college and postcollege life. The partners are often cut off from teen-age or young-adult social life, and their chances of attaining leadership in college groups are reduced. Their finances often do not permit as much recreation as other college students and older married couples enjoy. Both partners are likely to miss fulfilling experiences that add zest to living.

THE "INDEPENDENT CHILD" MARRIAGE

Some difficulties of college marriage can be avoided if the parents decide to subsidize the young couple's education (Cox, 1968, p. 53). Modern parents frequently recognize that they may not be able to prevent their children's marriage and may decide to support them until they finish college. Both partners can then continue in school and can share similar experiences while building their intellectual capacities. They have more time together because they do not have to work to meet their financial obligations, or at least they have to work less.

But another kind of problem arises. The children's financial dependence forces them into incongruent roles. That is, they are married as are independent adults yet receiving support as children do. All too often the parents or in-laws think that they are entitled to some control over the young couple's behavior in return for support, which causes resentment in the children. As Cox has put it, "There are very few fathers who, while straining to send several hundred dollars a month to help their child through college, would not object if he decided to use it to buy a new car" (1968, p. 54).

The possibilities for stress are many. It may range from the young man's nagging sense of inadequacy to open parental manipulation of their children's behavior and goals. Probably the best course is for parents to minimize the conditions of their support but to make clear those that they do impose. The children in turn should recognize these obligations and try to fulfill them as best they can.

General Indicators of Marital Happiness

Research findings on marital adjustment and satisfaction are certainly not yet conclusive. There are many difficulties in measuring facets of marriage accurately. Furthermore, most such research has been limited to middle-class subjects; the very rich and the very poor have rarely been sampled. L. J. Bischof (1969) and Pikunas (1969) have reviewed many studies in attempts to discover the factors related to marital adjustment. There appears to be general agreement that satisfactory adult marriages are not very romantic, "happily ever after" relationships. Rather, most couples appear to be willing to work together and to invest themselves in making their marriages work. They change their behavior to meet the challenges presented by close relationships.

SIMILARITIES AND DIFFERENCES BETWEEN PARTNERS

There seem to be some similarities between partners who remain married: similarities in age, social and economic background, talent, skills, religion, and race. Similar backgrounds appear to promote more stable marriages by contributing to fuller understanding and a tendency to enjoy the same activities. Such a couple's value systems are likely also to be rather similar, so that serious disagreements arise less often. One young woman therapeutic client exemplified the difficulties that can arise from differences in social, economic, and educational levels. A college graduate with intellectual interests, she had married a man from a lower socioeconomic background with only a high-school education. He would not, or could not, become interested in intellectual matters. In order not to hurt him she avoided bringing up such matters for many years and tried to relate to him in areas with which he was familiar and to participate in activities (some of which they both enjoyed) of his choosing. After several years, however, she could no longer suppress her desire to expand intellectually, and she enrolled in graduate school nearby. Her husband objected to her spending time away from him, and the disruption eventually led to divorce.

On the other hand, there is some evidence that different needs may deepen a couple's relationship. If one partner is dependent and the other strives for independence, their complementary needs may promote marital adjustment. If both have a strong dependency need, however, there may be a continual struggle over who is going to do what for whom. It is unlikely that either will feel that his needs are being met.

Current findings thus suggest that compatible couples are alike in some ways but not in others. Similarities in general background characteristics seem to promote positive marital adjustment; similarities in personal needs do not necessarily, although some, like a need for orderliness, may.

RELATIONS WITH PARENTS

Some findings have suggested that a person's experiences in his own family are related to the subsequent happiness of his marriage. Especially, there is a positive relationship between happiness in his parents' marriage and happiness in his own. An individual who feels close emotional ties with the parent of the opposite sex and does not have conflicts with either parent tends to make more satisfactory marital adjustments. These findings support the notion that children behave as do their parents, in their affectionate relationships as in other areas, because of learning and identification.

REASONS FOR DIVORCE

Marital unhappiness does not always lead to divorce. Some couples live together in misery for many years, whereas others separate for what seem to be minor reasons. Divorce is often contrary to moral or religious values and is therefore not a clear indicator of marital discord.

The reasons why people divorce are not simple to describe. Each instance must be examined individually. Nevertheless, Bischof (1969) has listed some of the more common variables that appear in conjunction with divorce.

Infidelity is often the direct stimulus for divorce proceedings. It may follow from many causes: a sense of unfulfillment in marriage, an exaggerated need to prove one's sexual identity, the discovery that another person is more compatible than one's mate, and so on. Regardless of cause, finances may largely determine whether a couple files for divorce or accepts a "living arrangement" that accommodates the extramarital relationship. Difficulties in breaking old ties and habits, emotional stress on the couple and other family members, and difficulties in separating from children and explaining divorce to them may also stand in the way.

Divorce seems most frequent at two particular stages of marriage: in the first two years and when the couple reaches its early forties. Early divorces usually result from an inability to cope with the initial problems of living together, financial strain, or disillusionment about partners. When a couple reaches its forties it can often afford a divorce, and the children are old enough not to suffer greatly from it. The husband may recognize that his physiological prime is passing and may seek out another woman to reassure himself that he is still the man that he used to be. This tendency is reflected in the fact that divorced men often marry women who are younger than their first wives are. On the other hand, the woman in her forties may feel that her personal worth is denied when her children no longer need her. She may therefore try to "mother" her husband, making demands on him that tend to alienate him. The woman, of course, may also seek the divorce for similar reasons or in response to her husband's behavior.

SEXUAL ADJUSTMENT

American culture places great emphasis on sex, both concealing and revealing it. It is a commonly acknowledged fact that advertisers recognize the importance of sex in drawing attention to their clients' products; recently magazines specializing in open sexuality have been thriving. It is little wonder that many individuals consider sex one of the most important factors in a personal relationship. The adolescent or young adult who is experiencing emotional arousal associated with sexual behavior for the first time is especially prone to letting sex overshadow all other considerations. Not infrequently young married couples, who may be free for the first time to experiment sexually without trepidation, find sex the focus of their relationships. Difficulties in sexual performance may have devastating psychological effects. In fact, pressure to perform well sexually is frequently a major source of stress that leads to performance difficulties.

Most couples that have been married for some time will agree that their initially active experimentation eventually gave way to a more stable and less active sex life. As one psychologist has put it:

> It should come as no surprise to any intelligent thinker about human behavior that sexual orgasms and sexual play diminish as the human gets older. So do most things. The overt form of sexual behavior may be considered to be supplanted by everyday intimacies. It is not a question of sublimation but of embellishment, diversifications, and greater subtlety. As the adjusted husband and wife well know, marriage is not one long sexual orgy, but marriage is mortgages, PTA meetings, parental pressures, and the like. (Bischof, 1969, p. 91)

Nevertheless, even though sex may receive disproportionate attention in our society, sexual compatibility *is* important in marriage, as the damaging effects of frigidity or impotence attest. Life can go on, perhaps with little disturbance if little importance has been placed on sex from the beginning, but the closeness and satisfaction associated with mutual sexual experiences do add to the fulfillment in marriage.

SEX DIFFERENCES

Some differences between male and female sexual behavior and associated cultural expectations have been examined in earlier chapters.

Development of identity is one area of such differences: Male identity is focused on achievement, assertiveness, and independence, whereas female identity emphasizes relatedness and social competence. These attitudes are generally reflected in sexual behavior, though we should always be aware that there is a wide range of individual variation. Men usually expect, and are expected, to be the aggressors in sexual activities. Females are generally less dominant and more passive. This broad generalization is not meant to suggest that individuals who vary from these patterns are abnormal or poorly adjusted.

Men, especially young men, are more likely to be sexually aroused by a wide range of stimuli than are women. Furthermore, they are likely to become aroused more quickly. Again individuals vary widely, however.

Although a man is likely to enjoy sexual activity for itself, a woman may have greater need for affection along with it. This difference follows naturally from the differences in identity formation.

We have also seen that the sex drive is greater in males than in females, especially during adolescence. (This difference does not necessarily reflect a biological difference between the sexes but may result from social training.) Although the drive reaches its peak earlier in men than in women, the general level of activity remains at least as high in men as in women as the years pass. Nevertheless, there are some indications that women's sex drive remains fairly constant during the adult years and increases slightly in middle age. After a couple has been married a long time, if the man's drive level decreases and his wife's remains constant or increases, problems may arise. Because a man's sense of worth is often associated with his sexual prowess he is likely to feel inadequate when his wife requires more sexual attention than he can comfortably give. The result may be conflict and marital disintegration.

The middle-aged male does not attain erection as easily or as spontaneously as he did when he was younger, nor does he reach orgasm as readily. He may find it necessary to indulge in a greater variety of sex play in order to reach full erection and orgasm; some of these activities his wife may consider evidence of instability or disgusting. Her negative responses may threaten her husband's sense of masculinity and cause him to seek satisfaction with another partner. On the other hand, a wife's inability to arouse her husband as she could when she was younger can generate insecurity about her own sexual attractiveness. Her husband's reduced responsiveness and requests for unfamiliar sexual activities may lead to confusion and conflict.

Aside from obvious anatomical differences between men and women, the main differences in sexual behavior can be accounted for by cultural training. To say that women in general are more likely to be inhibited and to harbor guilt over sexual relations is to miss the point of individual differences. Although it appears true that cultural training of women generally emphasizes sexual restrictions more than it does for men, some women do develop much freer and more sensible attitudes toward sexual behavior than do some men. The individual's response to his previous training is the crucial factor. There are men, for example, who are sexually impotent because of anxiety generated by their childhood training and perhaps more women who are frigid for the same reasons. The freer partner of any couple should be sensitive to the possible psychological effects of insisting on equally free responses from the other. Discussing the problem in an easy and open manner and showing understanding are probably as effective in overcoming difficulties and promoting future sexual compatibility as is any other technique. Once the difficulty is openly recognized a "slow and easy" approach should lead a couple to an eventually satisfying relationship.

TECHNIQUES OF SEXUAL AROUSAL

In the past social attitudes have dictated that the topic of arousing techniques be omitted from textbooks. Considering the importance of sexual adjustment and the increasing social freedom to discuss sexual matters, the author has concluded that sexual technique merits free discussion. Probably every imaginable means for bringing about sexual arousal and enhancing sexual intercourse has been tried. There is no prescribed way in which any particular couple or individual can achieve maximum arousal and orgasm. Probably the only sensible basic rule is that both partners should be comfortable within their value frames. From a psychological, though not always a legal, point of view, any sexual activity between a husband and wife is acceptable as long as both find it rewarding and beneficial to their relationship. But investigators of sexual behavior agree that some techniques generally produce positive effects.

J. L. McCary (1967) has begun his discussion of sexual techniques by stressing the importance of making oneself as attractive as possible to one's partner at all times. He does not mean that a person must be beautiful but that he should be neat and clean at all times.

> A man who is overweight, chronically unshaven, and slovenly dressed, and whose breath reeks of tobacco or alcohol, can hardly expect to be considered a desirable bed partner—even after a session with shower, toothbrush, and razor late in the evening, because his wife's memories of his earlier unattractiveness will simply detract from the excitement of the experience. Similarly a woman who neglects to make up her face, sits around home in bathrobe and curlers, allows herself to become significantly overweight or underweight, permits even faint urine, vaginal, or underarm odors to emanate or does not often shave her legs and underarms, is setting the stage for a loss of respect, admiration, and even love; sexual failure cannot be then far behind. (McCary, 1967, p. 148)

McCary has also suggested that personal characteristics like courtesy, kindness, and sensitivity to one's partner's needs are important. He has recommended that the partners start with clear and free communication about their likes and dislikes in techniques so that they will be more likely to satisfy each other.

Aside from such personal considerations, various approaches and settings can contribute to satisfactory sex relations.

> Too often sexual acts become ritualized, stale, and unimaginative, engaged in only to provide relief to physical urgency. Couples who wish to preserve delight and vigor in their sexual interaction will work as consistently on this aspect of their marriage as on any other. . . . A husband who impulsively sweeps his wife into his arms in the middle of a happy afternoon and carries her off to the bedroom and makes wild love to her, or the couple who occasionally has sexual intercourse while taking their shower, or the wife who surprises her husband by appearing in his study wearing nothing but a smile and [carrying] two cold, very dry martinis—these couples are not likely to find sex dull even after years of marriage. (McCary, 1967, p. 149)

Techniques of sexual arousal all focus on areas of the body called "erogenous zones." These areas have comparatively high concentrations of nerve endings. Although individuals vary in the particular areas that they find most arousing, men and women have essentially the same ones. Stimulation of the erogenous zones is most likely to arouse sexual desire. The most sensitive areas are, of course, the genitals and the areas immediately around them, including thighs, buttocks, and abdomen. Sensitive areas not associated with the genitals are the breasts (especially the nipples), the arm pits, the small of the back, the shoulders, the neck, the earlobes, the scalp, the eyelids, and especially the mouth, the tongue, and the nose.

It is beyond the scope of this book to go into detail about various techniques of arousal. There are excellent marriage manuals (for example, McCary, 1967) that do so. Basically all techniques incorporate stimulation of erogenous zones by hands or mouth or both; if the partners can be open with each other about their desires, they will discover which methods, timing, and areas of the body are most exciting to them.

There are also many possible positions for sexual intercourse. Again, the basic rule is that any position should be considered acceptable as long as it is agreeable and mutually satisfying to the partners. Although the laws in some states restrict certain types of sexual behavior, even between man and wife, an objective psychological appraisal does not justify them. This textbook is not intended to encourage people to break the laws (though most of them are rarely if ever enforced today), but it seems important to note that they are based upon the superstitions and moral prejudices of the past. McCary has expressed the opinion of most investigators of human sexuality:

> Most of the "shoulds" and "should nots" of sexual behavior are contingent on—and only on—the mutual pleasure, comfort, and satisfaction of the two people involved. Each must be just as aware of the needs of his spouse as he is of his own before coition can be truly successful. Therefore, experimentation and variation in coital positions assume major importance in the effort to achieve an optimal fulfillment of the rights and desires of each partner. (1967, p. 162)

Many illustrated books (for instance, Harkel, 1969) demonstrating the variety of coital positions are on the market today. There are four basic positions and many possible variations of each. The four positions are man above, woman above, side by side, and rear entry.

PROBLEMS IN SEXUAL FUNCTIONING

It is no secret that sexual activity has been associated with taboos, restrictions, and guilt in American society, as well as in others. Although physiological difficulties may sometimes cause sexual inadequacies, most result, even in elderly people, from the association of anxiety with sexual activity.

More attention has probably been directed toward ineffective sexual responses in men because of the importance of virility in masculine identity and the fact that intercourse is almost impossible if the man does not attain erection. Failure in sexual activities is usually devastating to a man's identity. His concern nearly always creates even greater problems because of the resulting increase in his anxiety about sexual encounters. As our culture places less emphasis on the woman's capacity for sexual satisfaction and because intercourse can be completed whether she is aroused or not, there is a tendency to be less concerned about the quality of her response. Nevertheless, if either partner is not finding sexual fulfillment his marriage loses a positive part of its potential.

The most common sexual difficulties in man are inability to achieve erection or to maintain it until orgasm, ejaculation just before or very quickly after entering the vagina, and inability to reach orgasm even with an erection.

The most common problem for women is frigidity. A woman may never or rarely achieve climax during sexual intercourse, or she may feel some discomfort or disgust about sexual activities in general. The amount of difficulty varies widely in specific cases.

The classical insight psychotherapies, in which therapists attempt to discover unconscious reasons, have not been very successful in overcoming such sexual problems. The comparatively new approaches of behavior therapy (see Chapter 7) are achieving much greater success. W. H. Masters and V. E. Johnson (1961, 1965) have treated couples experiencing difficulties in their sexual relationships. Their approach requires the couple to attend their institute for a period of eight to ten days (unmarried couples may attend, and prostitutes are furnished for some single people).

The therapist begins by taking a complete medical, sexual, and psychological history of each partner. He interviews each partner alone and then the couple together. From all this material he obtains an idea of the sexual problem. Usually the roots can be traced to childhood learning from puritanical parental attitudes, which have been further reinforced during adolescence. Masters and Johnson concentrate wholly on the present in their therapy, however. They prescribe practice sessions at the clinic and homework assignments. They establish short-term goals based on progress each day. Beside trying to promote the partners' comfort with each other's bodies, they also try to change attitudes that detract from effective sexual performance.

For example, the woman who is afraid of losing control is threatened by erotic arousal and unwittingly turns herself off. She may shift her positions or push her husband into a different one that terminates the stimulation leading to orgasm. A woman whose spouse does not satisfy her may stretch out on the bed and challenge him through her gestures, posture, and even sometimes words: "Okay, now give me an orgasm. I dare you. You failed last time, and you're going to fail again tonight." This attitude, of course, not only interferes with her own eroticism but is also likely to arouse anxiety in her partner and thus decrease his ability to perform. A man may take a similar attitude toward his wife, and by insisting on greater responsiveness accomplish nothing but distress, which reduces her response even more.

The most common fear among men is "fear of performance." Many men have been led to believe that they should be potent no matter what the situation, the time, and so on. This attitude engenders fear in a man when he fails to have an erection or loses one in a particular situation. The man who can "laugh it off" and expects failures of this sort once in a while usually regains his potency in a very short time. The man who responds with horror is, however, likely to develop strong anxiety in response to sexual stimuli. This response may effectively reduce his chances for erotic arousal. He begins to worry more and more about his sexual performance and becomes less and less involved in the actual sexual encounter. Only his body is in the bed, but his mind is outside watching, and waiting fearfully, for his penis to fail to rise.

Masters and Johnson usually assign exercises that help the partners to become more comfortable with nudity and free exploration of each other's bodies. As treatment progresses the couple's assignments bring them closer to satisfying coitus. The results of this approach have been highly encouraging: approximately 90 percent success with couples treated.

SOME SEXUAL MYTHS

Considering the uneasiness about sexual matters in our culture, it is not surprising that many myths and fallacies about sexual behavior have grown up. A long list of them has been presented by McCary (1967). We shall describe only a few of the most common ones here.

THERE IS A MYTH THAT EACH PERSON IS ALLOTTED A LIMITED NUMBER OF SEXUAL EXPERIENCES, that just so much sexual fluid and so many orgasms are "built into" the body; if he uses them up too quickly his sexual activity will cease while he is still young. This idea is completely false. The male does not "run out" of semen or sperm. In a healthy body they are easily and quickly manufactured. Nor will a woman become frigid from having too many orgasms. In fact, results show just about the opposite (Masters and Johnson, 1966). People who are sexually active throughout their lives tend to be active longer into old age. Individuals differ in their sex drives, but there is no evidence that a person who is sexually active "runs out" of sexual capacity.

THERE IS ANOTHER MYTH THAT THERE ARE TWO KINDS OF FEMALE ORGASMS, VAGINAL AND CLITORIAL   Masters and Johnson have discovered that this notion is invalid. Only stimulation of the clitoris produces orgasmic responses in women. The stimulation may be direct manual or other manipulation, or indirect kneading of the tissue around the clitoris by the penis during coitus. Psychoanalysts have assumed for years that only "mature" women have vaginal orgasms and that clitoral orgasms are a sign of sexual inadequacy. These psychoanalytic notions probably reflect the cultural training of women, rather than sexual inadequacy or immaturity. That is, vaginal penetration better fulfills psychological needs and thus produces more gratification for some women than does clitoral stimulation alone, though other women prefer direct stimulation of the clitoris. The guilt and sense of inadequacy experienced by many women who do not detect much difference between orgasms associated with penile penetration and with manual manipulation of the clitoris are unnecessary. In fact, such feelings can disrupt sexual functioning. Women vary widely in their orgasmic responses. Some have multiple orgasms, others may have orgasms similar to those of men, and still others are ranged between.

THERE IS STILL ANOTHER MYTH THAT INTERCOURSE IS NOT ADVISABLE DURING MENSTRUATION AND MAY IN FACT BE DANGEROUS This belief appears to be based on ancient notions that menstrual fluids hold unusual powers, most of them dangerous. More recently cultural emphasis on cleanliness and the puritanical idea that the sex organs are dirty have reinforced this myth. Except for discomfort there is no reason for people not to engage in coitus during menstruation. The woman's sex drive normally does not diminish, menstrual blood is perfectly harmless, and there is no danger that penile penetration will damage the woman.

FINALLY, THERE IS THE MYTH THAT A MAN WITH A LARGE PENIS IS MORE POTENT THAN IS ONE WITH A SMALL PENIS AND THAT A LARGE PENIS IS MORE SATISFYING TO WOMEN Any effects associated with the size of the penis in either sex must be explained by psychological expectations. Research has shown that the size of the man's penis has practically no relation to his ability to satisfy a woman sexually. There are exceptions: A woman may believe this myth and therefore be more aroused, or the penis may be large enough to cause the woman pain. Women vary in their responses to internal pressure from the penis; some experience added pleasure when the cervix is stimulated, and others report pain. It is true, however, that a penis with a larger circumference is more likely to knead the woman's external sexual tissues during coital movements, which may enhance her erotic pleasure.

AGING AND SEXUAL FUNCTION

As a person grows older there are some changes in sexual functioning. They need not be disturbing unless an individual has a strong desire to "hang on" to youth and refuses to face the fact that life is passing.

As we have noted, the male sex drive tends to decline very gradually after adolescence. J. Bernard (1956) has noted that middle-aged men appear to have integrated sex into their total personality more completely than younger men have. In selecting a mate, for instance, a middle-aged man is more likely to love a woman before she becomes a sexual partner, whereas a young groom loves his wife partly because she is a sexual object. Other qualities are more important to the middle-aged man, and sex becomes an area of less concern. We do not know whether this change is a sign of fading virility or of greater wisdom in appraising a potential partner. It is probably a combination of both. For females there is generally less focus in their identities on sexual performance. They are therefore more likely to consider other factors important in their youth and in later years. As we noted above, however, they may respond with insecurity when they fail to arouse their aging mate.

Men pass through a climacteric that eventually ends in sterility but not necessarily in impotence. The physiological changes occur very slowly. The climacteric may progress over three decades—the forties, fifties, and sixties and sometimes even into the seventies. In contrast to the female menopause, the male climacteric is accompanied by few physical discomforts, and the overall effects on behavior and attitudes are less striking. It is therefore unlikely that emotional problems associated with middle age in men are a direct response to physiological changes. They usually result instead from fear of a loss of virility, which is often important to masculine identity. It is not unusual for middle-aged men to go through periods in which they seek to recapture their youth by seeking young female companions. Although it is often true that a new sexual partner will have a temporary stimulating effect on a man's sex drive, the linear decrease in his drive does not alter significantly. "In short, the middle-aged man is kidding himself if he feels he has regained his youthful vigor in the bedroom" (Bischof, 1969, p. 94).

Masters and Johnson's experiments (1966) have added to our knowledge of sexuality in older people. Most of their information has been obtained through actual observation of intercourse, but some of it has come from interviews. A subsample of thirty-nine men and thirty-four women fifty-one years old or older was included in their observational sample, and sociosexual histories were taken from another 212 older men and 152 older women. Because of the limited size of the subsample the findings should be regarded as mere indications, rather than as established biological facts. Nevertheless, the general conclusions are worthy of consideration.

THE FEMALE   Masters and Johnson have concluded that there is no specific time limit on female sexual activity. A healthy older woman is likely to maintain a normal sex drive. Her capacity for sexual activity may, of course, be indirectly reduced by all the psychological and physiological changes associated with aging. Erection of the nipples during coitus follows the same pattern as in younger women, but the degree of erection is usually less. The "sex flush," a change in skin color observed in younger women as they approach orgasm, is less common in older women. Postmenopausal women may complain of a need to urinate immediately after coitus and of burning sensations accompanying urination. Although there is wide variation in clitoral response during coitus in women of all ages, postmenopausal women continue to show the patterns typical of younger women. Women over forty experience the same vaginal contractions during orgasm that younger women do, but the duration is usually shorter.

It seems that the aging woman's main adjustment is to a slower response to sexual stimulation and the need for more stimulation in order to achieve orgasm. Nevertheless, there is evidence that increased sexual desire and activity occur during the late forties and early fifties. Some women enjoy a "second honeymoon" phase that may be far more satisfying than was the first honeymoon.

Sexual capacity is associated with regularity of effective stimulation and the opportunity for coital activity. Without them sexual desires may decrease. Masters and Johnson's interview material further supports this notion. Women who have had happy, well-adjusted, and stimulating marriages usually pass through menopause and the subsequent period with little or no interruption of their interest in sex or of the frequency of their sexual activity.

THE MALE Wide variation is also common among men over sixty. Furthermore, each individual varies in his capacity and performance. In men sexuality in old age is also related to the consistency of previous sexual expression. If a man is not stimulated for long periods of time his sexual responsiveness may disappear. As long as physical incapacities do not intervene and sexual activity is maintained through the years, men can continue some form of active sexual expression into the seventies and eighties. But sexual adequacy in men does sharply decrease after fifty.

The aging man takes twice to three times as long to have an erection as does a young man, regardless of the technique of stimulation. Furthermore, full erection may not occur until just before ejaculation, especially in men over sixty. The pressure to ejaculate and consequently the distance that the seminal fluid is expelled decrease by about half as men pass fifty. Ejaculation usually occurs in a single stage, rather than in the two stages observed in younger men. After ejaculation the sixty-year-old man's penis becomes flaccid within seconds.

Masters and Johnson have remarked that the most constant factor associated with loss of sexual interest and performance is "monotony in the sexual relationship." This factor was not reported, however, for the female.

Masters and Johnson's interview sample suggested several additional reasons for decreased ability of older men to engage in sex. They may be over-concerned with occupational achievement and accumulating wealth, or physical and mental fatigue may reduce both sexual appetites and sexual activities. Excessive consumption of alcohol or food seems to lessen sexual arousal; very high alcohol consumption seems to produce complete impotence and absence of sexual desire. Fear of failure is another important factor. It is closely associated with cultural emphasis on male aggressiveness and sexual potency. A man may voluntarily withdraw from sexual activity completely after experiencing impotence, no matter what the circumstances, for he may feel safer to celibate than facing the shattering experience of inadequacy.

All these data suggest some adjustment difficulties. The close association between a man's sense of worth and his sexual prowess is clear. Recognition that he is approaching old age, coupled with an actual change in his sexual performance, can arouse great anxiety about his self-image. When his wife's sexual behavior changes little or her drive increases, his anxiety response may be even stronger. He may seek sexual stimulation outside marriage or withdraw from sexual activity and compensate by increasing his efforts in other areas. If his wife is unaware of these possibilities, she may try to shame him into having sex, which only increases his personal difficulties and further strains their relationship. If, however, both parties are able to treat sexual activity openly they can face natural changes. They may then continue to enjoy their sexual relationship, developing techniques to add variety and increase stimulation.

PARENTHOOD

The importance of parents in a child's development and how parents respond to their growing children have been described in earlier chapters. In the middle years the parents' interest in child care and training give way before the child's growing independence. A mutual exchange between parents and child may slowly develop as the child enters adult roles.

THE EMPTYING NEST

Many parents enjoy their children more and more as the latter move through adolescence. Parents and children come to a mutual understanding and appreciation of each other's interests and activities. Many parents regret that adolescence is so short, for their offspring too soon complete their education or job training and move away to establish their own families and individual lives. Some investigators call this period the "time of the emptying nest" (Pikunas, 1969). Parents who have not prepared for their children's departures may find themselves in a void. They may feel that their own lives have lost meaning and that their usefulness has ended. They may blame each other or expect each other to fill the void. Conflicts that have been masked or put aside in favor of their children's development may now come into the open. The couple may be directly faced for the first time with their own difficulties.

Another result of the emptying nest is that parents may almost inadvertently and without awareness depend upon their children for personal gratification. The newly independent child may feel that his parents are demanding too much of his time. Vacations for him and his wife may have to be forgone in favor of expected visits to their parents. In fact, the parents may let it be known that their children owe them visits in return for all the years spent in raising them. Such demands almost invariably lead to trouble between children and their parents.

Other conflicts are also common. Many in-law problems can be traced to aging parents' attempts to generate guilt in their children so that they pay more attention to their parents. A son may, for example, feel obligated to spend much of his time with his parents. His wife, who may wish to visit her own parents for the same reasons, is understandably distressed. The young people begin to dislike each other's parents, and marital conflict usually follows. Although many young couples try to hide their negative feelings from in-laws, such feelings are usually detected. The needs of the lonely aging couple are thus intensified by fear of emotional abandonment, and they increase the pressure on their children. The entire problem grows worse.

Parents who have anticipated the emptiness after their children leave are more likely to develop interests to replace child-oriented activities. They now have the time to participate in community organizations and civic efforts that can stimulate personal development and feelings of self-worth. They can develop closer relationships with their mates, relatives, and friends and enjoy hobbies, travel, and social functions. They are thus usually also able to develop more rewarding adult relationships with their children.

Our discussion so far suggests that stress inevitably follows when children leave home, but often the opposite is true. Many couples look forward to their freedom, knowing that they will have the chance to develop more fully their personal attributes and interests and to enjoy their mutual companionship. They can probably afford to do many things that they could not do earlier. The middle-aged couple may discover an exhilarating freedom that cements its relationship and opens opportunities for new relationships with people of similar interests and attitudes.

GRANDPARENTHOOD

From the forties on grandchildren begin to arrive. Grandma and Grandpa have been traditionally considered benign, gray-haired angels, but this picture is changing (Bischof, 1969). The extended family is becoming less and less a reality in American culture. Grandparents are increasingly "modern." They maintain well-kept homes, travel widely, and associate with their own friends. They are more likely to be "swinging" people.

> There is less and less of the so-called family reunion than there has been in the past. Supplanting this is the gathering of a single family unit usually during vacation time and under the auspices of the grandparents who wish to bring all the children together for one short, hectic, frenetic, and reacquaintance time. Neutral ground provides less disruption of the pattern of any single family involved. Not too infrequently the grandparents may pay a large proportion of the vacation resort bill. (Bischof, 1969, p. 129)

Grandchildren may simply add to the fulfillment of a couple's expanding lives during the middle and late years.

An older couple that seeks fulfillment through its children, however, may also make demands on the grandchildren. Grandparents may make their children feel guilty for not bringing the grandchildren to see them oftener. They may even offer bribes to the grandchildren or to their own children to encourage visits. Many grandparents are financially able to provide material pleasures to the grandchildren, but what could be free, pleasurable giving may turn to manipulation under some circumstances. For example, the wife's parents visit her unexpectedly and may take her shopping, replenish her wardrobe, and purchase furnishings for her home. At their own home they may keep exciting and expensive toys for the grandchildren. The child can use them if he visits, and therefore he may press his parents to take him to Grandma's house.

If grandparents really want to help their children through the financial stresses of early marriage, they will not attach "strings" to their gifts. Instead of taking their daughter on a buying spree, for example, they can simply send her a check with their blessings. Arrangements to visit can be made ahead of time, so that they are convenient for all. Toys can be given to grandchildren on birthdays and other holidays, but keeping them at Grandma's house suggests selfish motives.

Open communication should exist among all parties when it comes to financial help and gifts. Many young men dislike accepting money, which may imply that they are not meeting the needs of their families sufficiently. It is usually best for the grandparents to discuss their children's needs realistically with them to determine how they can help.

The illnesses and infirmities associated with old age can create problems for the aging couple's children, who feel obliged to help but at the same time must struggle to find the time and sometimes the money that is needed. Nor is it easy for an elderly person who is ill, and often frightened, not to lean on his children for support. Each family must discuss the matter and try to find a solution that will involve the least hardship for all, especially if the elderly person has experienced mental deterioration and cannot join in rational decision making.

If the older person has contacts with others his own age it is easier for him to accept gracefully the decline in his physical and mental powers. Obviously, family strains will then be reduced. Yet elderly people tend to isolate themselves unnecessarily because of their inability to accept aging, increasing their need for support from immediate family members.

One elderly gentleman who remained in good physical health through his early seventies was very interested in golf. For many years he and his friends had enjoyed close companionship through their golfing associations, and he prided himself on being the oldest active member of the local country club. His inability to accept aging, however, had been apparent for several years. His skills had gradually declined, and his scores had slowly risen. But he could not admit that his poor scores were the result of physical changes. He tried new clubs, blamed occupational worries, and so on. In his mid-seventies he developed mild heart trouble that required him not to overexert himself. But he continued playing golf as he always had until one hot day his friends had to help him back to the clubhouse and drive him home. After that he played only a few times, and it was obvious that active participation was too strenuous for him, especially on very warm or very cold days. His friends pleaded with him to ride around with them in a golf cart until he was tired. They tried unsuccessfully to persuade him to join them for lunch and postgolf activities. He could not, however, accept dependence upon them. His answer to their requests was, "If I can't drive myself to the course and play the way I used to, I won't go at all." His major social activity thus ceased completely. Increasingly he turned inward, became more and more concerned with his physical well-being, and finally almost completely isolated himself from others.

ADJUSTMENT TO INCREASING AGE

In this section we shall examine some of the more important adjustment tasks associated with adulthood. Four broad functional areas—vocational development, social development, physical deterioration, and changes in self-concept and personality—are included. We shall discuss each of these areas in relation to four rather arbitrary phases of adulthood: early, middle, and late adulthood, and old age. There is no specific age range for each phase nor do specific individuals enter any stage at the same time of life.

Early adulthood is the stage at which the individual attempts to integrate himself into the adult culture. The roles of childhood and adolescence are replaced by roles requiring participation in occupational, social, and political organizations. Middle adulthood spans about fifteen years of a person's life, usually from around thirty or thirty-five to around forty-five or fifty. For many individuals these years are the most productive of their lives. Significant progress usually occurs in vocational, marital, civic, and socioeconomic spheres. The emotional intensity of life experiences begins to decline during this phase, and the gains made in earlier years are consolidated. The late adult years are often characterized by attempts to maintain the same levels of performance and participation that had been achieved earlier. Physical and cognitive deterioration begin to accelerate moderately during these years. It is the period of menopause for women and the climacteric for men. Late adulthood usually ends between sixty and seventy, if not before. Old age is marked by increasing physical and mental decline ending in death. It is characterized by changes in physical and intellectual capacities as rapid as those during adolescence. Adjustments must therefore also be frequent and rapid. During old age there appears to be a reciprocal withdrawal from younger people. Old age is often a difficult period for the individual and those close to him (Cummings and Henry, 1961; Maddox, 1964).

VOCATIONAL TASKS

EARLY ADULTHOOD

Early adulthood is generally characterized by attempts to establish oneself in an occupation and then to advance. Because most young adults seek material comforts and are usually not able to afford them, vocational success may mean primarily financial gain to them. When someone asks how a young person is "doing," he usually means how is he doing financially. A job is likely to be evaluated according to its salary, rather than its potential for self-fulfillment.

Early adulthood is also a period of learning skills and information that will help the person to advance in his occupation. Job changes are not unusual, as some positions turn out to be unsatisfactory and others with higher salaries are offered.

The young person may also become aware for the first time that occupational advancement is not going to be as easy as he had anticipated. He finds that he must compete with well-established older people, and he often runs up against promotion policies based on seniority, rather than on ability. To an ambitious young person the recognition that he must wait a great deal longer or expend a great deal more energy than he had expected, can be most disheartening. Resulting conflict may drastically affect other areas of his life. For example, he may develop a generally defeatist attitude, become "sour," or take out his disappointment at home.

MIDDLE ADULTHOOD

In middle adulthood a person usually reaches his peak occupational status. Advancement often levels off around the age of forty, except in some fields of business, some professions, and some government positions. Adults in unskilled and semiskilled vocations especially find that their lack of training and technical knowledge limits their advancement; they may be forced to make frequent job changes and to accept intermittent layoffs because of automation and seasonal operations. The failure of these people to achieve permanent employment is reflected in lower social status. Hostility is likely to be their response. In vocations in which further specialization and progress are possible, however, the middle-aged adult can progress and easily maintain his morale.

LATE ADULTHOOD

In late adulthood the individual must recognize that his working career will soon end. His physical and cognitive capacities may begin to fail, and his expertise may be becoming obsolete. It frequently becomes clear that higher aspirations are unlikely to be satisfied. Some people at this age find themselves embarrassed by having to compete with younger people who are efficient specialists though less experienced with life. A typical expectation in late adulthood is that of vocational expertise. To maintain feelings of self-worth it is necessary to measure up to this expectation in one's own eyes and those of others.

Women are often freed from household chores in late adulthood and would like to work. Finding employment may be quite difficult, however. Even women who have been technically or professionally trained have often neglected their skills and must take refresher courses or additional training in order to compete on the job market. Starting new vocations or working at lower levels than their previous training called for may be very difficult.

OLD AGE

In old age most people experience definite losses in efficiency or even complete inability to work. Even when an older person can still do his job well he may be forced to retire whether he likes it or not. Retirement is a major challenge for many elderly people, especially those who have not planned for it by developing other interests, hobbies, and activities. They may suffer feelings of not being needed or of being unproductive. Their empty time may be spent in self-concern and unhappiness. Many people, of course, look forward to retirement and find old age quite fulfilling. They pursue avocations, spend more time with friends and relatives, or do the traveling that they have always wanted to do. Health, previous interests, flexibility of personality, and financial security help to determine the effects of retirement on the individual.

SOCIAL FUNCTIONING

EARLY ADULTHOOD

The main social task in early adulthood is to obtain acceptance in the adult community. The young adult, however, frequently has neither the financial means nor the social connections to participate in many community organizations or social groups. Often a young couple's spare time is taken up with the responsibilities of child rearing and establishing a home. Social contacts may therefore be limited to people of its own age who live nearby. There are other patterns too, especially among young people in the professions, but even they spend much of their time in establishing themselves.

Young people who have been leaders in their adolescent peer groups often want to become leaders in adult groups as well. To their consternation, however, they may find that older adults rebuff their attempts or adopt "wait and see" attitudes (Pikunas, 1969). Adults usually do not grant young people positions of leadership until they have proved that they can contribute as followers. They are "on probation." Adults usually believe (justly or not) that young people should gain more maturity before they are given leadership. On the other hand, young adults must actually begin to carry their share of social responsibilities in adult society if they expect its privileges. The young person who cannot control his ambition to lead may find his personal relations suffering. Not that conforming to the group is the best or only way to achieve status within it. On the contrary, leadership is more frequently achieved by people who are inner-directed. They are free to challenge the group when its decisions do not satisfy their own principles, values, and ideals. And, although they recognize the importance of contributing to the group, they are not controlled by it.

MIDDLE ADULTHOOD

Group membership usually reaches its peak in middle adulthood, and social activities increase. Parents enter groups related to their children's activities, and the opportunities for leadership increase with experience and broadening friendships within the community. As more time becomes available a person's interest in civic and political affairs rises as well. Civic and political activities, unlike social activities in general, are likely to continue with advancing age.

One major task of middle adulthood is preparation for later adult years and old age. Participation in active sports and other competitive endeavors begins to decline in favor of more sedentary and uncompetitive diversions like listening to music and visiting historic sites. The individual has the opportunity to develop interests that will prepare him for fulfilling and productive experiences in his later years. Creative, constructive, and uncompetitive activities, as opposed simply to time-killing ones, can be developed.

LATE ADULTHOOD

In the late adult years social contacts generally begin to diminish, for declining energy and physical capacity often render them less satisfying than they used to be. A person finds himself at social gatherings where many of the people are younger. Their interests are frequently different from his, and they are more likely to be abreast of current events than he is. He may find it difficult to participate in conversations because the topics are unfamiliar or because his hearing has deteriorated.

Nevertheless, active participation in both individual and group activities is important to him if he is to maintain a sense of belonging and self-esteem. The additional free time that follows from lighter vocational demands or early retirement can be filled with various interests. Late adulthood is an especially appropriate time for developing artistic and intellectual interests: in writing, painting, crafts, and so on. Older people can also engage in volunteer work that is helpful to others and serves to maintain their own sense of personal worth. Participation in church, charitable organizations, or civic activities can be personally gratifying, as well as offering opportunities for social interaction (Donahue *et al.*, 1958). The individual who withdraws from social contacts, for whatever reasons, will find himself increasingly isolated and unfulfilled. The probability that he will spend his remaining years in loneliness and sadness increases.

OLD AGE

Social isolation is usually greater in old age than at any other time of adult life. The elderly person is more likely to feel fulfilled if he maintains social contacts in which new ideas, interests, attitudes, and information can be exchanged. Social contacts offer one avenue for avoiding complete withdrawal and the focus on inner concerns that seem to occur in so many elderly people. The emotional stimulation of personal contacts is also necessary to prevent increasing emotional "blandness." Furthermore, satisfaction of the elderly person's needs for recognition, love, belonging, and status also depend upon his interactions with others.

PHYSICAL DETERIORATION

EARLY ADULTHOOD

Physical deterioration is not usually a problem for the young adult. He is in the prime of physical life, and active sports may be important to him. Young adults have high energy levels and can sustain prolonged physical output, recovering rapidly after large expenditures of energy. At this time of life worry over physical health is rare.

MIDDLE ADULTHOOD

During the middle adult years the body continues to function near its optimum, but a very gradual impairment may be noticed. At around forty visual acuity is likely to decline suddenly. Many people begin to wear glasses for reading and other fine work. A progressive loss of hearing for high-pitched tones may become noticeable after forty. Recovery from illness is slower and more difficult as age increases. General metabolism also often begins to slow down in the early forties, and consequently large weight gains are not unusual. Other metabolic disturbances may also begin to show up, and for that reason thorough physical examinations are recommended periodically even when one feels well. Strength and psychomotor speed decrease moderately. Diseases of the kidneys and respiratory or circulatory difficulties become more common. Sports that require high expenditures of energy become more difficult. Individuals who have characteristically preferred these activities may find themselves losing an important source of personal worth. Although many of these changes are barely perceptible in the early part of middle adulthood self-examination typically reveals that they are beginning.

Cognitive declines may also become noticeable in middle adulthood, but they are usually more gradual. Memory may be slightly affected. A person finds that he is writing more notes to himself. Quick thinking may not be as easy as it was in the past, and a more organized approach on problems and new situations may be adopted.

The greatest impact in middle adulthood comes not from actual physical deterioration but from the recognition that it is occurring. This recognition leads the individual to question his self-concept.

LATE ADULTHOOD

Physical decline continues in the late adult years, including the menopause for women and the climacteric for men. For many women menopause is not particularly difficult, but for others it may be quite upsetting. They may experience marked excitement, hot flashes, sweating, dizziness, extreme sensitivity to heat and cold, and other unsettling symptoms associated with chemical changes in their bodies. The more gradual the menopausal changes are, the more time a woman has to become used to them and to develop a new image of herself. She may need assistance from her husband and children in working through this phase of her life.

Cognitive decline is likely to begin during late adulthood. Vascular difficulties reduce blood flow to the brain; a person's failing interest in intellectual and cultural concerns may speed cognitive deterioration. The individual who keeps his interest in intellectual activities, assuming that other physical factors do not interfere, is more likely to maintain them through late adulthood.

OLD AGE

In old age general health becomes precarious. Chronic diseases become more frequent and severe. The declines that were noted in earlier years now increase and are more debilitating. Biological aging is marked by a slower metabolic rate; a person's capacity for energy exchange is thus reduced. Consequently, energy resources necessary for self-expression are gradually curtailed. The old person does not recover easily from overactivity. A gradual atrophying of muscle and tissue occurs because of the reduced supply of blood through hardening vessels. It results in loss of strength in muscles and vital organs like the brains, lungs, and heart. Sensory motor coordination gradually decreases, and reaction time increases. Gross body movements may become awkward; an old person finds it difficult to carry himself as he did when he was younger. His attractiveness to others is thus reduced.

It becomes especially clear in old age that the weakest system in the body will determine the person's ability to function. The system that "wears out" first will most often result in death. Physical impairments tend gradually to restrict the individual's environment. He becomes hesitant to enter activities that may overstrain him or to travel to places where medical attention is not readily available. Reduced vision may hinder his ability to read and to keep up with current events. Losses in hearing restrict his capacity for verbal communication. In general, an old person loses mobility because of his physical deterioration. His ability to relate to others and to his culture may therefore be drastically restricted.

Cognitive abilities may decline severely during old age. Loss of memory is often noticeable, especially memory of recent events and when an elderly person tries to recall a recent occurrence he may supplement his memory with imagination (with or without awareness), which often leads others to believe that he is out of contact with reality. Memory of long-ago events, however, is often quite clear, so that an old person often refers to such events as if they were quite recent. It also becomes increasingly difficult for the elderly to accept new ideas and ventures because their failing alertness makes it difficult to make decisions. A loss of orientation, even to familiar surroundings, may be very disconcerting to the old person and to those who have known him during his younger years. The combination of physical and cognitive declines in old age thus sets the stage for mutual rejection between the elderly and others. If deterioration impairs independent functioning to a great degree, the old person must be cared for either at home or in an institution.

SELF-CONCEPT AND PERSONALITY DEVELOPMENT

EARLY ADULTHOOD

In the early adult years the person continues to establish the identity that he has been building through late adolescence. Because of his associations in the social and vocational worlds he usually begins to recognize himself as part of a larger totality. More practical goals replace some of his earlier ambitions, and his self-knowledge deepens in many ways, as he recognizes more clearly the realities of living. In general he begins to "settle down." His interests become more stable, and he himself comes to recognize that he is on his own and that he can demonstrate his independence with some certainty. As he establishes himself in various areas (vocational, social, marital) he also begins to form a fairly consistent self-concept and habitual modes of personal functioning. His particular characteristics will vary, of course, depending upon his experiences. The stability that Ron, whom we discussed in Chapter 1, gained in early adulthood was noticeable. His vocational interests and goals were beginning to crystallize, he began to appraise his personal characteristics more realistically, and he could then emphasize some of his more adaptive traits. His ability to relate comfortably to others was thus increasing as was his comfort in relating to himself. His culture also became less threatening; he was, in fact, beginning to make positive gains through use of opportunities that it presented.

MIDDLE ADULTHOOD

One of the most difficult tasks in the middle adult years is to recognize that one is beginning to age. Noticing that progress at work or in a hobby is more difficult to attain, finding it more difficult to learn than it once was, experiencing less satisfaction in familiar recreational pursuits, and experiencing exhaustion after large expenditures of energy are all indications that old age is more than an abstract possibility. Around forty the recognition that one is only holding on or is losing ground may become painful. Expectations of advancement in status and the hope that some unexpected windfall will turn up begin to fade. Many people respond with anxiety and concern. They may try inappropriate activities in hopes of recapturing their youth or to prove that they are not aging. An individual may feel that he is facing his "last chance" at life. Life itself may begin to seem purposeless. Some individuals try to resolve the problem by returning to activities that were rewarding when they were younger. A man acquires a young girl friend, another runs off to the woods in search of the thrills that he experienced as a boy, a woman adopts current teenage clothing: All offer examples of maneuvers to avoid recognizing that age is happening to *them*.

Many adults in their early forties go through a period of striving harder and realigning themselves. They may renew their striving for vocational advancement, but they frequently meet obstacles. Positive outcomes seldom follow, and individuals are forced to recognize the limits of their success. One response that is rarely helpful in the long run is to blame oneself or others for not having made appreciable gains. It helps to avoid recognition that one's current status may be appropriate to one's capabilities and efforts but only for a while.

Emotional detachment may be important to objective evaluation of one's life at this time. The reduced emotional intensity associated with middle adulthood may enable a person to rely more on his rational judgment. Meeting this challenge tends to lead to more consistency in personal traits. Uncertainty over lasting values and goals lessens, and some inflexibility often becomes noticeable. The individual begins to rely more on habitual response patterns that have been successful in the past. As he moves into his late adult years, order and consistency become more prevalent in his functioning.

LATE ADULTHOOD

Most people in their late adult years still consider themselves middle-aged for some time. They often try to convince others and themselves that they are still capable of doing many of the same things that they did when they were younger. Continuing as active as they were earlier is, however, quite difficult. Many therefore reverse their attitudes and deliberately slow down and seek additional comforts. Their self-concepts change to those of old people, with all the associated drawbacks in a "youth culture."

Their lives must be reorganized to some degree. They recognize that their ability to learn new things has declined, and they therefore dread learning. They must also unlearn old habits (Lehman, 1953), which is equally difficult. Older people who remain ambitious nevertheless find that they meet with less success and may develop a tendency to blame others or society at large, refusing to face their own declining abilities.

In late adulthood the final stabilization of the personality occurs. Personal rigidity progresses, and the individual becomes increasingly resistant to change. More and more he relies on the past and on habit, and he rarely compromises with new fads, fashions, and so on (Neugarten *et al.*, 1964). Expectations for the future may decline rather rapidly. The past, or rather recollections of it, is increasingly important in his life. His goals switch to maintaining status, rather than to raising it.

OLD AGE

A major task in old age is to maintain personality integration so that independent functioning is possible. Old people who have in the past shown desire to learn when the opportunity existed, are now rewarded with interests in life, rather than complete self-concern. Those who have faced the reality of aging earlier and have acquired the abilities, interests, and skills necessary to cope with novel situations and new problems are more likely to make the adjustments required in old age satisfactorily. Individuals who have failed to grasp the complexity of modern living and those who limited themselves unnecessarily when they were younger are likely to experience earlier personality disintegration. "Early senility is a frequent result appearing in later years of adulthood or early in old age. Many such individuals finish their lives in mental and similar institutions" (Pikunas, 1969, p. 372).

People who cannot accept aging or adjust to its changes often show an intensification of undesirable traits that were apparent but not disruptive earlier. Selfishness and attitudes of superiority become marked. They may boast of past accomplishments and seek respect from others to bolster their failing self-esteem.

Many elderly people begin to dramatize minor injuries and symptoms and focus totally on their physical functioning. Of course, some of their concern is realistic. Death is approaching, and their bodies are deteriorating. Yet exaggerated self-interest can help them to avoid unpleasant obligations like doing their own shopping and can also promote concern and attention from others. The older person's increased sensitivity to danger and his worries about his body can greatly inhibit his activities and promote withdrawal.

Rapid physical and social changes in old age are likely to increase the need for respect, affection, security, and self-esteem. But satisfaction of these needs is often difficult to obtain. For various reasons other people do not want to be bothered. The elderly may consequently become very demanding and cause even more friction in their social relationships. Their ability to relate to other people becomes even more restricted.

The elderly person must reorganize his self-concept to view himself realistically. To the extent that it does not correspond with actual facts, he will experience problems in living. New interests are often necessary as earlier ones become impossible to pursue. The old person must recognize, however, that as aging continues even some of his new interests must be given up. The essential attitude for optimum adjustment to old age is flexibility—precisely the characteristic that tends to disappear with age. Nevertheless, new areas of interest are almost always available as sources of personal satisfaction. When we recall the elderly golfer, we can see how his response to his failing abilities led to self-imposed restrictions and failure to find other sources of gratification.

Another extremely difficult change in the old person's self-concept involves accepting dependence. For financial or physical reasons many old people must depend upon their children, and the parent-child roles are reversed to a large degree. The question that an old person must face is to what extent he can or should relinquish his personal freedom in such circumstances. To what extent will he be a burden or nuisance to those who care for him. There are no simple answers to such questions. The most satisfactory solution varies with each individual and depends upon his capacities and attributes, as well as on those of his potential helpers.

The elderly must also relinquish the control and power that they have previously held in the community or family. Younger people are now fully mature and their own abilities are declining. The elderly are thus faced with still another social change that requires further realignment of self-concepts.

SUMMARY

Some of the most important tasks that confront adults have been examined in this chapter, especially those associated with marriage. People marry for many reasons. Ideally, a couple would evaluate objectively its compatibility before marrying, but for many reasons it usually does not. Of course, psychologists themselves are uncertain about what makes couples compatible. It has been fairly well established, however, that people who marry quite young generally have less chance for successful marriages. There are several reasons why: They are often not mature enough to deal effectively with personal problems, limited finances cause strains, and premarital pregnancy often forces the marriage. Marital happiness generally appears related to both similarities in socioeconomic backgrounds, education, and interests and to differences in personality traits that permit the partners to complement each other.

Sexual adjustment is important in marriage. Men and women differ in their sexual needs and activity. Men are generally more active and reach their peak sex drive in adolescence; a gradual decline follows. Techniques of sexual arousal are focused mainly on stimulation of the erogenous zones. Women generally require more emotional closeness than men do to enjoy sex fully. There are four basic positions of sexual intercourse: man on top, woman on top, side by side, and rear entry. Many variations on each are possible. Both men and women suffer from sexual inadequacies. Men may be impotent, either fail to attain erections or to ejaculate prematurely. Women may be frigid in varying degrees, ranging from mild displeasure during coitus to a complete aversion to sex. Highly successful treatment methods for problems of sexual adjustment are currently being developed.

Men and women also differ in their responses to aging as it affects sexual behavior. A woman's sex drive remains about the same and may even increase at about forty, whereas the man's drive slowly but steadily declines. Both sexes, however, are capable of sexual activity into the seventies and eighties, as long as physical and emotional problems do not interfere. There are many sexual myths that have no basis in fact. It is not true, for example, that the size of the penis determines a woman's satisfaction or that there is a limited supply of sexual fluid that will be used up early if a person is sexually very active.

Adults must adjust to vocational progress. In early adulthood their major tasks are to establish themselves and to strive for advancement. An adult usually reaches his peak vocational performance during middle adulthood and may have to face the possibility that he has reached his limit, regardless of earlier aspirations. Late adulthood is a time when physical skills begin to weaken, and earlier training may become obsolete. Further advancement is even less possible, and one's own expectations of expertise generate stress. Voluntary or forced retirement must be faced in old age. Other activities must then replace vocational ones.

Social adjustments also vary with age. The young person has less opportunity to enter some adult social activities because of his financial status and the amount of time that he must spend in advancing vocationally and establishing a home. Middle adulthood is the peak of social activity for most people. The scope of one's participation expands, and increasing civic participation is likely. Positions of leadership become more accessible in middle adulthood. In late adulthood energetic and competitive activities are replaced by intellectual, sedentary, and artistic endeavors. It is a time to develop new interests that will make old age satisfying. In old age the individual has fewer social contacts than at any other time in his life. Failing health and other factors tend to limit his interactions and to restrict his capacity for social exchange.

The young adult is little concerned about physical deterioration—he is in his physical prime. Toward the end of middle adulthood, however, he usually begins to notice changes in his vision, hearing, and capacity for energy expenditure. He must begin to plan for a less active life and old age. In late adulthood physical changes become even more noticeable, and the individual is almost forced to recognize and to plan for old age. Physical deterioration accelerates in old age and calls for many rapid adjustments. Effective functioning in the earlier years can be most helpful in preventing complete withdrawal and morbid self-centeredness.

A person's self-concept and personality also change with age. In early adulthood he usually consolidates the identity that he began to form in adolescence. He begins to "settle down" as he gains a more realistic view of life, and his earlier idealism is usually modified. In middle adulthood he must cope, often for the first time, with the idea that he will become old. Realigning his self-concept may be quite difficult and is often accompanied by efforts to prove that he is still young. Late adulthood is a time for reappraisal. The personality becomes more rigid and habit patterns that were successful in earlier years become more inflexible. In old age the individual's major task is to maintain personality integration. He must relinquish most of his control and power, and he may have to depend on others for his care. Some old people become self-centered and demanding, which only increases their isolation from others and their community.

References

Allport, G. W. *Personality: A psychological interpretation.* New York: Holt, 1937.

Anderson, H. H. & Anderson, G. L. Social development. In L. Carmichael (Ed.), *Manual of child psychology.* New York: Wiley, 1954.

Argyris, C. Conditions for competence acquisition and therapy. *Journal of Applied Behavioral Science,* 1968, **4,** 147–177.

Axline, V. M. *Play therapy.* Boston: Houghton Mifflin, 1947.

Ayllon, T. & Azrin, N. *The token economy: A motivational system for therapy and rehabilitation.* New York: Appleton, 1968.

Bach, G. R. The marathon group: Intensive practice of intimate interaction. *Psychological Reports,* 1966, **18,** 995–1002.

Baldwin, A. L. The effect of home environment on nursery school behavior. *Child Development,* 1949, **20,** 40–62.

Baldwin, A. L. *Theories of child development.* New York: Wiley, 1967.

Ball, T. S. Behavior shaping of self-help skills in the severely retarded child. In J. Fisher & R. E. Harris (Eds.), Reinforcement theory in psychological treatment—A symposium. *California Department of Mental Hygiene Research Monograph,* 1966, **8,** 15–24.

Bandura, A. *Principles of behavior modification.* New York: Holt, 1969.

Bandura, A. & Walters, R. H. *Social learning and personality development.* New York: Holt, 1963.

Barron, F. *Creative person and creative process.* New York: Holt, 1969.

Barry, H., Child, I. L. & Bacon, M. K. Relation of child training to subsistence economy. *American Anthropologist,* 1959, **61,** 51–63.

Bayley, N. Individual patterns of development. *Child Development,* 1956, **27,** 45–74.

Bennett, E. L., Diamond, M. C., Krech, D. & Rosenzweig, M. R. Chemical and anatomical plasticity of the brain. *Science,* 1964, **146,** 610–619.

Bergin, A. E. Some implications of psychotherapy research for therapeutic practice. *Journal of Abnormal Psychology,* 1966, **71,** 235–246.

Bernard, J. *Remarriage: A study of marriage.* New York: Holt, 1956.

Bettelheim, B. Individual and mass behavior in extreme situations. *Journal of Abnormal and Social Psychology,* 1943, **38,** 417–452.

Bindrim, P. Nudity as a quick grab for intimacy in group therapy. *Psychology Today,* 1969, **3,** 25–28.

Bischof, L. J. *Adult psychology.* New York: Harper, 1969.

Block, J. Studies in the phenomenology of emotions. *Journal of Abnormal and Social Psychology*, 1957, **54**, 358–363.

Blum, G. S. *Psychodynamics: The science of unconscious mental forces*. Belmont, Calif.: Wadsworth, 1966.

Blum, R. H. *Utopiates: The use and users of LSD-25*. New York: Atherton, 1964.

Bombard, A. *The voyage of the Hérétique*. New York: Simon & Schuster, 1954.

Bowlby, J. *Maternal care and mental health*. Geneva: World Health Organization, 1951.

Brannon, R. C. Gimme that old-time racism. *Psychology Today*, 1970, **3**, 42–44.

Brown, R. W. *Social psychology*. New York: Free Press, 1965.

Burton, A., ed. *Modern psychotherapeutic practice*. Palo Alto, Calif.: Science and Behavior, 1967.

Button, A. D. *The authentic child*. New York: Random House, 1969.

Camus, A. *The Stranger*. New York: Random House, 1946.

Carmichael, L., Roberts, S. D. & Wessel, N. Y. A study of the judgment of manual expression as presented in still and motion pictures. *Journal of Social Psychology*, 1937, **8**, 115–142.

Cholden, L. *Lysergic acid diethylamide and mescaline in experimental psychiatry*. New York: Grune & Stratton, 1956.

Clark, D. F. The treatment of monosymptomatic phobia by systematic desensitization. *Behavior Research and Therapy*, 1963, **1**, 63.

Coe, W. C. Dick and his parents—A case study. Paper presented at the workshop "The Troubled Adolescent and His Family" sponsored by the University of California Medical School Division of Continuing Education, Mendocino, Calif., March 1970a.

Coe, W. C. A family operant program. Paper presented at the annual meeting of the Western Psychological Association, Los Angeles, May 1970b.

Coe, W. C. A behavioral approach to disturbed family interactions. *Psychotherapy: Research, Theory and Practice*, in press.

Coe, W. C., Curry, A. E. & Kessler, D. R. Family interactions of psychiatric patients. *Family Process*, 1969, **8**, 119–130.

Coleman, J. C. *Personality dynamics and effective behavior*. Glenview, Ill.: Scott, Foresman, 1960.

Coleman, J. C. *Abnormal psychology and modern life*. (3rd ed.) Glenview, Ill.: Scott, Foresman, 1964.

Committee on Adolescence—Group for the Advancement of Psychiatry. *Normal adolescence: Its dynamics and impact*. New York: Scribner's, 1968.

Cox, F. D. *Youth, marriage, and the seductive society*. Dubuque, Ia.: Brown, 1968.

Cummings, E. & Henry, W. E. *Growing old: The process of disengagement*. New York: Basic Books, 1961.

Dollard, J. L. & Miller, N. E. *Personality and psychotherapy*. New York: McGraw-Hill, 1950.

Donahue, W. (Ed.) *Free time: Challenge to later maturity*. Ann Arbor: University of Michigan Press, 1958.

Douvan, E. & Adelson, J. *The adolescent experience*. New York: Wiley, 1966.

Douvan, E. A. & Kaye, C. *Adolescent girls*. Ann Arbor, Mich.: Survey Research Center, University of Michigan, 1957.

Dunlap, K. *Habits: Their making and unmaking*. New York: Liveright, 1932.

Dusenberry, D. & Kroner, F. H. Experimental studies of the symbolism of voice and action: II. A study of the specificity of meaning in abstract tonal symbols. *Quarterly Journal of Speech*, 1939, **25**, 67–75.

Ekman, P. Communication through non-verbal behavior: A source of information about an interpersonal relationship. In S. S. Tomkins and C. E. Izzard (Eds.), *Affect, cognition and personality*. New York: Springer, 1965.

Ekman, P. & Friesen, W. V. Non-verbal behavior in psychotherapy research. In J. Shlien (Ed.), *Research on psychotherapy*. Vol. III. Washington, D.C.: American Psychological Association, 1967.

Epstein, S. & Smith, R. Thematic apperception, Rorschach content, and ratings of sexual attractiveness of women as measures of the sex drive. *Journal of Consulting Psychology*, 1957, **21**, 473–478.

Erikson, E. H. *Childhood and society*. New York: Atherton, 1963.

Eysenck, H. J. *Behavior therapy and the neurosis*. London: Pergamon, 1960.

Fairweather, G. W. (Ed.) *Social psychology in treating mental illness: An experimental approach*. New York: Wiley, 1964.

Fairweather, G. W. *Community life for the mentally ill*. New York: Aldine, 1967a.

Fairweather, G. W. *Methods for experimental social innovation*. New York: Wiley, 1967b.

Farson, R. E. Emotional barriers to education. *Psychology Today*, 1967, **1**(6), 25–31.

Fenichel, O. *The psychoanalytic theory of the neuroses*. New York: Norton, 1945.

Ferster, C. B., and Skinner, B. F. *Schedules of reinforcement*. New York: Appleton, 1957.

Flacks, R. Student activist: Result, not revolt. *Psychology Today*, 1967, **1**, 18–23, 61.

Frankl, V. E. *Man's search for meaning: An introduction to logotherapy*. Boston: Beacon, 1963.

Freud, A. *The ego and mechanisms of defense*. New York: International Universities Press, 1946a.

Freud, A. *The psychoanalytic treatment of children*. London: Imago, 1946b.

Freud, S. *Collected papers*, Vol. 3. London: Hogarth, 1950.

Fromm-Reichmann, F. *Principles of intensive psychotherapy*. Chicago: University of Chicago Press, 1950.

Gesell, A. *Infant and child in the culture of today*. New York: Harper, 1943.

Goddard, H. H. *The Kallikak family*. New York: Macmillan, 1912.

Graham, R. L. A teenager sails the world alone. *National Geographic*, 1968, **134**, 449–493.

Grahn, D. & Kratchman, J. Variation in neonatal death rate and birth rate in the U.S., and possible relations to environmental radiation, geology, and altitude. *American Journal of Human Genetics*, 1963, **15**, 329–352.

Griffin, J. H. *Black like me*. Boston: Houghton Mifflin, 1961.

Hadden, J. K. The private generation. *Psychology Today*, 1969, **3**(5), 32–35, 68–69.

Hall, C. S. & Lindzey, G. *Theories of personality*. New York: Wiley, 1957.

Harkel, R. L. *The picture book of sexual love*. New York: Cybertype, 1969.

Harlow, H. F., Harlow, M. K. & Meyer, D. R. Learning motivated by a manipulation drive. *Journal of Experimental Psychology*, 1950, **40**, 228–234.

Harris, G. T. The young are captives of each other: A conversation with David Riesman. *Psychology Today*, 1969, **3**, 28–31.

Harris, G. T. Religion in the age of Aquarius—A conversation with theologian Harvey Cox. *Psychology Today*, 1970, **3**, 45–47, 62–67.

Hebb, D. The effects of early experience on problem solving at maturity. *American Psychologist*, 1947, **2**, 306–307.

Hebb, D. D. *The organization of behavior.* New York: Wiley, 1949.

Hewitt, F. *The emotionally disturbed child in the classroom: A developmental strategy for educating children with maladaptive behavior.* Boston: Allyn & Bacon, 1968.

Hewitt, F., Taylor, F. & Artuso, A. An engineered classroom design with emotionally disturbed children. In G. Fargo, C. Behrns & P. Nolen (Eds.), *Behavior modification in the classroom.* Belmont, Calif.: Wadsworth, 1970.

Hilgard, E. R. *Theories of learning.* New York: Appleton, 1956.

Hilgard, E. R. & Atkinson, R. C. *Introduction to psychology.* (4th ed.) New York: Harcourt, 1967.

Hull, C. L. *Principles of behavior.* New York: Appleton, 1943.

Hunt, J. M. Experience and the development of motivation: Some reinterpretations. *Child Development*, 1960, **31**, 489–504.

Hunt, J. M. *Intelligence and experience.* New York: Ronald, 1961.

Inhelder, B. & Piaget, J. *The growth of logical thinking.* New York: Basic Books, 1958.

Jacobson, E. *Anxiety and tension control.* Philadelphia: Lippincott, 1964.

Jersild, A. T. *In search of self.* New York: Teachers College, Columbia University, 1952.

Kallman, F. J. & Roth, B. Genetic aspects of preadolescent schizophrenia. *American Journal of Psychiatry*, 1956, **112**, 599–606.

Keniston, K. Drug use and student values. In C. Hollander (Ed.), *Background papers on student drug involvement.* Washington, D.C.: National Student Association, 1967.

Kerr, C. Mary Harrington Hall interviews Clark Kerr. *Psychology Today*, 1967, **1**(6), 25–31.

Kessler, J. W. *Psychopathology of childhood.* Englewood Cliffs, N.J.: Prentice-Hall, 1966.

Kinsey, A. C., Pomeroy, W. B. & Martin, C. E. *Sexual behavior in the human male.* Philadelphia: Saunders, 1948.

Kinsey, A. C., Pomeroy, W. B., Martin, C. E. & Gebhard, P. H. *Sexual behavior in the human female.* Philadelphia: Saunders, 1953.

Klausner, S. Z. *Why man takes chances.* New York: Doubleday, 1968.

Knapp, P. H. *Expression of the emotions in man.* New York: International Universities Press, 1963.

Koch, H. L. Sissiness and tomboyishness in relation to sibling characteristics. *Journal of Genetic Psychology*, 1956, **88**, 231–244.

Krasner, L. & Ullman, L. *Research in behavior modification.* New York: Holt, 1965.

Krasner, L., Ullman, L. & Weiss, R. L. Distribution and validation of modal perception responses of normal and psychiatric subjects. Paper presented at the meeting of the American Psychological Association, New York, September 1961.

Kretschmer, E. *Physique and character*. New York: Harcourt, 1925.

Kroeber, T. C. The coping functions of the ego mechanisms. In R. W. White (Ed.), *The study of lives*. New York: Atherton, 1963.

Leeper, R. W. A study of a neglected portion of the field of learning: The development of sensory organization. *Journal of Genetic Psychology*, 1935, **46**, 41–75.

Lehman, H. C. *Age and achievement*. Princeton, N.J.: Princeton University Press, 1953.

Levy, D. M. Release therapy. *American Journal of Orthopsychiatry*, 1939, **9**, 913–936.

Lovibond, S. H. The mechanism of conditioning treatment of enuresis. *Behavior Research and Therapy*, 1963, **1**, 17.

Maddox, G. L., Jr. Disengagement theory: A critical evaluation. *Gerontologist*, 1964, **4**, 80–82.

Maslow, A. H. *Toward a psychology of being*. Princeton, N.J.: Van Nostrand, 1962.

Maslow, A. H. & Murphy, G. (Eds.), *Motivation and personality*. New York: Harper, 1954.

Masters, R. E. & Houston, J. *The varieties of psychedelic experience*. New York: Holt, 1966.

Masters, W. H. & Johnson, V. E. Treatment of the sexually incompatible family unit. *Minnesota Medicine*, 1961, **44**, 466–471.

Masters, W. H. & Johnson, V. E. Counseling with sexually incompatible marriage partners. In R. H. Clemer (Ed.), *Counseling in marital and sexual problems*. Baltimore: Williams & Wilkins, 1965.

Masters, W. H. & Johnson, V. E. *Human sexual response*. Boston: Little, Brown, 1966.

May, R., Angel, E. & Ellenberger, H. F. (Eds.) *Existence*. New York: Basic Books, 1958.

McCary, J. L. *Human sexuality: A contemporary marriage manual*. Princeton, N.J.: Van Nostrand, 1967.

McConnell, R. A. ESP and credibility in science. *American Psychologist*, 1969, **24**, 531–538.

Mcginnies, E. Emotionality and perceptual defense. *Psychological Review*, 1949, **56**, 244–251.

Mead, M. *Male and female*. New York: Morrow, 1949.

Merrill, B. A measurement of mother-child interaction. *Journal of Abnormal and Social Psychology*, 1946, **4**, 211–214.

Mintz, E. E. Time extended marathon groups. *Psychotherapy: Theory, Research, and Practice*, 1967, **4**, 65–70.

Mischel, W. & Grusec, J. E. The model's characteristics as determinants of social learning. *Journal of Personality and Social Psychology*, 1966, **4**, 211–214.

Monroe, R. L. *Schools of psychoanalytic thoughts*. New York: Holt, 1955.

Montgomery, R. *A gift of prophecy: The phenomenal Jeanne Dixon*. New York: Morrow, 1965.

Muller, P. *The tasks of childhood.* New York: McGraw-Hill, 1969.

Murray, H. A. *Explorations in personality.* New York: Oxford, 1938.

Mussen, P. Early socialization: Learning and identification. In G. Mandler, P. Mussen, N. Kogan & M. A. Wallach (Eds.), *New directions in psychology,* Vol. III, New York: Holt, 1967.

Mussen, P., Conger, J. J. & Kagan, J. *Childhood development and personality.* (3rd ed.) New York: Harper, 1969.

Mussen, P. & Rutherford, E. Parent-child relations and parental personality in relation to young children's sex-role preferences. *Child Development,* 1963, **34,** 589–607.

Mussen, P. & Distler, L. Masculinity, identification, and father-son relationships. *Journal of Abnormal and Social Psychology,* 1959, **59,** 350–356.

Neugarten, B. L. *et al. Personality in middle and late life: Empirical studies.* New York: Atherton, 1964.

Orne, M. T. & Scheibe, K. The contribution of nondeprivation factors in the production of sensory deprivation effects: The psychology of the "panic button." *Journal of Abnormal and Social Psychology,* 1964, **68,** 3–12.

Pavlov, I. P. *Conditioned reflexes.* Trans. by G. V. Anrep. New York: Liveright, 1927.

Pavlov, I. P. *Lectures on conditioned reflexes* (W. H. Grantt, Ed.). New York: International Publishers, 1928.

Piaget, J. *The origins of intelligence in children.* New York: International Universities Press, 1952.

Piaget, J. *The construction of reality in the child.* New York: Basic Books, 1954.

Piaget, J. *Judgment and reasoning in the child.* Paterson, N.J.: Littlefield, 1959.

Pikunas, J. *Human development: A science of growth.* New York: McGraw-Hill. 1969.

Postman, L., Bronson, W. & Gropper, G. Is there a mechanism of perceptual defense? *Journal of Abnormal and Social Psychology,* 1953, **48,** 215–225.

Riesman, D. The young are captives of each other: A conversation with David Riesman and George T. Harris. *Psychology Today,* 1969, **3** (5), 28–31, 63–67.

Rhine, J. B. & Hall, M. H. A conversation with J. B. Rhine and Mary Harrington Hall. *Psychology Today,* 1969, **2,** 20–28.

Rogers, C. *Client-centered therapy.* Boston: Houghton Mifflin, 1951.

Rogers, C. R. A theory of therapy, personality, and interpersonal relationships, as developed in the client-centered framework. In S. Koch (Ed.), *Psychology: A theory of science.* Vol. 3. New York: McGraw-Hill, 1959.

Rogers, C. R. *On becoming a person.* Boston: Houghton Mifflin, 1961.

Rogers, C. R. Community: The group comes of age. *Psychology Today,* 1969, **3,** 27–31.

Rogers, C. R. & Dymond, R. F. *Psychotherapy and personality change.* Chicago: University of Chicago Press, 1954.

Rogers, C. R., Gendlin, E. T., Kiesler, D. J. & Truax, C. B. (Eds.) *The therapeutic relationship and its impact.* Madison: University of Wisconsin Press, 1967.

Rogers, C. R. & Stevens, B. *Person to person: The problem of being human, a new trend in psychology.* Lafayette, Calif.: Real People Press, 1967.

Rokeach, M. Paradoxes of religious belief. *Trans-Action,* 1965, January–February, pp. 9–12.

Rokeach, M. Faith, hope, bigotry. *Psychology Today*, 1970, **3**, 33–37, 58.

Rosenthal, R. Self-fulfilling prophecy. *Psychology Today*, 1968, **2**, 44–51.

Rosenthal, R. & Jacobson, L. *Pygmalion in the classroom*. New York: Holt, 1968.

Sarbin, T. R. A new model of the behavior disorders. *Gawein*, 1962, **10**, 324–341.

Sarbin, T. R. Anxiety: Reification of a metaphor. *Archives of General Psychiatry*, 1964, **10**, 630–638.

Sarbin, T. R. A role theory perspective for community psychology: The structure of social identity. Address to the Mental Health Department, Oakland, Calif., Oct. 1967.

Sarbin, T. R. *Fybate lectures notes: Abnormal psychology*. Berkeley, Calif.: Fybate, 1968.

Sarbin, T. R. Ontology recapitulates philology: The mythic nature of anxiety. *American Psychologist*, 1968, **23**, 411–418.

Sarbin, T. R. Schizophrenic thinking: A role-theoretical analysis. *Journal of Personality*, 1969, **37**, 190–206.

Sarbin, T. R. & Allen, V. L. Role theory. In G. Lindzey & E. Aronson (Eds.), *Handbook of social psychology*, Vol. I. Reading, Mass.: Addison-Wesley, 1968. Pp. 488–567.

Sarbin, T. R. & Hardyck, C. D. Conformance in role perception as a personality variable. *Journal of Consulting Psychology*, 1955, **19**, 109–111.

Satir, V. *Conjoint family therapy*. Palo Alto, Calif.: Science and Behavior Books, 1964.

Schachter, S. & Singer, I. E. Cognitive, social and physiological determinants of emotional state. *Psychological Review*, 1962, **69**, 379–399.

Schaefer, E. S. & Bayley, N. Maternal behavior, child behavior, and their inter-correlations from infancy through adolescence. *Monographs of social research in child development*, 1963, **82** (3, Whole No. 87).

Schaefer, H. H. Investigations on operant conditioning procedures in a mental hospital. In J. Fisher & R. E. Harris (Eds.), Reinforcement theory in psychological treatment—A symposium. *California Department of Mental Hygiene Research Monograph*, 1966, **8**, 15–24.

Schaefer, H. & Martin, P. *Behavioral therapy*. New York: McGraw-Hill, 1969.

Scholsberg, H. Three dimensions of emotion. *Psychological Review*, 1954, **61**, 81–88.

Schutz, W. C. *Joy*. New York: Grove, 1967.

Scott, J. P. *Early experience and the organization of behavior*. Belmont, Calif.: Wadsworth, 1968.

Sears, R. R., Maccoby, E. & Levine, H. *Patterns of child rearing*. New York: Harper, 1957.

Sears, R. R., Raw, L. & Alpert, R. *Identification and child rearing*. Stanford, Calif.: Stanford University Press, 1965.

Sheldon, W. H. (with the collaboration of C. W. Dupertuis and E. McDermott) *Atlas of men: A guide for somatotyping the adult male at all ages*. New York: Harper, 1954.

Sheldon, W. H. (with the collaboration of S. S. Stevens) *The varieties of temperament: A psychology of constitutional differences*. New York: Harper, 1942.

Sheldon, W. H. (with the collaboration of S. S. Stevens and W. B. Tucker)

The varieties of human physique: An introduction to constitutional psychology. New York: Harper, 1940.

Shoben, E. J., Jr. Toward a concept of the normal personality. *American Psychologist,* 1957, **12,** 183–189.

Shostrom, E. L. Group therapy: Let the buyer beware. *Psychology Today,* 1969, **2,** 36–40.

Singer, M. & Wynn, L. C. Thought disorder and family relations of schizophrenics. *Archives of General Psychiatry,* 1965, **12,** 187–212.

Skinner, B. F. *The behavior of organisms: An experimental analysis.* New York: Appleton, 1938.

Skinner, B. F. *Walden two.* New York: Macmillan, 1948.

Slavson, S. R. *Child psychotherapy.* New York: Columbia University Press, 1952.

Solomon, P., Kubzansky, P. E., Leideman, P. H., Mendelson, J. H., Trumbel, R. & Wexler, D. (Eds.), *Sensory deprivation: A symposium held at Harvard Medical School in 1958.* Cambridge, Mass.: Harvard University Press, 1961.

Stampfl, T. G. & Levis, D. J. Essentials of implosive therapy: A learning-theory-based psychodynamic behavioral therapy. *Journal of Abnormal Psychology,* 1967, **72,** 496–503.

Stark, R., Foster, B. D., Glock, C. Y. & Quinley, H. Sounds of silence. *Psychology Today,* 1970, **3,** 38–41.

Stern, J. *Edward Cayce: The sleeping prophet.* New York: Doubleday, 1967.

Stone, J. L. & Church, J. *Childhood and adolescence.* New York: Random House, 1957.

Strong, E. K., Jr. *Vocational interests of men and women.* Stanford, Calif.: Stanford University Press, 1943.

Ullman, L. & Krasner, L. *Case studies in behavior modification.* New York: Holt, 1965.

Veen, F. van der. Basic elements in the process of psychotherapy: A research study. *Journal of Consulting Psychology,* 1967, **31,** 295–303.

Vernon, J. A. *Inside the black room.* New York: Potter, 1963.

Verville, E. *Behavior problems of children.* Philadelphia: Saunders, 1967.

Whalen, R. E. The determinants of sexuality in animals. In S. C. Plog & R. B. Edgerton (Eds.), *Changing perspectives in mental illness.* New York: Holt, 1969. Pp. 627–653.

White, R. W. Motivation reconsidered: The concept of competence. *Psychological Review,* 1959, **66,** 297–323.

Witkin, H. A., Dyk, R. B., Faterson, H. F., Goodenough, D. R. & Karp, S. A. *Psychological differentiation.* New York: Wiley, 1962.

Wolpe, J. *Psychotherapy by reciprocal inhibition.* Stanford, Calif.: Stanford University Press, 1958.

Wolpe, J. *The practice of behavior therapy.* New York: Pergamon, 1969.

Wolpe, J. & Lazarus, A. L. *Behavior therapy techniques.* New York: Pergamon, 1966.

Wrenn, R. L. & Ruiz, R. A. *The normal personality: Issues to insights.* Belmont, Calif.: Brooks/Cole, 1970.

Wyzanski, C. E., Jr. It is quite right that the young should talk about us as hypocrites: We are. *Saturday Review,* July 20, 1968, p. 14.

Yarrow, L. J. Separation from parents during early childhood. In M. L. Hoffman & L. W. Hoffman (Eds.), *Review of child development research*. New York: Russell Sage, 1964.

Zoellner, R. Confessions of a middle-aged moralist. *Commonweal*, June 7, 1968, pp. 352–355.

Index

A

Adjustment
  in adolescence (*see* Adolescence)
  in adulthood (*see* Adulthood; Aging)
  case example of, 4–10
  in the preschool years, 256–270
  as relatedness, 10–17
  in school child and preadolescent, 270–291
  tasks of the preschool child, 261–270
Adolescence
  choice of values in, 392–396
  criteria for, 334–336
  definition of, 336–337
  effects of physical changes in, 338–347
  and heterosexual relationships, 374–387
  interpersonal adjustments in early, 348–358
  See also Sexuality; Vocation
Adulthood
  and changes in self-concept and personality, 447–450
  and changes in social functioning, 443–445
  marriage in, 420–428
  physical deterioration in, 445–447
  sexual adjustment in, 428–438
  tasks of parenthood in, 438–441
  tasks with aging in, 441–450
  See also Vocation
Affect (*see* Emotion)
Aggression, 93
Aging
  adjustments to, 441–450
  changes in self-concept and personality with, 447–450
  and physical deterioration, 445–447
  See also Adulthood
Alcoholism, 42–43
Ambiguous stimuli, 73
Anal stage of development, 114

Anxiety
  as cognitive strain (Sarbin), 222–228
  in existentialism, 134–135
  the mythic nature of, 222–224
  in psychoanalysis, 105
  in Rogers' self theory, 157–158
Anxiety flooding, 190–191
Anxiety reactions, 59–60
Arithmetic, 280
Assertive training, 183–186
Authentic child, 314–318
Autism, 269, 320
Autonomic reactivity, 24
Aversive conditioning, 189–190

B

Basic personality, 300
Bed-wetting (*see* Enuresis)
Behavior modification
  basic assumptions of the therapist in, 173–174
  counterconditioning techniques in, 179–188
  techniques based on extinction in, 190–192
  techniques based on operant conditioning in, 192–204
Behavioral rehearsal, 184
Behavior shaping, 197–199
Beliefs (*see* Values)
Birth, 260–261
Birth order, 312–313
Body image, 347
Body types (*see* Somatotypes)

C

Cathexes, drive, counter-, hyper-, 95–96
Castration anxiety, 103

Castration complex, 103
Childhood schizophrenia (*see* Autism)
Clairvoyance (*see* Extrasensory perception)
Client-centered therapy, 160–164
Classical conditioning, concepts of, 175–179
Climacteric, 436, 445
Cognitive strain
    applied to schizophrenic thinking, 229–231
    a model of, 224–228
    as a substitute for anxiety, 222–228
Communication
    in disturbed families, 323–327
    levels of, 324–325
Competence motive, 46–47
Concordance method, 30
Conditioned response, 175–177
Conflict
    in deciding on an action, 71–72
    psychological, 207–209
    over value choices in adolescence, 396–397
Conscience, 269, 396
Constitutional theory, 25–28
Cotwin control method, 30–31
Countertransference, 119
Culture, as a demand in adjustment, 15–17

D

Dating, 378–382
Defense mechanisms (*see* Ego, defense mechanisms of)
Denial, 111
Depression (*see* Mood disorders)
Development
    cognitive stages in, 282–285
    effects of cultural and social factors on, 298–318
    effects of family on, 306–318
    effects of personal relations on, 303
    effects of physical determinants on, 294–298
    prenatal, 256–260
    rate of on adjustment, 343–344
Developmental time, 271–274
Discipline, in childhood, 310–311
Discrimination, in learning theory, 178–179
Displacement, 112
Divorce, 427–428
Down's syndrome, 34–36

Dreams, psychoanalytic interpretation of, 121–124
Drive-reduction theory (*see* Motives)
Drug addiction, 41–42
Drug abuse, 79, 235
    See also Psychedelic drugs
Drugs, use in college students, 411–415
    See also Psychedelic drugs

E

Education, and the generation gap, 406–411
Ego
    abilities of, 109–113
    coping mechanisms of, 109–113
    defense mechanisms of, 109–113
    primary autonomy of, 108
    the psychoanalytic concept of, 97
    secondary autonomy of, 108
    synthesizing function of, 108
Ego apparatuses, 108
Ego psychology, 107–116
Electra complex, 103
Embryo, 257
Emotion
    cues for labeling, 55–56
    disorders of, 56–61
    as a drive and incentive, 56
    labeling, 52–53
    and Rogers' self theory, 154–155
    and theories of psychophysiological disorders, 58–59
Empathy, 111–112
Encounter group (*see* Groups, for competence and growth)
Energy level, 25
Engineered classroom, 202–203
Enriched environment, 295
Enuresis, 265
Environmental psychology, 299
Erikson, E. H., eight stages of man, 113–117
E.S.P. (*see* Extrasensory perception)
Existentialism, 127–152
    concepts of, 130–136
    psychotherapy, 136–143
Extinction
    behavior modification techniques of, 190–192
    in classical conditioning, 177

Extrasensory perception
   clairvoyance, 76
   mental telepathy, 76
   precognition, 77–78

F

Family biography, 28
Family therapy, 322–331
   See also Development
Fetus, 257–258
Figure-ground perception, 66–67
Fixation, of psychic energy, 99
Frame of reference, 69
Freud, Sigmund, 90
   See also Psychoanalysis
Free association, technique of, 118
Functional autonomy of motives (*see*
      Motives)

G

Generation gap, 403–415
Genetics
   basic, 22–23
   specific effects on adjustment, 34–37
   See also Inheritance
Grandparenthood, 439–441
Groups, for competence and growth, 143–
      150
Guidance, of children, 310–311
Guilt, 135–136

H

Headaches (*see* Migraine headaches)
Heterosexual relationships
   in early adolescence, 355–357
   in late adolescence, 374–387
   See also Adulthood; Sexuality
Homosexuality, 346
   See also Sexuality, treatment for
      disorders in
Homeostasis, 92
Humanistic views, 127–170
Hypochondriasis, 228

I

Id, 96
   See also Psychoanalysis, concepts of
Identity
   in ego psychology, 115–116
   with a group, 16
   importance of vocation to, 365–366
   in late adolescence, 364–365
   as relatedness to self, 11
Idealism, in youth, 392
Identification
   psychoanalytic, 103
   in school age children, 285–291
   theories of, 288–291
Implosive therapy, 191
Independence, in early adolescence, 348–
      352
Inheritance, general effects on adjustment,
      23–25
   See also Genetics
Intelligence
   abilities of, 446
   changes in adolescence, 357–358
   effects of inheritance and environment
      on, 31–33
   Piaget's theory of, 280–285
   skills of the school child, 279–280
   See also I.Q.
Intellectualization, 110
Interview, 371
Introjection, 156
I.Q., 271
   See also Intelligence

L

Language, 265–266
Latency, stage of development, 104,
   115
Learning, effects of physical environment
      on, 294–296
Learning theory, 171–212
   and behavior modification, 173–174,
      179–192, 197–204
   and personality, 204–211
Libido, 93
Logotherapy, 141–143
Love, 374
L.S.D.-25, 79

M

Manic reaction (*see* Mood disorders)
Manipulation drive, 46
Marathon group (*see* Groups, for competence and growth)
Marriage
  in college, 424–426
  indicators of happiness in, 426–428
  reasons for, 421–423
  in young people, 423–424
Maslow, A. H., 51
Masochism, 41
Masturbation, 345, 375
Maternal drive, 45
Maternal expectations, 311–312
Maternal types, 308–310
Maturation, 261
Menopause, 445
Mental age, 272
Mental hospital, 241–250
Mental retardation, 198–199
Mental telepathy (*see* Extrasensory perception)
Mescaline, 78, 82–83
Migraine headaches, 57–58
Mongolism, 34–36
Mood disorder, 60–61
Morality
  early concepts of, 269–270
  and the generation gap, 405–406
Motivation
  drive-reduction theory of, 48
  incongruence-dissonance theory of, 47–48
  in role theory, 218
  in self theory, 154–155
  See also Motives; Needs
Motives
  functional autonomy of, 49
  in learning theory, 205
  physiological, 40–47
  social, 48–49
  See also Motivation; Needs

N

Narcotics, 261
  See also Drug addiction; Drug abuse
Nature–nurture issue
  as a function of heredity and environment, 33
  methods of studying the, 28–30

Needs
  hierarchy of, 51–52
  and motives, 49
  See also Motivation; Motives; Psychogenic needs
Negative practice, 190
Neurological handicap, 328
Neurosis, 173, 207, 209–210
Normal (*see* Normality)
Normality, definitions of, 17–19
Nude group (*see* Groups, for competence and growth)

O

Occupation (*see* Vocations)
Oedipal conflict, 102, 115
Operant conditioning
  basic concepts of, 192–197
  program in mental hospital with, 200–202
  See also Behavior modification
Opium addiction, 42
Oral stage of development, 113
Orgasm, 345–386
  See also Sexuality

P

Pain, 41
Parental attitudes, 306–308
Parenthood, 438–441
Parents, 348–352
Pedigree method, 28
Peer group
  in conflict with parental values, 396–397
  in early adolescence, 352–355
  and the school child, 275–276
  See also Adolescence
Penis (*see* Sexuality)
Penis envy, 103
Peptic ulcers, 57
Perception
  analogy with electronic computer, 65
  and categorization, 70
  and deciding on action, 71–72
  effects of previous experience on, 69–70
  effects of temporary needs and circumstances on, 71
  the process of, 65–73
  selectivity in, 67–68

Perception (*cont.*)
  and subjective frame of reference, 69
Perceptual defense, 67–68
Perceptual process, case example of, 72–73
Perceptual styles, 68
Personal adjustment (*see* Adjustment)
Personality
  changes with aging, 447–450
  Dollard and Miller's learning theory of,
    204–211
  See also Psychoanalysis; Role theory; Self
    theory
Personality development
  psychoanalytic stages of, 98–105
  See also Erikson, E. H.; Personality
Personality types
  psychoanalytic, 100, 102, 104, 105
  Sheldon's body types, 26–27
Peyote, 78, 79
Phallic stage of development, 115
Phenylketonuria (P.K.U.), 36–37
Phrenology, 25
Physical appearance, in relating to self, 12
Physical characteristics, inherited, 24–25
Piaget, J., 46, 280–285
P.K.U., 36–37
Play therapy, 318–322
Pleasure principle, 97
Preadolescence, adjustments of, 270–291
  See also School children
Precognition (*see* Extrasensory perception)
Preconscious, 94
Pregnancy
  premarital, 421
  See also Birth; Prenatal experiences
Prejudice, 70
Prenatal experiences, 258–259
Primal scene, 102
Projection, 111
Psilocybin, 79
Psi phenomena (*see* Extrasensory percep-
    tion; Psychokineses)
Psychedelic drugs, 78–84
  experience of, 81–84
  as a social movement, 80
  and symptoms of mental illness, 83–84
  therapeutic uses of, 80–81
  See also Drug abuse; Drugs, use in college
    students
Psychic energy, 96
Psychoanalysis
  and concepts of adjustment
    abnormal behavior, 106–107

Psychoanalysis (*cont.*)
  and concepts of adjustment (*cont.*)
    anxiety, 105–106
  and economic concepts
    instincts, 91–94
    psychic energy, 91
  and genetic concepts (stages of develop-
    ment), 98–105
  and structural concepts (id, ego, super-
    ego), 96–98
  and topographical concepts
    dynamics of consciousness, 95–96
    levels of consciousness, 94–95
  as a treatment, 116–124
Psychoanalysis, classical theory of, 89–107
Psychoanalyst, 120
Psychogenic needs, 49–51
  See also Needs
Psychokineses (P.K.), 78
Psychological tests, 372
Psychophysiological disorders, 57–59
  See also Hypochondriasis
Psychosexual stages of development,
    99–105, 209
    See also Erikson, E. H., eight stages
    of man
Psychosomatic disorders (*see* Psychophysi-
    ological disorders; Hypochondriasis)
Psychotomimetic drugs (*see* Psychedelic
    drugs)
Psychotherapy
  an eclectic approach to, 232–233
  with the family, 322–331
  nondirective, 164
  as play with children, 318–322
  and reflection of feelings, 162–164
  research in, 164–166
  for sexual problems, 433–434
  See also Behavior modification; Client-
    centered therapy; Existentialism;
    Logotherapy; Psychoanalysis;
    Sexuality
Puberty, 338–347
  See also Adolescence
Punishment, 195–196

R

Rationalization, 110
Reaction formation, 112
Reading, 279
Reality principle, 97

Regression, 99–100
Reinforcement
  in classical conditioning, 177
  schedules of, 193–195
Reinforcers, 195
Relaxation, training in, 179
Religion, 397–403
Repression, 96, 112–113, 129, 208
Resistance, in psychotherapy, 119
Respondent conditioning (*see* Classical
  conditioning)
Risk-taking, 56
Rogers, C. R., 19, 320
  See also Self theory; Client-centered
    therapy
Role, 215
Role theory, Sarbin's, 214–234
  concepts of, 215–221
  variables important to role enactment,
    217–221

S

Sadism, 41
Sarbin, T. R. (*see* Role theory)
Schizophrenia
  and sensory deprivation, 75
  thinking in, 229–231
  See also Autism
School children
  adjustments of, 270–291
  class placement of, 273–274
  developmental tasks of, 275–280
  learning and identification in, 285–291
  See also Preadolescence
School phobia, 276
School psychologist, 305
Self actualization, 154
Self concept
  and changes in adulthood, 447–450
  and mastery of physical skills, 278–279
  Rogers' theory of, 155–160
  according to role theory, 217–218
  See also Identity
Self awareness, the beginning of, 266–267
Self-fulfilling prophecy, 304–305
Self theory, Carl Rogers, 151–160
  recent emphasis, 166–169
Sense organs, 66
Sensitivity group (*see* Groups, for compe-
  tence and growth)
Sensory deprivation, 73–75

Sensory stimulation, 296–298
Sex role, in school age children, 276–278
Sexual attractiveness, 377–378
Sexuality
  and adjustments in adulthood, 428–438
  and aging, 435–438
  arousal of, 44
  arousal and expression in early adoles-
    cence, 344–346
  drive and, 43–44
  myths of, 434–435
  overt expression of in late adolescence,
    375–377
  physical development of in adolescence,
    338–341
  premarital, 382–387
  problems in, 432–434
  techniques of arousal, 430–432
  treatment of difficulties in, 186–189
  and vocational choice, 369–370
Sheldon, W. H. (*see* Constitutional theory)
Sibling method of study, 29–30
Skinner, B. F. (*see* Operant conditioning)
Socialization
  early development of, 267–269
  primary, 267
Social class, 300–303, 368–369, 376
Social innovation, 234–235
  an experimental model for, 236–238
  in a mental hospital, 241–250
  phases of, 238–241
Social roles, 302–303
  See also Role theory
Socioeconomic status, 300–303, 368–369
  See also Sexuality; Vocation
Somatotype, 26
Special education, 274
Stereotypes, 70
Student activists, 410–411
Student-centered teaching, 169
Student drug culture, 411–415
Subliminal perception, 66
Sublimation, 112
Superego, 98
  See also Psychoanalysis
Systematic desensitization, 179–183
  See also Behavior modification

T

Teaching machines, 203–204
Teachers, 303–304

Tests, projective, 68
  See also Psychological tests
T-group (*see* Groups, for competence and
      growth)
Thanatos, 93
Thrill seeking, 56
Toilet training, 101, 264–265
Transcendence, 133–134
  See also Existentialism
Transference, 119
  See also Psychoanalysis, as a treatment

Values (*cont.*)
  as demands in personal adjustment, 15
  religious, 397–403
Viscerogenic needs, 49
  See also Motivation; Motives; Needs
Vocation
  changes in with aging, 441–443
  characteristics of, 366–368
  choice of, 365–374
  counseling and guidance for, 370–374
  factors in choice of, 368–370

U

Ulcers, 57
Unconscious, 94–95, 207

W

Weaning, 262
Work (*see* Vocation)
Writing, 279–280

V

Z

Values
  choice of in late adolescence, 392–396

Zygote, 257